Java for Absolute Beginners

Learn to Program the Fundamentals the Java 9+ Way

Iuliana Cosmina

Apress®

Java for Absolute Beginners: Learn to Program the Fundamentals the Java 9+ Way

Iuliana Cosmina
Edinburgh, UK

ISBN-13 (pbk): 978-1-4842-3777-9 ISBN-13 (electronic): 978-1-4842-3778-6
https://doi.org/10.1007/978-1-4842-3778-6

Library of Congress Control Number: 2018964482

Copyright © 2018 by Iuliana Cosmina

This work is subject to copyright. All rights are reserved by the Publisher, whether the whole or part of the material is concerned, specifically the rights of translation, reprinting, reuse of illustrations, recitation, broadcasting, reproduction on microfilms or in any other physical way, and transmission or information storage and retrieval, electronic adaptation, computer software, or by similar or dissimilar methodology now known or hereafter developed.

Trademarked names, logos, and images may appear in this book. Rather than use a trademark symbol with every occurrence of a trademarked name, logo, or image we use the names, logos, and images only in an editorial fashion and to the benefit of the trademark owner, with no intention of infringement of the trademark.

The use in this publication of trade names, trademarks, service marks, and similar terms, even if they are not identified as such, is not to be taken as an expression of opinion as to whether or not they are subject to proprietary rights.

While the advice and information in this book are believed to be true and accurate at the date of publication, neither the authors nor the editors nor the publisher can accept any legal responsibility for any errors or omissions that may be made. The publisher makes no warranty, express or implied, with respect to the material contained herein.

Managing Director, Apress Media LLC: Welmoed Spahr
Acquisitions Editor: Steve Anglin
Development Editor: Matthew Moodie
Coordinating Editor: Mark Powers

Cover designed by eStudioCalamar

Cover image designed by Freepik (www.freepik.com)

Distributed to the book trade worldwide by Springer Science+Business Media New York, 233 Spring Street, 6th Floor, New York, NY 10013. Phone 1-800-SPRINGER, fax (201) 348-4505, e-mail orders-ny@springer-sbm.com, or visit www.springeronline.com. Apress Media, LLC is a California LLC and the sole member (owner) is Springer Science + Business Media Finance Inc (SSBM Finance Inc). SSBM Finance Inc is a **Delaware** corporation.

For information on translations, please e-mail editorial@apress.com; for reprint, paperback, or audio rights, please email bookpermissions@springernature.com.

Apress titles may be purchased in bulk for academic, corporate, or promotional use. eBook versions and licenses are also available for most titles. For more information, reference our Print and eBook Bulk Sales web page at http://www.apress.com/bulk-sales.

Any source code or other supplementary material referenced by the author in this book is available to readers on GitHub via the book's product page, located at www.apress.com/9781484237779. For more detailed information, please visit http://www.apress.com/source-code.

Printed on acid-free paper

*This book is dedicated to all men that told me
software engineering is not for women.*

And to that one professor that told me I'm not PhD material.

How do ya' like them apples?

Table of Contents

About the Author xiii

About the Technical Reviewer xv

Acknowledgments xvii

Introduction xix

Chapter 1: An Introduction to Java and Its History 1

Who This Book Is For... 2

How This Book Is Structured.. 3

Conventions 4

When Java Was Owned by Sun Microsystems... 5

    Why Is Java Portable? 8

    Sun Microsystem's Java Versions 10

Oracle Takes Over 15

What the Future Holds 21

Prerequisites 21

Chapter 2: Preparing Your Development Environment 23

Installing Java.. 24

The JAVA_HOME Environment Variable.. 29

    JAVA_HOME on Windows 30

    JAVA_HOME on macOS... 35

    JAVA_HOME on Linux 36

Installing Gradle... 37

Installing Git... 38

Installing a Java IDE 39

Summary.. 47

TABLE OF CONTENTS

Chapter 3: Getting Your Feet Wet 49
Using JShell 49
Java Fundamental Building Blocks 56
    Access Modifiers 60
    Introducing Modules 64
    Configuring Modules 67
    Determining the Structure: A Java Project 69
Explaining and Enriching the Hello World! Class 89
Summary 96

Chapter 4: Java Syntax 99
Base Rules of Writing Java Code 100
    Package Declaration 101
    Import Section 101
    Java "Grammar" 103
    Java Identifiers 106
    Java Comments 107
Java Object Types 107
    Classes 108
    Enums 125
    Interfaces 129
Exceptions 139
Generics 145
Java Reserved Words 147
Summary 151

Chapter 5: Data Types 153
Stack and Heap Memory 153
Introduction to Java Data Types 159
    Primitive Data Types 159
    Reference Data Types 161

Java Primitive Types 165
    The Boolean Type 165
    The char Type 166
    Integer Primitives 167
    Real Primitives 170
Java Reference Types 173
    Arrays 177
    The String Type 183
    Escaping Characters 187
    Wrapper Classes 189
    Date Time API 191
    Collections 196
    Concurrency Specific Types 201
Summary 206

Chapter 6: Operators 207

The Assignment Operator (=) 208
Explicit Type Conversion (type) and instanceof 211
Numerical Operators 214
    Unary Operators 214
    Binary Operators 217
    Relational Operators 223
    Bitwise Operators 227
    Bitwise NOT 227
    Bitwise AND 228
    Bitwise Inclusive OR 230
    Bitwise Exclusive OR 231
    Logical Operators 233
    Shift Operators 238
    The Elvis Operator 241
Summary 242

vii

TABLE OF CONTENTS

Chapter 7: Controlling the Flow 243

if-else Statement 244

switch Statement 250

Looping Statements 256

    for Statements.. 257

    while Statement 263

    do-while Statement 268

Breaking Loops and Skipping Steps 271

    break Statement.. 271

    continue Statement 273

    return Statement 275

Controlling the Flow Using try-catch Constructions 277

Summary... 280

Chapter 8: The Stream API 281

Introduction to Streams 281

Creating Streams 284

    Creating Streams from Collections... 284

    Creating Streams from Arrays... 287

    Creating Empty Streams.. 289

    Creating Finite Streams... 289

    Streams of Primitives and Streams of Strings 292

    A Short Introduction to Optional 295

How to Use Streams.. 298

    Terminal Functions: forEach and forEachOrdered 300

    Intermediate Operation filter and Terminal Operation toArray.................. 302

    Intermediate Operations map and flatMap and Terminal Operation collect 303

    Intermediate Operation sorted and Terminal Operation findFirst 306

    Intermediate Operation distinct and Terminal Operation count................ 306

    Intermediate Operation limit and Terminal Operations min and max 307

    Terminal Operations sum and reduce.. 307

    Intermediate Operation peek 308

    Intermediate Operation skip and Terminal Operations findAny, anyMatch,
    allMatch, and noneMatch 309

  Debugging Stream Code 310

  Summary 314

Chapter 9: Debugging, Testing, and Documenting 317

  Debugging 317

    Logging 318

    Logging with SLF4J and Logback 337

    Debug Using Assertions 345

    Step-by-Step Debugging 348

    Inspect Running Application Using Java Tools 351

  Accessing the Java Process API 362

  Testing 369

    A Small Introduction to Testing 370

    Test Code Location 371

    Application to Test 372

  Documenting 397

  Summary 408

Chapter 10: Making Your Application Interactive 409

  Reading Data from the Command Line 409

    Reading User Data Using System.in 410

    Using Scanner 411

    Reading User Data with java.io.Console 417

  Build Applications Using Swing 420

  Introducing JavaFX 432

  Internationalization 442

  Build a Web Application 450

  Summary 468

TABLE OF CONTENTS

Chapter 11: Working with Files 471

File Handlers 471

Path Handlers 478

Reading Files 482

    Using Scanner to Read Files.. 482

    Using Files Utility Methods to Read Files 484

    Using Readers to Read Files 485

    Using InputStream to Read Files 489

Writing Files 492

    Writing Files Using Files Utility Methods 492

    Using Writers to Write Files 495

    Using OutputStream to Write Files 499

Serialization and Deserialization... 502

    Binary Serialization 503

    XML Serialization... 507

    JSON Serialization 511

The Media API 513

Using JavaFX Image Classes 526

Summary... 529

Chapter 12: The Publish/Subscribe Framework 531

Reactive Programming and the Reactive Manifesto 532

Using the JDK Reactive Streams API 536

Reactive Streams Technology Compatibility Kit 548

Using Project Reactor 552

Summary... 558

Chapter 13: Garbage Collection 559

Garbage Collection Basics 560

    Oracle Hotspot JVM Architecture.. 560

    How Many Garbage Collectors Are There? 564

TABLE OF CONTENTS

Working with GC from the Code 571
    Using the finalize() Method 571
    Heap Memory Statistics 578
    Using Cleaner 584
    Preventing GC from Deleting an Object 587
    Using Weak References 591

Garbage Collection Exceptions and Causes 595

Summary 596

Index 599

About the Author

Iuliana Cosmina is currently a software engineer for NCR Edinburgh. She has been writing Java code since 2002. She has contributed to various types of applications, such as experimental search engines, ERPs, track and trace, and banking. During her career, she has been a teacher, a team leader, software architect, a DevOps professional, and a software manager.

She is a Spring-certified professional, as defined by Pivotal, the makers of Spring Framework, Boot, and other tools.

She considers Spring the best Java framework to work with.

When she is not programming, she spends her time reading, blogging, learning to play piano, travelling, hiking, or biking.

- You can find some of her personal work on her GitHub account at `https://github.com/iuliana`.
- You can find her complete CV on her LinkedIn account at `www.linkedin.com/in/iulianacosmina`.
- You can contact her at `Iuliana.Cosmina@gmail.com`.

About the Technical Reviewer

Wallace Jackson has been writing for leading multimedia publications about his work in new media content development since the advent of *Multimedia Producer Magazine* nearly two decades ago. He has authored a half-dozen Android book titles for Apress, including four titles in the popular Pro Android series. Wallace received his undergraduate degree in business economics from the University of California at Los Angeles and a graduate degree in MIS design and implementation from the University of Southern California. He is currently the CEO of Mind Taffy Design, a new media content production and digital campaign design and development agency.

Acknowledgments

Here I am again, the main author of a technical book for the third time.

This book was quite challenging to write, because I had to quickly adapt to changes made to the Java ecosystem. With the new six months interval release system, modules being introduced, and backward compatibility thrown out the window, I found myself with a project that stopped compiling and had to invest precious time into fixing it, understand why it broke in the first place, and eventually adapt the book.

Writing books for beginners is tricky, because as an experienced developer, it might be difficult to find the right examples and explain them in such a way that even a non-technical person would easily understand them. That is why I am profoundly grateful to Matthew Moodie and Mark Powers for all the support and advice they provided to keep this book at beginner level. We have been working together for four years and it has been a fruitful collaboration so far.

I would like to thank Wallace Jackson; his recommendations and corrections were crucial for the final form of the book.

Apress has published many of the books that I have read and used to improve myself professionally. It is a great honor to publish my fourth book with Apress, and it gives me enormous satisfaction to be able to contribute to the "making" of a new generation of Java developers.

I am grateful to all my friends who had the patience to listen to me complain about sleepless nights and writer's block. Thank you all for being supportive and making sure I still had some fun while writing this book. You have no idea how dear you are to me.

I am thankful to John Mayer still, as his music provided yet again, a great environment for my working nights.

A special thank you to Achim Wagner, whom I consider both a mentor and a dear friend. He provided me with an environment and support to grow as a professional and as a person, and I will miss working with him.

ACKNOWLEDGMENTS

A special thank you to the Bogza-Vlad family: Monica, Tinel, Cristina, and Stefan. You are all close to my heart and this book might have been released later without your support when I moved to Edinburgh.

And a very special thank-you in advance to all the passionate Java developers who will find mistakes in the book and be so kind to write me about them so I can provide an erratum and make this book even better.

Introduction

Even though I have been writing Java Applications since 2002 I don't think I've ever dived so deeply into the JVM as I did while writing this book. Most companies I've worked for had their own code base when I joined them, and my work was mostly related to designing, improving or maintaining one that already existed. It's like making brownies when you already have brownie mix. Writing this book has given me the opportunity to get down to basics and work with basic ingredients—so, making brownies using eggs, flower, cocoa, milk, and butter.

Java began in 1982 and was created by a handful of people. The most renowned name linked to the beginning of Java is James Gosling, also known as the father of Java, the language that is now used on over three billion devices. When Oracle bought Sun Microsystems, developers were worried about Java's future, especially since its main creator quit the company and went on to create what was thought to be Java's replacement: Scala. That will probably never happen. Java is still here.

Most banking applications are written in Java and because it is definitely dangerous and costly to migrate these applications, Java will be here in 50 years, if not more. Java began by making websites more dynamic and more entertaining, and ended up being the basis for applications run on ATMs, cashier machines, computers, and mobile devices. Sure, this would have been more difficult if Java wasn't cross-platform.

The first Java version was officially released in 1996. Since then, ten more versions have been released, with the latest one, Java 11, being released on 25th September 2018. The work on Java 12 has already begun and the early access build is already available.

This book was written with the intention to cover the fundamental elements of the language and of the JVM, especially the ones introduced in versions 9, 10, and 11. The book provides a complete overview of the most important Java classes in the JVM, all wrapped up in a multimodule project that compiles with Java 11 and Gradle 5.

INTRODUCTION

A group of reviewers has gone over the book, but if you notice any inconsistencies, please send an email to editorial@apress.com, or directly to the author, and corrections will be made and published in an erratum that will be uploaded to the official GitHub repository for the book. The example source code for this book can be found on GitHub or downloaded from the official book's product page, located at www.apress.com/in/book/9781484237779.

I truly hope you will enjoy using this book to learn Java as much as I enjoyed writing it.

CHAPTER 1

An Introduction to Java and Its History

Java is currently one of the most influential programming languages. It all started in 1990, when an American company that was leading the revolution in the computer industry decided to gather its best engineers together to design and develop a product that would allow them to become an important player in the new emerging Internet world. Among those engineers was James Arthur Gosling, a Canadian computer scientist who is recognized as the "father" of the Java programming language. It would take five years of design, programming, and one rename (from Oak to Java because of trademark issues), but finally in 1996, Java 1.0 was released for Linux, Solaris, Mac, and Windows.

You might have the tendency to skip this chapter altogether. But I think it would be a mistake. I was never much interested in the history of Java. I was using it for work. I knew that James Gosling was the creator and that Oracle bought Sun, and that was pretty much it. I never cared much about how the language evolved, where the inspiration came from, or how one version was different from another. I started learning Java at version 1.5, and I took a lot of things in the language for granted. So, when I was assigned to a project running on Java 1.4, I was quite confused, because I did not know why some of the code I wrote was not compiling. Although the IT industry is moving very fast, there will always be that one client that has a legacy application. And knowing the peculiarities of each Java version is an advantage, because you know the issues when performing a migration.

When I started doing research for this book, I was mesmerized. The history of Java is interesting because it is a tale of incredible growth, success of a technology, and how a clash of egos in management almost killed the company that created it. Because even if Java is the most used technology in software development, it is simply paradoxical that the company that gave birth to it no longer exists.

© Iuliana Cosmina 2018
I. Cosmina, *Java for Absolute Beginners*, https://doi.org/10.1007/978-1-4842-3778-6_1

CHAPTER 1   AN INTRODUCTION TO JAVA AND ITS HISTORY

This chapter covers each version of Java to track the evolution of the language and the Java virtual machine. You can find a timeline for versions 1.0 to 1.8 on the Oracle official site at http://oracle.com/edgesuite.net/timeline/java./. But first, I'll introduce the book.

Who This Book Is For

Most Java books for beginners start with the typical *Hello World!* example depicted here:

```
public class HelloWorld {
    public static void main(String[] args) {
        System.out.println("Hello World!");
    }
}
```

This code, when executed, prints *Hello World!* in the console. But if you have bought this book, it is assumed that you want to develop real applications in Java, and get a real chance when applying for a position as a Java developer. If this is what you want, if this is who you are, a beginner with the wits and the desire to make full use of this language's power, then this book is for you. And that is why to start this book, a complex example is used. We go over it in almost every section, when some part of it is clarified.

Java is a language with a syntax that is readable and based on the English language. So, if you have a logical thinking and a little knowledge of the English language, it should be obvious to you what the following code does without even executing it.

```
package com.apress.ch.one.hw;

import java.util.List;

public class Example01 {
  public static void main(String[] args) {
    List<String> items = List.of("1", "a", "2", "a", "3", "a");

    items.forEach(item -> {
        if (item.equals("a")) {
            System.out.println("A");
        } else {
```

```
            System.out.println("Not A");
        }
    });
  }
}
```

In this code example, a list of text values is declared; then the list is traversed, and when a text is equal to "a", the letter "A" is printed in the console; otherwise, "Not A" is printed.

If you are an absolute beginner to programming, this book is for you, especially because the sources attached to this book make use of algorithms and design patterns commonly used in programming. So, if your plan is to get into programming and learn a high-level programming language, read the book, run the examples, write your own code, and you should have a good head start.

If you already know Java, you can use this book too because it covers the specifics of Java versions 9, 10, and 11 (the EAP[1] release).

How This Book Is Structured

The chapter you are reading is an introductory one that covers a little bit of Java history, showing you how the language has evolved and a glimpse into its future. Also, the mechanics of executing a Java application are covered, so that you are prepared for **Chapter** 2. The next chapter shows you how to set up a development environment and introduces you to a simple application. In Chapters 3 to 7, the fundamental parts of the language are covered: packages, modules, classes, objects, operators, data types, statements, streams, lambda expressions, and so forth. Starting with Chapter 8 more advanced features are covered such as: interactions with external data sources: reading writing files, serializing/deserializing objects, testing and creating an interface. Chapter 12 is dedicated fully to the publish-subscribe framework introduced in Java 9. Chapter 13 covers the garbage collector.

The book is completed by the `java-for-absolute-beginners` project. This project is organized in modules (thus it is a multimodule project) that are linked to each other and must be managed by **Gradle**. Gradle is something we developers call a *build tool*, which is used to build projects. To build a project means transforming the code into something that can be executed. I chose to use multimodule projects for the books I write because it is easier to build them, and common elements can be grouped together, keeping the

---

[1]Early Access Program

configuration of the project simple and non-repetitive. Also, by having all the sources organized in one multimodule project, you get the feedback on whether the sources are working or not as soon as possible, and you can contact the author and ask him or her to update them.

Conventions

This book uses a number of formatting conventions that should make it easier to read. To that end, the following conventions are used within the book:

- code or concept names in paragraphs appear as follows:

    ```
    import java.util.List;
    ```

- code listings appear as follows:

    ```
    public static void main(String[] args) {
            System.out.println("Hello there young developer!");
    }
    ```

- logs in console outputs appear as follows:

    ```
    01:24:07.809 [main] INFO  c.a.Application - Starting Application
    01:24:07.814 [main] DEBUG c.a.p.c.Application - Running in debug mode
    ...
    ```

- ! This symbol appears in front of paragraphs that you should pay specific attention to.

- *Italic* font is used for metaphors, jocular terms and technical terms that the reader should pay special attention to because they are not explained in the current context, but they are covered in the book. Examples: "This was mentioned before at the end of Chapter 4 when *generics* were introduced." "The **stack** memory is used during execution (also referred to as at *runtime*)" or "Let's see how this is being done *under the hood*".

- **Bold** font is used for chapter references and important terms.

As for my style of writing, I like to write my books in the same way I have technical conversations with colleagues and friends: sprinkling jokes, giving production examples, and making analogies to non-programming situations. Because programming is just another way to model the real world.

When Java Was Owned by Sun Microsystems

The first version of Java was released in 1996. Up until that point, there was a small team named the **Green Team** that worked on a prototype language named Oak, which was introduced to the world with a working demo—an interactive handheld home entertainment controller called the Star7. The star of the animated touch-screen user interface was a cartoon character named **Duke**, created by one of the team's graphic artists, Joe Palrang. Over the years, Duke has become the official Java technology mascot, and every JavaOne conference has its own Duke mascot personality and the most simple version is depicted in Figure 1-1.

Figure 1-1. The Duke mascot (image source: `http://oracle.com`)

The **Green Team** released it to the world via the Internet, because that was the fastest way to create widespread adoptions. You can imagine that they jumped for joy every time somebody downloaded it, because it meant people were interested in it. And there are a few other advantages making software open source, like the fact that contributions and feedback come from a bigger and diverse number of people from all over the world. Thus, for Java, this was the best decision, as it shaped the language a lot of developers are using today. Even after 22 years, Java is still among the top-three most used programming languages.

CHAPTER 1   AN INTRODUCTION TO JAVA AND ITS HISTORY

The American company that started all of this was Sun Microsystems, founded in 1982. It guided the computer revolution by selling computers, computer parts, and software. Among their greatest achievements is the Java programming language. In Figure 1-2,[2] you can see the company logo that was used since Java's birth year until it was acquired by Oracle in 2010.

Figure 1-2. *The Sun Microsystems logo (image source:* `https://en.wikipedia.org/wiki/Sun_Microsystems`*)*

It is quite difficult to find information about the first version of Java, but dedicated developers that witnessed the birth of Java—when the web was way smaller and full of static pages—did create blogs and shared their experience with the world. It was quite easy for Java to shine with its applets that displayed dynamic content and interacted with the user. But because the development team thought bigger, Java became much more than a web programming language. Because in trying to make applets run in any browser, the team found a solution to a common problem: portability.

Nowadays, developers face a lot of headaches when developing software that should run on any operating system. And with the mobile revolution, things have become really tricky. In Figure 1-3, you see an abstract drawing of what is believed to be the first Java logo.

---

[2]The story behind the logo can be read here: `https://goodlogo.com/extended.info/sun-microsystems-logo-2385`. You can also read more about Sun Microsystems.

CHAPTER 1 ■ AN INTRODUCTION TO JAVA AND ITS HISTORY

Figure 1-3. The first Java logo, 1996–2003 (image source: http://xahlee.info/)

Java 1.0 was released at the first JavaOne conference—with over 6000 attendees. It started out as a language named Oak[3] that was really similar to C++ and was designed for handheld devices and set-top boxes. It evolved into the first version of Java, which provided developers some advantages that C++ did not.

- **security**: In Java, there is no danger of reading bogus data when accidentally going over the size of an array.

- **automatic memory management**: A Java developer does not have to check if there is enough memory to allocate for an object and then deallocate it explicitly; the operations are automatically handled by the garbage collector. This also means that pointers are not necessary.

- **simplicity**: There are no pointers, unions, templates, structures. Mostly anything in Java can be declared as a class. Also, confusion when using multiple inheritance is avoided by modifying the inheritance model and not allowing multiple class inheritance.

- **support for multithreaded execution**: Java was designed from the start to support development of multithreaded software.

- **portability**: A Java motto is *Write it once, run it everywhere*. This is made possible by the Java virtual machine, which is covered shortly.

---

[3]The language was named by James Gosling after the oak tree in front of his house.

7

CHAPTER 1 AN INTRODUCTION TO JAVA AND ITS HISTORY

All this made Java appealing for developers, and by 1997, when Java 1.1 was released, there were already approximatively 400,000 Java developers in the world. JavaOne had 10,000 attendees that year. The path to greatness was set. Before going further in our analysis of each Java version, let's clarify a few things.

Why Is Java Portable?

I mentioned a few times that Java is portable and that Java programs can run on any operating system. It is time to explain how this is possible. Let's start with a simple drawing, like the one in Figure 1-4.

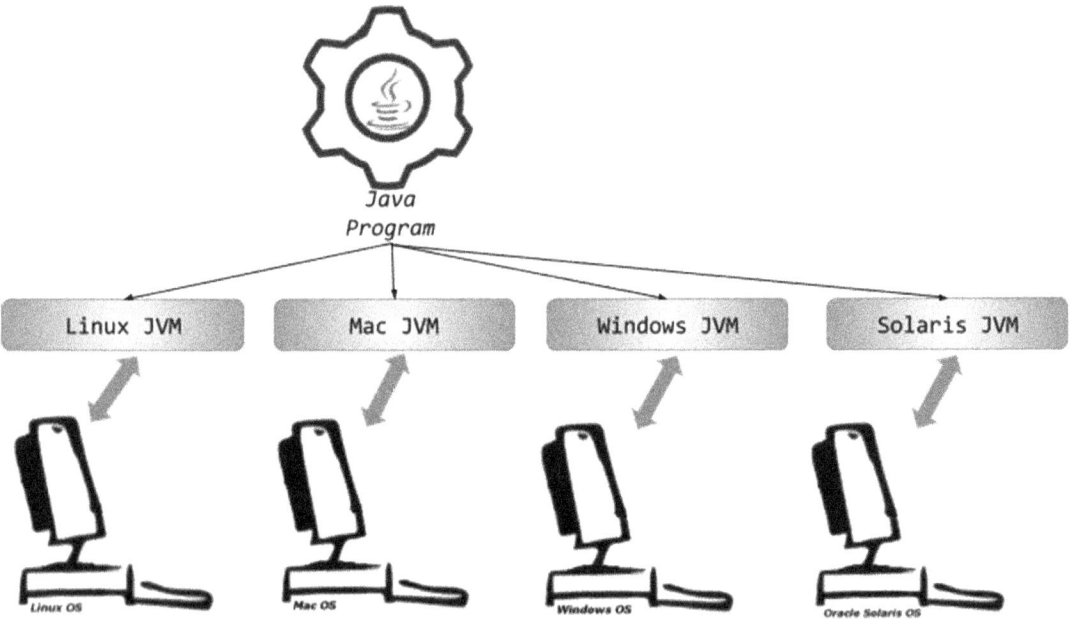

Figure 1-4. *What makes Java portable*

Java is what we call a high-level programming language that allows a developer to write programs that are independent of a particular type of computer. High-level languages are easier to read, write, and maintain. But their code must be translated by a compiler or interpreted into machine language (unreadable by humans because is it made up of numbers) to be executed, because that is the only language that computers understand.

In Figure 1-4, notice that on top of the operating systems, a JVM is needed to execute a Java program. JVM stands for Java virtual machine, which is an abstract computing machine that enables a computer to run a Java program. It is a platform-independent execution environment that converts Java code into machine language and executes it.

So, what is the difference between Java and other high-level languages? Well, other high-level languages compile source code directly into machine code that is designed to run on a specific microprocessor architecture or operating system, such as Windows or UNIX. What JVM does, it that is mimics a Java processor making it possible for a Java program to be interpreted as a sequence of actions or operating system calls on any processor regardless of the operating system.

And because the Java compiler was mentioned, we have to get back to Java 1.1, which was widely used, even as new versions were released. It came with an improved Abstract Window Toolkit (AWT) graphical API (collections of components used for building applets), inner classes, database connectivity classes (JDBC model), classes for remote calls (RMI), a special compiler for Microsoft platforms named JIT,[4] support for internationalization, and Unicode. Also, what made it so widely embraced is that shortly after Java was released, Microsoft licensed it and started creating applications using it. The feedback helped further development of Java, thus Java 1.1 was supported on all browsers of the time, which is why it was so widely deployed.

! A lot of terms used in the introduction of the book might seem foreign to you now, but as you read the book, more information is presented and these words will start to make more sense. For now, just keep in mind, that every new Java version, has something more than the previous version, and at that time, every new component is a novelty.

So, what exactly happens to developer-written Java code until the actual execution? The process is depicted in Figure 1-5.

---

[4]Just In Time

CHAPTER 1   AN INTRODUCTION TO JAVA AND ITS HISTORY

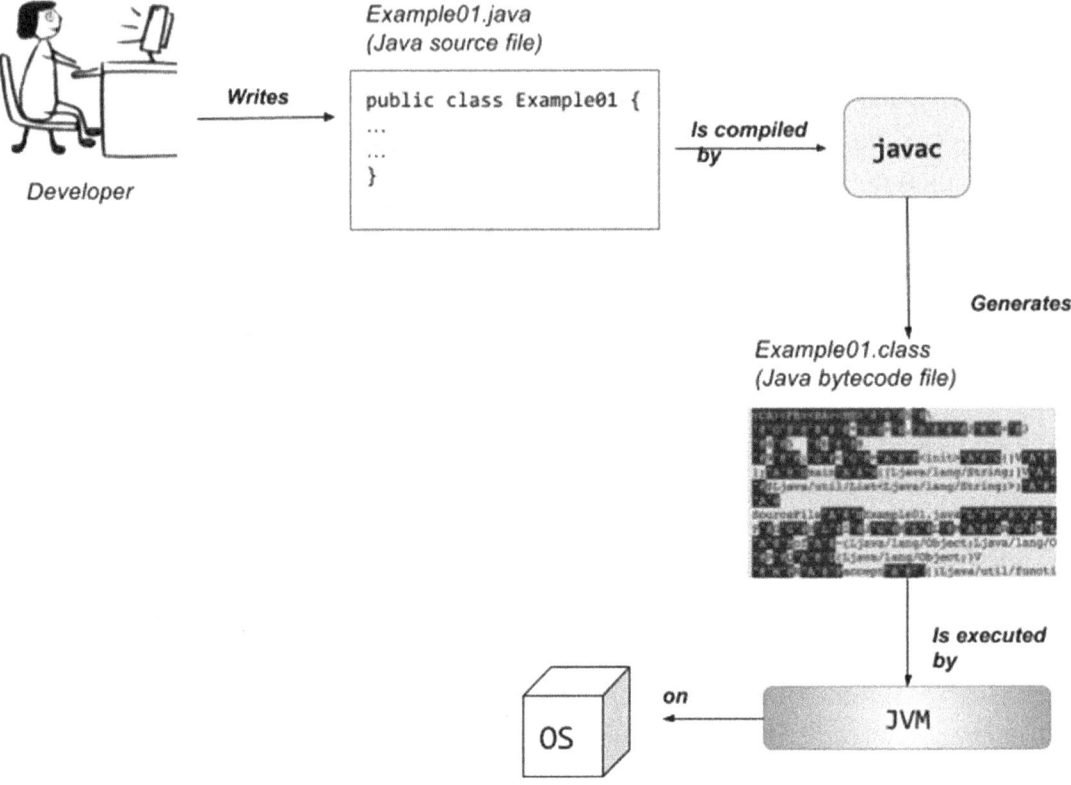

Figure 1-5.   From Java code to machine code

In Figure 1-5, you see that Java code is compiled and transformed to bytecode that is then interpreted and executed by the Java virtual machine on the underlying operating system. This is what Java is: a compiled and interpreted general-purpose programming language with a large number of features that make it well suited for the web. And now that we've covered how Java code is executed, let's go back to some more history.

Sun Microsystem's Java Versions

The first stable Java version released by Sun Microsystems could be downloaded from the website as an archive named JDK 1.0.2. JDK is an acronym for **J**ava **D**evelopment **K**it. This is the software development environment used for developing Java applications and applets. It includes the **J**ava **R**untime **E**nvironment (JRE), an interpreter (loader), a compiler, an archiver, a documentation generator, and other tools needed for Java development. We will get into this more when I cover how to install the JDK on your computer.

Starting with version 1.2, released in 1998, Java versions were given codenames.[5] The Java version 1.2 codename was **Playground**. It was a massive release and this was the moment when people started talking about **the Java 2 Platform**. Starting with this version, the releases up to J2SE 5.0 were renamed, and J2SE replaced JDK because the Java platform was now composed of three parts:

- J2SE (Java 2 Platform, Standard Edition), which later became JSE, a computing platform for the development and deployment of portable code for desktop and server environments

- J2EE (Java 2 Platform, Enterprise Edition), which later became JEE, a set of specifications extending Java SE with specifications for enterprise features such as distributed computing and web services

- J2ME (Java 2 Platform, Micro Edition), which later became JME, a computing platform for development and deployment of portable code for embedded and mobile devices

With this release, the JIT compiler became part of Sun Microsystem's JVM (which basically means turning code into executable code became a faster operation and the generated executable code was optimized), the Swing graphical API was introduced as a fancy alternative to AWT (new components to create fancy desktop applications were introduced), and the Java collections framework (for working with sets of data) was introduced.

J2SE 1.3 was released in 2000 with the codename **Kestrel** (maybe as a reference to the newly introduced Java sound classes). This release also contained Java XML APIs.

J2SE 1.4 was released in 2002 with the codename **Merlin**. This is the first year that the **J**ava **C**ommunity **P**rocess members were involved in deciding which features the release should contain, and thus, the release was quite consistent. This is the first release of the Java platform developed under the Java Community Process as JSR 59.[6] The following features are among those worth mentioning.

- Support for IPv6 (basically applications that run over a network can now be written to work using networking protocol IPv6).

---

[5]All codenames, for intermediary releases too, are listed here: http://www.oracle.com/technetwork/java/javase/codenames-136090.html#close

[6]If you want to see the contents and the list of Java Specification Requests, follow this URL: http://www.jcp.org/en/jsr/detail?id=59

- Non-blocking IO (IO is an acronym for input-output, which refers to reading and writing data— a very slow operation. Making IO non-blocking means to optimize these operations to increase speed of the running application.)

- Logging API (Operations that get executed need to be reported to a file or a resource, which can be read in case of failure to determine the cause and find a solution. This process is called logging and apparently only in this version components to support this operation were introduced.)

- Image processing API (Components developers can use this to manipulate images with Java code.)

Java's coffee cup logo made its entrance in 2003 (between releases 1.4 and 5.0) at the JavaOne conference. You can see it in Figure 1-6.[7]

Figure 1-6. *Java official logo 2003-2006 (image source:* `http://oracle.com`*)*

J2SE 5.0 was released in 2004 with the codename **Tiger**. Initially, it followed the typical versioning, and was named 1.5, but because this was a major release with a significant number of new features that proved a serious improvement of maturity, stability, scalability, and security of the J2SE, the version was labeled 5.0 and presented like that to the public, even if internally 1.5 was still used. For this version and the next two, it was considered that `1.x = x.0`. Let's list those features because most of them are covered in the book.

---

[7]The Java language was first named Oak. It was renamed to Java because of copyright issues. There are a few theories that you will find regarding the new name. There is one saying that the JAVA name is actually a collection of the initials of the names being part of the Green team: **J**ames Gosling, **A**rthur **V**an Hoff, and **A**ndy Bechtolsheim, and that the logo is inspired by their love of coffee.

- **Generics** provide compile-time (static) type safety for collections and eliminates the need for most type conversions (which means the type used in a certain context is decided while the application is running, we have a full section about this in **Chapter** 5).

- **Annotations**, also known as **metadata**, are used to tag classes and methods to allow metadata-aware utilities to process them (which means a component is labeled as something another component recognizes and does specific operations with it).

- **Autoboxing/unboxing** are automatic conversion between primitive types and matching object types (wrappers), also covered in **Chapter** 5.

- **Enumerations** define static final ordered sets of values using the `enum` keyword; covered in **Chapter** 5.

- **Varargs** are the last parameter of a method is declared using a type name followed by three dots (`String...`), which implies that any number of arguments of that type can be provided and is placed into an array; covered in **Chapter** 3.

- **Enhanced for each loop** is used to iterate over collections and arrays too; covered in **Chapter** 5.

- Improved semantics for multithreaded Java programs, covered in **Chapter** 7.

- **Static imports** are covered in **Chapter** 5.

- Improvements for RMI (not covered in the book), Swing (**Chapter** 10), concurrency utilities (**Chapter** 7), and introduction to the `Scanner` class; covered in **Chapter** 11.

Java 5 was the first available for Mac OS X (version 10.4) and the default version installed on Mac OS X (version 10.5). There were a lot of updates[8] released for this version to fix issues related to security and performance. It was a pretty buggy release, which is understandable since quite a lot of features were developed in only two years.

---

[8] Let's call them what they actually are: hotfixes.

CHAPTER 1   AN INTRODUCTION TO JAVA AND ITS HISTORY

In 2006, Java SE 6 was released with a little delay, with the codename **Mustang**. Yes, yet another rename. And yes, yet again a serious number of features were implemented in a short period of time and a lot of updates followed. This was the last major Java release by Sun Microsystems. Oracle acquired the company in January 2010. Let's take a look at the most important features in this release:

- Dramatic performance improvements for the core platform (applications run faster, need less memory or CPU to execute)

- Improved web service support (optimized components that are required for development of web applications)

- JDBC 4.0 (optimized components that are required for development of applications using databases)

- Java Compiler API (basically, from your code you can components that are used to compile code)

- Many GUI improvements, such as integration of SwingWorker in the API, table sorting and filtering, and true Swing double-buffering (eliminating the gray-area effect); basically, improvement of components used to create interfaces for desktop applications

In December 2008, Java FX 1.0 SDK was released. JavaFX is used to create graphical user interfaces for any platform, and the initial version was a scripting language. Until 2008, there were two ways to create a user interface in Java:

- **AWT** (Abstract Window Toolkit) components, which are rendered and controlled by a native peer component specific to the underlying operating system; that is why AWT components are also called *heavyweight components*.

- **Swing** components, which are called *lightweight* because they do not require allocation of native resources in the operating system's windowing toolkit. The Swing API is a complimentary extension of AWT.

In the first versions, it was never really clear if JavaFX would actually have a future and grow up to replace Swing. The management turmoil inside Sun did not help in defining a clear path for the project either.

Oracle Takes Over

Although Sun Microsystems won a lawsuit against Microsoft, in which they agreed to pay $20 million for not implementing the Java 1.1 standard completely, in 2008, the company was in such poor shape that negotiations for a merger with IBM and Hewlett-Packard began. In 2009, Oracle and Sun announced that they agreed on the price: Oracle would acquire Sun for $9.50 a share in cash; this amounted to a $5.6 billion offer. The impact was massive. A lot of engineers quit, including James Gosling, *the father of Java*, which made a lot of developers question the future of the Java platform.

Java SE 7, codename **Dolphin**, was the first Java version released by Oracle in 2011. It was the result of an extensive collaboration between Oracle engineers and members of the worldwide Java communities, like the OpenJDK Community and the Java Community Process (JCP). It contained a lot of changes, but still, a lot fewer than developers expected. Considering the long period between the releases, the expectations were pretty high. Project **Lambda**, which was supposed to allow usage of lambda expressions in Java (this leads to considerable syntax simplification in certain cases), and **Jigsaw** (making JVM and the Java application modular; there is a section in **Chapter** 3 about them) were dropped. Both were released in future versions. The following are the most notable features in Java 7.

- JVM support for dynamic languages with the new `invokedynamic` bytecode (basically, Java code can use code implemented in non-Java languages, such as C)
- Compressed 64-bit pointers (internal optimization of the JVM, so less memory is consumed)
- Small language changes grouped under project **Coin**
    - strings in `switch` (covered in **Chapter** 7)
    - automatic resource management in try-statement (covered in **Chapter** 5)
    - improved type inference for generics—the diamond <> operator (covered in **Chapter** 5)
    - binary integer literals (covered in **Chapter** 5)
    - multiple exceptions handling improvements (covered in **Chapter** 5)
- Concurrency improvements

- New I/O library (new classes added to read/write data to/from files, covered in **Chapter** 8)

- `Timsort` to sort collections and arrays of objects instead of `merge sort` (Sets of data that are ordered need to be sorted using an algorithm, basically, in this version, the algorithm was replaced with one that has better performance. Better performance usually means reducing of consumed resources: memory and/or CPU, or reducing the time needed for execution.)

It must have been difficult to pick up a project and update it with almost none of the original development team involved. That can be seen in the 161 updates that followed; most of them needed to fix security issues and vulnerabilities.

JavaFX 2.0 was released with Java 7. This confirmed that the JavaFX project had a future with Oracle. As a major change, JavaFX stopped being a scripting language and became a Java API. This meant that knowledge of the Java language syntax would be enough to start building user graphical interfaces with it. JavaFX started gaining ground over Swing because of its hardware-accelerated graphical engine called **Prism** that did a better job at rendering.

Java SE 8, codename **Spider**, was released in 2014, and included features that were initially intended to be part of Java 7. But, better late than never, right? Three years in the making, Java 8 contained the following key features.

- Language syntax changes

  - Language-level support for lambda expressions (functional programming features)

  - Support for default methods in interfaces (covered in **Chapter** 4)

  - New date and time API (covered in **Chapter** 5)

  - New way to do parallel processing by using streams (covered in **Chapter** 8)

- Improved integration with JavaScript (the Nashorn project). JavaScript is a web scripting language that is quite loved in the development community, so providing support for it in Java probably won Oracle a few new supporters.

- Improvements of the garbage collection process

CHAPTER 1   AN INTRODUCTION TO JAVA AND ITS HISTORY

Starting with Java 8, codenames were dropped to avoid any trademark-law hassles; instead, a semantic versioning that easily distinguishes major, minor, and security-update releases was adopted.[9] The version number matches the following pattern:

$MAJOR.$MINOR.$SECURITY

When executing `java -version` in a terminal (if you have Java 8 installed), you see something similar to the following log.

```
$ java -version
java version "1.8.0_162"
JavaTM SE Runtime Environment build 1.8.0_162-b12
Java HotSpotTM 64-Bit Server VM build 25.162-b12, mixed mode
```

In this log, the version numbers have the following meaning:

- The 1 represents the major version number, incremented for a major release that contains significant new features as specified in a new edition of the Java SE Platform Specification.

- The 8 represents the minor version number, incremented for a minor update release that may contain compatible bug fixes, revisions to standard APIs and other small features.

- The 0 represents the security level that is incremented for a security-update release that contains critical fixes, including those necessary to improve security. $SECURITY is not reset to zero when $MINOR is incremented, which lets the users know that this version is a more secure one.

- 162 is the build number.

- b12 represents additional build information.

This versioning style is quite common for Java applications, thus this versioning style was adopted to align with the general industry practices.

Java SE 9 was released in September 2017. The long-awaited **Jigsaw** project was finally here. The Java platform is finally modular.

---

[9]Java Enhancement Proposal 223: http://openjdk.java.net/jeps/223

> ! This is a big change for the Java world; it's not a change in syntax and it's not some new feature. It's a change in the design of the platform. Some experienced developers I know, who have used Java since its first years have difficulties adapting. It is supposed to fix some serious problems that Java has been living with for years (covered in **Chapter** 3). You are lucky because, as a beginner, you start from scratch, so you do not need to change the way you develop your applications.

The following are the most important features, aside the introduction of Java modules.[10]

- The Java Shell tool, an interactive command-line interface for evaluation declarations, statements, and expressions written in Java (covered in **Chapter** 3)

- Quite a few security updates

- Improved `try-with-resources`: final variables can now be used as resources (covered in **Chapter** 5)

- "_" is removed from the set of legal identifier names (covered in **Chapter** 4)

- Support for private interface methods (covered in **Chapter** 5)

- Enhancements for the Garbage-First (G1) garbage collector; this becomes the default garbage collector (covered in **Chapter** 13)

- Internally, a new more compact String representation is used (covered in **Chapter** 5)

- Concurrency updates (related to parallel execution, mentioned in **Chapter** 5)

- Factory methods for collections (covered in **Chapter** 5)

- Updates of the image processing API optimization of components used to write code that processes images

---

[10] A detailed description of all JDK 9 features can be found here: https://docs.oracle.com/javase/9/whatsnew/toc.htm#JSNEW-GUID-983469B6-9BB5-48CA-B71D-8D7012B2F3CA

Java 9 followed the same versioning scheme as Java 8, with a small change. The Java version number contained in the name of the JDK finally became the $MAJOR number in the version scheme. So, if you have Java 9 installed, when executing `java -version` in a terminal, you see something similar to the following log.

```
$ java  -version
java version "9.0.4"
JavaTM SE Runtime Environment build 9.0.4+11
Java HotSpotTM 64-Bit Server VM build 9.0.4+11, mixed mode
```

Java SE 10 (AKA Java 18.3) was released on March 20, 2018. Oracle changed the Java release style, so a new version is released every six months. Also, Java 10 uses the new versioning convention set up by Oracle: the version numbers follow a $YEAR.$MONTH format.[11] Apparently, this release versioning style is supposed to make it easier for developers or end users to figure out the age of a release so that they can judge whether to upgrade it to a newer release with the latest security fixes and additional features.

The following are a few features of Java 10.[12]

- A local-variable type inference to enhance the language to extend type inference to local variables (this is the most expected feature and is covered in **Chapter** 5)

- More optimizations for garbage collection (covered in **Chapter** 13)

- Application Class-Data Sharing to reduce the footprint by sharing common class metadata across processes (this is an advanced feature that won't be covered in the book)

- More concurrency updates (related to parallel execution, mentioned in **Chapter** 5)

- Heap allocation on alternative memory devices (The memory needed by JVM to run a Java program—called *heap memory*—can be allocated on an alternative memory device, so the heap can also be split between volatile and non-volatile RAM. More about memory used by Java applications can be read in **Chapter** 5.)

---

[11]Java Enhancement Proposal 322: http://openjdk.java.net/jeps/322
[12]The complete list can be found at http://openjdk.java.net/projects/jdk/10/ and the release notes containing the detailed list with API and internal changes can be found at http://www.oracle.com/technetwork/java/javase/10-relnote-issues-4108729.html10-relnote-issues-4108729.html

And since we've done this before, let's see what running `java -version` in a terminal shows for this Java version.

```
$ java -version
java version "10" 2018-03-20
JavaTM SE Runtime Environment 18.3 build 10+46
Java HotSpotTM 64-Bit Server VM 18.3 build 10+46, mixed mode
```

Java SE 11 (AKA Java 18.9)[13] (released on 25 September 2018) contains the following features:

- Removal of JEE advanced components used to build enterprise Java applications and Corba (really old technology for remote invocation, allowing your application to communicate with applications installed on a different computer) modules

- Local-variable syntax for lambda parameters allow the `var` keyword to be used when declaring the formal parameters of implicitly typed lambda expressions

- Epsilon, a low-overhead garbage collector (is a no-GC, so basically you can run an application without a GC), basically more optimizations to the garbage collection (covered in **Chapter** 13)

- More concurrency updates (related to parallel execution, mentioned in **Chapter** 5)

Aside from these changes, it was also speculated that a new versioning change should be introduced because the `$YEAR.$MONTH` format did not go so well with developers. (Why so many versioning naming changes, right? Is this really so important? Apparently, it is.) The proposed versioning change is similar to the one introduced in Java 9, and if you are curious, you can read a detailed specification for it at `http://openjdk.java.net/jeps/322`.

When this chapter was written, JDK 11 was available only via the early access program, which is why the "ea" string is present in the version name; it means *early access*. It is quite difficult to use it, as it is not supported by any editors or other build tools yet. By the time this book is released, Java 11 will be stable and ready to use and the sources for the book are updated accordingly on the GitHub repository.

---

[13]Details are at `http://openjdk.java.net/projects/jdk/11/`

```
$ java -version
java version "11-ea" 2018-09-18
JavaTM SE Runtime Environment 18.9 build 11-ea+2
Java HotSpotTM 64-Bit Server VM 18.9 build 11-ea+2, mixed mode
```

And this is where the details end. If you want more information on the first 20 years of Java's life, you can find it on Oracle's website.[14]

What the Future Holds

Java has dominated the industry for more than 20 years. It wasn't always at the top of the most-used development technologies, but it never left the top five since its existence. Even with server-side JavaScript smart frameworks, like Node.js, the heavy-lifting is still left to Java. Emerging programming languages like Scala and Kotlin run on the JVM, so maybe the Java programming language will suffer a serious metamorphosis in order to compete, but it will still be here.

The modularization possibility introduced in version 9 opens the gates for Java applications to be installed on smaller devices, because to run a Java application, we no longer need the whole runtime—only its core plus the modules the application was built with.

Also, there are a lot of applications written in Java, especially in the financial domain, so Java will still be here, because of legacy reasons and because migrating these titan applications to another technology is an impossible mission.

Java will probably survive and be on top for the next 10 to 15 years. It does help that it is a very mature technology with a huge community built around it. And the fact that is easy to learn and developer-friendly makes it remain the first choice for most companies. So, you might conclude at this point that learning Java and buying this book is a good investment.

Prerequisites

Before ending this chapter, it is only fair to tell you that to learn Java, you need to know or have a few things....

- Your way around an operating system, such as Windows, Linux or macOS

---

[14]The first 20 years of Java's life: http://oracle.com.edgesuite.net/timeline/java/

- How to refine your search criteria, because information related to your operating systems is not covered in the book; if you have issues, you must fix them yourself
- An Internet connection

If you already know Java, and you just bought this book out of curiosity or for the modules chapter, knowing about a build tool like Maven or Gradle is helpful, because the source code is organized in a multimodule project that can be fully built with one simple command. I've chosen to use a build tool because in this day and age, learning Java without one makes no sense; any company you apply to most definitely uses one.

Aside from the prerequisites that I listed, nothing else is needed. You do not need to know math, algorithms, or design patterns. Actually, you might end up knowing a few after you read this book.

This being said, let's dig in.

CHAPTER 2

Preparing Your Development Environment

To start learning Java, you need a few things installed on your computer. The following are the requirements:

- **Java** support on your computer (kinda' mandatory).

- An integrated development environment, also known as **IDE**, which is basically an application in which you write your code and that you use to compile and execute it.

    - The recommended IDE for this book is IntelliJ IDEA. You can go to their website to get the free community edition; for the purposes of the book, it will do.

    - Or, you can choose the most popular free IDE for Java development: Eclipse.

    - Or, you can try NetBeans,[1] which is the default choice for most beginners because it was bundled with the JDK until version 8.[2,3]

---

[1] Get it from here https://netbeans.org/
[2] See: http://www.oracle.com/technetwork/java/javase/downloads/jdk-netbeans-jsp-142931.html
[3] For Eclipse and NetbeansNetBeans, you will need to install a plugin for Gradle support.

- **Gradle** is a build tool used to organize projects, to easily handle dependencies, and make your work easier as your projects get bigger. (It is mandatory because the projects in this book are organized and built on a Gradle setup.)

- **Git** is a versioning system that you can use to get the sources for the book, and you can experiment with it and create your own version. It is optional because GitHub, which is where the sources for this chapter are hosted, supports direct download.[4]

To write and execute Java programs/applications, you only need the Java Development Kit installed. All other tools that I've listed here are only needed to make your job easier and to familiarize you with a real development job.

! You probably need administrative rights if you install these applications for all users. For Windows 10, you might even need a special application to give your user administrative rights so you can install the necessary tools. This book provides instructions on how to install everything—assuming your user has the necessary rights. If you need more information, the Internet is there to help.

If it seems like a lot, do not get discouraged; this chapter contains instructions on how to install and verify that each of tool is working accordingly. Let's start by making sure your computer supports Java.

Installing Java

Here you are with your computer and you can't wait to start writing Java applications. But first, you need to get yourself a JDK and install it. For this, you need an Internet connection to open `https://developer.oracle.com/java`.

---

[4]Also, I don't think there is a company that does not use a versioning system these days, so getting comfortable with Git could be a serious advantage when applying for a software developer position.

CHAPTER 2 PREPARING YOUR DEVELOPMENT ENVIRONMENT

Scroll down until you see the **Downloads** section. Click the Java SE link. The two links and their contents are depicted in Figure 2-1.

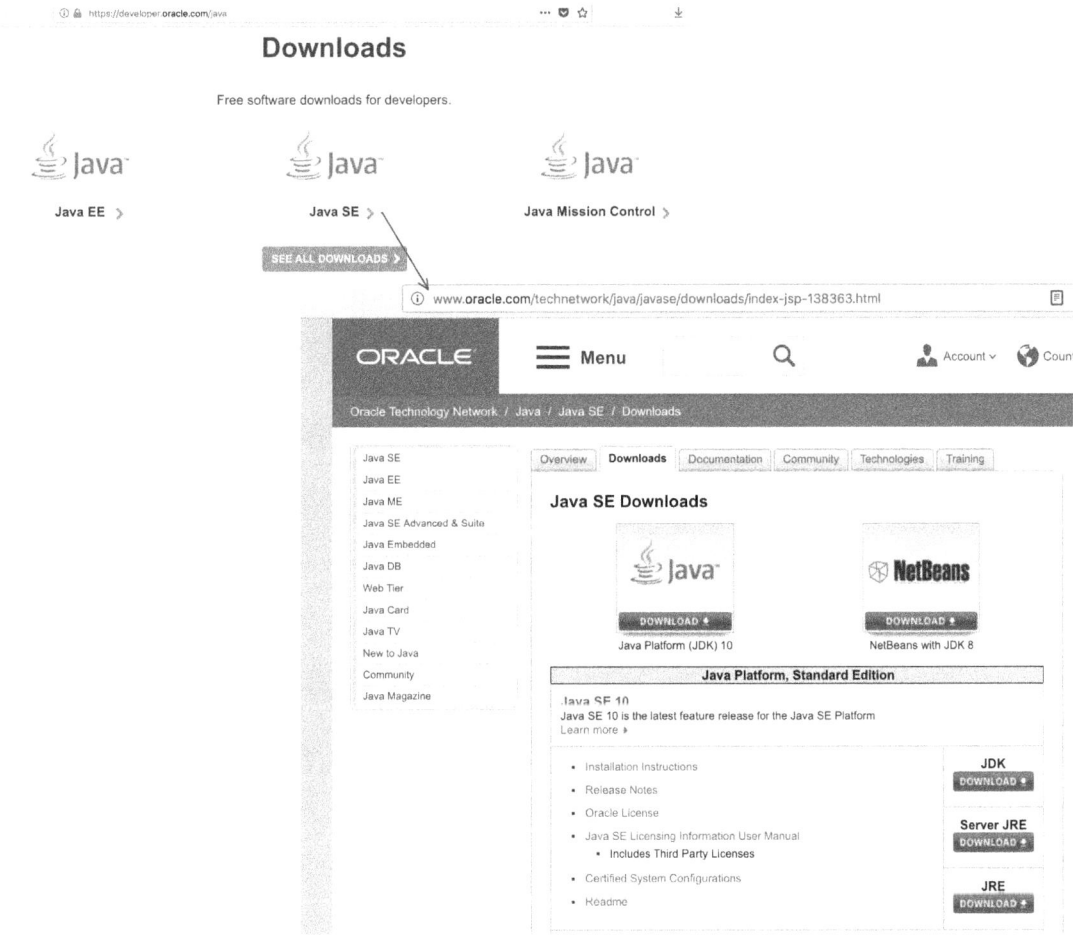

Figure 2-1. *Navigating the Oracle site to find the desired product, JDK in this case*

CHAPTER 2   PREPARING YOUR DEVELOPMENT ENVIRONMENT

On the Oracle site, you find the latest stable Java version. Click the **Download JDK** button. You should be redirected to the page depicted in Figure 2-2.

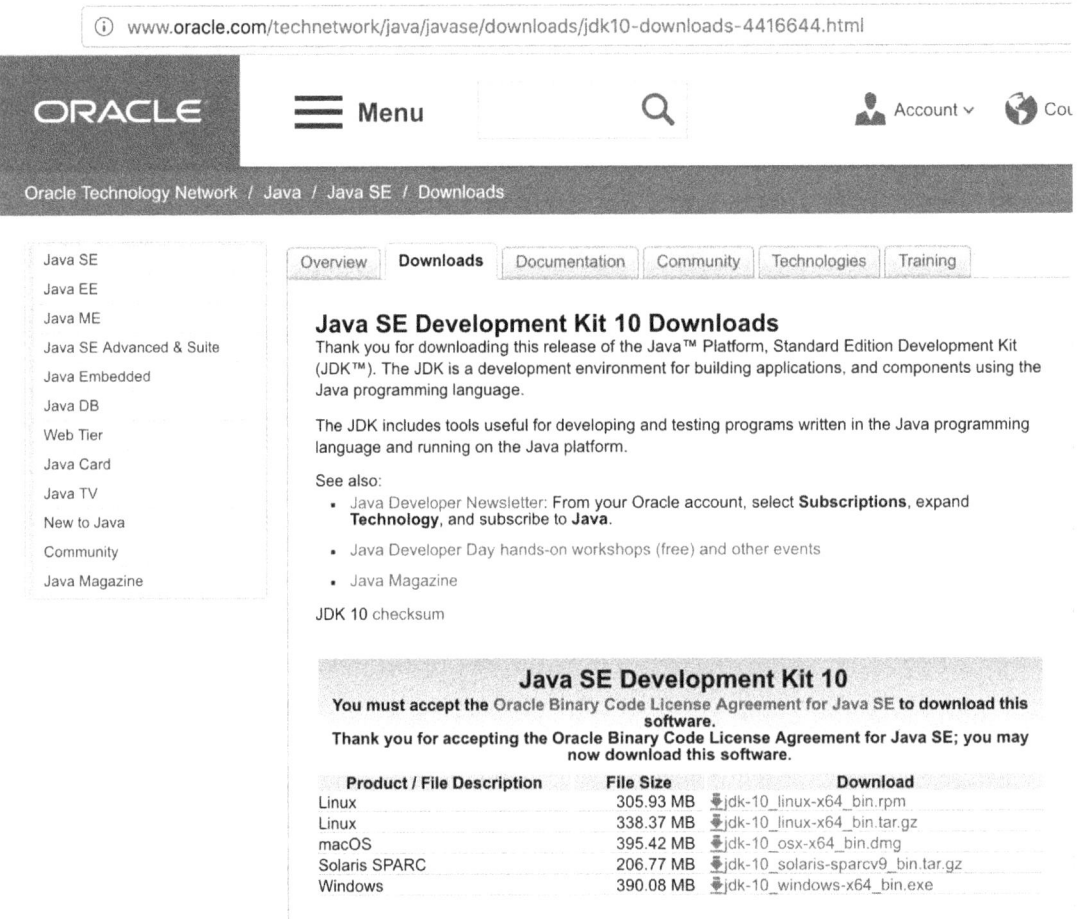

Figure 2-2. *The Oracle page where you can download the desired JDK*

As you can see, JDK is available for a few operating systems. You should download the one matching yours. For writing this book and the source code, I used a macOS computer, which means I download the JDK with the .dmg extension.

You need to accept the license agreement before being allowed to download the desired JDK. You can read it if you are curious, but basically, it tells you that you are allowed to use Java as long as you do not modify its original components. It also tells you that you are responsible for how you use it, so if you use it to write or execute dangerous applications, you are legally responsible.

If you want to get your hands on an early version of JDK that is not officially released yet, go to http://openjdk.java.net/projects/jdk/. Under **Releases**, versions 10 and 11, an early access (unstable) JDK 11 is available for download.

! This book covers Java specifics until Java 11, but that version was eight months away when this chapter was written, so some images and details might seem deprecated. Keep in mind that there are common details that remain the same from one version to the next, and those won't be reviewed and changed, as the only thing that is different is the version number. Since this book was planned to be released after Java 11 was released, it is recommended to download that version of the JDK to have full compatibility of the sources.

After you download the JDK, the next step is to install it. Just double-click it and click **Next** until finished. This works for Windows and macOS. The JDK is installed in a specific location.

In Windows, it is C:\ProgramFiles\Java\jdk-10.

In macOS, it is /Library/Java/JavaVirtualMachines/jdk-10.jdk/Contents/Home.

On Linux systems, depending on the distribution, the JDK install location varies. My preferred way is to get the *.tar.gz from the Oracle site that contains the full content of the JDK, unpack it, and copy it to a specific location. Also, my preferred location on Linux is /home/iuliana.cosmina/tools/jdk-10.jdk.

! Using a PPA (repository)[5] installer on Linux puts the JDK files where they are supposed to go on Linux automatically and updates them automatically when a new version is released using the Linux (Global) updater utility. But if you are using Linux proficiently, you've probably figured this out.

If you go to that location, you can inspect the contents of the JDK. In Figure 2-3, the contents of JDK 10 are on the left; the contents of the JDK 8 are on the right.

---

[5]Also known as a Package Manager

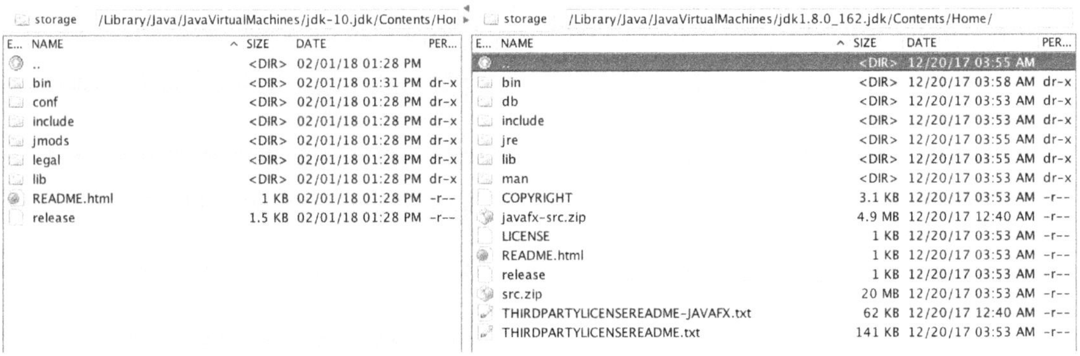

CHAPTER 2   PREPARING YOUR DEVELOPMENT ENVIRONMENT

Figure 2-3. JDK version 8 and ten contents comparison

I chose to make this comparison because, starting with Java 9, the content of the JDK is organized differently. Until Java 8, the JDK contained a directory called `jre` that contained a Java Runtime Environment (JRE) used by the JDK. The `lib` directory contains Java libraries and support files needed by development tools.

The `bin` contains a set of Java executables for running Java applications.

Starting in Java 9, the JRE was no longer isolated in its own directory. In the Figure 2-4, you see the contents of the JDK 10 on the left, and the contents of the JRE 10 on the right.[6]

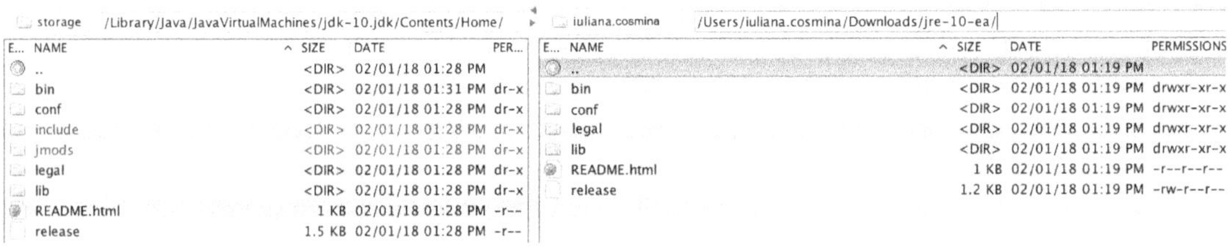

Figure 2-4. JDK 10 and JRE contents compared

---

[6]JDK and JRE 10 have the same directory structure introduced in version 9.

The directory structure depicted was introduced when Java 9 was released. You can read more about it on the official Oracle site.[7]

The most important thing you need to know about the JDK is that the `bin` directory contains executables and command-line launchers that are defined by the modules linked to the image, thus the JDK has a few of those extra compared to the JRE. The other directories are the `jmods` directory, which contains the compiled module definitions, and the `include` directory, which contains the C-language header files that support native-code programming with the Java Native Interface (JNI) and the Java Virtual Machine (JVM) Debug Interface.

The JAVA_HOME Environment Variable

The most important directory in the JDK is the `bin` directory, because that directory has to be added to the path of your system so you can call the Java executables from anywhere. This allows other applications to call them as well, without extra configurations steps needed. Most IDEs used for handling[8] Java code are written in Java, and they require knowing where the JDK is installed so that they can be run. This is done by declaring an environment variable named JAVA_HOME that points to the location of the JDK directory. To make the Java executables callable from any location within a system, you must add the `bin` directory to the system path. The next three sections explain how to do this on the three most common operating systems.

---

[7]The new directory structure introduced with Java 9 is explained in detail at https://docs.oracle.com/javase/9/install/installed-directory-structure-jdk-and-jre.htm#JSJIG-GUID-F7178F2F-DC92-47E9-8062-CA6B2612D350

[8]Includes operations like writing the code, analyzing the code, compiling it, and executing it.

CHAPTER 2 PREPARING YOUR DEVELOPMENT ENVIRONMENT

JAVA_HOME on Windows

To declare the JAVA_HOME environment variable on a Windows system, you need to open the dialog window for setting up system variables. On Windows systems, click the Start button; in the menu, there is a search box (or right-click the Start button for a context-menu and select Search). Enter the word **environment** in there (the first three letters should suffice) and the option should become available for clicking. These steps are depicted in Figure 2-5.

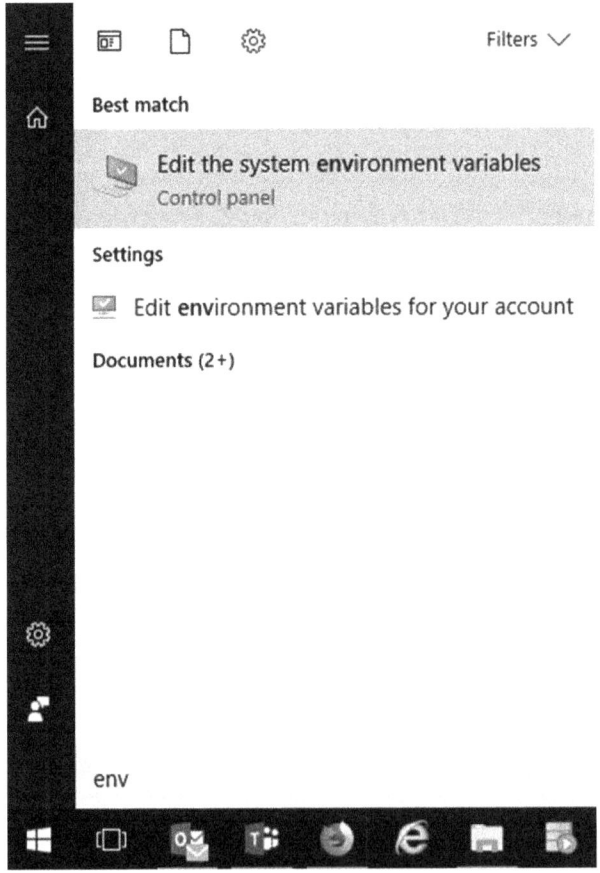

Figure 2-5. *Windows menu item to configure environment variables*

CHAPTER 2 PREPARING YOUR DEVELOPMENT ENVIRONMENT

After clicking that menu item, a window like the one shown in Figure 2-6 should open.

Figure 2-6. *First dialog window to set environment variables on Windows*

Click the **Environment Variables** button. Another dialog window opens, which is split into two sections: user variables and system variables. You are interested in **system variables** because that is where we declare JAVA_HOME. Just click the **New...** button and a small dialog window appears with two text fields; one requires you to enter the variable name–JAVA_HOME in this case, and one requires you to enter the path—to the JDK in this case. The second window and the variable information pop-up dialog window are depicted in Figure 2-7.

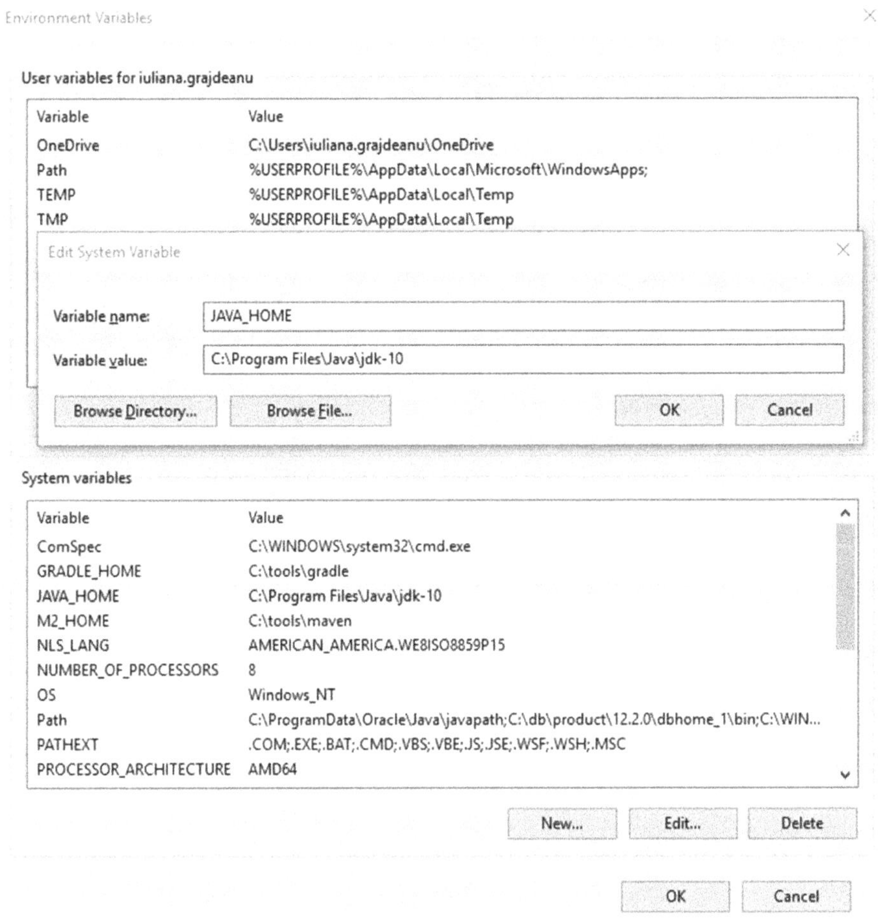

CHAPTER 2 PREPARING YOUR DEVELOPMENT ENVIRONMENT

Figure 2-7. Declaring JAVA_HOME as a system variable on Windows

After defining the JAVA_HOME variable, you need to add the executables to the system path. This can be done by editing the Path variable. Just select it from the **System Variables** list and click the **Edit...** button. Starting in Windows 10, each part of the Path variable is shown on a different line, so you can add a different line and add %JAVA_HOME%\bin on it. This syntax is practical because it takes the location of the bin directory from whatever location the JAVA_HOME variable contains. The dialog window is depicted in Figure 2-8.

CHAPTER 2 PREPARING YOUR DEVELOPMENT ENVIRONMENT

Figure 2-8. *Declaring the JDK executables directory as part of the system Path variable on Windows 10*

On older Windows systems, the contents of the Path variable are depicted in the dialog box shown in Figure 2-7, so you must add the %JAVA_HOME%\bin text in the **Variable value** text field, and separate it from the existing content by using a semicolon (;).

No matter which Windows system you have, you can check that you set everything correctly by opening **Command Prompt** and executing the set command. This lists all the system variables and their values. JAVA_HOME and Path should be there with the desired values. For the setup proposed in this section when executing **set** the output is depicted in Figure 2-9.

33

CHAPTER 2   PREPARING YOUR DEVELOPMENT ENVIRONMENT

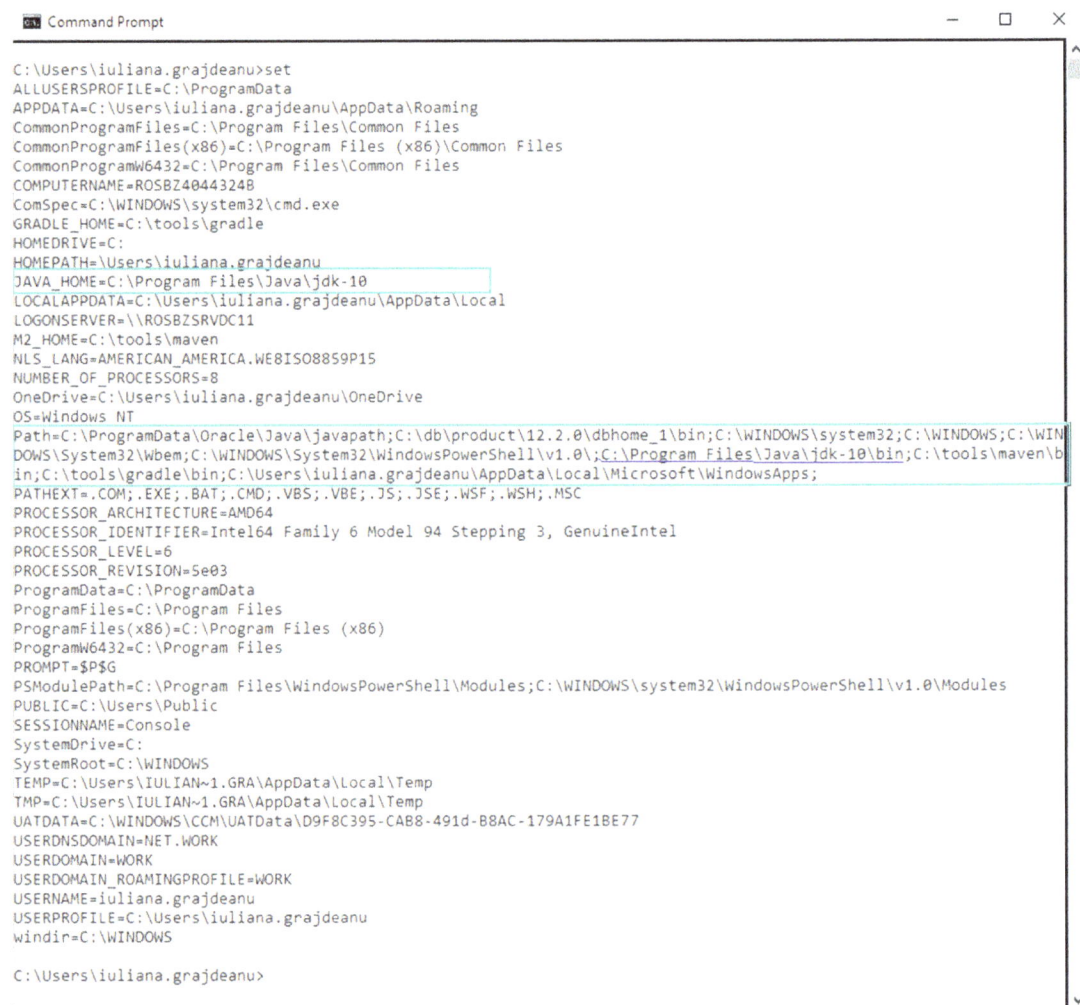

Figure 2-9. *Windows system variables listed with the **set** command*

If you execute the previous command and see the expected output and then execute java -version in the **command prompt**, it prints the expected result. You are all set.

```
...> java -version
java version "10-ea" 2018-03-20
Java(TM) SE Runtime Environment 18.3 (build 10-ea+42)
Java HotSpot(TM) 64-Bit Server VM 18.3 (build 10-ea+42, mixed mode)
```

JAVA_HOME on macOS

The location in which JDK is installed is `/Library/Java/JavaVirtualMachines/jdk-10.jdk/Contents/Home`. Your `JAVA_HOME` should point to this location. To do this for the current user, you can do the following:

1. In the `/Users/your.user` directory, create a file named `.bash_profile`.

2. In this file, write the following:

   `export JAVA_HOME=$(/usr/libexec/java_home -v10)`

   `export PATH=$JAVA_HOME/bin:$PATH`

On macOS, you can simultaneously install multiple Java versions. You can set which version is the one currently used on the system by obtaining the JDK location for the desired version by calling the `/usr/libexec/java_home` command and giving the Java version you are interested in as the argument. The result of executing the command is stored as a value for the JAVA_HOME variable.

On my system, I have JDK 8, 9, 10, and 11 installed. If I execute the command, giving an argument to each of the Java versions, look at what happens:

```
$ /usr/libexec/java_home -v11
/Library/Java/JavaVirtualMachines/jdk-11.jdk/Contents/Home

$ /usr/libexec/java_home -v10
/Library/Java/JavaVirtualMachines/jdk-10.jdk/Contents/Home

$ /usr/libexec/java_home -v9
/Library/Java/JavaVirtualMachines/jdk-9.0.4.jdk/Contents/Home

$ /usr/libexec/java_home -v1.8
/Library/Java/JavaVirtualMachines/jdk1.8.0_162.jdk/Contents/Home
```

Depending of the version given as argument, a different JDK location is returned. If you want to test the value of the JAVA_HOME, the echo command can help with that.

```
$ echo $JAVA_HOME
/Library/Java/JavaVirtualMachines/jdk-10.jdk/Contents/Home
```

The line export PATH=$JAVA_HOME/bin:$PATH adds the contents of the bin directory from the JDK location to the system patch. This means that I could open a terminal and execute any of the Java executables under it. For example, I could verify that the Java version set as default for my user is the expected one by executing java -version.

```
$ java -version
java version "10-ea" 2018-03-20
Java(TM) SE Runtime Environment 18.3 (build 10-ea+42)
Java HotSpot(TM) 64-Bit Server VM 18.3 (build 10-ea+42, mixed mode)
```

If you do all of this and java -version prints the expected result, you are all set.

JAVA_HOME on Linux

! If you are using Linux proficiently, you probably are using a PPA, so you can skip this section. But if you like to control where the JDK is and define your own environment variables, keep reading.

Linux systems are Unix-like operating systems. This is similar to macOS, which is based on Unix. Depending on your Linux distribution, installing Java can be done via the specific package manager or by directly downloading the JDK as a *.tar.gz archive from the official Oracle site.

If Java is installed using a package manager, the necessary executables are usually automatically placed in the system path at installation time. That is why in this book, we cover only the cases where you do everything manually, and choose to install Java only for the current user in a location such as /home/your.user/tools/jdk-10.jdk,[9] because covering package managers is not the object of the book after all.[10]

---

[9] Replaces your.user with your actual system username

[10] Linux users do not really need this section anyway.'☺

So, after downloading the JDK archive from the Oracle site and unpacking it at /home/your.user/tools/jdk-10.jdk, you need to create a file named either .bashrc or .bash_profile[11] in your user home directory and add the following to it.

export JAVA_HOME=/home/your.user/tools/jdk-10.jdk

export PATH=$JAVA_HOME/bin:$PATH

As you can see, the syntax is similar to macOS. To check the location of the JDK and the Java version, same commands mentioned in the macOS section can be used.

Installing Gradle

Gradle 5.x ** The sources attached to this book can be compiled and executed using the Gradle wrapper, which is a batch script on Windows and a shell script for other operating systems. When you start a Gradle build via the wrapper, Gradle automatically downloads and runs the build; thus you do not to really need to install Gradle. Instructions on how to do this can be found by reading the public documentation at www.gradle.org/docs/current/userguide/gradle_wrapper.html.

A good practice is to keep code and build tools separate, and for the project attached to this book this is the recommended way to go.

If you decide to use Gradle outside the editor, you can download the binaries only (or if you are curious, you can download the full package, which contains binaries, sources, and documentation) from the official site (www.gradle.org), unpack them, and copy the contents somewhere on the hard drive. Create a GRADLE_HOME environment variable and point it to the location where you have unpacked Gradle. Also, add %GRADLE_HOME%\bin for Windows, or $GRADLE_HOME/bin for Unix-based operating systems, to the general path of the system.

Gradle was chosen as a build tool for the sources of this book because of the easy setup, small configuration files, flexibility in defining execution tasks, and because it is practical to learn a build tool—because for medium-sized and large projects, they are a must-have.

---

[11]On some Linux distributions, the file might already exist, you just need to edit it.

! Verify that the version of Gradle the operating system sees is the one you just installed by opening a terminal (**Command Prompt** in Windows, and any type of terminal you have installed on macOS and Linux) and entering

```
gradle -version
```

You should see something similar to this:

```
------------------------------------------------------------
Gradle 5.0-20180826235923+0000
------------------------------------------------------------

Build time:   2018-08-26 23:59:23 UTC
Revision:     c2edb259761ee18f9a14e271f24ef58530b1300f

Kotlin DSL:   1.0-rc-3
Kotlin:       1.2.60
Groovy:       2.4.15
Ant:          Apache Ant (TM) version 1.9.11 compiled on March 23 2018
JVM:          10 (Oracle Corporation 10+46)
OS:           -- whatever operating system you have --
```

The preceding text is confirmation that Gradle commands can be executed in your terminal; thus, Gradle was installed successfully.

Installing Git

This is an optional section, but as a developer, being familiar with a versioning system is important, so here it is. To install Git on your system, just go to the official page at https://git-scm.com/downloads and download the installer. Open the installer and click **Next** until done. This works for Windows and macOS.[12] Yes, it is this easy. You do not need to do anything else.[13] For Linux, you can use your package manager or PPA to install Git.

---

[12]For macOS, you can use homebrew as well.

[13]Just in case, here is a page with instructions on how to install Git for all operating systems: https://gist.github.com/derhuerst/1b15ff4652a867391f03

To test that Git installed successfully on your system, open a terminal (**Command Prompt** in Windows, and any type of terminal you have installed on macOS and Linux) and run `git --version` to see the result that it is printed. It should be the version of Git that you just installed.

```
$ git -version
git version 2.15.1
```

Now that you have Git installed, you can get the sources for this book by cloning the official Git repository in a terminal or directly from the IDE. But more about this a little bit later.

Installing a Java IDE

The editor that I recommend, based on my experience of more than ten years, is IntelliJ IDEA. It is produced by a company called JetBrains. You can download this IDE from their official site at `www.jetbrains.com`. There is an Ultimate Edition available that you can use for free for 30 days; after that, you need to acquire a license. That is why I recommend you download and use the Community Edition,[14] because for the simple development involved in learning Java, this version suffices.

After you download the IntelliJ IDEA archive, double-click it to install it. After that, start it to do a couple of configurations. Just click the **Next** button until you get to the plugin selection step, which should be very similar to the one depicted in Figure 2-10.

---

[14]The IntelliJ IDEA download page is at `https://www.jetbrains.com/idea/download/`

CHAPTER 2 PREPARING YOUR DEVELOPMENT ENVIRONMENT

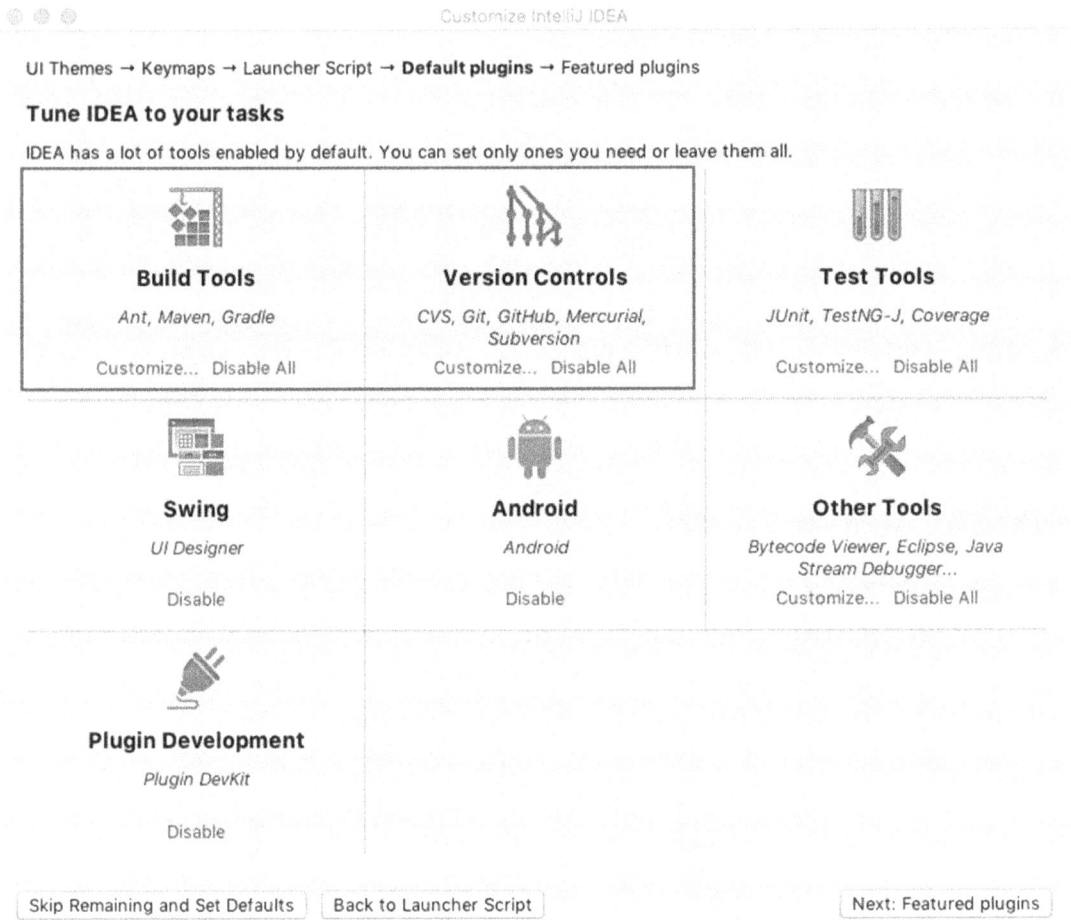

Figure 2-10. IntelliJ IDEA Community Edition configure plugins dialog section

In the previous image, two sections were underlined. The first section configures build tools. If you click **Customize…** button, the window should change to show you the plugins that are available for build tools. Make sure that the option for Gradle is checked, as depicted in Figure 2-11, then click the **Save Changes and Go Back** button.

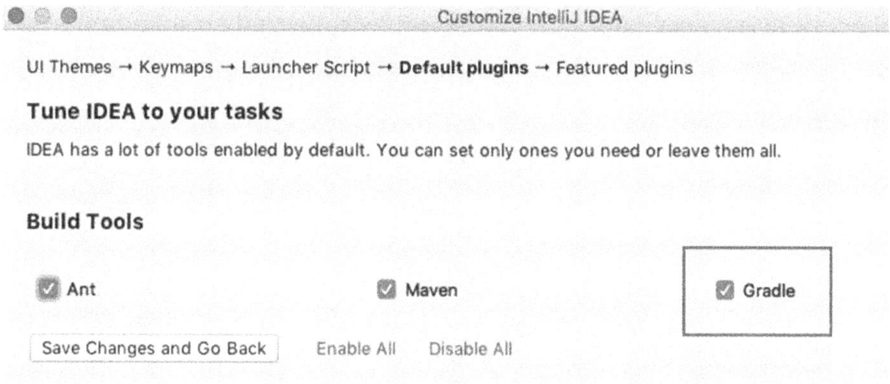

CHAPTER 2   PREPARING YOUR DEVELOPMENT ENVIRONMENT

Figure 2-11.   IntelliJ IDEA Community Edition configure Gradle plugin

The second section configures support for versioning control systems. If you click the **Customize...** button, the window should show you which plugins are available for versioning systems. Make sure that the options for Git and GitHub are checked, as depicted in Figure 2-12, and then click the **Save Changes and Go Back** button. If you go another step forward, you get to another plugin screen that offers you the possibility to install a plugin called **IDE Feature Trainer**. I think if you are a beginner, a plugin might be very useful. The window is depicted in Figure 2-13

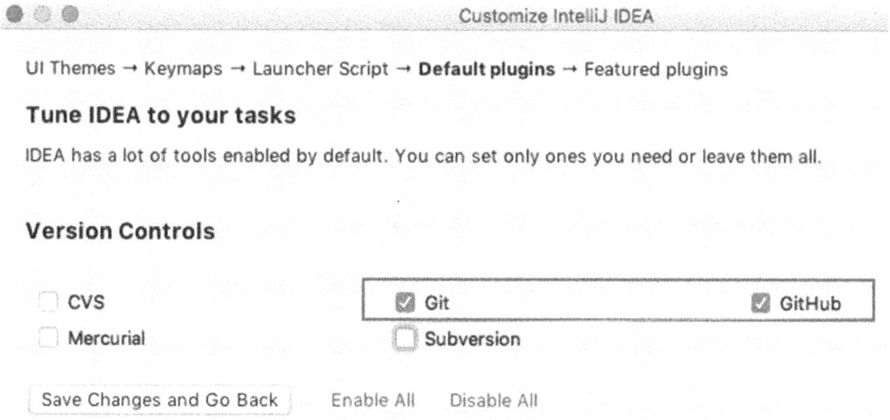

Figure 2-12.   IntelliJ IDEA Community Edition configure Git plugin

For the final step, click the **Install** button, and then **Start using IntelliJ IDEA**, and you are all set up and good to go. Your development environment is fully configured and ready for you to write your first Java program.

CHAPTER 2   PREPARING YOUR DEVELOPMENT ENVIRONMENT

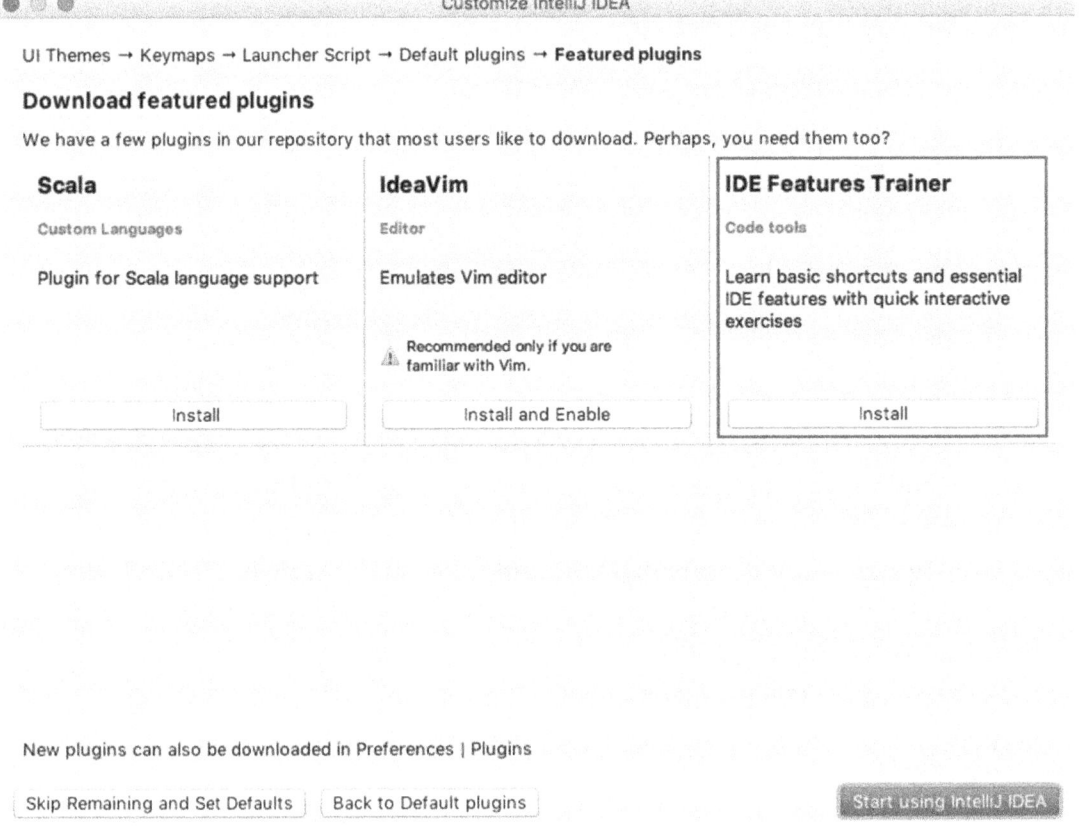

Figure 2-13. IntelliJ IDEA Community Edition configure IDE Feature Trainer plugin

But before doing that, let's also cover how to retrieve the sources for the book. There are three ways to get the sources for the book:

- Download the zipped package directly from GitHub.

- Clone the repository using a terminal (or Git Bash Shell in Windows) using the following command:

  ```
  git clone git@github.com:Apress/java-for-absolute-beginners.git
  ```

- Clone the project using IntelliJ IDEA. For this and cloning from the command line, you need a GitHub user. The following images show all the dialog windows that you see when cloning the project with IntelliJ IDEA. Figure 2-14 shows the window that you see after

CHAPTER 2 PREPARING YOUR DEVELOPMENT ENVIRONMENT

you start an IntelliJ IDEA instance that was never used. The project is hosted on GitHub, so from the **Check out from Version Control** menu, select **GitHub**. At this point, you to the next dialog window, depicted in Figure 2-15.

Figure 2-14. *IntelliJ IDEA first dialog window to clone the java-for-absolute-beginners project*

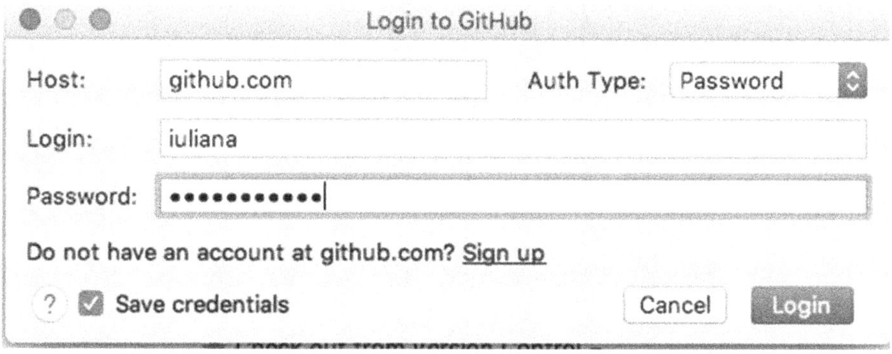

Figure 2-15. *IntelliJ IDEA second dialog window to clone the java-for-absolute-beginners project*

CHAPTER 2 PREPARING YOUR DEVELOPMENT ENVIRONMENT

This requires you to insert your GitHub username and password (Auth Type: **Password**). If you do not have a GitHub username, go to https://github.com to create one. After clicking the **Login** button, the window depicted in Figure 2-16 is shown.

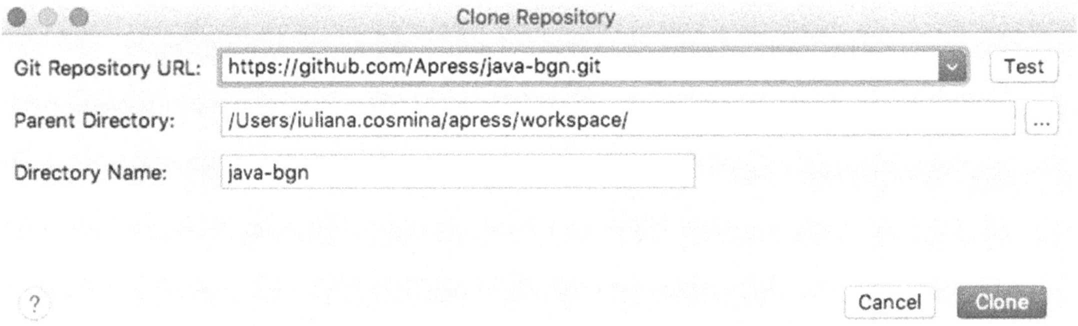

Figure 2-16. IntelliJ IDEA third dialog window to clone the java-for-absolute-beginners project

Click the **Clone** button and move on to the window depicted in Figure 2-17.

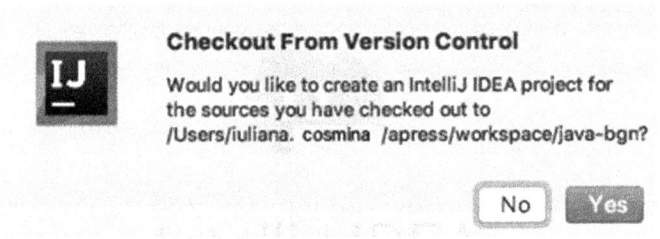

Figure 2-17. IntelliJ IDEA fourth dialog window to clone the java-for-absolute-beginners project

Click **Yes** because you definitely need an IntelliJ IDEA project for the sources. In Figure 2-18, IntelliJ IDEA has identified that the project might be configured with Gradle and recommends to **Import project from External model** and select Gradle. Do so and click **Next**.

CHAPTER 2 PREPARING YOUR DEVELOPMENT ENVIRONMENT

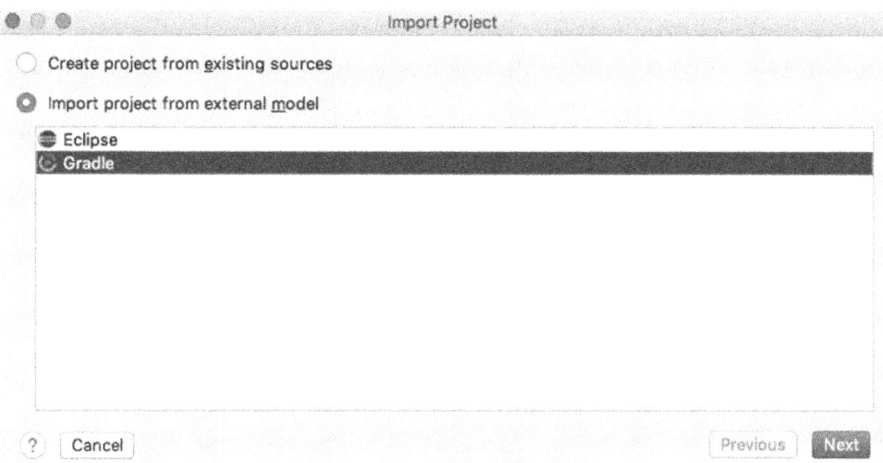

Figure 2-18. *IntelliJ IDEA fifth dialog window to clone the java-for-absolute-beginners project*

The window depicted in Figure 2-19 is the last image before having a full-blown local Gradle project. If you configured JAVA and Gradle properly, IntelliJ IDEA finds and selects them automatically for you.

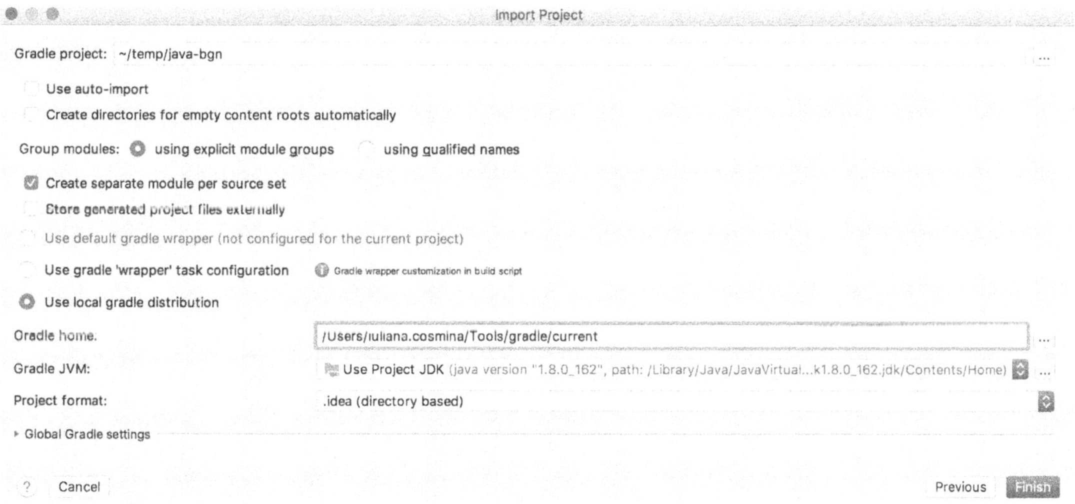

Figure 2-19. *IntelliJ IDEA last window to clone the java-for-absolute-beginners project*

CHAPTER 2   PREPARING YOUR DEVELOPMENT ENVIRONMENT

And this is it. Starting in the next chapter, some code snippets are presented; so go ahead and build the project. You can do this by executing the build task from Gradle project view. Figure 2-20 shows the IntelliJ IDEA editor with the project loaded and the Gradle view opened.

Figure 2-20. IntelliJ IDEA Gradle project view with Tasks node expanded

Summary

If any of instructions are unclear to you (or I missed something), do not hesitate to use the World Wide Web to search for answers. All the software technologies introduced in this chapter are backed up by documented and comprehensive official websites and by huge communities of developers eager to help. And in the worst-case scenario, you can always create an issue on the Apress GitHub official repository for this book, or drop me an email. I'll do my best to support you if need be.

But I think you will be fine. Java is hardly rocket-science.[15]☺

---

[15] Well, it wasn't until Java 9. But this book should make it easier for beginner developers.

CHAPTER 3

Getting Your Feet Wet

This is the last introductory chapter in the book. After this one, we get to the serious business. The previous chapter left you with a complete development environment configured for writing Java code. It is time to make use of it. The following topics are covered in this chapter:

- Using JShell
- Java fundamental building blocks: packages, modules, and classes
- Creating a Java project with IntelliJ IDEA
- Compiling and executing Java classes
- Packing a Java application into an executable jar
- Using Gradle to automate compiling and test execution

Using JShell

Introduced in Java 9, the Java Shell tool (JShell) is an interactive tool for learning the Java programming language and prototyping Java code. This means that you can write Java code and execute it in the console, without the need to save it to a file, which is later compiled into bytecode and then interpreted by the underlying OS as a sequence of instructions to run to execute it. JShell is quite late to the party, as scripting languages like Python and Node introduced similar utilities years ago, and JVM languages like Scala, Clojure, and Groovy adopted it some time ago. But, better late than never is still acceptable.

JShell is a Read-Eval-Print Loop (REPL), which evaluates declarations, statements, and expressions as they are entered, and then it immediately shows the results. It is practical to try new ideas and techniques quickly and without the need to have a complete development environment or an entire context for the code to be executed in.

© Iuliana Cosmina 2018
I. Cosmina, *Java for Absolute Beginners*, https://doi.org/10.1007/978-1-4842-3778-6_3

CHAPTER 3   GETTING YOUR FEET WET

JShell is a standard component of the JDK and the executable to start it, is in the bin directory located in the JDK installation directory. This means that all you have to do is open a terminal (Command Prompt in Windows, and any type of terminal you have installed on macOS and Linux) and type **jshell**. You should see something like this:[1]

```
$ jshell
  |  Welcome to JShell -- Version 10
  |  For an introduction type: /help intro
```

Go ahead and enter /**help** to view a list of all the available actions and commands.

```
jshell> /help
|  Type a Java language expression, statement, or declaration.
|  Or type one of the following commands:
|  /list <name or id>|-all|-start
|          list the source you have typed
|  /edit <name or id>
|          edit a source entry
|  /drop <name or id>
|          delete a source entry
...
|  /exit <integer-expression-snippet>
|          exit the jshell tool
...
```

To see exactly what JShell is doing, we can start it in verbose mode by adding -v as an argument when starting it. Let's play with a few numbers and see what happens. First, let's start the JShell in a verbose mode, so we'll have a report log of everything that JShell does when we insert statements. In your terminal, of enter **java -v**.

```
$ jshell -v
|  Welcome to JShell -- Version 10-ea
|  For an introduction type: /help intro
```

---

[1]Since this book covers Java notions up to Java 11, you can install JDK 11 and work with it, if it has been released by the time you get this book. While writing the book, I installed a new JDK as soon as it was available, but tried to keep the version 10 as a constant version throughout the book, as to avoid confusion.

50

In Java, values are assigned to sequences of characters named **variables**. (More about how to name them and use them in **Chapter** 4.) Next, let's create a variable of type integer (int in Java) and give it the value of 42. To do this, enter **int i=42**.

```
jshell> int i = 42
i ==> 42
|  created variable i : int
```

As you can see, the log message is clear and tells us that our command was executed successfully and the variable of type int was created. The line i ==> 42 lets us know that value 42 was assigned to the variable that we just created.

Let's declare another one named j. In the code snippet, below 35 is the value that we assign to it. But you can try different numbers if you want to.

```
jshell> int j = 35
j ==> 35
|  created variable j : int
```

As long as the JShell session is not closed, the two previous variables still exist, because we can further use them. Let's add them together. The + operator sums two integer variables in Java, just like in plain mathematics. Enter **i + j**.

```
jshell> i + j
$3 ==> 77
|  created scratch variable $3 : int
```

As you can see, we added two variables but we did not store the result in a third, thus JShell creates a **scratch variable** to store the result and print it in the log; but that variable cannot be used in later statements, because it does not have a name.

All seems fine: variables are created and operations are executed correctly. Anything that could be written in Java can be written in the JShell and executed.

! The building blocks of Java are named **classes**, which are pieces of code that model real-world objects and events. Classes contain two types of **members**: those modelling to states, which are the class variables, also named **fields** or **properties,** and those modelling behavior, named **methods**. JDK provides a lot of classes that model the base components needed to create most applications. Classes are covered in more detail in the next chapter and you create a lot of them while reading this book. Even if this terms and concepts seem foreign now, just be patient, and let them add up; they will make more sense later.

In JShell, JDK classes can be used like `java.lang.String` (programming components that you learn more about in **Chapter** 4), which is the Java class that represents text objects. And their methods can be called. Let's declare our first String variable.

```
jshell> String text = "this is a text";
text ==> "this is a text"
|  created variable text : String
```

We've just declared a variable of type String named text with the value of "this is a text". The String class has many methods you can call to modify a text, let's call one with an obvious effect. Type text.toUpperCase().

```
jshell> text.toUpperCase()
$6 ==> "THIS IS A TEXT"
|  created scratch variable $6 : String
```

The last statement is called a String method, which uppercases the variable contents. But let's see what happens when we introduce something that does not match the Java syntax. Let's call a method that does not exist for type String.

```
jshell> text.toAnotherUniverse()
|  Error:
|  cannot find symbol
|    symbol:   method toAnotherUniverse()
|  text.toAnotherUniverse()
|  ^--------------------^
```

CHAPTER 3   GETTING YOUR FEET WET

JShell is quite clear in telling us that the `toAnotherUniverse()` is unknown to it. Let's throw plain text in there. In the following, I tried `"what is this?"`.

```
jshell> what is this?
|  Error:
|  ';' expected
|  what is this?
|           ^
```

In the first statement, we tried calling a method that is not defined for the `String` class, and the error message was pretty relevant in regards to what we did wrong.

We can even create our own methods.

```
jshell> String createHello(String s){
   ...> return "Hello " + s;
   ...> }
|  created method createHello(String)
jshell> createHello(text)
$8 ==> "Hello this is a text"
|  created scratch variable $8 : String
```

Code completion[2] is also available in JShell. Take the `text` variable that we defined earlier, for example; if we enter **text** then put a "`.`" (dot) after it and then press the Tab key, the list of available methods is listed, as depicted in Figure 3-1. If you type a few letters from the method name, filtering is applied. JShell suggests only the method names that start with that combination of letters. Pretty helpful, right?

---

[2]Also called *code assistance*

CHAPTER 3　GETTING YOUR FEET WET

```
 | Goodbye
[iuliana.grajdeanu@ROSBZM4044324X ~ - $ jshell -v
 | Welcome to JShell -- Version 10-ea
 | For an introduction type: /help intro

jshell> String text="this is a text"
text ==> "this is a text"
 | created variable text : String

jshell> text.
charAt(              chars()              codePointAt(         codePointBefore(     codePointCount(
codePoints()         compareTo(           compareToIgnoreCase( concat(              contains(
contentEquals(       endsWith(            equals(              equalsIgnoreCase(    getBytes(
getChars(            getClass()           hashCode()           indexOf(             intern()
isEmpty()            lastIndexOf(         length()             matches(             notify()
notifyAll()          offsetByCodePoints(  regionMatches(       replace(             replaceAll(
replaceFirst(        split(               startsWith(          subSequence(         substring(
toCharArray()        toLowerCase(         toString()           toUpperCase(         trim()
wait(

jshell> text.to
toCharArray()   toLowerCase(   toString()      toUpperCase(

jshell> text.to
```

Figure 3-1. *JShell lists methods possible to call on a String variable*

If you want to see all variables you have declared in a JShell play session, you can do so by executing the /vars command.

```
jshell> /vars
 |    String text = "this is a text"
 |    List<String> units = []
 |    List<String> list1 = [One]
 |    File f = .
 |    Logger log = null
```

The preceding output corresponds to a sequence of statements executed in a JShell console that looks like this:

```
jshell> String text = "this is a text"
        text ==> "this is a text"
 | created variable text : String
jshell> List<String> units = new ArrayList<>()
        units ==> []
 | created variable units : List<String>
jshell> List<String> list1 = new ArrayList<>()
        list1 ==> []
 | created variable list1 : List<String>
```

```
jshell> list1.add("One");
        $4 ==> true
|  created scratch variable $4 : boolean
jshell> File f = new File(".")
        f ==> .
|  created variable f : File
jshell> import java.util.logging.LogManager;

jshell> import java.util.logging.Logger;

jshell> Logger l = LogManager.getLogManager().getLogger("sample");
l ==> null
|  created variable l : Logger
```

If you want to save all your input from a JShell session, you can do so by executing the /save [filename.java] command. It results in a file containing all Java statements that you have executed with JShell within that session.

```
String text="this is a text";
List<String> units = new ArrayList<>();
List<String> list1 = List.of("One");
File f = new File(".");
import java.util.logging.Logger;
import java.util.logging.LogManager;
Logger log = LogManager.getLogManager().getLogger("sample");
```

Also, assuming the preceding output is a list of Java statements exported by JShell to a file called sample.java, using the command /save sample.java, all of those statements can be executed into a new JShell session using the /open sample.java command. So, all variables will be created and we can use them in the new session.

There is a JShell complete user guide available on the Oracle official site if you are interested in trying every command and every feature it has to offer.[3]

If you have opened your JShell and tried yourself some of the commands listed in this section, you already got your feet wet with a little Java syntax. But there is a reason that there is an entire chapter for that, but until then, it is more helpful to know the building blocks of the Java ecosystem.

---

[3]Oracle JShell user guide: https://docs.oracle.com/javase/9/jshell/toc.htm

CHAPTER 3   GETTING YOUR FEET WET

Java Fundamental Building Blocks

! This is a consistent introduction into Java as a platform, but to write code confidently, you need to have a grasp of what happens *under the hood*, what the building blocks are, and how they are connected to each other. If you want, you can skip the next section altogether, but in the same way some new drivers need a little knowledge of how the engine works before grabbing the driving wheel, some people might feel more confident and in control when programming if they understand *the mechanics* a little. So, I wanted to make sure that anyone reading this book gets a proper start.[4]

To write Java applications, a developer must be familiar with the Java building blocks of the Java ecosystem. The core of this ecosystem is the **class**. There are other object types in Java, but classes are the most important because they represent the templates for the objects making up an application. A class groups **fields** and **methods**. When an object is created, the values of the fields define the state of the object and the methods describe its behavior.

! The Java object is a model of a real-world object. So, if we choose to model a car in Java, we choose to define fields that describe the car: manufacturer, modelName, productionYear, and speed. The methods of our car class describe what the car does; and a car does mainly two things: accelerates and brakes.

All object types are described in files with the `*.java` extension. Object types are organized in **packages**. A package is a logical collection of types, some of them are visible outside the package, and some of them are not, depending on their scope. A package is a hierarchy of directories, with the Java object types on the last level (usually, but now always).

---

[4]If you are worried that you will forget the keywords and meaning for modules, print the cheat sheet at `http://files.zeroturnaround.com/pdf/RebelLabs-Java-9-modules-cheat-sheet.pdf` and keep it handy.

Package names must be unique and their name should follow a certain template. Good practices say that to ensure unicity and meaning, you typically begin the name with your organization's Internet domain name in reverse order, then add various grouping criteria. In this project, package names follow the template depicted here:

com.apress.bgn.ch[*]+

This template begins with the reversed domain name for Apress publisher (www.apress.com), then a term identifying the book is added (bgn is a shortcut for *beginner*) and at last the ch plus the number of the package the source (usually) matches.

Starting with Java 5, each package can contain a file named package-info.java that contains a package declaration, package annotations, package comments, and Javadoc tags. The comments are exported to the Javadoc for that package and you learn how to generate that with Gradle later. The package-info.java must reside under the last directory in the package. So, if we define a com.apress.bgn.ch3 package, the overall structure and contents of the Java project looks like Figure 3-2.[5]

```
chapter03/
├── chapter03.iml
└── src
    └── com
        └── apress
            └── bgn
                └── ch3
                    ├── SimpleReader.java
                    └── package-info.java
```

Figure 3-2. *Java package contents*

The package-info.java contents could be similar to this:

```
/**
 * Contains classes used for reading information from various sources.
 * @since 1.0-SNAPSHOT
 * @author iuliana.cosmina
 * @version 1.0-SNAPSHOT
 */
@Deprecated
package com.apress.bgn.ch3;
```

---

[5]The chapter03.iml is an IntelliJ IDEA project file.

The files with *.java extension containing the object types definitions are compiled into files with *.class that are organized according to the package structure and packaged into one or more **JARs** (**J**ava **Ar**chives).[6] For the previous example, if we were to unpack the JAR resulted after the compilation and linkage, you would see what's shown in Figure 3-3.

```
chapter03-1.0-SNAPSHOT
├── META-INF
│   └── MANIFEST.MF
├── com
│   └── apress
│       └── bgn
│           └── ch3
│               ├── SimpleReader.class
│               └── package-info.class
```

Figure 3-3. *Contents of a sample JAR*

! package-info.java files are not mandatory, packages can be defined without them. They are useful mostly for documentation purposes.

The code in one package might span multiple JARs, meaning if you have more than one subproject[7] in your project you can have the same package name in more than once, containing different classes. A symbolic representation of all the preceding is depicted in Figure 3-4.

---

[6]When JARs are hosted on a repository, such as The Maven Public Repository, they are also called **artifacts**.

[7]I am deliberately avoiding the term *module* for now to avoid confusion between project modules and Java modules.

CHAPTER 3   GETTING YOUR FEET WET

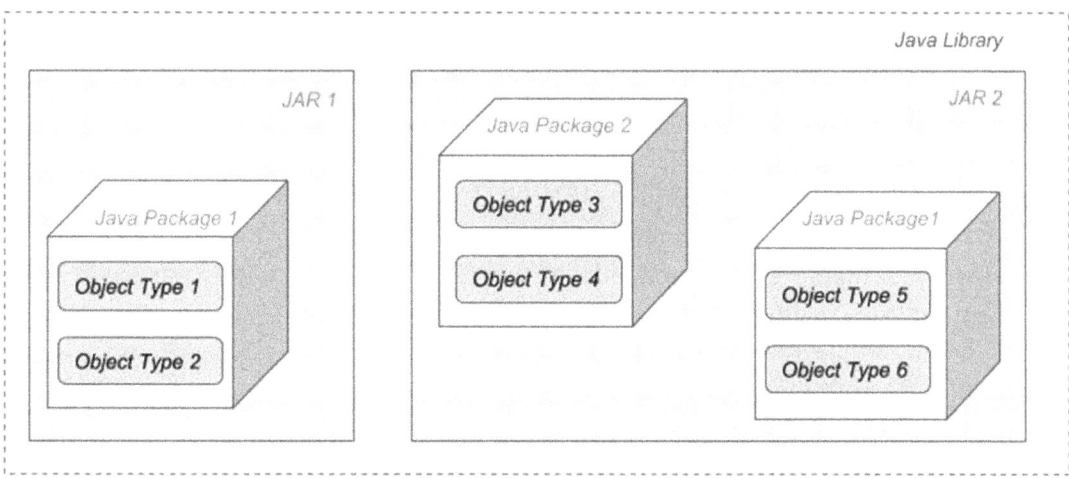

Figure 3-4. *Java building blocks*

A **library** groups one or more JARs.[8]

A Java application can make use of one or more libraries, and in order to be run, needs all of its dependencies (all the JARs) on the classpath. What does this mean? It means that to run a Java application, the JDK is needed, the dependencies (external JARs) and the application jars. Figure 3-5 depicts this quite clearly.

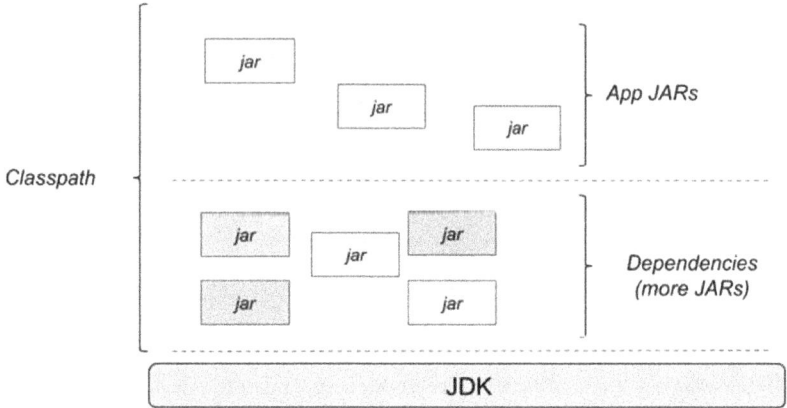

Figure 3-5. *Classpath of an application*

The JARs that make up an application classpath are (obviously) not always independent of each other. For 21 years this organization style was enough, but in complex applications there were a lot of complications caused by: packages scattered in

---

[8]The most popular are logging libraries like Log4J. (`https://logging.apache.org/log4j/2.x/`) and Logback (`https://logback.qos.ch/`)

59

multiple jars, transitive dependencies between jars, which sometimes leads to different versions of the same class on the classpath, missing transitive dependencies and accessibility problems. All these problems are grouped under one name **The Jar Hell**.[9] This problem was resolved in Java 9 by introducing another level to group packages, but we should expect that there is **The Module Hell** at some point in the future.

Before introducing modules, **access modifiers** should be mentioned because Java object types and members can declared with certain access rights within packages, and that is something important to understand before jumping into coding.

Access Modifiers

When you declare an object type in Java (let's stick to class because it is the only one mentioned so far), you can configure who should be able to use it. Access modifiers specify access to classes, and in this case, we say that they are used at the **top-level**. They can also specify access to class members, and in this case, they are used at **member-level**.[10]

At top-level only two access modifiers can be used: public and none.

A `top-level` class that is declared `public` must be defined in a Java file with the same name. So, the following class is defined in a file named `Base.java` stored under the `com.apress.bgn.ch0` package.

```
package com.apress.bgn.ch0;

//top-level access modifier
public class Base {
    ...
}
```

The contents of the class are not depicted for the moment and replaced with ... to stop you from losing focus. A public class is visible to all classes anywhere. So, a different class, in a different package can create an object of this type, like in the following sample code:

---

[9]A great article about **The Jar Hell** in case you want to know more, but you might want to read it later, after you have written a little code of your own. See https://tech-read.com/2009/01/13/what-is-jar-hell/

[10]I will not mention nested classes right now, as they are not really crucial for understanding this section. But in the downloadable Appendix, there is a small section about nested and local classes that you might find useful.

```
package com.apress.bgn.ch3;

import com.apress.bgn.ch0.Base;
import  org.apache.logging.log4j.LogManager;
import org.apache.logging.log4j.Logger;

public class Main {
   public static void main(String... args) {
           // creating an object of type Base
       Base base = new Base();
   }
}
```

! For now, let this affirmation sink in: **a public class is visible to all classes everywhere**.

The option to not use an access modifier it is called using the `default` or package-private modifier.[11] This means if a class has no access modifier, the class is only visible to classes defined in the same package. A class without an access modifier can be defined in any Java file, one that has the same name, or right next to the class that gives the file its name. So, if we were to declare a class named `HiddenBase` in the `Base.java` file as depicted in the following code snippet, trying to create an object of this type within the `Main` class is not possible, because this class is in a different package.

```
package com.apress.bgn.ch0;

public class Base {
        ...
}

class HiddenBase{
    // you cannot see me outside the package
}
```

---

[11]I know it seems confusing that there are two names referring to the lack of access modifiers, but as you might read other books or blog posts that refer to this situation, it is better to have all the possibilities listed here.

Sure, you can write the code, but the Java compiler will not compile it, and there is no bytecode to execute. Also, smart Java editors very clearly show you the error of your ways, by making your code red and refusing to provide any code assistance when writing it. Figure 3-6 depicts how IntelliJ IDEA tries to tell me that I'm doing something wrong in trying to access a `package-private` class.

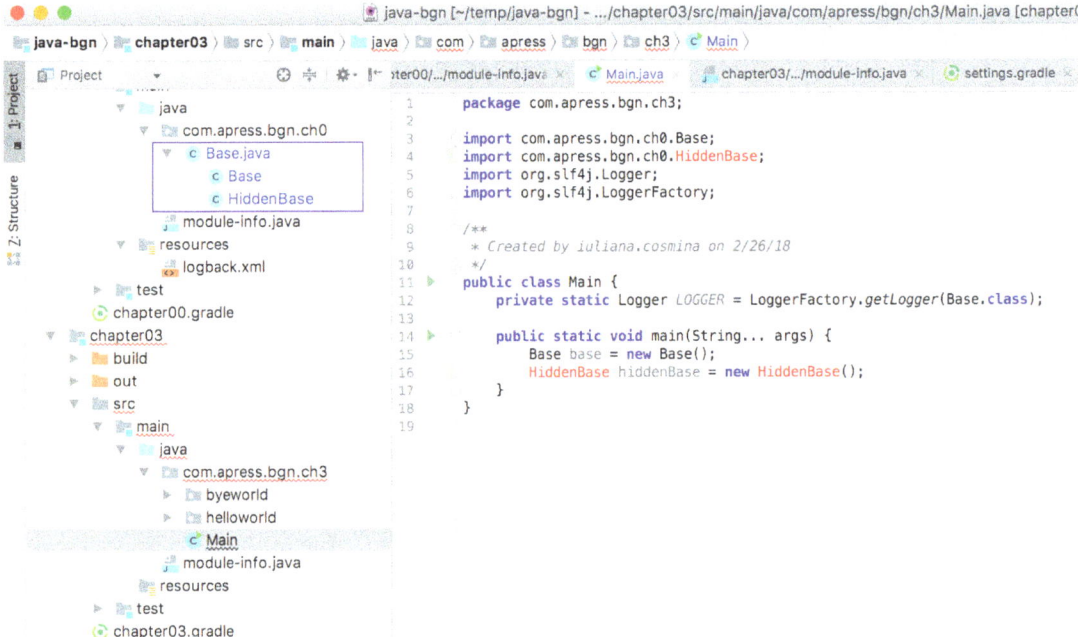

Figure 3-6. *IntelliJ IDEA hinting that access to a package-private class leads to a compilation error*

In the same figure, the file containing the two classes is depicted in a rectangle to attract your attention on how the editor is making it obvious that the two classes are defined in the same Java file.

! For now, take this affirmation and let it sink in: **a class with no access modifier is visible to all classes in the same package**.

Inside a class, the class members are defined: fields and methods.[12] Access modifiers can be applied to the class members as well, and at member-level, two more modifiers can be applied: `private` and `protected`. At member-level, the access modifiers have the following affects.

- `public`: The same as at top level, the member can be accessed from everywhere.
- `private`: The member can only be accessed from within its own class.
- `protected`: The member can only be accessed from within its own package or by any subclass[13] of its class in another package.
- `none`: The member can only be accessed from within its own package.

If it seems complicated, it's only until you begin writing code and getting used to it. On the official Oracle documentation page, there is a table with the visibility of members, depicted here in this book as Table 3-1.[14]

Table 3-1. *Member-Level Accessors*

Modifier	Class	Package	Subclass	World
public	Yes	Yes	Yes	Yes
protected	Yes	Yes	Yes	No
none (also referred to as default/package-private)	Yes	Yes	No	No
private	Yes	No	No	No

You will probably come back to this table once or twice after you start writing Java code. Everything in this table is still valid after the introduction of modules, but only once you properly configure module access, of course. 😊

---

[12]Aside from that, we can also define other Java object types, which are referred to as **nested**, but we'll cross that bridge when we come to it.

[13]Creating a subclass is covered in **Chapter 5**.

[14]I depicted the table to avoid the hassle of navigating to this URL: https://docs.oracle.com/javase/tutorial/java/javaOO/accesscontrol.html

CHAPTER 3   GETTING YOUR FEET WET

Introducing Modules

Starting with Java 9, a new concept was introduced: **modules**. They are used to group and encapsulate packages. Implementation of this new concept took more than ten years. The discussion about modules started in 2005, and it was proposed to be implemented for Java 7. Under the name **Project Jigsaw** an exploratory phase started in 2008. Java developers hoped a modular JDK would be available with Java 8, but it was made possible in Java 9, after three years of work (and almost seven year of analysis). Apparently, this is why the official release date for Java 9 was postponed to September 2017.[15]

Modules represent a new way to aggregate packages. A **module** is a way to group them and configure more granulated access to package contents.

A **module** is a uniquely named, reusable group of packages and resources (XML files) described by a file named `module-info.java`. This file contains the following information:

- the module's name
- the module's dependencies (that is, other modules this module depends on)
- the packages it explicitly makes available to other modules (all other packages in the module are implicitly unavailable to other modules)
- the services it offers
- the services it consumes
- to what other modules it allows reflection
- native code
- resources
- configuration data

In theory, module naming resembles package naming and follows the reversed-domain-name convention. In practice, make sure that the module name does not contain any numbers and that it reveals clearly what its purpose is. The `module-info.java` file is compiled into a **module descriptor**, which is a file named `module-info.`

---

[15]The full history of the Jigsaw project can be found at `http://openjdk.java.net/projects/jigsaw/`

class that is packed with classes into a plain old JAR file. The location of the file is in the root sources directory, outside of any package. For the example introduced earlier, a module-info.java was added and the new project structure is depicted in Figure 3-7.

```
chapter03/
└── src
    ├── main
    │   ├── java
    │   │   └── com
    │   │       └── apress
    │   │           └── bgn
    │   │               └── ch3
    │   │                   ├── SimpleReader.java
    │   │                   └── package-info.java
    │   └── module-info.java
    └── resources
```

Figure 3-7. *Structure of a Java 9 project*

As any file with the *.java extension, the module-info.java gets compiled into a *.class file. As the module declaration is not a part of Java object types declaration, module is not a Java keyword, so it can still be used when writing code for Java object types. For package, the situation is different, as every Java object type declaration must start with a package declaration. Take a look at the SimpleReader class, declared as follows.

package com.apress.bgn.ch3;

public class SimpleReader {

    private String source;
    ...
}

So, what does this actually mean? Where is the module and what is it? Well, in simple projects that are made of one root directory with sources, modules do not have to physically delimit or organize sources.[16] They are defined by the contents of the module-info.java file. So, starting with Java 9, what is shown in Figure 3-4 evolves into Figure 3-8.

---

[16]Unless you rename directories containing sources for a module to the module name. Having actual directories for modules is unavoidable when the sources in the root directory of a project must be split into different modules.

CHAPTER 3 GETTING YOUR FEET WET

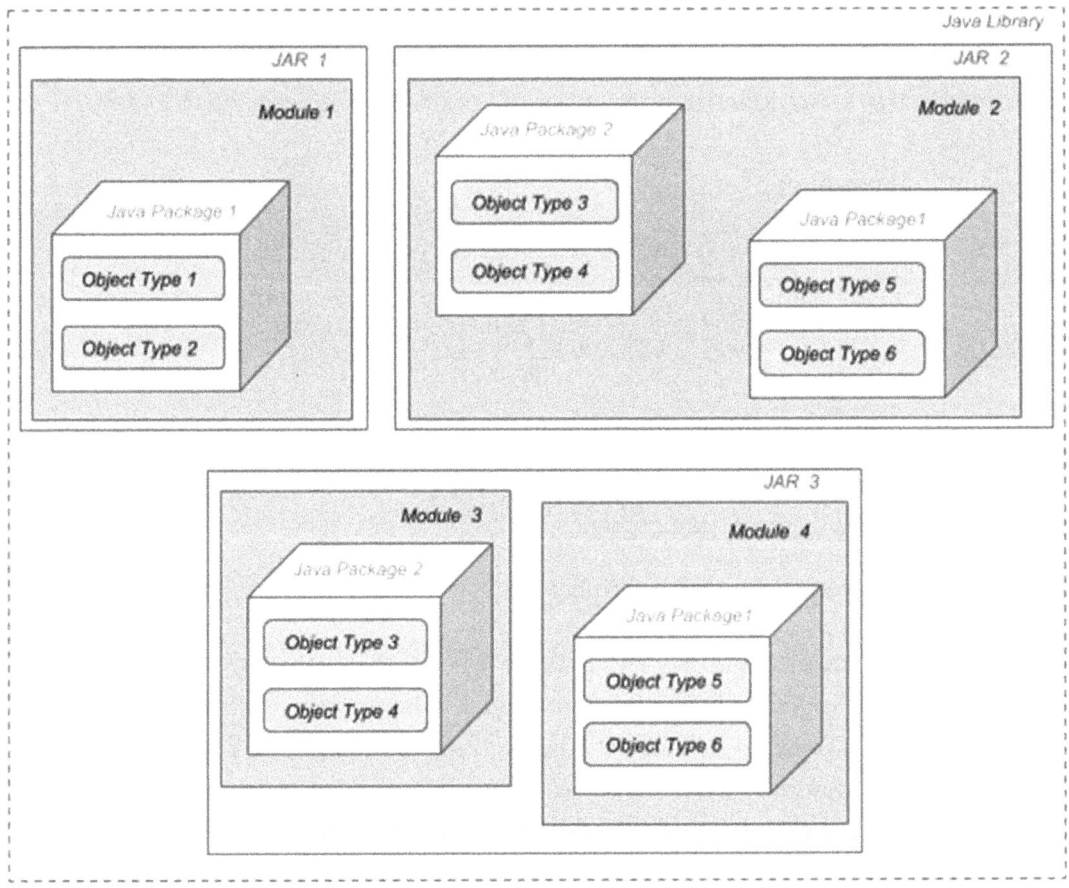

Figure 3-8. *Java building blocks, starting with Java 9*

In Figure 3-8, there is no need to create a directory for the module in JAR1 and JAR2. For JAR3, there are two modules archived in the same JAR; in this case, we need to explicitly separate their sources. The reason for this is the need to have two module-info.java files, and obviously no operating system allows two files in the same directory to have the same name. An example of such a project is covered in the **Appendix**, which is available as part of the book's source code download (https://github.com/apress/java-for-absolute-beginners).

The introduction of modules means the JDK is now divided into modules as well. This means that the Java platform is no longer a monolith that consists of a massive number of packages and making it challenging to develop, maintain, and evolve. The platform is now split into 95 modules that can be viewed by executing java --list-modules (the number might vary in Java later versions).

```
$ java --list-modules
java.base@10
```

```
java.compiler@10
java.datatransfer@10
java.desktop@10
...
```

Each module name is followed by a version string, @10, which means that the module belongs to Java 10.

So, if a Java application does not require all modules, a runtime can be created only with the modules that it needs, which reduces the runtime's size. The tool to build a smaller runtime customized to an application needs is called jlink, which is part of the JDK executables. It allows larger levels of scalability and increased performance.[17]

There are multiple benefits of introducing modules, that more experienced developers have been waiting for years to take advantage of. But configuring modules for bigger and more complex projects is no walk in the park, so for the time being, a simple configuration for a module containing one package is covered. After finishing this book, you are welcome to read the **Appendix**, where a more advanced module configuration is covered, with examples for each of the possible module configuration is presented.

The contents of the module-info.java can be as simple as the name of the module and two brackets.

```
module chapter.three {
}
```

Configuring Modules

Within those brackets, different module directives may be declared, using one of the following keywords:

- requires
- exports
- module
- open

---

[17] How to use **jlink** is not an object of this book. The focus of the book is learning the Java programming language; thus, the technical details of the Java platform will be kept to a minimum, just enough to start writing and executing code confidently.

- opens... to
- provides ... with
- transitive

Each of them covers a specific behavior, but for a beginner, the most important two are requires and exports.

Modules can depend on one another. For our example, classes inside the chapter.three module need access to packages, and classes in the chapter.zero module. Declaring a module dependency is done my using the requires keyword.

```
module chapter.three {
    requires chapter.zero;
}
```

The preceding dependency is an **explicit** one. But there are also implicit dependencies. For example, any module declared by a developer **implicitly** requires the JDK java.base module. This module defines the foundational APIs of the Java SE Platform, and no Java application could be written without it.

Declaring a module as required, means that that module is required at compile time and runtime. If a module is required only at runtime, the requires static keywords are used to declare the dependency. Keep that in mind for now; it will make sense when I talk about web applications.

But is it enough to declare our module as dependent of another? Does this mean that the dependent module can access all public types (and their nested public and protected types)? If you are thinking not, you are right. Just because a module depends on another, it does not mean it has access to the packages and classes that it needs to. This is because the module it depends on must be configured to expose its *insides*. How can that be done? In our case, we need to make sure module chapter.zero gives access to the required packages. This is done by customizing the module-info.java for this module by adding the exports directive, followed by the necessary package names.

```
module chapter.zero {
    exports com.apress.bgn.ch0;
}
```

By doing this we have given access to the `com.apress.bgn.ch0` package to any module that requires this package as a dependency. What if we do not want that?

! If you were curious and read the recommended **Jar Hell** article, you noticed that one of the concerns of working with Java sources packed in Jars, was security. Because even without access to Java sources, objects could be accessed, extended, and instantiated by adding a Jar as a dependency to an application. So, aside from providing a reliable configuration, better scaling, integrity for the platform, and improved performance, the goal for introduction of modules was better security.

What if we want to **limit the access to module contents** only to the `chapter.three` module? This can be done by adding the `to` keyword followed by the module name to the `exports` directive.

```
module chapter.zero {
    exports com.apress.bgn.ch0 to chapter.three;
}
```

More than one module can be specified to have access by listing the desired modules, separated by comma.

```
module chapter.zero {
    exports com.apress.bgn.ch0 to chapter.three, chapter.two;
}
```

And that's about all you need to know about modules for the moment.

Determining the Structure: A Java Project

! When this chapter was written, JDK 11 EAP has just been released. Shortly after, Gradle version 4.9 and IntelliJ IDEA version 2018.2 were released and they fully supported development using JDK 11. So, from this section onward Java 11 will be referred in the rest of the book.

69

There are a few ways Java projects can be structured. It depends on the project's scope and the build tool used.

You might wonder why does the project scope influence its structure because you expect there should be a standard for this, right? Well, there is more than one standard, and that is dependent on the project scope, because the scope, the reason for creating a Java project influences its size. And if a project is small, it might not require you to split the sources into subprojects, and you do not need a build tool either, and build tools come with their own standard way of organizing a project. Let's start with the smallest Java project ever, which should print Hello World! to the console.

The HelloWorld! Project in IntelliJ IDEA

As a side note, you do not even need a project because you have JShell. Open a terminal (Command Prompt for Windows) and JShell, and enter the `System.out.print("Hello World!")` statement.

```
$ jshell
|  Welcome to JShell -- Version 11-ea
|  For an introduction type: /help intro

jshell> System.out.print("Hello World!")
Hello World!
```

Since you installed IntelliJ IDEA, let's create a Java project and check what project structure the editor chooses for us. Start with the first IntelliJ IDEA and click the **Create New Project** option. A second dialog window appears on top with the types of projects that you can create listed on the left. The two dialog windows mentioned here are depicted in Figure 3-9.

CHAPTER 3   GETTING YOUR FEET WET

Figure 3-9. *Create an IntelliJ IDEA project*

Select Java project type from the left and click **Next**. (Do not select any of the additional libraries and frameworks, we are actually creating the smallest Java project possible.) In the next dialog window, the project name and location can be introduced. As we are creating a Java 11 project, you can notice at the bottom a section used to configure the Java module. This configuration window is depicted in Figure 3-10.

71

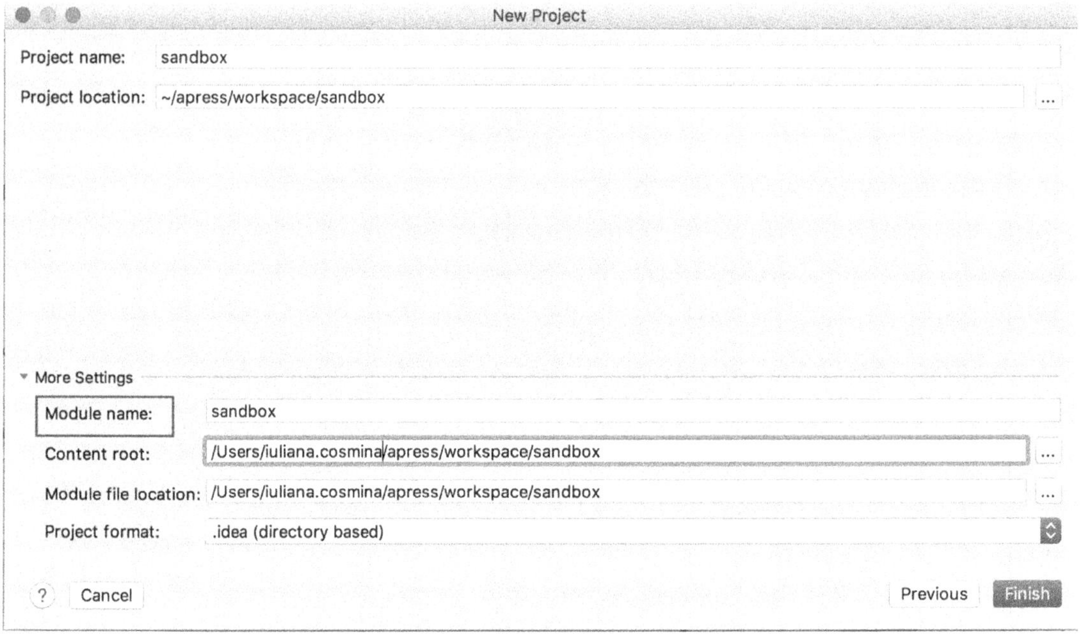

CHAPTER 3 GETTING YOUR FEET WET

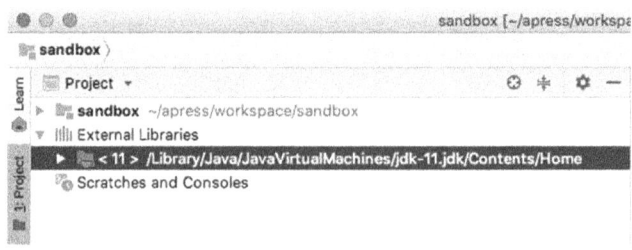

Figure 3-10. IntelliJ IDEA project configuration dialog window

After inserting the project and module name- we used `sandbox` for both project name and module name- click **Finish** and the next window should be the editor window, in which you can start writing code. If you expand the `sandbox` node on the left (that section is called *the project view*), you can see that the project is built using the JDK you have installed (in this case 11) and a `src` directory was created for you. Your project should look a lot like the one depicted in Figure 3-11.

Figure 3-11. IntelliJ IDEA project view

CHAPTER 3   GETTING YOUR FEET WET

Before writing code, let's check out what other project settings are available. IntelliJ IDEA provides you access to view and edit project properties through the **File ➤ Project Structure...** menu item. If you click it, a dialog window opens, similar to the one depicted in Figure 3-12.

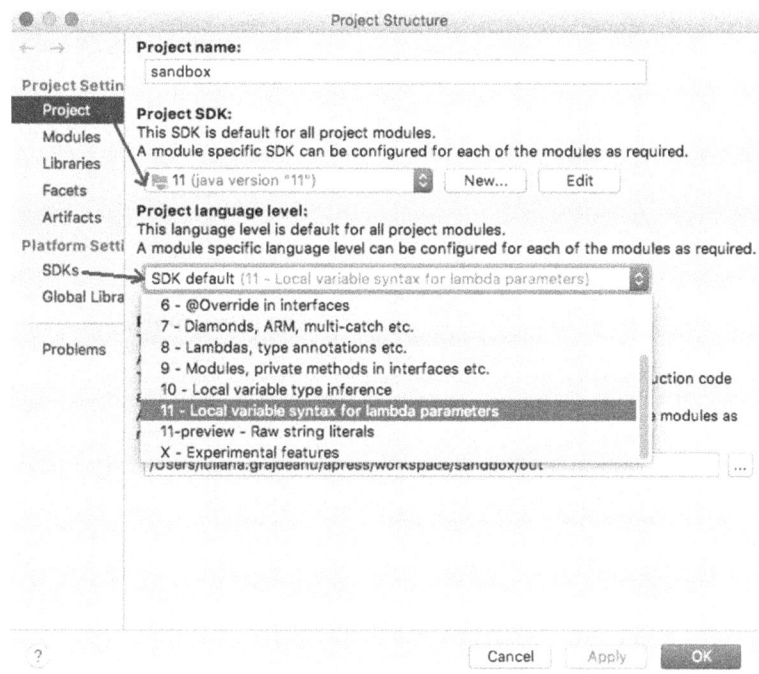

Figure 3-12. *IntelliJ IDEA project settings tab*

By default, the **Project** settings tab is opened. In Figure 3-12, there are two arrows attracting your attention to the **Project SDK:** section, which is depicting the JDK version for a Java project, and the **Project language level:** section. At the time this chapter was written, JDK 11 EA was the most recent version. The most recent version of IntelliJ IDEA supports syntax and code completion for Java 11, which is why it is depicted here. This is the meaning of the project language level setting.

If you switch to the tab named **Modules** you see the information depicted in Figure 3-13.

73

CHAPTER 3   GETTING YOUR FEET WET

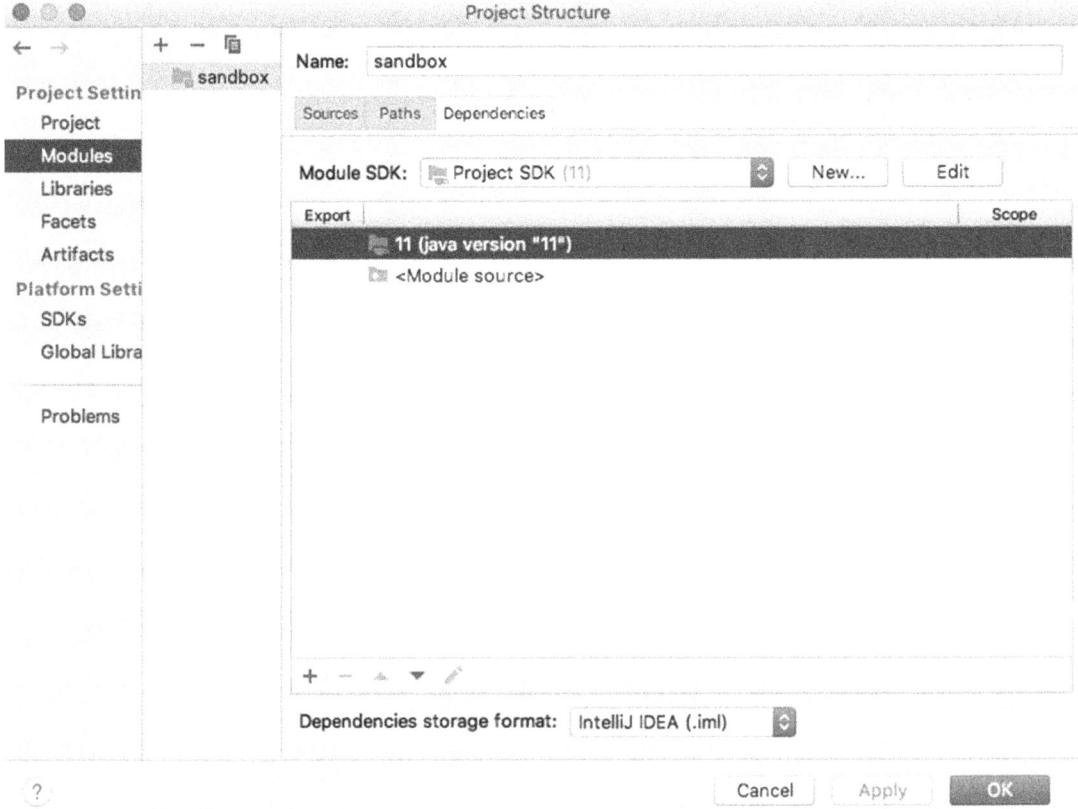

Figure 3-13. IntelliJ IDEA modules settings tab

! Let's clarify something first. The Modules tab does not show information about Java modules in your project. Aside from Java modules, that wrap packages together; a module is also a way to wrap up Java sources and resource files with a common purpose within a project. That is why, before Oracle introduced the `module` concept to modularize Java applications, the code making up these applications was already modularized by developers that needed to structure big projects in some practical way.

In the Modules tab, you can see the number of parts (modules) that a project has and the settings for each part. The `sandbox` has one part: one module named also `sandbox` and the source for this module is contained in the `src` directory. So, if we want to write a class that prints *Hello World!*, the file called `HelloWorld.java` must be placed under it. If you right-click the `src` directory, the menu depicted in Figure 3-14 appears.

CHAPTER 3   GETTING YOUR FEET WET

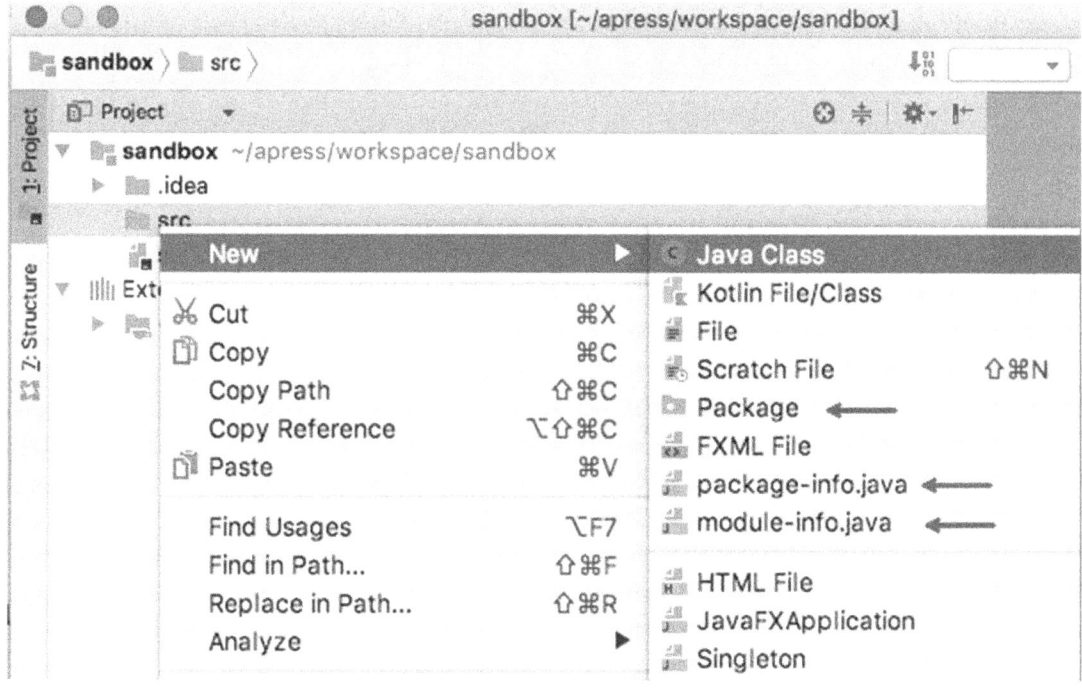

Figure 3-14. IntelliJ IDEA menu listing which Java objects can be created in the src directory

Aside from the Java Class option, there are a few red arrows showing you what other components can be in the `src` directory. Let's go ahead and create our class. Click the **Java Class** menu option, and after introducing the class name, expand the **Kind:** drop-down list. Figure 3-15 shows the expanded list.

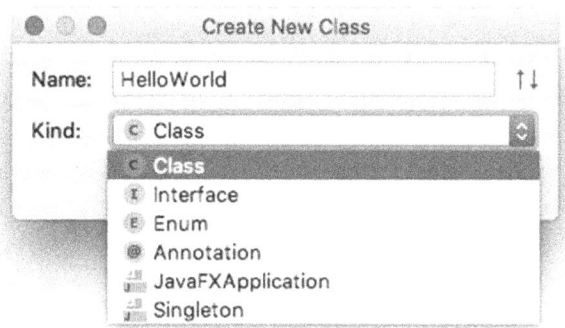

Figure 3-15. IntelliJ IDEA dialog windows to create a Java data type

75

The core building block of a Java application is the Java class, but there are other object types in Java. In the **Kind:** list, the four Java object types are listed. Each of them is explained in detail later; for now, select **Class** and click the **OK** button. You notice that a file named `HelloWorld.java` was created under the `src` directory and the contents of that file are quite simple.

```
/**
 * Created on 3/3/18.
 */
public class HelloWorld {

}
```

You have created your first Java class in your first simple Java project. It does nothing yet. But it can be compiled by selecting from the IntelliJ IDEA **Build** menu, the **Build Project** option, or by pressing a combination of keys, that is different for each operation system. Compiling the Build Project option produce the `HelloWorld.class` file, containing the bytecode. By default, IntelliJ IDEA stores compilation results into a directory named `out\production`. The menu option for compiling your project and the result are depicted in Figure 3-16. The menu option is marked with (1).

CHAPTER 3   GETTING YOUR FEET WET

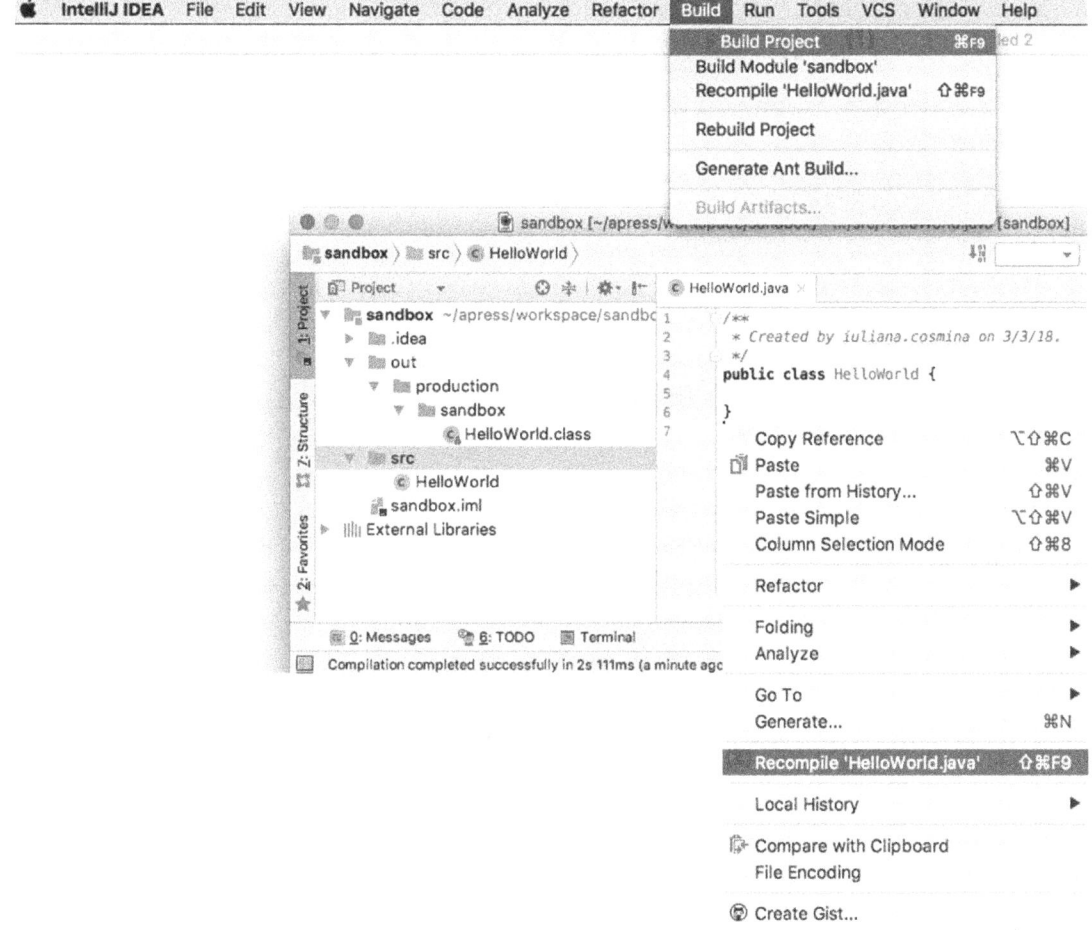

Figure 3-16. *IntelliJ IDEA—how to compile a Java project*

When you have more classes in your project, you can compile the one you modify by right-clicking the class body and choosing **Recompile [ClassName].java**, marked with (2) in Figure 3-16.

It is time we make the class print *Hello World!*. For that we need to add a special method to the class. Any Java desktop application has a special method named `main` that has to be declared in a top-level class. This method is called by the JRE to run the Java program/application and I call it the **entry point**. Without such a method, a Java project is a collection of classes that are not runnable, cannot be executed, and cannot perform certain functions. Imagine it this way: it's like having a car, but you have no way of starting it, because the ignition lock cylinder is missing. By for all intents and purposes,

77

it is a car, but it cannot perform the main purpose of a car, which is to take you somewhere. You can imagine the main method as the ignition lock cylinder, where the JRE inserts the key to get your application running. Let's add that method to the `HelloWorld` class.[18]

```
/**
 * Created on 3/3/18.
 */
public class HelloWorld {

    public static void main(String... args) {
        System.out.println("Hello World!");
    }
}
```

Now, let's run this class. In IntelliJ IDEA, you have also two options: from the Run menu choose the **Run '[ClassName]'** option, or right-click the class body and select **Run '[ClassName]'.main()** from the menu that appears.[19]

Figure 3-17, depicts the menu items that you can use to execute the class, as well as the result of the execution.

---

[18]Because IntelliJ IDEA is an awesome editor, you can generate the *main* method, by typing **psvm** and pressing the **Tab** key.

[19]Next to the Run menu item, a combination of keys is depicted that can be used to run the class.

CHAPTER 3　GETTING YOUR FEET WET

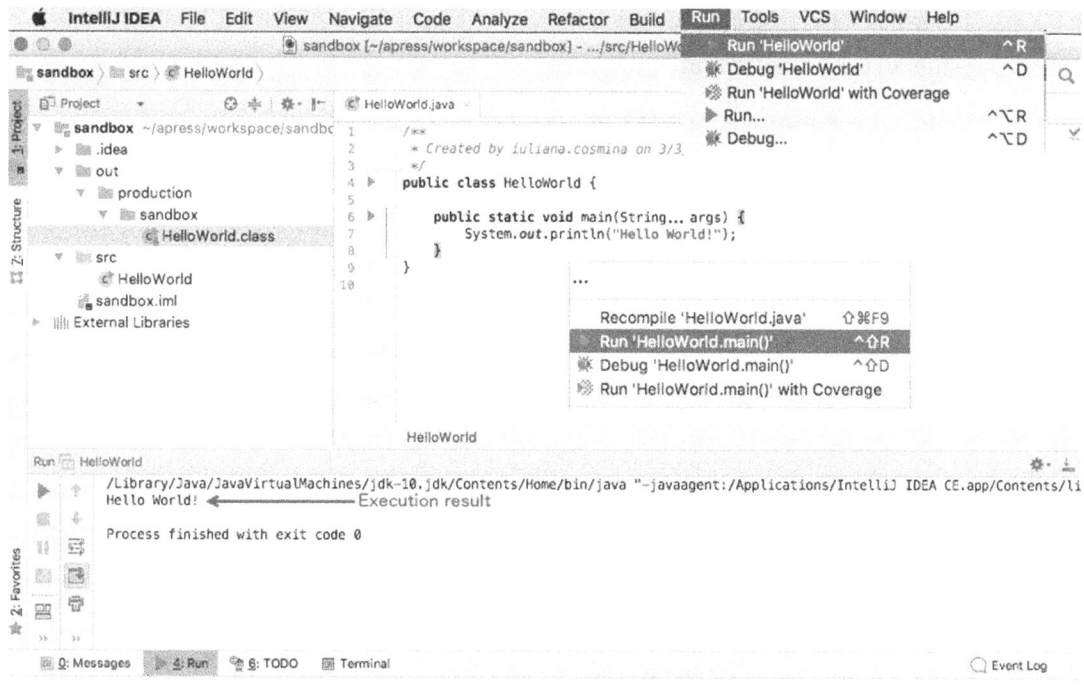

Figure 3-17. *IntelliJ IDEA—how to execute a Java class*

So, this is the most basic structure for a Java Project. This project is so simple that it can also be compiled manually from the command line. So, let's do that.

The HelloWorld! Project Compiled and Executed Manually

You've probably noticed the **Terminal** button in your IntelliJ IDEA. If you click that button, inside the editor a terminal window will be opened. For Windows it is a Command Prompt instance, for Linux and macOS are the default shell. And IntelliJ open your terminal right into your project root. The following explains what you have to do.

1. Enter the `src` directory by executing the following command:

   ```
   cd src
   ```

   `cd` is a command that works in Windows and Unix systems and is short for *change directory*.

2. Compile the `HelloWorld.java` file by executing:

   ```
   javac HelloWorld.java
   ```

79

CHAPTER 3 GETTING YOUR FEET WET

> javac is a JDK executable used to compile Java files that IntelliJ IDEA calls in the background.

3. Run the resulting bytecode from the `HelloWorld.class` file by executing:

   `java HelloWorld`

Figure 3-18 depicts the execution of those commands in a terminal in IntelliJ IDEA.

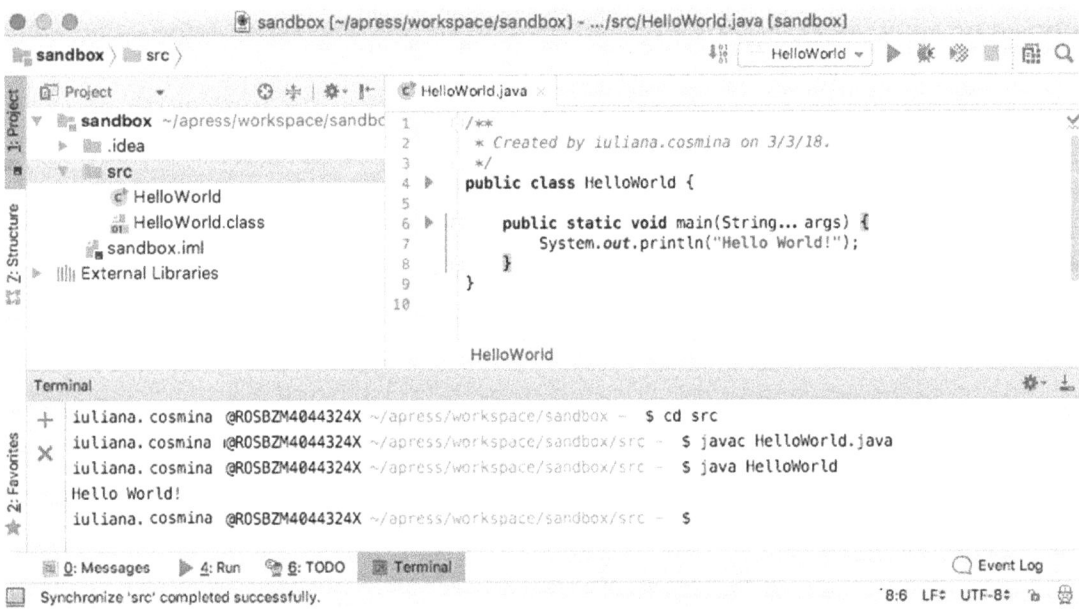

Figure 3-18. *Manually compile and run the HelloWorld class in a terminal inside IntelliJ IDEA*

Looks simple, right? And it actually is simple, because no packages or Java modules were defined. But wait, is that possible? Well, yes. If you did not define a package, the class is still part of an unnamed default package that is provided by default by the JSE platform for the development of small, temporary, and educational applications like the one you are building. So, let's make our project a little bit more complicated and add a named package for our class to be in.

CHAPTER 3   GETTING YOUR FEET WET

Putting the HelloWorld Class in a Package

In Figure 3-14, there is a **Package** option in the menu. So right-click the `src` directory and select it. A dialog window appears where you must enter the package name. Enter **com.sandbox**. Figure 3-19 shows the dialog windows. Even though the package was already created, I introduced the same name again to show how the IDE warns that you are trying to create a package with the same name.

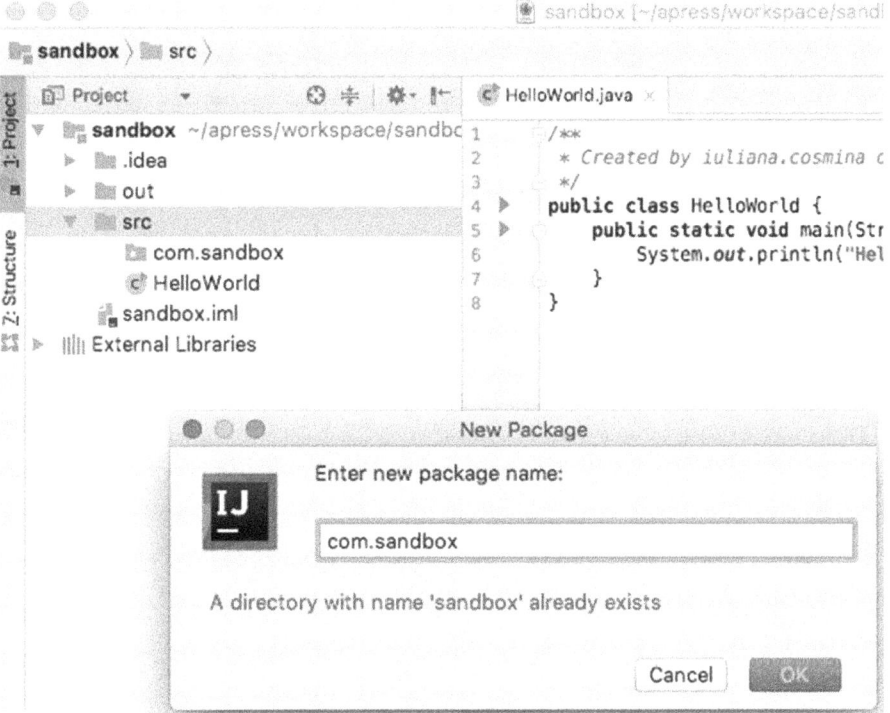

Figure 3-19. Create package in IntelliJ IDEA

So, we created the package, but the class is not in it. Well, the way to get it there, is to select it and drag it into it. A dialog window for moving the class appear, because the editor must modify the class to make it to belong to the package by adding a `package` statement. And it requires your approval for the operation. Figure 3-20 depicts this dialog window.

81

CHAPTER 3   GETTING YOUR FEET WET

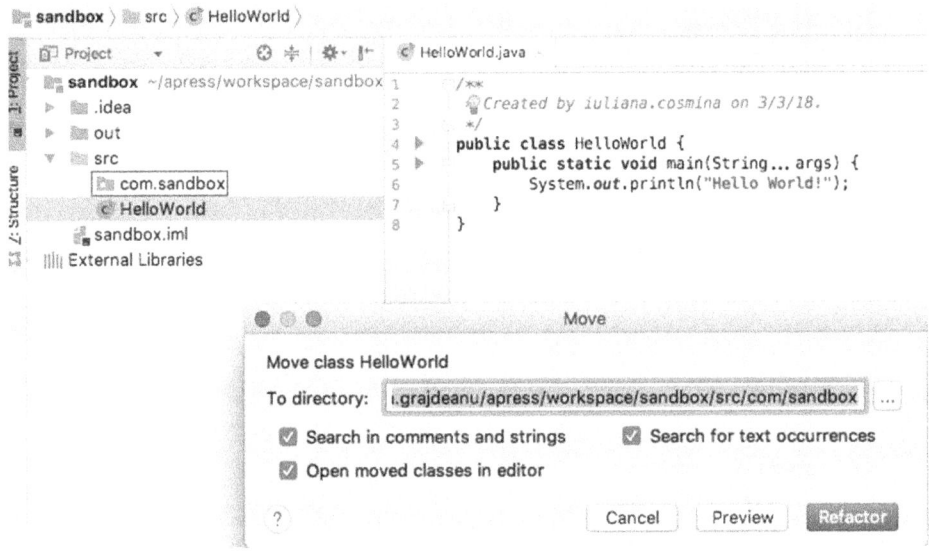

Figure 3-20. *Moving a class into a package in IntelliJ IDEA*

Click the **Refactor** button and look at what happens to the class. The class should now start with a package `com.sandbox;` declaration. If you rebuild your project, and then look at the directory structure, you see something similar to what is depicted in Figure 3-21.

```
iuliana.cosmina @ROSBZM4044324X ~/apress/workspace/sandbox ─ $ tree
.
├── out
│   └── production
│       └── sandbox
│           └── com
│               └── sandbox
│                   └── HelloWorld.class
├── sandbox.iml
└── src
    └── com
        └── sandbox
            └── HelloWorld.java

8 directories, 3 files
```

Figure 3-21. *New directory structure after adding the com.sandbox package*

If you compile and execute the class manually, you must consider the package now, so your commands change to

```
~/sandbox/src:   $ javac com/sandbox/HelloWorld.java
~/sandbox/src:   $ java com/sandbox/HelloWorld
Hello World!
```

But things do not end here, because we still have Java modules. So, what about that? How is our code running without a `module-info.java` file? Well, there is a default unnamed module, and all JARs, modular or not, and classes on the classpath are contained in it. This default and unnamed module exports all packages and reads all other modules. Because it does not have a name it cannot be required and read by named application modules. Thus, even if your small project seems to work with JDKs in versions 9 and higher, it cannot be accessed by other modules; but it works because it can access others. (This ensures backward compatibility with older versions of the JDK, but depending on the complexity of the project, compatibility is not always ensured.) This being said, let's add a module to our project.

Configuring the com.sandbox Module

Configuring a module is as easy as adding a `module-info.java` file under the `src` directory. In Figure 3-14, in the menu listed there is a `module-info.java` option and if you select that, the IDE generates the file for you. All is well and fine, and if you do not like the module name that was generated for you, you can change it. I changed it to `com.sandbox` to respect the module naming convention established by Oracle developers.

```java
/**
 * Created on 3/3/18.
 */
module com.sandbox {

}
```

What happens now that we have a module? Not much from the IDEs point of view. But if you want to compile a module manually, you have to know a few things. I compiled our module using the following command:

```
~/sandbox/src/: $ javac -d ../out/com.sandbox \
        module-info.java       \
        com/sandbox/HelloWorld.java
```

CHAPTER 3   GETTING YOUR FEET WET

! "\" is a macOS/Linux separator. On Windows, either write the whole command on a single line or replace "\" with "^".

Let me explain what I did there. The syntax to compile a module is this:

```
javac -d [destination location]/[module name] \
    [source  location]/module-info.java \
    [java files...]
```

The result of executing that command is that a directory named `com.sandbox` in the out directory is created—the module name. Under this directory, we have the normal structure of the `com.sandbox` package. The contents of the out directory are depicted in Figure 3-22.

Figure 3-22. *Java module com.sandbox compiled manually*

As you have noticed in this example, the module does not really exist until we compile the sources, because a Java module is more of a logical mode of encapsulating packages described by the `module-info.class` descriptor. The only reason the `com.sandbox` directory was created is that we specified it as argument in the `javac -d` command.

We have a compiled module, what do we do with it? We try to run the application obviously.

```
sandbox/: $ java --module-path out \
    --module   com.sandbox/com.sandbox.HelloWorld
Hello  World!
```

The syntax to execute a modular application is this:

```
java --module-path [destination location] \
    --module [module name] /[package name].HelloWorld
Hello  World!
```

Regarding the module name, doesn't it seem a little redundant? To me it sure looks like it, which is why I prefer not to create directories for modules unless I have more of them under the `src` directory. And we must talk about the standard naming conventions for modules. That is also another thing that might give developer headaches if they want to create directories for modules. In multiple blog articles and *Oracle Magazine* (September 2017), this is recommended.[20] But do not worry about it for now; the book's sources contain modules with simple names, and the module configuration is already in place for you.

Java Projects Using Build Tools (Mostly Gradle)

Maven is a build automation tool used primarily for Java projects. Although Gradle is gaining ground, Maven is still one of the most used build tools. Tools like Gradle and Maven are used to organize the source code of an application in interdependent project modules and configure a way to compile, validate, generate sources, test, and generate artifacts automatically. An artifact is a file, usually a JAR, that gets deployed to a Maven repository. A Maven repository is a location on an HDD where JARs are saved in a special directory structure.

The discussion about build tools must start with Maven, because this build tool standardized a lot of the terms we used in development today. Gradle respects a lot of Maven standard rules was chosen as the go-to build tool for the sources attached to this book, because it is easier to configure and the configuration files are reduced in size. A project split into multiple subprojects can be downloaded from GitHub, and built in the command line or imported into IntelliJ. This approach makes sure that you get quality sources that can be compiled at once. It is also practical, because I imagine you do not want to load a new project in IntelliJ IDEA every time you start reading a new chapter. Also, it makes it easier for me to maintain the sources and adapt them to a new JDK, and with Oracle releasing so often, I need to be able to do this quickly.

---

[20]*Oracle Magazine* from September 2017 can be accessed at `http://www.javamagazine.mozaicreader.com/SeptOct2017#&pageSet=29&page=0`

CHAPTER 3   GETTING YOUR FEET WET

The project you use to test the code written in this book and write your own code if you want to, is called `java-for-absolute-beginners`. It is a multimodule Gradle project. The first level of the project is the `java-for-absolute-beginners` project, that has a configuration file named `build.gradle`. In this file, all dependencies and their versions are listed. The child projects, the ones on the second level, are the modules of this project. And we call them *child* projects because they inherit those dependencies and modules from the parent project. In their configuration files, we can specify which dependencies are needed from the list defined in the parent. And these modules are a method of wrapping up sources for each chapter and that is why these modules are named `chapter00`, `chapter01`, and so forth. If a project is big and needs a lot of code to be written, the code is split again in another level of modules. Module `chapter05` is such a case, and is configured as a parent for the projects underneath it. In Figure 3-23, you see what this project looks like loaded in IntelliJ IDEA, and module `chapter05` is expanded so you can see the third level of modules. Each level is marked with the corresponding number.

CHAPTER 3 GETTING YOUR FEET WET

Figure 3-23. *Gradle multimodule-level structure*

Chapter 3 Getting Your Feet Wet

In the Appendix you can read a detailed explanation for the configuration of this Gradle project. For now, if you have loaded it into IntelliJ IDEA as you were taught in **Chapter** 2, you can make sure everything is working correctly by building it. Here's how you do it.

You can do it by using the IntelliJ IDEA editor, in the upper right side you should have a tab called **Gradle projects**.

If the projects are loaded as they are depicted in Figure 3-24, the project was loaded correctly. If the **Gradle projects** tab is not visible, look for a label like the one marked with (1), and click it.

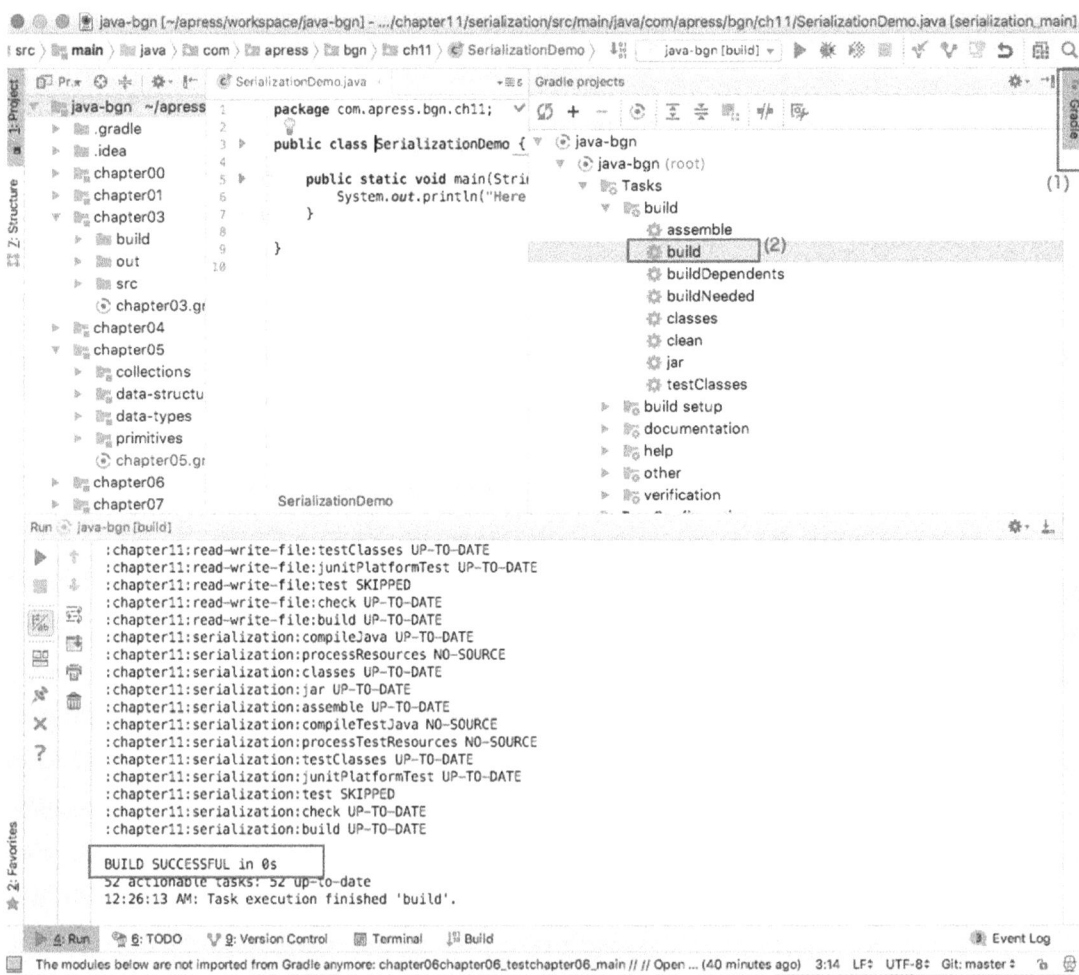

Figure 3-24. Gradle multimodule-level structure

Expand the java-for-absolute-beginners(root) node until you find the build task, marked with (2). If you double click it and in the view at the bottom of the editor you do not see any error, all your projects were built successfully.

The second way to make sure the Gradle project is working as expected is to build it from the command line. Open an IntelliJ IDEA terminal, and if you installed Gradle on the system path as explained in **Chapter** 2, enter **`gradle clean build`** and hit the **Enter** key. In the command line, you might see some warnings, if the Gradle plugin for supporting Java modules is still unstable when this book reaches you, but as long as the execution ends with BUILD SUCCESSFUL, everything is alright.

Aside from the sandbox project, all the classes, modules, and packages mentioned in this section are part of this project. chapter00 and chapter01 do not really contain classes specific to those chapters. I needed them to construct the Java module examples. IntelliJ IDEA sorts modules in alphabetical order, so the naming of the chapter modules was chosen this way. They are listed in the order that you should work with them. Until now, this chapter was focused on the building blocks of Java applications, and you created a class that prints *Hello World!* by following the instructions, but the details were not really covered. Let's do that now and enrich the class with new details.

Explaining and Enriching the Hello World! Class

We wrote a class named HelloWorld in our sandbox project. I propose you to add that class to the chapter03 module. Just copy it or create it under the com.apress.bgn.ch3.helloworld package, and let's analyze it first and then see what more can we do with it. In Figure 3-25, the class is depicted in the IntelliJ IDEA editor, and a few details about the IDE are underlined. Let's talk about the class first.

CHAPTER 3   GETTING YOUR FEET WET

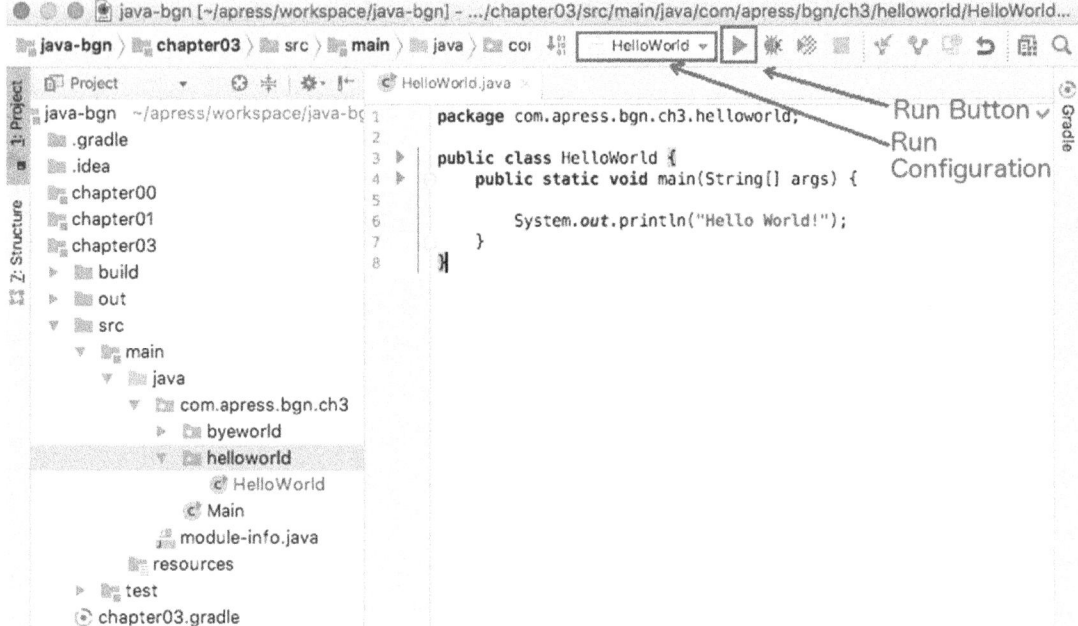

Figure 3-25. *Adding HelloWorld to the java-for-absolute-beginners project*

The following explains the lines that contain different statements.

- **the package declaration:** When classes are part of a package their code must start with this line that declares the package the class is part of. The `package` is a reserved keyword in Java and cannot be used for anything else but declaring a package.

- <empty for convenience> (left empty so the picture looks nicer)

- **the class declaration:** This is the line where we declare our class; it is `public` so it can be seen from everywhere; it is a `class` named `HelloWorld`. The body of a class is enclosed between curly brackets, and the opening bracket is on this line as well.

- **the main() method declaration:** In Java, a method signature is the method name and the number, type, and order of its parameters. A method also has a return type, as in the type of result it returns. But there is also a special type that can declare methods that do not return anything. In order of appearance, the following explains what every term of the `main()` method represents.

- **public:** A method accessor; the main method must be `public`; otherwise, JRE can't access it and call it.

- **static:** When an object of that class type is created, it has the fields and methods as declared by the class. The class is a template for creating objects. Because of the `static` keyword, the main method is not associated with an object of a class type, but with the class itself. More information about this in **Chapter** 4.

- **void:** This keyword is used here to tell us that the main method does not return anything, so it's like a replacement for "no type", because if nothing is returned there is no need for a type.

- **String[] args:** Methods are sometimes declared as receiving some input data, `String[] args` represents an array of text values. (Arrays are sets of data of fixed length; in mathematics they are known as a **one-dimension matrix** or **vector**.) `String` is the class representing text objects in Java. The [ ] means array and `args` is its name. But wait, we've run this method before and we did not need to provide anything! Well, it is not mandatory, but you'll see how you can give it arguments (values provided to the method, which are used by the code in its body) after this list.

! In previous code samples, you might have noticed that the main method was written like this:

```
public class HelloWorld {
    public static void main(String... args) {
        System.out.println("Hello World!");
    }
}
```

The three dots are referred to as `varargs` and allow you to pass more than one string to the method. It's an alternative way of writing this method and it is used in the book when the sources require some special formatting that involves [ ].

- **{:** The starting bracket of the `main()` method body.
- <empty for convenience> (left empty so the picture looks nicer).

- **System.out.println("Hello World!");**: A statement used for writing *Hello World* in the console.

- **}**: The closing bracket of the `main()` method body.

- **}**: The closing bracket for the class body.

If we execute this class, *Hello World!* gets printed in the console. Figure 3-17 shows how to execute a class with a `main()` method in it. After executing a class that way, IntelliJ IDEA automatically saves the configuration for that execution in a run configuration and displays it in a drop-down list next to a triangular green button that executes that class by clicking it. Both are placed on the IDE header and ostentatiously pointed to you in Figure 3-25. Those two elements are really important because a run configuration can be edited and added arguments for the JVM and the `main()` method. Let's first modify the `main()` method to do something with the arguments.

```java
package com.apress.bgn.ch3.helloworld;

public class HelloWorld {
    public static void main(String[] args) {
        System.out.println("Hello " + args[0] + "!");
    }
}
```

! Arrays are accessed using indexes of their elements, and the counting starts in Java from 0. Consequently, the first member of an array can be found at 0, the second at 1 and so on. But arrays can be empty, so in the previous code snippet, if no argument is specified, the execution of the program crash and in the console an explicit message are printed in red.

```
Exception in thread "main" java.lang.ArrayIndexOutOfBoundsException: 0
    at chapter.three/com.apress.bgn.ch3.helloworld.HelloWorld.
    main(HelloWorld.java:5)
```

When we try to access an empty array, or an element of an array that does not exist, Java programs crash and the JVM throws an object of type `ArrayIndexOutOfBoundsException` containing the line where the failure happened and the index of the element we were trying to access. Exception

CHAPTER 3   GETTING YOUR FEET WET

objects are used by the JVM to notify developers of exceptional situations when a Java execution does not work as expected and these objects contain information on where in the code it happened and what caused the problem.

The modification we did in the previous code snippet prints the text value provided as argument when executing the class. Let's modify the run configuration for this class and add an argument. If you click the small gray arrow next to the Run configuration name, a menu appears. Click **Edit Configurations...** and inspect the dialog window shown in Figure 3-26 .

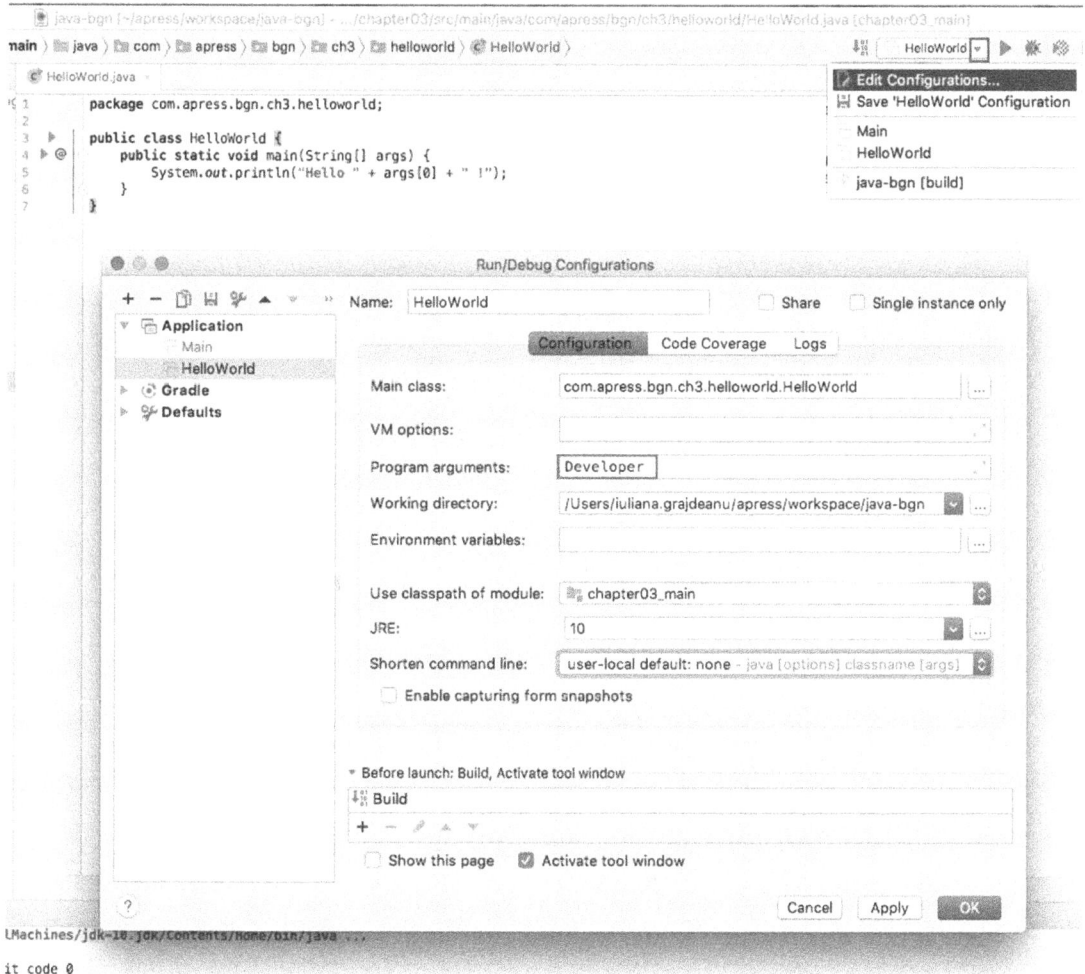

Figure 3-26. Customizing a Run configuration

In the image, the key elements were circled (well, enclosed in a rectangle actually, but you get the idea!). As you can see in the run configurations list in Figure 3-26, IntelliJ IDEA saves a few of your previous executions, including the Gradle `build` task, that you executed earlier in this chapter. In the left of the **Run/Debug Configurations** dialog windows, you can see the IntelliJ IDEA run configurations grouped by type. By default, the last run configuration is opened on the right of the window, in this case it should be the run configuration for the `HelloWorld` class. There are a lot of options you can configure for an execution and most of them have been automatically decided by the IDE. The **Program arguments:** text field is where your arguments for the `main()` method are introduced. In Figure 3-26, I introduced `Developer`. So, if you click the **Apply** button and then the **OK** button, and then execute the class, instead of *Hello World!* you should see now *Hello Developer!* in the console.

So what else can we do with our class? Remember the code the book started with? Let's put it in the main `main()` method.

```java
package com.apress.bgn.ch3.helloworld;

import   java.util.List;

public class HelloWorld {

    public static void main(String... args) {
        List<String> items = List.of("1", "a", "2", "a", "3", "a");
        items.forEach(item -> {
            if (item.equals("a")) {
                System.out.println("A");
            } else {
                System.out.println("Not A");
            }
        });
    }
}
```

The `import java.util.List;` statement is the only type of statement that can exist between a package and a class declaration. This statement is telling the Java compiler that object type `java.util.List` is used in the program. The `import` keyword is followed by the fully qualified name of the data type. A fully qualified name of a data type is made of the package name(`java.util`), a dot(.) and the simple name of the class(`List`).

Without it, the class will not compile. Try it; just put // in front of the statement, which turns the line into a comment that is ignored by the compiler. You will see the editor complaining by making any piece of code related to that list bright red.

The statement `List<String> items = List.of("1", "a", "2", "a", "3", "a");` creates a list of text values[21,22] that are then traversed, one by one, by the `forEach` method, and each of them are tested to see if they are equal to the "a" character.[23]

If you run the class now, you should see a sequence of `A` and `Not A` in the console, each on its own line.

```
Not  A
A
Not  A
A
Not  A
A
```

The code we have written until now uses a few types of objects to print a simple message in the console. The `List` object is used to hold a few `String` objects. The messages are printed using the `println()` method, that is called on the `out` object, that is a static field in the `System` class. And these are just the objects that are visible to you in the code. Under the hood, the `List` objects are processed by a `Consumer` object created on the spot that the lambda expression hides for simplicity.

```
package com.apress.bgn.ch3.helloworld;

import java.util.List;
[import  java.util.function.Consumer;]

public class HelloWorld {
    public static void main(String... args) {
        List<String> items = List.of("1", "a", "2", "a", "3", "a");
        items.forEach(new Consumer<String>() {
            @Override
```

---

[21]Creating lists this way was introduced in Java 9

[22]Specifying what type of elements are in a list by using <> was introduced in Java 5 and it's called **generics**

[23]The whole expression used to do this is called a **lambda expression**. This type of syntax was introduced in Java 8, together with the `forEach` method.

```
            public void accept(String item) {
                if (item.equals("a")) {
                    System.out.println("A");
                } else {
                    System.out.println("Not A");
                }
            }
        });
    }
}
```

It might look scary now, but I promise that this book introduces each concept in a clear context and compared with real life objects and events so you can understand it easily. And if that does not work, there are always more books, more blogs, and the official Oracle webpage for each JDK, which have good tutorials. Where there's a will, there's a way.

! Also, use your IDE! By clicking any object type in the code while pressing the Control/Command key, the code of the object class is opened, and you can see how that class was written and you can read the documentation for it directly in the editor. As an exercise do this for the `forEach` method and the `System` class.

Summary

In this chapter, you did the following tasks:

- Learned how to use JShell
- Learned about Java packages and actually created one
- Learned about Java accessors
- Learned about modules
- Created our first Java project with IntelliJ IDEA
- Wrote the code for our first program within IntelliJ IDEA
- … that we later compiled manually too

- Ran our first program (Hello World!)
- Added packages to it
- Configured a module for it
- … and compiled and executed it manually too
- Learned about Gradle and how it can make a developer's life easy

Many of the things you did in this chapter, you will probably do daily after getting a job as a Java developer—except for the time you'll spend hunting and fixing bugs in existing code. You will probably spend a lot of time reading documentation too, because the JDK has a lot of classes, fields, and methods that you can use to write an application. And with each released version, things change and you must keep yourself up-to-date. Brains have limited capacity, so no employer should ever expect you to know every JDK class and method; but work smart and keep the webpage[24] at `https://docs.oracle.com/javase/10/docs/api/` open in your browser. And when you have doubts about a JDK class or method, you can read about it on the spot.

---

[24]Currently, only the JDK 10 is available at `https://docs.oracle.com/javase/10/`

CHAPTER 4

Java Syntax

Languages are means of communication—verbal or written—between people. Whether they are natural or artificial, they are made of terms and have rules on how to use them to perform the task of communication. Programming languages are means of communicating with a computer. The communication with a computer is a written communication; basically, the developer defines some instructions to be executed, communicates them through an intermediary to the computer, and if the computer understands them, performs the set of actions, and depending on the application type, some sort of reply is returned to the developer.

In the Java language, communication is done through an intermediary—the Java virtual machine. The set of programming rules that define how terms should be connected to produce an understandable unit of communication is called **syntax**. Java borrowed most of its syntax from a programming language called C++, which has a syntax based on the C language. C syntax borrows elements and rules from languages that preceded it, but in essence, all of these languages are based on the natural English language.

Maybe Java got a little cryptic in version 8 because of the introduction of lambda expressions, but when writing a Java program, if you are naming your terms properly in the English language, the result should be code that is easily readable, like a story.

A few details were covered in **Chapter** 3; packages and modules were covered enough to give you a solid understanding of their purpose to avoid confusion with the organization of the project and aimless fumbling through the code. But as expected when it comes to actual code writing, the surface has been barely scratched. Thus, let's begin our deep dive into Java.

CHAPTER 4   JAVA SYNTAX

Base Rules of Writing Java Code

Before writing Java code, let's go over a few rules that you should follow to make sure your code actually works. Let's depict the class we ended **Chapter** 3 with by adding a few details.

```
01.  package com.apress.bgn.ch3.helloworld;
02.
03.  import java.util.List;
04.
05.  /**
06.   * this is a JavaDoc comment
07.   */
08.  public class HelloWorld {
09.      public static void main(String... args) {
10.          //this is a one-line comment
11.          List<String> items = List.of("1", "a", "2", "a", "3", "a");
12.          items.forEach(item -> {
13.          /* this is a
14.                  multi-line
15.             comment */
16.              if (item.equals("a")) {
17.                  System.out.println("A");
18.              } else {
19.                  System.out.println("Not A");
20.              }
21.          });
22.      }
23.  }
```

Next, I'll cover each rule in its own section.

Package Declaration

A Java file always starts with the **package declaration**. The package name can contain letters and numbers, separated by dots. Each part matches a directory in the path to the classes contained in it. The package declaration should reveal the name of the application and the purpose of the classes in the package. Let's take the package naming used for the sources of this book: `com.apress.bgn.ch4.basic`. If we split the package name in pieces, the meaning of each piece is described as follows.

- `com.apress` is the domain of the application, or who owns the application in this case
- `bgn` is the scope of the code, in this case the book it is written for (Java for Absolute **Begin**ners)
- `ch4` is the purpose of the classes in Chapter 4
- `basic` is a more refined level of the purpose for the classes, these classes are simple, used to depict basic Java notions

Import Section

The **import section** follows the package declaration. This section contains the fully qualified names of all classes, interfaces, and enums used within the file. Look at the following code sample.

```
package java.lang;

import java.io.Serializable;
import java.io.ObjectStreamField;
import java.io.UnsupportedEncodingException;
import java.lang.annotation.Native;
import java.nio.charset.Charset;
import java.util.ArrayList;
import java.util.Arrays;
import java.util.Comparator;
import java.util.Formatter;
import java.util.Locale;
...
```

```
public final class String
    implements Serializable, Comparable<String>, CharSequence {

    private  static  final  ObjectStreamField  serialPersistentFields  =
        new ObjectStreamField0;

    ...
}
```

It is a snippet from the official Java `String` class. Every import statement makes reference to the package and the name of a class used within the `String` class body.

Special import statements import static variables and static methods. Static variables and methods can be used without the need to instantiate a class. In the JDK, there is a class used for mathematical processes. It contains static variables and methods that can be used by developers to implement code that solves mathematical problems. Look at the following code.

```
package com.apress.bgn.ch4.basic;

import static java.lang.Math.PI;

import static java.lang.Math.sqrt;

public class Sample extends Object {
    public static void main(String... args) {
        System.out.println("PI value =" + PI);

        double result = sqrt(5.0);

        System.out.println("SQRT value =" + result);
    }
}
```

By putting `import` and `static` together, we can declare a fully qualified name of a class and the method or the variable we are interested in using in the code. This allows us to use the variable or method directly, without the name of the class it is declared in. Without the static imports, the code has to be rewritten like this:

```
package com.apress.bgn.ch4.basic;

import  java.lang.Math;

public class Sample extends Object {
```

```
        public static void main(String... args)  {
            System.out.println("PI value =" + Math.PI);

            double result = Math.sqrt(5.0);

            System.out.println("SQRT value =" + result);
        }
}
```

Another thing that you probably do when writing Java code is to **compact** import statements. Compacting imports is recommended when using multiple classes from the same package to write code, or multiple static variables and methods from the same class. When doing so, the import section of a file becomes really big and difficult to read. This is where compacting comes to help. Compacting imports means replacing all classes from the same package or variables and methods from the same class with a wildcard so only one import statement is needed. So, the Sample class becomes

```
package com.apress.bgn.ch4.basic;

import static java.lang.Math.*;

public class Sample extends Object {
    public static void main(String... args) {
        System.out.println("PI value  =" + PI);

        double result = sqrt(5.0);

        System.out.println("SQRT value =" + result);
    }
}
```

Java "Grammar"

Java is case sensitive, which means that you can write a piece of code as follows.

```
public class Sample {
    public static void main(String... args) {
        int mynumber = 0;
        int myNumber = 1;
```

```
        int Mynumber = 2;
        int MYNUMBER = 3;
        System.out.println(mynumber);
        System.out.println(myNumber);
        System.out.println(Mynumber);
        System.out.println(MYNUMBER);
    }
}
```

All four variables are different and the last lines print numbers: 0 1 2 3. You cannot declare two variables sharing the same name, in the same context (e.g., in the body of a method), because you would be basically redeclaring the same variable and the Java compiler does not allow this. If you try to do this, your code will not compile, and even IntelliJ IDEA will try to make you see the error of your ways by underlining the code in red and showing you a relevant message, like in Figure 4-1, where the mynumber variable is declared twice.

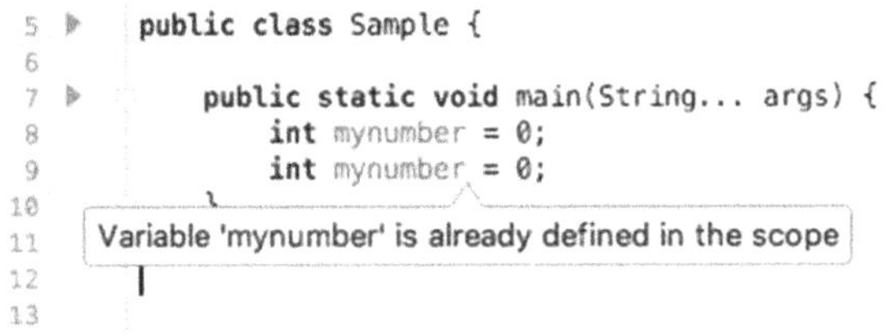

Figure 4-1. *Same statements example with error*

There is a set of **Java keywords** that can be used only for a fixed and predefined purpose in the Java code. A few of them have already been introduced: import, package, public, class. The rest of them are covered at the end of the chapter with a short explanation for each (see Tables 4-2 and 4-3).

CHAPTER 4 JAVA SYNTAX

Except for import, package, interface (or @interface), enum and class declarations, everything else in a Java source file must be declared between **curly brackets** ({}). These are called **block delimiters**. Take a look at the beginning of section 4.1. The brackets are used there to wrap up the following.

- contents of a class, also called the body of the class (brackets in lines 08 and 23)

- contents of a method, also called the body of a method (brackets in lines 09 and 22)

- a set of instructions to be executed together (brackets in lines 12 and 21)

Line terminators: code lines are usually ended in Java by the semicolon (;) symbol or by the ASCII characters CR, LF, or CR LF. Colons are used to terminate fully functioning statements, like the list declaration in line 11. If we have a really little monitor, and we are forced to split that statement on two subsequent lines to keep the code readable, the colon at its end tells the compiler that this statement that is correct only when taken together. Take a look at Figure 4-2.

```
1     package com.apress.bgn.ch4.basic;
2
3     import java.util.List;
4
5     public class Sample {
6
7         public static void main(String... args) {
8             List<String> items = List.of("1", "a", "2", "a", "3", "a");
9
10            List<String> others =
11                    List.of("1", "a", "2", "a", "3", "a");
12
13            List<String> badList = ;
14                    List.of("1", "a", "2", "a", "3", "a");
15        }
16    }
17
```

Figure 4-2. *Different statements samples*

The declaration of a list in line 8 is equivalent to the one in lines 10 and 11. The declaration in line 13 and 14 is intentionally written wrong—a colon is added in line 13, which ends the statement there; but that statement is not valid and the compiler complains about it when you try to compile that class by printing an exception saying: "Error:(13, 32) java: illegal start of expression". If the error message does not seem to fit the example, think about it like this: the problem for the compiler is not

105

the wrongful termination of the statement, but that after the = symbol, the compiler expects to find some sort of expression that produces the value for the `badList` variable, but instead it finds nothing.

Java Identifiers

An **identifier** is the name you give to an item in Java: a class, variable, method, and so forth. Identifiers must respect a few rules to allow the code to compile and also common-sense programming rules, called **Java coding conventions**. A few of them are listed below:

- an identifier cannot be one of the Java reserved words, or the code will not compile
- an identifier cannot be a boolean literal (`true, false`) or the `null` literal , or the code will not compile
- an identifier can be made of letters, numbers and any of _, $
- developers should declare their identifiers following the Camel case writing style, the practice of writing compound words or phrases such that each word or abbreviation in the middle of the phrase begins with a capital letter, with no intervening spaces or punctuation, making sure each word or abbreviation in the middle of the identifier name begins with a capital letter (e.g., `StringBuilder, isAdult`)

A **variable** is a set of characters that can be associated with a value. It has a type. The set of values that can be assigned to it are restricted to a certain interval group of values or must follow a certain form defined by that type. For example, `items` declared in line 11 is a variable of type `List`.

In Java, there are three types of variables.

- **fields** are variables defined in class bodies, outside of method bodies and that do not have the keyword `static` in front of them
- **local variables** are variables declared inside method bodies, they are relevant only in that context
- **static variables** are variables declared inside class bodies with the have the keyword `static` in front of them. If they are declared as public they are accessible globally.

Java Comments

Java comments refer to pieces of explanatory text that are not part of the code executed and are ignored by the compiler. There are three ways to add comments within the code in Java, depending on the characters used to declare them.

- `//` is used for single line comments (line 10)
- `/** ... */` Javadoc comments, special comments that are exported using special tools into the documentation of a project called Javadoc API (lines 05 to 07)
- `/* ... */` used for multiline comments (lines 13 to 15)

Java Object Types

When introducing the Java building blocks in **Chapter** 3, only class was mentioned to keep things simple. It was mentioned that there are other object types in Java. The expression **object type** is not really accurate and in this section, things become clearer.

Classes are templates for creating objects. Creating an object based on a class is called **instantiation** and the resulted object is referred to as **an instance of that class**. Instances are called **objects** because by default any class written by a developer implicitly extends class `java.lang.Object` if no other superclass is declared. So, the following class declaration

```
package com.apress.bgn.ch4.basic;

public class Sample {
}
```

is equivalent to

```
package com.apress.bgn.ch4.basic;

public class Sample extends Object {
}
```

Also, notice how importing the `java.lang` package is not necessary, because the `Object` class is the root class of the Java hierarchy, all classes (including arrays) must have access to extend it. And thus, the `java.lang` package is implicitly imported as well.

But aside from classes, there are other template types that can be used for creating objects in Java. The following sections introduce them and explain what they are used for. But let's do so in context.

Let's create a family of templates for defining humans. Most Java tutorials use templates for vehicles or geometrical shapes. I want to model something that anybody can easily understand and relate to. The purpose of the following sections is to develop Java templates that model different types of people. The only Java template that I've explained so far is the class, so let's continue with that.

Classes

The operation through which instances are created is called **instantiation**. So, to design a class that models a generic human, we should think about two things: human characteristics and human actions. So, what do all humans have in common? Well, a lot, but for the purpose of this section, let's choose three generic attributes: a name, age, and height. These attributes map in a Java class to variables called **fields** or **properties**.

Fields

So, our class looks like this (initially):

```
package com.apress.bgn.ch4.basic;

public class Human {
    String name;
    int age;
    float height;
}
```

In the code sample, the **fields** have different types, depending on which values should be associated with them. For example, `name` can be associated with a text value, like "John", and text is represented in Java by the `String` type. The `age` can be associated with numeric integer values, so is of type `int`. And for the purpose of this section, we've considered that the height of a person is a rational number like 1.9, so we used the special Java type for this kind of value: `float`.

So, now we have a class modelling some basic attributes of a human. How do we use it? We need a `main()` method and we need to instantiate the class. In the next code snippet, a human named John is created.

```java
package com.apress.bgn.ch4.basic;

public class BasicHumanDemo {

    public static void main(String... args) {
        Human human = new Human();
        human.name = "John";
        human.age = 40;
        human.height  =  1.91f;
    }
}
```

To create a `Human` instance, we use the `new` keyword. Next, we call a special method called a `constructor`. I've covered methods before, but this one is special. (Some programmers do not even consider it a method.) The most obvious reason for that is it wasn't defined anywhere in the body of the `Human` class. So, where is it coming from? Well, it's a default constructor that is automatically generated by the compiler unless an explicit one is declared. A class cannot exist without a constructor; otherwise, it cannot be instantiated. That is why the compiler generates one if none was explicitly declared. The default constructor, calls `super()` that invokes the `Object` no argument constructor that initializes all fields with default values. This can be tested by the following example.

```java
package com.apress.bgn.ch4.basic;

public class BasicHumanDemo {

    public static void main(String... args) {
        Human human = new Human();
        System.out.println("name: " + human.name);
        System.out.println("age:  " +  human.age);
        System.out.println("height: " + human.height);
    }
}
```

What do you think will happen when you run the previous code? If you think that some default values (neutral) printed, you are absolutely right. The following is the output of the previous code.

```
name: null
age: 0
height: 0.0
```

The numeric variables were initialized with 0, and the `String` value was initialized with `null`. The reason for that is that the numeric types are primitive data types and `String` is an object data type. The `String` class is part of the `java.lang` package, which is one of the predefined Java classes that creates objects of type `String`. It is a special data type that represents text objects. We'll go deeper into data types in the following chapter.

Class Variables

Aside attributes that are specific to each human in particular, all humans have something in common: a lifespan, which is assumed to be 100 years. It would be redundant to declare a field called *lifespan*, because it has to be associated with the same value for all human instances. So, we declare a field using the `static` keyword in the Human class, which has the same value for all Human instances and that is initialized only once. And we can go one step further and make sure that value never changes during the execution of the program by adding the `final` modifier in front of its declaration as well. This way we created a special type of variable called a **constant**. The new Human class looks like this:

```
package com.apress.bgn.ch4.basic;

public class Human {
    static final int LIFESPAN = 100;

    String name;

    int age;

    float height;

}
```

The `LIFESPAN` variable is also called a **class variable**, because it is not associated with instances but with the class. This is clear in the following example.

```java
package com.apress.bgn.ch4.basic;

public class BasicHumanDemo {
    public static void main(String... args) {
        Human john = new Human();
        john.name = "John";

        Human jane = new Human();
        jane.name = "Jane";

        System.out.println("John's lifespan = " + john.LIFESPAN);
        System.out.println("Jane's lifespan = " + jane.LIFESPAN);

        System.out.println("Human lifespan = " + Human.LIFESPAN);
    }
}
```

When the `main()` method of the preceding class is executed, the following is printed, which proves everything that was mentioned before.

```
John's lifespan = 100
Jane's lifespan = 100
Human lifespan = 100
```

Encapsulating Data

The class we defined makes no use of access modifiers on the fields, which is not acceptable. Java is known as an object-oriented programming language (OOP), and thus, code written in Java must respect **the principles of OOP**. Respecting these coding principles ensures that the written code is of good quality and totally aligns with the fundamental Java style. One of the OOP principles is **encapsulation**. The encapsulation principle refers to hiding of data implementation by restricting access to it using special methods called **accessors (getters)** and **mutators (setters)**.

Basically, any field of a class should have private access, and access to it should be controlled by methods that can be intercepted, tested, and tracked to see where they were called. Getters and setters are a normal practice to have when working so objects that most IDEs have a default options to generate them, including IntelliJ IDEA. Right-click inside the class body and select the **Generate** option to see all possibilities and select **Getters and Setters** to generate the methods for you. The menu is depicted in Figure 4-3.

After making the fields private, and generating the getters and setter the Human class now looks like this:

```java
package com.apress.bgn.ch4.basic;

public class Human {
    static final int LIFESPAN = 100;

    private String name;

    private int age;

    private float height;

    public String getName() {
        return name;
    }

    public void setName(String name) {
        this.name = name;
    }

    public int getAge() {
        return age;
    }

    public void setAge(int age) {
        this.age = age;
    }

    public float getHeight() {
        return height;
    }
```

CHAPTER 4 JAVA SYNTAX

```
    public void setHeight(float height) {
        this.height = height;
    }
}
```

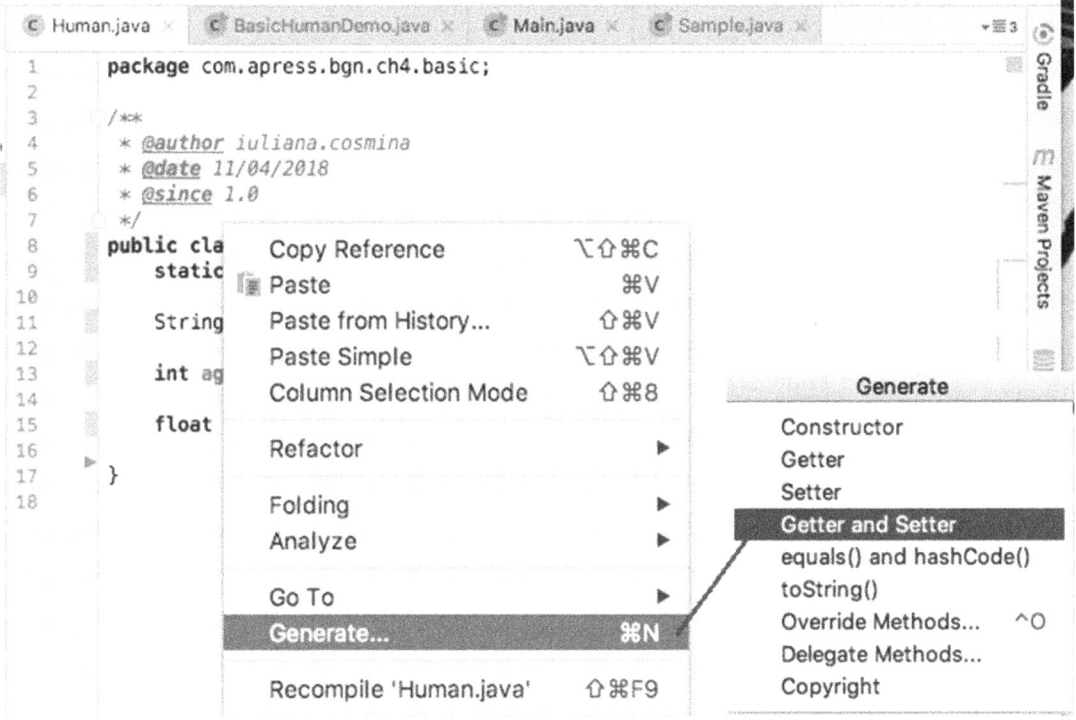

Figure 4-3. *IntelliJ IDEA code generation menu. Generate...* ➤ *Getter and Setter submenu*

So, you may be wondering what `this` is. As the word says, it is a reference to the current object. So, `this.name` is the value of the field `name` of the current object. Inside the class body, `this` accesses fields for the current object, when there are parameters in methods that have the same name. And as you can see, the setters and getters that IntelliJ IDEA generates have parameters that are named the same as the fields.

Getters are the simplest methods declared without any **parameter**. They return the value of the field they are associated with. Their naming convention uses the `get` prefix and the name of the field they access, with the first letter uppercased.

113

Setters are methods that return nothing. They declare as a parameter a variable with the same type that needs to be associated to the field. Their names are made of the *set* prefix and the name of the field they access, with its first letter uppercased. Figure 4-4 depicts the setter and getter for the **name** field.

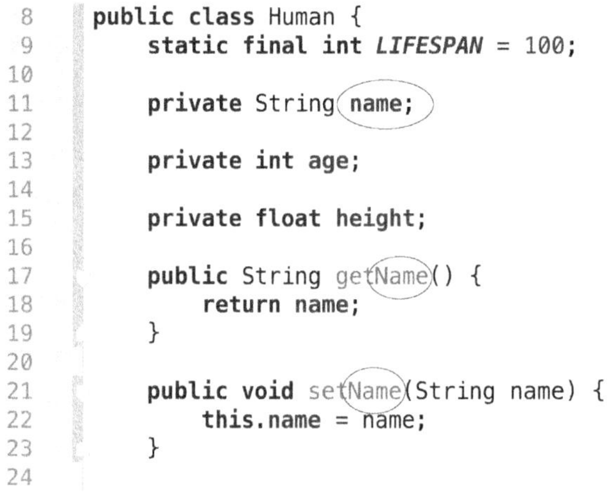

```
 8   public class Human {
 9       static final int LIFESPAN = 100;
10
11       private String name;
12
13       private int age;
14
15       private float height;
16
17       public String getName() {
18           return name;
19       }
20
21       public void setName(String name) {
22           this.name = name;
23       }
24
```

Figure 4-4. *Setter and getter methods used for the name field*

This means that when instantiating the Human class, we have to use the setters to set the field values and the getters to access those values. Thus, our class BasicHumanDemo becomes

```
package com.apress.bgn.ch4.basic;

public class BasicHumanDemo {

    public static void main(String... args) {
        Human human = new Human();
        human.setName("John");
        human.setAge(40);
        human.setHeight(1.91f);

        System.out.println("name: " + human.getName());
        System.out.println("age: " + human.getAge());
        System.out.println("height: " + human.getHeight());
    }
```

Methods

Since getters and setters are methods it is time to start the discussions about methods too. A method is a block of code characterized by returned type, name, and parameters that describes an action done by or on the object that makes use of the values of its fields and/or arguments provided. An abstract template of a Java method is depicted as follows.

```
[accessor] [returned type] [name] type1 param1, type2 param2, ... {
  // code
  [ [maybe] return val]
}
```

Let's create a method for the Human class that computes and prints how much time a human still has to live by making use of his age and the LIFESPAN constant. Because the method does not return anything, the return type used is void, a special type that tells the compiler that the method does not return anything and we have no return statement in the method body.

```java
package com.apress.bgn.ch4.basic;

public class Human {
    static final int LIFESPAN = 100;

    private String name;
    private int age;
    private float height;

    /**
     * compute and prints time to live
     */
    public void computeAndPrintTtl(){
        int ttl = LIFESPAN - this.age;
        System.out.println("Time to live: " + ttl);
    }
        ...
}
```

> ! There is a Java coding convention in the naming of constants that recommends using only uppercase letters, underscores, and numbers.

The preceding method definition does not declare any parameters, so considering we have a Human instance we can call the method like this:

```
Human human = new Human();
human.setName("John");
human.setAge(40);
human.setHeight(1.91f);
human.computeAndPrintTtl();
```

And we expect it to print Time to live: 60, which actually happened. Now, let's modify the method to return the value instead of printing it.

```
package com.apress.bgn.ch4.basic;

public class Human {
    static final int LIFESPAN = 100;

    private String name;
    private int age;
    private float height;

    /**
     * @return time to live
     */
    public int getTimeToLive(){
        int ttl = LIFESPAN - this.age;
        return ttl;
    }
        ...
}
```

Calling the method do nothing in this case, we have to modify the code to save the returned value and print it.

```
Human human = new Human();
human.setName("John");
human.setAge(40);
human.setHeight(1.91f);
int timeToLive = getTimeToLive();
System.out.println("Time  to  live: " + timeToLive);
```

Both methods introduced here declare no parameters, so they are called without providing any arguments. We won't cover methods with parameters, as the setters are more than obvious. Let's skip ahead.

Constructors

Now we've done it. We can no longer use `human.name` without the compiler complaining about it. But still, it is annoying to call all of those setters to set the properties; something should be done about that. Remember the implicit constructor? Well, let's create an explicit one that has parameters for each of the fields we are interested in.

```
public class Human {
    static final int LIFESPAN = 100;

    private String name;
    private int age;
    private float height;

    public Human(String name, int age, float height) {
        this.name = namc;
        this.age =  age;
        this.height   =   height;
    }
    ...
}
```

In the preceding example, you can see that the constructor does not include a `return` statement, even if the result of calling a constructor is the creation of an object. Constructors are different from methods in that way. By declaring an explicit constructor, the default constructor is no longer generated. So, creating a Human instance by calling the default constructor does not work anymore; the code no longer compiles because the default constructor is no longer generated.

```
Human human = new Human();
```

To create a Human instance, we now have to call the new constructor and provide proper arguments in place of the parameters, having the same types as declared.

```
Human human = new Human("John", 40, 1.91f);
```

But what if we do not want to be forced to set all fields using this constructor? It's simple, we define another with only the parameters that we are interested in. Let's define a constructor that only sets the name and the age for a Human instance.

```java
public class Human {
    static final int LIFESPAN = 100;

    private String name;
    private int age;
    private float height;

    public Human(String name, int age) {
        this.name = name;
        this.age = age;
    }

    public Human(String name, int age, float height) {
        this.name = name;
        this.age = age;
        this.height = height;
    }
    ...
}
```

And this is where we stumble upon an OOP principle called **polymorphism**. The term is Greek and translates to *one name, many forms*. Polymorphism manifests itself by having multiple methods all with the same name, but slightly different functionality. There are two basic types of polymorphism: **overriding**, also called **run-time polymorphism**, and **overloading**, which is referred to as **compile-time polymorphism**. The second type of polymorphism applies to the preceding constructors, because we have two of them, one with a different set of parameters that looks like it is an extension of the simpler one.

So, we have some code duplication in the previous example, and there is a common sense programming principle called **DRY**[1] (Don't Repeat Yourself!) that the following example clearly defies. So, let's fix that by using the `this` keyword.

```java
public class Human {
    static final int LIFESPAN = 100;

    private String  name;
    private int age;
    private float height;

    public Human(String name, int age) {
        this.name = name;
        this.age  =  age;
    }
    public Human(String name, int age, float height) {
        this(name, age);
        this.height  =  height;
    }
    ...
}
```

Yes, constructors can call each other by using `this(...)`. So now, we can use both constructors to create `Human` instances. If we use the one that does not set the height, the `height` field is implicitly initialized with the default value for type `float`.

---

[1] Also one of the clean coding principles; read more about it at https://blog.goyello.com/2013/01/21/top-9-principles-clean-code/

Now, our class is generic; we could even say that it models a Human class in an abstract way. If we were to try to model humans with certain skill sets or abilities, we must enrich this class. Let's say we want to model musicians and actors. This means we need to create two new classes. The Musician class is depicted in the following; getters and setters for the fields are skipped.

```java
public class Musician {
    static final int LIFESPAN = 100;
    private String name;
    private int age;
    private float height;
    private String musicSchool;
    private String  genre;
    private List<String> songs;
    ...
}
```

The Actor class is depicted next; getters and setters for the fields are also skipped.

```java
public class Actor {
    static final int LIFESPAN = 100;
    private String name;
    private int age;
    private float height;
    private  String  actingSchool;
    private List<String> films;
    ...
}
```

There are more than a few common elements between the two classes. One of the clean coding principles requires developers to avoid code redundancy. This can be done by designing the classes by following two OOP principles: **inheritance** and **abstraction**.

Abstraction

Abstraction is an OOP principle that manages complexity. Abstraction decomposes complex implementations and defines core parts that can be reused. In our case, common fields of the `Musician` and `Actor` classes can be grouped in the `Human` class that we defined earlier in the chapter. The `Human` class can be viewed as an abstraction, because any human in this world is more than his name, age, and height. So, there is no need to create `Human` instances, because a human is represented by something else, like passion, purpose, and skill. A class that does not need to be instantiated, but groups together fields and methods for other classes to inherit, or provide a concrete implementation for is modelled in Java by an abstract class. Thus, we modify the `Human` class to make it `abstract` first. And since we are abstracting this class, let's make the `LIFESPAN` constant public so we can access it from anywhere and make the `getTimeToLive` method abstract.

```java
package com.apress.bgn.ch4.basic;

public abstract class Human {
    public static final int LIFESPAN = 100;

    private String name;
    private int age;
    private float height;

    public Human(String name, int age) {
        this.name = name;
        this.age  =  age;
    }

    public Human(String name, int age, float height) {
        this(name, age);
        this.height  =  height;
    }

    /**
     * @return time to live
     */
    public abstract int getTimeToLive();
...
// setters & getters for fields in this class
}
```

An abstract method like getTimeToLive() is declared in the example; it is a method missing the body. This means that within the Human class, there is no concrete implementation for this method, only a skeleton—a template that extending classes must provide a concrete implementation for.

Oh, but wait, we kept the constructors! Why did we do that if we are not allowed to use them anymore? And we aren't, because Figure 4-5 shows what IntelliJ IDEA does with the BasicHumanDemo class Figure 4-5.

```java
package com.apress.bgn.ch4.basic;

/**
 * @author iuliana.cosmina
 * @date 21/04/2018
 * @since 1.0
 */
public class BasicHumanDemo {

    public static void main(String... args) {
        Human human = new Human( name: "John", age: 40, height: 1.91f);

        Syst 'Human' is abstract; cannot be instantiated ));
        System.out.println("age: " + human.getAge());
        System.out.println("height: " + human.getHeight());

    }
}
```

Figure 4-5. *Java compiler error when trying to instantiate an abstract class*

We kept the constructors because they can help further abstracting behavior. The Musician and Actor classes must be rewritten to extend the Human class. This is done by using the extends keyword when declaring the class and specifying the class to be extended, also called the **parent class** or **superclass**. The resulting class is called a **subclass**. When extending a non-abstract class, the subclass **inherits** all the fields and concrete methods declared in the superclass.

When extending an abstract class, the subclass must provide a concrete implementation for all abstract methods, and must declare their own constructors, which eventually make use of the constructors declared in the abstract class. These constructors can be called by using the keyword super. The same goes for methods, but not for fields, unless they have the proper access modifier.

Let's see what the `Musician` class looks like when making use of abstraction and inheritance.

```java
package com.apress.bgn.ch4.basic;

import java.util.List;

public class Musician extends Human {

    private String musicSchool;

    private String genre;

    private List<String> songs;

    public Musician(String name, int age, float height,
            String musicSchool, String genre) {
        super(name, age, height);
        this.musicSchool = musicSchool;
        this.genre = genre;
    }

    public int getTimeToLive() {
        return (LIFESPAN - getAge()) / 2;
    }
...
// setters & getters for fields in this class
}
```

The `songs` field was not used as a parameter in the constructor for simplicity reasons here.

The `Musician` constructor calls the constructor in the superclass to set the properties defined there. Also, notice the full implementation provided for the `getTimeToLive()` method.

The `Actor` class is rewritten in a similar manner. You find a proposal implementation in the sources for the book, but try to write your own before looking in the `com.apress.bgn.ch4.basic` package.

Figure 4-6 shows the `Human` class hierarchy, as generated by IntelliJ IDEA.

CHAPTER 4 JAVA SYNTAX

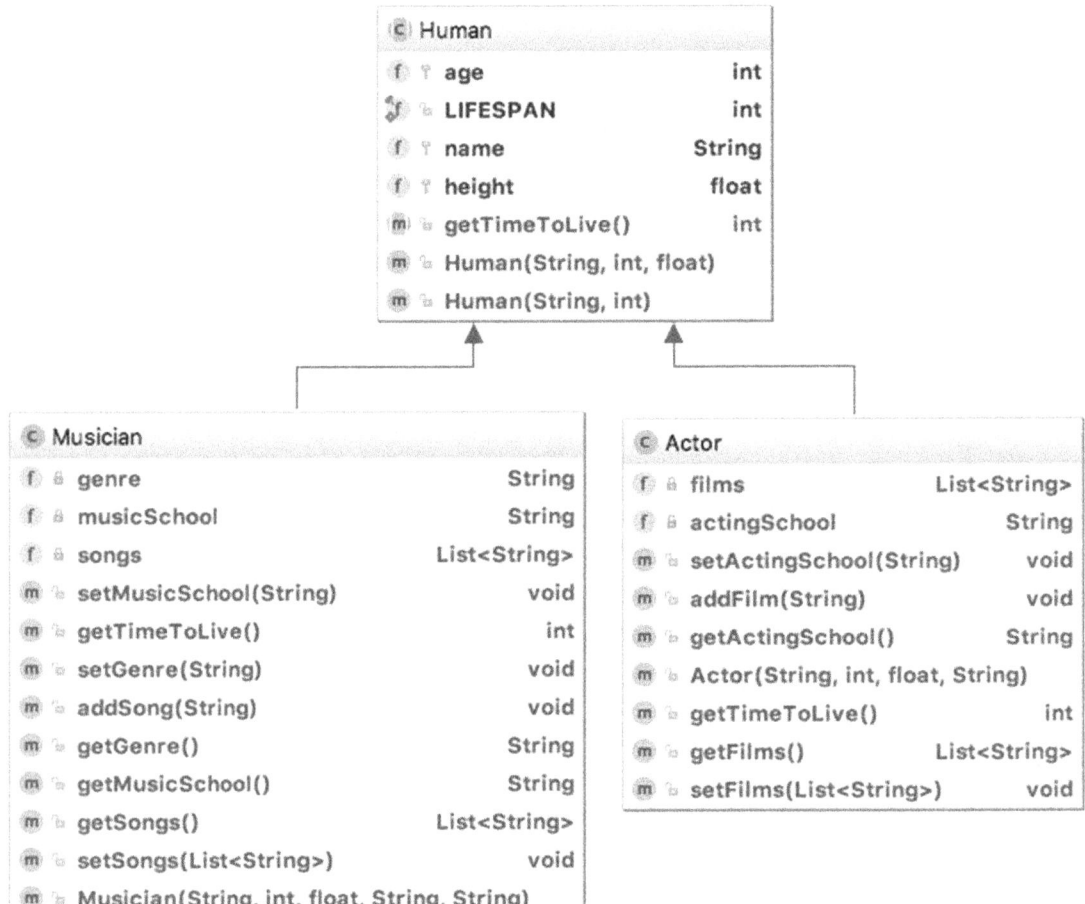

Figure 4-6. *UML diagram generated by IntelliJ IDEA*

The UML diagram clearly shows the members of each class and the arrows point to the superclass. UML diagrams are useful tools in designing class hierarchies and defining logic of applications. If you want to read more about them and the many types of UML diagrams that there are, you can do so at www.uml-diagrams.org.

After covering so much about classes and how to create objects, we need to cover other Java important components that create even more detailed objects, which can then be used to implement more complex applications. Our Human class is missing quite a few attributes, like gender for example. A field that models the gender of a person can only have values from a fixed set of values. It used to be two, but because we are living in a brave new world that is fond of political correctness, we cannot limit the set of values for genders to two; so we introduce a third, called *UNDEFINED*. This means that we must introduce a new class to represent a gender that is limited to being instantiated three times. This would be tricky to do with a typical class. So, in Java version 1.5, **enums** were introduced.

Enums

The enum type is a special class type. It defines a special type of class that can only be instantiated a fixed number of times. An enum declaration, groups all instances of that enum. All of them are constants. So, the Gender enum can be defined as shown in the following piece of code.

```
package com.apress.bgn.ch4.basic;

public enum Gender {
    FEMALE,
    MALE,
    UNDEFINED
}
```

An enum cannot be instantiated externally. An enum is by default final, thus it cannot be extended. Remember how by default every class in Java implicitly extends class Object? Every enum in Java implicitly extends class java.lang.Enum<E> and in doing so, every enum instance inherits special methods that are useful when handling enums.

As an enum is a special type of class, it can have fields and a constructor that can only be private, as enum instances cannot be created externally. The private modifier is not needed explicitly, as the compiler knows what to do. Let's modify our Gender enum to add an integer field that is the numerical representation of each gender and a String field that is the text representation.

```
package com.apress.bgn.ch4.basic;

public enum Gender {
    FEMALE(1, "f"),
    MALE(2, "m") ,
    UNDEFINED(3, "u");

    private int repr;
    private String descr;
```

CHAPTER 4   JAVA SYNTAX

```
    Gender(int repr, String descr) {
        this.repr = repr;
        this.descr = descr;
    }

    public int getRepr() {
        return repr;
    }

    public String getDescr() {
        return descr;
    }
}
```

But wait, what would stop us from declaring setters and modifying the field values? Well, nothing. If that is what you need to do you can do it. But **this is not a good practice**. Enum instances, should be constant. So, what we can do is to not create setters, and make sure the values of the fields never change by declaring them `final`. When we do so, the only way the fields can be initialized is by calling the constructor, and since the constructor cannot be called externally, the integrity of our data is ensured. So, our enum becomes

```
package com.apress.bgn.ch4.basic;

public enum Gender {
    FEMALE(1, "f"),
    MALE(2, "m") ,
    UNDEFINED(3, "u");

    private final int repr;
    private final String descr;

    Gender(int repr, String descr) {
        this.repr = repr;
        this.descr = descr;
    }

    public int getRepr() {
        return repr;
    }
```

```java
        public String getDescr() {
            return descr;
        }
    }
```

Methods can be added to enums, and each instance can override them. So, if we add a method called getComment() to the Gender enum, every instance inherits it. But the instance can override it. Let's see what that looks like.

```java
package com.apress.bgn.ch4.basic;

public enum Gender {
    FEMALE(1, "f"),
    MALE(2, "m") ,
    UNDEFINED(3, "u"){
        @Override
        public String comment() {
            return "to be decided later: " + getRepr() + ", " + getDescr();
        }
    };

    private final int repr;
    private final String descr;

    Gender(int repr, String descr) {
        this.repr = repr;
        this.descr = descr;
    }

    public int getRepr() {
        return repr;
    }

    public String getDescr() {
        return descr;
    }

    public String comment() {
        return repr + ": " + descr;
    }
}
```

If we were to print the values returned by the comment() method for each instance, we would see the following.

```java
package com.apress.bgn.ch4.basic;

public class Sample extends Object {
    public static void main(String... args) {
        System.out.println(Gender.FEMALE.comment());
        // prints '1: f'
        System.out.println(Gender.MALE.comment());
        // prints '2: m'
        System.out.println(Gender.UNDEFINED.comment());
        //prints 'to be decided later: 3, u'
    }
}
```

We're going to be playing with enums in future examples as well. Just remember that whenever you need to limit the implementation of a class to a fixed number of instances, enums are the tools for you. And now because we introduced enums, our Human class can also have a field of type Gender.

```java
package com.apress.bgn.ch4.basic;

public abstract class Human {
    public static final int LIFESPAN = 100;

    protected String name;

    protected int age;

    protected float height;

    private Gender gender;

    public Human(String name, int age, Gender gender) {
        this.name = name;
        this.age = age;
        this.gender = gender;
    }
```

```
    public Human(String name, int age, float height, Gender gender) {
        this(name, age, gender);
        this.height = height;
    }
    ...
}
```

In previous sections, **interfaces** were mentioned as one of the Java tools used to create objects. It is high time I expand the subject.

Interfaces

One of the most common Java interview questions is, "What is the difference between an interface and an abstract class?" This section provides you the most detailed answer to that question. An **interface** is not a class, but it does help create classes. An interface is fully abstract; it has no fields, only method definitions (skeletons). A class can implement an interface, and unless the class is abstract, it is forced to provide concrete implementations for them. Each method declared inside an interface is implicitly public and abstract, because methods need to be abstract to force implementing classes to provide implementations and are public, so classes have access to do so.

The only methods with concrete bodies in an interface are static methods and starting with Java 8, **default** methods. The interfaces cannot be instantiated, they do not have constructors.

Interfaces that declare no method definitions are called **marker** interfaces and have the purpose to mark classes for specific purposes. The most renowned Java marker interface is `java.io.Serializable`, which marks objects that can be serialized(their state can be saved to a binary file).

An interface can be declared in its own file as a top-level component, or nested inside another component. There are two types of interfaces: normal interfaces and annotations.

The difference between abstract classes and interfaces, and when one or the other should be used, becomes relevant in the context of **inheritance**. Java supports only single inheritance. This means a class can only have one superclass. This might seem like a limitation, but let's consider a simple example. Let's modify the previous hierarchy and imagine a class called `Performer` that should extend the `Musician` and `Actor` classes. If you need a real human that can be modelled by this class, think of David Duchovny, an actor who recently got into music.

Figure 4-7 shows the class hierarchy.

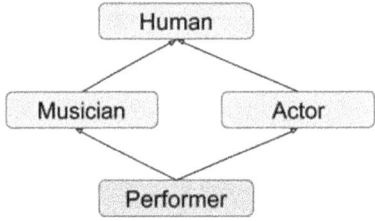

Figure 4-7. *Diamond class hierarchy*

The hierarchy in Figure 4-7 introduces something called **the diamond problem**, and the name is inspired by the shape formed by the relationships between classes. What is actually wrong with the design? If both `Musician` and `Actor` extend `Human`, and inherit all members from it, which member does `Performer` inherit and from where? Because it cannot inherit members of the `Human` class twice - this would make this class useless and invalid. So, what is the solution? As you probably imagine, given the title of this section: **interfaces**.

What has to be done is to turn methods in classes `Musician` and `Actor` into method skeletons and transform those classes into interfaces. The behavior from the `Musician` is moved to a class called, let's say `Guitarist`, which extends the `Human` class and implement the `Musician` interface. For the `Actor` class, something similar can be done, but I'll leave that as an exercise for you. Some help is provided by the hierarchy shown in Figure 4-8.

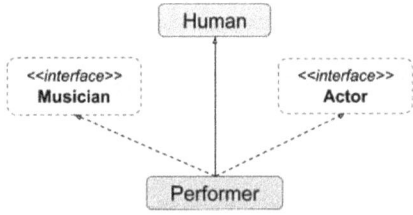

Figure 4-8. *Java hierarchy with interfaces for Performer class*

The `Musician` interface contains only method templates mapping what a musician does. It does not go into detail to model how. The same goes for the `Actor` interface. In the following code snippet, you can see the bodies of the two interfaces.

```
// Musician.java
package com.apress.bgn.ch4.hierarchy;

import java.util.List;
```

```java
public interface Musician {
    String getMusicSchool();
    void setMusicSchool(String musicSchool);
    List<String> getSongs();
    void setSongs(List<String> songs);
    String getGenre();
    void setGenre(String genre);
}

// Actor
package com.apress.bgn.ch4.hierarchy;

import java.util.List;

public interface Actor {
    String getActingSchool();
    void setActingSchool(String actingSchool);
    List<String> getFilms();
    void setFilms(List<String> films);
    void addFilm(String filmName);
}
```

The fields have been removed because they cannot be part of the interfaces; all that is left are the method templates. The `Performer` class is depicted in the next code snippet.

```java
package com.apress.bgn.ch4.hierarchy;

import java.util.List;

public class Performer extends Human
    implements Musician, Actor {

    private String musicSchool;

    private String genre;

    private List<String> songs;

    private String actingSchool;

    private List<String> films;
```

CHAPTER 4 JAVA SYNTAX

```java
    public Performer(String name, int age, float height, Gender gender) {
        super(name, age, height, gender);
    }

    @Override
    public int getTimeToLive() {
        return (LIFESPAN - getAge()) / 2;
    }

    public String getMusicSchool() {
        return musicSchool;
    }

    public void setMusicSchool(String musicSchool) {
        this.musicSchool = musicSchool;
    }

    public List<String> getSongs() {
        return songs;
    }

    public void setSongs(List<String> songs) {
        this.songs = songs;
    }

    public void addSong(String song) {
        this.songs.add(song);
    }

    public String getGenre() {
        return genre;
    }

    public void setGenre(String genre) {
        this.genre = genre;
    }

    public String getActingSchool() {
        return actingSchool;
    }
```

```java
    public void setActingSchool(String actingSchool) {
        this.actingSchool = actingSchool;
    }

    public List<String> getFilms() {
        return films;
    }

    public void setFilms(List<String> films) {
        this.films = films;
    }

    public void addFilm(String filmName) {
        this.films.add(filmName);
    }
}
```

What you are left with from this example is that using interfaces **multiple inheritance** is possible in Java, and that classes extend classes and implement interfaces. But inheritance applies to interfaces too. For example, both `Musician` and `Actor` interface can extend an interface named `Artist` that contains template for behavior common to both. For example, we can combine the music school and acting school into a generic school and define the setters and getters for it as method templates. The `Artist` interface is depicted as follows with `Musician`.

```java
// Artist.java
package com.apress.bgn.ch4.hierarchy;

public interface Artist {
    String getSchool();
    void setSchool(String chool);
}
```

```java
// Musician.java
package com.apress.bgn.ch4.hierarchy;

import java.util.List;
```

```java
public interface Musician extends Artist {
    List<String> getSongs();
    void setSongs(List<String> songs);
    String getGenre();
    void setGenre(String genre);
}
```

Hopefully, you understood the idea of multiple inheritance, when it is appropriate to use classes, and when to use interfaces in designing your applications. It is time to fulfill the promise made in the beginning of this section and list the differences between abstract classes and interfaces. You can find them in Table 4-1.

Table 4-1. Differences Between Abstract Classes and Interfaces in Java

Abstract Class	Interface
Can have non-abstract methods	Can only have abstract and (since Java 8 default methods, since Java 9 private methods)
Single inheritance: a class can only extend one class	Multiple inheritance: a class can implement more than one interface.
Can have final, non-final, static and non-static variables	Can only have static and final fields.
Declared with **abstract class**	Declared with **interface**.
Can extend another class using keyword **extends** and implement interfaces with keyword **implements**	Can only extend other interfaces (one or more) using key-word **extends**.
Can have non-abstract, protected or private members	All members are method definitions and are by default abstract and public. (Except default methods, starting with Java 8 and private methods, starting with Java 9.)
If a class has an abstract method, it must be declared itself abstract	(No correspondence)

Default Methods

One problem with interfaces is that if you modify their bodies to add new methods, most likely, the code stops compiling because the classes implementing the interfaces do not provide concrete implementations for the new methods declared in the interfaces. Sure, a solution would be to declare the new methods in a new interface and then creating new classes that implement both new and old interfaces.

The methods interfaces expose make up an API (application programming interface) and when developing applications, the aim is to design applications and their components to have a stable API. This rule is described in the **open closed principle**, which is one of the five SOLID programming principles.[2] This principle states that you should be able to extend a class without modifying it. Thus, modifying the interface a class implements, extends the class behavior, but only if the class is modified to provide a concrete implementation for the new methods. So, implementing interfaces, tends to lead to breaking this principle. So, how can we avoid this in Java?

In Java 8, a solution for this was finally introduced: **default methods**. Starting with Java 8, methods with a full implementation can be declared in interfaces as long as they are declared using the `default` keyword.

Let's consider the previous example: the `Artist` interface. Any artist should be able to create something, right? So, he or she should have a creative nature. Given the world we are living in, I won't mention names, but some of our artists are actually products of the industry, so they are not creative themselves. So, the realization that we should have a method that tells us if an artist has a creative nature or not, came way after we decided our hierarchy, which is depicted in Figure 4-9.

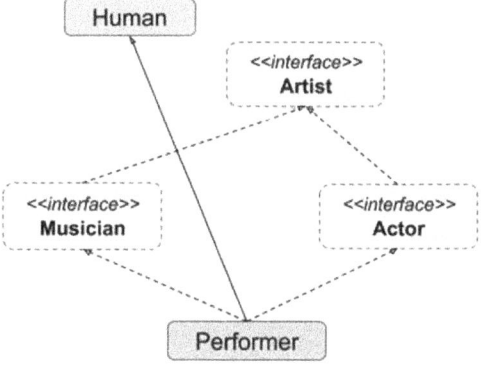

Figure 4-9. *Java hierarchy with more interfaces for Performer class*

---

[2]A good article is at `https://hackernoon.com/solid-principles-made-easy-67b1246bcdf`

CHAPTER 4   JAVA SYNTAX

If we add a new method template to the `Artist` interface, the `Performer` class causes a compile error. IntelliJ IDEA makes it clear that our application does not work anymore by showing a lot of things in red, as depicted in Figure 4-10.

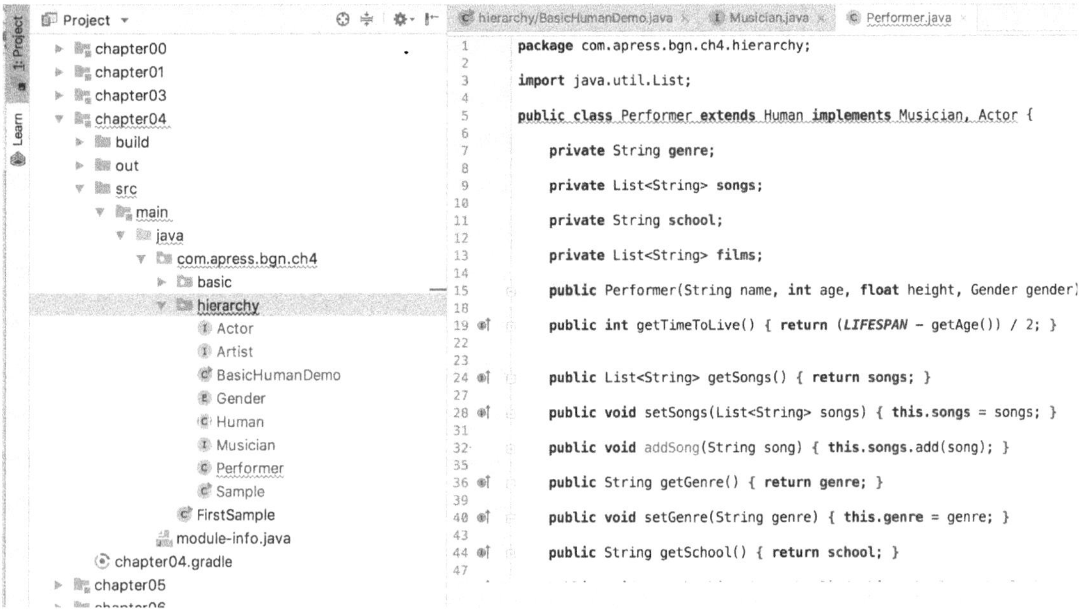

Figure 4-10.   Java broken hierarchy

The compiler errors that we see are caused by our decision to add a new method, named `isCreative`, to the `Artist` interface. It is underlined in the following code snippet.

```
package com.apress.bgn.ch4.hierarchy;

public interface Artist {
    String getSchool();

    void setSchool(String school);

    boolean isCreative();
}
```

To get rid of the compiling errors we'll transform the `isCreative` method into a default method that returns `true`, because every artist should be creative.

```
package com.apress.bgn.ch4.hierarchy;

public interface Artist {
    String getSchool();

    void setSchool(String school);

    default boolean isCreative(){
        return true;
    }
}
```

Now, the code should compile again. If we need to add more than one default method to an interface and the methods have some implementation in common, that code can be isolated starting with Java 9 into a private method that can be called from the default methods. So basically, starting from Java 9, full blown methods can be part of an interface, as long as they are declared private.

Annotation Types

An annotation is defined in a similar way to an interface; the difference is that the `interface` keyword is preceded by the *at* sign (@). Annotation types are a form of interfaces, and most times, they are used as markers. For example, you've probably noticed the `@Override` annotation. This annotation is automatically placed by intelligent IDEs when classes extending or implementing interfaces are generated automatically. It's declaration in the JDK is depicted in the following code snippet.

```
package java.lang;

import java.lang.annotation.*;

@Target(ElementType.METHOD)
@Retention(RetentionPolicy.SOURCE)
public @interface Override {}
```

Annotations that do not declare any property are called **marker** or **informative** annotations. They are needed only to inform other classes in the application, or developers of the purpose of the components they are placed on. They are not mandatory and the code compiles without them.

In Java 8, an annotation named @FunctionalInterface was introduced. This annotation was placed on all Java interfaces that can be used in **lambda expressions**.

```
 package java.lang;

import java.lang.annotation.*;
@Documented
@Retention(RetentionPolicy.RUNTIME)
@Target(ElementType.TYPE)
public @interface FunctionalInterface {}
```

Lambda expressions were also introduced in Java 8 and they represent a compact and practical way of writing code that was borrowed from languages like Groovy and Ruby.

Functional Interfaces are interfaces that declare a single abstract method. Because of this, the implementation of that method can be provided on the spot, without the need to create a class to define a concrete implementation.

Let's imagine the following scenario: we create an interface named Operation that contains a single method.

```
package com.apress.bgn.ch4.lambda;

@FunctionalInterface
public interface Operation {
    float execute(int a, int b);
}
```

We'll next create a class named Addition.

```
package com.apress.bgn.ch4.lambda;

public class Addition implements Operation {

    @Override
    public float execute(int a, int b) {
        return a + b;
    }
}
```

And if we want to test it, we need yet another class.

```
package com.apress.bgn.ch4.lambda;

public class OperationDemo {
    public static void main(String... args) {
        Addition addition = new Addition();
        float  result = addition.execute(2,5);
        System.out.println("Result is " + result);
    }
}
```

Using lambda, the `Addition` class is no longer needed, and the instantiation and the method call can be replaced with

```
package com.apress.bgn.ch4.lambda;

public class OperationDemo {
    public static void main(String... args) {
        Operation addition2 = (a, b) -> a + b;
        float result2 = addition2.execute(2, 5);
        System.out.println("Lambda Result is " + result2);
    }
}
```

Lambda expressions can be used for a lot of things. I'll cover them throughout the book, whenever code can be written in a more practical way using them.

Exceptions

Exceptions are special Java classes that are used to intercept special unexpected situations during the execution of a program so that the developer can implement the proper course of action. These classes are organized in a hierarchy that is depicted in Figure 4-11.

CHAPTER 4   JAVA SYNTAX

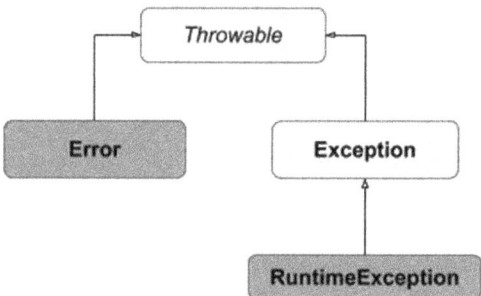

Figure 4-11. *Java Exception hierarchy*

Throwable is the superclass of all errors that can be thrown in a Java application. The exceptional situations can be caused by hardware failures (e.g., trying to read a protected file), by missing resources (e.g., trying to read a file that does not exist), or by bad code. Bad developers tend to do this: when in doubt, catch a throwable. You should definitely try to avoid this because the Error class that notifies the developer about a situation that the system cannot recover from is a subclass of it. Let's start with a simple example. We define a method that calls itself (its technical name is **recursive**), but we'll design it badly to call itself forever and cause the JVM to run out of memory.

```
package com.apress.bgn.ch4.ex;

public class ExceptionsDemo {

    // bad method
    static int rec(int i){
        return rec(i*i);
    }

    public static void main(String... args) {
        rec(1000);
        System.out.println("An error happened.");
    }
}
```

If we run the class, *An error happened* is not printed. Instead, the program ends abnormally by throwing a StackOverFlowError and states the line where the problem is (in our case, the line where the recursive method calls itself).

```
Exception in thread "main" java.lang.StackOverflowError
        at chapter.four/com.apress.bgn.ch4.ex.ExceptionsDemo.
        recExceptionsDemo.java:7
        at chapter.four/com.apress.bgn.ch4.ex.ExceptionsDemo.
        recExceptionsDemo.java:7
        ...
```

`StackOverFlowError` is a subclass of `Error`, and is caused by the defective recursive method that was called. Sure, we could modify the code, treat this exceptional situation, and execute whatever has to be executed next.

```
package com.apress.bgn.ch4.ex;

public class ExceptionsDemo {
...
    public static void main(String... args) {
        try {
            rec(1000);
        } catch (Throwable r) {
        }
        System.out.println("An error happened.");
    }
}
```

In the console, you see only the *An error happened* text, but no trace of the error, which is why we caught it and decided not to print any information about it. This is also a bad practice called **exception swallowing**, never do this! Also, the system should not recover from this, as the result of any operation after an error is thrown is unreliable. That is why, as a rule of thumb, **never catch a throwable!!**

The `Exception` class is the superclass of all exceptions that can be caught and treated, and the system can recover from them. The `RuntimeException` class is the superclass of exceptions that are thrown during the execution of the program, so the possibility of them being thrown is not known when the code is written. Let's consider the following code sample.

CHAPTER 4 JAVA SYNTAX

```java
package com.apress.bgn.ch4.ex;

import com.apress.bgn.ch4.hierarchy.Performer;

public class ExceptionsDemo {
    public static void  main(String... args) {
        Performer p = PerformerGenerator.get("John");

        System.out.println("TTL: " + p.getTimeToLive());
    }
}
```

Let's suppose we do not have access to the code of the `PerformerGenerator` class. We know that if we call the `get(..)` method with a name, it returns a `Performer` instance. So, we write the preceding code and try to print the performer time to live. What happens if the performer is not initialized with a proper object, because the get("John") method call returns null? The outcome is depicted in the next code snippet.

```
Exception in thread "main" java.lang.NullPointerException
        at chapter.four/com.apress.bgn.ch4.ex.ExceptionsDemo.
        mainExceptionsDemo.java:10
```

But if we are smart developers, or a little paranoid, we can prepare for this case, catch the exception and throw an appropriate message or perform there a dummy initialization, in case the performer instance is used in some other way later in the code.

```java
package com.apress.bgn.ch4.ex;

import com.apress.bgn.ch4.hierarchy.Performer;

public class ExceptionsDemo {
    public static void main(String... args) {
        Performer p = null;//PerformerGenerator.get("John");
        try {
            System.out.println("TTL: " + p.getTimeToLive());
        } catch (Exception e) {
            System.out.println("The performer was not initialised properly
                because of: " + e.getMessage() );
        }
    }
}
```

The exception that was thrown is of type `NullPointerException`, a class that extends `RuntimeException`, so a `try/catch block` is not mandatory. This type of exceptions are called **unchecked exceptions**, because the developer is not obligated to check for them. The `NullPointerException` is the exception type Java beginner developers get a lot because they do not have the "paranoia sense" developed enough to always test objects with unknown origin before using them.

There is another type of exceptions that are called **checked exceptions**. This is any type of exception that extends `Exception`—including custom exception classes declared by the developer—that are declared as explicitly thrown by a method. In this case, when invoking that method, the compiler forces the developer to treat that exception or throws it forward. Let's use a mock implementation for `PerformerGenerator`.

```
package com.apress.bgn.ch4.ex;

import com.apress.bgn.ch4.hierarchy.Gender;
import com.apress.bgn.ch4.hierarchy.Performer;

public class PerformerGenerator {

    public static Performer get(String name)
            throws EmptyPerformerException {
        return new Performer(name,40, 1.91f, Gender.MALE);
    }
}
```

The `EmptyPerformerException` is a simple custom exception class that extends the `java.lang.exception` class.

```
package com.apress.bgn.ch4.ex;

public class EmptyPerformerException extends Exception {
    public EmptyPerformerException(String message) {
        super(message);
    }
}
```

We declared that the `get(..)` method might throw `EmptyPerformerException`; and without a `try/catch` block wrapping that method call a compiler error is thrown, as depicted in Figure 4-12.

CHAPTER 4   JAVA SYNTAX

Figure 4-12. Java compiler error caused by checked exception

How do we fix it? Well, we write the code to catch it and print a relevant message.

```
package com.apress.bgn.ch4.ex;

import com.apress.bgn.ch4.hierarchy.Performer;

public class ExceptionsDemo {
    public static void main(String... args) {
        try {
            Performer p = PerformerGenerator.get("John");
            System.out.println("TTL: " + p.getTimeToLive());
        } catch (EmptyPerformerException e) {
            System.out.println("Cannot use an empty performer
                because of " + e.getMessage());
        }
    }
}
```

And since we are talking about exceptions, the `try/catch` block can be completed with a `finally` block. The contents of the `finally` block are executed if the exception is thrown further, or if the method returns normally. The only situation in which the `finally` block is not executed is when the program ends in an error.

144

```java
package com.apress.bgn.ch4.ex;

import com.apress.bgn.ch4.hierarchy.Performer;

public class ExceptionsDemo {

    public static void main(String... args) {
        try {
            Performer p = PerformerGenerator.get("John");
            System.out.println("TTL: " + p.getTimeToLive());
        } catch (EmptyPerformerException e) {
            System.out.println("Cannot use an empty performer!");
        } finally {
            System.out.println("All went as expected!");
        }
    }
}
```

During this book, we write code that ends in exceptional situations, so we'll have the opportunity to expand the subject when your knowledge is a little more advanced.

Generics

Until now we talked only of object types and java templates used for creating objects. But what if we would need to design a class with functionality that applies to multiple types of objects? Since every class in Java extends the `Object` class, we can create a class with a method that receives a parameter of type `Object`, and in the method we can test the object type. Take this for granted; it is covered later.

In Java 5, the possibility to use a type as parameter when creating an object was introduced. The classes that are developed to process other classes are called **generics**.

When writing Java applications, you most likely need at some point to pair up values of different types. The simplest version of a `Pair` class that can hold a pair of instances of any type is listed in the following code snippet.

```java
package com.apress.bgn.ch4.gen;
public class Pair<X, Y> {

        protected X   x;
        protected Y   y;
```

```java
        private Pair(X x, Y y) {
                this.x = x;
                this.y = y;
        }
        public X x() {
                return x;
        }
        public Y y() {
                return y;
        }
        public void x(X x) {
                this.x = x;
        }
        public void y(Y y) {
                this.y = y;
        }
        ...
        public static <X, Y> Pair<X, Y> of(X x, Y y) {
                return new Pair<>(x, y);
        }
    @Override public String toString() {
        return "Pair{" + x.toString() +", " + y.toString() + '}';
    }
}
```

Let's test it! Let's create a pair of `Performer` instances, a pair of a `String` and a `Performer` instance, and a pair of `Strings` to check if this is possible. The `toString()}` method is inherited from the `Object` class and overridden in the `Pair` class to print the values of the fields.

```
package com.apress.bgn.ch4.gen;
```

```
import com.apress.bgn.ch4.hierarchy.Gender;
import com.apress.bgn.ch4.hierarchy.Performer;
```

```java
public class GenericsDemo {
    public static void main(String... args) {
        Performer john = new Performer("John", 40, 1.91f, Gender.MALE);
        Performer jane = new Performer("Jane", 34, 1.591f, Gender.FEMALE);

        Pair<Performer, Performer> performerPair = Pair.of(john, jane);
        System.out.println(performerPair);

        Pair<String, String> stringPair = Pair.of("John", "Jane");
        System.out.println(stringPair);

        Pair<String, Performer> spPair = Pair.of("John", john);
        System.out.println(spPair);

        System.out.println("all good.");
    }
}
```

If you execute the preceding class, you see something like the log depicted, as follows.

```
Pair{com.apress.bgn.ch4.hierarchy.Performer@1d057a39com.apress.bgn.ch4.
              hierarchy.Performer@26be92ad}
Pair{JohnJane}
Pair{Johncom.apress.bgn.ch4.hierarchy.Performer@1d057a39}
all good.
```

The `println` method expects its argument to be a `String` instance, the `toString()` method is called on the object given if argument if the type is not `String`. If the `toString` method was not overridden, the one from the `Object` class is called that returns the fully qualified name of the object type and something called a **hashcode**, which is a numerical representation of the object.

Java Reserved Words

Table 4-2 and Table 4-3 list Java keywords that can be used only for their fixed and predefined purposes in the language. This means they cannot be used as identifiers; you cannot use them as names for variables, classes, interfaces, enums, or methods.

CHAPTER 4　JAVA SYNTAX

Table 4-2. *Java Keywords (part 1)*

Method	Description
abstract	Declares a class or method as abstract—as in any extending or implementing class, must provide a concrete implementation.
assert	Test an assumption about your code. Introduced in Java 1.4, it is ignored by the JVM, unless the program is run with "-ea" option.
boolean byte char short int long float double	Primitive type names
break	Statement used inside loops to terminate them immediately.
continue	Statement used inside loops to jump to the next iteration immediately.
switch	Statement name to test equality against a set of values known as cases.
case	Statement to define case values in a switch statement.
default	Declares a default case within a switch statement. Also used to declare default values in interfaces. And starting with Java 8, it can be used to declare default methods in interfaces, methods that have a default implementation.
try catch finally throw throws	Keywords used in exception handling.
class interface	Keywords used in classes and interfaces declarations.
extends implements	Keywords used in extending classes and implementing interfaces.

(*continued*)

Table 4-2. (*continued*)

Method	Description
enum	Keyword introduced in Java 5.0 to declare a special type of class that defines a fixed set of instances.
const	Not used in Java; a keyword borrowed from C where it declares constants, variables that are assigned a value, which cannot be changed during the execution of the program.
final	The equivalent of the const keyword in Java. Anything defined with this modifier, cannot change after a final initialization. A final class cannot be extended. A final method cannot be overridden. A final variable has the same value that was initialized with throughout the execution of the program. Any code written to modify final items, lead to a compiler error.

Table 4-3. *Java Keywords (part 2)*

Method	Description
do	Keywords to create loops:
while	do{..} while(condition),
for	while(condition){..}, for(initialisation;condition;incrementation){..}
goto	Another keyword borrowed from C, but that is currently not used in Java, because it can be replaced by labeled break and continue statements
if	Creates conditional statements:
else	if(condition) {..} else {..} else if (condition) {..}
import	Makes classes and interfaces available in the current source code.
instanceof	Tests instance types in conditional expressions.
native	This modifier indicates that a method is implemented in native code using JNI (Java Native Interface).

(*continued*)

Table 4-3. (*continued*)

Method	Description
new	Creates java instances.
package	Declares the package the class/interface/enum/annotation is part of and it should be the first Java statement line.
public private protected	Access-level modifiers for Java items (templates, fields, or methods).
return	Keyword used within a method to return to the code that invoked it. The method can also return a value to the calling code.
static	This modifier can be applied to variables, methods, blocks, and nested classes. It declares an item that is shared between all instances of the class where declared.
stricfp	Used to restrict floating-point calculations to ensure portability. Added in Java 1.2.
super	Keyword used inside a class to access members of the super class.
this	Keyword used to access members of the current object.
synchronized	Ensures that only one thread executes a block of code at any given time. This avoids a problem cause "race-condition"[3].
transient	Marks data that should not be serialized.
volatile	Ensures that changes done to a variable value are accessible to all threads accessing it.
void	Used when declaring methods as a return type to indicate that the method does not return a value.
_(underscore)	Cannot be used as an identifier starting with Java 9.

---

[3] A detailed article describing this problem and ways to avoid it can be found here: https://devopedia.org/race-/condition/-software

Summary

The most often used elements of the Java language were introduced in this chapter, so that nothing you find in future code samples should surprise you, and you can focus on learning the language properly.

- Syntax mistakes prevent java code from being transformed into executable code. This means the code is not compiling.

- Static variables can be used directly when declaring classes if static import statement are used.

- Java identifiers must respect naming rules.

- Comments are ignored by the compiler and there are three types of comments in Java.

- Classes, interfaces, and enums are Java components used to create objects.

- Abstract classes cannot be instantiated, even if they can have constructors.

- Interfaces could only contain method templates until Java version 8, when default methods were introduced. And starting with Java 9 they can contain full implemented methods as long as they are declared private and are being called only from default methods.

- Enums are special types of classes that can only be instantiated a fixed number of times.

- In Java, there is no multiple inheritance using classes.

- Interfaces can extend other interfaces.

- Java defines a fixed number of keywords, called **reserved keywords**, which can be used only for a specific purposes. They are covered in the previous section.

CHAPTER 5

Data Types

In Chapter 4, a lot of Java code was written, but when designing classes, only the most simple data types were used: a few numeric ones and text. In the JDK, a lot of data types are declared for a multitude of purposes: for modelling calendar dates, for representing multiple types of numeric, for manipulating texts, collections, files, database connections, and so forth. Aside from JDK, there are libraries created by other parties that provide even more functionality. But the data types provided by the JDK are fundamental ones, the bricks every Java application is built from. Of course, depending on the type of application you are building, you might not need all of them. For example, I've never had the occasion to use the `java.util.logging.Logger` class. Most applications that I've worked on were already set up by a different team when I came along, and they were using external libraries like Log4j or Logback, or logging abstractions like Slf4j.

This section covers the basic Java data types that you need to write about 80% of any Java application.

Stack and Heap Memory

Java types can be split in two main categories: **primitive** and **reference** types. Java code files are stored on the HDD, Java bytecode files as well. Java programs run on the JVM, which is launched as a process by executing the `java` executable. During execution, all data is stored in two different types of memory named: `stack` and `heap` that are allocated for a program's execution by the operating system.

The **stack** memory is used during execution(also referred to as *at runtime*) to store method primitive local variables and references to objects stored in the heap. A **stack** is also a data-structure represented by a list of values that can only be accessed at one end, also called a **LIFO** order, which is an acronym for **L**ast **I**n, **F**irst **O**ut. The name fits, because every time a method gets called, a new block is created in the stack memory to hold local variables of the method: primitives and references to other objects in the method.[1]

Each JVM execution thread has its own stack memory, and its size can be specified using JVM parameter `-Xss`. If too many variables are allocated, or the method being called is recursive and badly designed, the condition to return is never fulfilled, and thus keeps calling itself forever. You run into a `java.lang.StackOverFlowError`, which means there is no stack memory left, because every method call causes a new block to be created on the stack.

The **heap** memory is used at runtime to allocate memory for objects and JRE classes. Objects are instances of JDK classes or developer defined classes. Any object created with `new` is stored inside the heap memory. Objects created inside the heap memory can be accessed by all threads of the application. Access and management of the heap memory are a little more complex and is covered more in **Chapter 13**. The `-Xms` and `-Xmx` JVM parameters set the initial and maximum size of the heap memory for a Java program during execution. The heap size may vary, depending on the number of objects created by the program, and if all heap memory allocated to a Java program is full, then a `java.lang.OutOfMemoryError` is thrown.

The JVM parameters are useful because during development, you might have to write code that solves complex problems and that needs a bigger than usual stack or heap memory, so instead of relying on the default sizes, you can set your own. Stack and heap default values are platform-specific. If you are interested in these values, check out the official documentation at https://docs.oracle.com/cd/E13150_01/jrockit_jvm/jrockit/jrdocs/refman/optionX.html, which covers all JVM parameters and default values. You can open the link in your browser and search for `-Xss`, `-Xms`, or `-Xmx`.

The `java.lang.String` class is the most used class in the Java programming language. Because text values within an application might have the same value, for efficiency reasons this type of objects are managed a little different within the heap. In the heap there is a special memory region called the **StringPool** where all the `String`

---

[1]When the call ends, the block is removed (popped out) and new blocks are created for methods being called after that. The first element in a stack it's called *head*. Operations performed on a stack have specific names: adding an element to the stack is called a *push* operation, inspecting the first element in the stack is called a *peek* or *top* operation and extracting the first element in the stack, its head, is called *pop*.

instances are stored by the JVM. This had to be mentioned here because the following piece of code that is analyzed to explain how memory is managed in Java contains a definition of a String instance, but the String Pool and other details about the String data type is covered in detail in its own section later in the chapter.

Let's consider the following executable class, and imagine how the memory is organized during the execution of this program.

```
01.  package com.apress.bgn.ch5;
02.
03.  import java.util.Date;
04.
05.  public class PrimitivesDemo {
06.
07.      public static void main(String... args) {
08.          int i = 5;
09.          int j = 7;
10.          Date d = new Date();
11.          int result = add(i, j);
12.          System.out.print(result);
13.          d = null;
14.      }
15.
16.      static int add(int a, int b) {
17.          String mess = new String("performing add ...");
18.          return a + b;
19.      }
20.  }
```

Can you figure out which variables are saved on the stack and which are on the heap? Let's go over the program line by line to see what is happening.

- As soon as the program starts, Runtime classes that JVM need are loaded in the heap memory.

- The `main()` method is discovered in **line 07** so a stack memory is created to be used during the execution of this method.

- Primitive local variable in **line 08**, `i=5`, is created and stored in the stack memory of `main()` method.

CHAPTER 5　DATA TYPES

- Primitive local variable in **line 09**, j=7, is created and stored in the stack memory of main() method. At this point, the program memory looks like what's depicted in Figure 5-1.

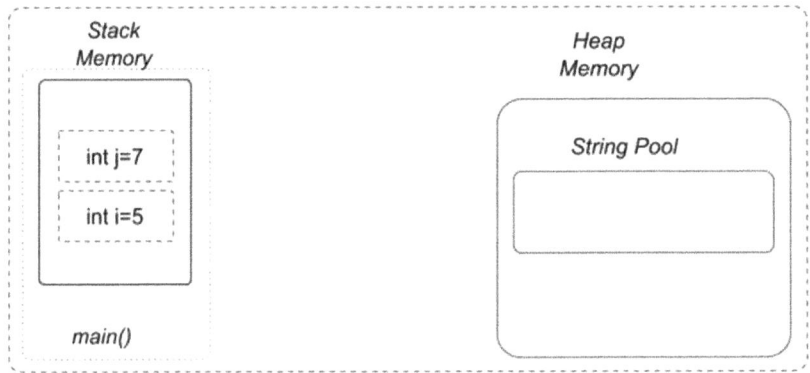

Figure 5-1. Java stack and heap memory, after declaring two primitive variables

- In **line 10** an object of type java.util.Date is declared, so this object is created and stored in the heap memory and a reference named d is saved on the stack. At this point, the program memory looks like what's depicted in Figure 5-2.

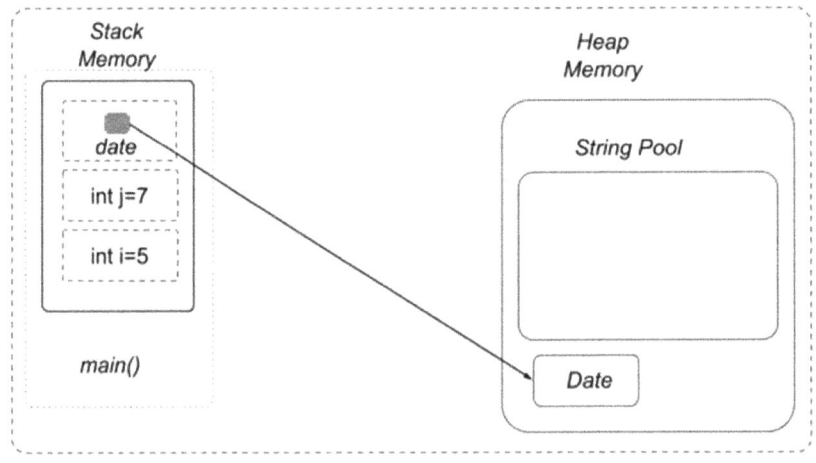

Figure 5-2. Java stack and heap memory, after declaring two primitive variables and an object

CHAPTER 5　DATA TYPES

- In **line 11** method add() is called with arguments i and j. This means their values is copied into the local variables for this method named a and b and these two is stored in the memory block for this method.

- Inside the add(..) method body, in **line 17** a String instance is declared. So, the String object is created in the heap memory, in the String Pool memory block, and the reference named mess is stored, in the stack, in the memory block for this method. At this point, the program memory looks like what's shown in Figure 5-3.

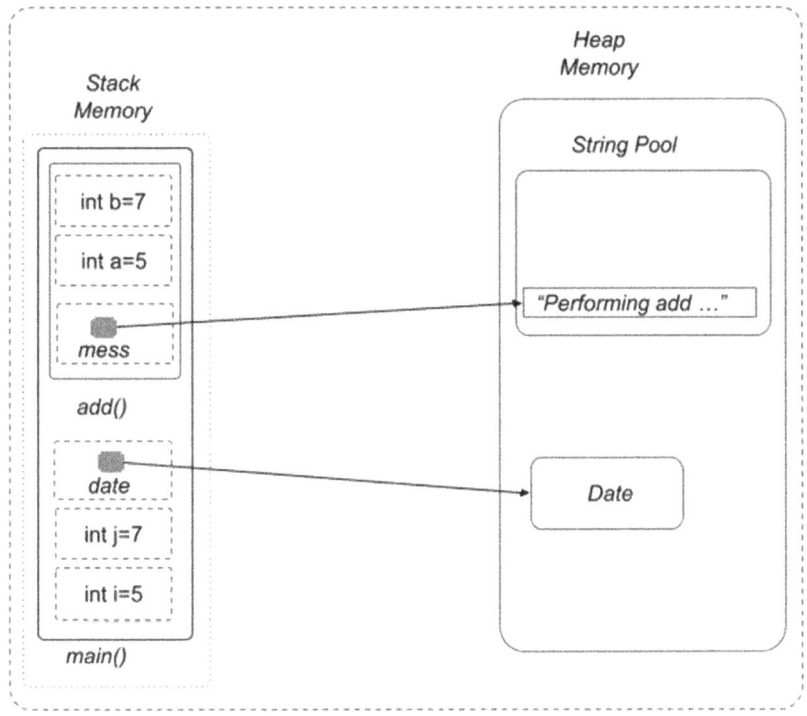

Figure 5-3. Java stack and heap memory, after calling the add(..) method

- Also in **line 11**, the result of the execution of the add(..) method is stored in the local variable named result. Because at this point, the add(..) method has finished its execution, its stack block is discarded. Thus we can conclude that variables that are stored on the stack exist for as long as the function that created them is running. At this point in the stack memory of main() method the result variable is saved.

157

CHAPTER 5   DATA TYPES

- In **line 12**, the print method is called, but we'll skip the explanation for this line for simplicity reasons.

- In **line 13**, the d reference is assigned a null value, which means, the object of type Date is now only in the heap, and it is not linked to the execution of the main method in any way. Look at it like this: in that line, we are basically telling the JVM that were are no longer interested in that object, which means the space containing it can be **collected** and used to store other objects.

At this point, the program memory looks like what's shown in Figure 5-4.

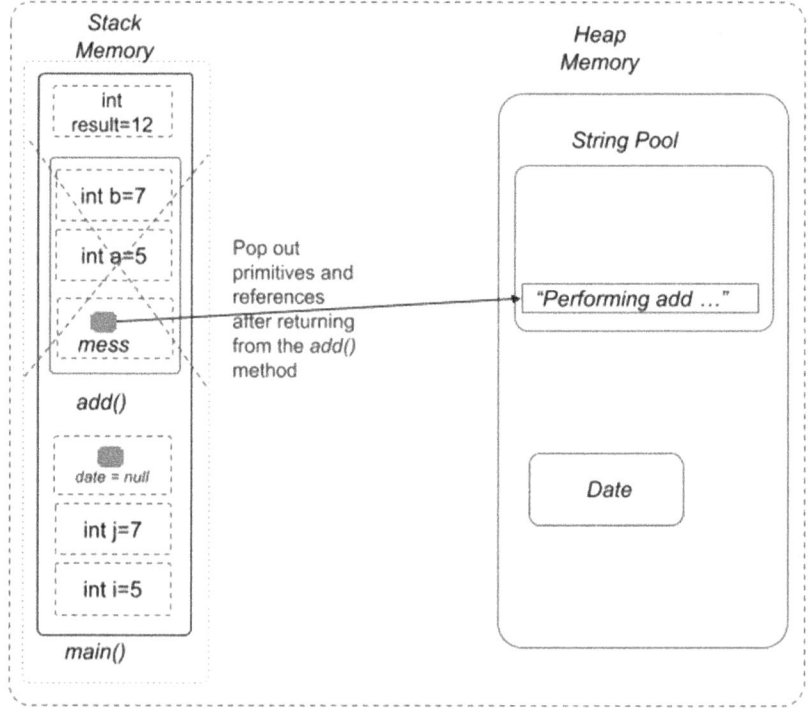

Figure 5-4. Java stack and heap memory, before the ending of the main(..) *method execution*

After the program exits all memory contents are discarded.

! When applying for a Java developer position, you will most likely be asked about the differences between stack and heap memory. So, if you think that the previous section did not clarify this for you, please feel free to consult additional resources.[2]

Introduction to Java Data Types

The previous example showed that data types in Java can be split into two big groups based on where they are stored during execution: primitive types and reference types. I'll introduce them briefly and explain their most important members later.

Primitive Data Types

Primitive types are defined by the Java programming language as special types that do not have a supporting class and are named by their reserved keyword. Variables of these types are saved on the stack memory and when values are assigned to them using the = (equals) operator, the value is actually copied. So, if we declare two primitive variables of type int, as in the following code listing, we end up with two variables, k and q, both having the same value: 42.

```
package com.apress.bgn.ch5;

public class PrimitivesDemo {

    public static void main(String... args) {
        int k - 42;
        int q = k;

        System.out.println("k = " + k);
        System.out.println("q = " + q);
    }
}
```

---

[2]A very good article about this subject is at https://www.journaldev.com/4098/java-heap-space-vs-stack-memory

CHAPTER 5 DATA TYPES

When passed as arguments to other methods, the values of primitive values are copied and used without the initial variables being modified. This can be proved by creating a method to swap the values of two int variables. The following is the code for the method.

```java
package com.apress.bgn.ch5;

public class PrimitivesDemo {

    public static void main(String... args) {
        int k = 42;
        int q = 44;

        swap(k, q);

        System.out.println("k = " + k);
        System.out.println("q = " + q);
    }

    static void swap(int a, int b) {
        int temp = a;
        a = b;
        b =  temp;
    }
}
```

So, what do you think is printed as values for k and q? If you thought the output is the same as the following, you are correct.

```
k = 42
q = 44
```

This happens because in Java passing arguments to a method is done through their value, which means for primitives, changing the formal parameter's value doesn't affect the actual parameter's value. If you read the previous section, you can already imagine what happens on the stack. When the swap() method is called a new stack memory block is created to save the values used by this method. During the execution of the method, the values might change, but if they are not returned and assigned to variables in the calling method, the values are lost when the method execution ends. Figure 5-5 depicts the changes that take place on the stack during the execution of the code previously listed. As you can obviously notice, the heap memory is not used at all.

CHAPTER 5 DATA TYPES

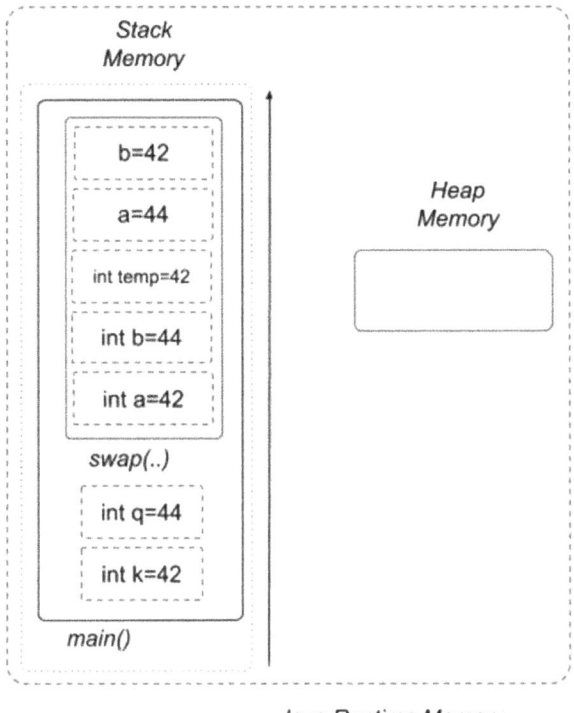

Figure 5-5. Java passing primitive arguments by value

Reference Data Types

There are four **reference types** in Java:

- class types
- interface types
- enums
- array types

Reference types are different from primitive types as these types are instantiable (except interfaces). Objects of these types are created by calling constructors, and variables of these types are references to objects stored in the heap. Because the references are stored on the stack as well, even if we modify the previous code to use references, the behavior is the same. Let's introduce a class named IntContainer, whose only purpose is to wrap primitive values into objects.

161

```java
package com.apress.bgn.ch5;

public class IntContainer {

    private int value;

    public IntContainer(int value) {
        this.value = value;
    }

    public int getValue() {
        return value;
    }

    public void setValue(int value) {
        this.value  =  value;
    }
}
```

And now we create two objects of this type and two references for them and rewrite the swap method.

```java
package com.apress.bgn.ch5;

public class ReferencesDemo {
    public static void main(String... args) {
        IntContainer k = new IntContainer(42);
        IntContainer q = new IntContainer(44);

        swap(k,q);

        System.out.println("k = " + k.getValue());
        System.out.println("q = " + q.getValue());
    }

    static void swap(IntContainer a, IntContainer b) {
        IntContainer temp = a;
        a = b;
        b = temp;
    }
}
```

If we run the main(..) method, you notice that we still get

k = 42
q = 44

How can this be explained? In the same manner, Java still uses the same style of arguments passing by value, only this time, the value of the reference is the one passed. Figure 5-6 depicts what is going on in the memory managed by the JVM for the execution of the previous code.

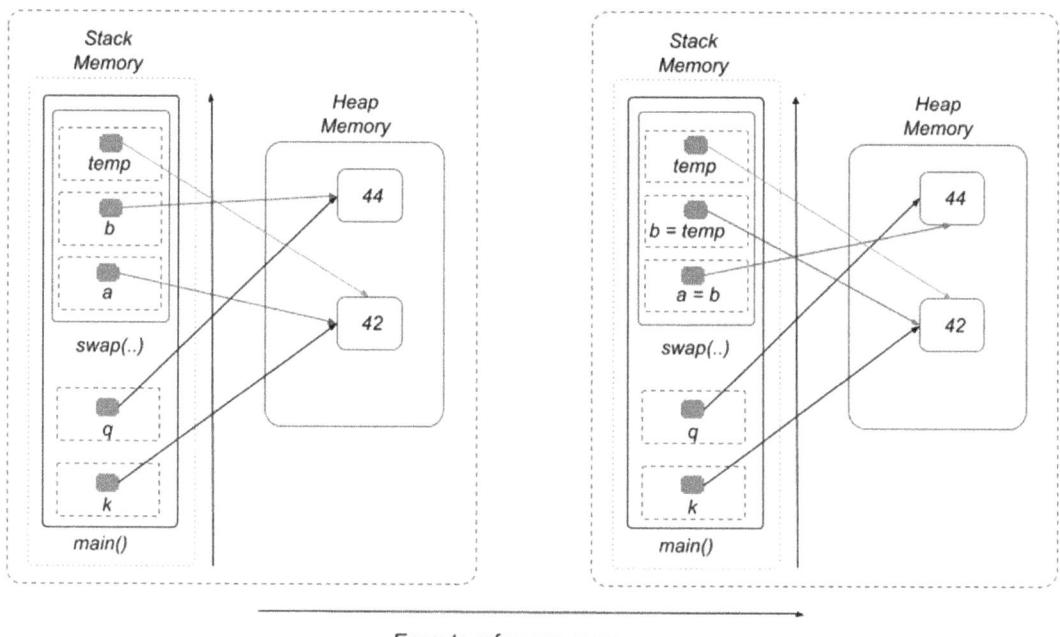

Figure 5-6. *Java passing reference arguments by value*

In a similar manner, the references to the objects are interchanged in the body of the swap(..) method, but they have no effect on the k and q references, and neither on the objects they point to in the heap. To really exchange the values, we need to exchange the content of the objects by using a new object. Look at the following new version of the swap(..) method.

```
package com.apress.bgn.ch5;

public class ReferencesDemo {
```

CHAPTER 5   DATA TYPES

```
public static void main(String... args) {
    IntContainer k = new IntContainer(42);
    IntContainer q = new IntContainer(44);

    swap(k,q);

    System.out.println("k = " + k.getValue());
    System.out.println("q = " + q.getValue());
}
static void swap(IntContainer a, IntContainer b) {
    IntContainer temp = new IntContainer(a.getValue());
    a.setValue(b.getValue());
    b.setValue(temp.getValue());
}
}
```

By making use of setters and getters, we exchange the values of the objects, because the references are never modified inside the body of the method. Figure 5-7 depicts what happens within the memory during execution of the previous piece of code.

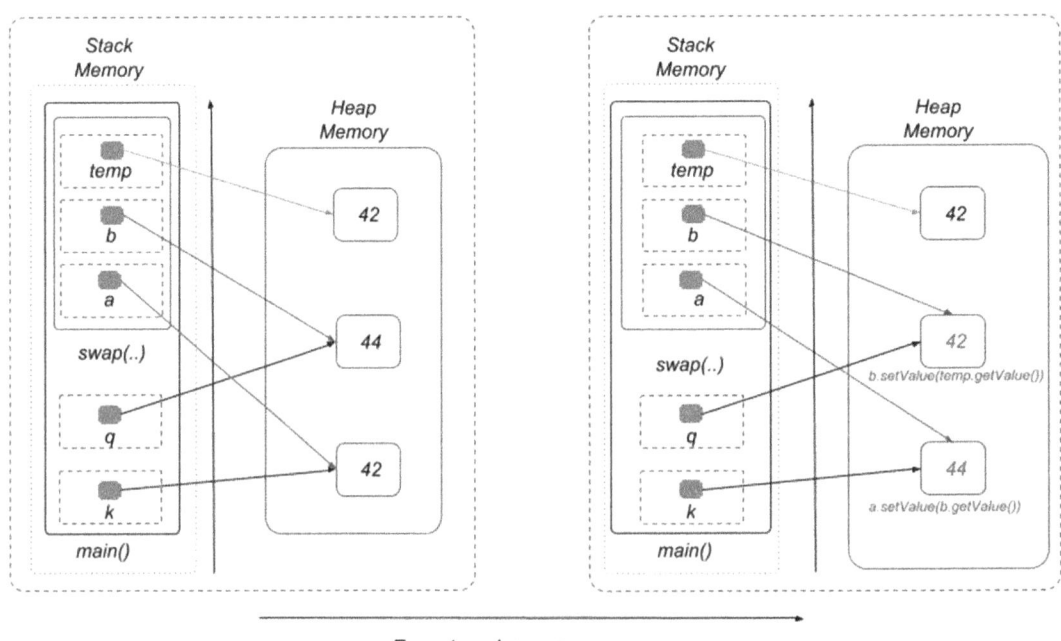

Figure 5-7. Java passing reference arguments by value, swapping object contents

CHAPTER 5 DATA TYPES

Maybe this example was introduced too early, but it was needed so you could witness as early as possible the major differences between primitive and reference types. We'll list all the differences in the summary, until then, let's introduce the most used data types in Java.

Java Primitive Types

Primitive types are the basic types of data in Java. Variables of this type can be created by directly assigning values of that type, so they are not instantiated.(That would be pretty difficult to do since these types are not backed up by a class) In Java there are 8 types of primitive types, six of them used to represent numbers, one to represent characters and one to represent boolean values. Primitive types are predefined into the Java language and they have names that are reserved keywords. Primitive variables can have values only in the interval or dataset that is predefined for that type. When declared as fields of a class at instantiation time, a default value specific to the type is assigned to the field. Primitive values do not share state with other primitive values.

Most Java tutorials introduce the numeric types first, but this book starts with the non-numerics.

The Boolean Type

Variables of this type can have only one of the two accepted values: `true` and `false`. This type of variable is used in conditions to decide a course of action. The values `true` and `false` are themselves reserved keywords. **Default value** for a boolean variable is `false`.

Another observation: when a field is of type `boolean` the getter for it has a different syntax. It is not prefixed with `get` but with `is`. This makes sense because of what boolean values are used for. They model properties with only two values. For example, let's say we are writing a class to model a conversion process. A boolean field marks the process state as done or still in process. If the name of the field is `done`, a getter named `getDone()` would be pretty unintuitive and stupid, but one named `isDone()` would be quite the opposite. Let's write that class and also add a main method to test the default value of the `done` field.

```
package com.apress.bgn.ch5;

public class ConvertProcess {
    /* other fields and methods */
```

```
    private boolean done;
    public boolean isDone() {
        return done;
    }
    public void setDone(boolean done) {
        this.done = done;
    }
    public static void main(String... args) {
        ConvertProcess cp = new ConvertProcess();
        System.out.println("Default value = " + cp.isDone());
    }
}
```

And as expected, the output printed is

```
Default value = false
```

The boolean type is not compatible with any other primitive type, assigning a boolean value to an int variable by simple assignment(using =) is not possible. Explicit conversion is not possible either. So, writing something like the following causes a compilation error.

```
boolean f = false;
int fi = (int) f;
```

We'll be adding more information about this type in **Chapter** 6.

The char Type

The char type represents characters. The values are 16-bit unsigned integers representing UTF-16 code units. The interval of the possible values for char variables is : from '\u0000' to '\uffff' inclusive, as numbers this means: from 0 to 65535. This means that we can try to print the full set of values. As the representation of the characters is numeric, this means we can convert int values from interval to char values. The following code snippet, prints all the numeric values of the char interval and their matching characters.

```
package com.apress.bgn.ch5;

public class CharLister {
    public static void main(String... args) {
        for (int i = 0; i < 65536; ++i ) {
            char c = (char) i;
            System.out.println("c[" + i + "]=" + c);
        }
    }
}
```

! The last char value the for loop statement prints is 65535. The 65536 value is used as an upper maximum value. So, if i=65336, then nothing gets printed and the execution of the statement ends. The for loop is covered in detail in Chapter 8: Controlling the flow.

Depending on the operating system, some of the characters might not be supported, so they won't be displayed, or they are replaced with a bogus character. The same goes for whitespace characters.

If you think the interval dedicated to represent characters is too big, scroll the console and you will understand why. The UTF-16 character set contains all numbers as characters, all separators, characters from Chinese, Arabic and a lot more symbols.[3]

Integer Primitives

In the code samples used so far to introduce Java language basics, we mostly used variables of type int, but there is more than one numeric primitive type in Java. Java defines six primitive numeric types, and each of them has a specific internal representation, on a certain number of bits, which means that there is a minimum and a maximum value. There are four numeric types to represent integer values and two numeric types to represent real numbers. Figure 5-8 shows the integer types and the interval of the values for each of them.

---

[3]A complete list of the symbols and their meanings can be found at https://www.fileformat.info/info/charset/UTF-16/list.htm

CHAPTER 5   DATA TYPES

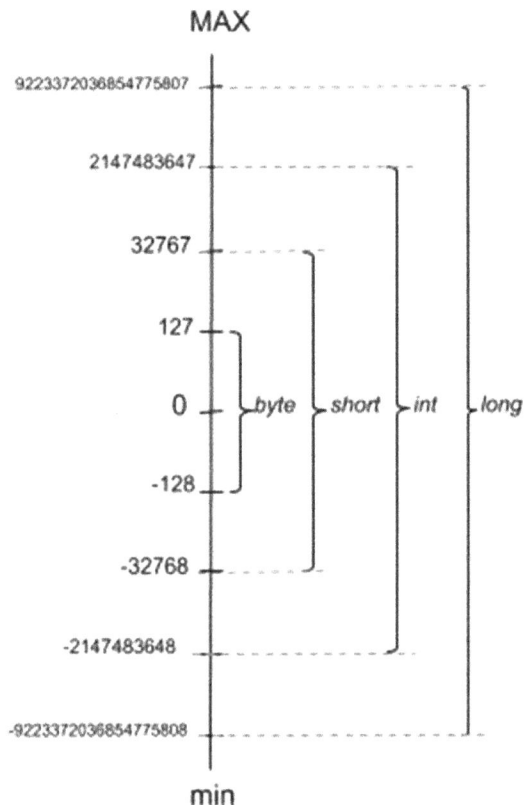

Figure 5-8. *Java numeric types to represent integer values*

Anything in a computer is represented using bits of information, each bit can only have a value of 1 or 0, which is why it is called *binary representation.* Binary representation is not the focus of this book, but a short mention is made because it is important. You might be wondering now why the binary representation was chosen for our computers? Well, primarily because data (in memory and on storage) is stored using a series of ones (on) and zeros (off) binary representations; also binary operations are really easy to do, and this makes computers very fast. Let's take math for example, we widely use the decimal system, which is made of 10 unique digits, from 0 to 9. Internally computers use a binary system, which uses only two digits: 0 and 1. To represent numbers bigger than 1, we need more bits. So, in a decimal system we have: 0, 1, 2 , 3, 4, 5, 6, 7, 8, 9, 10, 11, and so forth, in a binary system to represent numbers we only have two digits, so we'll have: 0, 1, 10, 11, 100, 101, 110, 111, 1000, and so forth. If you imagine a box in which you can only put ones and zeroes to represent numbers like a computer does, you need more as the numbers get bigger. A bit can only have two values, so the number of values to represent it is defined by a power of 2. Look at Figure 5-9.

CHAPTER 5 DATA TYPES

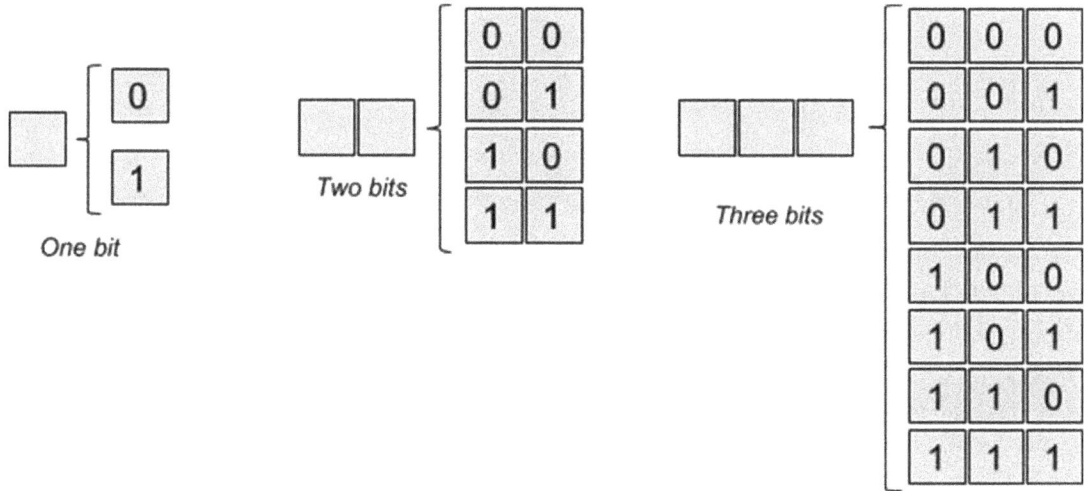

Figure 5-9. *Binary numeric representation*

So, on one bit we can represent two values, which is 2^1, on two bits we can represent four values, which is 2^2 and so on. So, that is how we refer to Java primitive numeric types representation boundaries, sometimes including a bit for the sign as well. Thus, the following list contains the integer primitive types and their boundaries.

- byte represents numbers between -2^7 and 2^7-1 inclusive ([-128, 127]). Default value for a byte field is 0 and is represented on 8 bits.

- short represents numbers between -2^{15} and $2^{15} - 1$ inclusive ([-32768, 32767]). The values interval for this type is a superset of the byte values interval, thus a byte value can be safely assigned to a short variable without the need for an explicit conversion. This goes for all types that have the values interval a superset of the one for the byte type. In the next code snippet, a byte value is assigned to a short variable and the code compiles and when executed prints 23.

  Default value for a short field is 0 and is represented on 16 bits.

  ```
  byte bv = 23;
  short sbv = bv;
  System.out.println("byte to short: " + sbv);
  ```

- int represents integer numbers between -2^{31} and $2^{31}-1$ inclusive ([-2147483648, 2147483647]). Default value for a byte field is 0 and is represented on 32 bits.

CHAPTER 5 DATA TYPES

- long represents integer numbers between -2^{63} and $2^{63} - 1$ inclusive ([-9223372036854775808, 9223372036854775807]) Default value for a byte field is 0 and is represented on 64 bits.

! In practice sometimes the need to work with integer numbers outside the interval long appears. For this situations, in Java a special class (yes a class, not a primitive type) was defined and is named BigInteger that allocates just as much memory is needed to store a number of any size. Operations with BigInteger might be slow, but this is the trade off to work with huge numbers.

Real Primitives

Real numbers are useful because most prices and most arithmetic operations executed by programs do not result in an integer number. Real numbers contain a decimal point and decimals after it. To represent real numbers in Java, two primitive types (called **floating-point types**) are defined: float and double. Let's discuss each of them in a little more detail.

- float represents single-precision 32-bit format IEEE 754 values as specified in IEEE Standard for Binary Floating-Point Arithmetic, ANSI/IEEE Standard 754-1985 (IEEE, New York).The default value is 0.0. A floating-point variable can represent a wider range of numbers than a fixed point variable of the same bit width at the cost of precision. Because of this values of type int or long can be assigned to variables of type float. What is actually happening and why the loss of precision? Well, a number is represented as a floating-point number and an exponent, which is a power of 10. So, when the floating-point number is multiplied with 10 at this exponent power, the initial number should result. Let's take the maximum long value, assign it to a float variable, and check what is printed.

```
float maxLongF = Long.MAX_VALUE;
System.out.println("max long= " + Long.MAX_VALUE);
System.out.println("float max long= " + maxLongF);
```

The Long.MAX_VALUE is a final static variable that has the maximum long value assigned to it: 9223372036854775807. The preceding code prints the following.

```
max long= 9223372036854775807
float max long= 9.223372E18
```

As you can see, the maxLongF number should be equal to 9223372036854775807, but because it is represented as a smaller number and a power of 10, precision is lost. Because if we were to reconstruct the integer number by multiplying 9.223372 with 10^{18} gives us 9223372000000000000. So yeah, close, but not close enough. So, what are the interval edges for float? Float represents real numbers between $1.4E^{-45}$ and $2^{128} * 10^{38}$.

- double represents single-precision 64-bit format IEEE 754 values as specified in IEEE Standard for Binary Floating-Point Arithmetic, ANSI/IEEE Standard 754-1985 (IEEE, New York) and represents numbers between $4.9E^{-324}$ and $2^{127} * 10^{308}$. The default value is 0.0.

! Values 0 and 0.0 are different in Java. To a normal user, they both mean zero, but in mathematics, the one with the decimal point is more precise. Still in Java we are allowed to compare an int value to a float value, and if we compare 0 and 0.0, the result is that they are equal. Also positive zero and negative zero are considered equal; thus the result of the comparison 0.0==-0.0 is true.

Developers cannot define a primitive type by defining it from scratch or by extending an existing primitive type. Type names are **reserved Java keywords**, which cannot be redefined by a developer. It is prohibited to declare fields, methods, or class names that are named as those types.

A variable that we intend to use must be declared first. When it is declared, a value can be associated as well. For primitive values, a number can be written in many ways. The following shows a few samples of how numeric values can be written when variables are initialized or assigned afterward.

```
package com.apress.bgn.ch5;

public class NumericDemo {
    private byte b;
    private short s;
```

CHAPTER 5   DATA TYPES

```java
    private int i;
    private long l;
    private float f;
    private double d;

    public static void main(String... args) {
        NumericDemo nd = new NumericDemo();

        nd.b = 0b1100;
        System.out.println("Byte binary value: " + nd.b);

        nd.i = 42 ;     // decimal case

        nd.i = 045 ;    // octal case - base 8
        System.out.println("Int octal value: " + nd.i);

        nd.i = 0xcafe ; // hexadecimal case - base 16
        System.out.println("Int hexadecimal value: " + nd.i);

        nd.i = 0b10101010101010101010101010101011;
        System.out.println("Int binary value: " + nd.i);

        //Java 7 syntax
        nd.i = 0b1010_1010_1010_1010_1010_1010_1010_1011;
        System.out.println("Int binary value: " + nd.i);

        nd.l = 1000_000l; // equivalent to 1000_000L
        System.out.println("Long value: " + nd.l);

        nd.f = 5;
        System.out.println("Integer value assigned to a float variable: 
" + nd.f);

        nd.f = 2.5f; // equivalent to nd.f =    2.5F;
        System.out.println("Decimal value assigned to a float variable: 
" + nd.f);

        nd.d = 2.5d; // equivalent to  nd.d = 2.5D;
        System.out.println("Decimal value assigned to a double variable: 
" + nd.f);
    }
}
```

Starting with Java 7, the "_" is permitted to be used when declaring numeric values to group digits and increase clarity. When running the previous code, the following is printed.

```
Byte binary value: 12
Int octal value: 37
Int hexadecimal value: 51966
Int binary value: -1431655765
Int binary value: -1431655765
Long value: 1000000
Integer value assigned to a float variable: 5.0
Decimal value assigned to a float variable: 2.5
Decimal value assigned to a double variable: 2.5
```

Since no formatting is done when the variables are printed, the values depicted in the console are in the decimal system.

For now, this is all that can be said about the primitive types. Each of the primitive types has a matching reference type defined within the JDK, and converting a primitive value to its equivalent reference is called boxing and the reverse process is called unboxing. In certain situation those processes are done explicitly, but more about that later.

Java Reference Types

Java Reference Types were described earlier to highlight the differences between primitive and reference types. It is now time to expand that description and give some examples of the most used JDK reference types when programming.

Objects or *instances* are created using the new keyword followed by the call of a constructor. The constructor is a special member of a class, used to create an object by initializing all fields of the class with their default values, or values received as arguments. A class instance is created by calling the class constructor (one of them, because there might be more than one defined within the class). So, considering the example that we had in **Chapter** 4, the Performer class, to declare a reference to an object of type Performer the following expression is used.

```
Performer human = new Performer("John", 40, 1.91f, Gender.MALE);
```

CHAPTER 5   DATA TYPES

The interface reference types cannot be instantiated, but objects of class types that extend that interface can be assigned to references of that interface type. The hierarchy used in **Chapter** 4 is depicted in Figure 5-10.

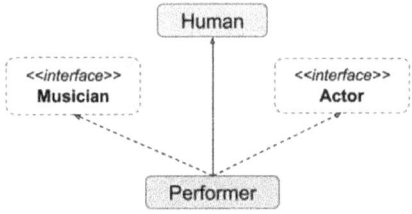

Figure 5-10. *Class and interface hierarchy*

Based on this hierarchy, the following four statements are valid and they compile.

```
package com.apress.bgn.ch5;

import com.apress.bgn.ch4.hierarchy.*;

public class ReferencesDemo {
    public static void main(String... args) {
        Performer performer = new Performer("John", 40, 1.91f, Gender.MALE);
        Human human = new Performer("Jack", 40, 1.91f, Gender.MALE);
        Actor actor = new Performer("Jean", 40, 1.91f, Gender.MALE);
        Musician musician = new Performer("Jodie", 40, 1.71f, Gender.
        FEMALE);
    }
}
```

In the example, we created four objects of type Performer and assigned them to different reference types, including two interface reference types. If we were to inspect the stack and heap contents for the preceding method, Figure 5-11 shows what we would find. (Figure 5-11)

CHAPTER 5   DATA TYPES

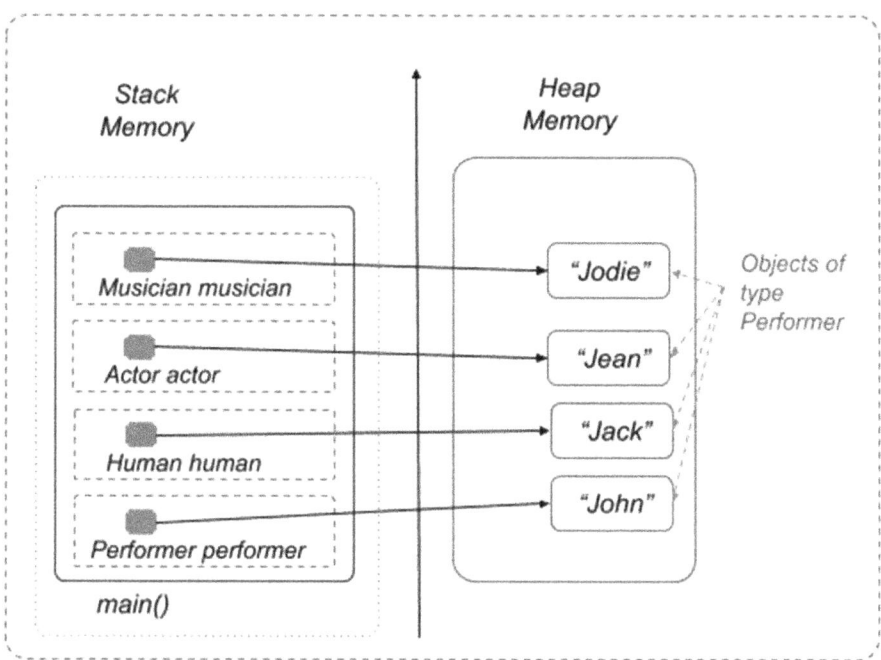

Figure 5-11. *Multiple reference types*

All the references in the previous example point to different objects in the heap, but the following code is possible as well.

```
package com.apress.bgn.ch5;

import com.apress.bgn.ch4.hierarchy.*;

public class ReferencesDemo {
    public static void main(String... args) {
        Performer performer = new Performer("John", 40, 1.91f, Gender.MALE);
        Human human = performer;
        Actor actor = performer;
        Musician musician = performer;
    }
}
```

175

CHAPTER 5 DATA TYPES

In the code snippet, we've created only one object, but multiple references to it, of different types. If we were to inspect the stack and heap contents for the preceding method, Figure 5-12 shows what we would find.

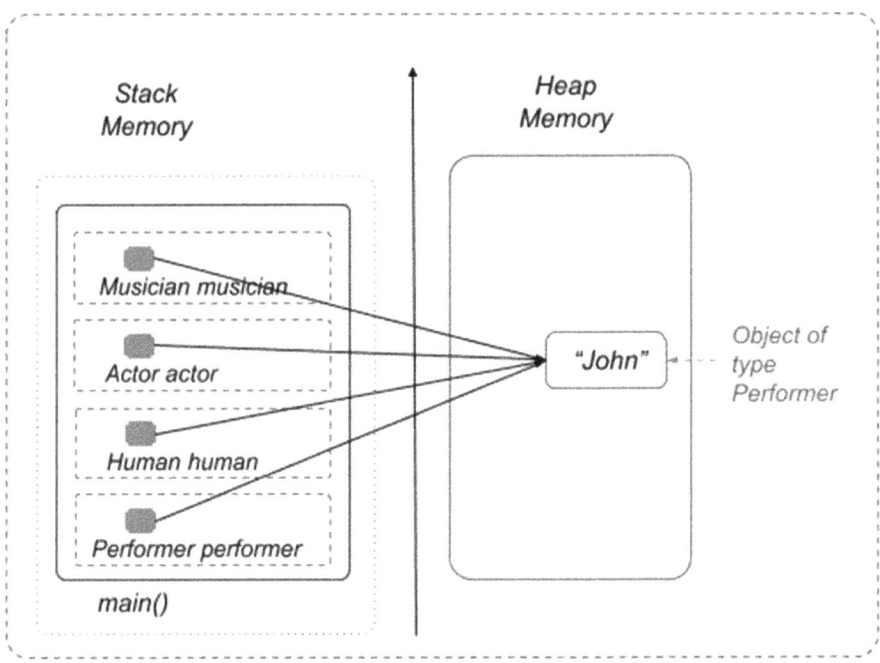

Figure 5-12. *Multiple reference types, second example*

References can only be of the super-type of an assigned object, so the assignments in the following code snippet will not compile.

```
package com.apress.bgn.ch5;

import com.apress.bgn.ch4.hierarchy.*;

public class ReferencesDemo {
    public static void main(String... args) {
        Performer performer = new Performer("John", 40, 1.91f, Gender.MALE);
        Human human = performer;
        Actor actor = performer;
        Musician musician = performer;
```

```
        //these will not compile!!!
        performer = musician;
        //or
        performer = human;
        //or
        performer = actor;
    }
}
```

The reason for that is that the methods are called on the reference, so the object the reference is pointing to must have those methods. So, if a reference is of type `Performer` and `getSongs()` gets called on it, an object of type actor, like in the last line of code will not have that method. That is why the Java compiler complains, and that is why smart editors notify you by underlining the statement with a red line.

Sure, an explicit conversion can be made: `performer = (Performer) actor;`, and this convinces the compiler that all is well, but this only causes an exception at runtime.

Arrays

The new keyword can also be used to create arrays. In a similar manner, it creates objects. An **array** is a data structure that holds a group of variables together. Its size is defined when it is created, and it cannot be changed.

Each variable can be accessed using an index that starts at 0 and goes up to the length of the array to –1. Arrays can hold primitive and reference values. Let's declare a few arrays to show you how versatile and useful they are. Let's declare first an array field and check what is happening with it when an object is created.

```
package com.apress.bgn.ch5;

public class ArraysDemo {

    int array[];

    public static void main(String... args) {
        ArraysDemo ad = new ArraysDemo();
        System.out.println("array was initialized with " + ad.array);
    }
}
```

What do you think is printed in the console when the preceding code is executed? If you assumed that the `ad.array` field is initialed with `null`, you were right.

Arrays are reference types, and thus when left to the JVM to initialize fields of this type with a default value, `null` is used, as this is the typical default value for reference types.

The `null` keyword represents a non-existing value. A reference that is assigned this value does not have a concrete object assigned to it; it does not point to an object in the heap. That is why when writing code, if an object is used (through its reference, of course) before being initialized, a `NullPointerException` is thrown. This is why developers test equality to `null` before using the object (or array). Let's modify the previous example to do that.

```
package com.apress.bgn.ch5;

public class ArraysDemo {

    int array[];

    public static void main(String... args) {
        ArraysDemo ad = new ArraysDemo();

        if (ad.array == null) {
            System.out.println("array unusable");
        }
    }
}
```

Why do we need the `null` keyword to mark something that does not exist yet? Because it is common practice in programming to declare a reference first and initialize it only when first time used. This is useful, especially for objects that tend to be large in size, and the process is called **lazy loading**.

Back to arrays. Let's properly initialize the array field previously declared and give it a size to see what happens.

```
1.  package com.apress.bgn.ch5;
2.
3.  public class ArraysDemo {
4.
5.      public static void main(String... args) {
```

```
6.          int[] array = new int[2];
7.          for (int i = 0; i < array.length; ++i) {
8.              System.out.println("array["+ i +"]= " + array[i]);
9.          }
10.     }
11. }
```

The initialization of the Array takes place in line 6 and the size of the array is 2. The size of the array is given as a parameter to what it looks like a constructor call, only instead of parentheses, square brackets are used. By setting the dimension of the array to 2, we are telling the JVM that two adjacent memory locations must be put aside for this object to store two `int` values in. And because, no values were specified as the array contents, what do you think they are filled with when the array is created? Well, this is a simple one: the previous array is defined to be made of two `int` values, so when the array is initialized, the default value for the `int` type is used. Figure 5-13 depicts what happens in the stack and heap memory when the previous code is executed.

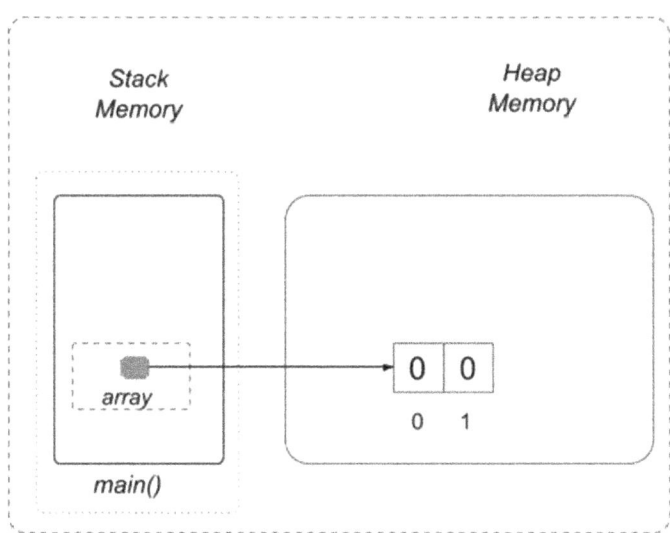

Figure 5-13. *Declaring an int array of size 2*

In lines 7 to 9, a `for` loop prints the values of the array. The `int i` variable is what we call an index variable and traverses all values of the array in increments of 1 in each step of the loop. The `array.length` is the property containing the size of the array, how many elements the array contains. As you probably expected, the output printed in the console is

CHAPTER 5 DATA TYPES

```
array[0]= 0
array[1]= 0
```

To put values in an array, we have the following choices.

- We access the element directly and we set the value.

```
array[0] = 5;
array[1] = 7;
//or
for (int i = 0; i < array.length; ++i) {
    array[i] = i;
}
```

- We initialize the array explicitly with the values we intend to store.

```
int another[] = {1,4,3,2};
```

Arrays can contain references as well. The following code sample depicts how a Performer array can be used.

```
package com.apress.bgn.ch5;

import com.apress.bgn.ch4.hierarchy.*;
public class PerformerArrayDemo {
    public static void main(String... args) {
        Performer[] array = new Performer[2];
        for (int i = 0; i < array.length; ++i) {
            System.out.println("performer[" + i + "]= " + array[i] );
        }

        array[0] = new Performer("John", 40, 1.91f, Gender.MALE);
        array[1] = new Performer("Julianna", 35, 1.61f, Gender.FEMALE);

        for (int i = 0; i < array.length; ++i) {
            System.out.println("performer[" + i + "]= " + array[i].
            getName() );
        }
    }
}
```

And because depicting the memory contents makes it more clear what happens with our array and objects, I give to you Figure 5-14.

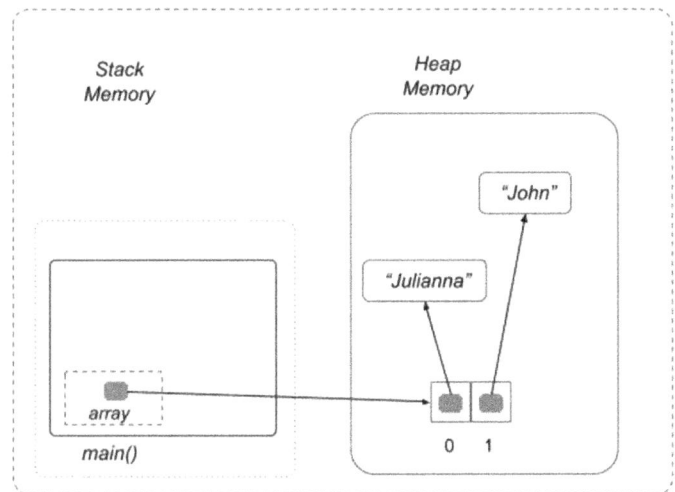

Figure 5-14. *Declaring an array of Performers with size 2*

So yeah, we have an array of references, and the object they point to can be changed during the program.

Arrays can be multidimensional. If you studied advanced math, you probably remember the *matrix* concept, which was a rectangular array arranged in rows and columns. In Java, you can model matrices by using arrays. If you want a simple matrix with rows and columns, you define an array with two dimensions.

```java
package com.apress.bgn.ch5;

public class MatricesDemo {
    public static void main(String... args) {
        // bi-dimensional array: 2 rows, 2 columns
        int[][] intMatrix = {{1, 0}, {0, 1}};

        int[][] intMatrix2 = new int[2][2];
        for (int i = 0; i < intMatrix2.length; ++i) {
            for (int j = 0; j < intMatrix2[i].length; ++j) {
                intMatrix2[i][j] = i + j;
                System.out.print(intMatrix[i][j] + " ");
            }
```

```
            System.out.println();
        }
    }
}
```

But you can get multidimensional and define as many coordinates as you want. The next code snippet defines only three of them.

```
package com.apress.bgn.ch5;

public class MatricesDemo {
    public static void main(String... args) {
        // cubical matrix, with three coordinates
        int[][][] intMatrix3 = new int[2][2][2];
        for (int i = 0; i < intMatrix3.length; ++i) {
            for (int j = 0; j < intMatrix3[i].length; ++j) {
                for (int k = 0; k < intMatrix3[i][j].length; ++k) {
                    intMatrix3[i][j][k] = i + j + k;
                    System.out.print("["+i+", "+j+", " + k + "]");
                }
                System.out.println();
            }
            System.out.println();
        }
    }
}
```

When it comes to arrays, make them as big as you need them and your memory allows, but make sure to initialize them and make sure in your code that you do not try to access indexes outside the allowed range. If the size of an array is **N**, then its last index is **N-1** and its first is **0**. Try to access any index outside that range and an exception of type java.lang.ArrayIndexOutOfBoundsException is thrown at runtime. So writing code like this

```
int array = new int[2];
array[5] =7;
```

causes your program to crash at runtime, and the following is printed in the console.

```
Exception in thread "main" java.lang.ArrayIndexOutOfBoundsException:
    Index 5 out of bounds for length 2
at chapter.five.collections/com.apress.bgn.ch5.ArraysDemo.main(ArraysDemo.java:56)
```

For easier handling of arrays in Java, there is a special class: `java.util.Arrays`. This class provides utility methods to sort and compare arrays, search elements, and convert their content to text or a stream, so that they can print without writing the tedious for loop.

```
int array = new int2;
 System.out.println(Arrays.toString(ad.array));
//or
Arrays.stream(array).forEach(ai -> System.out.println(ai));
//or using methods reference
Arrays.stream(array).forEach(System.out::println);
//sorting
Arrays.sort(another);
```

Feel free to modify the code provided for this chapter to try some of those methods.

The String Type

The next special Java type on our list is `String`. You've seen it being used quite often until now, without a detailed explanation. Together with the primitive `int`, this is one of the most used types in Java. String instances model texts and perform all kinds of operations on them. The `String` type is a special type, because **objects of this type are given special treatment by the JVM**. If you remember the first image with memory contents, `String` objects are allocated in the heap in a special place called the `String Pool`. This section is dedicated to it; the `String` type is covered in detail, and a lot of your questions you might have about this type should get answered.

Until now `String` variables were declared in this book like this:

```
String name= "John";
```

CHAPTER 5 DATA TYPES

But the `String` class has many constructors to initialize `String` variables. The following is a set of `String` variables being declared and initialized.

```
package com.apress.bgn.ch5.refs;

public class StringDemo {

    public static void main(String... args) {
1.      String  text1 = null;
2.
3.      String text21 = "two";
4.      String text22 = "two";
5.      String text23 = new String ("two");
6.
7.      String piece1 = "t";
8.      String piece2  = "wo";
9.      String text24 = piece1 + piece2;
10.
11.     char[] twoCh = {'t', 'w', 'o'};
12.     String text25 = new String(twoCh);
    }
}
```

Lines 3, 4, 5, 9, and 11 all define a `String` object with the same content *two*. We intentionally did that, creating multiple `String` objects with the same value. In real life applications, especially in this big data hype period, applications handle a lot of data, most of it text form. So, being able to compress the data and reuse it would reduce the memory consumption, also reducing memory access attempts also increases speed by reducing processing, which in turn reduces costs.

Before continuing this section, I have to discuss what **object equality** means in Java. Objects are handled in Java using references to them. The == operator compares references; but if we want to compare the objects, we must use the `equals()` method. This is a special method inherited from the `Object` class.

In Java `String` instances are immutable, which means they cannot be changed once created. This means that the JVM can reuse existing values to form new string values, without consuming additional memory. This process is called *interning*. One copy of each text value (literal) is saved to a special memory region called `String Pool`. When a new String variable is created and a value is assigned to it, the JVM first searches the pool for a string of equal value. If found, a reference to this memory address is returned, without allocating additional memory. If not found, it'll be added to the pool and its reference is returned.

This being said, considering the preceding sample code, we expect for `text21` and `text22` variable to point to the same String object in the pool, which means references are equal too. Let's test that.

```java
package com.apress.bgn.ch5.refs;

public class StringDemo {

    public static void main(String... args) {
        String text21 = "two";
        String text22 = "two";

        if (text21 == text22) {
            System.out.println("Equal References");
        } else {
            System.out.println("Different References");
        }

        if (text21.equals(text22)) {
            System.out.println("Equal Objects");
        } else {
            System.out.println("Different Objects");
        }
    }
}
```

When running the preceding code, the following is printed in the console, proving the previous affirmations and the existence of the String pool.

```
Equal References
Equal Objects
```

Figure 5-15 shows an abstract representation of the memory contents when the code is executed.

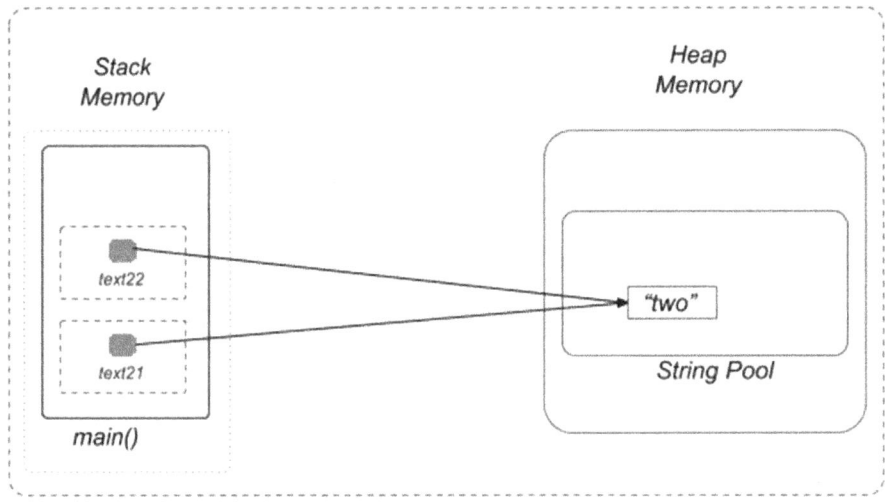

Figure 5-15. String Pool example

When a new String object is created using the new operator, the JVM allocate new memory for a new object and store it in the heap, so the String pool won't be used. This results in every String object created like this having its own memory region with its own address. That is why if we were to compare variable text22 and variable text23, from the initial code sample, we would expect their references to be different, but the objects should be equal. Let's test that.

```
package com.apress.bgn.ch5.refs;

public class StringDemo {
    public static void main(String... args) {
        String text22 = "two";
        String text23 = new String ("two");

        if (text22 == text23) {
            System.out.println("Equal References");
        } else {
            System.out.println("Different References");
        }
```

```
        if (text22.equals(text23)) {
            System.out.println("Equal Objects");
        } else {
            System.out.println("Different Objects");
        }
    }
}
```

When running the preceding code, the following is printed in the console, proving everything that was mentioned before.

```
Different References
Equal Objects
```

I leave it up to you to imagine what the stack and heap memory look like in the previous example.[4]

The `String Pool` has a default size of 1009. Starting with Java 6, its size can be modified using the `-XX:StringTableSize`.

** Lines 11 and 12 in the initial code sample depict how a `String` instance is created from a `char[3]` array. Until Java 8, internally that was the initial representation for String: arrays of characters. A character is represented on 2 bytes, which means a lot of memory was consumed for *Strings*. In Java 9, a new representation was introduced called **Compact String**, which uses `byte[]` or `char[]` depending on the content. This means that the memory consumed by your `String` processing application is significantly lower starting with Java 9.

Escaping Characters

There are special characters that cannot be part of a `String` value. As you have probably noticed, `String` values are defined between double quotes (`"sample"`) and this makes the "(double quote) character unusable as a value. To use it as a `String` value, it has to

---

[4]If you want to check if you understood memory management and Strings correctly, you are welcome to draw your own picture and sent it to the author for a review and a technical discussion.

CHAPTER 5 DATA TYPES

be *escaped*. Aside from this character there is also the \(backslash) and the \a(alert). Figure 5-16 shows how IntelliJ IDEA tries to tell you that you cannot use those characters in the content of a String value.

```
28      package com.apress.bgn.ch5.refs;
29
30      /**
31       * @author Iuliana Cosmina
32       * since 1.0
33       */
34      public class StringDemo {
35
36          public void sample(String args) {
37              String text332 = "Special " character ";
38              String text331 = "Special \" character";
39
40              String text341 = "Special \ character";
41              String text342 = "Special \\ character";
42
43              String text351 = "Special \a character";
44              String text352 = "Special \\a character";
45          }
46      }
```

Figure 5-16. *Code samples with special characters*

To escape those characters, a backlash must be inserted before them. The '(single quote) must be escaped as well when used as a character value.

char quote = '\'';

There are some other Java escape sequences that can be used in String values to get a certain effect, which are listed in Table 5-1.

Table 5-1. *Java Escape Sequences*

Escape Sequence	Effect
\n	Create a new line (often called the newline character)
\t	Create a tab
\b	Create a backspace character (which might delete the preceding character, depending on the output device)
\r	Return to the start of the line (but do not make a new line, the equivalent of the Home key on the keyboard)
\f	Form feed (move to the top of the next page for printers)

The newline \n and the tab \t character are used often in programming to properly format console output. If we define a `String` instance like the following,

```
String perf = "The singers performing tonight are: \n\t Paolo Nutini \n\t Seth MacFarlane
    \n\t John Mayer";
```

When printed in the console, the text is formatted to look like this:

```
The singers performing tonight are:
        Paolo Nutini
        Seth MacFarlane
        John Mayer
```

Wrapper Classes

Each primitive type has a corresponding reference type. Before covering each of them and explaining why they are needed, please take a look at Table 5-2. The Java wrapper classes wrap a value of the primitive type with the same name.

Table 5-2. Java Primitive and Equivalent Reference Types

Primitive	Class
byte	java.lang.Byte
short	java.lang.Short
int	java.lang.Integer
long	java.lang.Long
float	java.lang.Float
double	java.lang.Double
boolean	java.lang.Boolean
char	java.lang.Char

In addition, these classes provide methods for converting primitive values to `String` and vice versa, as well as constants and methods useful when dealing with primitive types that need to be treated as objects. The numeric wrapper classes are related, all of them extend the `Number` class, as depicted in Figure 5-17.

CHAPTER 5   DATA TYPES

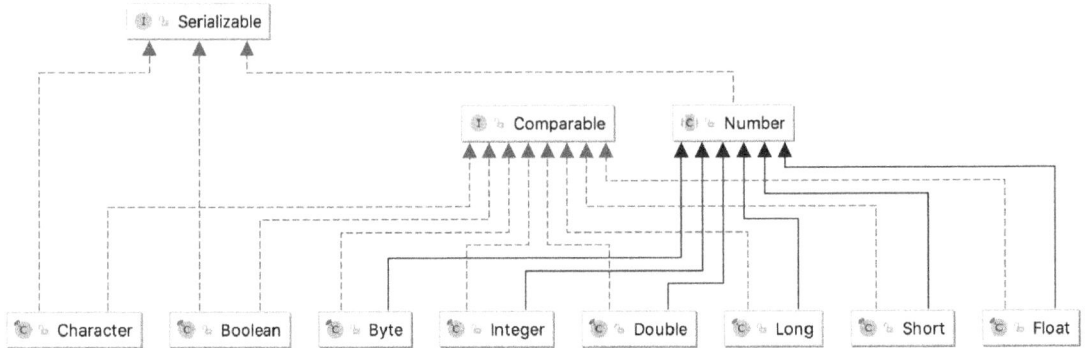

Figure 5-17.   *Wrapper classes hierarchy*

The following code samples mostly use the Integer class, but the other numeric wrapper classes can be used in a similar way. The JVM knows how to convert a primitive int into an Integer object automatically when needed, operation that is called **boxing** and from an Integer object to a primitive int, operation that is called **unboxing**. The following code sample contains a few operations with Integer and int values.

```
package com.apress.bgn.ch5.refs;

public class WrapperDemo {
    public static void main(String... args) {
        // upper interval boundary for int
        Integer max =  Integer.MAX_VALUE;
        System.out.println(max);

        //unboxing
        int pmax =  max;

        //boxing
        Integer io = 10;

        //creating primitive utility method
        //exception is thrown, if string is not a number
        int i1 = Integer.parseInt("11");

        //constructor deprecated in Java 9
        //exception is thrown, if string is not a number
        Integer i2 = new Integer("12");
```

```
        //exception is thrown, if string is not a number
        Integer i3 = Integer.valueOf("12");

        //convert int into to String
        String s0 = Integer.toString(13);

        //convert int to float
        float f0 = Integer.valueOf(14).floatValue();

        //creating string with binary representation of number 9 (1001)
        String  s1  = Integer.toBinaryString(9);

        //introduced in Java 1.8
        Integer i4 = Integer.parseUnsignedInt("+15");

        //method to add to integers
        int sum = Integer.sum(2, 3);

        //method to get the bigger value
        int maximum = Integer.max(2, 7);
    }
}
```

The Character and Boolean types are a little bit different, because these types are not numeric, so they cannot be converted to any numeric value. They cannot be converted one to another either. Oracle provides really good documentation for its classes, so if you are curious about using these two types, check out the official JDK API documentation at https://docs.oracle.com/javase/10/docs/api/index.html?overview-summary.html.

Date Time API

A lot of applications make use of calendar date types to print the current date, deadlines, and birthdays. No matter what application you decide to build you most likely need to use calendar dates. Until Java 8, the main class to model a calendar date was java.util.Date. There are a few problems with this class and others involved in handling calendar dates. But before we get into that, let's see how we can get the current date, create a custom date, and print certain details.

CHAPTER 5　DATA TYPES

```java
package com.apress.bgn.ch5;

import java.util.Date;
import java.text.SimpleDateFormat;

public class CalendarDateDemo {
    public static void main(String... args) {
        SimpleDateFormat sdf = new SimpleDateFormat("dd-MM-yyyy");
        Date currentDate = new Date();
        System.out.println("Today: " + sdf.format(currentDate));

        //deprecated since 1.1
        Date johnBirthday = new Date(77, 9, 16);
        System.out.println("John's Birthday: " + sdf.format(johnBirthday));

        int day = johnBirthday.getDay();
        System.out.println("Day: " + day);
        int month = johnBirthday.getMonth() + 1;
        System.out.println("Month: " + month);
        int year = johnBirthday.getYear();
        System.out.println("Year: " + year);
    }
}
```

Getting the current date is simple; just call the default constructor of the `Date` class.

```java
Date currentDate = new Date();
```

The contents of the `currentDate` can be displayed directly, but usually an instance of `java.text.SimpleDateFormat` is used to format the date to a pattern that is country specific. The formatter can also be used to convert a `String` with that specific format intro a `Date` instance. Of course, if the text does not match the pattern of the formatter, a specific exception is thrown (type: `java.text.ParseException`)

```java
SimpleDateFormat sdf = new SimpleDateFormat("dd-MM-yyyy");
System.out.println(currentDate);
System.out.println("Today: " + sdf.format(currentDate));
Date johnBirthday = sdf.parse("16-10-1977");
```

To create a Date instance from the numbers representing a date: year, month and day, a constructor that takes those values as arguments can be used, although that constructor has been deprecated since Java 1.1, and the recommended way is to use the sdf.parse(..) method. The constructor has a few particularities regarding its arguments.

- changes the technical meaning again the year argument must be the intended year value from which 1900 is subtracted
- the months are counted from 0, so the month to give as an argument, must be the month we want −1

The code to construct a Date from the numeric values for the year, month, and day is depicted as follows.

```
//deprecated since 1.1
Date johnBirthday = new Date(77, 9, 16);
System.out.println("John's Birthday: " + sdf.format(johnBirthday));
//it prints: John's Birthday: 16-10-1977
```

If we want to extract the year, month, and day of the month from the date, there are methods for that: the method to extract the day of the month is named getDate().

```
try {
     johnBirthday = sdf.parse("16-10-1977");
} catch (ParseException e) {
    e.printStackTrace();
}
System.out.println("John's Birthday: " + sdf.format(johnBirthday));

//day of the month
int day = johnBirthday.getDate();
System.out.println("Day: " + day);

int month = johnBirthday.getMonth() + 1;
System.out.println("Month: " +  month);

int year = johnBirthday.getYear();
System.out.println("Year: " + year);
```

CHAPTER 5   DATA TYPES

If you inspect the `CalendarDateDemo` class in the IntelliJ IDEA editor, you notice that some constructors and methods are written with a strikethrough font. This means that they are deprecated and might be removed in future versions of Java and thus they should not be used. That is why there is another way to do all of that: use the `java.util.Calendar` class. The code to do the same as before, but using the `Calendar` class is listed next.

```
package com.apress.bgn.ch5;

import java.util.Calendar;
import java.util.Date;
import java.util.GregorianCalendar;
import java.text.SimpleDateFormat;

public class CalendarDateDemo {
    public static void main(String... args) {
        SimpleDateFormat sdf = new SimpleDateFormat("dd-MM-yyyy");
        Calendar calendar = new GregorianCalendar();
        Date currentDate = calendar.getTime();
        System.out.println("Today: " + sdf.format(currentDate));

        calendar.set(1977, 9, 16);
        Date johnBirthday = calendar.getTime();
        System.out.println("John's Birthday: " + sdf.format(johnBirthday));

        int day = calendar.get(Calendar.DAY_OF_MONTH);
        System.out.println("Day: " + day);
        int month = calendar.get(Calendar.MONTH);
        System.out.println("Month: " + month);
        in year = calendar.get(Calendar.YEAR);
        System.out.println("Year: " + year);
    }
}
```

Unfortunately some of the peculiarities remain, as the central class for representing dates is still the `java.util.Date`, but at least we are not using anything deprecated anymore.

The java.util.Date class and the java.text.SimpleDateFormat class are not thread safe, so in complex applications with multiple execution threads, developers must synchronize access to those type of objects explicitly. Objects of those types are not immutable, and working with time zones is a pain. That is why in Java 8, a new API to model calendar-date operations was introduced. It is better designed, and date instances are thread-safe and immutable. The central classes for the API are java.time.LocalDate and java.time.LocalDateTime, used to model calendar dates and calendar dates with time. Let's see how the code to get the current date and to create a custom date looks with the new API.

```java
package com.apress.bgn.ch5;

import java.time.LocalDate;
import java.time.LocalDateTime;
import java.time.Month;

public class CalendarDateDemo {
    public static void main(String... args) {
        LocalDateTime currentTime = LocalDateTime.now();
        System.out.println("Current DateTime: " + currentTime);
        LocalDate today = currentTime.toLocalDate();
        System.out.println("Today: " + today);

        LocalDate johnBd = LocalDate.of(1977, Month.OCTOBER, 16);
        System.out.println("John's Birthday: " + johnBd);

        int day = johnBd.getDayOfMonth();
        System.out.println("Day: " + day + ", " + johnBd.getDayOfWeek());
        int month = johnBd.getMonthValue();
        System.out.println("Month: " + month + ", " + johnBd.getMonth());
        int year = johnBd.getYear();
        System.out.println("Year: " + year);
    }
}
```

To get the current date and time a static method named now() is called, which returns an instance of type LocalDateTime. This instance can get the current date by calling toLocalDate().

To create a custom date, the actual year and day of month can be used as parameters and the month can be specified using one of the values of the `java.time.Month` enum.

Extracting information regarding a date can be done easily by calling methods with intuitive names. Look at the getDayOfMonth() and getDayOfWeek() methods in the previous snippet. Their name reflects exactly what data they are returning.

The `LocalDate` and `LocalDateTime` classes simplify the development where time zones are not required. Working with time zones is an advanced subject, so it won't be covered in this book.

Collections

Among the most important family types in JDK are collections. Classes and interfaces in the collections family model common data collections, such as sets, lists, and maps. All the classes are stored under package `java.util` and can be split into two categories: tuples and collections of key-value pairs. The tuples are unidimensional sets of data: if the values are unique, any class implementing the `java.util.Set` interface should be used to model them, if not any class implementing the `java.util.List` interface should be used. For collections of key-value pairs classes, implementations of `java.util.Map` should be used.

Starting with Java 1.5 collections have become generic, which allows developers more precision and security when working with them. Before Java 1.5, collections could contain any type of objects. Developers can still write code like this:

```
package com.apress.bgn.ch5;

import com.apress.bgn.ch4.hierarchy.Gender;
import com.apress.bgn.ch4.hierarchy.Performer;

import java.util.*;

public class CollectionsDemo {
    public static void main(String... args) {
        List objList = new ArrayList();
        objList.add("temp");
        objList.add(Integer.valueOf(5));
        objList.add(new Performer("John", 40, 1.91f, Gender.MALE));
    }
}
```

When you iterate this list, it is difficult to determine which objects you are handling without complicated code analyzing the type of each object. This was mentioned at the end of **Chapter** 4 when *generics* were introduced. The code to iterate the list and process the elements is depicted next to show you why this is a bad idea and bad practice in this day and age of Java.

```java
package com.apress.bgn.ch5;

import com.apress.bgn.ch4.hierarchy.Gender;
import com.apress.bgn.ch4.hierarchy.Performer;

import java.util.*;

public class CollectionsDemo {

    public static void main(String... args) {
        List objList = new ArrayList();
        objList.add("temp");
        objList.add(Integer.valueOf(5));
        objList.add(new Performer("John", 40, 1.91f, Gender.MALE));

        for (Object obj : objList) {
            if (obj instanceof String) {
                System.out.println("String object = " + obj.toString());
            } else if (obj instanceof Integer) {
                Integer i = (Integer)obj;
                System.out.println("Integer object = " + obj.toString());
            } else {
                Performer p = (Performer) obj;
                System.out.println("Performer object = " + p.getName());
            }
        }
    }
}
```

Maybe this is not clear to you now, but to use the contents of the list, you have to know all the types of objects that were put in the list. This might be doable when you are working on a small project, but in a bigger project with multiple developers involved, this can get messy really fast.

CHAPTER 5   DATA TYPES

This is where *generics* come to help. Generics help define at compile time what types of objects should be put into a collection, and thus, if the wrong object type is added to the collection, the code no longer compiles. Both lists and sets implement the same interface: java.util.Collection<T>, which means their API is almost the same. Figure 5-18 shows a simplified hierarchy of the collections with the most used classes and interfaces in programming Figure 5-18.

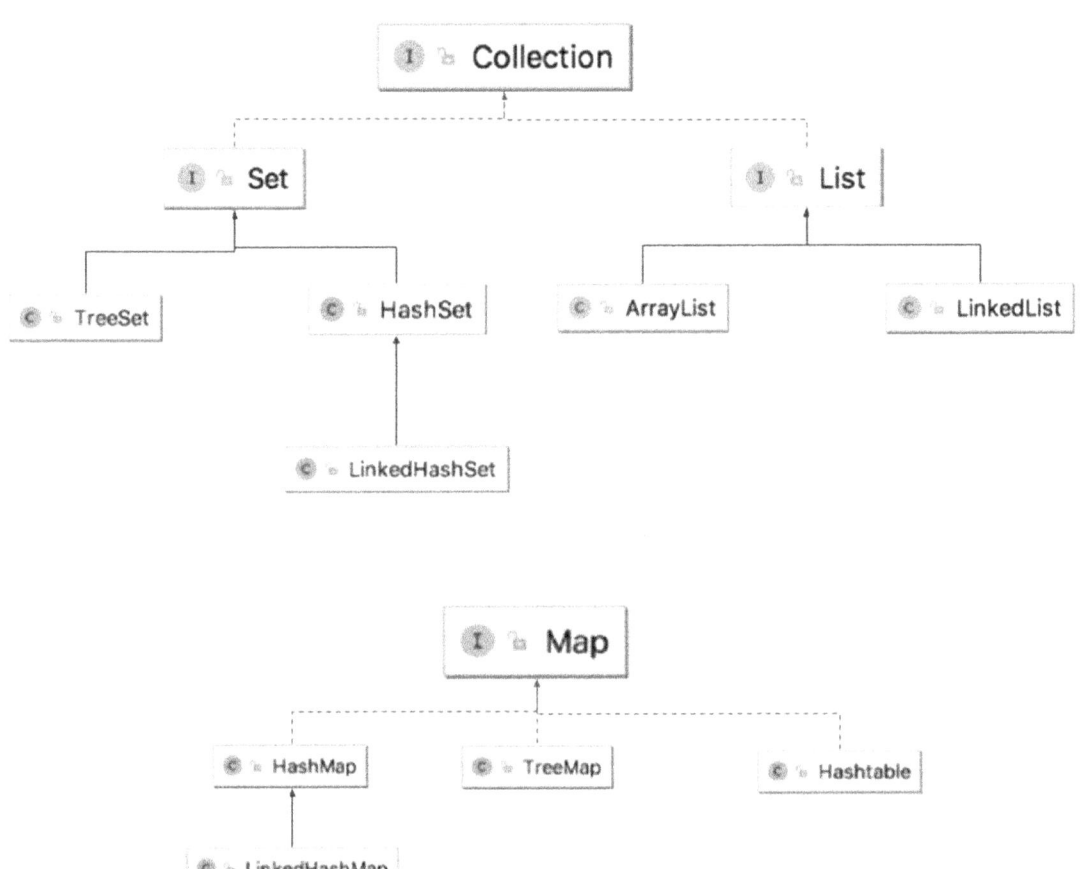

Figure 5-18. *Collection hierarchy*

Let's start with a list example.

```
package com.apress.bgn.ch5;

import java.util.*;

public class CollectionsDemo {
```

```
    public static void main(String... args) {
        List<String> stringList = new ArrayList<String>();
        stringList.add("one");
        stringList.add("two");
        stringList.add("three");

        for (String s : stringList) {
            System.out.println(s);
        }
    }
}
```

A `List` contains an unsorted collection of non-unique data, null elements included. In the example, we declared a reference of type `List<T>` and an object of type `ArrayList<T>`. We did this because as all implementations have the same API, we could easily switch `ArrayList<T>` with `LinkedList<T>` and the code still works. **Declaring abstract references is a good programming practice**.

```
List<String> stringList = new ArrayList<String>();
stringList = new LinkedList<String>();
```

The syntax in the previous examples are pre-Java 1.7, when the <> **(diamond operator)** was introduced. This allowed more simplification of collections initializations, because it only required declaring the type of the elements in the list only in the reference declaration. So, the two lines in the previous code snippet became

```
List<String> stringList = new ArrayList<>();
stringList = new LinkedList<>();
```

Every new Java version has added changes to the collection framework starting with Java 1.5. In Java 1.8, support for lambda expressions was added with a default method named `forEach` in the `java.lang.Iterable<T>` interface, which is extended by the `java.lang.Collection<T>`. So, the code to print all the values in the list, as we did previously using a `for` loop, can be replaced with

```
stringList.forEach(element -> System.out.println(element));
```

CHAPTER 5　DATA TYPES

In Java 9, yet another improvement was introduced: factory methods for collections. Our collection was populated with elements by repeatedly calling `add(..)`, which is a little redundant, especially since we have the full collection of elements we want to put in the list. That is why in Java 9 methods to create collection objects in one line of code were introduced; for example,

```
List<String> stringList = List.of("one", "two", "three");
```

The resulting `List<T>` is an immutable collection; it can no longer be modified, and elements cannot be added or removed from it.

Moving closer to the present, in Java 10, support for **local variable type inference** was added, which means that we no longer have to explicitly specify the reference type, because it is automatically be inferred based on the object type, so the following declaration

```
List<String> stringList = List.of("one", "two", "three");
```

becomes

```
var stringList = List.of("one", "two", "three");
```

Similar code can be written with `Set<T>`, `HashSet<T>`, and `TreeSet<T>`, and similar methods exist for the `Set<T>` classes.

Map implementations come with a few differences because they model collections of key-value pairs; so this case is treated separately. The following code snippet depicts the creation, initialization of a map that uses keys of type `String` and values of type `Integer`. The syntax is Java 6.

```java
package com.apress.bgn.ch5;

import java.util.*;

public class CollectionsDemo {
    public static void main(String... args) {
        Map<String, Integer> stringMap = new HashMap<String, Integer>();
        stringMap.put("one", 1);
        stringMap.put("two", 2);
        stringMap.put("three", 3);
```

```
        for (Map.Entry<String, Integer> entry : stringMap.entrySet()) {
            System.out.println(entry.getKey() + ":  " + entry.getValue());
        }
    }
}
```

From the `for` loop, you can infer that a map is a collection of `Map.Entry<K, V>` elements. If we were to move ahead to the Java 1.7 syntax, the declaration of the map changes to

```
  Map<String, Integer> stringMap = new HashMap<>();
```

In Java 1.8, traversal and printing values in maps became more practical.

```
stringMap.forEach((k,v) -> System.out.println(k + ": " + v));
```

And in Java 9, declaring and populating a map became easier.

```
Map<String, Integer> stringMap = Map.of("one", 1,"two", 2, "three", 3);
```

And local variable type inference works for maps too.

```
var stringMap = new HashMap<String, Integer>();
```

The JDK classes for working with collections, cover a wide range of functionality, such as sorting, searching, merging collections, intersections, and so on. As the book advances, the context of the code samples widen, and we are able to use collections to solve real-life problems. So, other methods are covered and working code samples are provided.

Concurrency Specific Types

A Java program can have more than one execution thread. By default, when a Java program is executed, a thread is created for the code that is called from the `main` method and a few other utility threads are created and executed in parallel for JVM related things. These threads can easily be accessed using static utility methods defined in the `java.lang.Thread` class. The following code sample does just that: extracts the references to the `Thread` instances and prints their name in the console.

CHAPTER 5   DATA TYPES

```
package com.apress.bgn.ch5;

public class ListJvmThreads {
    public static void main(String... args) {
        var threadSet = Thread.getAllStackTraces().keySet();
        var threadArray = threadSet.toArray(new Thread[threadSet.size()]);

        for (int i = 0; i < threadArray.length; ++i) {
            System.out.println("thread name: " + threadArray[i].getName());
        }
    }
}
```

The output produced by running the code in JDK 11 prints the following.

```
thread name: Reference Handler
thread name: Monitor Ctrl-Break
thread name: Finalizer
thread name: main
thread name: Signal Dispatcher
thread name: Common-Cleaner
```

The thread named main is the thread that executes the developer written code. The developer can write code to start its own threads from the main thread. The simplest way to create a custom thread is to create a class that extends the Thread class. The Thread class implements an interface named Runnable that declares a single method named run(). The Thread class declares a method named start(). When this method is called, the body of the run() method is executed in a separate execution thread.[5] Thus, when extending the Thread class, the run() method must be overridden.

The following example depicts a class named CounterThread. The contents of the run() method is designed to pause the execution from time to time by calling the Thread.sleep(..) utility method. The body of the method is wrapped in two lines of code that print the name of the thread and a starting message and the name of the thread and an ending message. This is necessary to slow down the execution of this type of thread, so that we can clearly see they are executed in parallel.

---

[5]Sure, the internal of thread management is much more complicated, but this section scratches the surface.

```java
package com.apress.bgn.ch5;

public class CounterThread extends Thread {
    @Override
    public void run() {
        System.out.println(this.getName() + " started...");
        for (int i = 0; i < 10; ++i) {
            try {
                Thread.sleep(i * 10);
            } catch (InterruptedException e) {
                e.printStackTrace();
            }
        }
        System.out.println(this.getName() + " ended.");
    }
}
```

To test our thread class is as simple as instantiating it a few times and calling the start() method.

```java
package com.apress.bgn.ch5;

public class ThreadDemo {
    public static void main(String... args) {
        for (int i = 0; i < 10; ++i) {
            new CounterThread().start();
        }
    }
}
```

In the example, ten instances of class CounterThread were created and the start() method was called for each of them. When the previous code is executed, a log similar to the following should print in the console.

```
Thread-0 started...
Thread-3 started...
Thread-8 started...
Thread-9 started...
```

```
Thread-7 started...
Thread-6 started...
Thread-1 started...
Thread-2 started...
Thread-4 started...
Thread-5 started...
Thread-4 ended.
Thread-1 ended.
Thread-9 ended.
Thread-7 ended.
Thread-5 ended.
Thread-8 ended.
Thread-0 ended.
Thread-6 ended.
Thread-2 ended.
Thread-3 ended.
```

Another way to create threads is by creating a class that implements the `Runnable` interface. This is useful when we want to customize the execution in the `run` method a little more and maybe extend another class. Or, considering that the `Runnable` declares one method, lambda expressions can be used too. Let's declare the equivalent `Runnable` implementation.

```java
package com.apress.bgn.ch5;

import static java.lang.Thread.*;

public class CounterRunnable implements Runnable {
    @Override
    public void run() {
        System.out.println(Thread.currentThread().getName() + " started...");
        for (int i = 0; i < 10; ++i) {
            try {
                Thread.sleep(i * 10);
            } catch (InterruptedException e) {
                e.printStackTrace();
            }
```

```
        }
        System.out.println(Thread.currentThread().getName() + " ended.");
    }
}
```

Because we no longer have access to the name of the thread, to print it we must use another utility method `Thread.currentThread()` to retrieve a reference to the current thread in execution. The `Thread` class provides a constructor with a parameter of type `Runnable`, this means it can be called with any argument of a type that implements `Runnable`. And thus, to create threads using `CounterRunnable`, code similar to the following example can be written.

```
package com.apress.bgn.ch5;

public class LambdaRunnableDemo {
    public static void main(String... args) {
        for (int i = 0; i < 10; ++i) {
            new Thread(new CounterRunnable()).start();
        }
    }
}
```

If this code is run, we'll get a similar output.

This is a good candidate for using lambda expressions, because `Runnable` can be implemented on the spot. So, the previous code can also be written as follows.

```
for (int i = 0; i < 10; ++i) {
        new Thread(
        //Runnable implemented on the spot
        () -> {
            System.out.println(currentThread().getName() + " started...");
            for (int j = 0; j < 10; ++j) {
                try {
                    sleep(j * 10);
                } catch (InterruptedException e) {
                    e.printStackTrace();
                }
            }
```

```
            System.out.println(currentThread().getName() + " ended.");
    }).start();
}
```

Java provides thread management classes that can create and manage threads, so the developer mustn't declare the threads explicitly. The concurrency framework is a subject too advanced for this book, but if this section has made you curious, the Oracle Concurrency tutorial is at https://docs.oracle.com/javase/tutorial/essential/concurrency/index.html.

Summary

In this chapter, you learned how memory for a Java program is administered by the JVM and the basics of the most used Java data types. We discussed the following.

- how the memory is managed during the execution of a Java program
- the differences between primitive and reference types
- how many primitive types are defined in Java
- why the String type is special
- how to work with calendar dates
- how arrays are declared and used
- how null is used
- how to declare and use collection implementations

If some of the examples in this chapter seem complicated, do not be discouraged. It is difficult to explain certain concepts without providing working code that you can execute, test, and even modify yourself. Unfortunately, this requires the use of concepts introduced in later chapters (e.g., `for` and `if` statements). Make a note of every concept that it is not clear now, and the page number, and return to this chapter after you read about the concept in more detail later in the book.

CHAPTER 6

Operators

The previous chapters covered the basic concepts of Java programming. You were taught how to organize your code, how your files should be named, and which data types you can use, depending on the problem you are trying to solve. You were taught how to declare fields, variables, and methods and how they were stored in memory to help you design your solutions so that resource consumption is optimal.

In this chapter, you learn to combine declared variables using *operators*. Most Java operators are the ones you know from math, but because programming involves types other than numeric, extra operators with specific purposes were added. Table 6-1 lists all Java operators with their category and scope.

Table 6-1. *Java Operators*

Category	Operator	Scope
casting	*(type)*	explicit type conversion
unary, postfix	expr++, expr–	post increment/decrement
unary, prefix	++expr, expr	pre increment/decrement
unary, logical	!	negation
unary, bitwise	~	bitwise complement performs a bit-by-bit reversal of an integer value
multiplicative, binary	*, /, %	for numeric types: multiply, divide, and return remainder
additive, binary	+, -	for numeric types: addition, subtraction; "+" also used for String concatenation

(*continued*)

CHAPTER 6 OPERATORS

Table 6-1. (*continued*)

Category	Operator	Scope
bit shifting, binary	>>, <<, >>>	for numeric types: move bits to the right, left, and right ignoring the sign
conditional, relational	instanceof	tests whether the object is an instance of the specified type (class or subclass or interface)
conditional, relational	==, !=, <, >, <=, >=	equals differs from, lesser than, greater than, less than or equals, greater than or equals
AND, binary	&	bitwise logical AND
exclusive OR, binary	^	bitwise logical XOR
inclusive OR, binary	|	bitwise logical OR
conditional, logical AND	&&	
conditional, logical OR	||	
conditional, ternary	? :	also called *the Elvis operator*
assignment	=, +=, -=, *=, /= %=, &=, ^=, <<= >>=, >>>=, |=	simple assignment, combined assignments

Let's start this chapter with the most common operator in programming: the assignment operator (=).

The Assignment Operator (=)

This operator is the most used in programming, as nothing can be done without it. Any variable that you create, regardless of the type, primitive or reference has to be given a value at some point in the program. Setting of a value using the assignment operator is quite simple: on the left side of the operator you have the variable name and on the right it is a value. The only condition for an assignment to work is that the value matches the type of the variable.

CHAPTER 6 OPERATORS

To test this operator, you can play a little using `jshell`; make sure that you start it in verbose mode so you can see the effect of your assignments.

```
$ jshell -v
|  Welcome to JShell -- Version 11-ea
|  For an introduction type: /help intro
[jshell> int i = 0;
i ==> 0
|  created variable i : int

[jshell> i = -4;
i ==> -4
|  assigned to i : int

jshell> String sample = "text"
[sample ==> "text"
|  created variable sample : String

[jshell> List<String> list = new ArrayList<>()
list ==> []
|  created variable list : List<String>

[jshell> list = new LinkedList<>();
list ==> []
|  assigned to list : List<String>
```

In the previous example, we declared primitive and reference values and assigned and reassigned values to them. Assignment of values with types that mismatch the initial type is not permitted. In the following code sample, we are trying to assign a text value to a variable that was previously declared as having the `int` type.

```
[jshell> int i = 0;
i ==> 0
|  created variable i : int

[jshell> i = -4;
i ==> -4
|  assigned to i : int
```

209

```
[jshell> i = "gigi pedala"
|  Error:
|  incompatible types: java.lang.String cannot be converted to int
|  i = "gigi pedala"
|      ^-----------^
```

Introduction of type inference in JDK 10 does not affect this, and the type of the variable is inferred depending on the type of the first value assigned. This means that you cannot declare a variable using the `var` keyword without specifying an initial value. This excludes the `null` value, as it cannot be used to declare a type. This can be forced though by casting the `null` value to the type we are interested in.

```
[jshell> var j;
|  Error:
|  cannot infer type for local variable j
|    (cannot use 'var' on variable without initializer)
|  var j;
|  ^----^

[jshell> var j = 5;
j ==> 5
|  created variable j : int

[jshell> var sample2 = "bubulina"
sample2 ==> "bubulina"
|  created variable sample2 : String

// yes, this actually works !
[jshell> var funny = (Integer) null;
funny ==> null
|  created variable funny : Integer
```

This is all that can be said about the assignment operator. Other details are covered later with the composed assignment operators.

Explicit Type Conversion (type) and instanceof

We coupled these two operators in the same section, because it is easier to provide code samples that are identical to what you use frequently in your job as a developer. (should you decide to go in this direction).

It is better to keep the reference type as generic as possible to allow changing of the concrete implementation without breaking the code, but sometimes, we might need to group objects together, but execute different code depending of their types. Remember the `Performer` hierarchy mentioned in the previous chapter? We're going to make use of these types here to show you how to use these operators. In case you do not want to go back to the previous chapter to see the hierarchy, 6-1 here it is again in Figure 6-1, but with a twist: we added an extra class named `Graphician`, which implements the `Artist` interface and extends the `Human` class.[1]

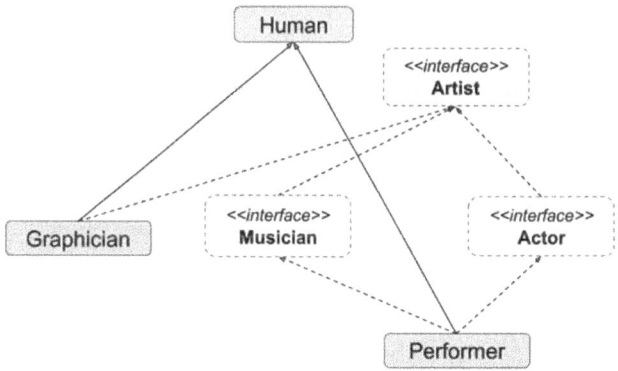

Figure 6-1. *The Performer hierarchy*

In the following code sample, an object of type `Musician` and one of type `Graphician` are created and both are added into a list containing references of type `Artist`. We can do this because, both types implement the interface `Artist`.

```
package com.apress.bgn.ch6;
```

```
import com.apress.bgn.ch4.hierarchy.*;
```

```
import java.util.ArrayList;
import java.util.List;
```

---

[1]The implementation of the new class is not relevant for this chapter, so it won't be detailed here.

CHAPTER 6   OPERATORS

```
public class OperatorDemo {

    public static void main(String... args) {
        List<Artist> artists = new ArrayList<>();

        Musician john = new Performer("John", 40, 1.91f, Gender.MALE);
        List<String> songs = List.of("Gravity");
        john.setSongs(songs);
        artists.add(john);

        Graphician diana = new Graphician("Diana", 23, 1.62f, Gender.FEMALE, "macOs"); artists.add(diana);

        for (Artist artist : artists) {
            if (artist instanceof Musician) { \\ (*)
                Musician musician = (Musician) artist; \\(**)
                System.out.println("Songs: " + musician.getSongs());
            } else {
                System.out.println("Other Type: " + artist.getClass());
            }
        }
    }
}
```

The line marked with (*) shows how to use the `instanceof` operator. This operator tests whether the object is an instance of the specified type. (class, subclass or interface). It is used in writing conditions to decide which code block should be executed.

The line marked with (**) does an explicit conversion of an reference. Since the `instanceof` operator helped figure out that the object the reference points to is of type `Musician`, we can now convert the reference to the proper type so methods of class `Musician` can be called.

But what happens if an explicit conversion fails? For this we try to convert the previously declared `Graphician` reference to `Musician`. So, we'll add the following line.

```
Musician fake = (Musician) diana;
```

The compiler won't complain, but this does not change the fact that Graphician has no relation to the Musician type, so the code will not run, and a special exception is thrown in the console to tell you what went wrong. The error message printed in the console is explicit and is depicted in the next log snippet.

```
Exception in thread "main" java.lang.ClassCastException:
  chapter.six/com.apress.bgn.ch6.Graphician cannot be cast to
  chapter.four/com.apress.bgn.ch4.hierarchy.Musician
       at chapter.six/com.apress.bgn.ch6.OperatorDemo.mainOperatorDemo.java:24
```

The message clearly states that the two types are not compatible and the package and module names are included.

But explicit conversion is not limited to reference types, it works for primitives too. Any variable of a type with values in a smaller interval can be converted to a type of a bigger interval, without explicit conversion. But the reverse is possible too by using explicit conversion, but if the value is too big, bits is lost and the value is… unexpected. Look at the following examples of conversions between byte and int.

```
[jshell> byte b = 2;
b ==> 2
|  created variable b : byte

[jshell> int i = 10;
i ==> 10
|  created variable i : int

[jshell> i = b
i ==> 2
|  assigned to i : int

[jshell> b = i
|  Error:
|  incompatible types: possible lossy conversion from int to byte
|  b = i
|      ^
```

```
[jshell> b = (byte) i
b ==> 2  // all good, because value is in byte interval
|  assigned to b : byte

[jshell> i = 300000
i ==> 300000
|  assigned to i : int

[jshell> b = (byte) i
b ==> -32   // oops! value outside byte interval
|  assigned to b : byte
```

So, as a general rule, use explicit conversion to widen the scope of a variable, not to narrow it, as narrowing it can lead to unexpected results.

Numerical Operators

This section groups all operators that are mostly used on numerical types. The numerical operators you know from math: +, -, /. Comparators are found in programming too, but they can be combined to obtain different effects.

Unary Operators

Unary operators require only one operand, and they affect the variable they are applied to.

Incrementors and Decrementors

In Java(and some other programming languages) there are unary operator called *incrementors* (++) and *decrementors* (--). These operators are placed before or after a variable to increase or decrease its value by 1. They are usually used in loops as counters to condition the termination of the loop. When they are placed before the variable, they are called `prefixed` and when are placed after it they are called `postfixed`.

When they are prefixed, the operation is executed on the variable, before the variable is used in the next statement. The following code sample tests this affirmation.

```
package com.apress.bgn.ch6;

public class UnaryOperatorsDemo {
    public static void main(String... args) {
        int i  = 1;
        int j = ++i;
        System.out.println("j is " + j + ", i is " + i);
    }
}
```

The expected result of the preceding code is that j=2, because the value of the i variable is modified to 2, before it is assigned to j. Thus, the expected output is j is 2, i is 2.

When they are postfixed, the operation is executed on the variable, after the variable is used in the next statement. The following code sample tests this affirmation.

```
package com.apress.bgn.ch6;

public class UnaryOperatorsDemo {
    public static void main(String... args) {
        i = 1;
        j = i++;
        System.out.println("j is " + j + ", i is " + i);
    }
}
```

The expected result of the preceding code is that j=1, because the value of the i variable is modified to 2, after it is assigned to j. Thus, the expected output is j is 1, i is 2.

The decrementor operator can be used in a similar manner, the only effect is that the variable is decreased by 1. Try to modify the UnaryOperatorsDemo to use the -- operator instead.

Sign Operators

Mathematical operator + is used on a single operator to indicate that a number is positive(redundant and mostly never used). So basically,

```
int i = 3;
```

Is the same as

```
int i = +3;
```

Mathematical operator - declares negative numbers.

```
[jshell> int i = -3
i ==> -3
|  created variable i : int
```

Or it negates an expression.

```
[jshell> int i = -3
i ==> -3
|  created variable i : int

[jshell> int j = - ( i + 4 )
j ==> -1
|  created variable j : int
```

As you can see in the example, the result of the (i + 4) is 1, because i = -3, but because of the - in front of the parentheses, the final result that is assigned to the j variable is -1.

Negation Operator

There are two more unary operators, and their role is to negate variables. Operator ! applies to boolean variables, and it is used to negate them. So, true becomes false and false becomes true.

```
[jshell> boolean t = true
t ==> true
|  created variable t : boolean

[jshell> boolean f = !t
f ==> false
|  created variable f : boolean

[jshell> boolean t2 = !f
t2 ==> true
|  created variable t2 : boolean
```

Binary Operators

Let's start with the ones you probably know from math.

- + adds two variables

```
[jshell> int i = 4
i ==> 4
|  created variable i : int

[jshell> int j = 6
j ==> 6
|  created variable j : int

[jshell> int k = i + j
k ==> 10
|  created variable k : int

[jshell> int i = i + 2
i ==> 6
|  modified variable i : int
|    update overwrote variable i : int
```

The last statement `int i = i + 2` has the effect of incrementing the value of i with 2 and there is a little redundancy there. That statement can be written without mentioning i twice, because its effect is to increase the value of i with 2. This can be done by using the += operator, which is composed of the assignment and the addition operator. The optimal statement is `i += 2`.

The + operator can also be used to concatenate `String` instances, or `String` instances with other types. The JVM decides how to use the + operator depending on the context. Let's look at the following example.

```
package com.apress.bgn.ch6;

public class ConcatenationDemo {
    public static void main(String... args) {
        int i1 = 0;
        int i2 = 1;
        int i3 = 2;
```

```
        System.out.println(i1 + i2 + i3);
        System.out.println("Result1 = " + (i1 + i2) + i3);
        System.out.println("Result2 = " + i1 + i2 + i3);
        System.out.println("Result3 = " + (i1 + i2 + i3));
    }
}
```

If the preceding code executed the following is displayed in the console.

1. 3
2. Result1 = 12
3. Result2 = 012
4. Result3 = 3

I'll explain.

- The result in line 1 can be explained as follows: because all operands are of type `int` JVM adds the terms as normal and the `println` function prints this result.

- The result in line 2 can be explained as follows: parentheses were added to isolate the addition of two terms (i1+i2). Because of this, the JVM executes the addition between the parentheses as a normal addition between to `int` terms. But after that, what we are left with is `"Result1 = " + 1 + i3`, and this operation includes a `String` operand, which means the + operator must be used as a concatenation operator, because adding a number with a text value does not work otherwise.

- The result in line 3 should be obvious at this time; we have three `int` operands, and a `String` operand, and thus the JVM decides that the context of the operation cannot be numeric, so concatenation is required.

- The result in line 4 can be explained in a similar way as line 2; the parentheses are used to ensure that the context of the operation is numeric, and thus the three operands are added.

This is a typical example to show how JVM decides the context for operations involving the + operator that you might find in other Java tutorials as well. But the int variables can be replaced with float or double variables and the behavior is similar.

- **-** subtracts two variables, or subtracts a value from a variable. The following shows how this operator and the -= operator, which is composed of the assignment and the subtraction operator, are used.

```
[jshell> int i = 4;
i ==> 4
|  created variable i : int

[jshell> int j = 2;
j ==> 2
|  created variable j : int

[jshell> int k = i - j
k ==> 2
|  created variable k : int

[jshell> int i = 4
i ==> 4
|  modified variable i : int
|    update overwrote variable i : int

[jshell> i = i - 3;
i ==> 1
|  assigned to i : int

[jshell> int i = 4
i ==> 4
|  modified variable i : int
|    update overwrote variable i : int

[jshell> i -= 3
$9 ==> 1
|  created scratch variable $9 : int
```

CHAPTER 6 OPERATORS

- * multiplies two variables, or multiplies a value with a variable. It is used in similar statements as + and -, and there is a composed operator *= that can be used to multiply the value of a variable and assign it on the spot.

```
[jshell> int i = 4
i ==> 4
|  created variable i : int

[jshell> int j = 2
j ==> 2
|  created variable j : int

[jshell> int k =    i * j
k ==> 8
|  created variable k : int

[jshell> int i = 4;
i ==> 4
|  modified variable i : int
|    update overwrote variable i : int

[jshell> i = i * 3
i ==> 12
|  assigned to i : int

[jshell> int i = 4
i ==> 4
|  modified variable i : int
|    update overwrote variable i : int

[jshell> i *= 3
$7 ==> 12
|  created scratch variable $7 : int
```

- / divides two variables, or divides a value by a variable. It is used in similar statements as + and -, and there is a composed operator /= that can be used to divide the value of a variable and assign it on the spot. The result of a division is named *quotient* and it is assigned to the variable on the left side of the assignment sign("="). When the operands are integers, the result is an integer too, and the *remainder* is discarded.

```
[jshell> int i = 4
i ==> 4
|  created variable i : int

[jshell> int j = 2
j ==> 2
|  created variable j : int

[jshell> int k = i / j
k ==> 2
|  created variable k : int

[jshell> int i = 4
i ==> 4
|  modified variable i : int
|    update overwrote variable i : int

[jshell> int i = i / 3
i ==> 1
|  modified variable i : int
|    update overwrote variable i : int

[jshell> int i = 4
i ==> 4
|  modified variable i : int
|    update overwrote variable i : int

[jshell> i /= 3
$7 ==> 1
|  created scratch variable $7 : int
```

CHAPTER 6   OPERATORS

- % is also called the *modulus* operator divides two variables, but the result is the remainder of the division. The operation is called *modularization* and there is also a composed operator %= that is used to divide the value of a variable and assign the remainder on the spot.

```
[jshell> int i = 4
i ==> 4
|  created variable i : int

[jshell> int j = 3
j ==> 3
|  created variable j : int

[jshell> int k = i % j
k ==> 1
|  created variable k : int

[jshell> int i = 4
i ==> 4
|  modified variable i : int
|    update overwrote variable i : int

[jshell> i = i % 3
i ==> 1
|  assigned to i : int

[jshell> int i = 4
i ==> 4
|  modified variable i : int
|    update overwrote variable i : int

[jshell> i %= 3
$7 ==> 1
|  created scratch variable $7 : int
```

The modulus operator returns the remainder, but, what happens when the operands are real numbers? And what if the remainder is a real number with an infinite numbers of decimals after the decimal point?

```java
package com.apress.bgn.ch6;

public class ModulusDemo {
    public static void main(String... args) {
        float f = 1.9f;
        float g = 0.4f;
        float h = f % g;
        System.out.println("remainder = " + h);
    }
}
```

Well, some rounding is done. The text printed in the console is `remainder = 0.29999995` which can be rounded to 0.3, for some cases. But rounding can be dangerous when the data is used for sensitive operations, like determining the volume of a tumor for a robot to operate on, or determining the perfect trajectory for a rocket to be sent to Mars. So, rounding can be problematic, because it causes a loss of precision.

Relational Operators

In certain cases, when designing the solution for a problem, you need to introduce conditions to drive and control the execution flow. Conditions require the evaluation of a comparison between two terms using a comparison operator. In this section all comparison operators used in java is described and code samples is provided. Let's proceed.

- `==` tests equality of terms. Because in Java a single equals (=) sign assigns values, a solution needed to be find to test equality, so the developers just duplicated the "=" operator. We have used `for` loops before to depict how to use certain types or statements, even if they are to be covered only in the next chapter, because the code samples presented to you should be compliable and runnable. In the following code sample, you see an example of testing the `==` comparator in searching for value 2 in an array. If the value is found, the index is printed in the console.

    ```java
    package com.apress.bgn.ch6;

    public class ComparisonOperatorsDemo {
    ```

```
    public static void main(String... args) {
        int[] values = {1, 7, 9, 2, 6,};

        for (int i = 0; i < values.length; ++i) {
            if (values[i] == 2) { \\(*)
                System.out.println("Fount 2 at index: " + i);
            }
        }
    }
}
```

The condition in the line marked with (*) is evaluated and the result is a boolean value. When the result is `false`, nothing is done, but if the result is `true` the index is printed. Because the result is of type boolean, if you make a mistake and instead you use = instead of ==, the code will not compile. You have to be extra careful when comparing boolean values though.

The == sign works just fine for primitives; for reference types, you need to use the `equals()` method that was covered in **Chapter 5**.

- `!=` tests inequality of terms. It is the opposite of the == operator. As an exercise, modify the previous example to print a message when the array value is not 2. This operator also works on reference types. But if you want to test inequality of references values you have to use an expression similar to: !a.equals(b)

- `<` and `<=` have the same purpose as the one you probably learned in math class. The first one (<) tests if the item on the left of the operator is less than the one on the right. The next one (<=) tests if the item on the left of the operator is less or equal to the one on the right. This operator cannot be used on reference types.

- `>` and `>=` have the same purpose as the one you probably learned in math class. The first one (>) tests if the item on the left of the operator is greater than the one on the right. The next one (>=) tests if the item on the left of the operator is greater or equal to the one on the right. This operator cannot be used on reference types.

Almost all numeric operators can be used on variables of different primitive (and wrapper) types, as they are automatically converted to type that has a wider interval representation or unboxed to the appropriate type in the case of wrapper types. The following code reflects a few situations, but in practice, you might need to make even more extreme decisions that do not always abide to the common-sense rules of programming or follow good practices.

```java
package com.apress.bgn.ch6;

public class MixedOperationsDemo {
    public static void main(String... args) {
        byte b = 1;
        short s = 2;
        int i = 3;
        long l = 4;

        float f = 5;
        double d = 6;
        int ii = 6;

        double resd = l + d;
        long   resl = s + 3;
        //etc

        if (b <= s) {
            System.out.println("byte val < short val");
        }

        if (i >= b) {
            System.out.println("int val >= byte val");
        }

        if (l > b) {
            System.out.println("long val > byte val");
        }

        if(d > i) {
            System.out.println("double val > byte val");
        }
```

CHAPTER 6 OPERATORS

```
            if(i == i) {
                System.out.println("double val == int val");
            }
        }
    }
}
```

Make sure that if you are ever in a situation where you need to make shady things (non-optimal code constructs) like these to test a lot, and think about your conversions well, especially when floating-point types are involved, because, for example, the following piece of code can have unexpected results.

```
package com.apress.bgn.ch6;

public class DecimalPointDemo {
    public static void main(String... args) {
       float f1 = 2.2f;
          float f2 = 2.0f;
          float f3 = f1 * f2;
          if (f3 == 4.4) {
              System.out.println("expected float value of 4.4");
          } else {
              System.out.println("unexpected value of " + f3);
          }
      }
}
```

If you expect the message *expected float value of 4.4* to be printed in the console, you will be surprised. Any IEEE 754 floating-point number representation presents issues because some numbers that appear to have a fixed number of decimals in the decimal system actually have an infinite number of decimals in the binary system. So, we cannot compare floats and doubles using ==. One of the solutions that is easiest to implement is to use the compare method provided by the wrapper class; in this case, Float.compare.

```
package com.apress.bgn.ch6;

public class DecimalPointDemo {
    public static void main(String... args) {
       float f1 = 2.2f;
          float f2 = 2.0f;
```

```
        float f3 = f1 * f2;
        if (Float.compare(f3,4.4f) == 0) {
            System.out.println("expected float value of 4.4");
        } else {
            System.out.println("unexpected value of " + f3);
        }
    }
}
```

Using the previous example, the expected message is now printed in the console: *expected float value of 4.4.*

Bitwise Operators

In Java there are a few operators that are used at bit level to manipulate variables of numerical types. Bitwise operators are used to change individual bits in an operand. Bitwise operations are faster and usually use less power because of the reduced use of resources. They are most useful in programming visual applications, games, where color, mouse clicks, and movements can be quickly determined using bitwise applications.

Bitwise NOT

The ~ operator is sort of a binary negator. It performs a bit-by-bit reversal of an integer value. Of course, this affects all bits used to represent the value. So, if we declare

```
byte b1 = 10;
```

the binary representation is 00001010. The `Integer` class provides a method named `toBinaryString` that can print the binary representation of the previously defined variable, but it won't print all the bits, because the method doesn't know on how many bits we want the representation on. So, we need to use a special `String` function to format the output. The following code snippet prints the b value in binary on 8 bits.

```
System.out.println("decimal:" + b1);
String str = String.format("%8s", Integer.toBinaryString(b1 & 0xFF))
        .replace(' ', '0');
System.out.println("binary:" + str);
```

If we apply the ~ operator on the b value, the binary value resulted is 11110101. The fist bit is the sign bit, and value one corresponds to -. So, the number is -11, as displayed in the following code.

```
byte b2 = (byte) ~b1;
System.out.println("decimal:" + b2);
String str2 = String.format("%8s", Integer.toBinaryString(b2 & 0xFF))
        .replace(' ', '0');
System.out.println("binary:" + str2);
```

In the previous example, you probably noticed this statement:

```
byte b2 = (byte) ~b1
```

You are expecting an explanation. The bitwise complement expression operator requires an operand that is convertible to a primitive integral type, or a compile time error occurs. Internally, Java uses one or more bytes to represent values. The ~ operator converts its operand to the int type, so it can use 32-bits when doing the complement operation; this is needed to avoid loss of precision. That is why an explicit cast to byte is needed in the previous example.

And because everything is clearer with images, Figure 6-2 shows the effect of the ~ on the bits of the b1 variable in parallel with its value.

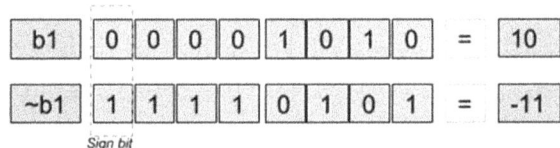

Figure 6-2. *The effect of the operator on every bit*

Bitwise AND

The bitwise AND operator is represented by & and what is does is to compare two numbers bit by bit and if the bits on each position have the value of 1, the bit in the result is 1. The following code sample, depicts the result of the & operator.

CHAPTER 6 OPERATORS

```
package com.apress.bgn.ch6;

public class BitwiseDemo {
    public static void main(String... args) {
        byte b1 = 117; // 01110101
        byte b2 = 95;  // 01011111

        byte result = (byte) (b1 & b2); // 01010101

        System.out.println("b1:"+ b1);
        System.out.println("b2:"+ b2);
        System.out.println("---------");
        String str = String.format("%8s", Integer.toBinaryString(result & 0xFF))
                .replace(' ', '0');
        System.out.println("result:" + result);
        System.out.println("binary result:" + str);
    }
}
```

We are using the same `String.format(..)` method to display the bits of the result of applying the & to the b1 and b2 operators. The preceding code prints the following.

```
b1:117
b2:95
---------
result:85
binary result:01010101
```

But the effect of the & operator is seen best in Figure 6-3. The 01010101 value is the binary representation of number 85.

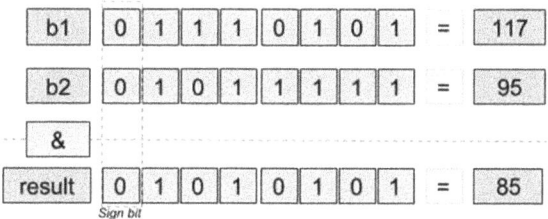

Figure 6-3. *The effect of the & operator on every bit*

CHAPTER 6 OPERATORS

For practical reasons, the composed operator &= is available in Java, so that the bitwise AND operation can be done on the same variable on which the result is assigned.

```
[jshell> byte b1 = 10
b1 ==> 10
|  created variable b1 : byte

[jshell> b1 &= 2
$2 ==> 2
|  created scratch variable $2 : byte
```

Bitwise Inclusive OR

The bitwise OR operator is represented by | and what is does is to compare two numbers bit by bit and if at least one of the bits is 1, the bit in the result is 1. The following code sample, depicts the result of the | operator.

```
package com.apress.bgn.ch6;

public class BitwiseDemo {
    public static void main(String... args) {
        byte b1 = 117; // 01110101
        byte b2 = 95;  // 01011111

        byte result = (byte) (b1 | b2);   // 01111111

        System.out.println("b1:"+ b1);
        System.out.println("b2:"+ b2);
        System.out.println("---------");
        String str = String.format("%8s", Integer.toBinaryString
        (result & 0xFF))
                .replace(' ', '0');
        System.out.println("result: " + result);
        System.out.println("binary result: " + str);
    }
}
```

We are using the same `String.format(..)` method to display the bits of the result of applying the | to the b1 and b2 operators. The preceding code prints the following.

```
b1:117
b2:95
---------
result: 127
binary result: 01111111
```

But the effect of the | operator is seen best in Figure 6-4. The 01010101 value is the binary representation of number 127.

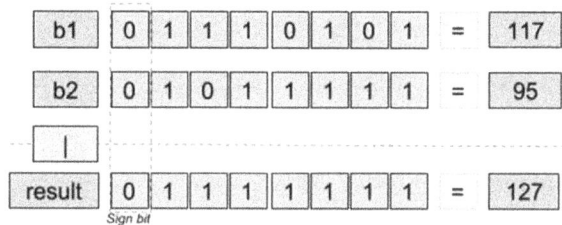

Figure 6-4. *The effect of the | operator on every bit*

For practical reasons, the composed operator |= is available in Java, so that the bitwise inclusive OR operation can be done on the same variable on which the result is assigned.

```
[jshell> byte b1 = 10
b1 ==> 10
|  created variable b1 : byte

[jshell> b1 |= 2
$4 ==> 10
|  created scratch variable $4 : byte
```

Bitwise Exclusive OR

The bitwise XOR operator is represented by ^ and what is does is to compare two numbers bit by bit and if the values are different, the bit in the result is 1. The following code sample, depicts the result of the ^ operator.

CHAPTER 6 OPERATORS

```
package com.apress.bgn.ch6;

public class BitwiseDemo {
    public static void main(String... args) {
        byte b1 = 117; // 01110101
        byte b2 = 95;  // 01011111

        byte result = (byte) (b1 ^ b2);   // 00101010

        System.out.println("b1:"+ b1);
        System.out.println("b2:"+ b2);
        System.out.println("---------");
        String str = String.format("%8s", Integer.toBinaryString
        (result & 0xFF))
            .replace(' ', '0');
        System.out.println("result: " + result);
        System.out.println("binary result: " + str);
    }
}
```

We are using the same `String.format(..)` method to display the bits of the result of applying the ^ to the b1 and b2 operators. The preceding code prints the following.

```
b1:117
b2:95
---------
result:  42
binary result: 00101010
```

But the effect of the ^ operator is seen best in Figure 6-5. The 00101010 value is the binary representation of number 42.

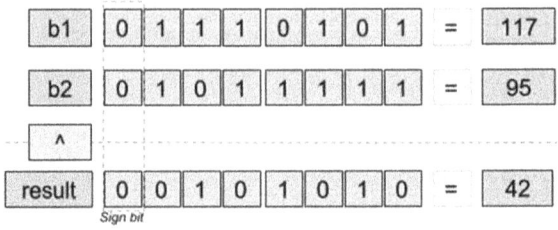

Figure 6-5. *The effect of the ^ operator on every bit*

For practical reasons, the composed operator ^= is available in Java, so that the bitwise exclusive OR operation can be done on the same variable on which the result is assigned.

```
[jshell> byte b1 = 10
b1 ==> 10
|  created variable b1 : byte

[jshell> b1 ^= 2
$6 ==> 8
|  created scratch variable $6 : byte
```

Logical Operators

When designing conditions for controlling the flow of the execution of a program, sometimes there is need for complex conditions to be written, composed conditions constructed from multiple expressions. There are four operators that are used to construct complex conditions; two of them are bitwise operations that can be reused: &(AND) and |(OR); but they require evaluation of all the parts of the condition. The operators &&(AND) and ||(OR) have the same effect as the other ones, but the difference is they do not require evaluation of all the expression, which is why they are also called **shortcut** operators. To explain the difficult behavior of these operators, there is a typical example. Basically, we declare a list of ten terms (some of them null) and a method to generate a random index, used to select an item from the list. Then we test the selected element from the list to see if it is not null and equal to an expected value. If both conditions are true, then a message is printed in the console. Let's start with the first example.

```java
package com.apress.bgn.ch6;

import java.util.ArrayList;
import java.util.List;
import java.util.Random;

public class LogicalDemo {
    static List<String> terms = new ArrayList<>() {{
        add("Rose");
        add(null);
        add("River");
        add("Clara");
        add("Vastra");
```

CHAPTER 6 OPERATORS

```
            add("Psi");
            add("Cas");
            add(null);
            add("Nardhole");
            add("Strax");
        }};

    public static void main(String... args) {
        for (int i = 0; i < 20; ++i) {
            int rnd = getRandomNumber();
            String term = terms.get(rnd);
            System.out.println("Generated index: " + rnd);
            if (term != null & term.equals("Rose")) { \\(*)
                System.out.println("Rose was  found");
            }
        }
    }

    private static int getRandomNumber() {
        Random r = new Random();
        return r.nextInt(10);
    }
}
```

To make sure we get the expected result, we repeat the operation of selecting a random term 20 times. In the line marked with (*), the & composes the two expressions. So, the text "Rose was found" should be printed in the console only if the value of the term variable is not null and equal to *Rose*. So, when the preceding code is run, expect to see something like this in the console.

```
Generated index: 8
Exception in thread "main" java.lang.NullPointerException
Generated index: 4
        at chapter.six/com.apress.bgn.ch6.LogicalDemo.mainLogicalDemo.java:57
Generated index: 7
```

But, think about it like this: if the term is null, should we even evaluate the equality to *"Rose"*, especially since calling a method on a null object causes a runtime error?

234

CHAPTER 6 OPERATORS

Obviously not, which is why the & is not suitable for this case. If the term is null, it fails the first condition; there is no point in evaluating the second. And so, enter the && shortcut operator that does exactly this. This works because when using the logical AND operator, if the first term is false, it does not really matter what the second term is equal to, the result is always false. So, we can correct the previous code sample as follows.

```java
package com.apress.bgn.ch6;

import java.util.ArrayList;
import java.util.List;
import java.util.Random;

public class LogicalDemo {
    static List<String> terms = new ArrayList<>() {{
        add("Rose");
        add(null);
        ..
    }};

    public static void main(String... args) {
        for (int i = 0; i < 20; ++i) {
            int rnd = getRandomNumber();
            String term = terms.get(rnd);
            System.out.println("Generated index: " + rnd);
            if (term != null && term.equals("Rose")) { \\(*)
                System.out.println("Rose  was  found");
            }
        }
    }

    private static int getRandomNumber() {
        Random r = new Random();
        return r.nextInt(10);
    }
}
```

So, when the preceding code is executed, no exception is thrown, because if the term is null, the second condition is not evaluated.

CHAPTER 6 OPERATORS

Let's modify the previous code sample, but this time, let's print the message if we find a null or if we find *"Rose"*.

```
package com.apress.bgn.ch6;

import java.util.ArrayList;
import java.util.List;
import java.util.Random;

public class LogicalDemo {
    static List<String> terms = new ArrayList<>() {{
        add("Rose");
        add(null);
        ..
    }};
    public static void main(String... args) {
        for (int i = 0; i < 20; ++i) {
            int rnd = getRandomNumber();
            String term = terms.get(rnd);
            System.out.println("Generated index: " + rnd);
            if (term == null | term.equals("Rose")) { \\(*)
                System.out.println("Rose was found");
            }
        }
    }

    private static int getRandomNumber() {
        Random r = new Random();
        return r.nextInt(10);
    }
}
```

If we run the previous code, the use of | throws a NullPointerException because this operator requires both expressions to be evaluated. So, if term is null, calling .equals(...) causes the exception to be thrown. So, to make sure that the code works as expected, the | must be replaced with ||, which shortcuts the condition and does not evaluate the second expression. This works because when using the logical OR operator, if the first term is true, it does not really matter what the second term is equal to; the result is always true. We'll leave that as an exercise for you.

CHAPTER 6 OPERATORS

Of course, conditions can be made up from more than one expression and more than one operator, whether it is && or ||. Take a look at the following examples.

```java
package com.apress.bgn.ch6;

import java.util.ArrayList;
import java.util.List;
import java.util.Random;

public class LogicalDemo {
    static List<String> terms = new ArrayList<>() {{
        add("Rose");
        add(null);
        ..
    }};

    public static void main(String... args) {
        for (int i = 0; i < 20; ++i) {
            int rnd = getRandomNumber();
            String term = terms.get(rnd);
            if (rnd == 0 || rnd == 1 || rnd <= 3) {
                System.out.println(rnd + ": this works...");
            }

            if (rnd > 3 && rnd <=6 || rnd < 3 && rnd > 0) {
                System.out.println(rnd + ": this works too...");
            }
        }
    }

    private static int getRandomNumber() {
        Random r = new Random();
        return r.nextInt(10);
    }
}
```

Beware of conditions that become too complex, make sure you cover that piece of code with a lot of tests. When writing complex conditions it is possible that some expressions become redundant, and IntelliJ IDEA and other smart editors display warnings of dead code on expressions that are redundant and unused.

CHAPTER 6 OPERATORS

Shift Operators

The shift operators are operators working at bit level. Because moving bits around is a sensitive operation, the only requirement of these operands is for arguments to be integers. The operand to the left of the operator is the number that is shifted, and the operand to the right of the operator is the number of bits that is shifted. There are three shift operators in Java, and each of them can be composed with the assignment operator to do the shifting and assign the result to the original variable on the spot. Let's analyze each of them separately.

- << shift left. Given a number represented in binary, this operator shifts bits to the left. Let's look at the following piece of code.

```
public class ShiftDemo {
    public static void main(String... args) {
        byte b1 = 12; // 00001100
        byte result = (byte) (b1 << 3);
        str = String.format("%8s", Integer.
        toBinaryString(result & 0xFF))
            .replace(' ', '0');
        System.out.println("result: " + result); // 01100000
    }
}
```

When bits are shifted to the left, the remaining positions are filled with 0. Also, the number becomes bigger, and the new value is its old value multiplied with -2^N, where N is the second operand. When the preceding code is executed, the following output is printed in the console.

```
b1: 12
binary result: 00001100
result:  96
binary result: 01100000
```

The preceding code can be written like this: b <<= 3, using the composed operators, without the need to declare another variable.

So, the result is $12 * 2^3$. The way that the bits shifted is shown in Figure 6-6.

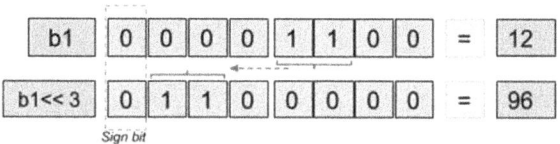

Figure 6-6. *The effect of the « operator*

- **»** shift right. Given a number represented in binary, this operator shifts bits to the right. Let's look at the following piece of code.

```
public class ShiftDemo {
    public static void main(String... args) {
        byte b1 = 96; // 01100000
        byte result = (byte) (b1 >> 3);
        str = String.format("%8s", Integer.
        toBinaryString(result & 0xFF))
              .replace(' ', '0');
        System.out.println("result: " + result); // 00001100
    }
}
```

When bits are shifted to the right, the remaining positions are filled with 0 if the number is positive. If the number is negative, the remaining positions are replaced with 1. This is done to preserve the sign of the number. Also, the number becomes smaller, and the new value is its old value divided by -2^N, where N is the second operand. When the preceding code is executed, the following output is printed in the console.

b1: 96
binary result: 01100000
result: 12
binary result: 00001100

The preceding code can be written like this: b >>= 3, using the composed operators, without the need to declare another variable.

CHAPTER 6 OPERATORS

So, the result is 96 / 2^3. And the way that the bits shifted for a positive number and a negative number is displayed in Figure 6-7.

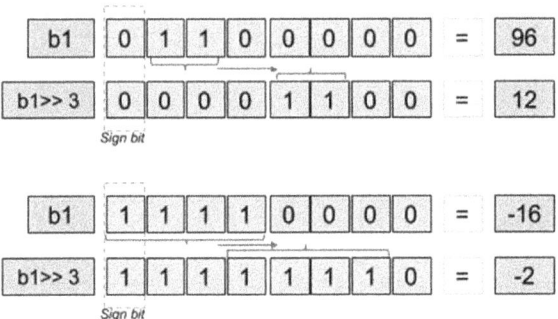

Figure 6-7. The effect of the » operator

- **>>>** unsigned shift right. Also called **logical shift**. Given a number represented in binary, this operator shifts bits to the right, together with the sign bit, and the remaining positions are replaced with zero. This is why, the result is always a positive number. Let's look at the following piece of code.

```
public class ShiftDemo {
    public static void main(String... args) {
        byte b1 = -16; // 11110000
        byte result = (byte) (b1 >>> 3);
        str = String.format("%8s", Integer.
        toBinaryString(result & 0xFF))
                .replace(' ', '0');
        System.out.println("result: " + result); // 00011110
    }
}
```

When the preceding code is executed, the following output is printed in the console.

```
b1: -16
binary result: 11110000
result:   30
binary result: 00011110
```

240

The preceding code can be written like this: b >>>= 3, using the composed operators, without the need to declare another variable.

And the way that the bits shifted is displayed in Figure 6-8.

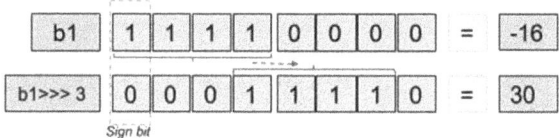

Figure 6-8. *The effect of the > > > operator*

As all bitwise operators, shifting operators promote char, byte, or short type variables to int, which is why an explicit conversion is necessary. As you have probably noticed, shifting bits on negative numbers is tricky, it is easy for the resulted number to be outside the interval of allowed values for a type, and an explicit conversion can lead to loss of precision or serious anomalies. So, why use them? Because they are fast. Make sure to test intensively when using shifting operators.

The Elvis Operator

The *Elvis operator* is the only ternary operator in Java. Its function is equivalent to a java method that tests a condition and depending of the outcome, returns a value. The following is a template for the Elvis operator.

```
variable = (condition) ? val1 : val2
```

The following if statement is equivalent.

```
variable = methodName(..)

type methodName(..) {
        if (condition) {
                return val1;
        } else {
                return val2;
        }
}
```

The reason this operator is called *the Elvis operator* is because the question mark resembles Elvis Presley's hair, and the column resembles the eyes. Let's see it in action.

```
[jshell> int a = 4
a ==> 4
|  created variable a : int

[jshell> int result = a > 4 ? 3 : 1;
result ==> 1
|  created variable result : int

[jshell> String a2 = "test"
a2 ==> "test"
|  created variable a2 : String

[jshell> var a3 = a2.length() > 3 ? "hello": "bye-bye"
a3 ==> "hello"
|  created variable a3 : String
```

This operator is practical when you have a simple `if` statement that contains only one expression per branch, because using this operator you can compact the whole thing in one expression, one line of code. Make sure that when using it, the readability of the code is improved, because from a performance point of view, there is no difference between an `if` statement and the equivalent Elvis operator expression. Another advantage of using the Elvis operator is that the expression can initialize a variable in a single in-line statement.

Summary

In this chapter, you learned that

- Java has a lot of operators, simple and composed.
- Bitwise operators are fast, but dangerous.
- The + operator does different things in different contexts.
- Java has a ternary operator that accepts three operands: a boolean expression and two objects of the same type. The result of the evaluation of the boolean expression decides which operand is the result of the statement.

The purpose of this chapter is to make you familiar with all the operators that are used throughout the book, to help you understand the provided solutions, and even to design and write your own.

CHAPTER 7

Controlling the Flow

The previous chapters covered ways to create statements and which operators to use. Sometimes, elements of logic were added to make the code runnable for you. This chapter is dedicated to explain how to manipulate the execution of your code using fundamental programming—conditional and repetitive statements.

A solution and an algorithm can be represented using flowcharts. Most of the programming that we've done until this chapter contained declaration and printing statements—simple one-step statements. Take the following piece of code.

```
package com.apress.bgn.ch7;

public class Main {

    public static void main(String... args) {
    String text = "sample";
    System.out.println(text);
    }
}
```

If we were to design a flowchart for it, the schema would be simple and linear, no decision and no repetition, as depicted in Figure 7-1.

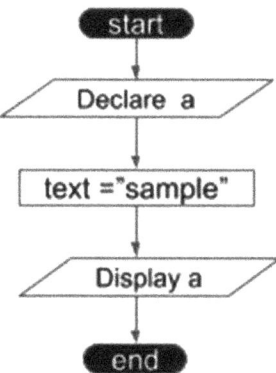

Figure 7-1. *Simple flowchart sample*

But resolving real-life problems requires often a more complicated logic than that, so more complicated statements are necessary. Before getting into that, let's describe the components of a flowchart, because they will be used a lot during this chapter. Table 7-1 lists flowchart elements.

Table 7-1. Flowchart Elements

Shape	Name	Scope
	Terminal	Indicates beginning or end of a program, and contains a text relevant to its scope.
	Flowline	Indicates the flow of the program, the order of operations.
	Input/Output	Indicates declaration of variables and outputting values.
	Process	Simple process statement: assignment, change of values, and so forth.
	Decision	Shows a conditional operation that decides a certain path of execution.
	Predefined Process	This element indicates a process defined else-where.
	On-page Connector	This element is usually labeled and indicates the continuation of the flow on the same page.
	Off-page Connector	This element is usually labeled and indicates the continuation of the flow on a different page.
	Comment (Or annotation)	When a flow or an element requires extra explanation it is introduced using this type of element.

The flowchart elements presented in this table are pretty standard; you will probably find very similar elements used in any programming course or tutorial. After this consistent introduction, it is only fit to get into it.

if-else Statement

The most simple decisional flow statement in Java is the `if-else` statement. (probably in other languages too) You've probably seen the `if-else` statement in code samples in the previous chapters. There was no way to avoid it, because providing runnable code that encourages you to write your own is important. But in this section the focus is strictly on this type of statement.

Let's imagine this scenario: we run a Java program with a numeric argument provided by the user. If the number is even, we print EVEN in the console; else, we print ODD. The flowchart matching this scenario is depicted in Figure 7-2.

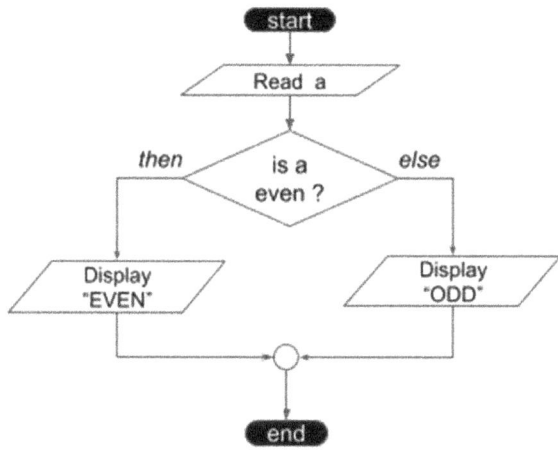

Figure 7-2. if-else flowchart sample

The condition is evaluated to a `boolean` value, if the result is `true` the statement corresponding to the `if` branch is executed, if the result is `false`, the statement corresponding to the `else` branch is executed.

The Java code that implements the process described by this flowchart is depicted in the following code snippet.

```java
package com.apress.bgn.ch7;

public class IfFlowDemo {
    public static void main(String... args) {
        //Read a
        int a = Integer.parseInt(args0);

        if (a % 2 == 0) { // is even
            //Display EVEN
            System.out.println("EVEN");
```

```
        } else {
            //Display ODD
            System.out.println("ODD");
        }
    }
}
```

To run this class with different arguments, you must create an IntelliJ IDEA launcher and add your argument in the **Program arguments** text field, as explained at the beginning of this book. Each Java statement in the previous code snippet was paired with a comment matching the flowchart element to make the implementation clear. The fun thing is that not both branches of an `if` statement are mandatory. Sometimes you want to print something if a value matches a condition, but you are not interested in what happens otherwise. For example, given a user provided argument, we want to print a message if the number is negative, but we are not interested in printing or doing anything else if the number is positive. The flowchart for that is depicted in Figure 7-3.

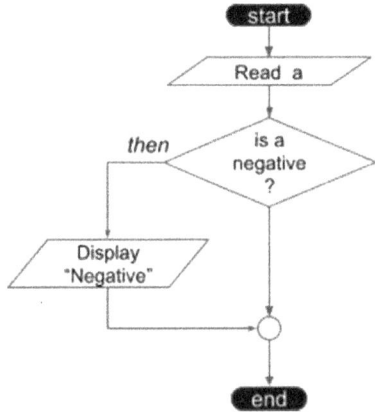

Figure 7-3. if flowchart sample, missing the else branch

And the Java code looks like this:

```
package com.apress.bgn.ch7;

public class IfFlowDemo {

    public static void main(String... args) {
        //Read a
        int a = Integer.parseInt(args0);
```

```
    if (a < 0) {
        System.out.println("Negative");
    }
  }
 }
}
```

And in the same way that the statement can be made simple, in the same way, is we need it, we can link more `if-else` statements together. Let's consider the following example: the user inserts a number from 1 to 12, and we have to print the season the month with that number corresponds to. How would the flowchart look like? Do you think Figure 7-4 fits the scenario?

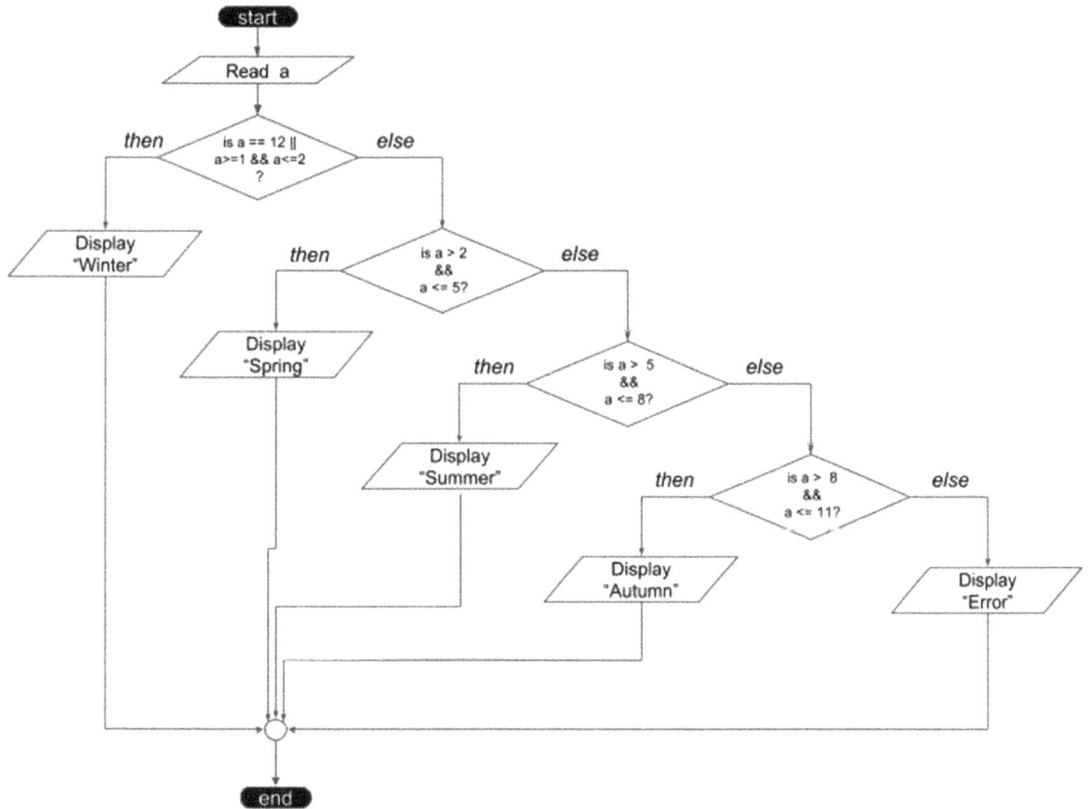

Figure 7-4. *Complex if-else flowchart sample*

Looks complicated, right? Wait until you see the code matching that diagram, that is depicted in this next code snippet.

CHAPTER 7 CONTROLLING THE FLOW

```java
package com.apress.bgn.ch7;

public class SeasonDemo {
    public static void main(String... args) {
    //Read a
    int a = Integer.parseInt(args[0]);

    if(a == 12 || (a>=1 && a<= 2)) {
        System.out.println("Winter");
    } else {
        if (a>2 && a <= 5 ) {
        System.out.println("Spring");
        } else {
        if (a>5 && a <= 8 ) {
            System.out.println("Summer");
        } else {
            if (a>8 && a <= 11 ) {
            System.out.println("Autumn");
            } else {
            System.out.println("Error");
            }
        }
        }
    }
    }
}
```

Looks ugly, right? But, fortunately, Java provides a way to simplify it, especially because it makes no sense having so many `else` blocks that only contain another `if` statement. The simplified code connects the `else` statements with the contained `if(s)` statements. And the code ends up looking like the following code snippet.

```java
package com.apress.bgn.ch7;

public class SeasonDemo {
    public static void main(String... args) {
    //Read a
    int a = Integer.parseInt(args0);
```

```
    if (a == 12 || (a >= 1 && a <= 2)) {
        System.out.println("Winter");
    } else if (a > 2 && a <= 5) {
        System.out.println("Spring");
    } else if (a > 5 && a <= 8) {
        System.out.println("Summer");
    } else if (a > 8 && a <= 11) {
        System.out.println("Autumn");
    } else {
        System.out.println("Error");
    }
  }
}
```

Any argument given by the user that is not in the [1,12] causes the program to print Error. You can test it for yourself if you want by modifying your IntelliJ IDEA launcher. The elements to focus on are underlined in Figure 7-5.

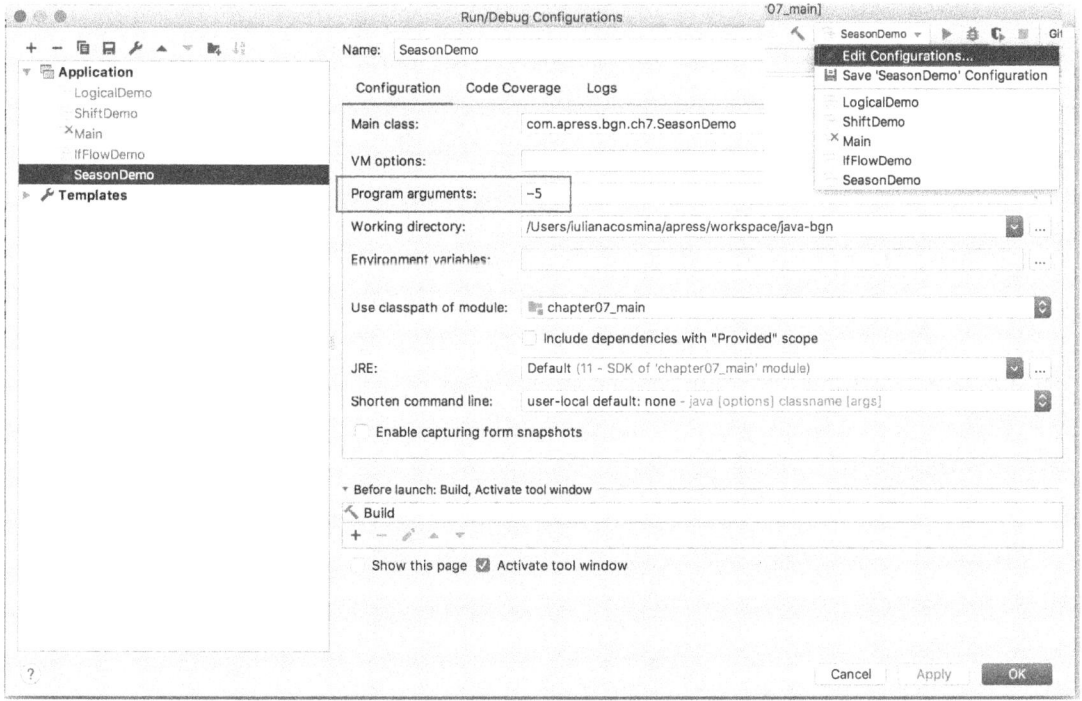

Figure 7-5. *IntelliJ IDEA launcher and parameters*

CHAPTER 7 CONTROLLING THE FLOW

switch Statement

When a value requires different actions for a fixed set of values, the `if` might get more complex, the more the set of values increases. In this case the more suitable statement is the `switch` statement. Let's look at the code first, and then check what more can be improved.

```
package com.apress.bgn.ch7;

public class SeasonSwitchDemo {
    public static void main(String... args) {
    //Read a
    int a = Integer.parseInt(args[0]);

    var season = "";
    switch (a) {
        case 1:
        season = "Winter";
        break;
        case 2:
        season = "Winter";
        break;
        case 3:
        season = "Spring";
        break;
        case 4:
        season = "Spring";
        break;
        case 5:
        season = "Spring";
        break;
        case 6:
        season = "Summer";
        break;
        case 7:
        season = "Summer";
        break;
```

```
            case 8:
            season = "Summer";
            break;
            case 9:
            season = "Autumn";
            break;
            case 10:
            season = "Autumn";
            break;
            case 11:
            season = "Autumn";
            break;
            case 12:
            season = "winter";
            break;
            default:
            System.out.println("Error");
        }
        System.out.println(season);
    }
}
```

Hm… that does not look very practical, at least not for this scenario. Before showing how the switch statement can be written differently, let's explain the structure and logic of it first. The general template of a switch statement is

```
switch ([onvar]) {
    case [option]:
    [statement;]
    break;
    ...
    default:
    [statement;]
}
```

The terms in square brackets are detailed in the following list.

- `[onvar]` is the variable that is tested against the `case` statements to select a statement. It can be of any primitive type, enumerations and starting with Java 7, `String`. Clearly the `switch` statement is not limited by conditions evaluated to `boolean` results, which allows for a lot of flexibility.

- `case [option]` is a value the variable is matched upon to make a decision regarding the statement to execute. A `case` as the keyword states.

- `[statement]` is a statement or a groups of statements to execute when `[onvar] == [option]`. Considering that there is no `else` branch, we have to make sure that only the statement(s) corresponding to the first match is executed, which is where the `break;` statement comes in. The `break` statement stops the current execution path and moves the execution point to the next statement outside the statement that contains it. I'll cover it later in the chapter. Without it, after the first match, all subsequent cases are traversed, and statements corresponding to them are executed.

  So, if we execute the preceding program and we provide number 7 as an argument, the text *Summer* is printed. But if the `break` statements for case 7 and 8 are commented, the output changes to *Autumn*.

- `default [statement;]` is a statement that is executed when no match on a `case` has been found, the `default` case does not need a `break` statement. If the previous program is run with any number outside the `[1-12]` interval, `Error` is printed because the default statement is executed.

Now that you understand how `switch` works, let's look at how we can reduce the previous statement. The month example is suitable here, because it can further be modified to show how the `switch` statement can be simplified, when a single statement should be executed for multiple cases. In our code, writing each assignment statement three times is a little redundant. `switch` can be written in a different way to avoid that by grouping the cases. The code is depicted next.

```java
package com.apress.bgn.ch7;

public class SeasonSwitchDemo {
    public static void main(String... args) {
        //Read a
        int a = Integer.parseInt(args0);

        var season = "";
        switch (a) {
            case 1:
            case 2:
            case 12:
            season = "winter";
                break;
             case 3:
             case 4:
             case 5:
             season = "Spring";
             break;
             case 6:
             case 7:
             case 8:
             season = "Summer";
                break;
             case 9:
             case 10:
             case 11:
             season = "Autumn";
             break;
             default:
             System.out.println("Error");
        }
        System.out.println(season);
    }
}
```

The grouping in this case represents the alignment of the cases that require the same statement to be executed, and writing it only once in the last one. This still looks a little weird, but this is the only way to reduce the statement repetition. The behavior in the previous case is possible because each case without a `break` statement is followed by the next case statement.

In Java 7, the `switch` statement started supporting `String` values. The main problems with `switch` supporting `String` values is that there is always a risk of `NullPointerExceptions` being thrown, because the `equals` method is used to test matching of the items, and the variable used in the switch statement can be null. Also, because equals is used, the comparison is case sensitive. If we modify the previous example and ask the user for a text representing the month, and use `switch` to decide the season to print, unless we use the exact text in case options that the user will use when writing the argument, we won't get the expected result.

The code changes to

```
package com.apress.bgn.ch7;

public class StringSwitchSeasonDemo {
    public static void main(String... args) {
       //Read a
       String a = args0;

       var season = "";
       switch (a) {
         case "january":
         case "february":
         case "december":
         season = "winter";
         break;
         case "march":
         case "april":
         case "may":
         season = "Spring";
         break;
```

```
        case "june":
        case "july":
        case "august":
        season = "Summer";
        break;
        case "september":
        case "october":
        case "november":
        season = "Autumn";
        break;
        default:
        System.out.println("Error");
    }
    System.out.println(season);
  }
}
```

If we run the previous program with the "january" argument, the text "winter" is printed in the console. If we run it with argument "january", the text "Error" is printed in the console. And if we run it with null, a NullPointerException is thrown in the line where the switch statement begins.

And this is all that can be said about the switch statement. In practice, depending on the solution you are trying to develop, you might decide to use a combination of if and switch statements.

Unfortunately because of its peculiar logic and its flexible number of options, it is difficult to draw a flowchart for the switch statement, but nevertheless I've tried and it's depicted in Figure 7-6.

CHAPTER 7 CONTROLLING THE FLOW

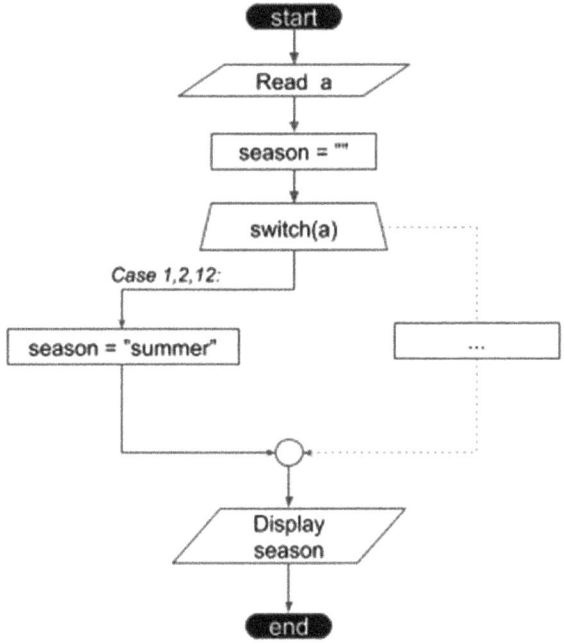

Figure 7-6. *The switch statement flowchart*

Looping Statements

Sometimes in programming, we need repetitive steps that involve the same variables. To write the same statement over and over again to get the job done would be ridiculous. Let's take the example of sorting an array of integer values. The most known algorithm to do this and the one that is taught first in programming courses because it is simple is called *bubble sort*. The algorithm compares the elements of an array, two by two and if they are not in the correct order it swaps them. It goes over the array again and again until no more swaps are needed. The effects of the algorithm are depicted in Figure 7-7.

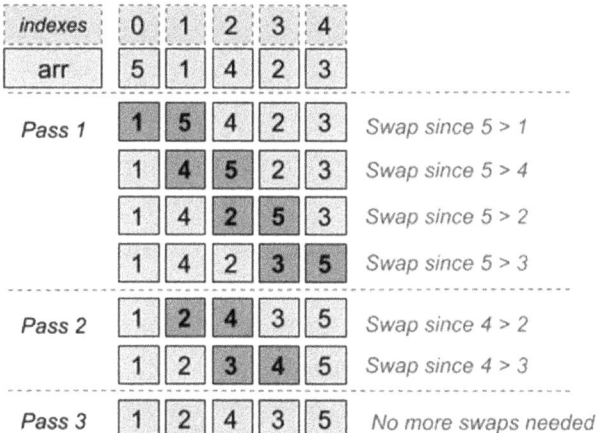

Figure 7-7. Bubble sort phases and effect

This algorithm performs two types of loops; one iterates each element of the array using indexes. And this traversal is repeated until no swaps are necessary. In Java this algorithm can be written in more than one way using different looping statements. But we'll get there, let's take it slow.

There are three types of looping statements in Java.

- `for` statement
- `while` statement
- `do-while` statement

The `for` looping statement is the most used, but `while` and `do-while` have their uses as well.

for Statements

For is recommended for iterating on objects like arrays and lists that can be counted. For example, traversing an array and printing each one of its values is as simple as depicted in the following code sample.

```
package com.apress.bgn.ch7;

public class ForLoopDemo {
    public static void main(String... args) {
        int arr[] = {5, 1, 4, 2, 3};
```

CHAPTER 7   CONTROLLING THE FLOW

```
      for (int i = 0; i < arr.length; ++i) {
         System.out.println("arr[" + i + "] = " + arr[i]);
      }
    }
}
```

Based on the previous example, a flowchart for the for statement can be drawn and it is depicted in Figure 7-8. The following code snippet depicts the for loop template.

```
for ([int_expr]; [condition];[step]){
      [code_block]
}
```

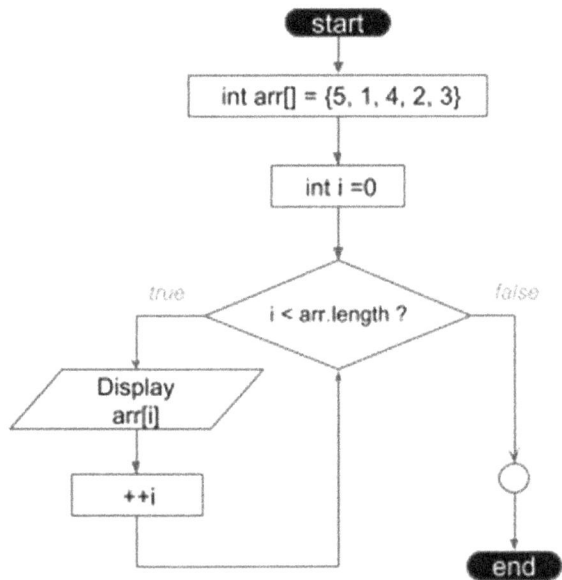

Figure 7-8. The for statement flowchart

Each of the terms between square brackets have a specific purpose that is explained next.

- **[init_expr]** is an initialization expression that sets the initial value of the counter used by this loop. It ends with ; and is not mandatory, as the initialization can be done outside the statement, especially if we are interested in using the counter variable later in the code and outside the statement. The preceding code can be written like this:

CHAPTER 7 CONTROLLING THE FLOW

```java
package com.apress.bgn.ch7;

public class ForLoopDemo {
    public static void main(String... args) {
        int arr[] = {5, 1, 4, 2, 3};
        int i = 0;
        for (; i < arr.length; ++i) {
            System.out.println("arr[" + i + "] = " + arr[i]);
        }
        System.out.println("Loop exited with index: " + i);
    }
}
```

- **[condition]** is the termination condition of the loop, as long as this condition is evaluated to true, the loop will continue executing. The condition ends with ; and funny enough, it is not mandatory either, as the termination condition can be placed inside the code to be executed repeatedly by the loop. So, the preceding code can be modified further and written like this:

```java
package com.apress.bgn.ch7;

public class ForLoopDemo {
    public static void main(String... args) {
        int arr[] = {5, 1, 4, 2, 3};
        int i = 0;
        for (; ; ++i) {
            if (i >= arr.length) {
            break;
            }
            System.out.println("arr[" + i + "] = " + arr[i]);
        }
        System.out.println("Loop exited with index: " + i);
    }
}
```

- **[step]** is the step expression or increment that increases the counter on every step of the loop. It should end in ;, but it is often dropped, and as you probably already expected, it is not mandatory either, as nothing stops the developer from manipulating the counter inside the code block. So, the preceding code can also be written like this:

```
package com.apress.bgn.ch7;

public class ForLoopDemo {
    public static void main(String... args) {
    int arr[] = {5, 1, 4, 2, 3};
    int i = 0;
    for (; ;) {
        if (i >= arr.length) {
        break;
        }
        System.out.println("arr[" + i + "] = " + arr[i]);
        ++i;
    }
    System.out.println("Loop exited with index: " + i);
    }
}
```

The modification of the counter does not have to be done inside the code; it can be done in the termination condition, but the initialization expression and the termination condition must be modified accordingly to fit the purpose. The code depicted next has the same effect as all the samples before it.

```
package com.apress.bgn.ch7;

public class ForLoopDemo {
    public static void main(String... args) {
    int arr[] = {5, 1, 4, 2, 3};
    for (int i = -1; i++ < arr.length -1;) {
            System.out.println("arr[" + i + "] = " + arr[i]);
    }
```

```
            System.out.println("Loop exited with index: " + i);
        }
}
```

The step expression does not have to be an incrementation. It can be any expression that modifies the value of the counter. Instead of ++i or i++, you can use i= i+1, or i=i+3, or even decrementation if the array of list is traversed starting with a bigger index. Any mathematical operations that keep the counter in the boundaries of the type it was declared and within the indexes range can be used safely.

- **[code_block]** is a block of code executed repeatedly, in every step of the loop. If there is no exit condition within this code, this block of code is executed by as many times as the counter passes the termination condition.

This is the basic form of the for looping statement, but in Java there are other ways to iterate a group of values. Let's say that instead of an array, we have to iterate over a list.

```
package com.apress.bgn.ch7;

import java.util.List;

public class ForLoopDemo {
    public static void main(String... args) {
      List<Integer> list = List.of(5, 1, 4, 2, 3);
      for (int j = 0; j < list.size(); ++j) {
         System.out.println("list[" + j + "] = " + list.get(j));
      }
    }
}
```

The code seems somehow impractical and that is why List<> instances can be traversed with a different type of for statement that was known as forEach until Java 8. You will see immediately why, but first let's look at forEach.

```
package com.apress.bgn.ch7;

import java.util.List;
```

CHAPTER 7   CONTROLLING THE FLOW

```java
public class ForLoopDemo {
    public static void main(String... args) {
      List<Integer> list = List.of(5, 1, 4, 2, 3);
      for (Integer item : list) {
        System.out.println(item);
      }
    }
}
```

This type of for statement is also called as having *enhanced syntax* and basically executes the code block for each item in the collection used in its expression. This means it works on any implementation of Collection interface and it works on arrays too. So, the example code is written like this:

```java
package com.apress.bgn.ch7;

public class ForLoopDemo {
    public static void main(String... args) {
      int arr[] = {5, 1, 4, 2, 3};
      for (int item : arr) {
        System.out.println(item);
      }
    }
}
```

Clearly the best part in this case is that we no longer need a termination condition, or counter at all. Starting with Java 8, the name *forEach* is no longer needed for the for statement with enhanced syntax, because the forEach default method was added to all Collection extensions. Combine that with lambda expressions and the code to print the elements of a list becomes

```java
package com.apress.bgn.ch7;

import java.util.List;

public class ForLoopDemo {
    public static void main(String... args) {
      List<Integer> list = List.of(5, 1, 4, 2, 3);
      list.forEach(item -> System.out.println(item));
      //or
```

```
        list.forEach(System.out::println);
    }
}
```

Pretty neat, ha? But wait, there's more, it works on arrays too, but a small conversion to suitable implementation BaseStream is necessary first. But it is provided by the Arrays utility class that was enriched in Java 8 with methods to support lambda expressions. So yeah, the code with the arr array can be written (starting in Java) 8 like this:

```
package com.apress.bgn.ch7;

public class ForLoopDemo {
    public static void main(String... args) {
    int arr[] = {5, 1, 4, 2, 3};
        Arrays.stream(arr).forEach(System.out::println);
    }
}
```

In Java 11, all the preceding examples compile and execute just fine, so use whatever syntax you prefer most when writing your solutions.

while Statement

The while statement is different from the for statement in that there is not a fixed number of steps that have to be executed, so a counter is not always needed. The number of repetitions of a while statement executes depends only on how many times the continuation condition that controls this number is evaluated to true. So, the generic template for this statement is depicted in the following listing:

```
while ([eval(condition)] == true) {
 [code_block]
}
```

A while statement does not really require an initialization statement either, as it can be inside the code block, or outside the statement. The while statement can replace the for statement, but the advantage of the for statement is that it encapsulates the initialization, the termination condition and the modification of the counter in a single block, so it's more concise. The array traversal code sample can be rewritten using the while statement; the code is listed next.

CHAPTER 7 CONTROLLING THE FLOW

```
package com.apress.bgn.ch7;

public class WhileLoopDemo {
    public static void main(String... args) {
    int arr[] = {5, 1, 4, 2, 3};
    int  i=0;
    while(i < arr.length){
        System.out.println("arr[" + i + "] = " + arr[i]);
        ++i;
    }
    }
}
```

As you can see, the declaration and initialization of the counter variable, `int i=0;` is done outside the statement and the incrementation of the counter is done inside the code block to be repeated. Basically at this point, if we design the flowchart for this scenario, it will look the same as the `for` statement depicted in Figure 7-9.

And as incredible as it sounds, the [condition] is not mandatory either, as it can be replaced directly with `true`. But in this case, you have to make sure that there is an exit condition inside the block of code that executes at some point; otherwise, the execution will most likely end with an error. And this condition must be placed at the beginning of the block of code to prevent the execution of the useful logic in a situation where it shouldn't be. For our simple example, we do not want to call `System.out.println` for an element with an index outside the array range.

```
package com.apress.bgn.ch7;

public class WhileLoopDemo {
public static void main(String... args) {
   int arr[] = {5, 1, 4, 2, 3};
    int  i=0;
   while(true){
       if (i >= arr.length) {
       break;
       }
```

264

```
            System.out.println("arr[" + i + "] = " + arr[i]);
            ++i;
        }
    }
}
```

The while statement is best used when we are working with a resource that is not always online. Let's say we are using a remote database for our application that is in a network that is unstable. Instead of giving up trying to save our data after the first timeout, we could try until we succeed, right? This is done by using a while statement that tries to initialize a connection object in its code block. And the code looks roughly like this:

```
package com.apress.bgn.ch7;

import java.sql.*;

public class ConnectionTester {
    public static void main(String... args) throws Exception {

    Connection con = null;
    while (con == null) {
        try {
        Class.forName("com.mysql.cj.jdbc.Driver");
        con = DriverManager.getConnection(
            "jdbc:mysql://localhost:3306/sample", "root", "pass");
        } catch (Exception e) {
        System.out.println("Connection refused. Retrying in 5 seconds ...");
        Thread.sleep(5000);
        }
    }
    // con != null, do something
    Statement stmt = con.createStatement();
    ResultSet rs = stmt.executeQuery("select * from test");
    while (rs.next()) {
        System.out.println(rs.getInt(1) + "  " + rs.getString(2));
    }
    con.close();
    }
}
```

CHAPTER 7 CONTROLLING THE FLOW

The problem with this code is that it runs forever; if we want to give up trying after a certain time, we must introduce a variable that counts the number of tries and then exits the loop using a break statement.

```java
package com.apress.bgn.ch7;

import java.sql.*;

public class ConnectionTester {
    public static final int MAX_TRIES = 10;

    public static void main(String... args) throws Exception {
        int cntTries = 0;
        Connection con = null;
        while (con == null && cntTries < MAX_TRIES) {
            try {
            Class.forName("com.mysql.cj.jdbc.Driver");
            con = DriverManager.getConnection(
                "jdbc:mysql://localhost:3306/sample", "root", "pass");
            } catch (Exception e) {
            ++cntTries;
            System.out.println("Connection refused. Retrying in 5 seconds ...");
            Thread.sleep(5000);
            }
        }
        if (con != null) {
            // con != null, do something
            Statement stmt = con.createStatement();
            ResultSet rs = stmt.executeQuery("select * from test");
            while (rs.next()) {
            System.out.println(rs.getInt(1) + " " + rs.getString(2));
            }
            con.close();
        } else {
            System.out.println("Could not connect!");
        }
    }
}
```

So, as a rule of thumb, **always make sure there is an exit condition when using looping statements**.

And since we've covered all the statements needed to implement the bubble sort algorithm depicted in Figure 7-9, let's see what the code looks like. Be aware that, this algorithm can be written in many ways, but the following code best matches the explanation provided earlier. So, while there are elements in the array that are not in the proper order, the array is traversed again and again and adjacent elements are swapped to fit the desired order (ascending, in this case).

```java
package com.apress.bgn.ch7;

import java.util.Arrays;

public class BubbleSortDemo {
    public static final int arr[] = {5, 1, 4, 2, 3};

    public static void main(String... args) {
    boolean swapped = true;
    while (swapped) {
        swapped = false;
        for (int i = 0; i < arr.length - 1; ++i) {
        if (arr[i] > arr[i + 1]) {
            int temp = arr[i];
            arr[i] = arr[i + 1];
            arr[i + 1] = temp;
            swapped = true;
        }
        }
    }
    Arrays.stream(arr).forEach(System.out::println);
    }
}
```

When run, the code swaps elements of the `arr` array until they are all in ascending order, so the last line in the code prints the modified `arr`:

1
2
3
4
5

do-while Statement

The `do-while` statement is similar to the `while`, with one difference, the continuation condition is evaluated after executing the code block. This causes for the code block to be executed at least once, unless there is a an exit condition embedded in it. The generic template for this statement is depicted in the following listing:

```
do {
 [code_block]
} while ([eval(condition)] == true)
```

Most times statements `while` and `do-while` can be easily interchanged, and sometimes a minimum change of the logic of the code block is needed. For example, traversing an array and printing the values of its elements can be written using `do-while` as well, without changing the code block. Figure 7-9 shows the two implementations side by side: the `while` on the left and `do-while` on the right.

```
WhileLoopDemo.java                                  DoWhileDemo.java
/.../                                               /.../
package com.apress.bgn.ch7;                         package com.apress.bgn.ch7;

/**                                                 /**
 * @author Iuliana Cosmina                           * @author Iuliana Cosmina
 * since 1.0                                         * since 1.0
 */                                                 */
public class WhileLoopDemo {                        public class DoWhileDemo {

    public static void main(String... args) {           public static void main(String... args) {
        int arr[] = {5, 1, 4, 2, 3};                        int arr[] = {5, 1, 4, 2, 3};
        int i=0;                                            int i = 0;

        while(i < arr.length){                              do {
            System.out.println("arr[" + i + "] = " + arr[i]);   System.out.println("arr[" + i + "] = " + arr[i]);
            ++i;                                                ++i;
        }                                                   } while (i < arr.length);
    }                                                   }
}                                                   }
```

Figure 7-9. *while and do-while implementation for printing elements of an array*

The flowchart for these two examples (see Figure 7-10) reveals the different logic between the two statements.

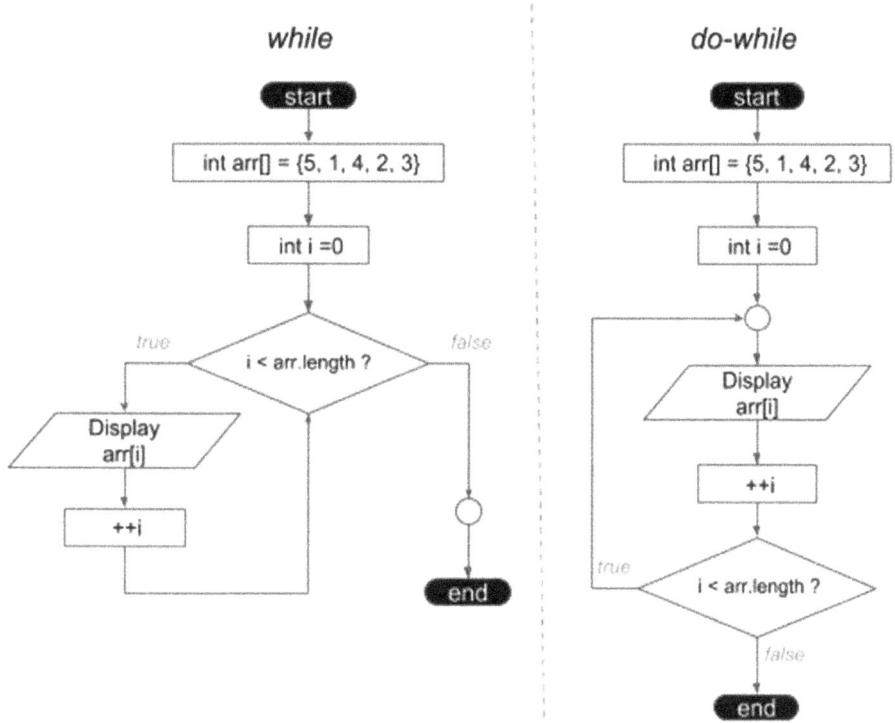

Figure 7-10. *Comparison between while and do-while statements flowcharts*

The do-while statement works best when the code block must be executed at least once; otherwise, we evaluate the condition once unnecessarily. Remember the code sample that was trying to connect to a database that was in an unstable network? Well, when while was used, the execution started by testing if the connection is not null, but the connection was not even initialized yet.

```
Connection con = null;
while (con == null) {
    Class.forName("com.mysql.cj.jdbc.Driver");
    con = DriverManager.getConnection(
    "jdbc:mysql://localhost:3306/sample", "root", "pass");
    ...
}
```

CHAPTER 7 CONTROLLING THE FLOW

This implementation, although functional, is a little redundant and the logic is not following programming best practices. More suitable would be a do-while implementation, one that avoids testing if the con instance is null, considering that it clearly is, as in the following.

```java
package com.apress.bgn.ch7;

import java.sql.*;

public class DoConnectionTester {
    public static final int MAX_TRIES = 10;

    public static void main(String... args) throws Exception {

        int cntTries = 0;
        Connection con = null;
        do {
            try {
                Class.forName("com.mysql.cj.jdbc.Driver");
                con = DriverManager.getConnection(
                    "jdbc:mysql://localhost:3306/sample", "root", "pass");
            } catch (Exception e) {
                ++cntTries;
                System.out.println("Connection refused. Retrying in 5 seconds ...");
                Thread.sleep(5000);
            }
        } while  (con == null && cntTries < MAX_TRIES);
        if (con != null) {
            // con != null, do something
            Statement stmt = con.createStatement();
            ResultSet rs = stmt.executeQuery("select * from test");
            while (rs.next()) {
            System.out.println(rs.getInt(1) + "   " + rs.getString(2));
            }
            con.close();
```

```
        } else {
            System.out.println("Could not connect!");
        }
    }
}
```

Sure, skipping the evaluation of the condition is not a big optimization, but in a big application, every little optimization counts.

Breaking Loops and Skipping Steps

In the previous examples, I mentioned that exiting a loop using the `break` statement. There are three ways to manipulate the behavior of a loop:

- The `break` statement exits the loop, and if accompanied by a label, it breaks the loop that is labeled with it; this is useful when we have more nested loops, because we can break form any of the nested loops, not just the one containing the statement.

- The `continue` statement skips the execution of any code after it and continues with the next step.

- The `return` statement is used to exit a method, so if the loop, or `if` or `switch` statement is within the body of a method, it is used to exit the loop as well. In regards to best practices, usage of `return` statements to exit a method should not be abused as they might make the execution flow difficult to follow.

break Statement

The `break` statement can only be used within `switch`, `for`, `while`, and `do-while` statements. You have already seen how it can be used within the `switch` statement; let's look at how to use it in all the others.

Breaking out of a `for`, `while` or `do-while` loop can be done using the `break` statement, but it must be controlled by an exit condition; otherwise, no step is executed. In the following code sample, we print only the first three elements, even if the `for` loop should traverse all of them. If we get to the index equal to 3, we exit the loop.

CHAPTER 7   CONTROLLING THE FLOW

```java
package com.apress.bgn.ch7;

public class ManipulationDemo {
    public static final int arr[] = {5, 1, 4, 2, 3};

    public static void main(String... args) {

        for (int i = 0; i < arr.length ; ++i) {
            if  (i == 3) {
            System.out.println("Bye bye!");
            break;
            }
            System.out.println("arr[" + i + "] = " + arr[i]);
        }
    }
}
```

If we have a case of nested loops, a label can be used to decide the looping statement to break out of. As an example, in the following code we have three nested for loops, and we exit the middle loop when all indexes are equal.

```java
package com.apress.bgn.ch7;

public class ManipulationDemo {
    public static final int arr[] = {5, 1, 4, 2, 3};

    public static void main(String... args) {

      for (int i = 0; i < 2; ++i) {
        HERE: for (int j = 0; j < 2; ++j) {
        for (int k = 0; k < 2; ++k) {
            System.out.println("(i, j, k) = (" + i + "," + j + "," + k + ")");
            if (i == j && j == k) {
            break HERE;
            }
          }
         }
       }
      }
}
```

The label used in the code sample is named HERE, and it precedes the for statement that is exited when the condition is fulfilled and follows the break statement. Writing label names in all all-caps letters is considered a best practice in development as it avoids confusing labels with variables or class named when reading the code.

To make sure this works, you can take a look in the console to see that all combinations of (i,j,k), including the ones with i = j = k and all after it, are no longer printed. In this case, all sets beginning with 0 are skipped, which is what is in the console.

(i, j, k) = (1,0,0)
(i, j, k) = (1,0,1)
(i, j, k) = (1,1,0)

continue Statement

The continue statement does not break a loop, but can be used to skip certain steps based on a condition. So it basically, stops the current step of the loop and moves to the next one, so you could say that this statement continues the loop. Let's continue experimenting with the array traversal example, and this time, let's skip from printing the elements with odd indexes by using the continue statement.

```
package com.apress.bgn.ch7;

public class ManipulationDemo {
    public static final int arr[] = {5, 1, 4, 2, 3};

    public static void main(String... args) {
      for (int i = 0; i < arr.length; ++i) {
        if (i % 2  != 0) {
        continue;
        }
        System.out.println("arr[" + i + "] = " + arr[i]);
      }
    }
}
```

CHAPTER 7 CONTROLLING THE FLOW

This statement must be conditioned; otherwise, the loop will iterate uselessly. The continue statement can be used with labels too. Let's take a similar example to the three nested for loops used earlier, but this time, when the k index is equal to 1, nothing is printed and we skip to the next step of the loop enclosing the k loop.

```
package com.apress.bgn.ch7;

public class ManipulationDemo {
    public static final int arr[] = {5, 1, 4, 2, 3};

    public static void main(String... args) {
      for (int i = 0; i < 3; ++i) {
        HERE:
        for (int j = 0; j < 3; ++j) {
        for (int k = 0; k < 3; ++k) {
            if (k == 1) {
            continue HERE;
            }
            System.out.println("(i, j, k) = (" + i + "," + j + "," + k + ")");
        }
        }
      }
    }
}
```

To make sure this works, you can take a look in the console to see that what combinations are printed. We clearly notice that no combination with k=1 or k=2 has printed.

```
(i, j, k) = (0,0,0)
(i, j, k) = (0,1,0)
(i, j, k) = (0,2,0)
(i, j, k) = (1,0,0)
(i, j, k) = (1,1,0)
(i, j, k) = (1,2,0)
(i, j, k) = (2,0,0)
(i, j, k) = (2,1,0)
(i, j, k) = (2,2,0)
```

! The usage of labels to break out of loops is frowned upon in the Java community, because jumping to a label resembles the goto statement that still can be found in certain old school programming languages. goto is a Java reserved keyword, because this statement used to exist in the first version of the JVM, but it was later removed. Using jumping makes code less readable, less testable and promotes bad design. That is why goto was removed in later versions, but any need of such operation can be implemented break and continue statements.

return Statement

The return statement is an easy one. It can be used to exit the execution of a method body. If the method returns a value, the return statement is accompanied by the value returned. The return statement can be used to exit any of the statements mentioned in this section. It can represent a smart way to shortcut the execution of a method, as the execution of the current method stops and processing continues from the point in the code that called the method.

Let's look at a few examples. First let's write a method that finds the first even element in an array; if found, the method returns its index; otherwise, it returns -1.

```java
package com.apress.bgn.ch7;

public class ReturnDemo {
    public static final int arr[] = {5, 1, 4, 2, 3};

    public static void main(String... args) {
        int foundIdx = findEven(arr);
        if (foundIdx != -1) {
            System.out.println("First even is at: " + foundIdx);
        }
    }
```

```
    public static int findEven(int ... arr) {
    for (int i = 0; i < arr.length; ++i) {
        if (arr[i] %2 == 0) {

            return i;
            }
        }
    return -1;
        }
}
```

Let's write the same method but using a while statement.

```
package com.apress.bgn.ch7;

public class ReturnDemo {
    public static final int arr[] = {5, 1, 4, 2, 3};

    public static void main(String... args) {
    int foundIdx = findEven(arr);
    if (foundIdx != -1) {
        System.out.println("First even is at: " + foundIdx);
        }
    }

    public static int findEven(int ... arr) {
    int i = 0;
    while (i < arr.length) {
        if (arr[i] % 2 == 0) {

            return i;
            }
            ++i;
        }
    return -1;
        }
}
```

The return statement can be used in any situation where we want to terminate the execution of a method if a condition is met.

Controlling the Flow Using try-catch Constructions

Exceptions and `try-catch` statements were already mentioned in this book, but not as tools to control flow execution. Before we skip to explanations and examples, let's first discuss the general template of a `try-catch-finally` statement.

```
try {
 [code_block]
} catch ([exception_block]} {
 [handling_code_block]
} finally {
 [cleanup_code_block]
}
```

I'll explain each of these components.

- `[code_block]` is the code block to execute.

- `[exception_block]` is a declaration or more of an exception type that can be thrown by the `[code_block]`.

- `[handling_code_block]` - an exception being thrown marks an unexpected situation, which must be handled, once the exception is being caught, this piece of code is executed to *treat it*, whether by trying to return the system to a normal state or by logging details about the cause of the exception.

- `[clean_up_code]` is a block of code releases resources or sets objects to null so that they are eligible for collection.

Now that you know how a `try-catch-finally` works, you can probably imagine how to use it to control the execution flow. Basically, within the `[code_block]`, you can explicitly throw exceptions and decide how they are treated.

Considering the array that we have been using until now, we'll design our piece of code based on it again. First, let's write a piece of code that throws an exception when an even value is found.

CHAPTER 7 CONTROLLING THE FLOW

```java
package com.apress.bgn.ch7.ex;

public class ExceptionFlowDemo {
    public static final int arr[] = {5, 1, 4, 2, 3};

    public static void main(String... args) {
    try {
        checkNotEven(arr);
        System.out.println("Not found, all good!");
    } catch (EvenException e) {
        System.out.println(e.getMessage());
    } finally {
        System.out.println("Cleaning up arr");
        for (int i = 0; i < arr.length; ++i) {
        arr[i] = 0;
        }
    }
    }

    public static int checkNotEven(int... arr) throws EvenException {
    for (int i = 0; i < arr.length; ++i) {
        if (arr[i] % 2 == 0) {
        throw new EvenException("Did not expect an even number at " + i);
        }
    }
    return -1;
    }
}
```

The EvenException type is a custom exception type written for this specific example and its implementation is not relevant here. If we execute this piece of code the following is printed.

```
Did not expect an even number at 2
Cleaning up arr
```

By throwing an exception, we've directed the execution to the handling code, so *Not found, all good!* was not printed, and because we have a `finally` block that was executed as well.

So, yeah, you can mix-and-match: use different types of exceptions, have multiple `catch` blocks—whatever you need to solve your problem. At a previous company that I worked for, I stumbled upon a piece of code that was validating a document and throwing different types of exceptions depending on the validation check that was not passed and in the `finally` block we had a code that was converting the error object to PDF. The code looks similar to this:

```
...
ErrorContainter errorContainer = new ErrorContainter();
try {
        validate(report);
} catch (FileNotFoundException | NotParsable e) {
        errorContainer.addBadFileError(e);
} catch (InvestmentMaxException e) {
        errorContainer.addInvestmentError(e);
} catch (CreditIncompatibilityException e) {
        errorContainer.addIncompatibilityError(e);
} finally {
        if (errorContainer.isEmpty()) {
            printValidationPassedDocument();
        } else {
            printValidationFailedDocument(errorContainer);
        }
}
...
```

The code in the `finally` code block was complex and totally not recommended to be in there. But sometimes in the real world, the solutions do not always respect best practices, or even common sense practices. And when dealing with legacy code, you might find yourself in the position to write crappy but functional code that must be delivered fast. Because, sure programming is awesome, but in the eyes of some managers, results are more important. If you are lucky enough to get a job at a company that is looking to build on the code in the future or hand it to other team members, you might actually end up with a manager that favors best practices. Just remember to do your best, and document everything properly and you'll be fine.

CHAPTER 7 CONTROLLING THE FLOW

Summary

This chapter covered one of the most important things in development: how to design your solutions, the logic of it. You've also been introduced to what flowcharts are and their components, as tools for deciding how to write your code and how to control execution paths. And finally, you've learned which statements to use and when. A few Java best practices were discussed, so that you are able to design the most suitable solutions to your problems.

Java provides

- simple and more complex ways to write `if` statements
- a `switch` statement that works with any primitive type, enumerations and starting with Java 7, `String` instances
- a few ways to write `for` statements
- how to use `forEach` methods and streams to traverse a collection of values
- `while` statement, used when a step must be repeated until a condition is met
- `do-while` statement, used when a step must be repeated until a condition is met, but the step is repeated at least once, because the continuation condition is evaluated after it
- how to manipulate loop behavior by using statements like `break`, `continue`, and `return`
- how to control the execution flow by using `try-catch-finally` constructions

CHAPTER 8

The Stream API

The term *stream* has more than one meaning, as explained on Dictionary.com.

- a body of water flowing in a channel or watercourse, as a river, rivulet, or brook
- a steady current in water, as in a river or the ocean
- any flow of water or other liquid or fluid
- a current or flow of air, gas, or the like
- **a continuous flow or succession of anything**
- prevailing direction; drift
- *In digital technology* - **a flow of data**, as an audio broadcast, a movie, or live video, transmitted smoothly and continuously from a source to a computer, mobile device, and so forth.

In the software development context the definitions that are closest to a stream are the fifth and part of the seventh (highlighted in bold). I software development a *stream* is a sequence of objects from a source that supports aggregate operations. In your mind, you would be saying right now: so, is it similar to a collection? Well... not quite.

Introduction to Streams

Consider a really big collection of songs that we want to analyze. We want to find all songs with duration of at least 300 seconds. We want to save the names of these songs in a list and sort them by decreasing order of their duration. Assuming we already have the songs in a list, the code looks like this:

```
List<Integer> songList = ...
List<Song> resultedSongs = new ArrayList<>();
```

CHAPTER 8   THE STREAM API

```
for (Song song: songList) {
    if (song.getDuration() >= 300) {
        resultedSongs.add(song);
    }
}
Collections.sort(resultedSongs, new Comparator<Song>(){
    public int compare(Song s1, Song s2){
        return s2.getDuration().compareTo(s1.getDuration());
    }
});
System.out.println(resultedSongs);
List<String> finalList = new ArrayList<>();
for (Song song: resultedSongs) {
    finalList.add(song.getTitle());
}
System.out.println(finalList);
```

One of the problems with this code is that processing large collections is not really efficient. Also, we are traversing lists over and over again and performing checks to get to a final result. Wouldn't it be nice if we could just link all of those operations together and execute them on the initial list?

Enter Java 8 and the new **Stream** abstraction that represents a sequence of elements that can be processed sequentially or in parallel and supports aggregate operations. Because of the latest evolutions in hardware development, CPUs have become more powerful and more complex, containing multiple cores that can process information in parallel. To make use of these hardware capabilities in Java the Fork Join Framework was introduced. And in Java 8, the *Stream API* was introduced to support parallel data processing, without the boiler-code of defining and synchronizing threads. The central interface of the *Stream API* is the `java.util.stream.BaseStream`. Any object with stream capabilities is of a type that extends it. A stream does not store elements itself, it is not a data structure, it is used to compute elements and serve them on-demand to a function or a set of aggregate functions. Serving the elements in a sequence involves an internal automatic iteration. Functions that return a stream can be chained in a *pipeline*, and are called *intermediate operations*. They are used to process elements of a stream and return the result as a stream to the next function in the pipeline. Functions that return a result that is not a stream are called *terminal operations* and are obviously present at the end of a pipeline. As a quick example before getting deeper, the previous code can be written like this using streams:

```
List<String> finalList = songList.stream().filter(s -> s.getDuration()>= 300)
    .sorted(Comparator.comparing(Song::getDuration).reversed())
    .map(Song::getTitle)
    .collect(Collectors.toList());
System.out.println(finalList);
```

Yup, programming with streams is awesome. The *Stream API* concept allows developers to transform collections into streams, and write code to process the data in parallel and then getting the results into a collection.

Because working with streams is a sensitive way of programming; I recommend designing the code by taking every possibility in mind. NullPointerException is one of the most common exceptions to be thrown in Java. In Java 8, the class Optional<T> was introduced to avoid this type of exceptions. Stream<T> instances are used to store an infinite instances of type T, while Optional<T> is an instance that might or might not contain an instance of type T. Because both of these implementations are basically wrappers for other types, they are covered together.

! For practical reasons, Stream instances are referred in this chapter as *streams*, in a similar manner as List instances are referred as *lists* and collection instances as *collections*, and many more.

! You might notice that the term *function* was introduced and refers to the methods called on streams or their arguments. This is because working with streams allows for Java code to be written in **functional programming** style. Java is an **object-oriented programming** language, and the **object** is its core term. In functional programming, the core term is *pure function*. Code is written by composing pure functions, which avoids shared states, takes advantage of immutable data, and avoids the side effects of processing contamination.[1]

---

[1] The following is a very good article about the functional programming paradigm and I gladly recommend you to read it: https://medium.com/javascript-scene/master-the-javascript-interview-what-is-functional-programming-7f218c68b3a0

CHAPTER 8 THE STREAM API

Creating Streams

Before having fun and optimizing our code using streams let's see how we can create them. To create a stream, we need a source. That source can be anything: a collection (list, set or map), an array, I/O resources used as input (such as files, databases, or anything that can be transformed into a sequence of instances).

A stream does not modify its source, so multiple stream instances can be created from the same source and used for different operations.

Creating Streams from Collections

In the introduction of the chapter, in the last snippet of code we were introduced to one method of creating a stream from a list. Starting with Java 8, all collection interfaces and classes were enriched with default methods that return streams. In the following code sample, we take a list of integers and transform it into a stream by calling its `stream()` method. After having a stream, we traverse it using the `forEach` method to print the values in the stream and the name of the execution thread this code is executed on. Why, the thread name you ask? You see shortly.

```
package com.apress.bgn.ch8;

import java.util.List;

public class StreamsDemo {
    public static void main(String... args) {
        List<Integer> bigList = List.of( 50, 10, 250, 100 ...);

        bigList.stream()
            .forEach(i ->
                System.out.println(Thread.currentThread().getName() + ": " + i)
            );
    }
}
```

The previous code creates a stream of integer elements. The Stream interface exposes a set of methods that each Stream implementation provides a concrete implementation for. The most used is the forEach method that iterates over the elements in the stream. The forEach method requires a parameter of type java.util.function.Consumer<T>.

! A *consumer* is what we call in this book an inline implementation of the java.util.function.Consumer<T> functional interface. This means it has only has one method that a class implementing it has to provide a concrete implementation for. The method named accept(T t), takes a stream element of type T as argument, processes it and returns nothing.

This method is called for each element in the stream, and the T is the type of the elements in the stream. The implementing class is basically declared inline by only mentioning the body of the method. The JVM does the rest, because of the magic of lambda expressions. Without them, you would have to write something like this:

```
import java.util.function.Consumer;
...
bigList.stream()
      .forEach(new Consumer<Integer>() {
          @Override
            public void accept(Integer i) {
               System.out.println(Thread.currentThread().getName() + ": " + i);
            }
});
```

Actually, this was the way you would write code before lambda expressions were introduced in Java 8. If you needed to create a single object of a class type implementing a specific interface, in a singular place in the application, you could choose to write a contraption like that, which looks like you are instantiating the interface; the result of that code is called an **anonymous class**. Lambda expressions simplified this process a lot, but only for a category of interfaces named *functional interfaces,* which define a single method and are annotated with the @FunctionalInterface annotation (starting in Java 8).

CHAPTER 8 THE STREAM API

In the previous example, the implementation prints the thread name and the value of the element. The following is the result is of running that code.

```
main: 50
main: 10
main: 250
main: 100
...
```

The fact that each number is prefixed with `main` means that all integers in the stream are processed sequentially by the same thread, and is the main thread of the application.

! For practical reasons, there is no need to call `stream()` for collections when a sequential stream is needed only for traversal, because the `forEach` method defined for them does the job well. So the preceding code can be reduced to

```java
bigList.forEach(i ->
      System.out.println(Thread.currentThread().getName() + ": " + i)
);
```

The name of the thread was printed because there is another way to create a stream by calling the `parallelStream()` method. The only difference is that the returned stream is a parallel stream. This means that each element of the stream is processed on a different thread. Of course, this means the implementation of the `Consumer` must be thread-safe and not contain code that involves instances that are not meant to be shared amongst threads. The code to print the value of a stream element, does not affect the value of the element returned by the stream, not other external object, so it is safe to parallelize. So let's use `parallelStream()` instead of `stream` to create a stream and print the elements of the stream using the same `Consumer` implementation.

```java
package com.apress.bgn.ch8;

import java.util.List;
import java.util.function.Consumer;

public class StreamsDemo {
    public static void main(String... args) {
        List<Integer> bigList = List.of( 50, 10, 250, 100 ...);
```

```
        bigList.parallelStream()
            .forEach(i ->
                System.out.println(Thread.currentThread().getName() + ": " + i)
        );
    }
}
```

If we execute the code in the console, we see something similar to the output, but slightly different.

```
ForkJoinPool.commonPool-worker-9: 94
ForkJoinPool.commonPool-worker-7: 10
ForkJoinPool.commonPool-worker-5: 40052
ForkJoinPool.commonPool-worker-3: 50
ForkJoinPool.commonPool-worker-13: 74
ForkJoinPool.commonPool-worker-9: 200
ForkJoinPool.commonPool-worker-11: 250
ForkJoinPool.commonPool-worker-7: 83
ForkJoinPool.commonPool-worker-3: 23
...
```

The first thing you notice is the thread name, we no longer have one, but a lot of them all named ForkJoinPool.commonPool-worker-**. This tells us that all stream elements are processed on different threads, but all of them are part of the same *pool*. A thread pool is created by the JVM in this case to contain a few thread instances, used to process all elements in the stream in parallel. The advantage of using a thread pool is that the threads can be reused, so no new thread instances need to be created and this optimizes the execution time a little, but it is visible only in more complex solutions. If you look at the number associated to each thread, the number at the end of the thread name, you can see that the numbers sometimes repeat. This basically means the same thread was reused to process another stream element.

Creating Streams from Arrays

The streams we have used so far, were created from a List instance. The same syntax can be used for Set instances as well.

CHAPTER 8 THE STREAM API

But streams can be created from arrays as well. Look at the following piece of code.

```java
package com.apress.bgn.ch8;

import java.util.Arrays;
public class ArrayStreamDemo {

    public static void main(String... args) {
        int[] arr = { 50, 10, 250, 100 ...};

        Arrays.stream(arr).forEach(
            i -> System.out.println(Thread.currentThread().getName() + ": " + i)
        );
    }
}
```

The static method `stream(int[] array)` from the utility class `Arrays` creates a stream of primitives. For arrays that contain objects, the method called is `stream(T[] array)` (where T is a generic type) that is replaced with the type of the elements in the array. Streams generated from arrays can be parallelized by calling the `parallel` methods, which exist for parallel streams as well. So, the following code can be parallelized, as shown.

```java
package com.apress.bgn.ch8;

import java.util.Arrays;
public class ArrayStreamDemo {

    public static void main(String... args) {
        int[] arr = { 50, 10, 250, 100 ...};

        Arrays.stream(arr).parallel().forEach(
            i -> System.out.println(Thread.currentThread().getName() + ": " + i)
        );
    }
}
```

For both cases, the output is the same as in the previous examples, so there is no need to depict it again.

The novelty with arrays is that a stream can be created form a part of the array by specifying the start and the end indexes for the array chunk.

```
Arrays.stream(arr, 3,6).forEach(
   i -> System.out.println(Thread.currentThread().getName() + ": " + i)
);
```

Creating Empty Streams

When writing Java code, a good practice is to write methods that return objects by avoiding returning `null` to reduce the possibility of `NullPointerExceptions` being thrown. When methods return streams, the preferred way is to return an empty stream. This can be done by calling the static `Stream.empty()` method of the `Stream` interface. The following method, receives a list of `Song` instances as a parameter and returns a stream using it as a source. If the list is `null` or empty, an empty stream is returned.

```
public static Stream<Song> asStream(List<Song> inputList) {
        if (inputList == null || inputList.isEmpty()) {
            return Stream.empty();
        } else {
            return inputList.stream();
        }
}
```

Creating Finite Streams

Aside from creating streams from actual sources, streams can be created on the spot by calling stream utility methods like `Stream.generate()` or `Stream.builder()`.

The `builder()` method should be used when we want to build a limited stream with a fixed sets of known values. This method returns an instance of `java.util.stream.Stream.Builder<T>`, an internal interface that declare a default method named `add(..)` that needs to be called to add the elements of the stream. To create the `Stream` instance, its `build` method must be finally called. The `add(..)` method returns a reference to the `Builder` instance so it can be chained with any other methods of this class. The following code is a sample of how the `builder()` method can be used to create a finite stream of `Integer` values.

CHAPTER 8   THE STREAM API

```
Stream<Integer> built = Stream.<Integer>builder()
    .add(50).add(10).add(250).build();
```

As the `Builder` interface is a generic one, it is mandatory to specify a type argument, as the type of the elements in the stream. Also, the `builder()` method is generic and requires the type to be provided as a parameter in front of it, right before being called. If no type is specified the default `Object` is used.

To create a stream, the `generate(..)` method can also be used. This method receives as a parameter an instance of type `java.util.function.Supplier<T>` instance.

! A *supplier* is what we call in this book an inline implementation of the `java.util.function.Supplier<T>` functional interface. This interface requires a concrete implementation to be provided for its single method named `get()`. This method should return the element to be added to the stream.

So, if we want to generate a stream of integers, a proper implementation for `get()` should return a random integer. The expanded code is depicted next; no lambda expressions are used to make it clear that the `get(..)` receives as a parameter a `Supplier<Integer>` instance created on the spot.

```
Stream<Integer> generated = Stream.generate(
        new Supplier<Integer>() {
            @Override
            public Integer get() {
                Random rand = new Random();
                return rand.nextInt(300) + 1;
            }
        }
).limit(15);
```

The `limit` method limits the number of elements generated by the supplier to 15; otherwise, the generated stream is infinite. If we make use of lambda expressions, the previous code reduces to

```
Stream<Integer> generated = Stream.generate(
    () -> new Random().nextInt(300) + 1
).limit(15);
```

But this is not all; if Supplier<Integer>.get() always returns the same number, no matter how useless it is, it can be done and the previous code becomes

```
Stream<Integer> generated = Stream.generate( () -> 5).limit(15);
```

If more control is needed over the elements in the stream, the iterate(..) method can be used. It was introduced in Java 9 and using this method is like having a for statement generate the entries for the stream. The method receives as arguments an initial value called a seed, a *predicate* that determines when the iteration should stop, and an iteration step.

! A *predicate* is an inline implementation of the functional interface java.util.function.Predicate<T> that declares a single method that returns a boolean value. The implementation of this method should test its single argument of type T against a condition and return true if the condition is fulfilled and false if not.

In the following example, stream elements are generated, starting from 0, using a step of 5 and they are generated as long as the values are lesser than 50, as defined by the predicate.

```
Stream<Integer> iterated = Stream.iterate(0, i -> i < 50 , i -> i + 5);
```

As with the for statement, the termination condition is not mandatory and there is an iterate(...) method version that does not require a predicate, but in this case the limit(...) method must be used to make sure the stream is finite.

```
Stream<Integer> iterated = Stream.iterate(0,    i -> i + 5).limit(15);
```

The first element of the stream is the seed value.

In Java 9 aside from limit() there is another way to control the numbers of values in a stream: the takeWhile(..) operation. This method takes the longest set of elements from the original stream that matches the predicate received as argument, starting with the first element. This works fine for ordered streams, but if the stream is unordered the result is, any set of elements that match the predicate, including an empty one. Let's see it in action! The first code sample uses takeWhile(..) on a stream of integers and returns a stream with elements that divide by 3.

```
Stream<Integer> forTaking = Stream.of( 3, 6, 9, 11, 12, 13, 15);
forTaking.takeWhile(s -> s % 3 == 0)
   .forEach(s -> System.out.print(s + " "));
```

The code prints *3 6 9* because this is the first set of elements that match the given predicate. If `takeWhile(..)` is called on an unordered stream, the result is unpredictable. The result might be *3 6 9* or *12 36 18 42*, as the result is a subset of any elements matching the predicate. So the result of `takeWhile(..)` on an unordered stream is non-deterministic.

```
Stream<Integer> forTaking = Stream.of( 3, 6, 9, 2, 4, 8, 12, 36, 18, 42, 11, 13);
forTaking.parallel().takeWhile(s -> s % 3 == 0)
   .forEach(s -> System.out.print(s + " "));
```

The `takeWhile(..)` operation is the "sister" of the `dropWhile(..)`; and does exactly the reverse of what `takeWhile(..)` does: it returns, for an ordered stream, a stream consisting elements after dropping the longest set of elements that match the predicate. So in the following example, we expect the following elements to be printed in the console: *11 12 13 15*

```
Stream<Integer> forDropping = Stream.of( 3, 6, 9, 11, 12, 13, 15);
forDropping.dropWhile(s -> s % 3 == 0 )
    .forEach(s -> System.out.print(s + " "));
```

The result of this operation for unordered streams is also non-deterministic, as the operation can drop any set, including the empty one.

If these two operations are executed on parallel streams, the only thing that changes is the order in which the elements are printed, but the result sets contain the same elements.

Streams of Primitives and Streams of Strings

When we first created a stream of primitives, we used an `int[]` array as a source. But streams of primitives can be created in a different way, because the *Stream API* contains more interfaces with default methods to make programming with streams practical. Figure 8-1 shows the `Stream` hierarchy. The `IntStream` interface can be used to create primitive streams of integers. This interface exposes many methods to do so, some of them inherited from `BaseStream`. An `IntStream` instance can be created from a few values specified on the spot, either by using the builder(), generate(), or iterate() methods or by using the of method, as depicted next.

IntStream intStream0 = IntStream.builder().add(0).add(1).add(2).add(5).build();

IntStream intStream1 = IntStream.of(0,1,2,3,4,5);

An IntStream instance can be created by giving the start and end of an interval as arguments to the range() and rangeClosed(). Both of them generate elements for the stream, with a step of 1, only the last one includes the upper range of the interval as a value.

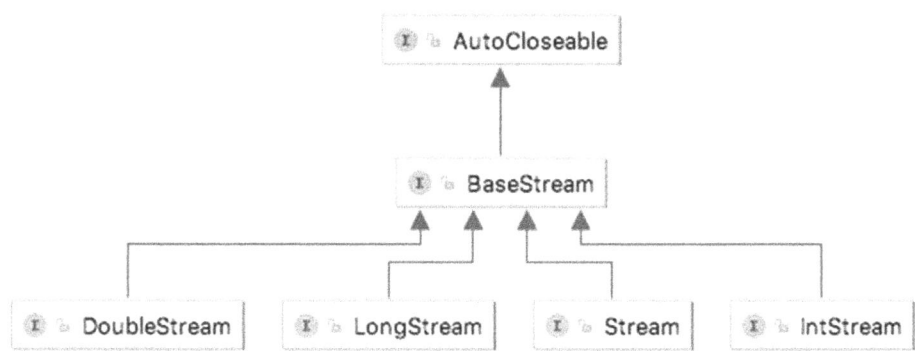

Figure 8-1. Stream API interfaces

intStream2 = IntStream.range(0, 10);

intStream3 = IntStream.rangeClosed(0, 10);

Also, in Java 1.8 the java.util.Random class was enriched with a method named ints that generates a stream of random integers. It declares a single argument that represents the number of elements to be generated and put in the stream, but there is a form of this method without the argument that generates an infinite stream.

Random random = new Random();
intStream = random.ints(5);

All the methods mentioned for IntStream can generate LongStream instances, because equivalent methods are defined in this interface. There are no range methods for DoubleStream, but there is the of() method, builder(), generate() and so on. Also, the java.util.Random class was enriched in Java 1.8 with the doubles() method that generates a stream of random double values. It declares a single argument that represents the number of elements to be generated and put in the stream, but there is a form of this method without the argument that generates an infinite stream. In the following code snippet, a few ways of creating streams of doubles are depicted.

```
DoubleStream doubleStream0 = DoubleStream.of(1, 2 , 2.3, 3.4, 4.5, 6);

Random random = new Random();
DoubleStream doubleStream1 = random.doubles(3);

DoubleStream doubleStream2 = DoubleStream.iterate(2.5, d -> d = d + 0.2).
limit(10);
```

For streams of char values there is no special interface, but IntStream can be used just fine.

```
IntStream intStream = IntStream.of('a','b','c','d');
intStream.forEach(c -> System.out.println((char) c));
```

Another way to create a stream of char values is to use a String instance as a stream source.

```
IntStream charStream = "sample".chars();
charStream.forEach(c -> System.out.println((char) c));
```

In Java 8, the java.util.regex.Pattern was enriched with stream specific methods too; as a class used to process String instances, it is the proper place to add these methods after all. A Pattern instance can be used to split an existing String instance and return the pieces as a stream using the splitAsStream(..) method.

```
Stream<String> stringStream = Pattern.compile(" ")
        .splitAsStream("live your life");
```

The contents of a file can also be returned as a stream of strings using the Files.lines(..) utility method.

```
String inputPath = "chapter08/src/main/resources/songs.csv";
Stream<String> stringStream = Files.lines(Path.of(inputPath));
```

The sections so far have shown you how to create all types of streams; the next sections show you how to use them to process data.

> ! If you feel the need to associate stream instances with real objects to make sense of them, I recommend the following: imagine a finite stream(like one created from a collection) as the water dripping from a mug when inclined. The water in the mug will end eventually, but while the water drips, it forms a stream. An infinite stream is like a river that has a fountain head, it flows continuously. (well, unless a serious drought dries the river, of course)

A Short Introduction to Optional

The `java.util.Optional<T>` instances are the Schrödinger[2] boxes of the Java Language. They are very useful because they can be used as a return type for methods to avoid returning a `null` value, and cause either a possible `NullPointerException` to be thrown, or the developer using the method to write extra code to treat the possibility of an exception being thrown. `Optional<T>` instances can be created in similar way to streams.

There is an `empty()` method for creating an optional value of any type that does not contain anything.

```
Optional<Song> empty = Optional.empty();
```

There is an `of()` method used to wrap an existing object into an `Optional<T>`.

```
Optional<Long> value = Optional.of(5L);
```

Considering that these type of instances were designed to not allow `null` values and the way the `Optional<T>` instance was created previously, what would stop us to write something like the following?

```
Song song = null;
Optional<Song> nullable = Optional.of(song);
```

The compiler wouldn't, but when the code is executed at runtime, a `NullPointer Exception` is thrown. Still, if we really need an `Optional<T>` instance to permit null values, it is possible, there's an utility method was introduced in Java 9 just for that.

```
Song song = null;
Optional<Song>  nullable = Optional.ofNullable(song);
```

---

[2]Read about it at https://en.wikipedia.org/wiki/Schr%C3%B6dinger%27s_cat

CHAPTER 8 THE STREAM API

Now that we have `Optional<T>` instances, what can we do with them? We use them. Let's take a look at the following code.

```
package com.apress.bgn.ch8;

import com.apress.bgn.ch8.util.MediaLoader;
import com.apress.bgn.ch8.util.Song;

import java.util.List;

public class OptionalDemo {
    public static void main(String... args) {
        List<Song> songs = MediaLoader.loadSongs();
        song = findFirst(songs, "B.B. King");
        if(song != null && song.getSinger().equals("The Thrill Is Gone")) {
            System.out.println("Good stuff!");
        } else {
            System.out.println("not found!");
        }
    }

    public static Song findFirst(List<Song> songs, String singer) {
        for (Song song: songs) {
            if (singer.equals(song.getSinger())) {
                return song;
            }
        }
        return null;
    }
}
```

The `findFirst(..)` method looks for the first song in the list that has the singer equal to "B.B. King", returns it and prints a message if found, and another if not. You can notice the nullability test and iteration of the list. In Java 8, both of them are no longer necessary.

```
Optional<Song> opt = songs.stream()
    .filter(s -> "B.B. King".equals(s.getSinger()))
    .findFirst();
opt.ifPresent(r -> System.out.println(r.getTitle()));
```

296

If the `Optional<T>` instance is not empty, the song title is printed, otherwise, nothing is printed, and the code continues from that point on without an exception being thrown. But what if we want to print something when the `Optional<T>` instance is empty? In Java 11, we can do something about that, because a method named `isEmpty()` was introduced to test the `Optional<T>` instance contents.

```
  Optional<Song> opt = songs.stream()
     .filter(s -> "B.B. King".equals(s.getSinger()))
     .findFirst();
if(opt.isEmpty()) {
    System.out.println("Not found!");
}
```

But wait, this is a little bit… not right. Can't we have a method to call on an `Optional<T>` to get the exact behavior as an `if-else` statement? Well, that was possible starting with Java 9; the `ifPresentOrElse(..)` that takes as arguments a consumer to process the contents of the `Optional<T>` instance when is not empty and a `Runner` instance to execute when the `Optional<T>` instance is empty.

```
Optional<Song> opt = songs.stream()
        .filter(ss -> "B.B. King".equals(ss.getSinger())).findFirst();
opt.ifPresentOrElse(
    r -> System.out.println(r.getTitle()),
    () -> System.out.println("Not found!")) ;
```

If the `Optional<T>` instance is not empty, its contents can be extracted by calling the `get()` method.

```
Optional<Song> opt2 = songs.stream()
   .filter(ss -> "Rob Thomas".equals(ss.getSinger()))
   .findFirst();
System.out.println("Found Song " + opt2.get());
```

The code does not print anything when the desired object is not found. But if we want to print a default value for example, we can do that as well using a method named `orElse()`.

```
Optional<Song> opt = songs.stream()
    .filter(ss -> "B.B. King".equals(ss.getSinger()))
    .findFirst();
opt.ifPresent(r -> System.out.println(r.getTitle()));

Song defaultSong = new Song();
defaultSong.setTitle("Untitled");

Song s = opt.orElse (defaultSong);
System.out.println("Found: " + s.getTitle());
```

If we were interested to throw a specific exception when the Optional<T> is empty, there is a method for that as well, named orElseThrow(..)

```
Optional<Song> opt = songs.stream()
    .filter(s -> "B.B. King".equals(s.getSinger()))
    .findFirst();
Song song = opt.orElseThrow(IllegalArgumentException::new);
```

As you probably noticed in the code samples, Optional<T> and Stream<T> can be combined to write practical code to solve complex solutions. As there are a lot of methods that can be applied to Optional<T> and Stream<T> instances as well, the next sections introduce them for streams and randomly make reference to Optional<T> as well.

How to Use Streams

After creating a stream, the next thing is to process the data on the stream. The result of that processing is another stream that can be further processed as many times as needed. There are a few methods to use to process a stream and return the result as another stream. These methods are called *intermediate operations*. The methods that do not return a stream but actual data structures, or nothing, are named *terminal operations*. All these are defined in the Stream interface. The key feature of streams is that the processing of data using streams is only done when the *terminal operation* is initiated and elements from source are consumed only as needed. So you could say that the whole stream process is well, lazy. Lazy loading of source elements and processing them when needed allows significant optimizations.

After the previous affirmations, you probably realized that the `forEach` method that was used to print values from the streams is a terminal operation. But there are a few that you'll likely need for the most common implementations.

This chapter started with an example of Song instances, but the Song class was not listed yet. You can see its contents in the following code listing.

```java
package com.apress.bgn.ch8.util;

public class Song {
    private Long id;
    private String singer;
    private String title;
    private Integer duration;
    private AudioType audioType;

    ... //getters and setters
    ... // toString
}
```

The `AudioType` is an enum containing the types of audio files and is depicted in the following code snippet.

```java
package com.apress.bgn.ch8.util;

public enum AudioType {
    MP3,
    FLAC,
    OGG,
    AAC,
    M4A,
    WMA
}
```

And now that the data type that is used on the following stream examples is depicted, the data should be depicted as well. In the example in the book, the data is contained into a file named `songs.csv`. The CSV extension denotes a *comma separated file*, and each Song instance matches a line in the file. Each line contains all the property values of each Song instance, separated by columns. Other separators can be used, semi-colons were used here for practical reasons(that is the default supported by the library reading the data). The contents of the file are depicted next.

```
ID;SINGER;TITLE;DURATION;AUDIOTYPE
01;John Mayer;New Light;206;FLAC
02;John Mayer;My Stupid Mouth;225;M4A
03;John Mayer;Vultures;247;FLAC
04;John Mayer;Edge of Desire;333;MP3
05;John Mayer;In Repair;372;MP3
05;Rob Thomas;Paper Dolls;185;MP3
07;The Script;Mad Love;207;MP3
08;Seth MacFarlane;No One Ever Tells You;244;MP3
09;Nat King Cole;Orange Colored Sky;154;MP3
10;Vertical Horizon;Forever;246;MP3
11;Mario Lanza;Temptation;141;M4A
12;Jack Radics;No Matter;235;MP3
13;George Michael;Fastlove;306;MP3
14;Childish Gambino;Freaks And Geeks;227;M4A
15;Bill Evans;Lover Man;304;MP3
16;Darren Hayes;Like It Or Not;381;MP3
17;Stevie Wonder;Superstition;284;MP3
18;Tony Bennett;It Had To Be You;196;MP3
19;Tarja Turunen;An Empty Dream;322;MP3
20;Lykke Li;Little bit;231;M4A
```

Each line in the file is transformed into a Song instance by using classes in a library named Josefa.[3] This library is not the topic of this book, but if you are interested, you can use the link in the footnote to get more information from the official site.

Terminal Functions: forEach and forEachOrdered

And now we are ready to start playing with streams. Assuming the songs stream provides all instances declared, let's first print all the elements on the stream.

```
package com.apress.bgn.ch8;

import com.apress.bgn.ch8.util.Song;
import com.apress.bgn.ch8.util.StreamMediaLoader;
```

---

[3]JSefa (Java Simple exchange format API) is a simple library for stream-based serialization of Java objects to XML, CSV, and FLR. More about it at http://jsefa.sourceforge.net/

```
import java.util.List;
import java.util.stream.Stream;

public class MediaStreamTester {
    public static void main(String... args) {
        Stream<Song> songs = StreamMediaLoader.loadSongs();
        songs.forEach(song -> System.out.println(song));
    }
}
```

Because we are using Java 11 by now, we can make use of method references introduced in Java 8. Method references are a shortcut for cases when a lambda expression does nothing else than call a method, so the method can be referred by name directly. So this line

```
songs.forEach(song -> System.out.println(song));
```

becomes

```
songs.forEach(System.out::println);
```

The `forEach(..)` method receives an instance of `Consumer<T>` as an argument. In the two previous examples, the implementation of the `accept()` method contained only a call to `System.out.println(song)` and that is why the code is so compact, but if the implementation of this method would contain more statements then the compact code previously written would not be possible.

Instead of printing the songs directly, let's first uppercase the singer name. The code would look like this:

```
songs.forEach(new Consumer<Song>() {
  @Override
   public void accept(Song song) {
        song.setSinger(song.getSinger().toUpperCase());
        System.out.println(song);
   }
});
```

Of course, it can be simplified using lambda expressions.

```
songs.forEach(song -> {
    song.setSinger(song.getSinger().toUpperCase());
    System.out.println(song);
});
```

The sister function, forEachOrdered(..), does the same thing as forEach(..), with one little difference, ensure that the elements on the stream is processed element is processed in encounter order, if such order is defined, even if the stream is a parallel one. So basically the following two lines, print the songs in the same order.

```
songs.forEach(System.out::println);
songs.parallel().forEachOrdered(System.out::println);
```

Intermediate Operation filter and Terminal Operation toArray

In the following example, we select all MP3 songs and save them to an array. Selecting all MP3 songs is done using the filter(..) method. This method receives an argument of type Predicate<? super T> that defines a condition that the elements of the stream must pass to be put into the array that results by calling the terminal method named toArray(..).

The toArray(..) receives an argument of type IntFunction<A[]>. This type of function takes an integer as argument and generates an array of that size, which is populated by the toArray() method.

The code to filter the MP3 entries and put them into an array of type Song[] is depicted next.

```
Song sarray = songs.filter(s -> s.getAudioType() == AudioType.MP3)
        .toArray(Song::new);
```

Intermediate Operations map and flatMap and Terminal Operation collect

In the following example we process all the songs and calculate the duration in minutes. To do this, we use the `map` method to associate each song with the method processing it. This result is a stream of `Integer` values. All of its elements are added to a `List<Integer>` using the `collect(..)` method. This method accumulates the elements as they are processed into a `Collection` instance.

```java
package com.apress.bgn.ch8.util;
public class SongTransformer {
    public static int processDuration(Song song) {
        int secs = song.getDuration();
        return secs/60;
    }
}
...
List<Integer> durationAsMinutes =  songs
    .map(SongTransformer::processDuration)
    .collect(Collectors.toList());
```

The `map(..)` method receives an argument of type `Function<T,R>` which is basically a reference to a function to apply on each element of the stream. The function we applied in the previous example takes a song element from the stream, gets its duration and transforms it into minutes and returns it.

The reference to it can be written as

```java
Function<Song,Integer> fct = SongTransformer::processDuration;
```

The first generic type is the type of the element processed and the second is the type of the result returned.

A version of the `filter` method is defined for the `Optional` type and can be used to avoid writing complicated `if` statements, together with the `map` method. Let's assume we have a `Song` instance and we want to check if it is more than three minutes and less than 10 minutes long. Instead of writing an `if` statement with two conditions connected by an AND operator, we can use an `Optional<Song>` and those two methods to do the same.

CHAPTER 8   THE STREAM API

```
public static boolean isMoreThan3Mins(Song song) {
    return Optional.ofNullable(song)
        .map(SongTransformer::processDuration)
        .filter(d -> d >= 3)
        .filter(d -> d <= 10)
        .isPresent();
}
```

So, the map(..) is quite powerful, but it has a small flaw. If we take a look at its signature in the Stream.java file, this is what we see:

`<R> Stream<R> map(Function<? super T, ? extends R> mapper);`

So, if the map function is applied to each element in the stream and returns a stream with the result, which is placed into another stream that contains all results, the collect(...) method is called on a Stream<Stream<Integer>>. The same goes for Optional<T>, the terminal method is called on a <Optional<Optional<T>>>. When the objects are simple, like we have here Song instances, the map(..) method works quite well, but if the objects in the original stream are more complex, let's say a List<List<Integer>>, things get complicated. In a case like this the map method should be replaced with flatMap. The easiest way to show the effects of the flatMap(..) is to apply it exactly on a List<List<Integer>>. Let's take a look at the following example.

```
List<List<Integer>> testList = List.of (List.of(2,3), List.of(4,5),
List.of(6,7));
System.out.println(processList(testList));
...
public static List<Integer> processList( List<List<Integer>> list) {
    List<Integer> result = list
        .stream()
        .flatMap(Collection::stream)
        .collect(Collectors.toList());
    return result;
}
```

The flatMap(..) method receives as argument a reference to a method that takes a collection and transforms it into a stream, the most simple way to create a Stream<Stream<Integer>>. The flatMap(..) does its magic and the result is

304

transformed into `<Stream<Integer>>` and the elements are then collected by the `collect` method into a `List<String>`. The operation of removing the useless stream wrapper is called *flattening*.

Another way to see the effect of the `flatMap(..)` method is to write a simpler example with `Optional`. Let's say we need a function that transforms a string into an integer and if the string is not a valid number we want to avoid returning null. This means that our function must take a string and return `Optional<Integer>`.

```
Function<String, Optional<Integer>> toIntOpt = OptionalDemo::toIntOpt;
 ...
public static Optional<Integer> toIntOpt(String string) {
        try {
            return Optional.of(Integer.parseInt(string));
        } catch (NumberFormatException e) {
            return Optional.empty();
        }
}
```

Now that we have our function, let's use it.

```
Optional<String> str = Optional.of("42");
Optional<Optional<Integer>> resInt = str.map(toIntOpt);

// flatten it
Optional<Integer> desiredRes = resInt.orElse(Optional.empty());
System.out.println("finally: " + desiredRes.get());
```

If we want to get to the `Optional` instance that we are really interested in, we have to get rid of the external `Optional` wrapper. If we use `flatMap(..)`, we do not need to do that.

```
Optional<String> str = Optional.of("42");
Optional<Integer> desiredRes = str.flatMap(toIntOpt);
System.out.println("boom: " + desiredRes.get());
```

So yeah, there is a slight difference between these two methods, which you probably would have never investigated; as in most cases when working with streams the `map()` method is usually terminated with `collect(..)`.

Intermediate Operation sorted and Terminal Operation findFirst

As the name says the `sorted()` method has something to do with sorting. When called on a stream, it creates another stream with all the elements of the initial stream, but sorted in their natural order. If the type of elements on the stream is not comparable (the type does not implement `java.lang.Comparable`, a `java.lang.ClassCastException` is thrown). And since we are going to use this method to get a stream of sorted elements, we use `findFirst()` to get the first element in the stream. This method returns an `Optional<T>`, because the stream might be empty.

```
List<String> pieces = List.of("some","of", "us", "we're", "hardly",
"ever", "here");
String first = pieces.stream().sorted().findFirst().get();
System.out.println("First from sorted list: " + first);
```

This code prints ever because that is the first element in the sorted stream.

Intermediate Operation distinct and Terminal Operation count

The `distinct()` method takes a stream and generates a stream with all the distinct elements of the original stream. And because we need a terminal function, let's use `count()`; as the name says, this function counts the elements of the stream.

```
List<String> pieces = List.of("as","long", "as", "there", "is",
      "you", "there", "is", "me");
long count = pieces.stream().distinct().count();
System.out.println("Elements in the stream: " + count);
```

If the code is run, the number printed is 6, because after removing the duplicate terms (as, there, is), we are left with six terms.

Intermediate Operation limit and Terminal Operations min and max

The `limit(..)` method was used in this chapter before to transform a infinite stream into a finite one. As it transforms a stream into another stream, clearly this is an intermediate function. To see it in action, we will use a stream of integers and we'll use as terminal methods two mathematical functions: to calculate the minimum of the elements in the stream - `min()` and to calculate the maximum of the elements fn the stream - `max()`. How to use these functions together is depicted in the following code snippet.

```
Stream<Integer> ints = Stream.of(5,2,7,9,8,1,12,7,2);
ints.limit(4).min(Integer::compareTo)
     .ifPresent(min -> System.out.println("Min is: " + min));
// Prints "Min is: 2"

Stream<Integer> ints = Stream.of(5,2,7,9,8,1,12,7,2);
ints.limit(4).max(Integer::compareTo)
     .ifPresent(max -> System.out.println("Max is: " + max));
// Prints "Max is: 9"
```

Terminal Operations sum and reduce

Let's consider the scenario: we have a finite stream of Song values and we want to calculate the sum of their durations. The code to do this is depicted in the following listing, and the use of another stream terminal function that can be used only on numeric streams.

```
Stream<Song> songs = StreamMediaLoader.loadSongs();
Integer totalDuration = songs
        .mapToInt(Song::getDuration)
        .sum();
```

The same result can be obtained using the `reduce(..)` function.

```
Stream<Song> songs = StreamMediaLoader.loadSongs();
Integer totalDuration = songs
        .mapToInt(Song::getDuration)
        .reduce(0, (a, b) -> a + b);
```

The reduce functions takes two arguments.

- The identity argument represented the initial version of the reduction and the default result if there are no elements in the stream

- The accumulator function takes two parameters; the operation is applied on to get a partial result (in this case is the addition of those two elements)

So basically, every time an element of the stream is processed, the accumulator returns a new value that is the result of adding the processed element with the previous partial result. So, if the result of the process is a collection, the accumulator's result is a collection, so every time a stream element is processed a new collection would be created. This is pretty inefficient, so in scenarios like this the collect function is more suitable.

Intermediate Operation peek

This function is special because it really doesn't affect the stream results in any way. The peek function returns a stream consisting of the elements of the stream it is called on while also performing for each element the operation specified by its Consumer<T> argument. This means that this function can be used to debug stream operations.

Let's take our stream of Song instances and filter them by their duration. Select all the ones with a duration >300 seconds, and then get their titles and collect them in a list. The following code shows how to do this.

```
Stream<Song> songs = StreamMediaLoader.loadSongs();
List<String> result = songs.filter(s -> s.getDuration() > 300)
    .map(Song::getTitle)
    .collect(Collectors.toList());
```

Before the map call, a peek call can be introduced to check if the filtered elements are the ones you expect. Another peek call can be introduced after to inspect the mapped value.

```
Stream<Song> songs = StreamMediaLoader.loadSongs();
List<String> result = songs.filter(s -> s.getDuration() > 300)
    .peek(e -> System.out.println("\t Filtered value: " + e))
    .map(Song::getTitle)
    .peek(e -> System.out.println("\t Mapped value: " + e))
    .collect(Collectors.toList());
```

Intermediate Operation skip and Terminal Operations findAny, anyMatch, allMatch, and noneMatch

These are the last operations discussed in this chapter, so they are coupled together because the skip operation might affect the result of the others.

The findAny() returns an Optional<T> instance that contains the first element of the stream or an empty Optional<T> instance when the stream is empty. When the stream is parallel, the function returns a random element of the stream wrapped into an Optional<T>. Because the stream of songs we've been using so far is not a parallel one, we create a parallel stream by calling the intermediate function parallel().

```
Stream<Song> songs = StreamMediaLoader.loadSongs();
Optional<Song> optSong = songs.parallel().findAny();
optSong.ifPresent(System.out::println);
```

The anyMatch(..) method receives an argument of type Predicate<T> and returns a boolean true value if there is any elements in the stream that match the predicate, and false otherwise. It works on parallel streams as well. The scenario the next code covers is to return true id any of the songs in our stream has a title containing the word *Paper*.

```
Stream<Song> songs = StreamMediaLoader.loadSongs();
boolean b = songs
        .anyMatch(s -> s.getTitle().contains("Paper"));
System.out.println("Are there songs with title containing 'Paper'? " + b);
```

The code prints true because there is song on the list called *Paper Dolls*. But, if we want to change that result, all we have to do is skip processing the first six elements in the original stream by calling skip(6). Yes, this method works on parallel streams as well.

```
Stream<Song> songs = StreamMediaLoader.loadSongs();
boolean b = songs.parallel()
        .skip(6)
        .anyMatch(s -> s.getTitle().contains("Paper"));
System.out.println("Are there songs with title containing \"Paper\"? " + b);
```

And so, if the first six elements in the original stream were not processed, now the previous code returns false. There is another function that analyses all elements of a stream checking if they all match a single predicate, and that method is called

CHAPTER 8   THE STREAM API

allMatch(..). In the next code sample, we check if all Song instances have duration bigger than 300. The function returns a boolean, and the value is true of all Song instances match the predicate and false otherwise. For our example, we are obviously expecting a false value, because not all of our Song instances have the duration field value bigger than 300.

```
Stream<Song> songs = StreamMediaLoader.loadSongs();
boolean b = songs.allMatch(s -> s.getDuration() > 300);
System.out.println("Are all songs longer than 5 minutes? " + b);
```

The pair of this function is a function named noneMatch and does exactly the opposite thing: takes a predicate as an argument and returns a boolean. The value of this boolean is true if none of the stream elements match the predicate provided as argument, and false otherwise. In the next code sample, we check using the noneMatch if there is no Song instance with duration > 300 and we expect the result to be false.

```
Stream<Song> songs = StreamMediaLoader.loadSongs();
boolean b = songs.noneMatch(s -> s.getDuration() > 300);
System.out.println("Are all songs shorter than 5 minutes? " + b);
```

Debugging Stream Code

The peek(..) method can be used for a light debugging, more like logging the changes that happen on stream elements between one stream method call and another. A more advanced way to debug streams is provided by the IntelliJ IDEA editor; starting on May 11, 2017, this editor includes a specialized plugin, called the Java Stream Debugger, for stream debugging.[4]

I am assuming that you already have a version of IntelliJ IDEA that is more recent than 2017, so you should already have this plugin. To use it, you have to place a breakpoint on the line where a stream processing chain is defined. Figure 8-2 shows a piece of code representing the processing of a stream of Song instances executed in debug and a breakpoint paused the execution in line 44. When the execution is paused the Stream debugger view can be opened by clicking the button that is surrounded in the red rectangle.

---

[4]Official blogpost from JetBrains, the company that created and maintains IntelliJ IDEA https://plugins.jetbrains.com/plugin/9696-java-stream-debugger?platform=hootsuite

CHAPTER 8　THE STREAM API

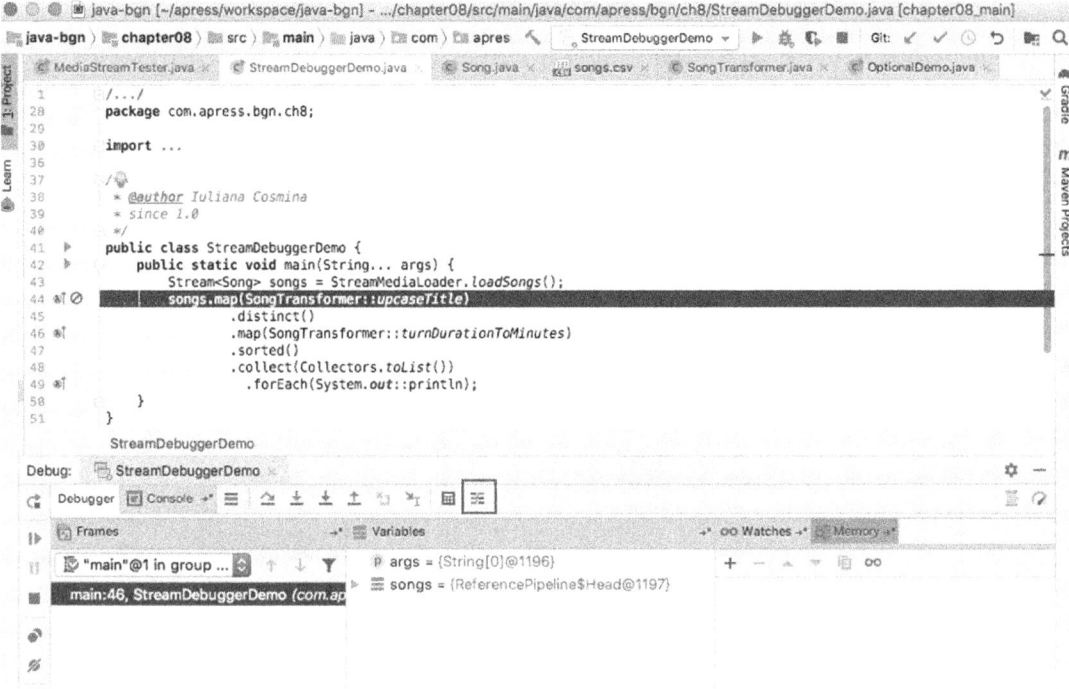

Figure 8-2. *Debugging*

If you click the debugger button shown in Figure 8-2, a pop-up window appears; it has a tab for each operation of the stream processing. Figure 8-3 shows the tabs and their methods underlined and linked to each other.

CHAPTER 8 THE STREAM API

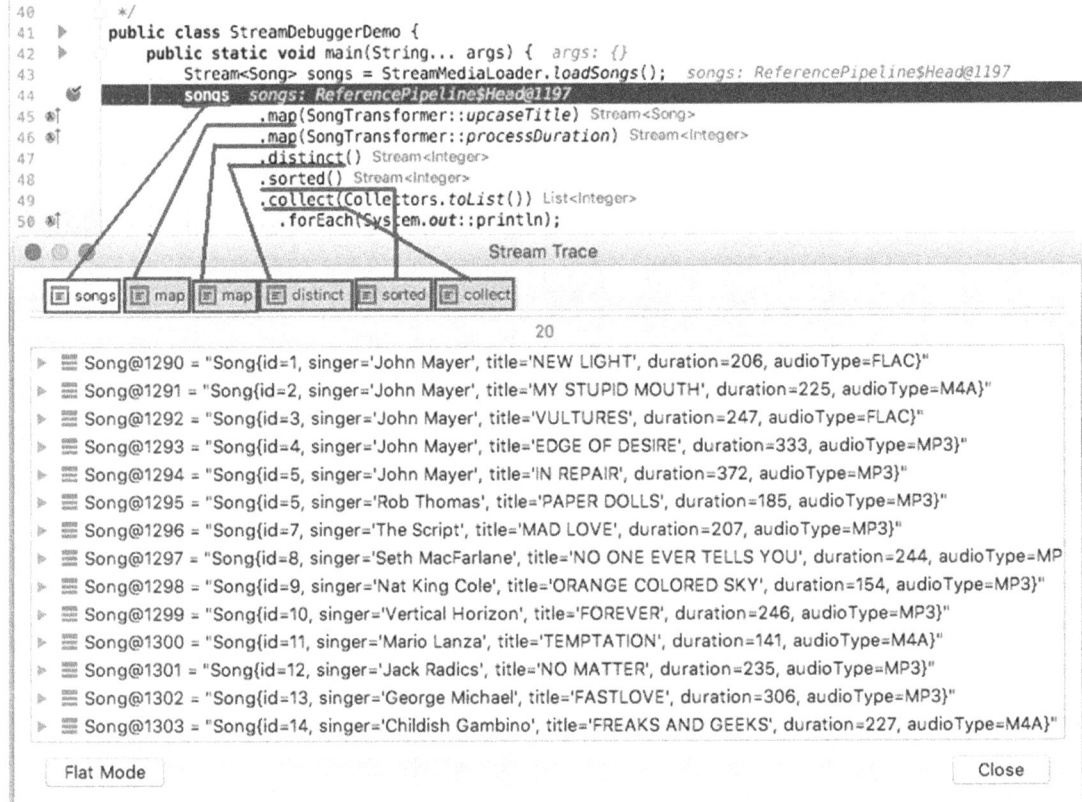

Figure 8-3. The Java Stream Debugger window

In each of the tabs, the text box on the left contains the elements on the original stream and on the text box on the right contains the resulting stream with its elements. For operations that reduce the number of elements or change their order there are lines from one set of elements to the other. The first map method transforms the song titles to their uppercase versions. The second map method transforms the duration of the songs in minutes and returns a stream of integers. The distinct method produces a new stream that contains only the distinct elements, and this operation's effect is depicted nicely in Figure 8-4.

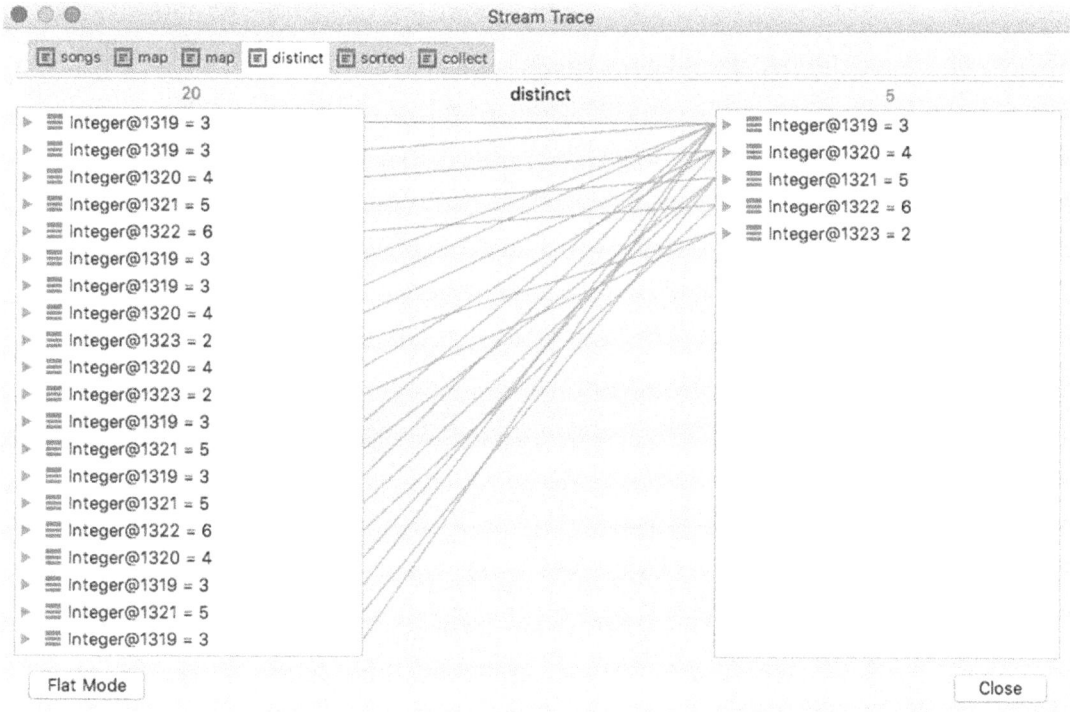

Figure 8-4. *The distinct() operation in the IntelliJ IDEA stream debugger*

The next operation is sorted() that sort the entries on the stream returned by the distinct() operation. The reordering of the elements and adding them to a new stream is depicted in the debugger also and in Figure 8-5.

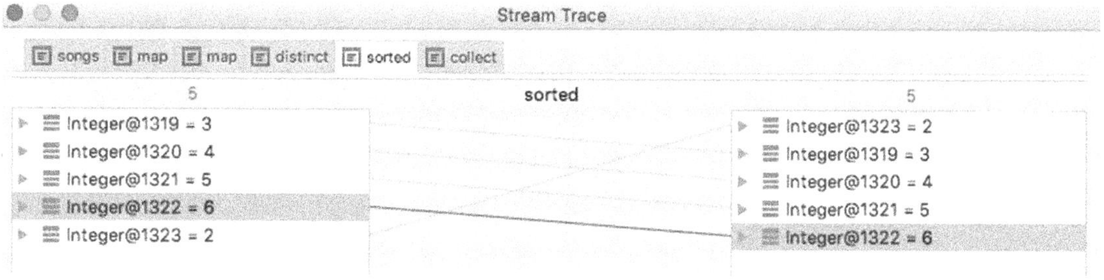

Figure 8-5. *The sorted() operation in the IntelliJ IDEA stream debugger*

Of course, after inspecting the results in the debugger, even if you want to continue the execution, this won't be possible, because all elements in the original stream and the resulting ones were consumed by the debugger, so the following exception is printed in the console.

```
Connected to the target VM, address: '127.0.0.1:64083', transport: 'socket'
Exception in thread "main" java.lang.IllegalStateException:
                        stream has already been operated upon or closed
Disconnected from the target VM, address: '127.0.0.1:64083',
transport: 'socket'
        at java.base/java.util.stream.AbstractPipeline.<init>AbstractPipe
        line.java:203
        at java.base/java.util.stream.ReferencePipeline.<init>ReferencePipe
        line.java:94
        at java.base/java.util.stream.ReferencePipeline$StatelessOp.<init>
                ReferencePipeline.java:696
        at java.base/java.util.stream.ReferencePipeline$3.<init>ReferencePi
        peline.java:189
        at java.base/java.util.stream.ReferencePipeline.
        mapReferencePipeline.java:188
        at chapter.eight/com.apress.bgn.ch8.StreamDebuggerDemo.
        mainStreamDebuggerDemo.java:45
```

Summary

After reading this chapter and running the provided code samples, it should be clear why the Stream API is so awesome. I like three things best: more compact and simple code can be written to solve problems without losing readability (`ifs` and loops can be avoided), parallel processing of data is possible without the boilerplate code required before Java 8 and the fact that code can be written in Functional Programming style. Also, the Stream API is more a declarative way of programming as most stream methods take arguments of type `Consumer<T>`, `Predicate<T>`, or `Function<T>`, which declare what should be done for each stream element, but the methods are not explicitly called from the developer written code.

This chapter also covered how to use `Optional<T>` instances to avoid `NullPointerExceptions` and writing `if` statements.

After you finished reading this chapter, you should have a pretty good idea about the following.

- how to create sequential and parallel streams from collections
- what empty streams are useful for
- terms to remember about streams:
  - sequence of elements
  - predicate
  - consumer
  - supplier
  - method reference
  - source
  - aggregate operations
  - intermediate operation
  - terminal operation
  - pipelining
  - internal automatic iterations
- how to create and use `Optional` instances

CHAPTER 9

Debugging, Testing, and Documenting

Development work does not only require you to write design the solution for a problem and write the code for it. To make sure your solution solves the problem, you have to test it. **Testing** involves making sure every component making up your solution behaves as expected in expected and unexpected situations.

The most practical way to test code is to inspect values of intermediary variables by **logging** them; print them in the console only in specific situations.

When a solution is complex, **debugging** provides the opportunity to pause the execution and inspect state of the variables. Debugging sometimes involves **breakpoints** and requires an IDE. Breakpoints are points where the application pauses its execution, and the inspection of variables can be performed.

After making sure your solution fits the requirements, you have to document it, especially if the problem that is being solved is one that requires complex code to solve it. Or if your solution might be a prerequisite for other applications, it is your responsibility to explain other developers how to use it.

This chapter covers a few ways to do all these, because these are key talents for a developer.

Debugging

Debugging is a process of finding and resolving defects or problems within a computer program. There are more debugging tactics, and depending of the complexity of an application, one or more can be used. The following is a list of those techniques.

- logging intermediary states of objects involved in the process and analyzing log files

CHAPTER 9 DEBUGGING, TESTING, AND DOCUMENTING

- interactive debugging using breakpoints to pause the execution of the program and inspect intermediary states of objects involved in the process
- testing
- monitoring at the application or system level
- analysis of memory dumps item profiling, a form of dynamic program analysis that measures the memory occupied by a program, or CPU used, duration of method calls, and so forth.

Let's start with the simplest way of debugging: logging.

Logging

In the real world, logging is a destructive process; it is the cutting and processing of trees to produce timber. In software programming, **logging** means writing log files that can be later used to identify problems in code. The simplest way to log information is to use the System.out.print method family, as depicted in Figure 9-1.

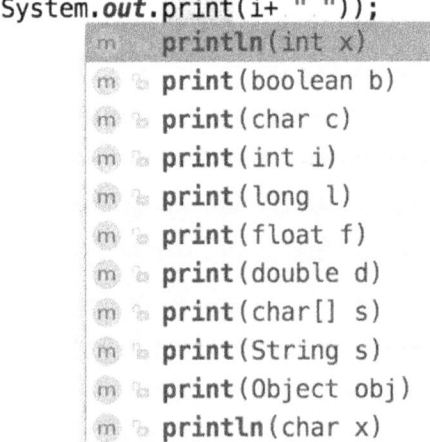

Figure 9-1. System.out.print class family

CHAPTER 9 DEBUGGING, TESTING, AND DOCUMENTING

For the examples in this chapter, we use a hierarchy of classes that provide methods to sort integer arrays. The class hierarchy is depicted in Figure 9-2.

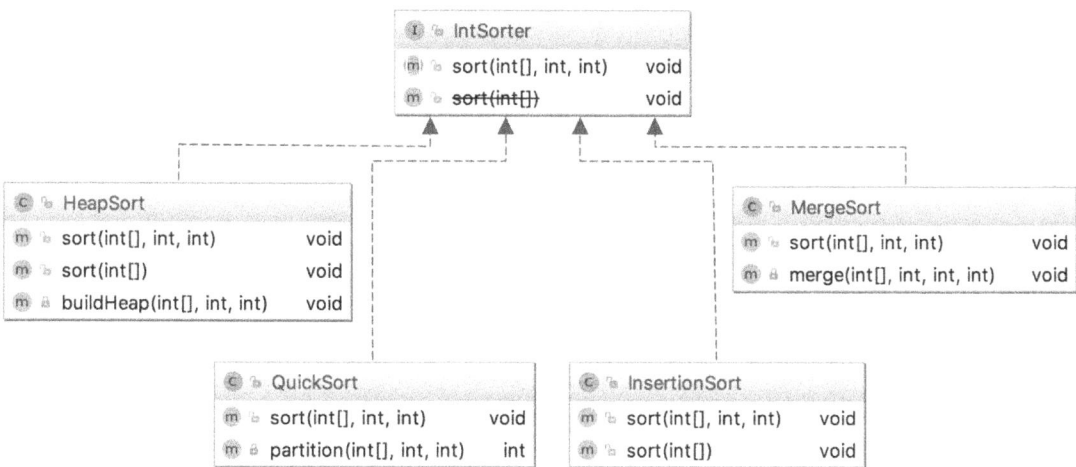

Figure 9-2. Sorting class hierarchy

We'll take first the MergeSort class and add System.out.print statements to log the steps of the algorithm. Merge sort is the name of a sorting algorithm with a better performance than bubble sort, and it works by splitting the array into two halves, then into smaller pieces, until it gets to the arrays of two elements that can be easily sorted. Then it starts merging the array pieces. This approach, of splitting the array repeatedly until sorting becomes a manageable operation is called **Divide et Impera** also known as **divide and conquer**. There are more algorithms that follow the same approach for solving a problem and merge sort is only the first of them that is covered in this book. Figure 9-3, shows what happens in every step of the merge-sort algorithm that we are going to implement.

CHAPTER 9   DEBUGGING, TESTING, AND DOCUMENTING

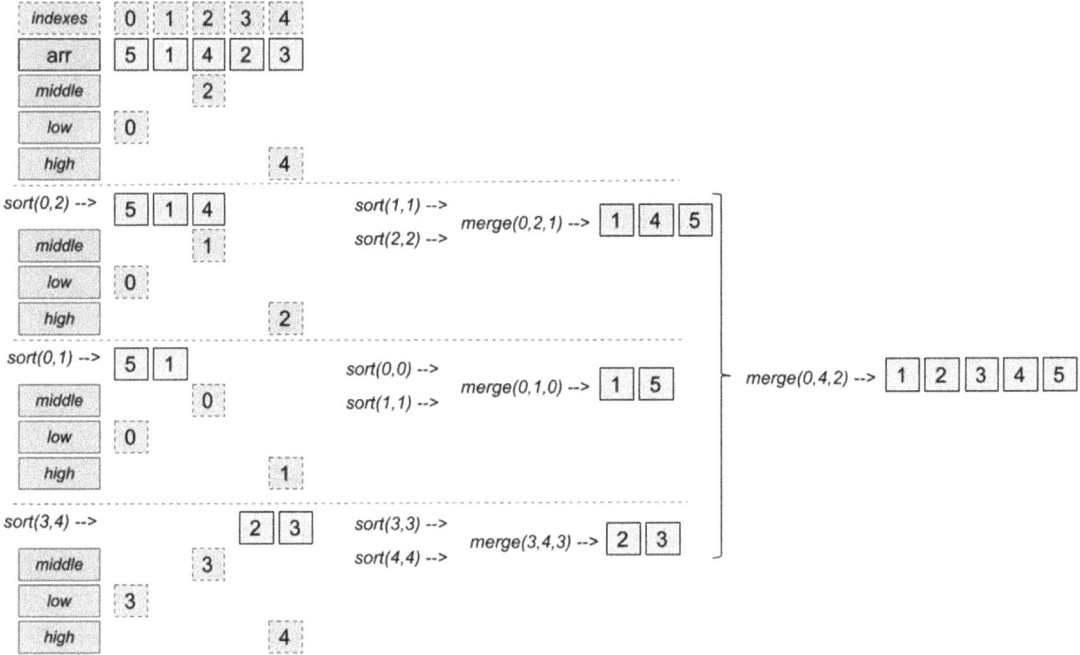

Figure 9-3. *Merge sort*

In each step of the algorithm the middle of the array is identified, and as long as the start index of the array the `low` value is smaller than the end index of the array to sort, the `high` value, we further split the array by calling the `sort(..)` method until we get to an array with one element. That is when the `merge(..)` method is called, aside from merging pieces of the array, it also sorts them during the merging. To write the code, we need to implement the two methods.

Listing 9-1. Logging with System.out.print

```
package com.apress.bgn.ch9.algs;

public class MergeSort implements IntSorter {
    public void sort(int[] arr, int low, int high) {
        if (low < high) {
            int middle = (low + high) / 2;
            sort(arr, low, middle);
            sort(arr, middle + 1, high);
            merge(arr, low, middle, high);
```

```
        }
    }
    private void merge(int arr[], int low, int middle, int high) {
        int leftLength = middle - low + 1;
        int rightLength = high - middle;

        int left[] = new int[leftLength];
        int right[] = new int[rightLength];

        for (int i = 0; i < leftLength; ++i) {
            left[i] = arr[low + i];
        }
        for (int i = 0; i < rightLength; ++i) {
            right[i] = arr[middle + 1 + i];
        }

        int i = 0, j = 0;

        int k = low;
        while (i < leftLength && j < rightLength) {
            if (left[i] <= right[j]) {
                arr[k] = left[i];
                i++;
            } else {
                arr[k] = right[j];
                j++;
            }
            k++;
        }

        while (i < leftLength) {
            arr[k] = left[i];
            i++;
            k++;
        }

        while (j < rightLength) {
            arr[k] = right[j];
```

CHAPTER 9 DEBUGGING, TESTING, AND DOCUMENTING

```
                j++;
                k++;
            }
        }
    }
}
```

This code might look scary, but it does exactly what is depicted in Figure 9-3; we just need a lot of variables to refer all the indexes we are using to arrange our elements in the proper order. To make sure our solution is properly implemented, it would be useful to see the values each method is called with and the array pieces that are being handled. We can do this by simply modifying our methods and adding a few `System.out.print` method calls.

```java
package com.apress.bgn.ch9.algs;

public class MergeSort implements IntSorter {

    public void sort(int[] arr, int low, int high) {
        System.out.print("Call sort of " + ": [" + low + " " + high + "] ");
        for (int i = low; i <= high; ++i) {
            System.out.print(arr[i] + " ");
        }
        System.out.println();
        if (low < high) {
            int middle = (low + high) / 2;
            sort(arr, low, middle);
            sort(arr, middle + 1, high);
            merge(arr, low, middle, high);
        }
    }

    private void merge(int arr[], int low, int middle, int high) {
        int leftLength = middle - low + 1;
        int rightLength = high - middle;

        int left[] = new int[leftLength];
        int right[] = new int[rightLength];
```

```
for (int i = 0; i < leftLength; ++i) {
    left[i] = arr[low + i];
}
for (int i = 0; i < rightLength; ++i) {
    right[i] = arr[middle + 1 + i];
}

int i = 0, j = 0;

int k = low;
while (i < leftLength && j < rightLength) {
    if (left[i] <= right[j]) {
        arr[k] = left[i];
        i++;
    } else {
        arr[k] = right[j];
        j++;
    }
    k++;
}

while (i < leftLength) {
    arr[k] = left[i];
    i++;
    k++;
}

while (j < rightLength) {
    arr[k] = right[j];
    j++;
    k++;
}

System.out.print("Called merge of: [" + low
        + " " + high + " " + middle + "], ");

for (int z = low; z <= high; ++z) {
    System.out.print(arr[z] + " ");
}
```

CHAPTER 9   DEBUGGING, TESTING, AND DOCUMENTING

```
            System.out.println();
    }
}
```

To test the output we need a class containing a `main(..)` method to execute the algorithm.

```
package com.apress.bgn.ch9;

import com.apress.bgn.ch9.algs.IntSorter;
import com.apress.bgn.ch9.algs.MergeSort;

import java.util.Arrays;

public class SortingDemo {
    public static void main(String... args) {
        int arr[] = {5,1,4,2,3};

        IntSorter mergeSort = new MergeSort();
        mergeSort.sort(arr, 0, arr.length-1);

        System.out.print("Sorted: ");
        Arrays.stream(arr).forEach(i -> System.out.print(i+ " "));
    }
}
```

If we run the preceding class, the intermediary values handled by `sort(..)` and `merge(..)` calls are printed in the console.

```
Call sort of : [0 4] 5 1 4 2 3
Call sort of : [0 2] 5 1 4
Call sort of : [0 1] 5 1
Call sort of : [0 0] 5
Call sort of : [1 1] 1
Called merge of: [0 1 0], 1 5
Call sort of : [2 2] 4
Called merge of: [0 2 1], 1 4 5
```

```
Call sort of : [3 4] 2 3
Call sort of : [3 3] 2
Call sort of : [4 4] 3
Called merge of: [3 4 3], 2 3
Called merge of: [0 4 2], 1 2 3 4 5
Sorted: 1 2 3 4 5
```

You can see that the console output matches the algorithm steps depicted in Figure 9-3; that output is clearly proof that the solution works as expected. But, there is a problem with the code now. Every time the sort(..) method is called, the output is printed, and if the sorting is only one step in a more complex solution, the output is not really necessary. It can even pollute the output of the bigger solution. Also, if the array is big, printing that output could affect the performance of the overall solution. So, a different approach should be considered, one that could be customized and decision made if the output should be printed or not. This is where logging libraries come in.

Logging with JUL

The JDK provides its own logger classes that are hosted under package `java.util.logging` that is why the logging module provided by the JDK is also called **JUL**. A Logger class instance is used to log messages. The logger instance should be provided a name when is created and log messages are printed by calling specialized methods that print messages at different levels. For the JUL module, the levels and their scope are listed next, but other logging libraries have similar logging levels.

- OFF   should be used to turn off all logging
- SEVERE – is the highest level, message indicates a serious failure
- WARNING - indicates that this message is being printed because of a potential problem
- INFO - indicates that this is an informational message
- CONFIG - indicates that this is a message containing configuration information
- FINE - indicates that this a message providing tracing information
- FINER - indicates that this is a fairly detailed tracing message

- FINEST - indicates that this is a very detailed tracing message
- ALL - all log messages should be printed

Loggers can be configured using XML or properties files and their output can be directed to external files. For the code sample introduced previously, let's replace all System.out.print method calls with logger calls. Let's start with the SorterJulDemo class.

```java
package com.apress.bgn.ch9;

import com.apress.bgn.ch9.algs.IntSorter;
import com.apress.bgn.ch9.algs.MergeSort;

import java.util.Arrays;
import java.util.logging.Logger;

public class SortingJulDemo {
    private static final Logger log =
            Logger.getLogger(SortingJulDemo.class.getName());

    public static void main(String... args) {
        int arr[] = {5,1,4,2,3};

        log.info("Sorting  an array with merge sort");
        IntSorter mergeSort = new MergeSort();
        mergeSort.sort(arr, 0, arr.length-1);

        StringBuilder sb = new StringBuilder("Sorted: ");
        Arrays.stream(arr).forEach(i -> sb.append(i).append(" "));
        log.info(sb.toString());
    }
}
```

In the code sample, a Logger instance was created by calling the static method Logger.getLogger(..). The recommended practice is for the logger to be named as the class it is logging messages for. Without any additional configuration, every message printed with log.info(..) is printed prefixed with the full system date, class name, and method name in front of it. Let's replace all System.out.print method calls with logger calls in the MergeSort class, and introduces a StringBuilder to construct longer messages before writing them with log.info(..).

```java
package com.apress.bgn.ch9.algs;

import java.util.logging.Logger;

public class MergeSort implements IntSorter {
    private static final Logger log =
            Logger.getLogger(SortingJulDemo.class.getName());

    public void sort(int[] arr, int low, int high) {
        StringBuilder sb = new StringBuilder("Call sort of ")
                .append(": [")
                    .append(low).append(" ").append(high)
                .append("] ");
        for (int i = low; i <= high; ++i) {
            sb.append(arr[i]).append(" ");
        }
        log.info(sb.toString());

        if (low < high) {

            int middle = (low + high) / 2;

            //sort lower half of the interval
            sort(arr, low, middle);
            //sort upper half of the interval
            sort(arr, middle + 1, high);

            // merge the two intervals
            merge(arr, low, middle, high);
        }
    }

    private void merge(int arr[], int low, int middle, int high) {
        ...
        StringBuilder sb = new StringBuilder("Called merge of: [")
                .append(low).append(" ").append(high).append(" ")
                 .append(middle)
                .append("],) ");
        for (int z = low; z <= high; ++z) {
            sb.append(arr[z]).append(" ");
```

CHAPTER 9 DEBUGGING, TESTING, AND DOCUMENTING

```
        }
        log.info(sb.toString());
    }
}
```

And now let's run the code and analyze the console output.

```
Jul 21, 2018 11:17:30 PM com.apress.bgn.ch9.SortingJulDemo main
        INFO: Sorting  an array with merge sort
Jul 21, 2018 11:17:30 PM com.apress.bgn.ch9.algs.MergeSort sort
        INFO: Call sort of : [0 4] 5 1 4 2 3
Jul 21, 2018 11:17:30 PM com.apress.bgn.ch9.algs.MergeSort sort
        INFO: Call sort of : [0 2] 5 1 4
Jul 21, 2018 11:17:30 PM com.apress.bgn.ch9.algs.MergeSort sort
        INFO: Call sort of : [0 1] 5 1
Jul 21, 2018 11:17:30 PM com.apress.bgn.ch9.algs.MergeSort sort
        INFO: Call sort of : [0 0] 5
Jul 21, 2018 11:17:30 PM com.apress.bgn.ch9.algs.MergeSort sort
        INFO: Call sort of : [1 1] 1
Jul 21, 2018 11:17:30 PM com.apress.bgn.ch9.algs.MergeSort merge
        INFO: Called merge of: [0 1 0],) 1 5
Jul 21, 2018 11:17:30 PM com.apress.bgn.ch9.algs.MergeSort sort
        INFO: Call sort of : [2 2] 4
Jul 21, 2018 11:17:30 PM com.apress.bgn.ch9.algs.MergeSort merge
        INFO: Called merge of: [0 2 1],) 1 4 5
Jul 21, 2018 11:17:30 PM com.apress.bgn.ch9.algs.MergeSort sort
        INFO: Call sort of : [3 4] 2 3
Jul 21, 2018 11:17:30 PM com.apress.bgn.ch9.algs.MergeSort sort
        INFO: Call sort of : [3 3] 2
Jul 21, 2018 11:17:30 PM com.apress.bgn.ch9.algs.MergeSort sort
        INFO: Call sort of : [4 4] 3
Jul 21, 2018 11:17:30 PM com.apress.bgn.ch9.algs.MergeSort merge
        INFO: Called merge of: [3 4 3],) 2 3
Jul 21, 2018 11:17:30 PM com.apress.bgn.ch9.algs.MergeSort merge
        INFO: Called merge of: [0 4 2],) 1 2 3 4 5
Jul 21, 2018 11:17:30 PM com.apress.bgn.ch9.SortingJulDemo main
        INFO: Sorted: 1 2 3 4 5
```

CHAPTER 9   DEBUGGING, TESTING, AND DOCUMENTING

The way log messages are written is decided by a special class called a formatter. When an explicit configuration is missing, the default formatter used is java.util.logging. SimpleFormatter that prints log messages exactly as shown in the previous listing. The messages are printed by default in the console and the class used for that is called a handler, and is java.util.logging.ConsoleHandler in this case. Both of these are configurable and can be replaced via a configuration file with more advanced classes or custom classes.

The previous log seems a little crowded and is not really clear. So, we must refine it by adding a proper configuration. The StreamFormatter class contains a field named format that can be initialized with a template for how the log messages should be written. So, let's remove the class and method name altogether because we have really specific messages in place anyway. The following code listing contains a simple configuration for JUL.

```
handlers=java.util.logging.ConsoleHandler
.level=ALL
java.util.logging.ConsoleHandler.level=ALL
java.util.logging.ConsoleHandler.formatter=java.util.logging.
SimpleFormatter
java.util.logging.SimpleFormatter.format=[%1$tF %1$tT] [%4$-4s] %5$s %n
```

This file should be loaded at the start of the execution using an instance of java. util.logging.LogManager and calling the readConfiguration(..) method, so the SortingJulDemo class is modified as follows.

```
public class SortingJulDemo {

    private static final Logger log =
        Logger.getLogger(SortingJulDemo.class.getName());

    static{
        try {
            LogManager logManager = LogManager.getLogManager();
            logManager.readConfiguration (
  new FileInputStream("./chapter09/src/main/resources/logging.properties"));
        } catch (IOException exception) {
            log.log(Level.SEVERE, "Error in loading configuration",exception);
        }
    }
```

CHAPTER 9 DEBUGGING, TESTING, AND DOCUMENTING

```
    public static void main(String... args) {
        // same code as before
        ...
    }
}
```

If we run our example again, the output changes to

```
[2018-07-21 23:58:29] [INFO] Sorting  an array with merge sort
[2018-07-21 23:58:29] [INFO] Call sort of : [0 4] 5 1 4 2 3
[2018-07-21 23:58:29] [INFO] Call sort of : [0 2] 5 1 4
[2018-07-21 23:58:29] [INFO] Call sort of : [0 1] 5 1
[2018-07-21 23:58:29] [INFO] Call sort of : [0 0] 5
[2018-07-21 23:58:29] [INFO] Call sort of : [1 1] 1
[2018-07-21 23:58:29] [INFO] Called merge of: [0 1 0],) 1 5
[2018-07-21 23:58:29] [INFO] Call sort of : [2 2] 4
[2018-07-21 23:58:29] [INFO] Called merge of: [0 2 1],) 1 4 5
[2018-07-21 23:58:29] [INFO] Call sort of : [3 4] 2 3
[2018-07-21 23:58:29] [INFO] Call sort of : [3 3] 2
[2018-07-21 23:58:29] [INFO] Call sort of : [4 4] 3
[2018-07-21 23:58:29] [INFO] Called merge of: [3 4 3],) 2 3
[2018-07-21 23:58:29] [INFO] Called merge of: [0 4 2],) 1 2 3 4 5
[2018-07-21 23:58:29] [INFO] Sorted: 1 2 3 4 5
```

Aside from `SimpleFormatter`, there is another class that can be used to format log messages named `XMLFormatter` that formats the messages as XML(Extensible Markup Language). The XML format of writing data is defined by a set of rules for encoding the data that is both human-readable and machine readable. Also, the set of rules makes it easy to validate and find errors.[1] And since for XML it makes no sense to be written in the console, let's use the `FileHandler` class to save the logs to a file. The modifications to add to the configuration file are shown next.

```
handlers=java.util.logging.FileHandler
java.util.logging.FileHandler.pattern=chapter09/out/chapter09-log.xml
.level=ALL
```

---

[1]More about XML here: https://en.wikipedia.org/wiki/XML

```
java.util.logging.ConsoleHandler.level=ALL
java.util.logging.ConsoleHandler.formatter=java.util.logging.XMLFormatter
```

With that configuration, when running the code, a `chapter09-log.xml` is generated located under `chapter09/out` and contains entries that look similar to the one depicted next.

```xml
<?xml version="1.0" encoding="UTF-8" standalone="no"?>
<!DOCTYPE log SYSTEM "logger.dtd">
<log>
<record>
  <date>2018-07-21T23:50:52.905961Z</date>
  <millis>1532217052905</millis>
  <nanos>961000</nanos>
  <sequence>0</sequence>
  <logger>com.apress.bgn.ch9.SortingJulDemo</logger>
  <level>INFO</level>
  <class>com.apress.bgn.ch9.SortingJulDemo</class>
  <method>main</method>
  <thread>1</thread>
  <message>Sorting  an array with merge sort</message>
</record>
...
</log>
```

The logging output can be customized also by providing a custom class, the only condition is for the class to extend the `java.util.logging.Formatter` class, or any of its JDK subclasses.

In the previous sample, we only had `log.info` calls because the code is basic and leaves no room for error; but let's modify the code to allow the user to insert the elements of the array. This requires code to be written to treat situations when the user does not insert proper data. Code to treat the case when the user does not provide any data and code to treat the case when user inserts bad data should be added to the class. If the user does not provide any data, a SEVERE log message should be printed and the application should terminate. If the user introduces invalid data, the valid data should be used and warning should be printed for elements that are not integers.

CHAPTER 9   DEBUGGING, TESTING, AND DOCUMENTING

This means that the SortingJulDemo class becomes

```java
package com.apress.bgn.ch9;

import com.apress.bgn.ch9.algs.IntSorter;
import com.apress.bgn.ch9.algs.MergeSort;

import java.io.FileInputStream;
import java.io.IOException;
import java.util.ArrayList;
import java.util.Arrays;
import java.util.List;
import java.util.logging.Level;
import java.util.logging.LogManager;
import java.util.logging.Logger;

public class SortingJulDemo {

    private static final Logger log =
            Logger.getLogger(SortingJulDemo.class.getName());

    static {
        try {
            LogManager logManager = LogManager.getLogManager();
            logManager.readConfiguration(new FileInputStream
                ("./chapter09/logging-jul/src/main/resources/logging.
                properties"));
        } catch (IOException exception) {
            log.log(Level.SEVERE, "Error in loading configuration",
            exception);
        }
    }

    public static void main(String... args) {
        if (args.length == 0) {
            log.severe ("No data to sort!");
            return;

        }
        int[] arr = getInts(args);
```

```java
        final StringBuilder sb = new
            StringBuilder("Sorting  an array with merge sort: ");

        Arrays.stream(arr).forEach(i -> sb.append(i).append(" "));
        log.info(sb.toString());

        IntSorter mergeSort = new MergeSort();
        mergeSort.sort(arr, 0, arr.length - 1);

        final StringBuilder sb2 = new StringBuilder("Sorted: ");
        Arrays.stream(arr).forEach(i -> sb2.append(i).append( " "));
        log.info(sb2.toString());
    }

    private static int[] getInts(String[] args) {

        List<Integer> list = new ArrayList<>();
        for (String arg : args) {
            try {
                int toInt = Integer.parseInt(arg);
                list.add(toInt);
            } catch (NumberFormatException nfe) {

                log.warning ("Element " + arg + " is not an
                    integer and cannot be added to the array!");

            }
        }
        int[] arr = new int[list.size()];
        int j = 0;
        for (Integer elem : list) {
            arr[j++] = elem;
        }
        return arr;
    }
}
```

CHAPTER 9   DEBUGGING, TESTING, AND DOCUMENTING

The `arr` array is no longer hardcoded in the `main(..)` method, but the values that this method receives as arguments become the array to be sorted and are converted from `String` values to `int` values by the `toInts(..)` method. The person executing this program can provide the arguments from the command line, but because we are using IntelliJ IDEA, there is an easier way to do that. If you now run the program without providing any arguments, the following is printed in the console.

[2018-07-22 01:34:37] [SEVERE] No data to sort!

The execution stops right there because there is nothing to sort. And since you've probably run this class a few times, IntelliJ probably created a launcher configuration that you can customize and provide arguments for the execution. E9-4, dit your configuration as shown in Figure 9-4 by adding the recommended values as program arguments.

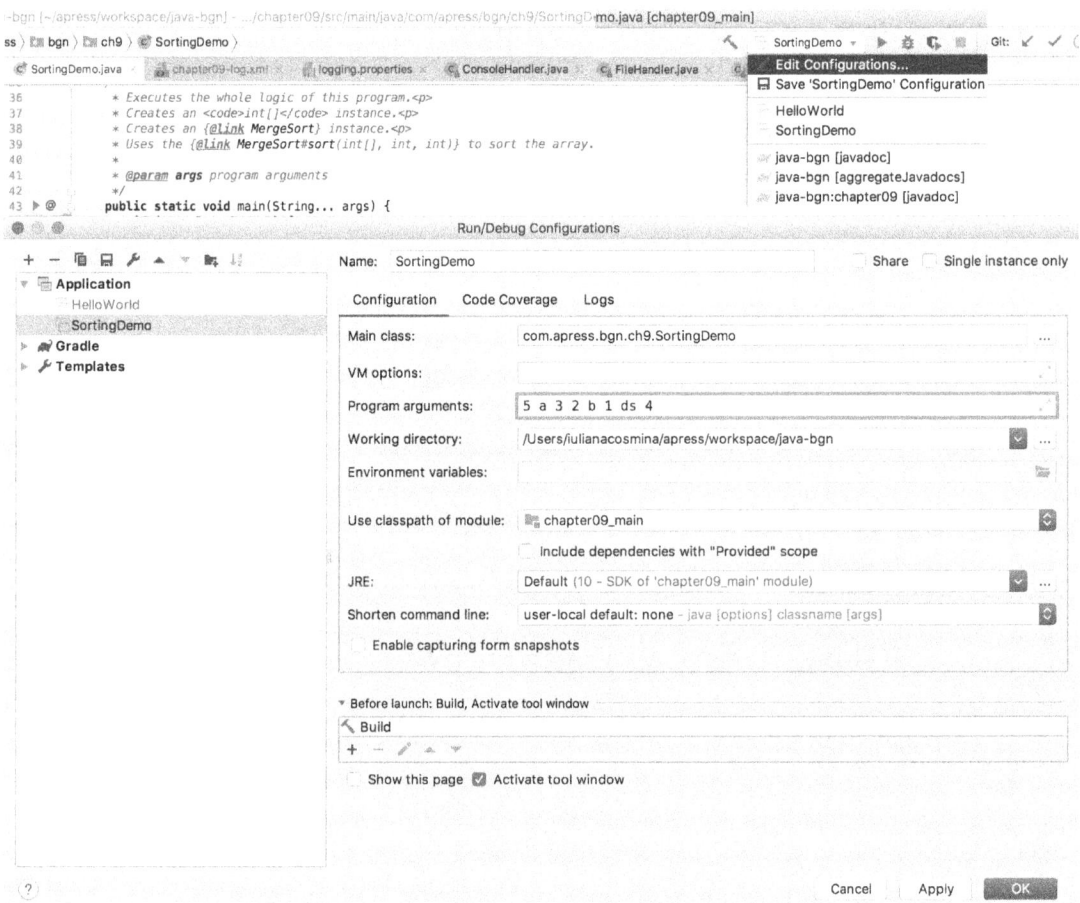

Figure 9-4. *IntelliJ IDEA launcher for the SortingJulDemo class*

Then, run the program and inspect the console log. You see a few extra log messages there with severity WARNING that are printed for values given as arguments that cannot be converted to int.

```
[2018-07-22 01:43:35] [WARNING] Element a is not an integer and cannot be added to the array!
[2018-07-22 01:43:35] [WARNING] Element b is not an integer and cannot be added to the array!
[2018-07-22 01:43:35] [WARNING] Element ds is not an integer and cannot be added to the array!
[2018-07-22 01:43:35] [INFO] Sorting  an array with merge sort: 5 3 2 1 4
[2018-07-22 01:43:35] [INFO] Call sort of : [0 4] 5 3 2 1 4
[2018-07-22 01:43:35] [INFO] Call sort of : [0 2] 5 3 2
[2018-07-22 01:43:35] [INFO] Call sort of : [0 1] 5 3
[2018-07-22 01:43:35] [INFO] Call sort of : [0 0] 5
[2018-07-22 01:43:35] [INFO] Call sort of : [1 1] 3
[2018-07-22 01:43:35] [INFO] Called merge of: [0 1 0],) 3 5
[2018-07-22 01:43:35] [INFO] Call sort of : [2 2] 2
[2018-07-22 01:43:35] [INFO] Called merge of: [0 2 1],) 2 3 5
[2018-07-22 01:43:35] [INFO] Call sort of : [3 4] 1 4
[2018-07-22 01:43:35] [INFO] Call sort of : [3 3] 1
[2018-07-22 01:43:35] [INFO] Call sort of : [4 4] 4
[2018-07-22 01:43:35] [INFO] Called merge of: [3 4 3],) 1 4
[2018-07-22 01:43:35] [INFO] Called merge of: [0 4 2],) 1 2 3 4 5
[2018-07-22 01:43:35] [INFO] Sorted: 1 2 3 4 5
```

Writing logs can affect performance, and in some cases, like when the application is running in a production system, we might want to refine the logging configuration to only important log messages that notify the risk of a problem and skip informational messages. In the previous configuration examples, there was a configuration line that enabled all log messages to be printed.

```
handlers=java.util.logging.ConsoleHandler
.level=ALL
java.util.logging.ConsoleHandler.level=ALL
java.util.logging.ConsoleHandler.formatter=java.util.logging.SimpleFormatter
java.util.logging.SimpleFormatter.format=[%1$tF %1$tT] [%4$-4s] %5$s %n
```

If we change the value of that property to OFF, nothing is printed. The log levels have integer values assigned to them, and those values can be used to compare the severity of the messages. As a rule, if you configure a certain level of messages, more severe messages are printed. So, if we set that property to INFO, warning messages are printed. The values for the severity levels of messages are defined in the `java.util.logging.Level` class, and if you open that class in your editor, you can see the integer values assigned to each of them.

...
```
    public static final Level OFF = new Level("OFF",Integer.MAX_VALUE,
    defaultBundle);
    public static final Level SEVERE = new Level("SEVERE",1000,
    defaultBundle);
    public static final Level WARNING = new Level("WARNING", 900,
    defaultBundle);
    public static final Level INFO = new Level("INFO", 800, defaultBundle);
    public static final Level CONFIG = new Level("CONFIG", 700,
    defaultBundle);
    public static final Level FINE = new Level("FINE", 500, defaultBundle);
    public static final Level FINER = new Level("FINER", 400,
    defaultBundle);
    public static final Level FINEST = new Level("FINEST", 300,
    defaultBundle);
```
...

So, in the previous configuration, if we change `.level=ALL` to `.level=WARNING`, then we would expect to see all log messages of levels WARNING and SEVERE. If we run the `SortingJulDemo` class with the previous arguments, we should see only the WARNING level messages.

```
[2018-07-22 15:46:19] [WARNING] Element a is not an integer and cannot be added to the array!
[2018-07-22 15:46:19] [WARNING] Element b is not an integer and cannot be added to the array!
[2018-07-22 15:46:19] [WARNING] Element ds is not an integer and cannot be added to the array!
```

To define log messaging formatting there are more ways: system properties can be used or programmatically a formatter can be instantiated and set on a logger instance. It really depends on the specifics of the application, but you might consider other options for logging, because JUL is known for its weak performance in multithreaded environments and most production applications use some other libraries. But when Java 7 was released, one of the announced features was improvements to the JUL module, so it might deserve a chance nowadays.

Another thing you have to take into account is that if the application you are building is a complex one, with a lot of dependencies, these dependencies might use different logging libraries, how do you configure and use them all? This is where a *logging facade* proves useful. And the next section shows you how to use the most renowned Java logging facade: SLF4J.

Logging with SLF4J and Logback

The most renowned Java logging facade is SLF4J[2] that serves as a logging abstraction for various logging frameworks. This means that you use the SLF4J classes, and behind the scenes all the work is done by a logging concrete implementation found in the classpath. The best part? You can change the logging implementation anytime, and your code still compiles and executes correctly, and there is no need to change anything in it.

In the code samples covered until now in this chapter, the code is seriously tied to JUL, if we want for some reason to change the logging library, we need to change the existing code as well. The first step is to change our code to use the SLF4J classes. Another advantage of using SLF4J is that the configuration is automatically read if the logging configuration file is on the classpath. So, the `LogManager` initialization block that we needed for JUL is not needed anymore, as long as the configuration file is named according to the standard of the concrete logging implementation used. So, let's see the code first.

package com.apress.bgn.ch9;

import org.slf4j.Logger;
import org.slf4j.LoggerFactory;

import java.util.Arrays;
import java.util.logging.Logger;

---

[2]Simple Logging Facade for Java (SLF4J) official site https://www.slf4j.org/

CHAPTER 9 DEBUGGING, TESTING, AND DOCUMENTING

```java
public class SortingJulDemo {

    private static final Logger log =
        LoggerFactory.getLogger(SortingSlf4jDemo.class);

    public static void main(String... args) {
        if (args.length == 0) {
            log.error ("No data to sort!");
            return;
        }

        int[] arr = getInts(args);

        final StringBuilder sb = new StringBuilder
                ("Sorting  an array with merge sort: ");

        Arrays.stream(arr).forEach(i -> sb.append(i).append(" "));
        log.debug (sb.toString());

        IntSorter mergeSort = new MergeSort();
        mergeSort.sort(arr, 0, arr.length - 1);

        final StringBuilder sb2 = new StringBuilder("Sorted: ");
        Arrays.stream(arr).forEach(i -> sb2.append(i).append( " "));
        log.info (sb2.toString());
    }
}
```

As you've probably noticed, the methods we are calling are a little bit different, which is because SLF4J defines an API that maps to the concrete implementation, but the methods depending on their names they are used to print log messages with specific purposes and at specific levels. I'll list them and provide a short explanation for each.

- info.error(..) logs messages at the ERROR level; usually these are messages that are used when there is a critical failure of the application and normal execution cannot continue. There is more than one form for this method, and exceptions and objects can be passed as arguments to it so that the state of the application at the moment of the failure can be assessed.

- `info.warn(..)` logs messages at the WARN level; usually these messages are printed to notify that the application is not functioning normally and there might be reason to worry, in the same way as the previous method, there is more than one form of for it, and exceptions and objects can be passed as arguments to better assess the current state of the application.

- `log.info(..)` logs messages at the INFO level; this type of messages is informational to let the user know that everything is OK.

- `info.debug(..)` logs messages at the DEBUG level; usually these messages are used to print intermediary states of the application and to check that things are going as expected; and in case of a failure, you can trace the evolution of the application objects.

- `log.trace(..)` logs messages at the TRACE level; this type of messages is informational of a very low importance.

The logging concrete implementation used for this example is called Logback,[3] which was chosen because it is the only library that works with SLF4J after the modules were introduced in Java 9. Logback is viewed as the successor of Log4j, another popular logging implementation, and it makes sense since the team that created it also worked on Log4j.[4] Logback implements SLF4J natively, so there is no need to add another bridge library. And it is faster because the Logback internals have been rewritten to perform faster on critical execution points. After modifying our classes to use SLF4J, all we have to do is add Logback as a dependency of our application and add a configuration file under the `resources` directory. The configuration file can be written in XML or Groovy. The standard requires for it to be named `logback.xml`. The next listing depicts the contents of this file for this sections' example.

```xml
<?xml version="1.0" encoding="UTF-8"?>
<configuration>

    <appender name="console" class="ch.qos.logback.core.ConsoleAppender">
        <encoder>
            <pattern>%d{HH:mm:ss.SSS} %-5level %logger{5} - %msg%n</pattern>
```

---

[3] Logback official site https://logback.qos.ch
[4] Log4j official site https://logging.apache.org/log4j

```
        </encoder>
    </appender>

    <logger name="com.apress.bgn.ch9" level="debug"/>

    <root level="info">
        <appender-ref ref="console" />
    </root>
</configuration>
```

The `ch.qos.logback.core.ConsoleAppender` class is used for writing log messages in the console and the `<pattern>` element defines the format of the log messages. Logback can format fully qualified class names by shortening package names to their initials thus, it allows for a compact logging without losing information. This makes Logback one of the favorite logging implementation of the Java development world at the moment.

The logging calls in the `MergeSort` class were all replaced with `log.debug(..)` because these messages are intermediary and not really informational, just samples of the state of the objects used by the application during the execution of the process. The general logging level of the application can be set using a `<root>` element to the desired level, but different logging levels can be set for classes or packages using `<logger>` elements.

So, if we run the `SortingSlf4jDemo` class with the previous configuration on the classpath, this is what is printed:

```
19:38:57.950 WARN  c.a.b.c.SortingSlf4jDemo -
    Element a is not an integer and cannot be added to the array!
19:38:57.951 WARN  c.a.b.c.SortingSlf4jDemo -
    Element b is not an integer and cannot be added to the array!
19:38:57.951 WARN  c.a.b.c.SortingSlf4jDemo -
    Element ds is not an integer and cannot be added to the array!
19:38:57.953 DEBUG c.a.b.c.SortingSlf4jDemo - Sorting  an array with merge sort: 5 3 2 1 4
19:38:57.953 DEBUG c.a.b.c.a.MergeSort - Call sort of : [0 4] 5 3 2 1 4
19:38:57.953 DEBUG c.a.b.c.a.MergeSort - Call sort of : [0 2] 5 3 2
19:38:57.953 DEBUG c.a.b.c.a.MergeSort - Call sort of : [0 1] 5 3
19:38:57.953 DEBUG c.a.b.c.a.MergeSort - Call sort of : [0 0] 5
```

CHAPTER 9   DEBUGGING, TESTING, AND DOCUMENTING

```
19:38:57.953 DEBUG c.a.b.c.a.MergeSort - Call sort of : [1 1] 3
19:38:57.953 DEBUG c.a.b.c.a.MergeSort - Called merge of: [0 1 0],) 3 5
19:38:57.953 DEBUG c.a.b.c.a.MergeSort - Call sort of : [2 2] 2
19:38:57.953 DEBUG c.a.b.c.a.MergeSort - Called merge of: [0 2 1],) 2 3 5
19:38:57.953 DEBUG c.a.b.c.a.MergeSort - Call sort of : [3 4] 1 4
19:38:57.953 DEBUG c.a.b.c.a.MergeSort - Call sort of : [3 3] 1
19:38:57.953 DEBUG c.a.b.c.a.MergeSort - Call sort of : [4 4] 4
19:38:57.954 DEBUG c.a.b.c.a.MergeSort - Called merge of: [3 4 3],) 1 4
19:38:57.954 DEBUG c.a.b.c.a.MergeSort - Called merge of: [0 4 2],) 1 2 3 4 5
19:38:57.954 INFO  c.a.b.c.SortingSlf4jDemo - Sorted: 1 2 3 4 5
```

The fully qualified class name com.apress.bgn.ch9.SortingSlf4jDemo was shortened to c.a.b.c.SortingSlf4jDemo.

The configuration file can be provided to the program as a VM argument, which means logging format can be configured externally. When launching the class, use -Dlogback.configurationFile=\temp\ext-logback.xml as a VM argument.

Logback can direct output to a file as well; all we have to do is add a configuration using the ch.qos.logback.core.FileAppender class and direct the output to the file by adding an <appender> element in the <root> configuration.

```xml
<?xml version="1.0" encoding="UTF-8"?>
<configuration>

    <appender name="file" class="ch.qos.logback.core.FileAppender">
        <file>chapter09/logging-slf4j/out/output.log</file>
        <append>true</append>
        <encoder>
            <pattern>%d{HH:mm:ss.SSS} %-5level %logger{5} - %msg%n</pattern>
        </encoder>
    </appender>

    <appender name="console" class="ch.qos.logback.core.ConsoleAppender">
        <encoder>
            <charset>UTF-8</charset>
            <pattern>%d{HH:mm:ss.SSS} %-5level %logger{5} - %msg%n</pattern>
        </encoder>
    </appender>
```

```
    <logger name="com.apress.bgn.ch9" level="debug"/>

    <root level="info">
        <appender-ref ref="file"/>
        <appender-ref ref="console" />
    </root>
</configuration>
```

In this example, we kept the original configuration because I wanted to give you a working example of log messages written to two destinations at once. But what if the log file becomes too big to open? Well, there's an approach for that. We can use a different class, which can be configured to write a file to a configured limit in size and then start another file. This class is named ch.qos.logback.core.rolling.RollingFileAppender and requires two arguments: an instance of a type that implements ch.qos.logback.core.rolling.RollingPolicy, which provides functionality to write a new log file (also called a *rollover*) and an instance of a type that implements ch.qos.logback.core.rolling.TriggeringPolicy that configures the conditions under which the rollover happens.

Also, a single instance of a type that implements both of the interfaces can configure the logger. Rolling over a log file means that the log file is renamed according to the configuration; usually, the last date that the file was accessed is added to its name, and a new log file is created, with the log file named configured (without any date information).

```
<?xml version="1.0" encoding="UTF-8"?>
<configuration scan="true">

  <appender name="r_file" class="ch.qos.logback.core.rolling.
  RollingFileAppender">
      <file>chapter09/logging-slf4j/out/output.log</file>
       <rollingPolicy class="ch.qos.logback.core.rolling.TimeBasedRollingPolicy">
         <fileNamePattern>
            chapter09/logging-slf4j/out/output_%d{yyyy-MM-dd}.%i.log
         </fileNamePattern>
```

```xml
        <timeBasedFileNamingAndTriggeringPolicy
                class="ch.qos.logback.core.rolling.SizeAndTimeBasedFNATP">
            <maxFileSize>10MB</maxFileSize>
        </timeBasedFileNamingAndTriggeringPolicy>
        <maxHistory>30</maxHistory>
    </rollingPolicy>

    <encoder>
       <charset>UTF-8</charset>
       <pattern>%d{HH:mm:ss.SSS} %-5level %logger{5} - %msg%n</pattern>
    </encoder>
 </appender>

 <appender name="console" class="ch.qos.logback.core.ConsoleAppender">
     <encoder>
         <pattern>%d{HH:mm:ss.SSS} %-5level %logger{5} - %msg%n</pattern>
     </encoder>
 </appender>

 <logger name="com.apress.bgn.ch9" level="debug"/>

 <root level="info">
     <appender-ref ref="r_file"/>
     <appender-ref ref="console" />
 </root>
</configuration>
```

So, the `<file>` element configures the location and the name of the log file. The `<rollingPolicy>` element configures the name the log file receive when log messages no longer be written in it using the `<fileNamePattern>`. In the previous configuration, the `output.log` file is renamed to `output_2018-07-22.log`, for example, and then a new `output.log` file is created daily. The `<timeBasedFileNamingAndTriggeringPolicy>` configures how big the `output.log` file should be before a new file is written. The configured size in the previous example is 10 MB. And if a log file grows bigger than 10 MB before the end of the day, the file is renamed to `output_2018-07-22.1.log`, an index is added to the name, and a new `output.log` is created. The `<maxHistory>` sets the lifespan of a log file, and in our case, it is 30 days.

Logging is a powerful tool; make sure not to abuse it because it can lead to performance problems and a lot of data that is difficult to analyze for useful information. Another thing worth noticing is in the previous code. `StringBuilder` instances are used to construct big log messages, which are printed at a certain level. What happens if logging for that level is disabled via configuration? If you guessed that time and memory are consumed by creating those messages, even if they are not logged, you are right. So, what do we do? The creators of SLF4J have thought of this as well and added methods to test if a certain logging level is enabled and those methods can be used in an `if` statement that wrap around the performance sensitive code. This being said the `SortingSlf4jDemo.main(..)` method becomes

```java
public static void main(String... args) {
    if (args.length == 0) {
        log.error("No data to sort!");
        return;
    }
    int[] arr = getInts(args);

    if (log.isDebugEnabled()) {
        final StringBuilder sb = new StringBuilder(
                "Sorting an array with merge sort: ");
        Arrays.stream(arr).forEach(i -> sb.append(i).append(" "));
        log.debug(sb.toString());
    }

    IntSorter mergeSort = new MergeSort();
    mergeSort.sort(arr, 0, arr.length - 1);

    if (log.isInfoEnabled()) {
        final StringBuilder sb2 = new StringBuilder("Sorted: ");
        Arrays.stream(arr).forEach(i -> sb2.append(i).append(" "));
        log.info(sb2.toString());
    }
}
```

In this code sample, if the SLF4J configuration for the `com.apress.bgn.ch9` package is set to info, the message starting with *Sorting an array with merge sort: ...* is no longer created nor printed, because the `log.isDebugEnabled()` returns `false`, so the code

CHAPTER 9 DEBUGGING, TESTING, AND DOCUMENTING

enclosed in the `if` statement is no longer executed. The `Logger` class contains `if..Enabled()` for any logger level.

And this is all that can be said in this section about logging. Remember to use it moderately, pay very much attention when you decide to log messages in loops and for big application always use a logging facade, meaning SLF4J.

Debug Using Assertions

Another tool to debug your code is using assertions. If you remember the section about Java keywords, you probably remember the `assert` keyword. The `assert` keyword writes an `assertion` statement that is a test of your assumptions on the program execution. In the previous examples, we had the user provide the input for our sorting program, so for our program to do the right thing, it is assumed that the user provide the proper input, this means, an array with size bigger than 1, because there is no point to run the algorithm for a single number. So, how does this assertion looks like in the code? The answer to this question is in the following code sample.

```java
package com.apress.bgn.ch9;

import com.apress.bgn.ch9.algs.IntSorter;
import com.apress.bgn.ch9.algs.QuickSort;

import java.util.Arrays;

import static com.apress.bgn.ch9.SortingSlf4jDemo.getInts;

public class AssertionDemo {
    public static void main(String... args) {
        int[] arr = getInts(args);

        assert arr.length > 1;

        IntSorter mergeSort = new QuickSort();
        mergeSort.sort(arr, 0, arr.length - 1);

        final StringBuilder sb2 = new StringBuilder("Sorted: ");
        Arrays.stream(arr).forEach(i -> sb2.append(i).append(" "));
        System.out.println(sb2.toString());
    }
}
```

CHAPTER 9 DEBUGGING, TESTING, AND DOCUMENTING

If you run this code without providing any arguments to the program, nothing happens, even if we have an `assertion` statement in it. The reason for this is that assertions need to be enabled using a VM argument: -ea. To specify this argument, you can add it to the command when executing from the command line; but since we've used the editor until now, you can add it in the **VM options** text box of the IntelliJ IDEA launcher, as depicted in Figure 9-5.

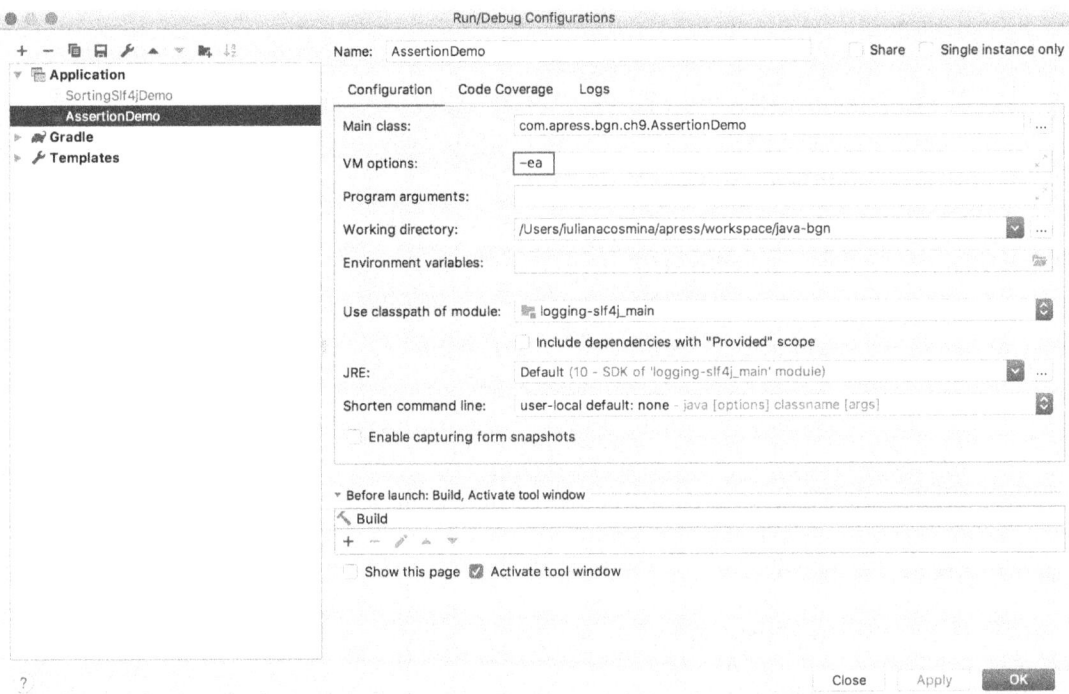

Figure 9-5. *IntelliJ IDEA launcher for the AssertionDemo class with the -ea VM argument set*

When assertions are enabled, running the previous code ends with an `java.lang.AssertionError` being thrown, because the expression of the assertions is evaluated to `false` because the `arr.length` is clearly not bigger than 1 when no argument is provided. Assertions have two forms. In the simple form, they only have the expression to evaluate; the assumption to test

```
assertion expression;
```

346

In this case, `java.lang.AssertionError` is being thrown. It prints the line of the assumption being made, which is clearly the wrong assumption for the current run of the program, with the module and the full classname.

```
Exception in thread "main" java.lang.AssertionError
    at chapter.nine.slf4j/com.apress.bgn.ch9.AssertionDemo.main
    (AssertionDemo.java:48)
```

The complex version of the assertion adds another expression to be evaluated, or a value in the stack to tell the user that the assumption was wrong.

```
assertion expression1 : expression 2;
```

So, if we replace

```
assert arr.length > 1;
```

with

```
assert arr.length > 1 : "Not enough data to sort!";
```

when `java.lang.AssertionError` is thrown, it depicts the *Not enough data to sort!* message, which makes it clear why the assertion statement is preventing the rest of the code from being executed.

```
Exception in thread "main" java.lang.AssertionError: Not enough data to sort!
    at chapter.nine.slf4j/com.apress.bgn.ch9.AssertionDemo.main
    (AssertionDemo.java:48)
```

Or we could just print the size of the array.

```
assert arr.length > 1 : arr.length;
```

Or both.

```
assert arr.length > 1 :
    "Not enough data to sort! Number of values: " + arr.length;
```

Assertions can be used before and after the piece of code that needs to be debugged. In the this case, the assertion was used as a precondition of the execution, because the failure of the assertion prevents code from being executed. But assertions can be used as post-conditions also to test the outcome of executing a piece of code.

In the previous code snippet, the assertion was used to test the correctness of the user provided input. In situations like this, the restriction of a valid input should be obeyed, whether assertions are enabled or not. Sure, if our array is empty or contains a single element, this is not a problem, as the algorithm is not executed, and this does not lead to a technical failure. There are a few rules to obey, or things to look for when writing code using assertions.

- **Assertions should not be used to check the correctness of arguments provided to public methods.** Correctness of arguments should be something tested in the code and a proper `RuntimeException` should be thrown and should not be avoidable.

- **Assertions should not be used to do work that is required for your application to run properly.** The main reason for this is that **assertions are disabled by default** and having them disabled leads to that code not being executed, so the rest of the application does not function properly because of the missing code.

- **For performance reasons, do not use expressions that are expensive to evaluate in assertions.** This rule requires no explanation, even if assertions are disabled by default, imagine that somebody enables them by mistake on a production application. That would be unfortunate, wouldn't it?

If you are interested in using assertions, keep in mind those three rules, and you should be fine.

Step-by-Step Debugging

If you do not want to write log messages, or use assertions, but you still want to inspect values of variables during the execution of a program. There is a way to do that using an IDE: pausing the execution using breakpoints and using the IDE to inspect variable contents or execute simple methods to check if your program is performing as expected.

A breakpoint is a mark set on an executable line of code (not a comment line, not an empty line and not a declaration). In IntelliJ IDEA, to set a breakpoint, you have to click the gutter area on the line you are interested in. Or select the line and from the **Run** menu select **Toggle Line Breakpoint**. When a breakpoint is in place, a red bubble appears on the line in the gutter section. Figure 9-6 shows a few breakpoints in IntelliJ IDEA.

CHAPTER 9 DEBUGGING, TESTING, AND DOCUMENTING

```
31  ▶ @    public static void main(String... args) {
32             if (args.length == 0) {
33                 log.error("No data to sort!");
34                 return;
35             }
36             int[] arr = getInts(args);
37
38             if (log.isDebugEnabled()) {
39                 final StringBuilder sb = new StringBuilder("Sorting an array with merge sort: ");
40  ●↑            Arrays.stream(arr).forEach(i -> sb.append(i).append(" "));
41                 log.debug(sb.toString());
42             }
43
44
45  ●          IntSorter mergeSort = new MergeSort();
46             mergeSort.sort(arr, low: 0, high: arr.length - 1);
47
48  ●          if (log.isInfoEnabled()) {
49                 final StringBuilder sb2 = new StringBuilder("Sorted: ");
50  ●↑            Arrays.stream(arr).forEach(i -> sb2.append(i).append(" "));
51                 log.info(sb2.toString());
52             }
53         }
54
55         /**
56          * Transforms a String[] to an int[] array
57          *
58          * @param args
59          * @return an array of integers
60          */
61  @      public static int[] getInts(String[] args) {
62             List<Integer> list = new ArrayList<>();
63  ●          for (String arg : args) {
```

Figure 9-6. IntelliJ IDEA breakpoints

Once the breakpoints are in place, when the application is executed in debug mode, it pauses on each of the lines. You can decide if you want to continue the step-by-step execution and inspect the values of the variables. IntelliJ IDEA is very helpful with this because it shows you the contents of every variable in each line of the code being executed. In Figure 9-7, the SortingSlf4jDemo class is running in debug mode and is paused during execution using breakpoints.

349

CHAPTER 9   DEBUGGING, TESTING, AND DOCUMENTING

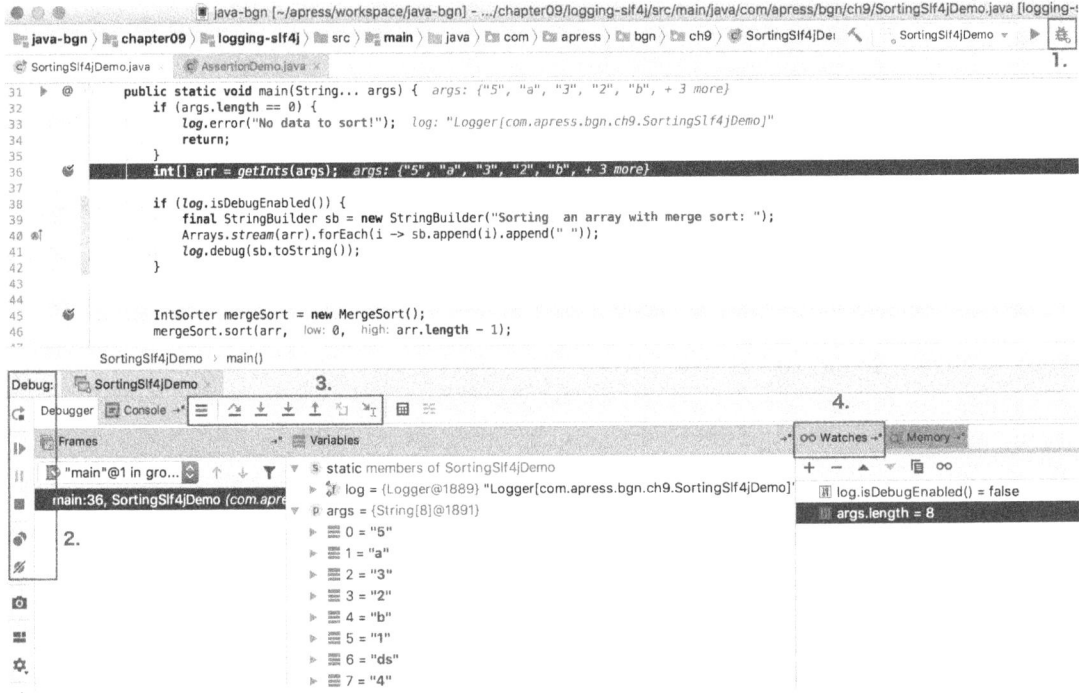

Figure 9-7. IntelliJ IDEA SortingSlf4jDemo class paused during execution

To run an application in debug mode, instead of starting the launcher normally, you can start it by clicking the green bug-shaped button (marked 1 in Figure 9-7) that is right next to the green triangle-shaped button that is normally used to run the application. The application runs and stops at the first line marked with a breakpoint. From that point on the developer can do the following things.

- Inspect values of the variables used on the line with the breakpoint by reading the values depicted by the editor there.

- Continue the execution until the next breakpoint by clicking the green triangle in the **Debug** section, marked 2 in Figure 9-7.

- Stop the execution by clicking the red square-shaped button in the **Debug** section, marked 2 in Figure 9-7.

- Disable all breakpoints by clicking red bubble cut diagonally shaped button in the **Debug** section, marked 2 in Figure 9-7.

- Continue execution to the next line of code by clicking the button with a 90-degree angle in the **Debugger** section, marked 3 in Figure 9-7.

CHAPTER 9   DEBUGGING, TESTING, AND DOCUMENTING

- Continue execution by entering the method in the current line of code by clicking the button with a blue arrow oriented down, in the **Debugger** section, marked 3 in Figure 9-7.

- Continue execution by stepping out of the current method by clicking the button with a blue arrow oriented up, in the **Debugger** section, marked 3 in Figure 9-7.

- Continue the execution to the line pointed at by the cursor by clicking the button with a diagonal arrow pointing to a cursor sign in the **Debugger** section, marked 3 in Figure 9-7.

- Evaluate your own expressions by adding them to the **Watches** section marked 4 in Figure 9-7. The only condition is that the expressions only use variables that are accessible in the context of the breakpoint line.

Most Java smart editors provide the means to run a Java application in debug mode; just make sure that you don't forget to clean up your **Watches** section from time to time, because if you add expressions that are expensive to evaluate there, it might affect the performance of the application. Also, be aware that expressions that use streams might make the application fail, as proven in Chapter 8.

Inspect Running Application Using Java Tools

Aside from the executables to compile Java code and execute or packaging of Java bytecode, the JDK provides a set of utility executables that can be used to debug and inspect the state of a running Java application. This section covers the most useful of them. without further ado, let's cover the most important ones.

jps

A Java application is assigned a process ID when it is running. This is how an operating system keeps track of all applications running in parallel at the same. You can see the process IDs in utilities, such as Process Explorer in Windows and Activity Monitor in macOS. But if you are comfortable with working in the console, you might prefer using the `jps` executable provided by the JDK because it only focuses on Java processes. When calling `jps` from the console, all Java process IDs are listed with the main class name or some details that are exposed by the application API that help you identify the application running. This is useful when an application crashes, but the process remains in a hanging state. This can be painful when the application uses resources such as files or network ports, because it might block them and prevent you from using them. When executing jps on my computer (I have a Mac) these are the Java processes I see running.

```
$ jps
21234 Launcher
18562
21235 SortingSlf4jDemo
3155 muCommander
21236 Jps
```

As you can see in the listing, jps does include itself in the output, because it is a Java process. The process with 21235 is the execution of the SortingSlf4jDemo class. The 21234 process is a launcher application that IntelliJ IDEA uses to start the execution of the SortingSlf4jDemo class. The process with ID 3155 is a Java application that is an alternative to Total Commander (a Windows file manager application). The 18562 process does not have any description, but at this point I can identify the process myself, because I know I have IntelliJ IDEA opened, which is itself a Java application.

The advantage of knowing the process IDs is that you can kill them when they hang and block resources. Let's assume that the process started by the execution of SortingSlf4jDemo ended up hanging. To kill a process, all operating systems provide a version of the kill command. For macOS and Linux, you should execute kill -9 [process_id]. For the preceding example, if I call kill -9 21235 and then call jps, I can see that that SortingSlf4jDemo process is no longer listed.

```
$ jps
21234 Launcher
18562
3155 muCommander
21257 Jps
```

I do still have the Launcher process, but that is a child process of IntelliJ IDEA so there is no point in killing it, because next time I run a main(..) in the IDE, the process is started again.

jps is a simple tool for this specific purpose, but sometimes when applications are installed on servers with minimal setup, it might be all you have. So, it's good to know it exists.

jcmd

The `jcmd` is another JDK utility that can be useful. It sends diagnostic command requests to the JVM, which can help troubleshoot and diagnose JVM and running Java applications. It must be used on the same machine where the JVM is running and the result of calling it without any commands is that it shows all Java processes currently running on the machine; it displays the process Ids and the command used to start their execution.

```
$ jcmd
3155 com.mucommander.muCommander
21369 jdk.jcmd/sun.tools.jcmd.JCmd
21355 org.jetbrains.jps.cmdline.Launcher /Applications/IntelliJ IDEA 2018.2 EAP
.app/Contents/lib/platform-api.jar:/Applications/IntelliJ IDEA 2018.2 EAP
.app/Contents/lib/jps-builders-6.jar:/Applications/IntelliJ IDEA 2018.2 EAP
...
.app/Contents/lib/netty-transport-4.1.25.Final.jar:/Applications/IntelliJ IDEA
21356 chapter.nine.slf4j/com.apress.bgn.ch9.SortingSlf4jDemo 5 a 3 2 b 1 ds 4
21326 org.jetbrains.idea.maven.server.RemoteMavenServer
```

The simplest command that you can run `jcmd` with is `help` on a running process, which depicts all additional commands you can use on that process. This works if the application is currently running and not paused using a breakpoint. Since the `SortingSlf4jDemo` was paused when I was writing this, I used the `muCommander` process as an example.

If I call `jcmd 3155 help` this is what I see:

```
$ jcmd 3155 help
3155:
The following commands are available:
JFR.configure
JFR.stop
JFR.start
JFR.dump
JFR.check
VM.log
VM.native_memory
VM.check_commercial_features
VM.unlock_commercial_features
ManagementAgent.status
```

ManagementAgent.stop
ManagementAgent.start_local
ManagementAgent.start
Compiler.directives_clear
Compiler.directives_remove
Compiler.directives_add
Compiler.directives_print
VM.print_touched_methods
Compiler.codecache
Compiler.codelist
Compiler.queue
VM.classloader_stats
Thread.print
JVMTI.data_dump
JVMTI.agent_load
VM.stringtable
VM.symboltable
VM.class_hierarchy
VM.systemdictionary
GC.class_stats
GC.class_histogram
GC.heap_dump
GC.finalizer_info
GC.heap_info
GC.run_finalization

GC.run
VM.info
VM.uptime
VM.dynlibs
VM.set_flag
VM.flags
VM.system_properties
VM.command_line
VM.version
help

It is not the objective of this book to cover them all, as these are advanced features of Java, but probably you have a basic idea of the scope of each command. As example, the following shows the output of calling jcmd 3155 GC.heap_info.

```
$ jcmd 3155 GC.heap_info
3155:
 garbage-first heap   total 48128K, used 11698K [0x00000006c0000000,
 0x00000007c0000000)
  region size 1024K, 1 young (1024K), 0 survivors (0K)
 Metaspace       used 35414K, capacity 35923K, committed 36864K, reserved 1081344K
  class space   used 4588K, capacity 4835K, committed 5120K, reserved 1048576K
```

If you remember, in **Chapter** 5 the different types of memory used by the JVM were discussed, and heap was the memory where all the objects used by an application were stored. This command prints the heap details: the amount that was used and reserved, the size of a region, and so forth. These details are covered more in detail in **Chapter 13**.

jconsole

jconsole is JDK utility that can be used to inspect various JVM statistics. To use it, you have to start it from the command line and connect it to a Java application that is already running. This application is quite useful, as it can connect to applications running on different machines also, as long as they are running in debug mode on a server and expose a port to connect to. To start a Java application in debug mode and expose a port for an external application, you have to start the application with the following VM parameters.

```
-agentlib:jdwp=transport=dt_socket,server=y,suspend=y,address=1044
```

The port can be any port really as long as it is bigger than 1024, because those are restricted by the operating system. The `transport=dt_socket` instructs the JVM that the debugger connections is made through a socket, the `address=1044` parameter informs it that the port number is 1044. The `suspend=y` instructs the JVM to suspend execution until a debugger is connected to it. To avoid that `suspend=n` should be used.

For our simple example and considering we use jconsole to debug a Java application on the same machine, we do not need all that. We need to start jconsole from the command line and look in the **Local Processes:** section and identify the Java process we are interested in debugging. Figure 9-8 shows the first JConsole dialog window.

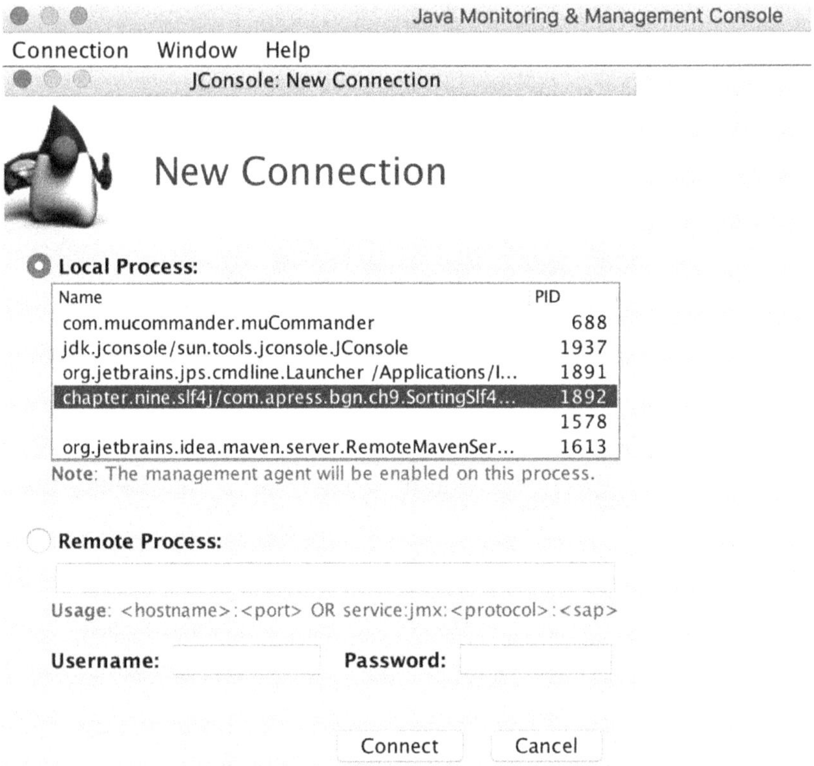

CHAPTER 9   DEBUGGING, TESTING, AND DOCUMENTING

Figure 9-8. JConsole first dialog window

When the process is running locally it can be easily identified because it is named using the module and the fully qualified main class name. When we use jconsole to debug locally, the application does not have to run in debug mode, but for an application as simple as ours we need to make a few tweaks to make sure that we can see a few statistics with jconsole, during the run of the application. A few Thread.sleep(..) statements were added to pause the execution enough for jconsole to connect. Also, we'll use a large array of data to make sure that the statistics are relevant.

```
public class SortingSlf4jDemo {

    private static final Logger log =
        LoggerFactory.getLogger(SortingSlf4jDemo.class);

      public static void main(String... args) throws Exception {
        Thread.sleep(3000);
```

CHAPTER 9 DEBUGGING, TESTING, AND DOCUMENTING

```
        Random random = new Random(5);
        IntStream intStream = random.ints(100_000_000,0,350);

        int[] arr =  intStream.toArray();

        if (log.isDebugEnabled()) {
            final StringBuilder sb =
                new StringBuilder("Sorting  an array with merge sort: ");
            Arrays.stream(arr).forEach(i -> sb.append(i).append(" "));
            log.debug(sb.toString());
        }

        Thread.sleep(3000);

        IntSorter mergeSort = new MergeSort();
        mergeSort.sort(arr, 0, arr.length - 1);

        if (log.isInfoEnabled()) {
            final StringBuilder sb2 = new StringBuilder("Sorted: ");
            Arrays.stream(arr).forEach(i -> sb2.append(i).append(" "));
            log.info(sb2.toString());
        }
    }
    ...
}
```

After doing the modifications, we'll start the application normally and connect jconsole to it. After a successful connection, a window like the one shown in Figure 9-9 is opens, and graphs of the JVM memory consumption, number of threads, of classes loaded and CPU usage are displayed.

CHAPTER 9 ■ DEBUGGING, TESTING, AND DOCUMENTING

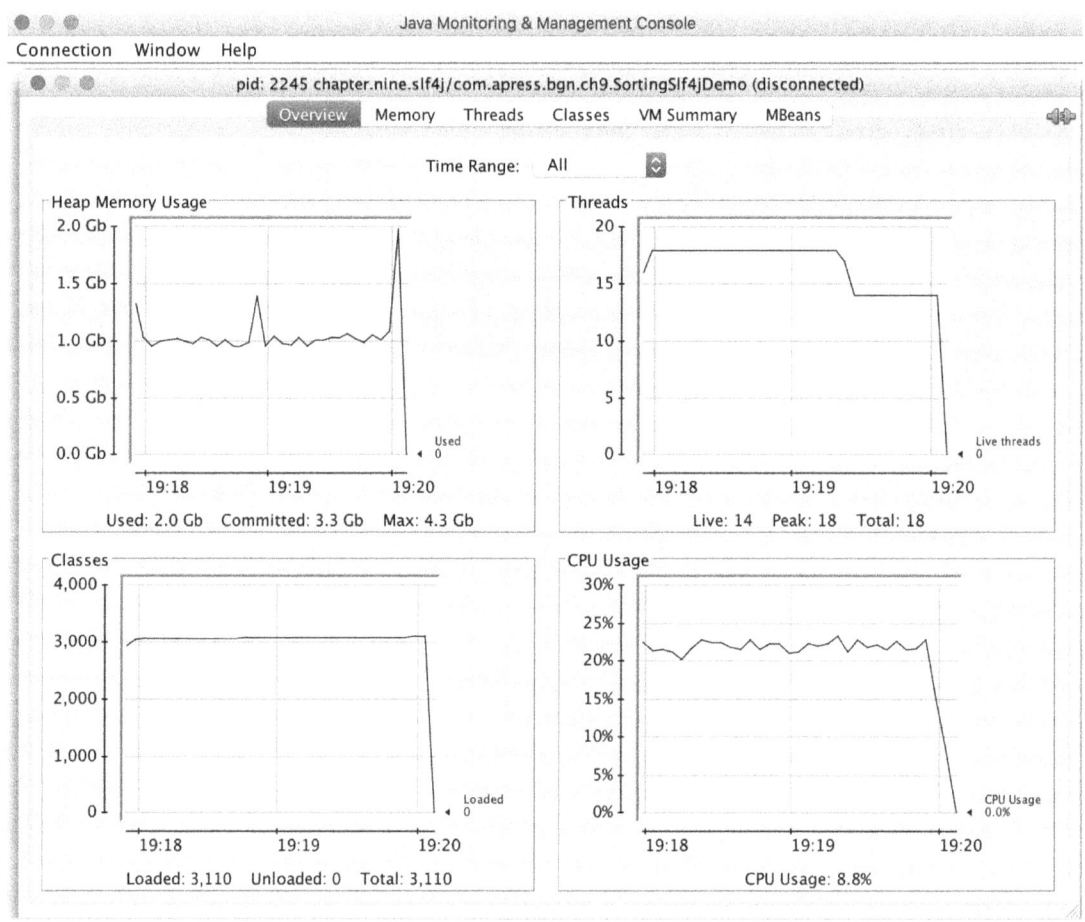

Figure 9-9. *JConsole statistics window*

There is a tab for each of these statistics that provides more information, and in a more complex application, this information can be used to improve performance, identify potential problems, or even estimate application behavior for desired cases. For our small application, the `jconsole` graphs do not reveal much, but if you really want to see valuable statistics, install an application like `mucommander`[5] use it for a while without closing it and then connect `jconsole` to it and have fun.

---

[5]The official MuCommander site is at `http://www.mucommander.com`

jmc

JMC is short for **Oracle Java Mission Control**. The jmc command starts an advanced Oracle application for debugging and analyzing JVM statistics for a running application. From its official description: *JMC is a tool suite for managing, monitoring, profiling, and troubleshooting your Java applications* that became part of the JDK utility tools family starting with version 7.

Similar to other tools, this utility identifies the Java processes currently running and provides the possibility to check out how much memory they require at specific times during execution, how many threads are running in parallel at a given moment in time, the classes loaded by the JVM, and how much processing power is required to run a Java application. The JMC has a friendlier interface and one of its most important components is the **Java Flight Recorder** that can be used to record all JVM activity while the application is running, all that data collected during this time being is then used to diagnose and profile the application.

To inspect the application while it is running, we open the JMC by running jmc from the command line, and then select the process that we recognize as the one running the SortingSlf4jDemo main class based on the same rule as before. We look for a process name containing the module name and the fully classified class name when we found it. We right-click it and select **Start JMX console**. You should see something similar to the image depicted in Figure 9-10.

CHAPTER 9   DEBUGGING, TESTING, AND DOCUMENTING

Figure 9-10. JMX console

As you probably noticed, the interface is definitely friendlier and the provided statistics are more detailed. Using JMC, everything that happens with the application and JVM during a run can be recorded and analyzed later, even if the application has stopped running since. The **Memory** tab provides a lot of information regarding the memory used by the application, including what types of objects are occupying it. The information for the memory occupied by `SortingSlf4jDemo` during its run is depicted in Figure 9-11.

CHAPTER 9   DEBUGGING, TESTING, AND DOCUMENTING

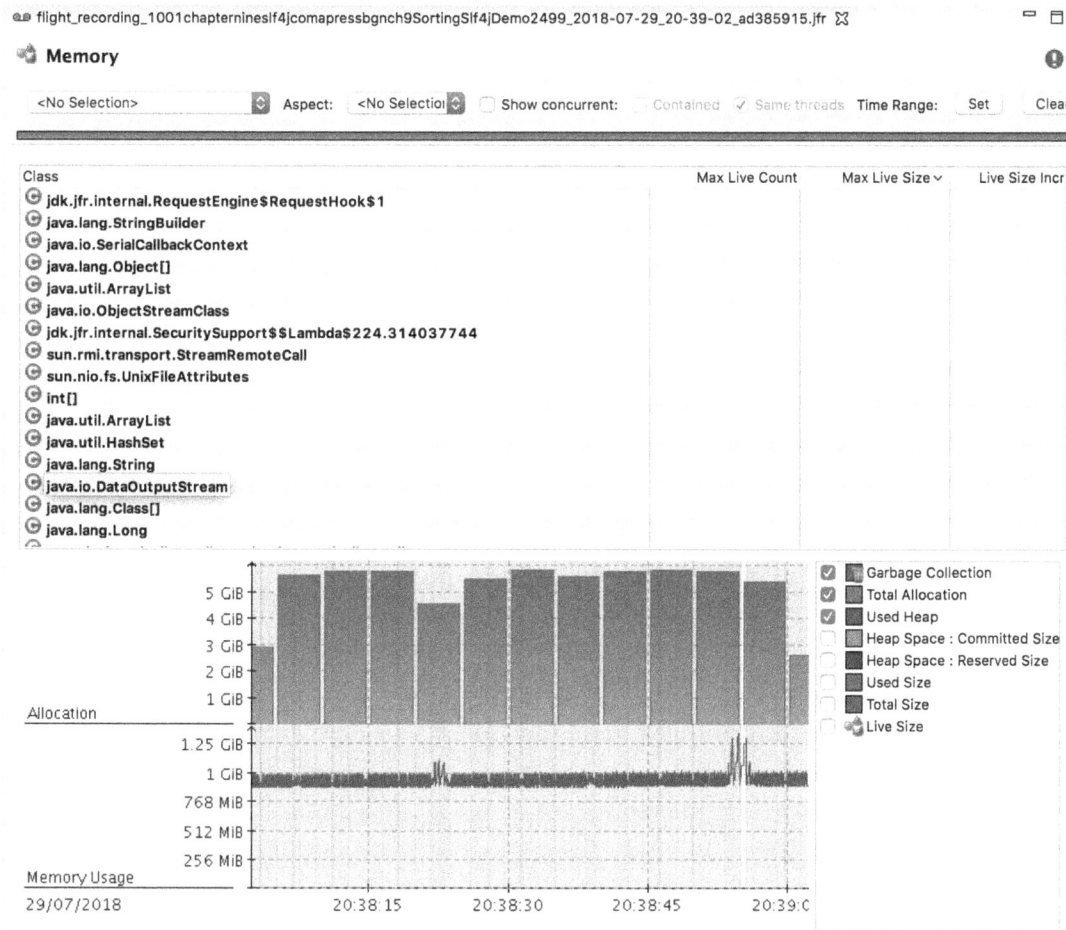

Figure 9-11. *JMX console ➤ the Memory tab*

To record this information during the application run, or for a limited period of time, in the **JVM Browser** expand the process node and select **Start Flight Recording**. A window is opened asking you to select a path where the recording is saved and the duration of the recording. The file has a .jfr extension and can be opened with the JMC for inspection. The flight recorder menu and the dialog to start recording data are depicted in Figure 9-12.

CHAPTER 9 DEBUGGING, TESTING, AND DOCUMENTING

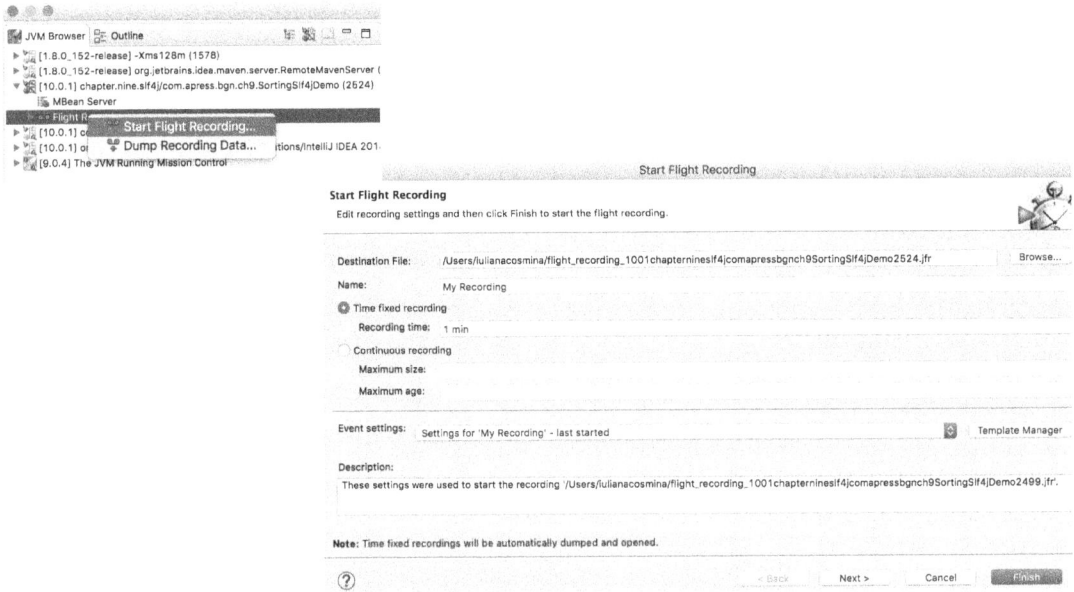

Figure 9-12. JMC Flight Recording menu and dialog window

The JMC subject is too advanced and broad for this section, an entire book could probably be written about its usage and how to interpret the statistics. So, I'll stop here and recommend this Oracle article if you want to dig deeper: www.oracle.com/technetwork/java/javaseproducts/mission-control/java-mission-control-1998576.html.

Accessing the Java Process API

Java 9 came with a lot of other improvements aside the Jigsaw modules, one of them being a new and improved Process API. The Java Process API allows you to start, retrieve information, and manage native operating system processes. The ability to manipulate processes was in former versions of Java, but it was rudimentary. Note how a process was created before Java 5.

```
package com.apress.bgn.ch9;

import org.slf4j.Logger;
import org.slf4j.LoggerFactory;
```

```java
import java.io.BufferedReader;
import java.io.InputStream;
import java.io.InputStreamReader;
import java.io.Reader;
import java.nio.charset.Charset;
import java.nio.charset.StandardCharsets;

public class ProcessCreationDemo {
    private static final Logger log =
        LoggerFactory.getLogger(ProcessCreationDemo.class);

    public static void main(String... args) {
        try {
            Process exec = Runtime.getRuntime()
              .exec(new String[] { "/bin/sh", "-c", "echo Java
              home:   $JAVA_HOME" });
            exec.waitFor();
             InputStream is = exec.getInputStream();
            StringBuilder textBuilder = new StringBuilder();
            try (Reader reader = new BufferedReader(new InputStreamReader
                    (is, Charset.forName(StandardCharsets.UTF_8.name())))) {
                int c = 0;
                while ((c = reader.read()) != -1) {
                    textBuilder.append((char) c);
                }
            }
            log.info("Process output -> {}", textBuilder.toString());
            log.info("process result: {}", exec.exitValue());
        } catch (Exception e) {
            e.printStackTrace();
        }
    }
}
```

Intercepting the output of a process that has started is a pain. We need to wrap a BufferedReader instance around the InputStream instance connected to the normal output of the process.

CHAPTER 9 DEBUGGING, TESTING, AND DOCUMENTING

The process API made things a little more practical. It has at its core a few classes and interfaces, all with names that start with the "Process" term. What we've done so far with Java executables, can be directly done by writing Java code. The interface that provides an API to access native processes is named ProcessHandle and is part of the core Java package java.lang. In a similar manner to the Thread class, there is a static method named current to call on this interface to retrieve the ProcessHandle instance of the current running process. Once we have this, we can use its methods to access more process information. The ProcessHandle provides several static utility methods to access native processes. Java code can be written to list all processes running on a computer and they can be sorted based on certain criteria. The following piece of code lists all the processes that were created by running the java command.

```
package com.apress.bgn.ch9;

import org.slf4j.Logger;
import org.slf4j.LoggerFactory;

import java.util.Arrays;
import java.util.Optional;
public class ProcessListingDemo {

    private static final Logger log = LoggerFactory.getLogger(ProcessDemo.class);

    public static void main(String... args) {
        Optional<String> currUser = ProcessHandle.current().info().user();

        ProcessHandle.allProcesses()
            .filter(ph -> ph.info().user().equals(currUser)
                && ph.info().commandLine().get().contains("java"))
            .forEach(p ->  log.info("PID: " + p.pid()));
                p.info() .arguments()
                  .ifPresent(s -> Arrays.stream(s)
                    .forEach(a -> log.info("\t {}", a)));

                p.info().command()
                    .ifPresent(c -> log.info("\t Command: {}", c));
        });
    }
}
```

CHAPTER 9　DEBUGGING, TESTING, AND DOCUMENTING

This code extracts the user from the current running process by obtaining its handle and calling `info()` to obtain an instance of `ProcessHandle.Info`, an interface that provides a set of methods to access snapshot information about the process as the command and arguments that were used to create the process. The output of the previous code is printed in the console. It should look similar to the following listing.

```
INFO  c.a.b.c.ProcessDemo - PID: 3077
INFO  c.a.b.c.ProcessDemo -     -Dlogback.configurationFile=
    chapter09/processapi/src/main/resources/logback.xml
INFO  c.a.b.c.ProcessDemo -     -javaagent:/Applications/IntelliJ IDEA
                                2018.2 EAP
    .app/Contents/lib/idea_rt.jar=57554:
    /Applications/IntelliJ IDEA 2018.2 EAP.app/Contents/bin
INFO  c.a.b.c.ProcessDemo -     -Dfile.encoding=UTF-8
INFO  c.a.b.c.ProcessDemo -     -p
INFO  c.a.b.c.ProcessDemo -     /Users/iulianacosmina/apress/workspace/
    java-bgn/chapter09/processapi/out/production/classes ...*.jar
INFO  c.a.b.c.ProcessDemo -     -m
INFO  c.a.b.c.ProcessDemo -     chapter.nine.processapi/com.apress.bgn.ch9.
                                ProcessDemo
INFO  c.a.b.c.ProcessDemo -         Command:
    /Library/Java/JavaVirtualMachines/jdk-10.0.1.jdk/Contents/Home/bin/java

INFO  c.a.b.c.ProcessDemo - PID: 3076
INFO  c.a.b.c.ProcessDemo -     -Xmx700m
INFO  c.a.b.c.ProcessDemo -     -Djava.awt.headless=true
INFO  c.a.b.c.ProcessDemo -     -Djdt.compiler.useSingleThread=true
...
INFO  c.a.b.c.ProcessDemo -     org.jetbrains.jps.cmdline.Launcher
INFO  c.a.b.c.ProcessDemo -     /Applications/IntelliJ IDEA 2018.2 EAP.app/
                                Contents/lib/...*.jar
INFO  c.a.b.c.ProcessDemo -     org.jetbrains.jps.cmdline.BuildMain
INFO  c.a.b.c.ProcessDemo -     127.0.0.1
INFO  c.a.b.c.ProcessDemo -     51833
INFO  c.a.b.c.ProcessDemo -     47353a1a-570c-4f45-85f9-91abcbb66e9a
INFO  c.a.b.c.ProcessDemo -
    /Users/iulianacosmina/Library/Caches/IntelliJIdea2018.2/compile-server
```

INFO c.a.b.c.ProcessDemo -   Command: /Library/Java/JavaVirtualMachines/jdk-10.0.1.jdk/Contents/Home/bin/java

In this log, only the IntelliJ IDEA launcher used to run the `ProcessDemo` class and the process spawned to run it were depicted, but the output could be much bigger. Also, some arguments were shortened, as it is useless to waste pages of the book with logs. Nevertheless, some depiction of the log format was necessary in case you never run the code yourself.

The previous code sample showed you roughly how to access native processes and print information about them. But, using the improved Java process API, new processes can be created, and commands of the underlying operation system can be started. For example, we can create a process that prints the value of the `JAVA_HOME` environment variable, and capture the output to display it in the IntelliJ console.

```java
  package com.apress.bgn.ch9;

import org.slf4j.Logger;
import org.slf4j.LoggerFactory;

public class ProcessCreationDemo {
    private static final Logger log =
        LoggerFactory.getLogger(ProcessCreationDemo.class);

    public static void main(String... args) {
        try {
            ProcessBuilder pb = new
               ProcessBuilder("/bin/sh", "-c", "echo Java home:  $JAVA_HOME")
                  .inheritIO();
            Process p = pb.start();
            p.onExit();
            CompletableFuture<Process> future =  p.onExit();
            int result = future.get().exitValue();
            log.info("Process result: {}", result);
        } catch (Exception e) {
            e.printStackTrace();
        }
    }
}
```

New processes can be created by using instances of `ProcessBuilder` that can receive as arguments a list of commands and values to use as arguments for them. The class has many constructors and methods with different signatures that can be used to create and start processes easily. The `inheritIO()` method sets the source and destination for the subprocess standard I/O to be the same as the current process. The `onExit()` method returns an `CompletableFuture<Process>` that can be used to access the process at the end of its execution to retrieve the exit value of the process. For a process terminating normally, the value should be 0(zero).

When a Java program creates a process, it becomes a child of the process that created it. To list all child processes, we need to make sure that they last a while, because once terminated, they obviously no longer exist. The following code sample creates three identical processes, each of them executing three Linux shell commands: the first is `echo "start"` to notify that the process has started execution, the second is `sleep 3` that pauses the process for 3 seconds, and the last one (`echo "done."`) is executed right before the process finishes its execution. Once the process has started, it can no longer be controlled, so to make sure that the child processes finish their execution, we'll ask the user to press a key to decide when the current process finishes execution by calling `System.in.read();`.

```java
package com.apress.bgn.ch9;

import org.slf4j.Logger;
import org.slf4j.LoggerFactory;

public class ProcessCreationDemo {
    private static final Logger log =
        LoggerFactory.getLogger(ProcessCreationDemo.class);

    public static void main(String... args) {
        try {
            List<ProcessBuilder> builders = List.of(
                    new ProcessBuilder("/bin/sh", "-c",
                        "echo \"start...\" ; sleep 3; echo \"done.\"").
                        inheritIO(),
                    new ProcessBuilder("/bin/sh", "-c",
                        "echo \"start...\" ; sleep 3; echo \"done.\"").
                        inheritIO(),
```

```
                new ProcessBuilder("/bin/sh", "-c",
                    "echo \"start...\" ; sleep 3; echo \"done.\"").
                    inheritIO()
            );
            builders.parallelStream().forEach(pbs -> {
                try {
                    pbs.start();
                } catch (Exception e) {
                    log.error("Oops, could not start process!", e);
                }
            });

            ProcessHandle ph = ProcessHandle.current();
            ph.children().forEach(pc -> {
                log.info("Child PID: {}", pc.pid());
                pc.parent().ifPresent(parent ->
                    log.info(" Parent PID: {}", parent.pid()));

            });
            System.out.println("Press any key to exit!");
            System.in.read();
        } catch (Exception e) {
            e.printStackTrace();
        }
    }
}
```

We have grouped the `ProcessBuilders` in a list and processed the instances using a parallel stream to make sure that all processes were started almost at the same time. We printed the results of each of them after termination to make sure all were executed correctly.

The `children()` method returns a stream containing `ProcessHandle` instances corresponding to the processes started by the current Java process.

The `parent()` method was called for each child `ProcessHandle` instance to obtain the `ProcessHandle` corresponding to the process that created it.

When running the previous code, in the console you should see an output similar to what is depicted in the next listing.

```
start...
start...
start...
22:29:04.593 [main] INFO com.apress.bgn.ch9.ProcessCreationDemo - Child
PID: 3966
22:29:04.594 [main] INFO com.apress.bgn.ch9.ProcessCreationDemo -    Parent
PID: 3962
22:29:04.594 [main] INFO com.apress.bgn.ch9.ProcessCreationDemo - Child
PID: 3965
22:29:04.594 [main] INFO com.apress.bgn.ch9.ProcessCreationDemo -    Parent
PID: 3962
22:29:04.594 [main] INFO com.apress.bgn.ch9.ProcessCreationDemo - Child
PID: 3964
22:29:04.594 [main] INFO com.apress.bgn.ch9.ProcessCreationDemo -    Parent
PID: 3962
Press any key to exit!
done.
done.
done.
```

The improved Java Process API provides a lot more control over running and spawned processes and in a practical manner. In the past, developers who needed to work with processes on a more advanced level resorted to native code. A full list of the Java process API improvements added in Java 9 can be found at https://docs.oracle.com/javase/9/core/process-api1.htm#JSCOR-GUID-6FAB2491-FD4E-42B4-A883-DCD181A1CE3E.

Testing

Debugging is a part of a software process called **testing** and involves identifying and correcting code errors. But avoiding technical errors is not enough, testing an application means much more than that. There is an organization providing very good materials for training and certifications for software testers. The **International Software**

Testing Qualifications Board (ISTQB) is a software testing qualification certification organization that operates internationally. It established a syllabus and a hierarchy of qualifications and guidelines for software testing.[6] If you think you are more interested in software testing then you should look into getting an ISTQB certification.

The ISTQB defines testing as "the process consisting of all lifecycle activities, both static and dynamic, concerned with planning, preparation and evaluation of software and related work products to determine that they satisfy specified requirements to demonstrate that they are fit for purpose and to detect defects."

This is a technical and academic definition. The definition that I propose is "the process of verifying that an implementation does what it is supposed to in the amount of time it is expected to, with an acceptable resources consumption and it does not break anything while doing so."

A Small Introduction to Testing

I want to be a developer. Why do I need to know all of these details about testing? The simple answer is because testing is a constant activity that is performed during every phase of the lifecycle of a software application. When the design is made, simulations are done and experienced people review the design to decide if it represents a proper solution for the problem and if it is realizable. When the code is written, it has to be tested to make sure the application does not crash and behaves as expected. Before delivery, there is a phase named acceptance testing when client representatives test the application in a controlled environment so every action is logged and problems identified. Testing can be done using debugging, using all the methods presented until now, but the disadvantage of debugging is that it is manual and repetitive. So, let's introduce a way to test the application that is a little bit more automated.

! Testing is an essential part of the development process and should start as early as possible, because the effort of fixing a defect grows exponentially with the time it takes to be discovered.[7]

---

[6]The ISTQB certification path: https://www.istqb.org/certification-path-root.html
[7]*Clean Code* by Robert Martin (Prentice Hall, 2008)

During the development phase, aside from writing the actual solution, you can also write code to test your solution. Those tests can run manually or by a build tool when you build your project. When writing your code, aside from thinking about the solution to solve the problem, you should also think about how to test the solution. This approach is called **TDD**, which is the acronym for **test-driven development**, a programming paradigm that states that you should think about how to test your solution, before implementing it, because if it is difficult to test, it probably is difficult to implement, maintain on the long run and extend to solve related problems.

The simplest tests are called **unit tests**, which test small units of functionality. If unit tests cannot be written easily, your design might be rotten. Unit tests are the first line of defense against failures. If unit tests fail, the foundation of your solution is bad.

The tests that span across multiple components, testing the communication between units of functionality and the results of their interactions against an expected results are called **integration tests**.

The last type of tests a developer should write are **regression tests**, which are tests that are run periodically to make sure that code that was previously tested still performs correctly after it is changed. These type of tests are crucial for big projects where code is written by a considerable number of developers, because sometimes dependencies among components are not obvious, and code one developer wrote might break another developer's code.

This section only shows you how to write unit tests using a Java library called JUnit. It describes a few typical testing components that a developer can build to set up a context for the unit tests. Thus, as my Scottish colleagues say, *let's get cracking!*

Test Code Location

As you probably remember, in **Chapter** 3 the `java-for-absolute-beginners` project structure was explained. The discussion about tests must start with the structure of the lowest level modules of the project, the ones that contain the source code and tests. Figure 9-13 shows the structure of the module containing the sources and test code for the module used in this section.

Chapter 9 Debugging, Testing, and Documenting

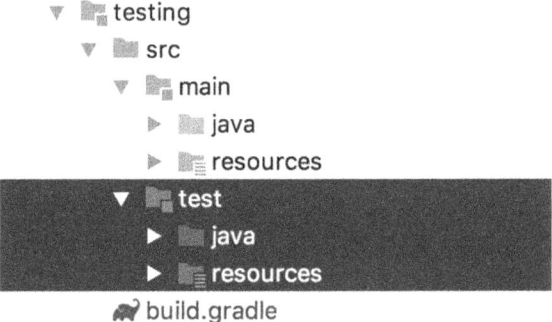

Figure 9-13. *The Gradle module structure*

The structure shown in Figure 9-13 can be explained as follows.

- The `src` directory contains all code and resources of the project. The contents are split into two directories `main` and `test`.

  - The `main` directory contains the source code and the application configuration files, split into two directories. The `java` directory contains the Java source code and the `resources` contains configuration files, non-executable text files(that can be written according to various formats: XML, SQL, CSV, etc.), media files, PDFs, and so forth. When the application is built and packed into a jar (or war or ear) only the files in the `java` directory are taken onto account, the `*.class` filed together with the configuration files are packed.

  - The `test` directory contains code used to test the source code in the `src` directory. The Java files are kept under the `java` directory and in the `resources` directory contains configuration files needed to build a test context. The contents of the `test` directory are not part of the project that is delivered to a client. They exist to help test the application during development.

Application to Test

For the examples in this section we build a simple application that uses an embedded Derby[8] database to store data. This is the production database. For the test environment the database is replaced with various pseudo-constructions that mimic the database

---

[8]If you are interested in finding our more about the Derby database, this is the official resource to go to: `https://db.apache.org/derby/`

CHAPTER 9   DEBUGGING, TESTING, AND DOCUMENTING

behavior. The application is rudimentary. An `AccountService` implementation takes data from the input and uses it to manage `Account` instances. The `Account` class is a very abstract an unrealistic implementation of a banking account. It has a `holder` field, which is the account owner, an `accountNumber` field, and an `amount` field. The `AccountService` implementation uses an `AccountRepo` implementation to perform all related database operations with `Account` instances using an implementation of `DBConnection`. The classes and interfaces that are making up this simple application and relationships between them are depicted in Figure 9-14.

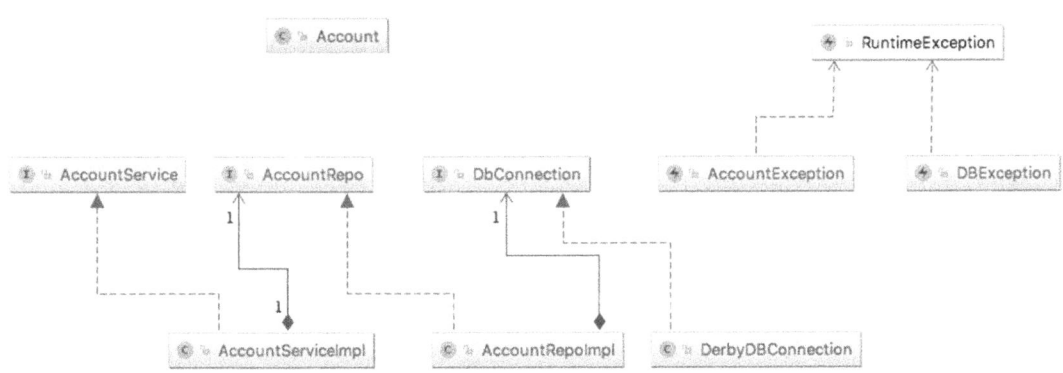

Figure 9-14. *Simple Account management application components*

The implementation of these classes is not relevant for this section, but if you are curious, you can find the full code on this book's official repository. So, let's start testing. The easiest way would be to write a main class and perform some account operations. But, we do not want that, once the application is in production we can no longer test new features on it, because there are risks of data corruption. Also, production databases are usually hosted on costly products, such as Oracle RDBMS (Oracle Relational Database Management System) or Microsoft SQL Server. They are not really appropriate for development, or testing. Also, the intention is to run tests automatically, so in-memory or implementations that can be instantiated are more suitable. So, let's start by testing our `AccountRepoImpl`.

Introducing JUnit

JUnit is undoubtedly the most used testing framework in the Java development world. At the end of 2017, JUnit 5[9] was released that is the next generation of this framework. It comes with a new engine, is compatible with Java 9+, and comes with a lot of lambda-based functionalities. JUnit provides annotations to mark test methods for automated execution, annotations for initialization and destruction of a test context and utility methods to practically implement test methods. There are multiple JUnit annotations that you can use. Five of them (and a utility class) represent the core of the JUnit framework, which is the best place to learn testing. Below each of them are a short description that builds a general picture of how JUnit can be used to test your application.

- `@BeforeAll` from package `org.junit.jupiter.api` is used on a `non-private static` method that returns `void` used to initialize objects and variables to be used by all test methods in the current class. This method is called only once, before all test methods in the class, so test methods should not modify these objects, because their state is shared and it might affect the test results. Eventually, the static fields to be initialized by the annotated method, can be `declared final`, so once initialized, they can no longer be changed. More than one method annotated with `@BeforeAll` can be declared in a test class, but what would be the point?

- `@AfterAll` from package `org.junit.jupiter.api` is the counterpart of `@BeforeAll`. It is also used to annotate `non-private static` methods that return `void`, but their purpose is to destroy the context the test methods were run in and perform cleanup actions.

- `@BeforeEach` from package `org.junit.jupiter.api` is used on `non-private non-static` methods that return `void` and as its name says, methods annotated with it are executed before every method annotated with `@Test`. These methods can be used to further customize the test context to populate objects with values that tests assertions in the test methods.

---

[9]Official JUnit 5 site: `https://junit.org/junit5/`

CHAPTER 9 DEBUGGING, TESTING, AND DOCUMENTING

- `@AfterEach` from package `org.junit.jupiter.api` is used on `public` non-`static` methods that return `void` and as its name says, methods annotated with it are executed after every method annotated with `@Test`.

- `@Test` from package `org.junit.jupiter.api` is used on `non-private` `non-static` methods that return `void` and as its name says, the method annotated with it is a test method. A test class can have one or more, depending on the class that is being tested.

- Utility class `org.junit.jupiter.api.Assertions` provides a set of methods that support asserting conditions in tests.

Another annotation that you might be interested to know it exists is `@DisplayName`. It is declared in the same package as all the others and receives a text argument that represents the test display name, which is displayed by the editor and in the resulting reports created by the build tool. Let's write a pseudo test class so you can get an idea of how test classes look.

```java
package com.apress.bgn.ch9.pseudo;

import org.junit.jupiter.api.*;
import org.slf4j.Logger;
import org.slf4j.LoggerFactory;

import static org.junit.jupiter.api.Assertions.assertFalse;
import static org.junit.jupiter.api.Assertions.assertTrue;

public class PseudoTest {

    private static final Logger log =
        LoggerFactory.getLogger(PseudoTest.class);

    @BeforeAll
    public static void loadCtx() {
        log.info("Loading general test context.");
    }

    @BeforeEach
    public  void setUp(){
        log.info("Prepare  single test context.");
    }
```

```java
@Test
@DisplayName("test one")
public void testOne() {
    log.info("Executing test one.");
    assertTrue(true);
}

@Test
@DisplayName("test two")
public void testTwo() {
    log.info("Executing test two.");
    assertFalse(false);
}

@AfterEach
public void tearDown(){
    log.info("Destroy  single test context.");
}

@AfterAll
public static void unloadCtx(){
    log.info("UnLoading general test context.");
}
}
```

Keeping in mind the information that you now have about these annotations, when running this class, we expect the log messages that each method prints to be in the exact order that we have defined, because the methods have been strategically placed in the previous code so the JUnit order of execution is respected. The only thing that cannot be guaranteed is the order the tests are executed in. Also parallel execution of tests is possible by adding a file named `junit-platform.properties` under `test\resources` that contains the following properties with values matching the hardware configuration.

```
junit.jupiter.execution.parallel.enabled=true
junit.jupiter.execution.parallel.config.strategy=fixed
junit.jupiter.execution.parallel.config.fixed.parallelism=8
```

CHAPTER 9 DEBUGGING, TESTING, AND DOCUMENTING

Most Java smart editors like IntelliJ IDEA provide you with an option to do so when you right-click the class. Figure 9-15 shows the menu option to execute a test class in IntelliJ IDEA.

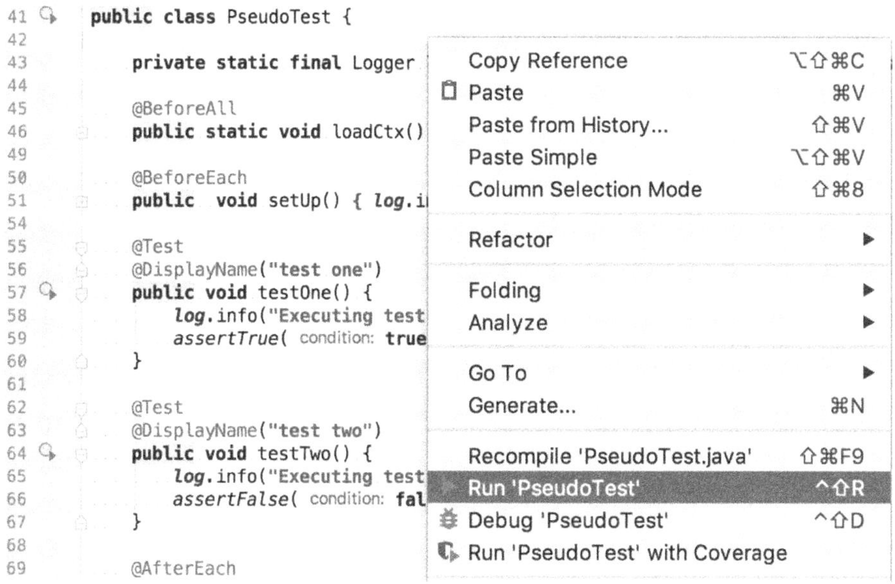

Figure 9-15. Menu option to execute a test class in IntelliJ IDEA

After right-clicking the class, select **Run 'PseudoTest.java'** from the menu that appears. The test class is executed. A launcher is created. Test classes can be executed in debug mode, and breakpoints can be used. When executing the previous class, even if the test methods are run in parallel, the output is consistent with the order of the methods matching the annotation specifications. To make sure that test methods are executed in parallel, the logger was configured to print the thread ID. The following is a sample output.

```
[1-worker-9] INFO  c.a.b.c.p.PseudoTest - Loading general test context.
[1-worker-9] INFO  c.a.b.c.p.PseudoTest - Prepare  single test context.
[1-worker-2] INFO  c.a.b.c.p.PseudoTest - Prepare  single test context.
[1-worker-2] INFO  c.a.b.c.p.PseudoTest - Executing test one.
[1-worker-9] INFO  c.a.b.c.p.PseudoTest - Executing test two.
[1-worker-2] INFO  c.a.b.c.p.PseudoTest - Destroy  single test context.
[1-worker-9] INFO  c.a.b.c.p.PseudoTest - Destroy  single test context.
[1-worker-9] INFO  c.a.b.c.p.PseudoTest - UnLoading general test context.
```

The `testOne()` method contains this line: `assertTrue(true);`, which is put there to show you how assertion methods look like. The `true` value is replaced with a condition in a real test. The same goes for the `assertFalse(false);` assertion in the `textTwo()` method.

And that's about all the space we can dedicate to JUnit in this book. But my honest recommendation is to look more into it, because a developer can write code, but a good developer knows how to make sure it works.

Using Fakes

A **fake** object is an object that has working implementations, but not the same as the production object. The code written to implement such an object has simplified functionality of the one deployed in production.

To test the `AccountRepoImpl` class, we have to replace the `DerbyDBConnection` with a `FakeDBConnection` that is not backed up by a database, but by something simpler, more accessible like a `Map`. The `DerbyDBConnection` uses a `java.sql.Connection` and other classes in that package to perform data operations on the Derby database.

The `FakeDBConnection` implement the `DBConnection` interface, so it can be passed to a `AccountRepoImpl` and all its methods is called on it.

The rule of thumb when writing tests and test supporting classes is to put them in the same packages with the objects tested or replaced, but in the `test/java` directory. But because we show you more than one approach of testing, each package is named accordingly. The package to test the application classes using fakes is named `com.apress.bgn.ch9.fake`.

Another rule of thumb when writing tests is to write a method to test the correct outcome of the method being tested, and one to test the incorrect behavior. In unexpected cases with unexpected data, your application behaves in unexpected ways, so although this seems paradoxical, you have to expect the unexpected and write tests for it.

The `AccountRepoImpl` class implements the basic methods to persist or delete an `Account` instance to/from the database. The implementation is depicted next.

```
package com.apress.bgn.ch9.repo;

import com.apress.bgn.ch9.Account;
import com.apress.bgn.ch9.db.DbConnection;

import java.util.List;
import java.util.Optional;
```

```java
public class AccountRepoImpl implements AccountRepo {

    private DbConnection conn;

    public AccountRepoImpl(DbConnection conn) {
        this.conn = conn;
    }

    @Override
    public Account save(Account account) {
        Account dbAcc = conn.findByHolder(account.getHolder());
        if(dbAcc == null) {
            return conn.insert(account);
        }
        return conn.update(account);
    }

    @Override
    public Optional<Account> findOne(String holder) {
        Account acc = conn.findByHolder(holder);
        if(acc != null) {
            return Optional.of(acc);
        }
        return Optional.empty();
    }

    @Override
    public List<Account> findAll() {
        return conn.findAll();
    }

    @Override
    public int deleteByHolder(String holder) {
        Account acc = conn.findByHolder(holder);
        conn.delete(holder);
        if(acc != null) {
            return 0;
        }
```

CHAPTER 9   DEBUGGING, TESTING, AND DOCUMENTING

```
        return 1;
    }
}
```

To test this method we need to provide a `DbConnection` implementation that simulates a connection to a database. This is where `FakeDBConnection` comes in.

```java
package com.apress.bgn.ch9.fake.db;

import com.apress.bgn.ch9.Account;
import com.apress.bgn.ch9.db.DBException;
import com.apress.bgn.ch9.db.DbConnection;

import java.util.ArrayList;
import java.util.HashMap;
import java.util.List;
import java.util.Map;

public class FakeDBConnection implements DbConnection {
    /**
     * pseudo-database {@code Map<holder, Account>}
     */
    Map<String, Account> database = new HashMap<>();

    @Override
    public void connect() {
        // no implementation needed
    }

    @Override
    public Account insert(Account account) {
        if (database.containsKey(account.getHolder())) {
            throw new DBException("Could not insert " + account);
        }
        database.put(account.getHolder(), account);
        return account;
    }
```

```java
    @Override
    public Account findByHolder(String holder) {
        return database.get(holder);
    }

    @Override
    public List<Account> findAll() {
        List<Account> result = new ArrayList<>();
        result.addAll(database.values());
        return result;
    }

    @Override
    public Account update(Account account) {
        if (!database.containsKey(account.getHolder())) {
            throw new DBException("Could not find account for " + account.
            getHolder());
        }
        database.put(account.getHolder(), account);
        return account;
    }

    @Override
    public void delete(String holder) {
        database.remove(holder);
    }

    @Override
    public void disconnect() {
        // no implementation needed
    }
}
```

The `FakeDBConnection` behaves exactly like a connection object that can be used to save entries to a database, search for them or delete them, only instead of a database is backed up by a `Map<String, Account>`. The map key is the holder's name, because in our database the holder name is used as an unique identifier for an `Account` entry in the table. Now, that we have the fake object, we can test that our `AccountRepoImpl` behaves as expected. Because of practical reasons only one method is tested in this section, but the full code is available on the official GitHub repo for the book.

The `deleteByHolder` method in the `AccountRepoImpl` deletes an account. If the entry is present, it deletes it and returns 0; otherwise, it returns 1. The `deleteByHolder` method is depicted in the next code snippet.

```java
package com.apress.bgn.ch9.repo;

import com.apress.bgn.ch9.Account;
import com.apress.bgn.ch9.db.DbConnection;

import java.util.List;
import java.util.Optional;

public class AccountRepoImpl implements AccountRepo {

    private DbConnection conn;

    public AccountRepoImpl(DbConnection conn) {
        this.conn = conn;
    }

    @Override
    public int deleteByHolder(String holder) {
        Account acc = conn.findByHolder(holder);
        conn.delete(holder);
        if(acc != null) {
            return 0;
        }
        return 1;
    }
    ...
}
```

CHAPTER 9 DEBUGGING, TESTING, AND DOCUMENTING

The test class is depicted next, and both cases are covered (when there is an entry to delete and when there isn't).

```java
package com.apress.bgn.ch9.fake;

import com.apress.bgn.ch9.Account;
import com.apress.bgn.ch9.db.DbConnection;
import com.apress.bgn.ch9.fake.db.FakeDBConnection;
import com.apress.bgn.ch9.repo.AccountRepo;
import com.apress.bgn.ch9.repo.AccountRepoImpl;
import org.junit.jupiter.api.*;
import org.slf4j.Logger;
import org.slf4j.LoggerFactory;

import static org.junit.jupiter.api.Assertions.assertEquals;
import static org.junit.jupiter.api.Assertions.assertTrue;

public class AccountRepoTest {
    private static final Logger log =
        LoggerFactory.getLogger(AccountRepoTest.class);
    private static DbConnection conn;

    private AccountRepo repo;

    @BeforeAll
    public static void prepare() {
        conn = new FakeDBConnection();
    }

    @BeforeEach
    public void setUp(){
        repo = new AccountRepoImpl(conn);

        // inserting an entry so we can test update
        repo.save(new Account("Pedala", 200, "2345"));
    }
```

```
    @Test
    public void testFindOneExisting (){
        Optional<Account> expected = repo.findOne("Pedala");
        assertTrue(expected.isPresent());
    }

    @Test
    public void testFindOneNonExisting(){
        Optional<Account> expected = repo.findOne("Dorel");
        assertFalse(expected.isPresent());
    }

    @AfterEach
    public void tearDown(){
        // delete the entry
        repo.deleteByHolder("Pedala");
    }

    @AfterAll
    public static void cleanUp(){
        conn = null;
        log.info("All done!");
    }
}
```

Notice how, we are creating exactly one entry that is added to our fake database before a test method is executed and deleted afterwards.

Now that we are sure the repository class does its job properly the next one to test is the `AccountServiceImpl`. To test this class we look into a different approach. Fakes, are useful but writing one for a class with complex functionality can be cost inefficient in regards to development time. In the next section, we'll look at *stubs*.

Using Stubs

A **stub** is an object that holds predefined data and uses it to answer test calls. An instance of `AccountServiceImpl` uses an instance of `AccountRepo` to retrieve data from the database or save data to a database. Considering we are writing unit tests, we want to cover the functionality of the service class, so we can write a **stub** class to simulate the behavior of `AccountRepo`. For the `AccountServiceImpl` instance to use it the stub must implement AccountRepo. In this section the tests cover the method createAccount(...) because there are multiple points of failure and we can write a lot of different tests for it. In the following code snippet the createAccount(...) method is depicted.

```java
package com.apress.bgn.ch9.service;

import com.apress.bgn.ch9.Account;
import com.apress.bgn.ch9.repo.AccountRepo;

import java.util.Optional;

/**
 * @author Iuliana Cosmina
 * @since 1.0
 */
public class AccountServiceImpl implements AccountService {

    AccountRepo repo;

    public AccountServiceImpl(AccountRepo repo) {
        this.repo = repo;
    }

    @Override
    public Account createAccount(String holder, String accountNumber,
        String amount) {
        int intAmount;
        try {
            intAmount = Integer.parseInt(amount);
        } catch (NumberFormatException nfe) {
            throw new InvalidDataException(
                "Could not create account with invalid amount!");
        }
        if (accountNumber == null ||
                accountNumber.isEmpty() || accountNumber.length() < 5
                || intAmount < 0) {
            throw new InvalidDataException(
                "Could not create account with invalid account number!");
        }
```

CHAPTER 9   DEBUGGING, TESTING, AND DOCUMENTING

```
        Optional<Account> existing = repo.findOne(holder);
        if (existing.isPresent()) {
            throw new AccountCreationException(
                "Account already exists for holder " + holder);
        }
        Account acc = new Account(holder, intAmount, accountNumber);
        return repo.save(acc);
    }
    ...
}
```

The `createAccount(..)` method takes as parameters the holder name, the number of the account to be created and the initial amount. All of them are provided as `String` instances intentionally, so that the method body contains a little bit of logic that would require serious testing. Let's analyze the behavior of the previous method and make a list with all possible returned values and returned exceptions.

- If the amount is not a number, an `InvalidDataException` is thrown.

- If the `accountNumber` argument is empty, an `InvalidDataException` is thrown.

- If the `accountNumber` argument is null, an `InvalidDataException` is thrown.

- If the `accountNumber` argument has less than five characters, an `InvalidDataException` is thrown.

- If the `amount` argument converted to a number is negative, an `InvalidDataException` is thrown.

- If there is an account for the `holder` argument already an `AccountCreationException` is thrown.

- If all the inputs are valid and there is no account for the `holder` argument, an `Account` instance is created, saved to the database, and the result is returned.

CHAPTER 9   DEBUGGING, TESTING, AND DOCUMENTING

So, if we were to be really obsessive about testing, we would have to write a test scenario for all of these cases. In the software world, there is something called *test coverage*, which is a process that determines whether test cases cover application code and how much of it. The result is a percentage value and companies usually define a test coverage percent[10] that represents a warranty of quality for the application. So, let's write all those tests methods, just for the practice. But before that, let's see what the repo stub looks like.

```java
  package com.apress.bgn.ch9.stub;

import com.apress.bgn.ch9.Account;
import com.apress.bgn.ch9.repo.AccountRepo;

import java.util.List;
import java.util.Optional;

public class AccountRepoStub implements AccountRepo {

    private  Integer option = 0;

   public synchronized void set(int val) {
        option = val;
    }

    @Override
    public Account save(Account account) {
        return account;
    }

    @Override
    public Optional<Account> findOne(String holder) {
        if(option == 0) {
            return Optional.of(new Account(holder, 100 ,"22446677"));
        }
        return Optional.empty();
    }
```

---

[10]A good read about test coverage, by Martin Fowler, one of the most renown Java gurus of this generation: https://martinfowler.com/bliki/TestCoverage.html

```
    @Override
    public List<Account> findAll() {
        return List.of(new Account("sample", 100, "22446677"));
    }

    @Override
    public int deleteByHolder(String holder) {
        return option;
    }
}
```

The `option` field can be used to change behavior of the stub to cover more test cases. This is useful when test methods are not executed in parallel. Test execution is done in parallel when time is of the essence, and if stubs are used, each method should instantiate and use its own stub to avoid collisions with other methods, which will most probably lead to test failures.

A negative test, passing for the situation when the input represents an invalid amount can be written in two way using JUnit. The two approaches only differ in how lambda expressions are used.

```
package com.apress.bgn.ch9.service;

import com.apress.bgn.ch9.Account;
import com.apress.bgn.ch9.service.stub.AccountRepoStub;
import org.junit.jupiter.api.*;

import static org.junit.jupiter.api.Assertions.assertEquals;
import static org.junit.jupiter.api.Assertions.assertThrows;

public class AccountServiceTest {

    private static AccountRepoStub repo;
    private AccountService service;

    @BeforeAll
    public static void prepare() {
        repo = new AccountRepoStub();
    }
```

CHAPTER 9 DEBUGGING, TESTING, AND DOCUMENTING

```java
    @BeforeEach
    public void setUp() {
        service = new AccountServiceImpl(repo);
    }

    @Test
    public void testNonNumericAmountVersionOne() {
        assertThrows(InvalidDataException.class,
                () -> {
                    service.createAccount("Gigi", "223311", "2I00");
                });
    }

    @Test
    public void testNonNumericAmountVersionTwo() {
        InvalidDataException expected = assertThrows(
                InvalidDataException.class, () -> {
                    service.createAccount("Gigi", "223311", "2I00");
                }
        );
        assertEquals("Could not create account with invalid amount!"
            , expected.getMessage());
    }
@AfterEach
    public void tearDown() {
        repo.set(0);
    }

    @AfterAll
    public static void destroy() {
        repo = null;
    }
}
```

The testNonNumericAmountVersionOne() method makes use of assertThrows that receives two parameters: the type of exception that is expected for the second parameter of type Executable to throw when executed. Executable is a functional interface defined in the org.junit.jupiter.api.function, which can be used in a lambda expression to get the compact test that you see.

389

CHAPTER 9 DEBUGGING, TESTING, AND DOCUMENTING

The testNonNumericAmountVersionTwo() method saves the result of the assertThrows(..) call, which allows for the message of the exception to be tested and to make sure that the execution flow worked exactly as expected.

The other tests are depicted in the following code snippet.

```
package com.apress.bgn.ch9.service;

import com.apress.bgn.ch9.Account;
import com.apress.bgn.ch9.service.stub.AccountRepoStub;
import org.junit.jupiter.api.*;

import static org.junit.jupiter.api.Assertions.assertEquals;
import static org.junit.jupiter.api.Assertions.assertThrows;

public class AccountServiceTest {

    private static AccountRepoStub repo;
    private AccountService service;

    @BeforeAll
    public static void prepare() {
        repo = new AccountRepoStub();
    }

    @BeforeEach
    public void setUp() {
        service = new AccountServiceImpl(repo);
    }

    @Test
    public void testEmptyAccountNumber() {
        InvalidDataException expected = assertThrows(
                InvalidDataException.class, () -> {
                    service.createAccount("Gigi", "", "2100");
                }
        );
        assertEquals("Could not create account with invalid account number!",
            expected.getMessage());
    }
```

```java
@Test
public void testNullAccountNumber() {
    InvalidDataException expected = assertThrows(
            InvalidDataException.class, () -> {
                service.createAccount("Gigi", null, "2100");
            }
    );
    assertEquals("Could not create account with invalid account number!",
        expected.getMessage());
}

@Test
public void testInvalidAccountNumber() {
    InvalidDataException expected = assertThrows(
            InvalidDataException.class, () -> {
                service.createAccount("Gigi", "11", "2100");
            }
    );
    assertEquals("Could not create account with invalid account number!",
        expected.getMessage());
}

@Test
public void testNegativeIntAmount() {
    InvalidDataException expected = assertThrows(
            InvalidDataException.class, () -> {
                service.createAccount("Gigi", "112233", "-2100");
            }
    );
    assertEquals("Could not create account with invalid account number!",
      expected.getMessage());
}
```

```java
    @Test
    public void testCreateAccount() {
        repo.set(1);
        Account expected = service.createAccount("Gigi", "112233", "2100");
        assertEquals("Gigi", expected.getHolder());
        assertEquals("112233", expected.getNumber());
        assertEquals(2100, expected.getSum());
    }

    @Test
    public void testCreateAccountAlreadyExists() {
        AccountCreationException expected = assertThrows(
                AccountCreationException.class, () -> {
                    service.createAccount("Gigi", "112233", "2100");
                }
        );
        assertEquals("Account already exists for holder Gigi",
            expected.getMessage());
    }

    @AfterEach
    public void tearDown() {
        repo.set(0);
    }

    @AfterAll
    public static void destroy() {
        repo = null;
    }
}
```

Similar methods can be written to test all other service methods. This is left as an exercise for you. Because there is one more test technique we have to cover in this chapter: using mocks.

Using Mocks

Mocks are objects that register calls they receive. During execution of a test, using assert utility methods, the assumption that all expected actions were performed on mocks are tested. Thankfully, code for mocks does not have to be written by the developer, there are three well-known libraries that provide the type of classes needed to test using mocks: Mockito,[11] JMock,[12] and EasyMock.[13] Also, if you are ever in need to mock static methods, the most common reason being bad design, there is PowerMock.[14]

Using mocks, you can jump directly to writing the tests. So, let's write two tests for the `createAccount(..)` method that focus on the repository class calling its methods, because the repository class is being replaced by a mock.

```java
package com.apress.bgn.ch9.mock;

import com.apress.bgn.ch9.Account;
import com.apress.bgn.ch9.repo.AccountRepo;
import com.apress.bgn.ch9.service.AccountCreationException;
import com.apress.bgn.ch9.service.AccountServiceImpl;
import com.apress.bgn.ch9.service.InvalidDataException;
import org.junit.jupiter.api.BeforeEach;
import org.junit.jupiter.api.Test;
import org.junit.jupiter.api.extension.ExtendWith;
import org.mockito.InjectMocks;
import org.mockito.Mock;
import org.mockito.junit.jupiter.MockitoExtension;

import java.util.Optional;

import static org.junit.jupiter.api.Assertions.*;
import static org.mockito.ArgumentMatchers.any;
import static org.mockito.Mockito.when;

@ExtendWith(MockitoExtension.class)
public class AccountServiceTest {
```

---

[11] Mockito official site: http://site.mockito.org/
[12] Official site for JMock: http://jmock.org/
[13] Official site for EasyMock: http://easymock.org/
[14] Official site for PowerMock: http://powermock.github.io/

```java
    @InjectMocks
    private AccountServiceImpl service;

    @Mock
    private AccountRepo mockRepo;

    @BeforeEach
    public void checkMocks() {
        assertNotNull(service);
        assertNotNull(mockRepo);
    }

    @Test
    public void testCreateAccount() {
        Account expected = new Account("Gigi", 2100, "223311");
        when(mockRepo.findOne("Gigi")).thenReturn(Optional.empty());
        when(mockRepo.save(any(Account.class))).thenReturn(expected);

        Account result = service.createAccount("Gigi", "223311", "2100");
        assertEquals(expected, result);
    }

    @Test
    public void testCreateAccountAlreadyExists() {
        Account expected = new Account("Gigi", 2100, "223311");
        when(mockRepo.findOne("Gigi")).thenReturn(Optional.of(expected));

        assertThrows(AccountCreationException.class,
                () -> {
                    service.createAccount("Gigi", "223311", "2100");
                });
    }
}
```

The tests are self-explanatory; the Mockito utility methods names make it easy to understand what is happening during a test execution. But how the mocks are created and injected, needs to be explained. So, let's do that! the `@ExtendWith(MockitoExtension.class)` is necessary for JUnit 5 tests to support Mockito annotations. Without it annotations like `@InjectMocks` and `@Mock` have no effect on the code.

CHAPTER 9 DEBUGGING, TESTING, AND DOCUMENTING

The `@Mock` annotation is to be used on references to mocks created by Mockito. The preferred way to work with mocks is to specify a reference of an interface type that is implemented by the real object type and the mock that is created for the test scenario. But `@Mock` can be placed on a concrete type reference as well, and the created mock is a subclass of that class.

The `@InjectMocks` annotation is used on the object to be tested, so that Mockito knows to create this object and inject mocks instead of the dependencies.

So, this is basically all you need to know to start using Mockito mocks in your test. Declaring the objects to be mocked and the object to be injected in is the only setup a class containing unit tests using mocks needs.

The body of test methods using mocks have a typical structure. The first lines must declare objects and variables passed as arguments to the method called on the object being tested or passed as arguments to Mockito utility methods that declare what mocks take as arguments and what they return. The next lines establish the behavior of the mock when its methods are called by the object to be tested. The following two lines depict this for the `findOne(..)` method. The first line creates an account object. The second lines define the behavior of the mock. When `mockRepo.findOne("Gigi")` is called, the previously created account instance is returned wrapped in an `Optional<T>` instance.

```
Account expected = new Account("Gigi", 2100, "223311");
when(mockRepo.findOne("Gigi")).thenReturn(Optional.of(expected));
```

There are many other libraries to make writing tests effortless for developers. Big frameworks like Spring provide their own testing library to help developers write tests for applications. Build tools like Ant, Maven, and Gradle can automatically run tests when the project is built, and generate useful reports related to the failures. Using Gradle, the project can be built by calling `gradle clean build` in the console. All test classes declared in the test module, are picked up automatically if they are named `*Test.java`. When writing tests, and not changing application code, you can run the tests only by calling `gradle test`. This is a configuration that can be changed by overloading the Gradle `test` task; you can look into that if you are curious.

The Gradle reports are in HTML format so they can be opened in the browser, and they look amazing. The reports are generated as a site with an `index.html` stat page, which are located at `java-bgn/chapter09/testing/build/reports/tests/test/index.html`.

I've chosen to fail a test intentionally so that you can see how that report looks like (see Figure 9-16).

CHAPTER 9 DEBUGGING, TESTING, AND DOCUMENTING

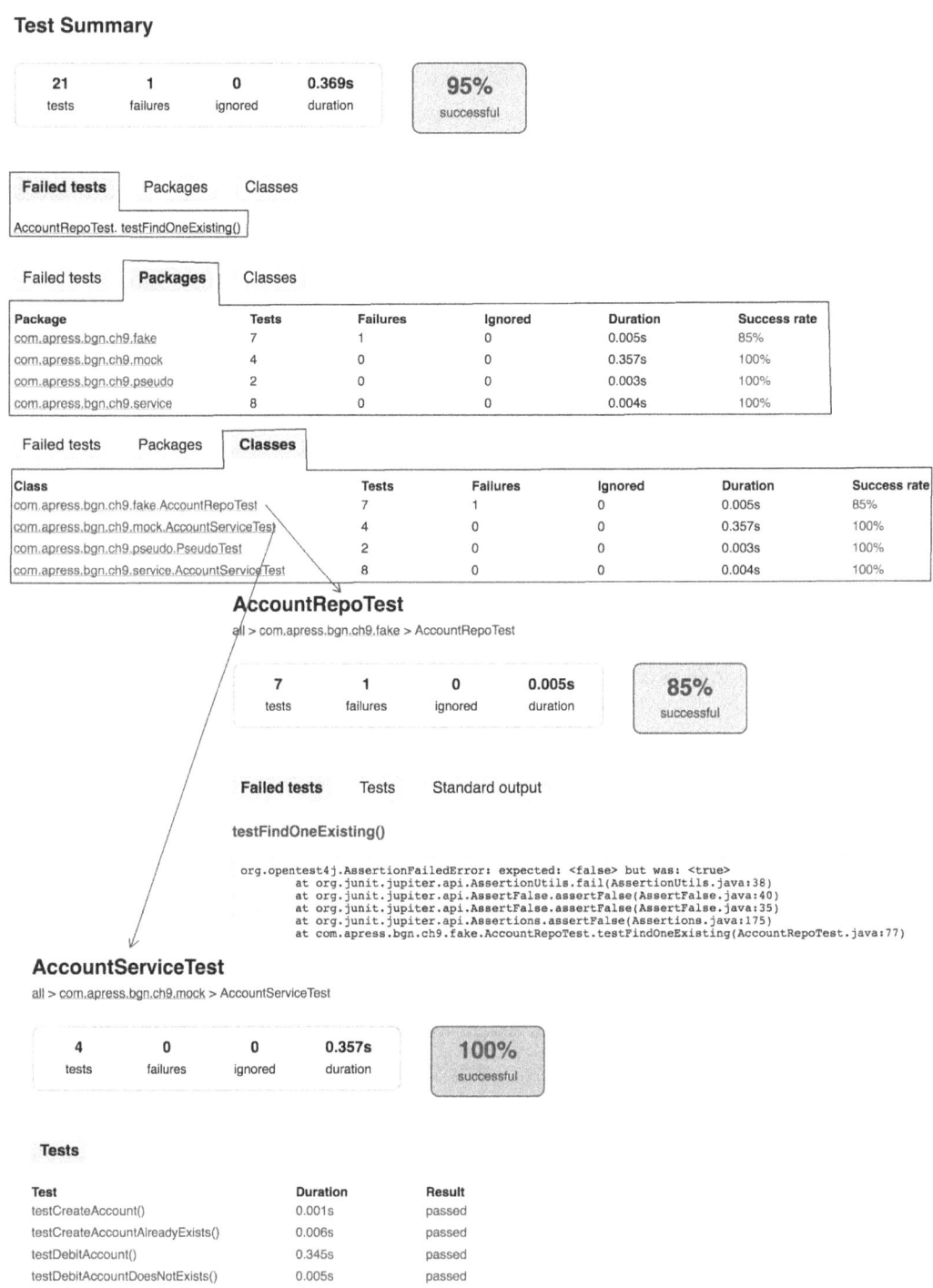

Figure 9-16. The Gradle test reports

To conclude this section, remember this: no matter how good a development team is, without a great testing team, the resulting application might actually be far away from an acceptable quality standard. So, if you ever come across companies that do not have a dedicated testing team, or at least a company culture that does not compromise in techniques such as code review and writing tests, think twice before accepting that job.

Documenting

In the software world, there is a joke about documentation that might not be to everybody's liking, but it is worth a mention.

> ! Documentation is like sex: when it's good, it is really, really good. And when it's bad, it's still better than nothing.

A common-sense rule and best practice of programming is to write code that is self-explanatory, so you won't need to write documentation. Basically, if you need to write too much documentation, you're doing it wrong. There are a lot of things you can do to avoid writing documentation, like using meaningful names for classes and variables, respect the language code conventions and many others. But when you are building a set of classes that is used by other developers, you need to provide a little documentation for the main APIs. Of course, if your solution requires a very complicated algorithm to be written, you might want to add comments here and there; although in this case, proper technical documentation with schemas and diagrams should be written too.

The Javadoc block comments are associated with a public class, interface, method body, or public field; sometimes even protected, if necessary. The Javadoc comments contain special tags that link documented elements together, or mark the different type of information. The Javadoc comments and their associated code can be processed by Javadoc tools, extracted, and wrapped into an HTML site that is called the Javadoc API of the project. The Gradle build tool that is used by this project exposes a task named `javadoc` that can be executed to generate the Javadoc API site for a module. To compact the documentation of a project with multiple modules a special plugin is needed.[15] Also, smart editors can access the documentation and display it when the developer tries to write code using the documented components.

---

[15]Same goes for Maven and any other Java build tool.

Let's start with a few examples of Javadoc comments to explain the most important tags used.

Whenever we create a class or interface, we should add Javadoc comments to explain their purpose, add the version of the application, and link existing resources. `IntSorter` is a hierarchy of classes implementing the `IntSorter` interface that provides implementations of different sorting algorithms. If these classes are used by other developers, one of them might want to add a customized algorithm to our hierarchy and a little information about the `IntSorter` interface would go a long way. In the following code snippet, a Javadoc comment was added to the `IntSorter` interface.

```
package com.apress.bgn.ch9.algs;

/**
 * Interface {@code IntSorter} is an interface that needs to be implemented
 * by classes that provide a method to sort an array of {@code int} values. <p>
 *
 * {@code int[]} was chosen as a type because this type
 * of values are always sortable.({@link Comparable})
 *
 * @author Iuliana Cosmina
 * @since 1.0
 */
public interface IntSorter {
        ...
}
```

In the Javadoc comments, HTML tags can be used to format information. In the previous code, `<p>` elements were used to make sure the comment is made of multiple paragraphs. The `@author` tag was introduced in JDK 1.0. It is useful when the development team is large, because if you end up working with somebody else's code, you know who to look for if issues appear. The `@since` tag provides the version of the application in which this interface was added. For an application that has had a long development and release cycle, this tag can be used to mark the elements of a specific version, so that a developer using the codebase of your application knows when elements were added; and in a rollback to a former version, knows where compile-time errors appear in the application.

CHAPTER 9 DEBUGGING, TESTING, AND DOCUMENTING

The best example here is the Java official Javadoc; let's take the `Optional<T>` interface, which was introduced in version 8. But more methods were added to it in versions 9, 10, and 11, and each of them are marked with the specific versions.

```
  package java.util;
...
 /**
...
 * @param <T> the type of value
 * @since 1.8
 */
public final class Optional<T> {
...
    /**
      ...
     * @since 9
     */
    public void ifPresentOrElse(Consumer<? super T> action, Runnable
    emptyAction) {
        if (value != null) {
            action.accept(value);
        } else {
            emptyAction.run();
        }
    }
    /**
      ...
     * @since 10
     */
    public T orElseThrow() {
        if (value == null) {
            throw new NoSuchElementException("No value present");
        }
        return value;
    }
```

399

CHAPTER 9 DEBUGGING, TESTING, AND DOCUMENTING

```java
    /**
     * If a value is  not present, returns {@code true}, otherwise
     * {@code false}.
     *
     * @return  {@code true} if a value is not present, otherwise {@code false}
     * @since   11
     */
    public boolean isEmpty() {
        return value == null;
    }
..
}
```

In the IntSorter example, you see the @code tag that was introduced in Java 1.5. It displays text in code form, using a special font and escaping symbols that might break the HTML syntax.(ex: < or >). The @link tag was added in Java 1.2 and inserts a navigable link to relevant documentation.

Now, let's document the method declarations to let the developer know what they should be used for.

```java
package com.apress.bgn.ch9.algs;

/**
 * Interface {@code IntSorter} is an interface that needs to be implemented
 * by classes that provide a method to sort an array of {@code int} values. <p>
 *
 * {@code int[]} was chosen as a type because this type

 * of values are always sortable.({@link Comparable})
 *
 * @author Iuliana Cosmina
 * @since 1.0
 */
public interface IntSorter {
```

```java
/**
 * Sorts {@code arr}
 *
 * @param arr int array to be sorted
 * @param low lower limit of the interval to be sorted
 * @param high higher limit of the interval to be sorted
 */
void sort(int[] arr, int low, int high);

/**
 * This method was used to sort arrays using BubbleSort
 * @deprecated As of version 0.1, because the
 *              {@link #sort(int[], int, int) ()} should be used instead.
 * To be removed in version 1.1
 * @param arr int array to be sorted
 */
@Deprecated (since= "0.1", forRemoval = true)
default void sort(int[] arr) {
    System.out.println("Do not use this! This is deprecated!!");
}
}
```

The IntelliJ IDEA editor (and other smart editors) generate small pieces of Javadoc for you. Once you have declared a class or method body that you want to document, type **/****, and press Enter. The generated block of comment contains the following.

- one or more `@param` tags with the parameter names, all is left for the developer to do is to add extra documentation to explain their purpose.

- if the method `returns` a value of a type different than `void` and `@return` is added, documentation must be provided by the developer to explain what the result represents and if there are special cases when a certain value is returned. And since we started using `Optional<T>` as a study case, here is the Javadoc of the `isPresent(..)` method.

CHAPTER 9   DEBUGGING, TESTING, AND DOCUMENTING

```
/**
 ...
 * @param predicate the predicate to apply to a value, if present
 * @return an {@code Optional} describing the value of this
 *         {@code Optional}, if a value is present and the value
           matches the
 *         given predicate, otherwise an empty {@code Optional}
 * @throws NullPointerException if the predicate is {@code null}
 */
public Optional<T> filter(Predicate<? super T> predicate) {
    Objects.requireNonNull(predicate);
    if (!isPresent()) {
        return this;
    } else {
        return predicate.test(value) ? this : empty();
    }
}
```

- if the methods declare an exception to be thrown, a @throws tag is generated together with the exception type, the developer's job is to explain when and why that type of exception is thrown.

```
/**
 ...
 * @param action the action to be performed, if a value is present
 * @throws NullPointerException if value is present and the
   given action is
 *         {@code null}
 */
public void ifPresent(Consumer<? super T> action) {
    if (value != null) {
        action.accept(value);
    }
}
```

The @link creates a documentation link to a class page, a method documentation section, or a field. In the previous sort method declaration example, we created a link to the other method in the interface.

CHAPTER 9   DEBUGGING, TESTING, AND DOCUMENTING

The @deprecated tag adds text explaining the reasons for deprecation, the version, and what to use instead. Javadoc generation tools take this text format it with italic and add it to the main description of the method.

And with this we have covered the most used tags when writing Javadoc comments. If you want to check out the complete list, you can find it at https://docs.oracle.com/javase/7/docs/technotes/tools/windows/javadoc.html#javadoctags. Javadoc documentation is a wide subject that could provide material for an entire book. We are just scratching the surface in this section and covering the basics so you have a good start.

To generate the HTML site for the logging-jul module, the easiest way to do it, is to open the Gradle project view, expand the **chapter09:logging-jul ➤ Tasks ➤ Documentation** node and under it we find the javadoc task, as depicted in Figure 9-17. To execute the task, we have to double-click it.

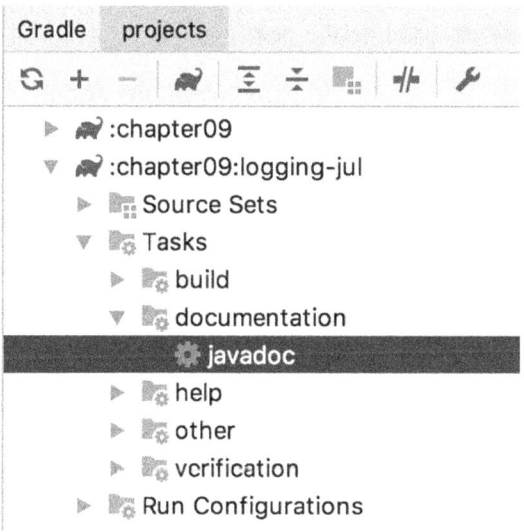

Figure 9-17. *The Gradle javadoc task*

```
00:22:17: Executing task 'javadoc'...

> Task :chapter09:logging-jul:compileJava
/Users/iulianacosmina/apress/workspace/java-bgn/chapter09/logging-jul/
  src/main/java/com/apress/bgn/ch9/algs/InsertionSort.java:59:
  warning: [removal] sort(int[]) in IntSorter has been deprecated and
  marked for removal
    public void sort(int[] arr) {
                ^
```

403

```
/Users/iulianacosmina/apress/workspace/java-bgn/chapter09/logging-jul/
  src/main/java/com/apress/bgn/ch9/algs/HeapSort.java:55:
  warning: [removal] sort(int[]) in IntSorter has been deprecated and
  marked for removal
    public void sort(int[] arr) {
                ^
2 warnings

> Task :chapter09:logging-jul:processResources
> Task :chapter09:logging-jul:classes
> Task :chapter09:logging-jul:javadoc

BUILD SUCCESSFUL in 2s
3 actionable tasks: 3 executed
00:22:19: Task execution finished 'javadoc'.
```

The `javadoc` task identifies the deprecated elements and prints a warning for the developer to see. After the successful execution of that task, `build` directory can be found under the `logging-jul` directory. That is where all Gradle tasks ran from IntelliJ IDEA store their results. In this directory there should be a **docs ➤ javadoc** directory hierarchy. And if we expand the **javadoc** hierarchy we should see all the files making up the Javadoc site of our module. The output to look forward to is depicted in Figure 9-18.

Figure 9-18. *Javadoc site generated by execution of the Gradle javadoc task*

Any site has a starting page and the default one is `index.html`. Right-click that file, and from the context sensitive menu that appears, select **Open in Browser** and select your preferred browser. If you think the page resembles the JDK official Javadoc page, you are not imagining it; the same Doclet API was used to generate that official one. For a detailed view of all the documentation in the module(project), click the **FRAMES** link. This redirects to a page that on the left; it has two frames: one with the packages of the project and one with the classes/interfaces/enums and the frame on the right, which displays information about every item clicked in frames on the left. You should be seeing something similar to the page depicted in Figure 9-19.

CHAPTER 9　DEBUGGING, TESTING, AND DOCUMENTING

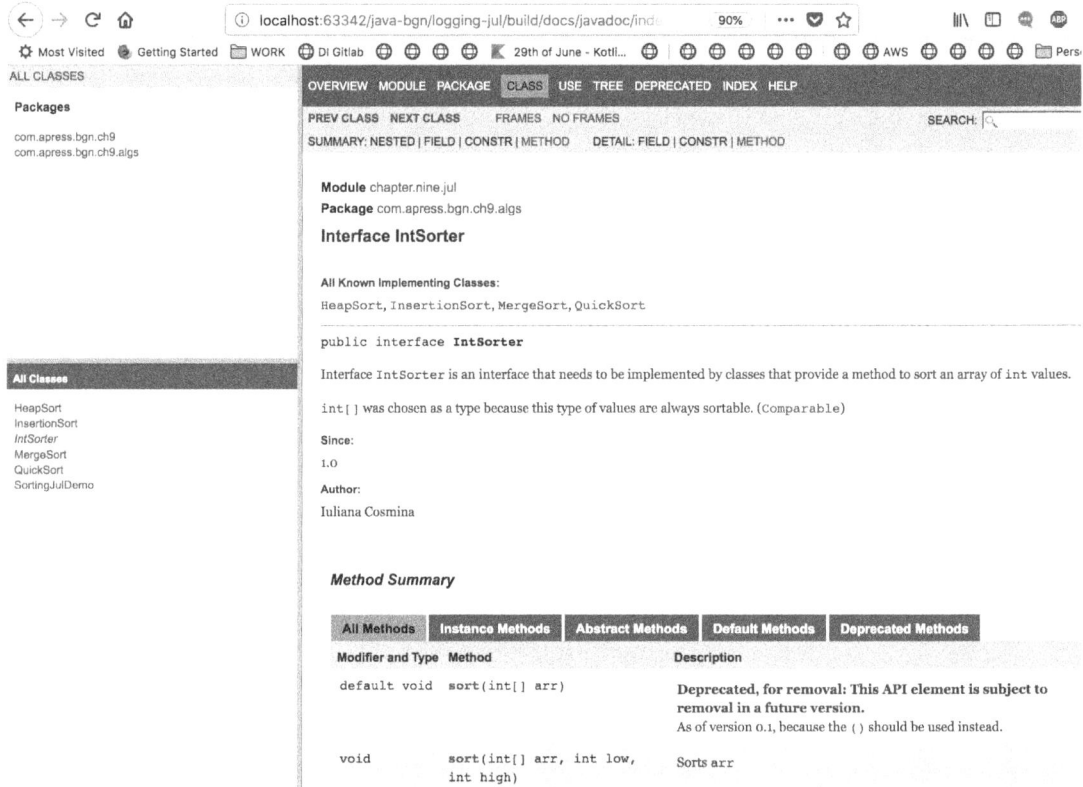

Figure 9-19. *Javadoc site generated by execution of the Gradle javadoc task, opened in the browser*

Javadoc documentation is picked up by IntelliJ IDEA and other smart editors, and depicted on the spot when the developer uses the documented components in the code. When selecting a class, method name, interface method, and so forth, most smart editors provide some kind of combination of keys that include F1, which the developer must press so that the documentation is depicted in a pop-up window. In IntelliJ IDEA, click an element and press F1, and the Javadoc documentation is shown in a pop-up window and formatted nicely, as depicted in Figure 9-20.

CHAPTER 9 DEBUGGING, TESTING, AND DOCUMENTING

```
/**
 * @author Iuliana Cosmina
 * @since 1.0
 */
public class DocDemo {
    public static void main(String... args) {
        IntSorter intSorter = new QuickSort();

        intSorter.|
    }
}
```

Figure 9-20. Javadoc information depicted in IntelliJ IDEA

You can view Javadoc information in a smart editor for any dependency of your project (including JDK classes) as long as the code is open source and the module exports the appropriate packages.

In Java 9, the Doclet API for generating Javadoc received an upgrade and a facelift. Before Java 9, developers complained about the performance issues of the old version, the cryptic API, the lack of support and the shallowness of it over all. In Java 9, most of the problems were resolved. A detailed description of improvements is at http://openjdk.java.net/jeps/221.

Documentation is really valuable and can make development practical and pleasant when it is really, really good. So, when writing code, document it as you expect the dependencies of your project to be.

You might probably have heard of the expression **RTFM**, which is an abbreviation for **Read The F***ing Manual!**. That expression is used a lot in software by experienced developers when working with newbie developers. Problem is, what should you do when there is no manual? Most companies on a deadline might have the tendency to allocate little or no time to documenting a project. So, this section was added to this book to emphasize the importance of documentation in software development, and teaching you how to write your documentation while you write your code, because you might not have time to do it afterwards.

CHAPTER 9   DEBUGGING, TESTING, AND DOCUMENTING

Summary

This chapter covered important development tools and techniques, the classes in JDK that provide support for them, and important Java libraries that could make your development job more practical and pleasant. The following is the complete list of topics.

- how to configure and use logging in a Java application
- how to log messages in the console
- how to log messages to a file
- how to use Java logging
- what a logging facade is and why it is recommended
- configuring and using SLF4J with Logback
- how to program using assertions
- how to debug using IntelliJ IDEA
- how to monitor and inspect JVM statistics while an application is running using various JDK tools: `jps`, `jcmd`, `jconsole`, and `jmc`
- how to use the Process API
- how to test an application using JUnit
- how to write tests using fakes
- how to write tests using mocks
- how to write tests using stubs
- how to document a Java application and generate documentation in HTML format

CHAPTER 10

Making Your Application Interactive

So far in the book input for our Java programs data was provided via arrays or variables that were initialized inside the code or via program arguments. But most applications nowadays require interaction with the user. The user can be provided access by entering a username and a password; the user is sometimes required to enter information to confirm his/her identity or to instruct the application what to do. Java supports multiple methods for user input to be read. In this chapter a few ways to build interactive Java applications are covered. Interactive Java application take their input either from the console, either from Java built interfaces, either desktop or web.

JShell is a command line interface, where a developer can enter variable declarations and one line statements that are executed when the Enter key is pressed. Command line interface shells like `bash` and terminals like Command Prompt from Windows can issue commands to programs in the form of successive lines of text. JShell was covered at the beginning of the book for the simple reason that it was a Java 9 novelty. The next sections cover how to read user-provided data and instructions using the command-line interface. The sections after that focus on building Java applications with a desktop/web interface.

Reading Data from the Command Line

This section is dedicated to reading user input from the command line, whether is the IntelliJ IDEA console, or if the program is run from an executable jar from any terminal specific to an operating system. In the JDK, there are two classes that can be used to read user data from the command line: `java.util.Scanner` and `java.io.Console` and this section cover them both in detail. Without further ado, let's get into it.

CHAPTER 10 MAKING YOUR APPLICATION INTERACTIVE

Reading User Data Using System.in

Before introducing logging in **Chapter 9** to print data in the console, methods under `System.out` were used. There is also a counterpart utility object named `System.in` used to read data from the console, data that a user of the program introduces to control the application flow. You might have noticed that until now all Java programs, when executed they would be started, they would process the data, would execute the declared statements and then they would terminate, exit gracefully or with an exception when something went wrong. The most simple and common way to pass decision of termination to the user is to end the main method with a call to `System.in.read()`. This method reads the next byte of data from the input stream and the program is paused until the user introduces a value, as the value is returned we can even save it and print it.

```java
import java.io.IOException;

public class ReadingFormStdinDemo {

    public static void main(String... args) throws IOException {
        System.out.print("Press any key to terminate:");

        int read = System.in.read();
        System.out.println("Key pressed: " + read);
    }
}
```

If you run the class using IntelliJ, you notice that the *Press any key to terminate:* message is printed and then the application just hangs. If you click the window where the message was printed and push any key, the byte value of the pressed key is printed and then the application terminates. So if you were to execute the previous code and press Enter, the following is what you see in the console.[1]

```
Press any key to terminate:
Key pressed: 10
```

But reading single bytes from the console is not really useful, right? Thankfully, there is another form of the `read(..)` method that saves the user entry into a byte array. But since the size is fixed, no matter how long the user entry, only what fits in the array is

---

[1]ASCII Table and Description `https://www.asciitable.com/`

saved. The final <Enter> that ends the entry is returned as an int value equal to 3, which is the code for *end of text*. So, the previous code changes to

```java
package com.apress.bgn.ch10;

import java.io.IOException;

public class ReadingFormStdinDemo {
    public static void main(String... args) throws IOException {
        System.out.print("Press any key to terminate:");

        byte[] b = new byte[3];
        int read = System.in.read(b);
        for (int i = 0; i < b.length; ++i) {
            System.out.println(b[i]);
        }
        System.out.println("Key pressed: " + read);
    }
}
```

And now the user input is saved in the byte[] b array. But, it is not useful to just read bytes, right? Well, let's look at how we can read full text and numeric values from the user: enter the java.util.Scanner class.

Using Scanner

The System.in variable is of type java.io.InputStream, which is a JDK special type extended by all classes representing an input stream of bytes. This means that System.in can be wrapped in any java.io.Reader extension so bytes can be read as readable data. But, the one that is really important is a class named Scanner from package java.util. An instance of this type can be created by calling its constructor and providing System.in as an argument. The Scanner class provides a lot of next..() methods that can be used to read almost any type from the console. In Figure 10-1, you can see the next..() methods list.

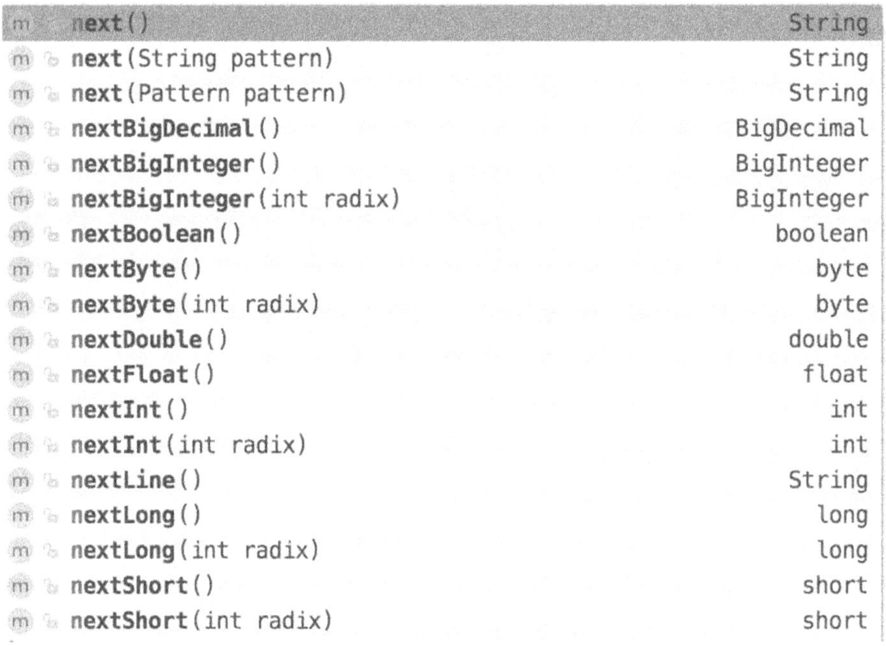

next()	String
next(String pattern)	String
next(Pattern pattern)	String
nextBigDecimal()	BigDecimal
nextBigInteger()	BigInteger
nextBigInteger(int radix)	BigInteger
nextBoolean()	boolean
nextByte()	byte
nextByte(int radix)	byte
nextDouble()	double
nextFloat()	float
nextInt()	int
nextInt(int radix)	int
nextLine()	String
nextLong()	long
nextLong(int radix)	long
nextShort()	short
nextShort(int radix)	short

Figure 10-1. Scanner methods for reading various types of data

The advantage of using Scanner to read data from the console is that the values read are automatically converted to the proper types, when possible. When it is not possible, a java.util.InputMismatchException is thrown. The following piece of code was designed so you can select the type of value you want to read by inserting a text and then the value. In the code, the appropriate method of the Scanner instance is called to read the value.

```
package com.apress.bgn.ch10;

import java.io.IOException;
import java.math.BigInteger;
import java.util.Scanner;

public class ReadingFormStdinDemo {

    public static final String EXIT = "exit";
    public static final String HELP = "help";
    public static final String BYTE = "byte";
    public static final String SHORT = "short";
    public static final String INT = "int";
```

```java
    public static final String BOOLEAN = "bool";
    public static final String DOUBLE = "double";
    public static final String LINE = "line";
    public static final String BIGINT = "bigint";
    public static final String TEXT = "text";

    public static void main(String... args) throws IOException {
        Scanner sc = new Scanner(System.in);
        String help = getHelpString();
        System.out.println(help);

        String input;
        do {
            System.out.print("Enter option: ");
            input = sc.nextLine();

            switch (input) {
case HELP:
    System.out.println(help);
    break;
case EXIT:
    System.out.println("Hope you had fun. Buh-bye!");
    break;
case BYTE:
    byte b = sc.nextByte();
    System.out.println("Nice byte there: " + b);
    sc.nextLine();
    break;
case SHORT:
    short s = sc.nextShort();
    System.out.println("Nice short there: " + s);
    sc.nextLine();
    break;
case INT:
    int i = sc.nextInt();
    System.out.println("Nice int there: " + i);
    sc.nextLine();
    break;
```

CHAPTER 10　MAKING YOUR APPLICATION INTERACTIVE

```java
            case BOOLEAN:
                boolean bool = sc.nextBoolean();
                System.out.println("Nice boolean there: " + bool);
                sc.nextLine();
                break;
            case DOUBLE:
                double d = sc.nextDouble();
                System.out.println("Nice double there: " + d);
                sc.nextLine();
                break;
            case LINE:
                String line = sc.nextLine();
                System.out.println("Nice line of text there: " + line);
                break;
            case BIGINT:
                BigInteger bi = sc.nextBigInteger();
                System.out.println("Nice big integer there: " + bi);
                sc.nextLine();
                break;
            case TEXT:
                String text = sc.next();
                System.out.println("Nice text there: " + text);
                sc.nextLine();
                break;
            default:
                System.out.println("No idea what you want bruh!");
                }

        } while (!input.equalsIgnoreCase(EXIT));
    }

    private static String getHelpString() {
        return new StringBuilder("This application helps you test various
        usage of Scanner. Enter type to be read next:")
```

```
    .append("\n\t help >  displays this help")
    .append("\n\t exit >  leave the application")
    .append("\n\t byte > read a byte")
    .append("\n\t short > read a short")
    .append("\n\t int > read an int")
    .append("\n\t bool > read a boolean")
    .append("\n\t double > read a double")
    .append("\n\t line > read a line of text")
    .append("\n\t bigint > read a BigInteger")
    .append("\n\t text > read a text value").toString();
    }
}
```

As you probably noticed in the code sample, most scanner methods are called together with a `nextLine()`, this is because every input you provide is made of the actual token and a new line character (the <Enter> pressed to end your input), and before you can enter your next value, you need to take that character from the stream as well.

Let's test the previous code a little.

```
This application helps you test various usage of Scanner. Enter type to be
read next:
        help >  displays this help
        exit >  leave the application
        byte > read a byte
        short > read a short
        int > read an int
        bool > read a boolean
        double > read a double
        line > read a line of text
        bigint > read a BigInteger
        text > read a text value
Enter option: byte
12
Nice byte there: 12
Enter option: bool
true
```

```
Nice boolean there: true
Enter option: line
some of us are hardly ever here
Nice line of text there: some of us are hardly ever here
Enter option: text
john
Nice text there: john
Enter option: text
the rest of us are made to disappear...
Nice text there: the
Enter option: double
4.2
Nice double there: 4.2
Enter option: int
AAAA
Exception in thread "main" java.util.InputMismatchException
        at java.base/java.util.Scanner.throwFor(Scanner.java:939)
        at java.base/java.util.Scanner.next(Scanner.java:1594)
        at java.base/java.util.Scanner.nextInt(Scanner.java:2258)
        at java.base/java.util.Scanner.nextInt(Scanner.java:2212)
        at chapter.ten/com.apress.bgn.ch10.ReadingFormStdinDemo.main(
            ReadingFormStdinDemo.java:78)
```

The output that is underlined in the listing, represents the test case for the `next()` method. This method should be used to read a single `String` token. The next token gets converted to a `String` instance, and the token ends when a whitespace is encountered. That is why, in the previous example the only read text ends up being *the*.

In the last case, the expected option is an integer value, but *AAAA* is entered, and that is why the exception is thrown.

When you need to repeatedly read the same type of values from the console you can peek at the value you want to read, and check it before reading it to avoid the `InputMismatchException` being thrown. For this particular scenario, each of the `next..()` methods has a pair method named `hasNext...()`. To show an example of how these methods can be used, let's add an option to the previous code to read a list of long values.

```
...
public static final String LONGS = "longs";
...
    String input;
        do {
            System.out.print("Enter option: ");
            input = sc.nextLine();

            switch (input) {
                case LONGS:
        List<Long> longList = new ArrayList<>();
        while (sc.hasNextLong()) {
            longList.add(sc.nextLong());
        }
        System.out.println("Nice long list there: " + longList);
        // else all done
        sc.nextLine();
        sc.nextLine();
        break;
    default:
        System.out.println("No idea what you want bruh!");
                }
        } while (!input.equalsIgnoreCase(EXIT));
...
```

Although seems weird, we need to call the nextLine() method twice. Once for the character that cannot be converted to long, so the while loop ends and once for the end of the line character, so the next read..() is the type of the following read value.

There are a few other methods in the Scanner class that can be used to filter the input and read only desired tokens, but the methods listed in this section are the ones you will probably use the most.

Reading User Data with java.io.Console

The java.io.Console class was introduced in Java version 1.6, one version later than Scanner; it provides methods to access he character-based console device, if any, associated with the current Java virtual machine. The methods of class java.io.Console can thus be also used to write to the console, not only read user input. If the JVM is started from a background process or a Java editor, the console will not be available, as the editor redirects the standard input and output streams to its own window. That is why if we were to write code using `Console` we can only test it by running the class or jar from a terminal by calling `java ReadingUsingConsoleDemo.class` or `java -jar using-console-1.0-SNAPSHOT.jar`. The console of a JVM, if available, is represented in the code by a single instance of the `Console` class, which can be obtained by calling `System.console()`.

```
console.
    readLine()                                    String
    flush()                                         void
    format(String fmt, Object... args)           Console
    printf(String format, Object... args)        Console
    reader()                                      Reader
    readLine(String fmt, Object... args)          String
    readPassword()                                char[]
    readPassword(String fmt, Object... args)      char[]
    writer()                                 PrintWriter
```

Figure 10.2. *Console methods*

Figure 10-2 shows the methods that can be called on the `console` instance.

The `read*(..)` methods are used to read user input from the console and `printf(..)` and `format(..)` are used to print text in the console. The special cases here are the two `readPassword(..)` methods that allow text to be read from the console, but not depicted while it is being written. This means that a Java application supporting authentication can be written without any actual user interface. Let's write a sample code to see all that in action.

```
package com.apress.bgn.ch10;

import java.io.Console;
import java.util.Calendar;
import java.util.GregorianCalendar;

public class ReadingUsingConsoleDemo {
    public static void main(String... args) {
        Console console = System.console();
```

```
        if (console == null) {
            System.err.println("No console found.");
            return;
        } else {
            console.writer().print("Hello there! (reply to salute)\n");
            console.flush();

            String hello = console.readLine();
            console.printf("You replied with: '" + hello + "'\n");

            Calendar calendar = new GregorianCalendar();
            console.format("Today is : %1$tm %1$te,%1$tY\n", calendar);

            char[] passwordChar =
            console.readPassword("Please provide password: ");
            String password =  new String(passwordChar);
            console.printf("Your password starts with '"
    + password.charAt(0) + "' and ends with '"
    + password.charAt(password.length()-1) + "'\n");
        }
    }
}
```

In the code sample, various methods to read and write data using the console were used to show you how they should be used.

The `console.writer()` returns an instance of `java.io.PrintWriter` that can be used to print messages to the console. The catch is that the messages are not printed until `console.flush()` is called. This means that more messages can be queued up by the `java.io.PrintWriter` instance and printed only when `flush()` is called or when its internal buffer is full.

The `console.format(..)` is called to print a formatted message, in this case a `Calendar` instance extracts the current date and print it according to the following template: `dd mm,yyyy` . Templates accepted by the `console` methods that use formatters are defined in the `java.util.Formatter` class.

And now the good part: running this code in IntelliJ is not possible, so we have to either execute the class or the jar in a terminal. The easiest way is to create an executable jar, Gradle creates one when `gradle clean build is executed`, because the configuration was setup for the generated jar to be executable and for the main class to be `ReadingUsingConsoleDemo`. The jar produced by Gradle can be found at `/chapter10/using-console/build/libs/using-console-1.0-SNAPSHOT.jar`. Open a terminal in IntelliJ IDEA if you want to by clicking the **Terminal** button, and go to the `libs` directory. Once there, execute `java -jar using-console-1.0-SNAPSHOT.jar` and have fun. In the following code listing, you can see the entries I used to test the program.

```
$ cd chapter10/using-console/build/libs/
$ java -jar using-console-1.0-SNAPSHOT.jar
Hello there! (reply to salute)
Salut!
You replayed with: 'Salut!'
Today is : 08 9,2018
Please provide password:
Your password starts with 'a' and ends with 'e'
```

And this is all you need to know about using the console, although once working on a real production-ready project, you might rarely need it.

Build Applications Using Swing

Swing is a GUI widget toolkit for Java. It is part of the JDK starting with version 1.2 and was developed to provide more pleasant looking and practical components for building user applications with complex interfaces with all types of buttons, progress bars, selectable lists, and so forth. Swing is based on an early version of something called **AWT** short for **Abstract Window Toolkit**, which is the original Java user-interface widget toolkit. AWT was pretty basic, and had a set of graphical interface components that were available on any platform, this means AWT was portable, but this did not imply that AWT code written on one platform would work on another, because of the platform specific limitations. AWT components depend on the native equivalent components, which is why they were called *heavyweight* components. Figure 10-3 shows a simple Java AWT application.

CHAPTER 10   MAKING YOUR APPLICATION INTERACTIVE

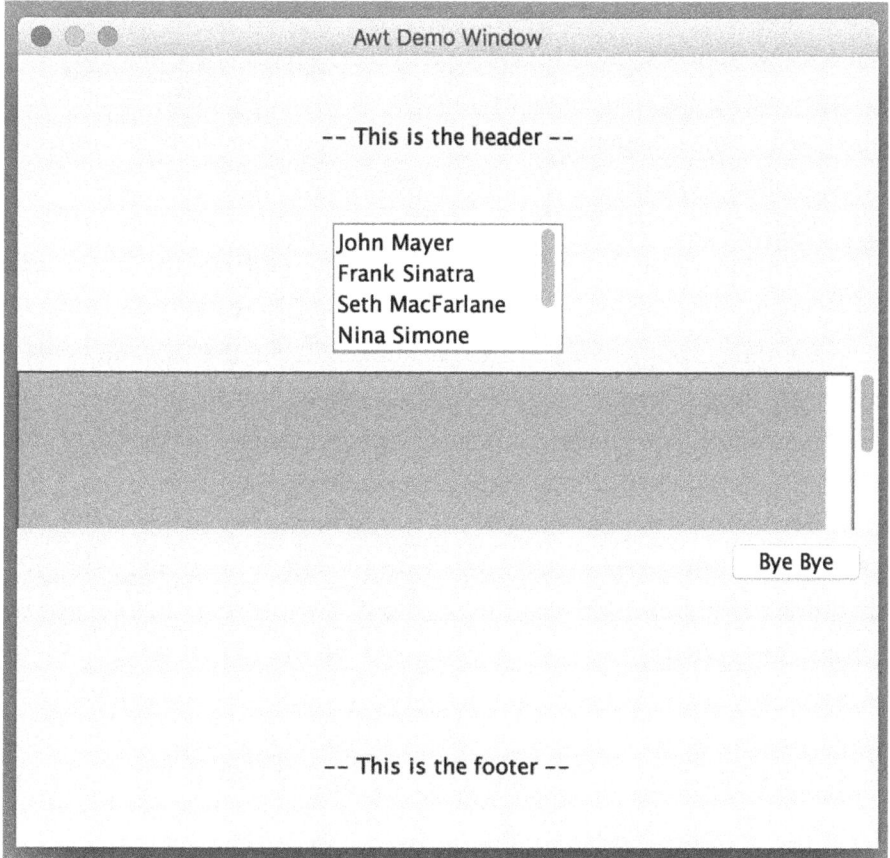

Figure 10-3. *Simple Java AWT application*

It's a simple window that contains a list, a text area and a button. The theme, also called the look-and-feel of the application, is the same as the operating system it was built on—macOS in the examples in this chapter— and it cannot be changed, AWT taps into the OS native graphical interface. If you run the same code on a Windows machine, the window will look different, because it will use the Windows theme.

Swing components are built in Java, follow the AWT model, but provide a pluggable look-and-feel. Swing is implemented entirely in Java and includes all features of AWT, but they are no longer depending on the native GUI, this is why Swing components are called *lightweight* components. Swing provides everything AWT does and also extends the set of components with higher-level ones such as tree view, list box, and tabbed panes. Also, the theme is pluggable and can be easily changed. This implies a much better portability than AWT applications, a possibility to write more complex application design with components that are not platform specific, and because Swing is an alternative to AWT, there was a lot more development done.

421

CHAPTER 10   MAKING YOUR APPLICATION INTERACTIVE

When web applications took flight, they were really ugly, because browsers had limited capabilities. AWT was introduced to build Java web applications called applets. Java applets were small applications that were launched from the browser and then executed within the JVM installed on the user's operating system in a process separate from the browser itself. That is why an applet can be run in a frame of the web page, a new application window, or standalone tools designed for testing applets. Java applets were using the GUI from the operating system, which made them prettier than the bulky initial look of HTML at the time. They are now deprecated and are scheduled to be removed in Java 11.

As for Java desktop applications written in Swing or AWT, they are rarely used anymore, and you might learn to build one during school, but are otherwise ... they are considered antique. Nevertheless, there are legacy applications used by certain institutions and companies that have had a long run in their business, which are built with Swing. I've seen Swing applications used by restaurants to manage tables and orders and I think most supermarkets use Swing applications to manage shopping items. And this is why this section exists in this book, because you might end up working on maintaining such application and it is good to know the basics, because Swing is still a part of the JDK. All Swing components (AWT too) are part of the `java.desktop` module so if you want to use Swing components you have to declare a dependence on this module. In the following configuration snippet, you can see that the module of our project that uses Swing declares its dependency on the `java.desktop` module by using the `requires` directive, in its `module-info.java`.

```
module chapter.ten.swing {
  requires java.desktop;
}
```

The application depicted in Figure 10-3 was build using AWT, this section covers building something similar in Swing and adding more components to it. The core class of any Swing application is named `JFrame` and instances of this type are used to create windows with border and title. So let's write some code to do just that.

```
package com.apress.bgn.ch10;

import javax.swing.*;
import java.awt.*;
```

CHAPTER 10   MAKING YOUR APPLICATION INTERACTIVE

```
public class SwingDemo extends JFrame {

    public static void main(String... args) {
        SwingDemo swingDemo = new SwingDemo();
        swingDemo.setTitle("Swing Demo Window");
        swingDemo.setSize(new Dimension(500,500));

        swingDemo.setVisible(true);
    }
}
```

In the code, an instance of `javax.swing.JFrame` is created, a title is set for it and we also set a size so when the window is created we can see something. To display the window, the `setVisible(true)` must be called on the `JFrame` instance. When you run the previous code, a window like the one depicted in Figure 10-4 is displayed. By default the window is positioned in the upper left corner of your main monitor, but that can be changed by using some Swing components to compute a position relative to the screen size. Determining size and position of a Swing window relative to screen size is only limited by the amount of math you are willing to get into. Figure 10-4 shows a simple Java Swing Window.

Figure 10-4. *Simple Java Swing application*

CHAPTER 10   MAKING YOUR APPLICATION INTERACTIVE

At this moment, if we close the displayed window, the application keeps running. Because by default, closing the window makes it invisible by calling `setVisible(false)`. If we want to change the default behavior to exiting the application we have to change the default operation performed when closing the window. This can be easily done by adding the following line of code after creating the `JFrame` instance.

```
swingDemo.setDefaultCloseOperation(JFrame.EXIT_ON_CLOSE);
```

The `JFrame.EXIT_ON_CLOSE` constant is part of a set of constants that define application behavior when the window is closed. This one declares that the application should exit when the window is closed. The other available options are depicted in the following list:

- `DO_NOTHING_ON_CLOSE` - does nothing, including closing the window.
- `HIDE_ON_CLOSE` - the default option, which causes `setVisible(false)` to be called.
- `DISPOSE_ON_CLOSE` - an application can have more than one window, this option exits the application when the last displayable window is closed.

Most Swing applications are written by extending the `JFrame` class to gain more control over its component, so the preceding code can also be written like this:

```java
package com.apress.bgn.ch10;

import javax.swing.*;
import java.awt.*;

public class SwingDemo extends JFrame {

    public static void main(String... args) {
        SwingDemo swingDemo = new SwingDemo();
        swingDemo.setDefaultCloseOperation(JFrame.EXIT_ON_CLOSE);
        swingDemo.setTitle("Swing Demo Window");
        swingDemo.setSize(new Dimension(500,500));

        swingDemo.setVisible(true);
    }
}
```

And now that we have a window, let's start adding components, because changing the look-and-feel is pointless if we do not have more components so we can notice the change. Each Swing application has at least one `JFrame` that is the root, the parent of all other windows, because windows can be created by using the `JDialog` class as well. The `JDialog` is the main class for creating a dialog window, a special type of window that contains mostly a message and buttons to select options. Developers can use this class to create a custom dialogs or use `JOptionPane` class methods to create a variety of dialog windows.

Back to adding components to a `JFrame` instance; components are added to a `JFrame` by adding them to its container. A reference to the `JFrame` container can be retrieved by calling `getContentPane()`. The default content pane is a simple intermediate container that inherits from `JComponent`, which extends `java.awt.Container` (Swing being an extension of AWT, most of its components are AWT extensions). For `JFrame`, the default content pane is an instance of `JPane`. This class has a field of type `java.awt.LayoutManager` that defines how other components are arranged in a `JPane`. The default content pane of a `JFrame` instance, uses a `java.awt.BorderLayout` as its layout manager, which splits a pane into five regions: EAST, WEST, NORTH, SOUTH, and CENTER. Each of the zones can be referred by a constant with a matching name defined in the `BorderLayout`. So if we would like to add an exit button to our application, we could add it to the south region by writing the following code.

```java
package com.apress.bgn.ch10;

import javax.swing.*;
import java.awt.*;
import java.awt.event.ActionEvent;
import java.awt.event.ActionListener;

public class SwingDemo extends JFrame {
    private JPanel mainPanel;
    private JButton exitButton;

    public SwingDemo(String title) {
        super(title);
        mainPanel = (JPanel) this.getContentPane();
        exitButton = new JButton("Bye Bye!");
        exitButton.addActionListener(new ActionListener() {
            @Override
```

```
            public void actionPerformed(ActionEvent e) {
System.exit(0);
            }
        });
        mainPanel.add(exitButton, BorderLayout.SOUTH);
    }

    public static void main(String... args) {
        SwingDemo swingDemo = new SwingDemo("Swing Demo Window");
        swingDemo.setDefaultCloseOperation(JFrame.DO_NOTHING_ON_CLOSE);
        swingDemo.setSize(new Dimension(500, 500));

        swingDemo.setVisible(true);
    }
}
```

Figure 10-5 shows the modified application. We've added an exit button in the SOUTH area of the content pane and underlined the overall region arrangement of the BorderLayout.

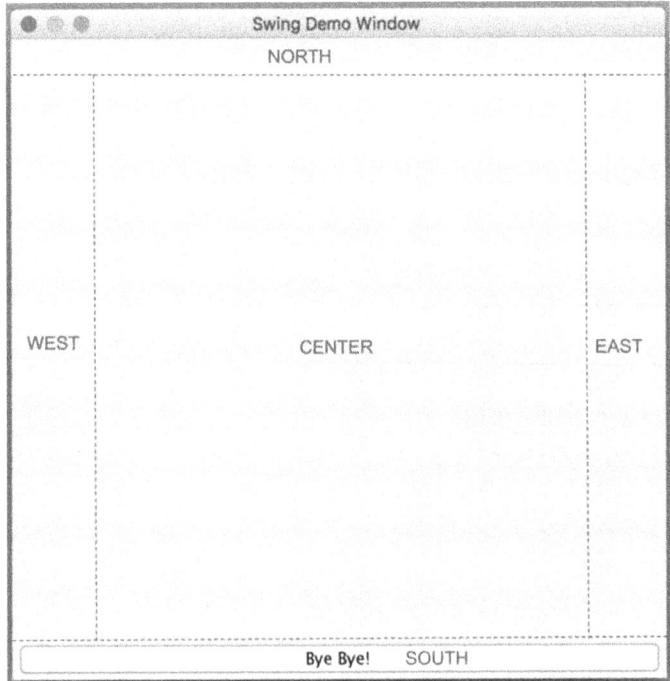

Figure 10-5. *Border layout zones*

Also, because the new button has to be the only way to exit our application, the set DefaultCloseOperation(JFrame.EXIT_ON_CLOSE); was replaced with setDefaultClose Operation(JFrame.DO_NOTHING_ON_CLOSE); and an java.awt.event.ActionListener instance was attached to the button, so it could record the event of the button being clicked and react accordingly, in this case exiting the application. Most Swing components support listeners that can be defined to capture events that are performed on the object by the user and react in a certain way.

As you can see, the button expands and fills the entire space of the region, because it inherits the dimension of the region. To avoid that, the button should be put in another container and that container should use a different layout: the FlowLayout. As the name implies, this layout allows for Swing components to be added in a directional flow, like in a paragraph. Adjustments can be made similar to a text formatting in text document and constants are defined for components being aligned: in the center (CENTER), left-justified (LEFT), and so forth. In the next code sample, we wrapped the exitButton in a JPanel that makes use of the FlowLayout.

```java
...
 public SwingDemo(String title) {
        super(title);
        mainPanel = (JPanel) this.getContentPane();

        exitButton = new JButton("Bye Bye!");
        exitButton.addActionListener(e -> System.exit(0));

        JPanel exitPanel = new JPanel();
        FlowLayout flowLayout = new FlowLayout();
        flowLayout.setAlignment(FlowLayout.RIGHT);
        exitPanel.setLayout(flowLayout);
        exitPanel.setComponentOrientation(ComponentOrientation.RIGHT_TO_LEFT);
        exitPanel.add(exitButton);

        mainPanel.add(exitPanel, BorderLayout.SOUTH);
    }
...
```

CHAPTER 10   MAKING YOUR APPLICATION INTERACTIVE

There are more layouts that can be used, but let's complete the application by adding a list with a number of entries and add a listener to it so when you click an element it is added to a text area in the center of the frame. A swing list can be created by instantiating the `JList<T>` class. This creates an object that displays a list of objects and allows the user to select one or more items. The swing `JList<T>` class contains a field of type `ListModel<T>` that manages the data contents displayed by the list. When created and elements were added, each object is associated with an index, and when the user selects an object the index can be used for processing as well. In the next snippet the `JList` object is declared, initialized, a `ListSelectionListener` is associated with it, to define the action to perform when an element from the list is selected. In our case the element value, must be added to a `JTextArea`, so this object is depicted in the code.

```java
  private static  String[] data = {"John Mayer", "Frank Sinatra",
      "Seth MacFarlane", "Nina Simone", "BB King", "Peggy Lee"};

  private JList<String> list;
  private JTextArea textArea;
...
        textArea = new JTextArea(50, 10);

        //NORTH
        list = new JList<>(data);
        list.addListSelectionListener(new ListSelectionListener() {
            @Override
            public void valueChanged(ListSelectionEvent e) {
  if (!e.getValueIsAdjusting()) {
     textArea.append(list.getSelectedValue() + "\n");
  }
            }
        });
        mainPanel.add(list, BorderLayout.NORTH);

        //CENTER
        JScrollPane txtPanel = new JScrollPane(textArea);
        textArea.setBackground(Color.LIGHT_GRAY);
        mainPanel.add(txtPanel, BorderLayout.CENTER);
  ...
```

CHAPTER 10 MAKING YOUR APPLICATION INTERACTIVE

If you click a list element, two things happen: the previous element is deselected, and one that was clicked the most recently is selected, so the selected element changes. The getValueIsAdjusting() method returns whether or not this is one in a series of multiple events, where changes are still being made, and we test if this method returns false to check that the selection has been already made, so we can get the value of the current selected element and add it to the text area.

Regarding the JTextArea instance, this one is added to a JScrollPane instance, which allows for the textArea contents to still be visible as it fills with text by providing a scrollbar or two, depending on the configuration. The JScrollPane can also be wrapped around a list with too many items to make sure all of them are accessible. Also, as we are not interested in user provided input via the text area, the setEditable(false); method is called.

Now that we have a more complex application, it is time to play with the look-and-feel of the application. Until now, we've used the default one, the one provided by the underlying Operation System. But with Swing, the look-and-feel can be configured as one of the defaults supported by the JDK or extra custom ones can be used, which are provided as dependencies in the project class path, or developers can create their own. To specify a look-and-feel explicitly, the following line of code must be added in the main method, before any swing component is created: UIManager.setLookAndFeel(..). This method receives as parameter a String value representing the fully qualified name of the appropriate subclass of look-and-feel. Although not necessary, you could specify explicitly that you want to use the native GUI by calling: UIManager.setLookAndFeel(UIManager.getCrossPlatformLookAndFeelClassName());. Knowing this, let's do something interesting. The UIManager class contains utility methods and nested classes used to manage look-and-feel for swing applications. One of this methods is getInstalledLookAndFeels(), which extracts the list of supported look-and-feels and returns them as a LookAndFeelInfo[]. Knowing this, let's list all the supported themes, add them to our list, and when the user selects one of them, let's apply them. Unfortunately, as swing is rarely used these days, there are not that many custom look-and-feels that we could use in our application. So, the only thing to do is to work with what JDK has. First, let's initialize the data array with the fully qualified class names.

```
private static  String[] data;
...
public static void main(String... args) throws Exception {
    UIManager.setLookAndFeel(UIManager.getCrossPlatformLookAndFeel
    ClassName());
```

429

```
        UIManager.LookAndFeelInfo[] looks = UIManager.getInstalledLookAnd
        Feels();
        data = new String[looks.length];
        int i =0;
        for (UIManager.LookAndFeelInfo look : looks) {
            data[i++] = look.getClassName();
        }

        SwingDemo swingDemo = new SwingDemo("Swing Demo Window");
        swingDemo.setDefaultCloseOperation(JFrame.DO_NOTHING_ON_CLOSE);
        swingDemo.setSize(new Dimension(500, 500));

        swingDemo.setVisible(true);
    }
...
```

Now, the `ListSelectionListener` implementation becomes a little complicated, because after selecting a new look and feel class, we have to call `repaint()` on the JFrame instance to apply the new look and feel, so we'll take the declaration out into its own class and provide the SwingDemo object as argument, so `repaint()` can be called on it, inside the `valueChanged(..)` method.

```
  private class LFListener implements ListSelectionListener {
        private JFrame parent;

        public LFListener(JFrame swingDemo) {
            parent = swingDemo;
        }

        @Override
        public void valueChanged(ListSelectionEvent e) {
            if (!e.getValueIsAdjusting()) {
  textArea.append(list.getSelectedValue() + "\n");
  try {
      UIManager.setLookAndFeel(list.getSelectedValue());
      Thread.sleep(1000);
      parent.repaint();
  } catch (Exception ee) {
```

```
            System.err.println(" Could not set look and feel! ");
        }
            }
        }
    }
}
```

If we run the modified program, and select each item in the list one by one, we should see the window look change a little bit. Figure 10-6 shows all windows side by side; the differences are barely noticeable, but they are there.

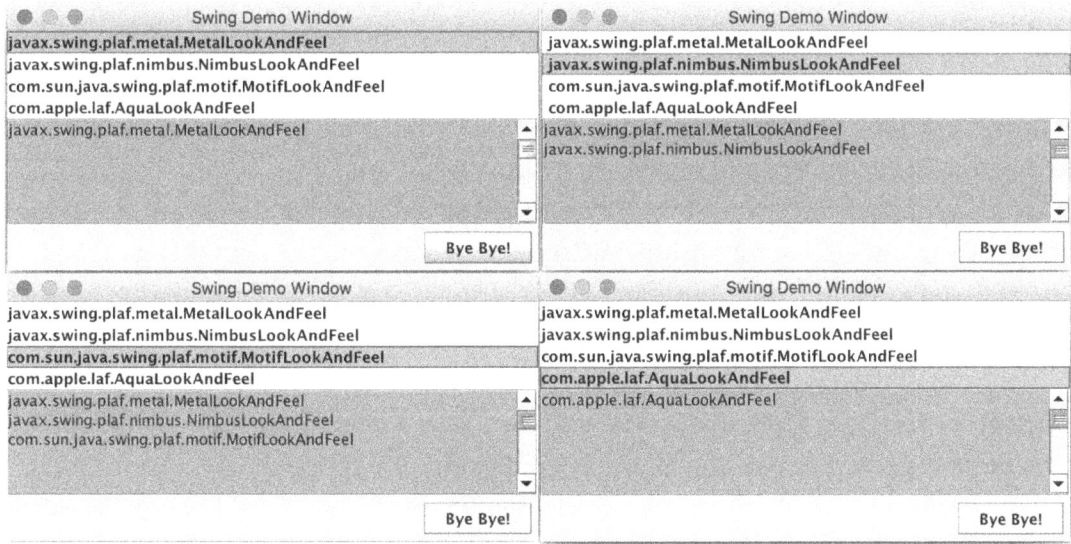

Figure 10-6. *Different Look And Feel provided by JDK*

This is what you can do with Swing components with a few lines of code. There are a lot more components that in the Swing library, but as it not really used anymore, as the focus is on web applications, this section has to end here. If you ever need to create or maintain a Swing application, Oracle provides an extensive tutorial with a lot of examples that you can directly copy/paste and adapt to your necessities.[2]

---

[2]Oracle extensive Swing tutorial: https://docs.oracle.com/javase/tutorial/uiswing/examples/layout/index.html

CHAPTER 10 MAKING YOUR APPLICATION INTERACTIVE

Introducing JavaFX

JavaFX Script was a scripting language designed by Sun Microsystems, forming part of the JavaFX family of technologies on the Java Platform. It was released shortly after JDK 6 in December 2008 and for a while developers expected it to be dropped because it really did not catch on that much, being a totally different language and all. But after acquiring Sun Microsystems, Oracle decided to keep it and they transformed it into the JavaFX library, which is a set of graphics and media packages that can be used by developers to design, create, test, debug, and deploy rich client applications that operate consistently across diverse platforms. And yes, mobile ones too. JavaFX is intended to replace Swing as the main GUI library of the JDK, but so far, both Swing and JavaFX have been part of all JDK versions until 10. That changed in JDK 11. Starting with JDK 11, JavaFX is available as a separate module, decoupled from the JDK. JavaFX is still not used as much as Oracle hoped, and separating it from the JDK might encourage the OpenJFX community to contribute with some innovative ideas, which might transform this library into an actual competitor for the other existing GUI toolkits on the market (e.g., Eclipse SWT[3]). So let's waste no time and start writing code to create an application similar to the previous one using JavaFX.

Being part of the JDK now, and having classes and other components, JavaFX code is currently normal Java code, so no more scripting. JavaFX components are defined under a list of `java.fx.*` modules. The following configuration snippet, shows that the module of our project that uses JavaFX declares its dependency on a few `java.fx` modules by using the `requires` directive, in its `module-info.java`.

```
module chapter.ten.javafx {
    requires javafx.base;
    requires javafx.graphics;
    requires javafx.controls;
    opens com.apress.bgn.ch10 to javafx.graphics;
}
```

---

[3]SWT is an open source widget toolkit for Java designed to provide efficient, portable access to the user-interface facilities of the operating systems on which it is implemented. More about it on the official site: https://www.eclipse.org/swt/

And because the JavaFX application launcher uses reflection to launch an application, you need to open the package containing the implementation; otherwise, an java.lang.IllegalAccessException is thrown, so that is why in the previous configuration the opens com.apress.bgn.ch10; exists.

Let's start with a simple window that has a closing option. I'll explain how it is executed because JavaFX is a little different from Swing and AWT. The code to display a plain square window is depicted next.

```
package com.apress.bgn.ch10;

import javafx.application.Application;
import javafx.scene.Scene;
import javafx.scene.layout.StackPane;
import javafx.stage.Stage;

public class JavaFxDemo extends Application {
    public static void main(String... args) {
        launch(args);
    }

    @Override
    public void start(Stage primaryStage) {
        primaryStage.setTitle("JavaFX Demo Window!");

        StackPane root = new StackPane();
        primaryStage.setScene(new Scene(root, 500, 500));
        primaryStage.show();
    }
}
```

The first thing you need to know is that the main class of the application must extend the javafx.application.Application class, because this is the entry point for a JavaFX application. This is required because JAVA FX applications are run by a new performance graphics engine named **Prism** that sits on top of the JVM. Aside from Prism, the graphic engine, JavaFX comes with its own windowing system named Glass, a media engine and a web engine. They are not exposed publicly, the only thing available to developers is the JavaFX API that provides access to any components you might need to build application with fancy interfaces. All of these engines are tied together by the

CHAPTER 10   MAKING YOUR APPLICATION INTERACTIVE

Quantum toolkit, which is the interface between these engines and the layer above in the stack. The Quantum toolkit manages execution threads and rendering.

The `launch(...)` method is a static method in the `Application` class that launches a standalone application. It is usually called from the main method and can only be called once; otherwise, a `java.lang.IllegalStateException` is thrown. The `launch` method does not return until the application is exited by closing all windows or calling `Platform.exit()`. The launch method creates an `JavaFxDemo` instance, calls the `init()` method on it and then calls `start(..)`. The `start(..)` method is declared `abstract` in the `Application` class, so the developer is forced to provide a concrete implementation.

A JavaFX application is built using components defined under the `javafx.scene` and has a hierarchical organization. The core class of the `javafx.scene` package is the `javafx.scene.Node` that is the root of the Scene hierarchy. Classes in this hierarchy provide implementations for all of the visual elements of the application's user interface. Because all of them have `Node` as a root class, visual elements are called **nodes**, which makes an application *a scene graph of nodes* and the initial node of this graph is called a *root*. Each node has an unique identifier, a style class and a bounding volume, and with the exception of the root node, each node in the graph has a single parent and zero or more children. Aside from that a node has the following properties.

- effects, such as blurs and shadow - useful when you hover with your mouse over the interface to make sure you click the right component
- opacity
- transformations - changing visual state or position
- event handlers - similar to listeners in Swing, used to define reaction on mouse, key and input method
- application specific state

The scene graph simplifies building rich interfaces a lot and, because it also includes graphics primitives as rectangles, text, images and media and also, animating various graphics can be accomplished by the animation APIs for package `javax.animation`. If you are interested in finding out more on what's under the hood of JavaFX, read the article at `https://docs.oracle.com/javafx/2/architecture/jfxpub-architecture.htm`, because the focus of this book is on how to do things rather than how they work, unless it really influences the design of your future solutions.

We've started again with a simple window. The first step is to add a button to quit the application. As rendering a JavaFX application involves a rendering engine, this means it has to shutdown gracefully, so calling System.exit(0) is no longer a preferred option. So the contents of the start(..) methods become the following.

```
...
public void start(Stage primaryStage) {
        primaryStage.setTitle("JavaFX Demo Window!");

        Button btn = new Button();
        btn.setText("Bye bye! ");
        btn.setOnAction(new EventHandler<ActionEvent>() {

            @Override
            public void handle(ActionEvent event) {
    Platform.exit();
            }
        });

        StackPane root = new StackPane();
        root.getChildren().add(btn);
        primaryStage.setScene(new Scene(root, 500, 500));
        primaryStage.show();
    }
...
```

If we run the JavaFxDemo class, the window depicted in Figure 10-7 pops up on your screen, and if you click the **Bye bye!** Button, the application is gracefully closed because of the Platform.exit(); call.

CHAPTER 10   MAKING YOUR APPLICATION INTERACTIVE

Figure 10-7. JavaFX Window Demo

But the button was just thrown in the window and put in the center by default because no code was written to position it. JavaFX supports arranging nodes[4] in a window in a manner similar to Swing, but JavaFX provides layout panes that support several different styles of layouts. The equivalent of a JPane with BorderLayout manager in JavaFX is a built-in layout named BorderPane. The BorderPane provides five regions where to place your nodes, with distribution similar to BorderLayout, but different names. Let's write the code to place our button in the bottom region in the right corner and then discuss more about it.

```
...
 public void start(Stage primaryStage) {
        primaryStage.setTitle("JavaFX Demo Window!");

        Button exitButton = new Button();
        exitButton.setText("Bye bye! ");
        exitButton.setOnAction(event -> Platform.exit());

        BorderPane borderPane = new BorderPane();
        HBox box = new HBox();
```

---

[4]It was mentioned that the root class for all Java FX components is named *Node*, so instead of components, Java FX components is referred as nodes in this section.

436

CHAPTER 10 MAKING YOUR APPLICATION INTERACTIVE

```
        box.setPadding(new Insets(10, 12, 10, 12));
        box.setSpacing(10);
        box.setAlignment(Pos.BASELINE_RIGHT);
        box.setStyle("-fx-background-color: #85929e;");
        box.getChildren().add(exitButton);
        borderPane.setBottom(box);

        StackPane root = new StackPane();
        root.getChildren().add(borderPane);
        primaryStage.setScene(new Scene(root, 500, 500));
        primaryStage.show();
    }
...
```

If we run the JavaFxDemo class the window depicted in Figure 10-8 pop up on your screen. The figure has been modified to show the regions of a BorderPane.

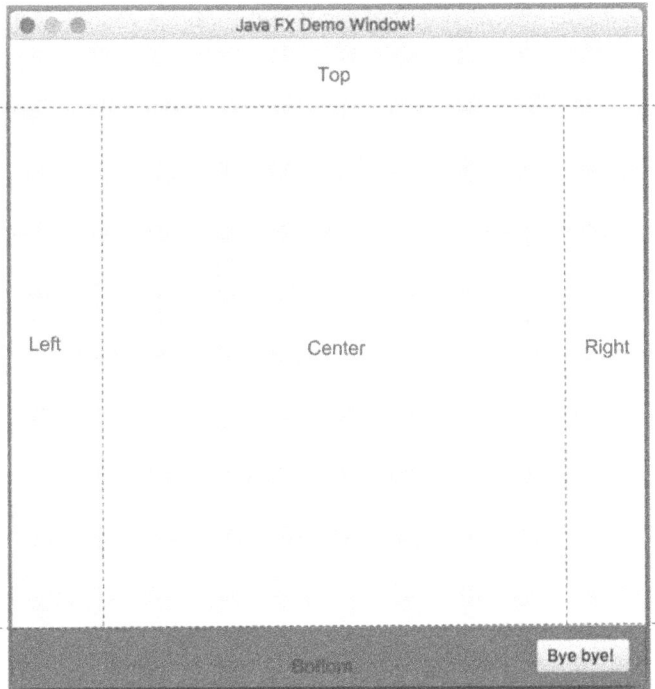

Figure 10-8. *JavaFX Window Demo*

The approach to decide where our button should be located is similar to Swing, with a few differences. The `BorderPane` has 5 regions named: Top, Bottom, Center, Left and Right. To place a node in each of those regions a `set*(..)` method for each of them has been defined: `setTop(..)`, `setBottom(..)`, `setCenter(..)`, `setLeft(..)` and `setRight(..)`. To further customize the position of the node, it should be placed in a `HBox` node, another JavaFX element that can be customized extensively. As you can see from the code, we are setting the background using CSS style elements, we customize the space between nodes in it and borders of the containing node by using an instance of class `Insets` and we customize the alignment of the contained nodes by calling `box.setAlignment(Pos.BASELINE_RIGHT)`. And there are a lot more things that `HBox` supports, so what you can do with a box is limited (mostly) only by your imagination.

So aside from all *making pretty* code in the preceding code sample, this was done: the *root* node became parent to a `BorderPane` node, in the bottom region of the `BorderPane`, a `HBox` was added, and this `HBox` instance became parent for a `Button`. This organization is hierarchic, with the button being the last node in the hierarchy.

Also, we avoided using a layer pane by styling the `HBox` node properly.

It is time to add the last functionality to our application: the text area and a list with selectable elements to add values to the text area. To create a text area in JavaFX is simple. The class is named in an clear manner: `TextArea`. We can directly add the node in the center region of the `BorderPane` because the JavaFX text area is scrollable by default. So there is no need to put it in a `ScrollPane`, although the class does exist in the `javafx.scene.control` package and is useful to display nodes inside it that make a form that is bigger than the window size. The following three lines of code create a node of type `TextArea`, declare it to not be editable, and add it to the center region of the `BorderPane`.

```
TextArea textArea = new TextArea();
textArea.setEditable(false);
borderPane.setCenter(textArea);
```

Next one is the list. The list is a little more complicated, but also a lot more fun to work with, because using JavaFX there is a lot you can do with a list. The class that needs to be instantiated to create a list object is named `ComboBox`. This class is just one of a bigger family of classes used to create lists, the root class being the abstract class `ComboBoxBase`. Depending on the desired behavior of the list, if we want support for single or multiple selection, if we want the list to be editable or not, the proper implementation should be chosen. In our case, the `ComboBox` class matches the requirements: we need a non-editable list, which supports single element section. A `ComboBox` has a `valueProperty()` method that returns the current user input. The user input can be based on a selection from a drop-down list or the input manually provided by the user when the list is editable. Let's see the code to add a list to the top section of the `BorderPane` and add a listener to record the selected value in the `TextArea` that we previously declared.

```
private static String[] data = {"John Mayer", "Frank Sinatra",
    "Seth MacFarlane", "Nina Simone", "BB King", "Peggy Lee"};
...
ComboBox<String> comboBox = new ComboBox<>();
comboBox.getItems().addAll(data);
borderPane.setTop(comboBox);

comboBox.valueProperty().addListener(
  new ChangeListener<String>() {
    @Override
      public void changed(ObservableValue<? extends String> observable,
          String oldValue, String newValue) {
          textArea.appendText(newValue + "\n");
      }
});
```

The `ComboBox` value field (accessed by calling `comboBox.valueProperty()`) is an `ObservableValue<T>` instance. The listener is an instance of type `ChangeListener<String>` is added to this instance by calling the `addListener(..)` method. Anytime the `comboBox` value field changes, the `changed(..)` method of the listener is called. The `changed(..)` method receives as argument the previous list selected value as well as the currently selected value, because who knows, maybe we have some logic that requires both.

In AWT and Swing, there was not much that you could do with a list visually. You had the look and feel and that was that. JavaFX supports more visual customization for nodes because it even supports CSS. That is why in the next section we'll make our `ComboBox` list interesting. In JavaFX each entry in a list is a cell that can be drawn differently. To do that, we have to add a `CellFactory` to this class, which creates an instance of `ListCell` for each item in a list. If a `CellFactory` is not specified the cells is created with the default style. Let's see the code first and explain more after.

CHAPTER 10 MAKING YOUR APPLICATION INTERACTIVE

```
comboBox.setCellFactory(
    new Callback<>() {
        @Override
        public ListCell<String> call(ListView<String> param) {
            return new ListCell<>() {
                {
    super.setPrefWidth(200);
                }

                @Override
                public void updateItem(String item, boolean empty) {
    super.updateItem(item, empty);
    if (item != null) {
        setText(item);
        if (item.contains("John") || item.contains("BB")) {
            setTextFill(Color.RED);
        } else if (item.contains("Frank") || item.contains("Peggy")) {
            setTextFill(Color.GREEN);
        } else if (item.contains("Seth")) {
            setTextFill(Color.BLUE);
        } else {
            setTextFill(Color.BLACK);
        }
    } else {
        setText(null);
    }
                }
            };
        }
    });
```

The `javafx.util.Callback` interface is a practical interface that can be used to declare a subsequent action for a certain action, if a callback is needed. In this case the subsequent action is doing the following: after a `String` value is added to the `ListView` of the `ComboBox` node (`ListView` is the visual, the interface type of a `ComboBox` that displays a horizontal or vertical list of items), a cell is being created and some piece of logic was inserted there to decide the color of the text depicted in the cell based on its value.

CHAPTER 10 MAKING YOUR APPLICATION INTERACTIVE

Inside the ListCell declaration there is a block of code that seems out of place.

```
{
     super.setPrefWidth(200);
}
```

The block is an interesting way to call a method from the parent class inside the declaration of an anonymous class. The setPrefWidth(200) is called here to make sure all the ListCell<> instances have the same size. The logic in the updateItem(..) is quite obvious, and thus it does not need any extended explanation. The result of adding the cell factory can be viewed in Figure 10-9.

And this is all the space we can give to JavaFX in this book. As long as you have a vague idea of why the JavaFX components are called *nodes*, you have a pretty good starting point. If you are curious, Oracle has some pretty good tutorials about it at https://docs.oracle.com/javase/8/javase-clienttechnologies.htm.

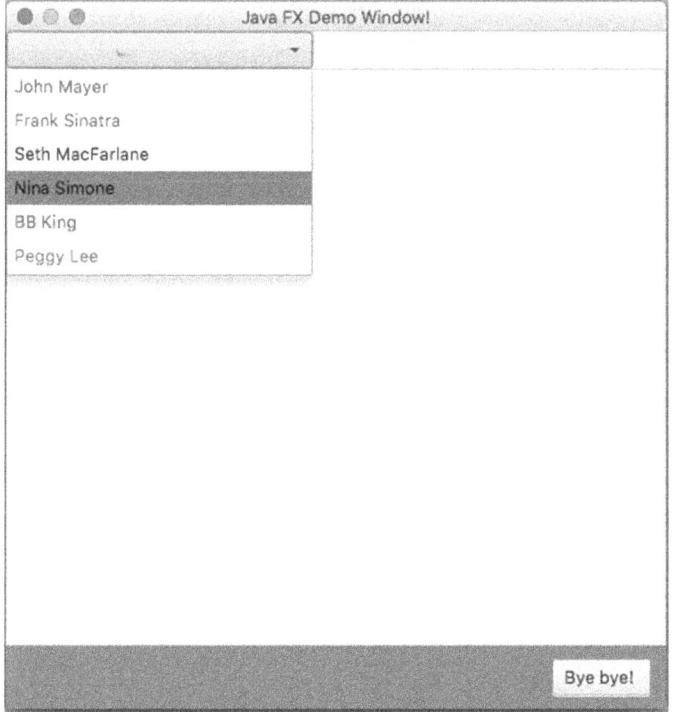

Figure 10-9. *JavaFX Colored ComboBox Demo*

CHAPTER 10 MAKING YOUR APPLICATION INTERACTIVE

Internationalization

Interactive applications are usually created to be deployed on more than one server and available 24/7 and in multiple locations. As not all of us speak the speak the same language, the key to convince people to become your clients and use your application is to build it in multiple languages. The process of designing an application so that it meets user needs in multiple countries and easily adapts to satisfy those needs is called *internationalization*. For example we can take the initial Google page. Depending on the location where it is accessed, it changes language according to that area. When you create an account, you can select the language you prefer. This does not mean that the Google has built a web application for each region, it's a single web application that displays text in different languages depending on the location. Internationalization should always be taken into consideration in the design phase of an application, because adding it later is difficult. We do not have a web application, but we are internationalizing a JavaFX application in this section.

When you start reading about internationalization you might notice that files or directories containing the internationalization property files are named `i18n`, which is because there are 18 letters between *i* and *n* in this word.

Internationalization is based on locale. **Locale** is the term given to a combination of language and region. The application locale is the one that decides which internationalization file customizes the application. The locale concept is implemented in Java by the `java.util.Locale` class and a `Locale` instance represents a geographical, political or cultural region. When an application depends on the locale we say that it is locale-sensitive, as most applications are nowadays. But selecting a locale can be something an user has to do as well. Each `Locale` can select the corresponding *locale resources*, these are files containing locale specific configurations. These files are grouped per locale and can usually be found under the `resources` directory. These resources are used to configure an instance of `java.util.ResourceBundle` that can manage locale-specific resources.

To build a proper use case for localization, the previous JavaFX application is modified; instead of singer names, the list contains a list of pet names with labels that can be translated in various languages. A list with the available languages is added, and when a language is selected from this list, a `Locale` static variable is set with the corresponding locale and the window is reinitialized so that all labels can be translated to the new language. Let's start by creating the *resource files*.

442

Resource files have the properties extension that contain a list of properties and values. Each line respects the following pattern: property_name=property_value, if it doesn't, it is not read. Each property name must be unique in the file, if there is a duplicate it is ignored and IntelliJ IDEA complains by underlining the property with red. For every language that needs to be supported, we need to create one property file that contains the same property names, but different values, as the values represent the translation of that value in each language. All files must have names that contain a common suffix and end with the language name and the country, separated by underscores, because these are the two elements needed to create a Locale instance. For our JavaFX application, we have three files, which are depicted in Figure 10-10.

Figure 10-10. *Resource Bundle with three resource files*

The suffix is global and this is our resource bundle name as well. This is made clear by IntelliJ IDEA, which figures out what our files are used for and depicts them in an obvious way. The contents of the files is depicted in Table 10-1.

Table 10-1. Contents of Resource Files

Property Name	Property value in global_en_GB	Property value in global_fr_FR	Property value in global_it_IT
English	English	Anglais	Inglese
French	French	Français	Francese
Italian	Italian	Italien	Italiano
Cat	Cat	Chat	Gatto
Dog	Dog	Chien	Cane
Parrot	Parrot	Chien	Pappagallo
Mouse	Mouse	Souris	Topo
Cow	Cow	Perroquet	Mucca
Pig	Pig	Porc	Maiale
WindowTitle	JavaFX Demo Window!	JavaFX Démo Fenêtre!	JavaFX Dimostratione Finestra!
Byebye	Bye bye!	Bye bye!	Ciao!
ChoosePet	Choose Pet:	Choisissez la langue:	Scegli la lingua:
ChooseLanguage	Choose Language:	Choisir un animal de compagnie:	Scegli un animale domestico

IntelliJ IDEA can help you edit resource bundle files easily and makes sure you are not missing any keys from any of them by providing a special view for them. When you open a resource file, in the bottom left corner you should see two tabs. One is called **Text** and when clicked, it allows you to edit a properties file as a normal text file. The other one is called **Resource Bundle** and when clicked, it opens a special view that has all the property names in the resource files and views from all resource files containing values for property names selected. Figure 10-11 shows this view and the values for the **Choose Language** property.

CHAPTER 10 MAKING YOUR APPLICATION INTERACTIVE

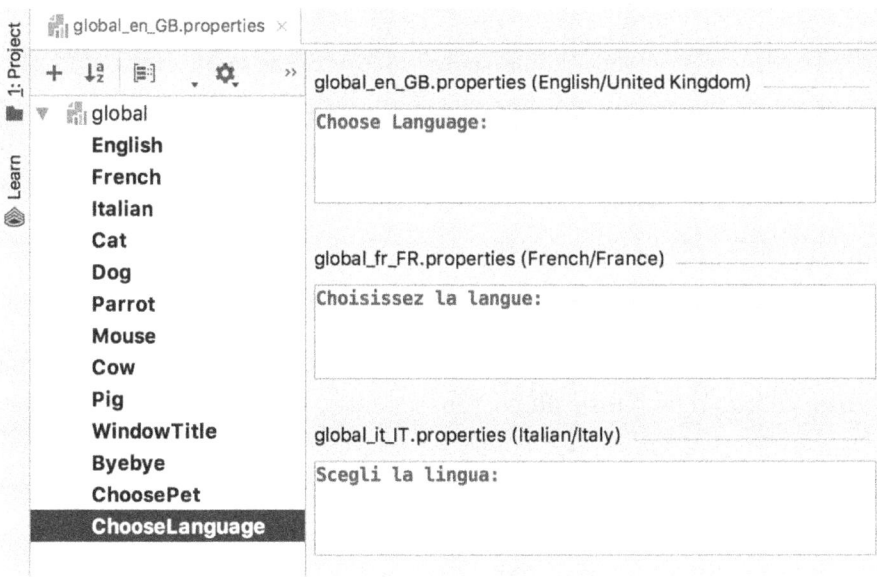

Figure 10-11. *Resource Bundle IntelliJ IDEA editor*

The property names can contain special characters as underscore and dots to separate parts of them. In this book example the property names are simple, because we only have so little of them. In bigger applications, property names usually contain a prefix that is relevant to their purpose, for example if the property value is a title the name is prefixed with title. For example, the property names in our files could be changed to the following:

```
English --> label.lang.english
French --> label.lang.french
Italian --> label.lang.italian
Cat --> label.pet.cat
Dog --> label.pet.dog
Parrot --> label.pet.parrot
Mouse --> label.pet.mouse
Cow --> label.pet.cow
Pig --> label.pet.pig
WindowTitle --> title.window
Byebye --> label.button.byebye
ChoosePet --> label.choose.pet
ChooseLanguage --> label.choose.language
```

445

Now that we have covered how the resource files should be written, let's see how they are used. To create a `ResourceBundle` instance, we first need a locale. Applications have a default locale that can be obtained by calling `Locale.getDefault()`, and a `ResourceBundle` instance can be obtained by using a bundle name and a locale instance, as depicted in the following code snippet.

```
Locale locale = Locale.getDefault();
ResourceBundle labels = ResourceBundle.getBundle("global", locale);
```

When a valid `ResourceBundle` is obtained, it can replace all hard-coded `String` instances with calls to return text values from the resource file matching the selected locale. So, every time we need to set a label for a node, instead of using the actual text, we use a call to `resourceBundle.getString("[property_name]")` to get the localized text.

When a JavaFX window is reloaded, all its nodes are re-created. To influence how, we need to add a couple of static properties to keep the selected locale set. So, for the application that we've build so far, after internationalizing it, the code looks like the one in the next listing.

```
package com.apress.bgn.ch10;

import javafx.*;

import java.io.File;
import java.net.URL;
import java.net.URLClassLoader;
import java.util.Locale;
import java.util.ResourceBundle;
public class JavaFxDemo extends Application {

    private static final String BUNDLE_LOCATION =
            "chapter10/using-javafx/src/main/resources";

    private static ResourceBundle resourceBundle = null;
    private static Locale locale = new Locale("en", "GB");
    private static int selectedLang = 0;

    public static void main(String... args) {
        Application.launch(args);
    }
```

```java
@Override
public void start(Stage primaryStage) throws Exception {
    loadLocale(locale);
    primaryStage.setTitle(resourceBundle.getString("WindowTitle"));

    String[] data = {resourceBundle.getString("Cat"),
            resourceBundle.getString("Dog"),
            resourceBundle.getString("Parrot"),
            resourceBundle.getString("Mouse"),
            resourceBundle.getString("Cow"),
            resourceBundle.getString("Pig")};

    BorderPane borderPane = new BorderPane();

    //Top
    final ComboBox<String> comboBox = new ComboBox<>();
    comboBox.getItems().addAll(data);

    final ComboBox<String> langList = new ComboBox<>();

    String[] languages = {
            resourceBundle.getString("English"),
            resourceBundle.getString("French"),
            resourceBundle.getString("Italian")};

    langList.getItems().addAll(languages);
    langList.getSelectionModel().select(selectedLang);

    GridPane gridPane = new GridPane();
    gridPane.setHgap(10);
    gridPane.setVgap(10);

    Label labelLang = new Label(resourceBundle.getString("Choose
    Language"));
    gridPane.add(labelLang, 0, 0);
    gridPane.add(langList, 1, 0);

    Label labelPet = new Label(resourceBundle.getString("ChoosePet"));
    gridPane.add(labelPet, 0, 1);
    gridPane.add(comboBox, 1, 1);
```

CHAPTER 10   MAKING YOUR APPLICATION INTERACTIVE

```java
borderPane.setTop(gridPane);

//Center
final TextArea textArea = new TextArea();
textArea.setEditable(false);
borderPane.setCenter(textArea);

comboBox.valueProperty().addListener((observable, oldValue, newValue)
        -> textArea.appendText(newValue + "\n"));

langList.valueProperty().addListener((observable, oldValue, newValue)
        -> {
    int idx = langList.getSelectionModel().getSelectedIndex();
    selectedLang = idx;
    if (idx == 0) {
        //locale = Locale.getDefault();
        new Locale("en", "GB");
    } else if (idx == 1) {
        locale = new Locale("fr", "FR");
    } else {
        locale = new Locale("it", "IT");
    }

    primaryStage.close();
    Platform.runLater(() -> {
        try {
            new JavaFxDemo().start(new Stage());
        } catch (Exception e) {
            System.err.println("Could not reload application!");
        }
    });
});

HBox box = new HBox();
box.setPadding(new Insets(10, 12, 10, 12));
box.setSpacing(10);
box.setAlignment(Pos.BASELINE_RIGHT);
```

CHAPTER 10 MAKING YOUR APPLICATION INTERACTIVE

```
        box.setStyle("-fx-background-color: #85929e;");
        Button exitButton = new Button();
        exitButton.setText(resourceBundle.getString("Byebye"));
        exitButton.setOnAction(event -> Platform.exit());
        box.getChildren().add(exitButton);
        borderPane.setBottom(box);

        //Bottom
        StackPane root = new StackPane();
        root.getChildren().add(borderPane);
        primaryStage.setScene(new Scene(root, 500, 500));
        primaryStage.show();
    }

    private void loadLocale(Locale locale) throws Exception {
        File file = new File(BUNDLE_LOCATION);

        URL[] url = {file.toURI().toURL()};
        ClassLoader loader = new URLClassLoader(url);

        resourceBundle = ResourceBundle.getBundle("global", locale, loader);
    }
}
```

You might be wondering why we used another way of loading the resource bundle and why the full relative path to the bundle location was used. Well, if we want the application to be runnable from the IntelliJ Interface, we have to provide a path relative to the execution context of the application. When the application is built and packed in a runnable Java archive, the resource files are part of it and in the classpath. But we run the application by executing the `main()` method in an Java IDE, the classpath is relative to the actual location of the project.

The following code snippet, restarts the scene by closing the `Stage`, then instantiating a `JavaFxDemo` object and calling `start(..)`. This means the whole hierarchical node structure is re-created; the only state that is kept is the one that was defined in static objects. This is needed for the locale setting, because the `start(..)` method execution now starts with a call to `loadLocale(locale)`, which selects the locale of the application and loads the `ResourceBundle` so that, all nodes can be labeled with texts returned by it.

```
primaryStage.close();
        Platform.runLater(() -> {
            try {
                new JavaFxDemo().start(new Stage());
            } catch (Exception e) {
                System.err.println("Could not reload application!");
            }
        });
```

The application we have built until now and played with is a simple one. If you ever need to build interfaces that are more complex and internationalization is needed, this means more than translations are configured. You might need to have files with different number and date formats, or multiple resource bundles. Internationalization is a big topic and an important one, as rarely an application is built nowadays to be used in a single region. But for a Java beginner, just knowing what the supporting classes are and how they can be used is a very good starting point.

Build a Web Application

Here we are. Things are getting serious. We are building a web application. A web application is an application that runs on a server and can be accessed using a browser. Until recently most Java applications needed web servers like Apache Tomcat, Glassfish, or Enterprise, and servers like JBoss (currently known as WildFly) or TomEE to be hosted on, so they could be accessed. You would write the web application, with the classes and HTML or JSP files, pack it in a WAR (Web ARchive) or an EAR (Enterprise ARchive), deploy it to a server, and start the server. The server would provide the context of the application and map requests to classes that would provide the answer to be served as responses. Assuming the application would be deployed on a Tomcat server, Figure 10-12 shows an abstract schema of the deployed application functionality.

CHAPTER 10   MAKING YOUR APPLICATION INTERACTIVE

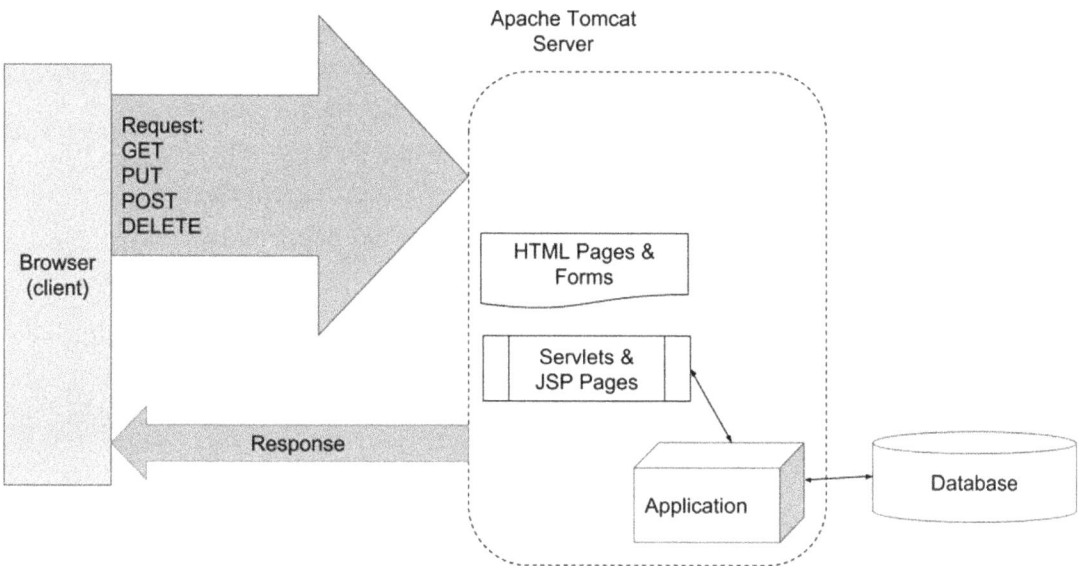

Figure 10-12. *Web application deployed on an Apache Tomcat server*

Requests to a web application can come from other clients than browsers, but because this section covers web applications, we'll assume all requests to our application come from a browser. Let me explain the Internet a little first.

The Internet is an information system made up of a lot of computers linked together. Some computers host application servers that provide access to applications, some computers access these applications and some do both. The communication between these computers is done over a network through a list of protocols: HTTP, FTP, SMTP, POP, and so forth. The most popular protocol is HTTP, which stands for **Hypertext Transfer Protocol** and it is an asymmetric request-response client-server protocol, this means that the client makes a request to the server and then the server sends a response. Subsequent requests have no knowledge of one another and they do not share any state, thus they are *stateless*. HTTP requests can be of different types, being categorized by the action they require the application on the server to perform, but there are four types that are more commonly used by developers (the ones listed in Figure 10-12 in the request arrow). I won't go into the details of request components because it is not really related to Java; I'll cover enough information to understand how a web application works. The following list contains the four most common request types and the responses a server generates for them:

451

- GET: Whenever a user enters a URL in the browser (e.g., http://mysite.com/index.html), the browser transforms the address into a request message and sends it to the web server. What the browser does can be easily viewed by opening the debugger view in Firefox. Click the **Network** tab, and access www.google.com. Figure 10-13 shows the Firefox debugger view showing the URL being requested and the contents of the Request message.

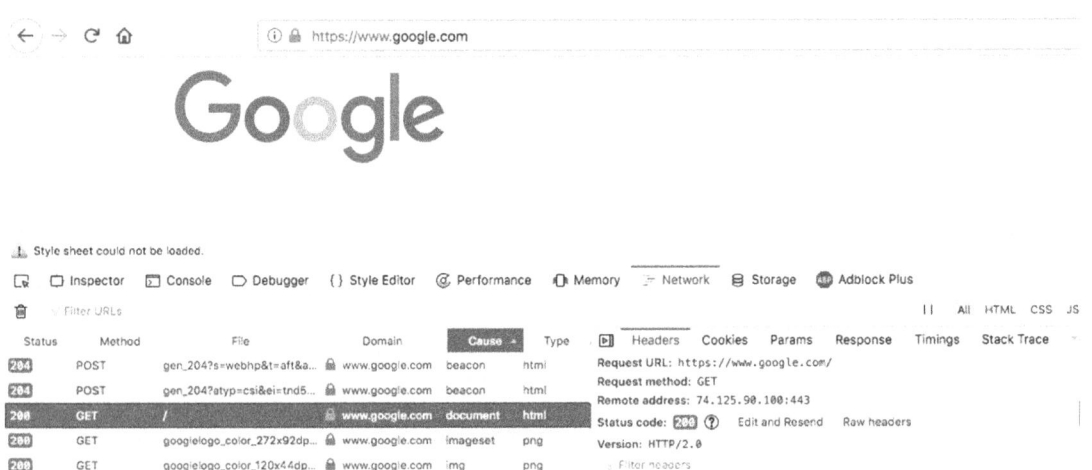

Figure 10-13. Network debugger view in Firefox

In the right part of the image, you can see the URL being requested, the type of request, also called a **request method**, which is GET in this case, and the **remote address** of the server where the request was sent to. There is also a **Raw headers** button that opens a view depicting the contents of the request and response as text. GET requests are used to retrieve something from the server, in this example, a web page. If the web page can be found, the response is sent with the page to be displayed by the browser and other attributes, such a status code, to communicate that all went fine. There is a list of HTTP status codes, the most important one is the 200 code, which means all went OK. In Figure 10-13, you can see that to display the page a lot of additional requests are done, after the initial request is replied, and all subsequent requests are successful, because the status returned by the server is put in the first column in the table and it's always 200.

- PUT: This type of request is used when data is sent to the server for storage. In enterprise applications, a PUT requests is interpreted as a request to update an existing object, and the request contains the updated version of the object and means to identify it.

- POST: This type of request is used when the server needs to be instructed to save data for storage as well. The difference from PUT request is that this data does not exist on the server yet. In enterprise applications a POST request is used to send credentials so the user can be authenticated, or to send data that creates a new object. When a POST request sends credentials the response status code is 200 when the user is authenticated and 401(Unauthorized) when the user credentials are not good, when a POST request sends data to be saved, the 201 status code is returned if the object was created.

- DELETE: This type of request is used when the server is asked to delete data. The response code is 200 when the deleting the data was successful, and any other error code related to the cause why it did not, otherwise.

There are a few other HTTP methods that are used in more complex applications. If you are curious about request methods, status codes, and HTTP basics, I confidently recommend the tutorial at www.ntu.edu.sg/home/ehchua/programming/webprogramming/http_basics.html. Now let's get back to writing Java web applications.

Until a while ago, we needed a server to host a web application but this is no longer the case. As databases were replaced for testing purposes and applications with minimum functionality with embedded databases, the same happened to web servers. If you want to quickly write a simple web application you have now the option of using an embedded server, like Jetty or Tomcat (the embedded version). For this section of the chapter, we'll use an embedded Tomcat server and we'll create a small web application that displays a simple HTML page. The code is depicted in the next listing.

```
package com.apress.bgn.ch10;

import org.apache.catalina.Context;
import org.apache.catalina.LifecycleException;
import org.apache.catalina.startup.Tomcat;

import java.io.File;
```

```
public class WebDemo {
    public static void main(String... args) throws LifecycleException {
        Tomcat tomcat = new Tomcat();
        tomcat.setBaseDir("chapter10/web-app/out");
        tomcat.setPort(8080);

        String contextPath = "/demo";
        String docBase = new File(".").getAbsolutePath();

        Context context = tomcat.addContext(contextPath, docBase);

        SampleServlet servlet = new SampleServlet();
        tomcat.addServlet(contextPath, servlet.getServletName(), servlet);
        context.addServletMapping(servlet.getUrlPattern(),
                servlet.getServletName());

        tomcat.start();
        tomcat.getServer().await();
    }
}
```

If you think it is simple, it really is. All we have to do to start an embedded server is to create a `Tomcat` instance and select the port we want to expose it on(in this case 8080) and specify a location for the Tomcat temp files. As we are running our `main(..)` method from IntelliJ, the context of the application is relative to the project directory, so the base directory for Tomcat is set as the `out` directory where IntelliJ IDEA stores compiled classes and other temporary files for this project. A Java web application needs a context path. The context path value is a part of the URL to access the application. An URL is made up of four parts.

- `protocol`: The application-level protocol used by client and server to communicate, (e.g., http, https, ftp, etc.).

- `hostname`: The DNS domain name (e.g., `www.google.com`) or IP address (e.g., 192.168.0.255) or any alias recognized in a network. For example when an application is accessed from the same computer the server is installed on either 127.0.0.1 can be used or *localhost*.

- port: The TCP port number the server is listening for incoming requests from clients. For web applications it usually is 8080, but most URLs do not contain this port as there are routing mechanisms in place to hide it.

- path and filename: The name and location of the resource, under the server document base directory. Users usually request to view specific pages hosted on servers, which is why URLs look like this: https://docs.oracle.com/index.html. But a very used practice is to hide the paths and file names by using internal mappings (called URL redirection) because of security reasons.

So where does the context path value come in? Well, when we have an embedded server declared like in the previous code sample, any files that are hosted by it can be accessed by using the http://localhost:8080/, but because a server can host more than one application, they must be a way to separate them, right? Here is where the context path value comes in handy. Because by setting the context path to /demo, the WebDemo application and the resources it provides to the users can be accessed at http://localhost:8080/demo/.

Java Web Applications are dynamic, the pages are generated from Java code using *Servlets* and *JSP(Java Server Pages)* pages. Because of that, Java Web Applications are not running on a server but inside a web container on the server. The web container provides a Java runtime environment for Java Web applications. Apache Tomcat is such a container running in the JVM; it supports execution of servlets and JSP pages. A **servlet** is a Java class that is a subclass of javax.servlet.http.HttpServlet. Instances of this type answer HTTP Requests within a web container. A JSP page is a file with .jsp extension that contains HTML and Java code. A JSP page gets compiled into a servlet by the web container the first time the page is accessed. In essence the *servlet* is the core element of a Java Web application. Also, the server must know that the servlet exists and how to identify it, this where the call tomcat.addServlet(contextPath, servlet.getServletName(), servlet); comes in, it basically says: add the servlet with name servlet.getServletName() to the application context with the contextPath value context path. Then, to associate an URL pattern to the servlet, the context.addServletMapping(servlet.getUrlPattern(), servlet.getServletName()); is called.

CHAPTER 10   MAKING YOUR APPLICATION INTERACTIVE

When a Java Web Application is running, all its servlets and JSP are running into its context, but they have to be added into the context in the code and mapped to an URL pattern. The requests URL that match that URL pattern will access that servlet. In the previous code sample, you can see that an instance of `SampleServlet` is created. It is a custom class extending `javax.servlet.http.HttpServlet` that overrides the `doGet(..)` method to return a response to the client for a GET request with `http://localhost:8080/demo/`. The code of this class is depicted next.

```java
package com.apress.bgn.ch10;

import javax.servlet.http.HttpServlet;
import javax.servlet.http.HttpServletRequest;
import javax.servlet.http.HttpServletResponse;
import java.io.BufferedReader;
import java.io.FileReader;
import java.io.IOException;
import java.io.PrintWriter;

public class SampleServlet extends HttpServlet {

    private final String servletName = "sampleServlet";
    private final String urlPattern = "/";

    @Override
    protected void doGet(HttpServletRequest request, HttpServletResponse response)
            throws IOException {
        PrintWriter writer = response.getWriter();
        try (BufferedReader reader = new BufferedReader(
         new FileReader("chapter10/web-app/src/main/resources/static/index.html"))) {
            String line = "";
            while ((line = reader.readLine()) != null) {
                writer.println(line);
            }
        }
    }
}
```

```
    @Override
    public String getServletName() {
        return servletName;
    }

    public String getUrlPattern() {     }
        return urlPattern;

}
```

The `urlPattern` property was added to this class for practical reasons to keep everything related to this servlet in one place. The same goes for `servletName`. If the intention was to instantiate this class multiple times to create multiple servlets, these two properties should be taken outside of it. Inside the `doGet(..)` method we only read the contents of the `index.html` file and we write them in the response object using the response `PrintWriter`.

As you can see, the `doGet(..)` method receives as arguments two objects: the `HttpServletRequest` instance is read and all contents of the request sent from the client can be accessed using appropriate methods, and the `HttpServletResponse` instance, that is used to add information to the response. In the previous code sample, we are just writing HTML code read from another file, but we can set the status also by calling `response.setStatus(HttpServletResponse.SC_OK);` Aside from the `doGet(..)` method there are `do*(..)` methods matching each HTTP method that declare the same type of parameters.

Another way to write the class (starting with Servlet 3.0) is depicted in the following code snippet:

```
package com.apress.bgn.ch10;

import javax.servlet.annotation.WebServlet;
import javax.servlet.http.HttpServlet;
import javax.servlet.http.HttpServletRequest;
import javax.servlet.http.HttpServletResponse;
import java.io.BufferedReader;
import java.io.FileReader;
import java.io.IOException;
import java.io.PrintWriter;
```

```
@WebServlet(
        name = "sampleServlet",
        urlPatterns = {"/"}
)
public class IndexServlet extends HttpServlet {

    @Override
    protected void doGet(HttpServletRequest request, HttpServletResponse 
    response)
            throws IOException {
        PrintWriter writer = response.getWriter();
        response.setStatus(HttpServletResponse.SC_OK);
        try (BufferedReader reader = new BufferedReader(
     new FileReader("chapter10/web-app/src/main/resources/static/index.
     html"))) {
            String line = "";
            while ((line = reader.readLine()) != null) {
                writer.println(line);
            }
        }
        writer.flush();
        writer.close();
    }
}
```

Using the @WebServlet annotation, we no longer need to have properties where we store the servlet name and URL pattern, but the Tomcat context needs to be modified a little to tell it to scan for classes annotated with @WebServlet. So, instantiating the servlet explicitly is no longer necessary. Neither is calling `tomcat.addServlet(..)` and `context.addServletMapping(..)`, because adding the servlet to the application context and mapping it is done automatically using the information provided by the @WebServlet annotation. But we do have to define where the compiled servlet classes are by declaring an `WebResourceSet` instance and adding it to the context resources.

```
import org.apache.catalina.Context;
import org.apache.catalina.WebResourceRoot;
import org.apache.catalina.startup.Tomcat;
```

CHAPTER 10 MAKING YOUR APPLICATION INTERACTIVE

```java
import org.apache.catalina.webresources.DirResourceSet;
import org.apache.catalina.webresources.StandardRoot;

import java.io.File;

public class WebDemo {

    public static void main(String... args) throws Exception {
        Tomcat tomcat = new Tomcat();
        tomcat.setBaseDir("chapter10/web-app/out");
        tomcat.setPort(8080);

        String contextPath = "/demo";
        String docBase = new File(".").getAbsolutePath();

        Context context = tomcat.addContext(contextPath, docBase);

        File webInfClasses = new File(root.getAbsolutePath(), "production/classes");
        WebResourceRoot resources = new StandardRoot(context);

        WebResourceSet resourceSet;
        if (webInfClasses.exists()) {
            resourceSet = new DirResourceSet(resources,
                "/WEB-INF/classes", webInfClasses.getAbsolutePath(), "/");
            System.out.println("loading WEB-INF resources from as '"
                + webInfClasses.getAbsolutePath() + "'");
        } else {
            resourceSet = new EmptyResourceSet(resources);
        }
        resources.addPreResources(resourceSet);
        context.setResources(resources);

        tomcat.start();
        tomcat.getServer().await();
    }
}
```

CHAPTER 10 MAKING YOUR APPLICATION INTERACTIVE

So this is how we handle servlets, but how do we handle JSP pages using an embedded server? First we have to create a directory where the JSP pages are. So the structure of our project must change as depicted in Figure 10-14.

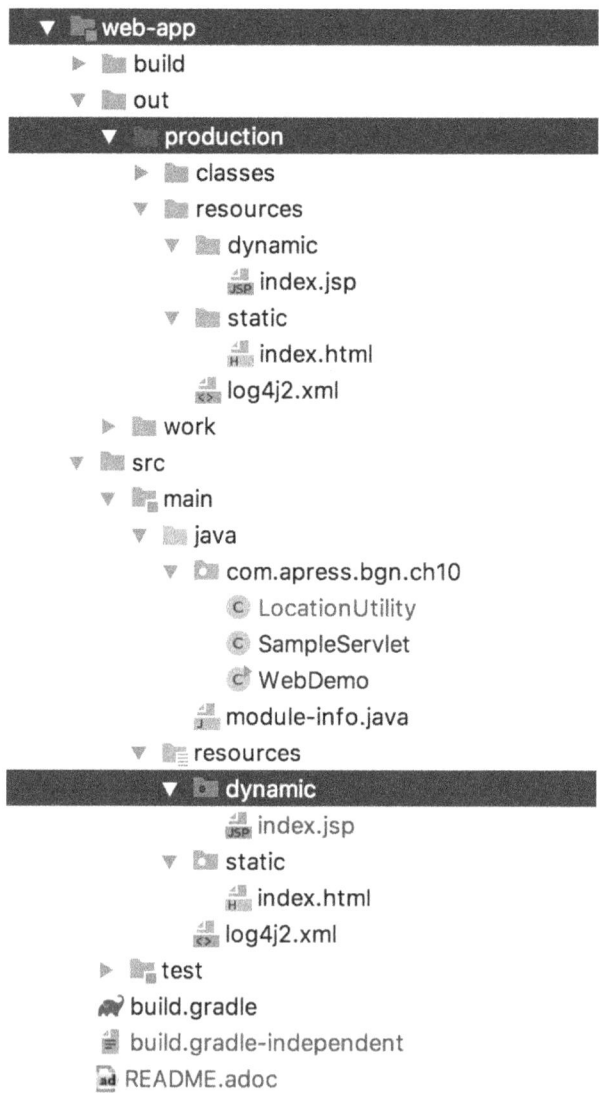

Figure 10-14. *Web application structure change*

As you can see, the `resource/dynamic` directory was added to place the JSP pages in. As our application is getting complicated it is time to clean it up a little and make paths relative to the execution path of the application, which is the `out` directory. So, we introduce the following class.

```
package com.apress.bgn.ch10;

import java.io.File;

public class LocationUtility {

    public static File getRootFolder() throws Exception {
        String executionPath = WebDemo.class.getProtectionDomain()
            .getCodeSource().getLocation().toURI().getPath().
            replaceAll("\\\\", "/");
        int lastIndexOf = executionPath.lastIndexOf("/production/");
        return lastIndexOf < 0 ? new File("") :
            new File(executionPath.substring(0, lastIndexOf));
    }
}
```

We now know that when IntelliJ IDEA compiles Gradle applications it creates under the `out` directory a directory named `production` containing compiled Java classes and resources, properly organized each in their own directory. So that is why, the root directory of the execution of our application is computed relative to that directory. As we've added an `index.jsp` page, we have to add a different URL pattern for `SampleServlet` and since we also added relative paths, the class code changes a little.

```
package com.apress.bgn.ch10;

import javax.servlet.annotation.WebServlet;
import javax.servlet.http.HttpServlet;
import javax.servlet.http.HttpServletRequest;
import javax.servlet.http.HttpServletResponse;
import java.io.BufferedReader;
import java.io.FileReader;
import java.io.IOException;
import java.io.PrintWriter;
```

CHAPTER 10 MAKING YOUR APPLICATION INTERACTIVE

```
@WebServlet(
        name = "sampleServlet",
        urlPatterns = {"/sample"}
)
public class SampleServlet extends HttpServlet {

    @Override
    protected void doGet(HttpServletRequest request, HttpServletResponse
    response)
            throws IOException {
        PrintWriter writer = response.getWriter();
        response.setStatus(HttpServletResponse.SC_OK);
        try (BufferedReader reader = new BufferedReader(
                new FileReader(LocationUtility.getRootFolder()
                  + "/production/resources/static/index.html"))) {
            String line = "";
            while ((line = reader.readLine()) != null) {
                writer.println(line);
            }
        } catch (Exception e) {
            writer.println(
             "<html><head><title>Web Application Demo [ERROR] </title></head>" +
              "<body><p style=\"color:#C70039\">Something went wrong." +
              "The page is not available. Error: " + e.getMessage()
              + "</p></body></html>");
            e.printStackTrace();
        }
        writer.flush();
        writer.close();
    }
}
```

And since we might get the path to index.html wrong, we made sure to display a proper message in the page. Next is to create a JSP page. There are two ways of writing JSP pages. *JSP scriptlets* are the simplest ones to use. They are pieces of Java code embedded in HTML code using *directive tags*. There are three type of directive tags.

CHAPTER 10 MAKING YOUR APPLICATION INTERACTIVE

- `<%@ page ... %>` directive used to provide instructions to the container. Instructions declared using this directive belong to the current page and can be used anywhere in the page. Such a directive can import Java types or define page properties; for example,

  ```
  <%@ page import="java.util.Date" %>
  <%@ page language="java" contentType="text/html; charset=US-ASCII"
      pageEncoding="US-ASCII" %>
  ```

- `<%@ include ... %>` directive includes a file during translation phase. Thus the current JSP file where this directive is used, is a composition of its content and the content of the file that is declared using this directive.

  ```
  <%@ include file = "footer.jsp" >
  ```

- `<%@ taglib ... %>` directive declares a tag library with elements that are used in the JSP page. This directive is important because it imports a library with custom tags and element that writes the JSP page. These tags provide dynamic functionality without the need for scriptlets.

The `index.jsp` page that we are using in this application is quite simple.

```
<%@ page import="java.util.Date" %>
<%@ page language="java" contentType="text/html; charset=US-ASCII"
    pageEncoding="US-ASCII" %>
<!DOCTYPE html PUBLIC "-//W3C//DTD HTML 4.01 Transitional//EN"
    "http://www.w3.org/TR/html4/loose.dtd">
<html>
    <head><title>Web Application Demo JSP Page</title></head>

    <body bgcolor=black>
    <p style="color:#ffd200"> Today is <%= new Date() %>  </p>
    </body>
</html>
```

The page displays today's date, and this is done by calling `new Date()`. We are using Java code in what it looks like an HTML page. Because those directives are in there at the

CHAPTER 10 MAKING YOUR APPLICATION INTERACTIVE

top of the page and the extension is .jsp, the container knows this file must be compiled into a servlet. The default page a web application opens with when its root domain is accessed, if nothing was mapped to the default URL pattern "/" is a file named index. html or index.htm or index.jsp in this case. So, aside from adding the file named index.jsp in the proper directory and then making sure the container can find the said application directory, there is nothing more to do so that when we access http:// localhost:8080/demo/ our page is displayed.

So let's see how the WebDemo class changes to make sure the index.jsp file is found and displayed properly.

```
package com.apress.bgn.ch10;

import org.apache.catalina.WebResourceRoot;
import org.apache.catalina.WebResourceSet;
import org.apache.catalina.core.StandardContext;
import org.apache.catalina.startup.Tomcat;
import org.apache.catalina.webresources.DirResourceSet;
import org.apache.catalina.webresources.EmptyResourceSet;
import org.apache.catalina.webresources.StandardRoot;

import java.io.File;
import java.nio.file.Files;
import static com.apress.bgn.ch10.LocationUtility.getRootFolder;

public class WebDemo {
    public static void main(String... args) throws Exception {
        File root = getRootFolder();
        Tomcat tomcat = new Tomcat();
        tomcat.setPort(8080);
        tomcat.setBaseDir(root.getAbsolutePath());

        File webAppFolder = new File(root.getAbsolutePath(),
                "production/resources/dynamic");
        if (!webAppFolder.exists()) {
            System.err.println("Could not find JSP pages directory!");
        }
        StandardContext context = (StandardContext) tomcat.
                addWebapp("/demo", webAppFolder.getAbsolutePath());
```

CHAPTER 10 MAKING YOUR APPLICATION INTERACTIVE

```
        context.setParentClassLoader(WebDemo.class.getClassLoader());

        File webInfClasses = new File(root.getAbsolutePath(), "production/
        classes");
        WebResourceRoot resources = new StandardRoot(context);

        WebResourceSet resourceSet;
        if (webInfClasses.exists()) {
            resourceSet = new DirResourceSet(resources, "/WEB-INF/classes",
                webInfClasses.getAbsolutePath(), "/");
        } else {
            resourceSet = new EmptyResourceSet(resources);
        }
        resources.addPreResources(resourceSet);
        context.setResources(resources);

        tomcat.start();
        tomcat.getServer().await();
    }
}
```

So now when we open http://localhost:8080/demo/ URL in the browser, you should see a simple message like the following.

Today is Mon Aug 20 01:41:29 BST 2018

Of course, the date is the one on your system.

? As an exercise for you, imagine how the Java servlet class would look like if you had to write it.

Since taglibs were mentioned, let's talk a little about them. The most basic tag library is the JSTL, which stands for **JSP Standard Tag Library**. Other more evolved tag libraries are provided by JSF (JavaServerFaces), Thymeleaf, or Spring. Tags defined in this library can be used to write JSP pages that change behavior. Depending on request attributes, they can be used to iterate, to test values, and for internationalization and formatting.

Based on the JSTL functions provided, the tags are grouped into five categories. They can be used in a JSP page only after specifying the appropriate directives. Next, the five directives are listed with the overall topic the tags cover.

- `<%@ taglib uri="http://java.sun.com/jsp/jstl/core" prefix="c" %>` JSTL Core tags provide support for displaying values, iteration, conditional logic, catch exceptions, URL, and forward or redirect response.

- `<%@ taglib uri="http://java.sun.com/jsp/jstl/fmt" prefix="fmt" %>` JSTL Formatting tags are provided for formatting of numbers, dates, and i18n support through locales and resource bundles.

- `<%@ taglib uri="http://java.sun.com/jsp/jstl/sql" prefix="sql" %>` JSTL SQL tags provide support for interaction with relational databases, but never do this, never use SQL in a web page because it is very easily hackable (look up *SQL Injection* on Google).

- `<%@ taglib uri="http://java.sun.com/jsp/jstl/xml" prefix="x" %>` JSTL XML tags provide support for handling XML documents, parsing, transformations and XPath expressions evaluation.

- `<%@ taglib uri="http://java.sun.com/jsp/jstl/functions" prefix="fn" %>` JSTL Function tags provide a number of functions that can be used to perform common operations such as text manipulations.

Now that we know the basic tag categories, which ones do you think we need to use to redesign our `index.jsp` page? If you thought about FMT and Core, you are right. Also, JSP pages that use taglibs are always backed up by a servlet that sets the proper attributes on the request that is used within the JSP page. So, let's modify the `index.jsp` page, as depicted next.

```
<%@ page language="java" contentType="text/html;
    charset=US-ASCII" pageEncoding="US-ASCII"%>
<%@ taglib uri="http://java.sun.com/jsp/jstl/fmt" prefix="fmt" %>
<%@ taglib uri="http://java.sun.com/jsp/jstl/core" prefix="c" %>
<!DOCTYPE html PUBLIC "-//W3C//DTD HTML 4.01 Transitional//EN"
    "http://www.w3.org/TR/html4/loose.dtd">
```

```
<html>
    <head>
        <title>Web Application Demo JSP Page</title>
    </head>
    <body bgcolor=black>
            <fmt:formatDate value="${requestScope.today}"
                    pattern="dd/MM/yyyy" var="todayFormatted"/>
        <p style="color:#ffd200"> Today is <c:out value="${todayFormatted}" /> </p>
    </body>
</html>
```

And while we are at it, let's rename it to make it obvious what it is used for, let's call it date.jsp and write a servlet class named DateServlet to add the today attribute to the request, which is formatted by the <fmt:formatDate> tag. The result is saved into the todayFormatted variable, which is later printed by the <c:out> tag.

```
package com.apress.bgn.ch10;

import javax.servlet.RequestDispatcher;
import javax.servlet.ServletException;
import javax.servlet.annotation.WebServlet;
import javax.servlet.http.HttpServlet;
import javax.servlet.http.HttpServletRequest;
import javax.servlet.http.HttpServletResponse;
import java.io.IOException;

import java.util.Date;

@WebServlet(
        name = "dateServlet",
        urlPatterns = {"/"}
)
public class DateServlet extends HttpServlet {
```

```
    @Override
    protected void doGet(HttpServletRequest request, HttpServletResponse
    response)
            throws IOException, ServletException {
        System.out.println(" ->>> Getting date ");
        request.setAttribute("today", new Date());
        RequestDispatcher rd = getServletContext().getRequestDispatcher
        ("/date.jsp");
        rd.forward(request, response);
    }
}
```

This is all. Now, we restart the application and the first page now displays: "Today is 20/08/2018", You will obviously see the date on your system when the code is run on your machine.

If you think writing Java Web applications is cumbersome you are right. Pure Java is tedious for such a task. Professional Java Web applications are usually written by using frameworks that make the job of creating pages and linking them to the backend easily. Even more, nowadays the tendency is to create interfaces in JavaScript(also using advanced CSS4, now many UI Designs can also be done 100% in CSS3 or CSS4) and communicate to a Java backend application hosted on an enterprise server using Web Service calls, usually REST. Anyway, look it up if you are curious, the subject is vast, but frameworks such as Spring make it easy to set up your environment and start developing.

Summary

This chapter covered important development tools and techniques, the classes in JDK that provide support, and important Java libraries that could make your development job more practical and pleasant. The JDK has never shined when it comes to GUI support, but JavaFX is an evolution from AWT and Swing, and it just might have a future. The following is a complete list of the topics.

- how to write an interactive console application
- how to write an interactive application with a Swing interface
- the basics of JavaFX architecture

CHAPTER 10   MAKING YOUR APPLICATION INTERACTIVE

- how to write an interactive application with a JavaFX interface
- how to internationalize your application
- how to write a web application using an embedded server
- what a servlet is
- what a JSP scriptlet is
- how to use taglibs to write JSP pages

CHAPTER 11

Working with Files

One of the most important functions in software is information organizing and storage, with the goal of using it and sharing it. Before computers were invented information was written on paper and stored in organized cabinets where it could be retrieved from manually. Software applications that run on computers do something similar. Information is written in files, files are organized in directories and in even more complex structures named databases. Java provides classes to read information from files and databases and classes to write files and write information to databases. In **Chapter 9**, a simple example using a Derby in-memory database was introduced to show you how heavy dependencies like databases can be mocked to allow faster unit testing. This chapter is not focused on using Java to perform database operations, but on how Java can be used to manipulate files.

File Handlers

Before showing you how to read or write files, I need to show you how to access them from the code, to check if they exist, to check their size and list their properties, and so forth. Enough with the literature—let's get cracking!

When working with files in Java, the most important class is the `java.io.File` class. This class is an abstract representation of a file and directory pathname. Instances of this class are called *file handlers* because they allow developers to handle files and directories in the Java code using references of this type, instead of complete pathnames. A `File` instance can be created by using different arguments.

The simplest way is to use the constructor that receives as an argument a `String` value containing the absolute file pathname. In the following code sample, the `printStats(..)` method prints file information. We use it a lot in this section, but the code won't be depicted again.

CHAPTER 11 WORKING WITH FILES

```java
package com.apress.bgn.ch11;

import org.slf4j.Logger;
import org.slf4j.LoggerFactory;

import java.io.File;

public class Demo {
    private static final Logger log = LoggerFactory.getLogger(Demo.class);

    public static void main(String... args) {
        File file = new File("/Users/iulianacosmina/apress/vultures.txt");
        printFileStats(file);
    }

    private static void printFileStats(File f) { if (f.exists()) {
        log.info("File Details:");
        log.info("Type : {}", f.isFile() ? "file" : "directory or symlink");
        log.info("Location :{}", f.getAbsolutePath());
        log.info("Parent :{}", f.getParent());
        log.info("Name : {}", f.getName());

        double kilobytes = f.length() / 1024; log.info("Size : {} ", kilobytes);

        log.info("Is Hidden : {}", f.isHidden());
        log.info("Is Readable? : {}", f.canRead());
        log.info("Is Writable? : {}", f.canWrite());
        }
    }
}
```

In the previous code snippet, the file handler instance is created by providing the absolute file pathname on my computer. If you want to run the code on your computer, you must provide a pathname to a file on your computer. If you are using Windows, keep in mind that the pathname contains the "\" character that is a special character in Java and must be escaped by doubling it.

The printStats(..) method makes use of a lot of methods that can be called on a file handler. The full list of methods that you can call is bigger. This list is in the official

API documentation https://docs.oracle.com/javase/10/docs/api/java/io/File.html. All the file handler methods are explained in the following list at: https://docs.oracle.com/javase/10/docs/api/java/io/File.html.

- isFile() returns true if the pathname points to a file and false if the pathname points to a directory or a symlink (a special type of file with the purpose to link to another file, can be useful when you want to shorten the pathname to a file and incredibly useful on Windows where the pathname length limit is of 256 characters). In the previous code sample, the method returns true, and the log prints:

  ```
  [main] INFO com.apress.bgn.ch11.Demo - Type : file
  ```

  If we want to see if the method works for a directory, we delete the file name from the pathname.

  ```
  File file = new File("/Users/iulianacosmina/apress");
  ```

  And then the log prints:

  ```
  [main] INFO com.apress.bgn.ch11.Demo - Type : directory or symlink
  ```

- getAbsolutePath() returns the absolute pathname to a file or a directory. When creating a file handler, the absolute pathname is not always needed, but in case you need to use it later, or to make sure the relative path was resolved correctly, this method is just what you need. The following piece of code creates a file handler to a file in the resources directory by using the path relative to the root project directory (in our case, the java-for-absolute-beginners directory).

  ```
  File d = new File("chapter11/read-write-file/src/main/resources/input/");
  ```

  And now the getAbsolutePath() method prints the full pathname.

  ```
  [main] INFO com.apress.bgn.ch11.Demo - Location :/Users/iulianacosmina/
          java-for-absolute-beginners/chapter11/read-write-
          file/src/main/resources/input/vultures.txt
  ```

The Java `File` class is quite powerful; it can also be used to point to a shared file on another computer. There is a special constructor for this which receives an argument of type `java.net.URI`, where URI stands for *Uniform Resource Identifier*. To test this constructor, select a file on your computer, and open it in a browser, so you can get its URI from the browser address bar.

```
try {
    URI uri = new URI("file:///Users/iulianacosmina/
    java-for-absolute-beginners/chapter11/"
    + "read-write-file/src/main/resources/input/vultures.
    txt"); f = new File(uri);
    printFileStats(f);
} catch (URISyntaxException use) {
    log.error("Malformed URI, no file there", use);
}
```

Because the URI might have an incorrect prefix or not exactly pointing to a file the URI constructor is declared to throw an `java.net.URISyntaxException`, which is why in the code, you must handle this as well. If an URI is used to create a file handler, the `getAbsolutePath()` method returns the absolute pathname of the file, on the computer and drive where the file is.

- `getParent()` returns the absolute path to the directory containing the file, because hierarchically, a file cannot have another file as a parent.

- `getName()` returns the file name. The file name contains the *extension* as the suffix after "." is called, indicates the type of file and what is intended to be used for.

- `length()` returns the length of the file in bytes. This method does not work for directories, as directories can contain files restricted to the user executing the program and exceptions might be thrown. So, if you ever need the size of a directory, you have to write the code yourself.

- isHidden() returns true if the file is not visible to the current user; otherwise, it returns else. On a macOS/Linux system, files with names starting with "." are hidden, so if we want to see that method returning true we must create a handler to one of the system configuration files, such as .bash_profile. So, calling the printStats(..) on a file handler created using a pathname to a hidden file results in an output similar to this:

```
[main] INFO com.apress.bgn.ch11.Demo - File Details:
[main] INFO com.apress.bgn.ch11.Demo - Type : file
[main] INFO com.apress.bgn.ch11.Demo - Location :/Users/
iulianacosmina/.viminfo [main] INFO com.apress.bgn.ch11.
Demo - Parent :/Users/iulianacosmina
[main] INFO com.apress.bgn.ch11.Demo - Name : .viminfo
[main] INFO com.apress.bgn.ch11.Demo - Size : 13.0 [main]
INFO com.apress.bgn.ch11.Demo - Is Hidden : true
[main] INFO com.apress.bgn.ch11.Demo - Is Readable? : true
[main] INFO com.apress.bgn.ch11.Demo - Is Writable? : true
```

- canRead() and canWrite() can secure files from normal users. Both methods return true when the use has the specific right on the file, and are false otherwise.

File handlers can be created for pathnames pointing to directories, which means there are available methods to call that are specific only to directories. The most common thing to do with a directory is to list its contents. The list() method returns a String array, containing the names of the files (and directories) under this directory. We can use a lambda expression to print the entries in the array.

```
Arrays.stream(d.list()).forEach(ff -> log.info("\t File Name : {}", ff));
```

But files names are not really useful in most cases, having a File array with file handlers to each of them would be better. That is why the listFiles() method was added in version 1.2.

```
Arrays.stream(d.listFiles()).forEach(ff ->
    log.info("\t File Name : {}", ff.getName()));
```

And this method has more than one form, because it filters the files and returns file handlers only for files matching a certain requirement when called with an instance of FileFilter.

```
Arrays.stream(d.listFiles(new FileFilter() {
    @Override
    public boolean accept(File pathname) {
    return pathname.getAbsolutePath().endsWith("yml")
        || pathname.getAbsolutePath().endsWith("properties");
    }
})).forEach(ff -> log.info("\t YML/Properties file : {}", ff.getName()));
```

The previous code sample is written in expanded form to make it clear that you should provide a concrete implementation for the accept(..) method. Using lambda expressions, the code can be simplified and made less prone to exceptions being thrown.

```
Arrays.stream(Objects.requireNonNull(
     d.listFiles(pathname -> pathname.getAbsolutePath()
     .endsWith("yml") || pathname.getAbsolutePath().endsWith("properties"))))
     .forEach(ff -> log.info("\t YML/Properties file : {}", ff.getName()));
```

In the previous example, we implemented the accept(..) to filter by extension, but the filter can involve anything really. But, when the filter you need strictly involves the file name, you can reduce the boilerplate by using the other version of the method, which receives a FilenameFilter instance as argument.

```
  Arrays.stream(d.listFiles(new FilenameFilter() {
     @Override
      public boolean accept(File dir, String name) {
     return name.contains("son");
     }
})).forEach(ff -> log.info("\t Namesakes : {}", ff.getName()));
```

Aside from listing properties of a file, a file handler can also be used to create a file. To create a file, the createNewFile() method must be called after creating a file handler with a specific pathname.

```
File created = new File(
   "chapter11/read-write-file/src/main/resources/output/created.txt");
if (!created.exists()) {
    try {
    created.createNewFile();
    } catch (IOException e) {
    log.error("Could not create file.", e);
    }
}
```

The exists() method returns true when the file hander is associated with a file, and false otherwise. It tests if the file we are trying to create is already there. If the file exists, the method has no effect. If the user does not have proper rights to create the file at the specified pathname, a SecurityException is thrown. In certain cases, we might need to create a file that needs only to be used during the execution of the program. This means we either have to create the file and delete it explicitly, or we can create a temporary file. Temporary files are created by calling createTempFile(prefix, suffix) and they are created in the temporary directory defined for the operating system. The prefix argument is of type String and the created file has the name starting with its value. The suffix argument is of type String as well and it specifies an extension for the file. The rest of the file name is generated by the operating system.

```
try {
    File temp = File.createTempFile("java_bgn_", ".tmp");
    log.info("File created.txt at: {}", temp.getAbsolutePath());
    temp.deleteOnExit();
} catch (IOException e) {
    log.error("Could not create temporary file.", e);
}
```

Files in the temporary directory of an operating system are periodically deleted by the operating system, but if you want to make sure it is deleted, you can explicitly call deleteOnExit() on the file handler for the temporary file. In the code sample, the absolute path to the file is printed to show the exact location where the temporary file was created and on a macOS system the full pathname looks very similar to this:

/var/folders/gg/nm_cb2lx72q1lz7xwwdh7tnc0000gn/T/java_bgn_14652264510049064218.tmp

A file can also be renamed using a Java file handler, there is a method for that called `rename(f)` that is called with a file handler argument, pointing to the location and desired name that the file should have. The method returns `true` if the renaming succeeded and `false` otherwise.

```
File file = new File(
    "chapter11/read-write-file/src/main/resources/output/sample/created.txt");
    File renamed = new File(
    "chapter11/read-write-file/src/main/resources/output/sample/renamed.txt");
boolean result = file.renameTo(renamed);
log.info("Renaming succeeded? : {} ", result);
```

Most methods in the `File` class throw `IOException` when things do not go as expected, because manipulating a file can fail because of a hardware problem, or an operating system problem. Methods that require special rights for accessing a file throw a `SecurityException` when things do not go as expected.

So, when writing Java applications that need to manipulate files, you must handle those as well. And now that the bases for working with file handlers have been covered, it is time for the next section.

Path Handlers

The `java.nio.file.Path` interface was introduced in Java 1.7 with the `java.nio.file.Files` and `java.nio.file.Paths` utility classes to provide new and more practical ways to work with files. They are part of the `java.nio` package; the word **nio** means *non-blocking input output*. A `Path` instance may be used to locate a file in a file system, thus represents a system dependent file path. `Path` instances are more practical than `File` because they can provide methods to acccss components of a path, to combine paths, and to compare paths.

`Path` instances cannot be directly created, because an interface cannot be instantiated, but the interface provides static utility methods to create them, and so does the class `Paths`. The simplest way to create a `Path` instance is to start with a file handler and call `Paths.get(fileURI)`.

```
package com.apress.bgn.ch11;

import org.slf4j.Logger;
import org.slf4j.LoggerFactory;
```

```java
import java.io.File;
import java.nio.file.Path;
import java.nio.file.Paths;
import java.util.Iterator;

public class PathDemo {
    private static final Logger log = LoggerFactory.getLogger(PathDemo.class);

    public static void main(String... args) {
    File file = new File(
        "chapter11/read-write-file/src/main/resources/input/vultures.txt");
    Path path = Paths.get(file.toURI());
    log.info(path.toString());
    }
}
```

Starting with Java 11, `Paths.get(file.toURI())` can be replaced with `Path.of(file.toURI())`.

The other way to create a `Path` instance is to use the other form of the `Paths.get(..)` which receives as arguments, multiple pieces of the path.

```java
Path composedPath = Paths.get("/Users/iulianacosmina/apress/workspace",
    "java-for-absolute-beginners/chapter11/read-write-file/src/main/
    resources/input",
    "vultures.txt");
log.info(composedPath.toString());
```

Both paths point to the same location, thus if compared with each other using the `compareTo(..)` method (because `Path` extends interface `Comparable<Path>`), the result returned is 0 (zero), which means the paths are equal.

```java
log.info("Is the same path? : {} ", path.compareTo(composedPath) ==0 ?
"yes" : "no");

// prints : INFO com.apress.bgn.ch11.PathDemo - Is the same path? : yes
```

In the next code sample, a few `Paths` methods are called on the path instance.

```java
log.info("Location :{}", path.toAbsolutePath());
log.info("Is Absolute? : {}", path.isAbsolute());
log.info("Parent :{}", path.getParent());
```

```
log.info("Root :{}", path.getRoot());
log.info("FileName : {}", path.getFileName());
log.info("FileSystem : {}", path.getFileSystem());
```

The list explains each method and its outcome:

- toAbsolutePath() returns a Path instance representing the absolute path of this path. When called on the path instance created, as it is already absolute, the method returns the path object the method is called on. Also, calling path.isAbsolute()returns true.

- getParent() returns the parent Path instance. So, calling this method on the path instance prints

    INFO com.apress.bgn.ch11.PathDemo - Parent :/Users/iulianacosmina/apress/workspace/java-for-absolute-beginners/chapter11/read-write-file/src/main/resources/input

- getRoot() returns the root component of this path as a Path instance. On a Linux or macOS system it prints "/", on Windows, something like "C:\".

- getFileName() returns the name of the file or directory denoted by this path as a Path instance, basically, the path is split by the system path separator, and the most far away from the root element is returned.

- getFileSystem() returns the file system that created this object, for macOS it is an instance of type

    sun.nio.fs.MacOSXFileSystem

Another useful Path method is resolve(..) This method takes a String instance that is a representation of a path and resolves it against the Path instance it is called on. This means that path separators are added according to the operating system the program runs on and a Path instance is returned.

```
Path chapterPath = Paths.get("/Users/iulianacosmina/apress/workspace",
    "java-for-absolute-beginners/chapter11");
Path filePath = chapterPath.resolve(
   "read-write-file/src/main/resources/input/vultures.txt");
log.info("Resolved Path :{}", filePath.toAbsolutePath());
```

The sample code prints the following:

INFO com.apress.bgn.ch11.PathDemo - Resolved Path : :/Users/iulianacosmina/apress/ workspace/java-for-absolute-beginners/chapter11/read-write-file/src/main/resources/input/vultures.txt

Using Path instances, writing code that manages files, or retrieves their properties becomes easier to write in combination with Files utility methods. The following code sample makes use of a few of these methods to print properties of a file, in the same way we did using a File handler.

```
Path outputPath = FileSystems.getDefault()
    .getPath("/Users/iulianacosmina/apress/workspace/" +
    "java-for-absolute-beginners/chapter11/read-write-file/src/main/
    resources/output/sample2");
try {
    Files.createDirectory(outputPath);
    log.info("Type: {}", Files.isDirectory(outputPath) ? "yes" : "no");

    Path destPath = Paths.get(outputPath.toAbsolutePath().toString(),
      "vultures.txt");
    Files.copy(path, destPath);
    double kilobytes = Files.size(destPath) / (double)1024;
    log.info("Size : {} ", kilobytes);
    Path newFilePath = Paths.get(outputPath.toAbsolutePath().toString(),
      "vultures2.txt");
    Files.createFile(newFilePath);
    log.info("Type: {}", Files.isRegularFile(newFilePath) ? "yes" : "no");
    log.info("Type: {}", Files.isSymbolicLink(newFilePath) ? "yes" : "no");

    log.info("Is Hidden: {}", Files.isHidden(newFilePath) ? "yes" : "no");
    log.info("Is Readable: {}", Files.isReadable(newFilePath) ? "yes" : "no");
    log.info("Is Writable: {}", Files.isWritable(newFilePath) ? "yes" : "no");

    Path copyFilePath = Paths.get("/Users/iulianacosmina/temp/",
    "vultures3.txt");
    Files.move(newFilePath, copyFilePath);
    log.info("Exists? : {}", Files.exists(copyFilePath)? "yes": "no");
    log.info("File moved to: {}", copyFilePath.toAbsolutePath());
```

```
    Files.deleteIfExists(copyFilePath);
} catch (FileAlreadyExistsException e) {
    log.error("Creation failed!", e);
} catch (IOException e) {
    log.error("Something unexpected happened!", e);
}
```

As you can see, the `Files` class provides a lot more functionality when working with files. Also, more specialized exceptions(types that extend `IOException`) are thrown depending on the operation, so the failure is obvious. For example,
`createFile(...)` throws a `java.nio.file.FileAlreadyExistsException` if the file already exists, it does not return a `Path` instance associated with it. `createDirectory(..)` has the same behavior and so does `move(..)`.

The `delete(..)` method that is not used here throws a `java.nio.file.NoSuchFileException` if the file to be deleted does not exist. To avoid an exception being thrown in the code sample, `deleteIfExists(..)` was used.

And the list of methods is even bigger, but since the size of this chapter is limited, you can check it out yourself on the official Javadoc API at https://docs.oracle.com/javase/10/docs/api/java/nio/file/Files.html.

Reading Files

Files are a succession of bits on a hard drive. A `File` handler does not provide methods to read the content of a file, but a group of other classes can be used to do so. Depending on what is needed to be done with the contents of a file, there is more than one way to read file contents in Java. Actually, there are a lot of ways and this section covers the most common.

Using Scanner to Read Files

The `Scanner` class was used to read input from the command line, but `System.in` can be replaced with `File` and `Scanner` methods to read the file contents.

```java
package com.apress.bgn.ch11;

import org.slf4j.Logger;
import org.slf4j.LoggerFactory;

import java.io.File;
import java.io.IOException;
import java.util.Scanner;

public class ReadingFilesDemo {
    private static final Logger log =
        LoggerFactory.getLogger(ReadingFilesDemo.class);

    public static void main(String... args) {
        File file = new File(
            "chapter11/read-write-file/src/main/resources/input/vultures.txt");
        String content = "";
        Scanner scanner;
        try {
            scanner = new Scanner(file);
            while (scanner.hasNextLine()) {
                content += scanner.nextLine() + "\n";
            }
            scanner.close();
            log.info("Read with Scanner--> {}", content);
            scanner.close();
    } catch (IOException e) {
            log.info("Something went wrong! ", e);
        }
    }
}
```

A Path instance can be used instead.

```java
scanner = new Scanner(Paths.get(file.toURI()), StandardCharsets.UTF_8.name());
```

CHAPTER 11   WORKING WITH FILES

Using Files Utility Methods to Read Files

Another way to read a file, when its size can be approximated and thus it would not be a problem storing its contents into a `String` object (there is enough memory) is to use the appropriate method of the `Files` class.

```
try {
    content = new String(Files.readAllBytes(Paths.get(file.toURI())));
    log.info("Read with Files.readAllBytes --> {}", content);
} catch (IOException e) {
    log.info("Something went wrong! ", e);
}
```

The advantage of using `Files.readAllBytes(..)` is that no loop is needed and we do not have to construct the `String` value line by line, because this method reads all the bytes in the files that can be given as an argument to the `String` constructor. The disadvantage is that no `Charset` is used, so the text value might not be the one we expect. But there is a way to overcome this; by calling `Files.readAllLines(..)`. It returns the file content as a list of `String` values, and has two forms, one of them declaring a `Charset` as a parameter.

```
try {
    List<String> lyricList = Files.readAllLines(Paths.get(file.toURI()),
        StandardCharsets.UTF_8);
    lyricList.forEach(System.out::println);
} catch (IOException e) {
    log.info("Something went wrong! ", e);
}
```

But what if we do not need a `List<String>`, but the one `String` instance? Well, in Java 11 there's a method for that and is called `readString`.

```
try {
    content = Files.readString(Paths.get(file.toURI()), StandardCharsets.UTF_8)
    log.info("Read with Files.readAllBytes --> {}", content);
} catch (IOException e) {
    log.info("Something went wrong! ", e);
}
```

Using Readers to Read Files

Before the fancy methods in the `Files` class, there were other ways, and you might find yourself in the position of using them, when you are not really interested saving everything you read from a file. Let's start with a contraption code that you would write up to Java 1.6 to read a file line by line.

```java
import java.io.BufferedReader;
import java.io.File;
import java.io.FileReader;

...

BufferedReader reader = null;
try {
    reader = new BufferedReader(new FileReader(
    new File("chapter11/read-write-file/src/main/resources/input/vultures.
    txt")));
    StringBuilder sb = new StringBuilder();
    String line;
    while ((line = reader.readLine()) != null) {
       if(!line.contains("Ooh")) {
         sb.append(line).append("\n");
       }
    }
    log.info("Read with BufferedReader --> {}", sb.toString() );
} catch (Exception e) {
    log.info("Something went wrong! ", e);
} finally {
   if(reader != null) {
     try {
        reader.close();
     } catch (IOException e1) {
        e1.printStackTrace();
     }
   }
}
```

Whoa, what is that, right? Before Java 1.7 if you wanted to read a file line by line, this is the code you had to write. You had to create a `File` handler. Then you needed to wrap the file handler into a `FileReader`. This type of instance could do the job of reading, but only in chunks of `char[]`, which is not very useful when you need the actual text. So, this instance needs to be wrapped into an instance of `BufferedReader` that provides this functionality by reading the characters in an internal buffer. So, the way it works, `reader.readLine()` is called until there is nothing more to read—the end of the file was reached and them we need to call `reader.close();` otherwise, a lock might be kept on the file and it becomes unreadable until a restart.

In Java 1.7, a lot of things made to reduce the boilerplate needed to manage files and file contents were introduced. One of those things was that all classes used to access file contents and that could keep a lock on the file were enriched by being declared to implement the `java.io.Closeable` interface that marked resources of these types as closable, and a `close()` method is invoked to release resources transparently by the JVM before execution ends. Also, in Java 7, *try-with-resources* was introduced. Making use of all these features, the code can be written like this:

```
import java.io.BufferedReader;
import java.io.File;
import java.io.FileReader;
...

try (BufferedReader reader = new BufferedReader(new FileReader(
      new File("chapter11/read-write-file/src/main/resources/input/
      vultures.txt")))){
    StringBuilder sb = new StringBuilder();
     String line;
     while ((line = reader.readLine()) != null) {
        if(!line.contains("Ooh")) {
           sb.append(line).append("\n");
            }
       }
     log.info("Read with BufferedReader --> {}", sb.toString() );
} catch (Exception e) {
         log.info("Something went wrong! ", e);
}
```

Still we have that ugly constructor within constructor thing that is quite ugly. Well, Java 8 comes to the rescue by introducing the `Files.newBufferedReader(Path)` method. So, the previous code becomes:

```java
import java.io.BufferedReader;
import java.io.File;
import java.io.FileReader;
...
File file = new File(
  "chapter11/read-write-file/src/main/resources/input/vultures.txt");
Path sourceFile = Paths.get(file.toURI());
try (BufferedReader reader = Files.newBufferedReader(sourceFile)){
    StringBuilder sb = new StringBuilder();
     String line;
     while ((line = reader.readLine()) != null) {
        if(!line.contains("Ooh")) {
            sb.append(line).append("\n");
             }
    }
    log.info("Read with BufferedReader --> {}", sb.toString() );
} catch (Exception e) {
            log.info("Something went wrong! ", e);
}
```

But still, by using a combination of lambda expressions, we could get a similar behavior when reading the file line by line:

```java
 List<String> lyricList = Files.readAllLines(Paths.get(file.toURI()),
     StandardCharsets.UTF_8)
     .stream()
     .filter(line -> !line.contains("Ooh"))
     .collect(Collectors.toList());
```

CHAPTER 11   WORKING WITH FILES

All we would have to do is traverse the lines and add everything to a `StringBuilder` and *voila!*, same result, less boilerplate. Or we can write it this way, using the `Files.lines(..)` introduced in Java 1.8 and get all contents as a stream:

```
Stream<String> lyricStream = Files.lines(file.toPath())
    .filter(s -> !s.contains("Ooh"));
    lyricStream.forEach(System.out::println);
```

The `BufferedReader` class is a member of a class group that extends the `Reader` class. It is an abstract class used for reading characters streams. The full hierarchy is depicted in Figure 11-1.

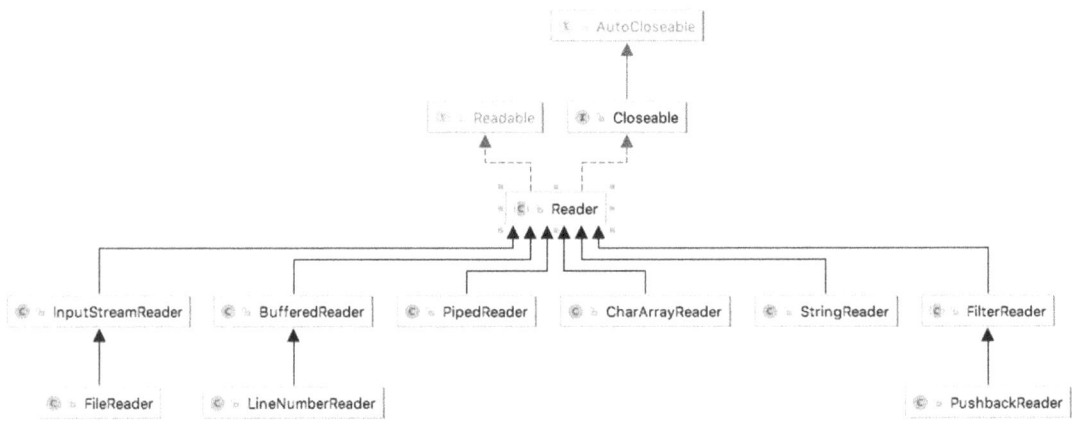

Figure 11-1. *Reader class hierarchy*

Character streams can have different sources, files being the most common. They provide sequential access to data stored in the file. The `BufferedReader` does not provide support for character encoding, but a `BufferedReader` can be based on another `Reader` instance, and the one that provides reading character streams and taking encoding into account is `InputStreamReader`. So, we can replace

```
try (BufferedReader reader = new BufferedReader(new FileReader(
  new File("chapter11/read-write-file/src/main/resources/input/vultures.txt")))){
    ...
}
```

with

```
import java.nio.charset.StandardCharsets;
import java.io.FileInputStream;
...
try (BufferedReader reader = new BufferedReader(new InputStreamReader(
  new FileInputStream(
      "chapter11/read-write-file/src/main/resources/input/vultures.txt"),
        StandardCharsets.UTF_8))){
    ...
}
```

But starting with Java 1.7, we don't have to do that anymore because there is a version of the `Files.newBufferedReader` that accepts a `Charset` instance as argument as well. So, the code can be safely replaces with the following.

```
try (BufferedReader reader = Files.newBufferedReader(sourceFile,
    StandardCharsets.UTF_8)){
    ...
}
```

In Java 11, the `Reader` was enriched with the `nullReader()` method, which returns a `Reader` instance that does nothing. This was requested by developers for testing purposes.

Using InputStream to Read Files

Classes in the `Reader` family are advanced classes for reading data as text. Files are a sequence of bytes, so classes are wrappers around classes in a family of classes used for reading byte streams. This becomes clear when trying to use the proper character encoding when reading text using the `BufferedReader`, as the `InputStreamReader` instance given as argument is based on a `java.io.FileInputStream` instance, a type that is a subclass of `java.io.InputStream`.

The root class of this hierarchy is `java.io.InputStream`, which is depicted in Figure 11-2.

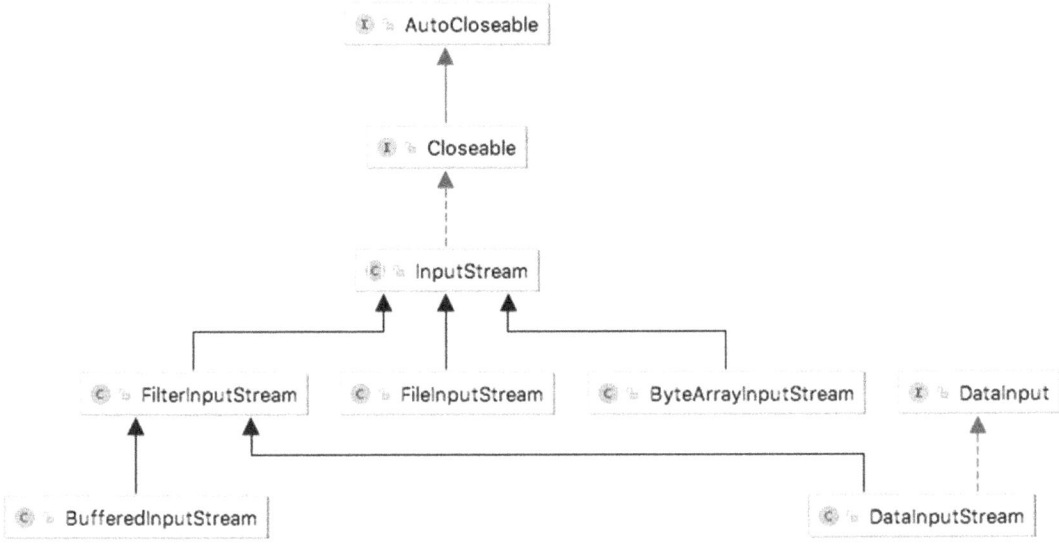

Figure 11-2. InputStream class hierarchy

The BufferedInputStream class is equivalent to BufferedReader for reading streams of bytes. The System.in that we used to read user data from the console is of this type, and the Scanner instance converts the bytes from its buffer into user understandable data. When the data we are interested in is not text that was stored using Unicode conventions, but raw numeric data (binary files such as images, media files, PDF's, etc.) classes for using streams of bytes are more suitable. Just for the purpose of showing you how it's done, we'll read the contents of the vultures.txt file using FileInputStream.

```
package com.apress.bgn.ch11.reading;

import org.slf4j.Logger;
import org.slf4j.LoggerFactory;

import java.io.File;
import java.io.FileInputStream;
import java.io.IOException;
public class FileInputStreamReadingDemo {
    private static final Logger log =
        LoggerFactory.getLogger(FileInputStreamReadingDemo.class);
```

```
    public static void main(String... args) {
        File file = new File(
            "chapter11/read-write-file/src/main/resources/input/vultures.txt");

        try {
            FileInputStream fis = new FileInputStream(file);
            byte[] buffer = new byte[1024];
            StringBuilder sb = new StringBuilder();
            while (fis.read(buffer) != -1) {
                sb.append(new String(buffer));
                buffer = new byte[1024];
            }
            fis.close();

            log.info("Read with FileInputStream --> {}", sb.toString() );
        } catch (IOException e) {
            log.info("Something went wrong! ", e);
        }
    }
}
```

If you run the code, you notice that the expected output is printed in the console; but after the text is printed a set of strange characters are printed too. On a macOS system, they look like what's shown in Figure 11-3.

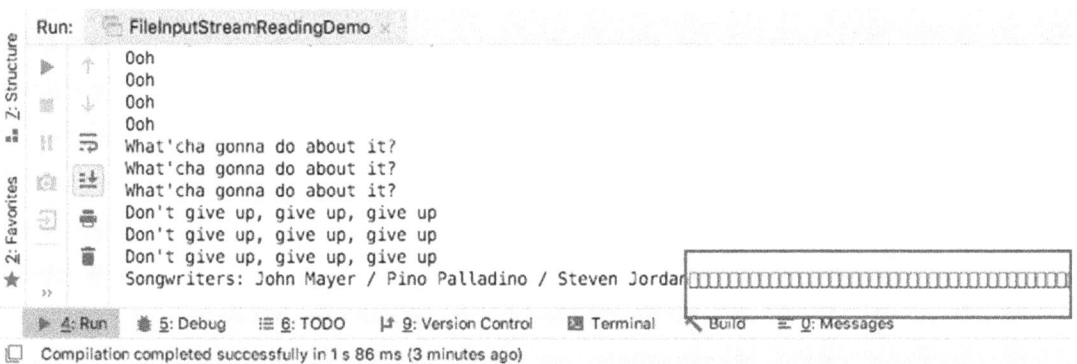

Figure 11-3. *Text read with FileInputStream*

Do you have any idea what those characters might be?

It's ok if you have no idea, I did not either the first time I had to use `FileInputStream` to read a file. Those characters appear there because the file size is not a multiple of 1024, so the `FileInputReader` ends up filling the rest of the last buffer with zeroes. A fix for this involves computing the size of the file in bytes and making sure we adapt the `byte[] buffer` size accordingly. You can try doing that as an exercise if you are in the mood for some coding. And now that we've shown you how to read file in a lot of ways, we can continue by showing you how to write files, since you already know how to create them.

In Java 11, the `InputStream` was also enriched with a method that returns an `InputStream` that does nothing named `nullInputStream()` method, for testing purposes.

Writing Files

Writing files in Java is similar to reading them, only different classes have to be used because streams are unidirectional, which means that a stream that is used for reading data cannot be used for writing data as well. Almost for any class or method of reading files there is one for writing files. Without further ado, let's start.

Writing Files Using Files Utility Methods

For smaller files, when we just need to write a bunch of bytes, the `Files.write(Path, byte[])` works fine.

```
package com.apress.bgn.ch11.writing;

import org.slf4j.Logger;
import org.slf4j.LoggerFactory;

import java.io.File;
import java.io.IOException;
import java.nio.file.Files;
import java.nio.file.Path;
```

```java
public class FilesWritingDemo {
    private static final Logger log =
        LoggerFactory.getLogger(FilesWritingDemo.class);

    public static void main(String... args) {
        File file = new File(
            "chapter11/read-write-file/src/main/resources/output/
            vultures.txt");

        byte[] data = "Some of us, we're hardly ever here".getBytes();
        try {
            Path dataPath = Files.write(file.toPath(), data);
            log.info("String written to {}", dataPath.toAbsolutePath());
        } catch (IOException e) {
            e.printStackTrace();
        }
    }
}
```

If the file already exists, the contents are simply overwritten.

In Java 11, the Files.writeString(..) method was introduced, which allows specifying a Charset when writing a String instance to a file; no conversion to bytes needed either.

```java
try {
    Path dataPath = Files.writeString(file.toPath(),
        "Some of us, we're hardly ever here",
        StandardCharsets.UTF_8);
    log.info("String written to {}", dataPath.toAbsolutePath());
} catch (IOException e) {
    e.printStackTrace();
}
```

There are three Files.write(..) methods in the Files class: the one used in the previous code snippet and two that can write collections of text values represented by any instance of type that extends CharSequence. The only difference between the two is that one of them also takes Charset as an argument.

CHAPTER 11 WORKING WITH FILES

```java
package com.apress.bgn.ch11.writing;

import org.slf4j.Logger;
import org.slf4j.LoggerFactory;

import java.io.File;
import java.io.IOException;
import java.nio.charset.StandardCharsets;
import java.nio.file.Files;
import java.nio.file.Path;
import java.util.List;

public class FilesWritingDemo {
    private static final Logger log =
        LoggerFactory.getLogger(FilesWritingDemo.class);

    public static void main(String... args) {
        List<String> dataList = List.of("Some of us, we're hardly ever here",
                "The rest of us, we're born to disappear",
                "How do I stop myself from",
                "Being just a number?");
        try {
            File file2 = new File(
              "chapter11/read-write-file/src/main/resources/output/vultures2.txt");
            Path dataPath = Files.write(file2.toPath(), dataList,
                StandardCharsets.UTF_8);
            log.info("String written to {}", dataPath.toAbsolutePath());
        } catch (IOException e) {
            e.printStackTrace();
        }
    }
}
```

And those are all the methods in the `Files` class that are used for writing files available in the `Files` class. Next, we look into writing files using classes in the `Writer` hierarchy.

Using Writers to Write Files

Similar to the Reader hierarchy for reading files, there is an abstract class named Writer, but before we get to that let's introduce the BufferedWriter, the correspondent of BufferedReader for writing files. This class too has an internal buffer, and when write methods are called, the arguments are stored into the buffer, and when the buffer is full, its contents are written to the file. The buffer can be emptied earlier by calling the flush() method. I definitely recommend calling this method explicitly before calling close() to make sure all output was written to the file. The next code snippet depicts how a list of String instances is written to a file.

```java
package com.apress.bgn.ch11.writing;

import org.slf4j.Logger;
import org.slf4j.LoggerFactory;

import java.io.BufferedWriter;
import java.io.File;
import java.io.FileWriter;
import java.io.IOException;
import java.util.List;

public class FilesWritingDemo {
    private static final Logger log =
        LoggerFactory.getLogger(FilesWritingDemo.class);

    public static void main(String... args) {
        File file = new File(
           "chapter11/read-write-file/src/main/resources/output/vultures.txt");
        List<String> lyricList =  List.of("Some of us, we're hardly ever here",
                "The rest of us, we're born to disappear",
                "How do I stop myself from",
                "Being just a number?");
        BufferedWriter writer = null;
```

```
        try {
            writer = new BufferedWriter(new FileWriter(file));
            for (String lyric : lyricList) {
                writer.write(lyric);
                writer.newLine();
            }
        } catch (IOException e) {
           log.info("Something went wrong! ", e);
        } finally {
           if(writer!= null) {
              try {
                  writer.flush();
                  writer.close();
              } catch (IOException e) {
                  log.info("Something went wrong! ", e);
              }
           }
        }
    }
}
```

Writing files is a sensitive operation, and the code contraption introduced earlier can fail for many reasons. That type of code is what you would write before Java 1.7, when try-with-resources reduced the boilerplate.

```
try (final BufferedWriter wr = new BufferedWriter(new FileWriter(file))){
    lyricList.forEach(lyric -> {
     try {
         wr.write(lyric);
       log.info("Something went wrong! ", e);wr.newLine();
       } catch (IOException e) {
          log.info("Something went wrong! ", e);
       }
    });
     wr.flush();
```

```
} catch (IOException e) {
    log.info("Something went wrong! ", e);
}
```

The only real simplification that can be done is by calling `Files.newBufferedWriter(..)` to avoid instantiating the `BufferedWriter` explicitly. This also adds in the advantage of deciding the charset of the file to be written.

```
try (final BufferedWriter wr = Files.newBufferedWriter(file.toPath(),
    StandardCharsets.UTF_8)){
        lyricList.forEach(lyric -> {
            try {
                    wr.write(lyric);
                    wr.newLine();
            } catch (IOException e) {
                    e.printStackTrace();
            }
        });
        wr.flush();
} catch (IOException e) {
    log.info("Something went wrong! ", e);
}
```

If we did not have the `Files.newBufferedWriter(..)` method, writing text values using a given charset would only be possible by using a different `Writer` class, the `OutputStreamWriter`.

```
try (final OutputStreamWriter wr = new OutputStreamWriter(
    new FileOutputStream(file), StandardCharsets.UTF_8)){
    lyricList.forEach(lyric -> {
    try {
            wr.write(lyric);
            wr.write("\n");
        } catch (IOException e) {
            e.printStackTrace();
        }
    });
    wr.flush();
```

```
} catch (IOException e) {
    log.info("Something went wrong! ", e);
}
```

If the file already exists, calling the write(..) method overrides the contents of the file. But this is not always needed, sometimes we just need to append new text to an existing file. BufferedWriter provides the append() method to do that.

```
try (final BufferedWriter wr = Files.newBufferedWriter(file.toPath(),
    StandardCharsets.UTF_8)){
        lyricList.forEach(lyric -> {
            try {
                wr.append(lyric);
                wr.append("\n");
            } catch (IOException e) {
                e.printStackTrace();
            }
        });
        wr.flush();
} catch (IOException e) {
    log.info("Something went wrong! ", e);
}
```

Now that the basics of using BufferedWriter have been covered, it's time to meet the Writer family, which is depicted in Figure 11-4.

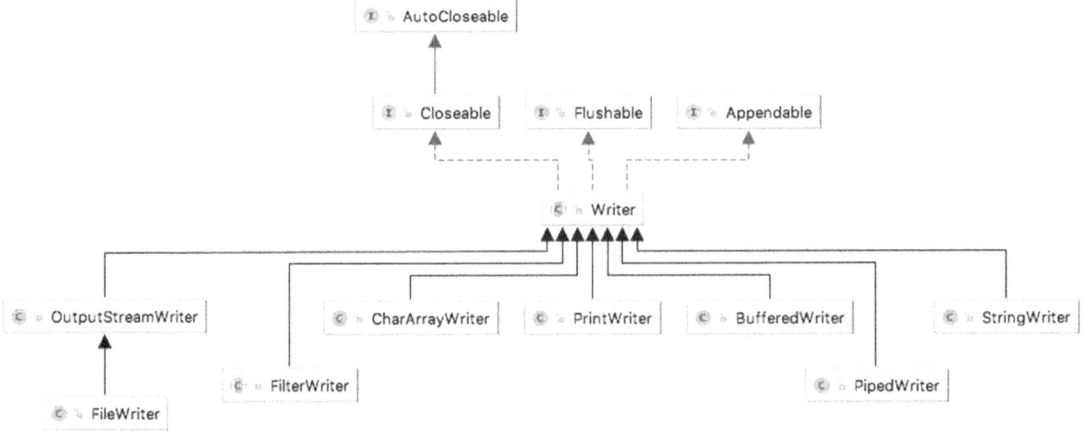

Figure 11-4. *The Writer class hierarchy*

The Writer class is abstract so it cannot be used directly, the appending API comes from the java.io.Appendable interface, which Writer implements. The other Writer classes are used for different purposes. As we've already seen, the OutputStreamWriter writes text using a special character set.

The PrintWriter writes formatted representations of objects to a text-output stream. (We used it to write HTML code in Chapter 10).

The StringWriter collects output into its internal buffer and write it to a String instance.

In Java 11, the Writer was enriched with the nullWriter() method, which returns a Writer instance that does nothing. This was requested by developers for testing purposes.

Using OutputStream to Write Files

Classes in the Writer family are advanced classes for writing data as text using character streams; but essentially, before data is written, it is turned into bytes. This means that files can be written by using stream of bytes as well. This probably became clear when trying to use the proper character encoding when writing text using the OutputStreamWriter, as the OutputStreamWriter instance given as argument is based on a FileOutputStream instance, a type that writes byte streams to a file.

The root class of this hierarchy is java.io.OutputStream, which is depicted in Figure 11-5.

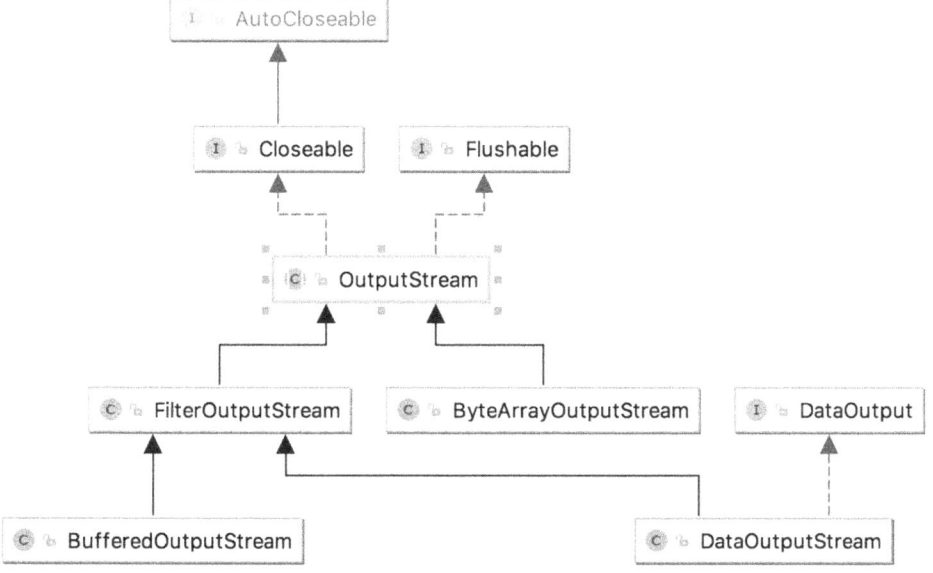

Figure 11-5. *OutputStream class hierarchy*

CHAPTER 11 WORKING WITH FILES

And since I mentioned `FileOutputStream`, let's see how we could use it to write the same list of entries that we have used before. The code is depicted in the following listing.

```
package com.apress.bgn.ch11.writing;

import com.apress.bgn.ch11.reading.FileInputStreamReadingDemo;
import org.slf4j.Logger;
import org.slf4j.LoggerFactory;

import java.io.File;
import java.io.FileNotFoundException;
import java.io.FileOutputStream;
import java.io.IOException;
import java.util.List;

public class FileOutputStreamWritingDemo {
    private static final Logger log =
        LoggerFactory.getLogger(FileOutputStreamWritingDemo.class);

    public static void main(String... args) {
        File file = new File(
            "chapter11/read-write-file/src/main/resources/output/vultures3.txt");

        List<String> lyricList =  List.of("Some of us, we're hardly ever here",
                "The rest of us, we're born to disappear",
                "How do I stop myself from",
                "Being just a number?");

        try (FileOutputStream output = new FileOutputStream(file)){
            lyricList.forEach(lyric -> {
                try {
                    output.write(lyric.getBytes());
                    output.write("\n".getBytes());
```

```
                } catch (IOException e) {
                    log.info("Something went wrong! ", e);
                }
            });
            output.flush();
        } catch (FileNotFoundException e) {
            log.info("Something went wrong! ", e);
        } catch (IOException e) {
            e.printStackTrace();
        }
    }
}
```

The OutputStream family class is used for writing streams of bytes that represent raw data, unreadable by users directly, such as the one contained in binary files like images, media, PDFs, and so forth. For example, the next piece of code, makes a copy of an image using FileInputStream to read it and FileOutputStream to write it.

```
package com.apress.bgn.ch11;

import org.slf4j.Logger;
import org.slf4j.LoggerFactory;

import java.io.*;
import java.nio.file.Files;

public class DuplicateImageDemo {

    private static final Logger log =
        LoggerFactory.getLogger(DuplicateImageDemo.class);

    public static void main(String... args) {
        File src = new File(
            "chapter11/read-write-file/src/main/resources/input/cat.jpg");
        File dest = new File(
            "chapter11/read-write-file/src/main/resources/output/cat1.jpg");
```

```
        try(FileInputStream fis = new FileInputStream(src);
            FileOutputStream fos = new FileOutputStream(dest)) {
            int content;
            while ((content = fis.read()) != -1) {
                fos.write(content);
            }
        } catch (FileNotFoundException e) {
            log.error("Something bad happened.", e);
        } catch (IOException e) {
            log.error("Something bad happened.", e);
        }
    }
}
```

But writing code like this is no longer necessary, thanks to the introduction of the `Files.copy(src.toPath(), dest.toPath())` method in Java 1.7.

In Java 11, the `OutputStream` was enriched with the `nullOutputStream()` method, which returns an `OutputStream` instance that does nothing. This was requested by developers for testing purposes.

And that's about all the space that I can allocate in this book for writing files using byte streams. Since there is a lot more to cover, two things before moving on…

- When working with multiple files, do not open too many at the same time, because some operating systems have a limit of how many files a process can open at the same time. If you end up going over that limit an `IOException` with a *Too many open files* message is thrown.

- We did not cover in this book, but take extra care when working with threads and files, because a file can be read by more than one thread simultaneously, but more threads writing to the same file can lead to unexpected results.

Serialization and Deserialization

Serialization is the name given to the operation of converting the state of an object to a byte stream so it can be sent over a network or written to a file and reverted back into a copy of that object. The operation to covert the byte stream back to an object is called

deserialization. Java Serialization has been a controversial topic, Java Platform Chief Architect Mark Reinhold describing it as a *horrible mistake* done in 1997. Apparently most Java vulnerabilities are somehow related to the way serialization is done in Java and there is a project named **Amber**[1] that is dedicated to remove Java serialization completely and allow developers to choose the serialization in a format of their choice.

Currently, things are unstable in Java; there were a lot of changes introduced in a short time that an industry addicted to backward compatibility was unable to adapt to. Sources in the next section might be unstable, but I will do my best to keep them at least compliable by the time the book is published, and I will maintain the repository and answer questions as much as possible.

Binary Serialization

The java.io.Serializable interface has no methods or fields and serves only to mark classes as being serializable. When an object is serialized, the information that identifies the object type is serialized as well. Most Java classes are serializable. Any subclass of a serializable class is by default considered serializable, but if any new fields are non-serializable an exception of type NotSerializableException is thrown. Classes written by developers that contain non-serializable fields must implement the Serializable interface and provide a concrete implementation for the following methods:

```
private void writeObject(java.io.ObjectOutputStream out)
    throws IOException;
 private void readObject(java.io.ObjectInputStream in)
    throws IOException, ClassNotFoundException;
 private void readObjectNoData()
    throws ObjectStreamException;
```

The writeObject method is used for writing the state of the object, so that the readObject method can restore it. The readObjectNoData method initializes the state of the object when the deserialization operation failed for some reason, so this method provides a default state despite the issues (e.g., incomplete stream, client application does not recognize the reserialized class, etc.). This method is not really mandatory if you are an optimist.

---

[1]Project Amber official page http://openjdk.java.net/projects/amber/

CHAPTER 11 WORKING WITH FILES

Also when making a class serializable, a static field of type `long` must be added as an unique identifier for the class to make sure both the application that sends the object as a byte stream and the client application receiving it have the same loaded classes. If the application that receives the byte stream has a class with a different identifier, a `java.io.InvalidClassException` is thrown. When this happens, this means the application was not updated, or you can even suspect fowl-play from a hacker. The field has to be named `serialVersionUID`, and if the developer does not explicitly add one, the serialization runtime will. The following code snippet depicts a class named `Singer` that contains serialization and deserialization methods.

```java
package com.apress.bgn.ch11;

import java.io.*;
import java.time.LocalDate;
import java.util.Objects;

public class Singer implements Serializable {
    private static final long serialVersionUID = 42L;

    private String name;

    private Double rating;

    private LocalDate birthDate;

    public Singer() {
        /* required for deserialization */
    }

    public Singer(String name, Double rating, LocalDate birthDate) {
        this.name = name;
        this.rating = rating;
        this.birthDate = birthDate;
    }

    private void writeObject(ObjectOutputStream out)
            throws IOException {
        out.defaultWriteObject();
    }
```

```java
    private void readObject(ObjectInputStream in)
        throws IOException, ClassNotFoundException {
        in.defaultReadObject();
    }

    private void readObjectNoData()
        throws ObjectStreamException {
        this.name = "undefined";
        this.rating = 0.0;
        this.birthDate = LocalDate.now();
    }

    @Override
    public String toString() {
        return "Singer{" +
                "name='" + name + '\"' +
                ", rating=" + rating +
                ", birthDate=" + birthDate +
                '}';
    }

    @Override
    public boolean equals(Object o) {
        if (this == o) return true;
        if (o == null || getClass() != o.getClass()) return false;
        Singer singer = (Singer) o;
        return Objects.equals(name, singer.name) &&
                Objects.equals(rating, singer.rating) &&
                Objects.equals(birthDate, singer.birthDate);
    }

    @Override
    public int hashCode() {
        return Objects.hash(name, rating, birthDate);
    }
}
```

CHAPTER 11 WORKING WITH FILES

Now that we have the class, let's instantiate it, serialize it, save it to a file and then deserialize the contents of the file into another object that we compare with the initial object.

```
package com.apress.bgn.ch11;

import org.slf4j.Logger;
import org.slf4j.LoggerFactory;

import java.io.*;
import java.time.LocalDate;
import java.time.Month;

public class SerializationDemo {

    private static final Logger log =
        LoggerFactory.getLogger(SerializationDemo.class);

    public static void main(String... args) throws ClassNotFoundException {
        LocalDate johnBd = LocalDate.of(1977, Month.OCTOBER, 16);
        Singer john = new Singer("John Mayer", 5.0, johnBd);

        File file = new File(
            "chapter11/serialization/src/main/resources/output/john.txt");
        try (ObjectOutputStream out =
            new ObjectOutputStream(new FileOutputStream(file))){
            out.writeObject(john);
        } catch (IOException e) {
            log.info("Something went wrong! ", e);
        }

        try(ObjectInputStream in =
            new ObjectInputStream(new FileInputStream(file))){
            Singer copyOfJohn = (Singer) in.readObject();
            log.info("Are objects equal? {}", copyOfJohn.equals(john));
            log.info("--> {}", copyOfJohn.toString());
        } catch (IOException e) {
            log.info("Something went wrong! ", e);
        }
    }
}
```

When the code is run, everything works as expected; the `writeObject` and the `readObject` are called by the `ObjectOutputStream`, `ObjectInputStream` respectively. If you want to test that they are called, you can add logging, or you can place breakpoints inside them and run the program in debug. If you open the `john.txt` you won't be able to understand much. The text written in there, does not make much sense, because it is binary, raw data. If you open the file, you might see something like what is depicted in Figure 11-6.

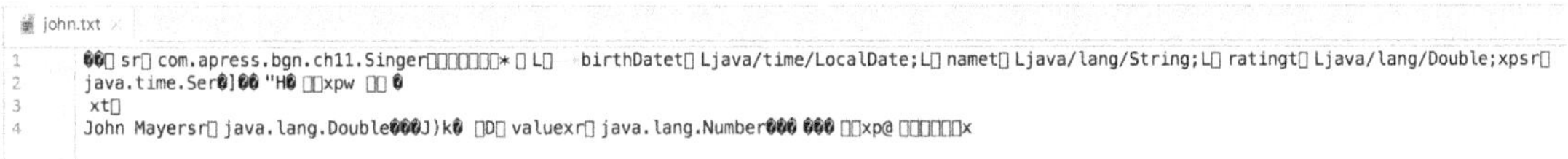

```
john.txt
1   �� sr  com.apress.bgn.ch11.Singer������* �L  birthDatet� Ljava/time/LocalDate;L� namet� Ljava/lang/String;L� ratingt� Ljava/lang/Double;xpsr�
2   java.time.Ser�]�� "H� �xpw �� �
3   xt�
4   John Mayersr� java.lang.Double���J)k� �D� valuexr� java.lang.Number��� ��� ��xp@ �����x
```

Figure 11-6. *Serialized Singer instance*

XML Serialization

But, Java serialization does not have to result in cryptic files, objects can be serialized to readable formats. One of the most used serialization format is XML and JDK provides classes to convert objects to XML and from XML back to the initial object. **Java Architecture for XML Binding (JAXB)** provides a fast and convenient way to bind XML schemas and Java representations, making it easy for Java developers to incorporate XML data and processing functions in Java applications. The operation to serialize an object to XML is named *marshalling*. The operation to deserialize an object form XML is called *unmarshalling*. For a class to be serializable to XML, it has to be decorated with JAXB-specific annotations.

- `@XmlRootElement(name = "...")` is a top-level annotation that is placed at class level to tell JAXB that the class name becomes an XML element at serialization time; if a different name is needed for the XML element, it can be specified via the `name` attribute.

- `@XmlElement(name = "..")` is a method or field level annotation that tells JAXB that the field or method name becomes an XML element at serialization time; if a different name is needed for the XML element, it can be specified via the `name` attribute.

- `@XmlAttribute(name = "..")` is a method or field level annotation that tells JAXB that the field or method name becomes an XML attribute at serialization time; if a different name is needed for the XML attribute, it can be specified via the `name` attribute.

JAXB was removed from JDK 11, so if you want to use it, you must add external dependencies. At the moment this chapter is being written it is also more than a little unstable, class com.sun.xml.internal.bind.v2.ContextFactory is part of the jaxb-impl library, which cannot be found on any public repository at the moment, at least not a version that was compiled with Java 11. The following is the code to make the Singer class serializable with JAXB.

```java
package com.apress.bgn.ch11.xml;

import javax.xml.bind.annotation.XmlAttribute;
import javax.xml.bind.annotation.XmlElement;
import javax.xml.bind.annotation.XmlRootElement;
import java.io.Serializable;
import java.time.LocalDate;
import java.util.Objects;

@XmlRootElement(name = "singer")
public class Singer implements Serializable {
    private static final long serialVersionUID = 42L;

    private String name;

    private Double rating;

    private LocalDate birthDate;

    public Singer() {
        /* required for deserialization */
    }

    public Singer(String name, Double rating, LocalDate birthDate) {
        this.name = name;
        this.rating = rating;
        this.birthDate = birthDate;
    }

    @XmlAttribute(name = "name")
    public String getName() {
        return name;
    }
```

```
    @XmlAttribute(name = "rating")
    public Double getRating() {
        return rating;
    }

    @XmlElement(name = "birthdate")
    public LocalDate getBirthDate() {
        return birthDate;
    }
...
}
```

Notice the location where the annotations were placed. Based on the placement of the annotation in the code when the john object is serialized, the following is what you find in the john.xml file.

```xml
<?xml version="1.0" encoding="utf-8"?>
<singer name="John Mayer" rating="5.0">
    <birthdate>1977-10-16T00:00:00Z</birthdate>
</singer>
```

More readable than the binary version, right? The next code snippet depicts the code that saves the Singer instance to the john.xml file; it loads it back into a copy, and then the two instances are compared.

```java
package com.apress.bgn.ch11.xml;

import org.slf4j.Logger;
import org.slf4j.LoggerFactory;

import javax.xml.bind.JAXBContext;
import javax.xml.bind.JAXBException;
import javax.xml.bind.Marshaller;
import javax.xml.bind.Unmarshaller;
import java.io.*;
import java.time.LocalDate;
import java.time.Month;
```

```java
public class JAXBSerializationDemo {

    private static final Logger log =
        LoggerFactory.getLogger(JAXBSerializationDemo.class);

    public static void main(String... args)
        throws ClassNotFoundException, JAXBException {
        LocalDate johnBd = LocalDate.of(1977, Month.OCTOBER, 16);
        Singer john = new Singer("John Mayer", 5.0, johnBd);

        File file = new File(
            "chapter11/serialization/src/main/resources/output/john.xml");
        JAXBContext jaxbContext = JAXBContext.newInstance(Singer.class);

        try {
            Marshaller marshaller = jaxbContext.createMarshaller();
            marshaller.setProperty(Marshaller.JAXB_FORMATTED_OUTPUT, true);
            marshaller.marshal(john, file);
        } catch (Exception e) {
            log.info("Something went wrong! ", e);
        }

        try {
            Unmarshaller unmarshaller = jaxbContext.createUnmarshaller();
            Singer copyOfJohn = (Singer) unmarshaller.unmarshal(file);
            log.info("Are objects equal? {}", copyOfJohn.equals(john));
            log.info("--> {}", copyOfJohn.toString());
        } catch (Exception e) {
            log.info("Something went wrong! ", e);
        }
    }
}
```

The class javax.xml.bind.JAXBContext is created by calling the newInstance static method and is given as argument a list of classes that will be handled (marshalled, unmarshalled) by this context instance. If none are specified, the JAXBContext only knows about spec-defined classes and those are the only ones that can be handled by the instance.

XML serialization has been dominating the development field for a lot of years, being used in most web services and remote communication. But XML files tend to become crowded, redundant and painful to read as they become bigger. So, a new format stole the show: JSON.

JSON Serialization

JSON(JavaScript Object Notation) is a lightweight data-interchange format. It is readable for humans and is easy for machines to parse and generate. JSON is the favorite format for data being used in JavaScript applications, for REST based application and is the internal format used by quite a few NoSQL databases. So, it is only appropriate that we show you how to serialize Java objects using this format as well. The advantage of serializing Java objects to JSON is that there is more than one library providing classes to do so, which means at least one of them is stable with Java 9+ versions.

The most preferred library for JSON serialization is the Jackson library[2], because it can convert Java objects to JSON objects and back again without much code being needed to be written. Unfortunately, no version compatible with Java 9+ had been released yet, so for this section, a less advanced library compatible with Java 9+ will be used.

JSON format is a collection of key-pair values. The values can be arrays, or collections of key-pairs themselves. Converting Java objects to JSON objects using the JSON library (yes, it's named exactly like that) is easy. We create a `JSONObject` and populate it with the field names and values of the `Singer` object, and then we convert the `JSONObject` to `String` and eventually write it to a file. In the following code sample, we skipped the writing to file part and we transform the `String` back into a copy of the initial `Singer` object.

```
package com.apress.bgn.ch11.json;
```

```
import com.apress.bgn.ch11.xml.Singer;
import org.json.JSONObject;
import org.slf4j.Logger;
import org.slf4j.LoggerFactory;
```

```
import java.time.LocalDate;
import java.time.Month;
import java.time.format.DateTimeFormatter;
```

---

[2]Official GitHub repository for the company that produces the Jackson library https://github.com/FasterXML

```java
public class JsonSerializationDemo {
    private static final Logger log =
        LoggerFactory.getLogger(JsonSerializationDemo.class);

        public static void main(String... args) {
            LocalDate johnBd = LocalDate.of(1977, Month.OCTOBER, 16);
            Singer john = new Singer("John Mayer", 5.0, johnBd);

            JSONObject jsonObject = new JSONObject();
            jsonObject.put("name", john.getName());
            jsonObject.put("rating", john.getRating());
            jsonObject.put("birthdate", john.getBirthDate().toString());
            String jsonData = jsonObject.toString(2);
            log.info("--> Serialized {}", jsonData);

            JSONObject readJson = new JSONObject(jsonData);
            Singer copyOfJohn = new Singer((String) readJson.get("name"),
                    Double.parseDouble(((Integer)readJson.get("rating")).
                    toString()),
                    LocalDate.parse((String)readJson.get("birthdate"),
                        DateTimeFormatter.ISO_LOCAL_DATE));
            log.info("Are objects equal? {}", copyOfJohn.equals(john));
            log.info("--> Deserialized {}", copyOfJohn);
        }
}
```

The number given as a parameter to the `jsonObject.toString(2);` method is an indentation value used to format the resulted text. When the previous program is executed, the output you can expect to see in the console should look very similar to this.

```
[main] INFO com.apress.bgn.ch11.json.JsonSerializationDemo - -->
Serialized {
  "birthdate": "1977-10-16",
  "name": "John Mayer",
  "rating": 5
}
```

```
[main] INFO com.apress.bgn.ch11.json.JsonSerializationDemo - Are objects
equal? true
[main] INFO com.apress.bgn.ch11.json.JsonSerializationDemo - -->
   Deserialized Singer{name='John Mayer', rating=5.0, birthDate=1977-10-16}
```

Theoretically this library provides a method to serialize an object directly by calling:

```
LocalDate johnBd = LocalDate.of(1977, Month.OCTOBER, 16);
Singer john = new Singer("John Mayer", 5.0, johnBd);
JSONObject jo = new JSONObject(john);
```

But the version that the project is currently using seems to have a bug and cannot actually do that. So, the only hope for developers that plan to write Java 9+ applications to use practical JSON serialization/deserialization is to either build one themselves, or to hope that a stable version of Jackson built with Java9+ is available soon.

The Media API

Aside from text data, Java can manipulate binary files such as images. The Java Media API contains a set of image encoder/decoder (codec) classes for several popular image storage formats: BMP, GIF (decoder only), FlashPix (decoder only), JPEG, PNG, PNM[3], TIFF, and WBMP.

In Java 9, the Java media API was transformed as well and functionality to encapsulate many images with different resolutions into a multiresolution image was added.

The core of the Java Media API is the `java.awt.Image` class that is the superclass to represent graphical images. The most important image classes and their relationships are depicted in Figure 11-7.

---

[3]The portable pixmap format (PPM), the portable graymap format (PGM) and the portable bitmap format (PBM) are image file formats designed to be easily exchanged between platforms. They are also sometimes referred to collectively as the portable any map format (PNM). More details at `https://en.wikipedia.org/wiki/Netpbm_format`

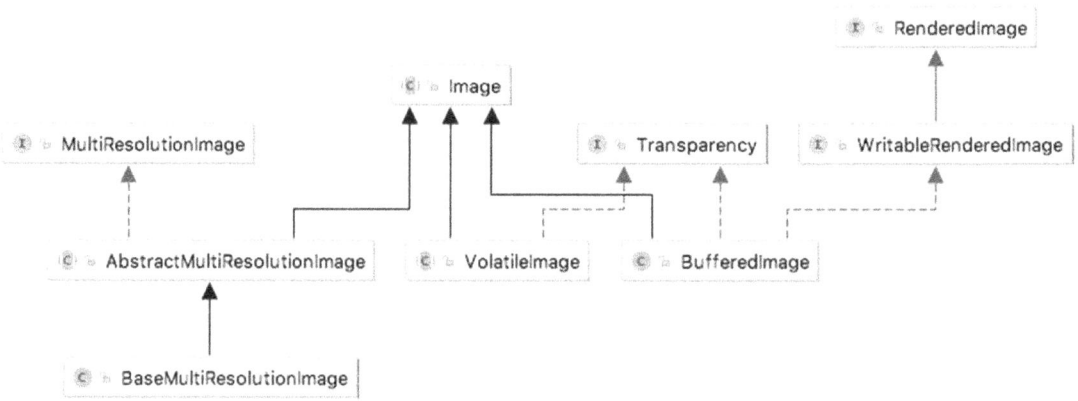

Figure 11-7. Image classes hierarchy

Although the `java.awt.Image` class is the most important in this hierarchy, the most used is `java.awt.BufferedImage`, which is an implementation with an accessible buffer of image data. It provides a lot of methods to create an image, to set its size and its contents, to extract its contents and analyze them, and so much more. In this section, we make use of this class to read and write images.

An image file is a complex file, aside from the picture itself, contains a lot of additional information, the most important nowadays is the location where that image was created. If you ever wondered how a social network proposes a check-in location for an image you are posting, this is where the information is found. This might not seem that important, but posting a picture of your cat, taken in your house, exposes your location to the whole world getting their hands on it. I'm not sure what you think about it, but to me this is terrifying. I used to post pictures of my cat sitting comfortable on the computer I am writing this book on now on my personal blog. I basically exposed my location and that of an expensive laptop to the whole world. Sure, most people do not care about my cat, nor the laptop, but somebody that might be looking to make an easy buck might. So, after a friendly and knowledgeable reader send me a private email telling be about something called EXIF data and how he knows where I live because of the last picture I've posted on my blog, I looked into it. A photo's EXIF data contains a ton of information about your camera, and where the picture was taken (GPS coordinates). Most smartphones embed EXIF data into pictures taken with their camera. Figure 11-8 shows the EXIF information depicted in the macOS **Preview** application.

CHAPTER 11   WORKING WITH FILES

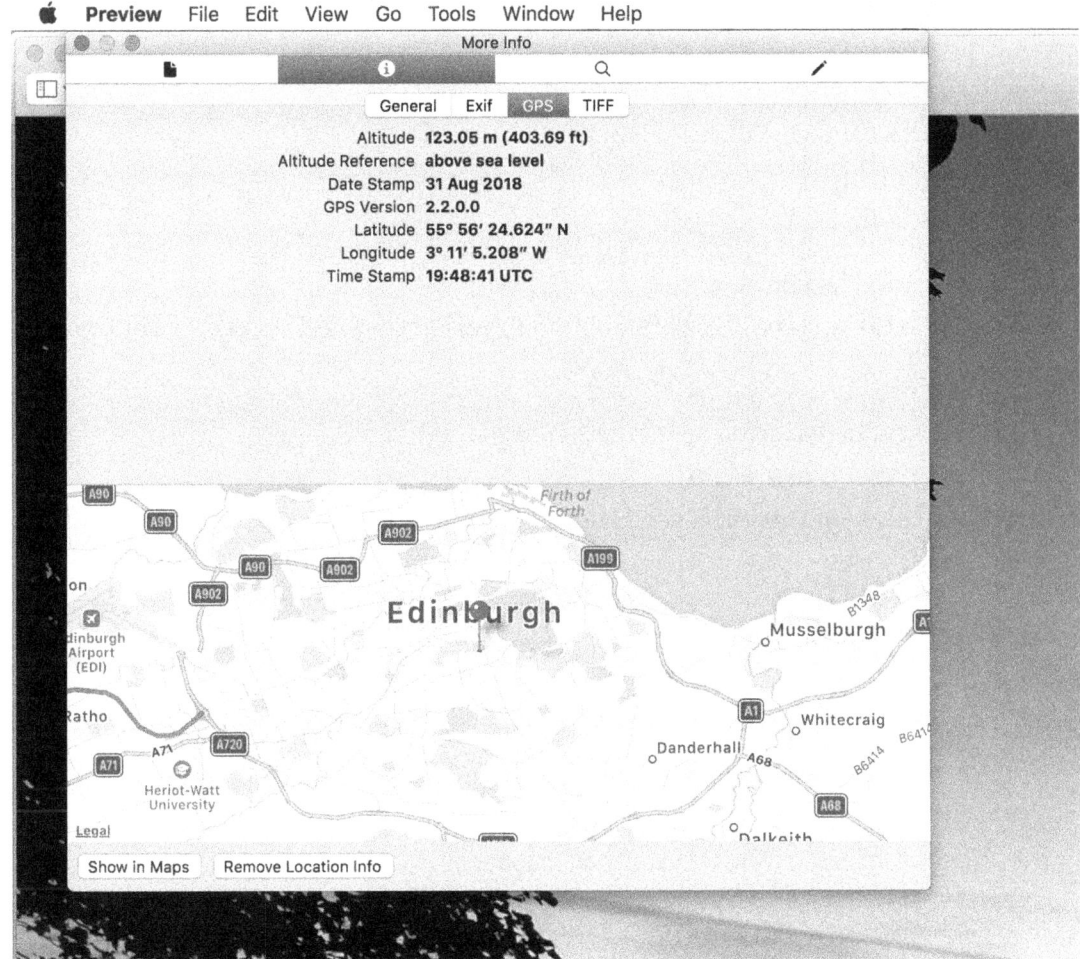

Figure 11-8. EXIF Information on a JPG image

The EXIF info contains the exact location (latitude and longitude included) where the picture was taken. **EXIF** stands for Exchangeable Image File Format. There are utilities to remove it, but when you post a lot of pictures on your blog (like I do), it takes too much time to clean them one by one. This is where Java comes in and I will share with you a snippet of code that I use to clean my pictures of EXIF data.

```
package com.apress.bgn.ch11;

import org.apache.commons.imaging.formats.jpeg.exif.ExifRewriter;
import org.slf4j.Logger;
import org.slf4j.LoggerFactory;
```

515

```
import javax.imageio.ImageIO;
import java.awt.*;
import java.awt.image.BaseMultiResolutionImage;
import java.awt.image.BufferedImage;
import java.io.*;
import java.util.List;

public class MediaDemo {
    private static final Logger log = LoggerFactory.getLogger(MediaDemo.
    class);

    public static void main(String... args) {
        File src = new File(
           "chapter11/media-handling/src/main/resources/scottish_sky.jpg");
        try {
            log.info(" --- Removing EXIF info ---");
            File destNoExif = new File(
              "chapter11/media-handling/src/main/resources/scottish_sky_
              noexif.jpg");
            removeExifTag(destNoExif, src);
         } catch (Exception e) {
            log.error("Something bad happened.", e);
        }
    }

    private static void removeExifTag(final File dest, final File src)
         throws Exception {
       new ExifRewriter().removeExifMetadata(src, new FileOutputStream(dest));
    }
}
```

To easily remove EXIF data, a utility class called `ExifRewriter` is used. It is part of a library named Sanselan created by Apache. This library is unmaintained, but since it doesn't have any dependencies, compiling it with JDK 11 works just fine. I've forked the GitHub repository and created my own branch named feature/jdk11-gradle-build at https://github.com/iuliana/sanselan. The artifact resulted by building that branch was added as a dependency to the project. That is why the `ExifRewriter.removeExifMetadata()` can be used. This method is given as an argument the source of the image and an OutputStream to a location where the new image should be saved. To test that the resulting image has no EXIF data, open it in an image viewer, any option that shows EXIF should either be disabled or should display nothing. In the Preview image viewer in macOS, the option is grayed out.

Now that we got that out of the way, let's resize the resulted image. To resize an image we need to create a BufferedImage instance from the original image to get the image dimensions. After that, we modify the dimensions and use them as arguments to create a new BufferedImage, which is populated with data by a java.awt.Graphics2D instance, a special type of class that renders 2D shapes, text, and images. The code is depicted in the next listing. And the method is called to create an image 25% smaller, an image 50% smaller, and an image 75% smaller.

```java
package com.apress.bgn.ch11;

import org.apache.commons.imaging.formats.jpeg.exif.ExifRewriter;
import org.slf4j.Logger;
import org.slf4j.LoggerFactory;

import javax.imageio.ImageIO;
import java.awt.*;
import java.awt.image.BaseMultiResolutionImage;
import java.awt.image.BufferedImage;
import java.io.*;
import java.util.List;

public class MediaDemo {
    private static final Logger log = LoggerFactory.getLogger(MediaDemo.class);

    public static void main(String... args) {
        File src = new File(
           "chapter11/media-handling/src/main/resources/scottish_sky.jpg");
        try {
            log.info(" --- Removing EXIF info ---");
            File destNoExif = new File(
              "chapter11/media-handling/src/main/resources/scottish_sky_noexif.jpg");
            removeExifTag(destNoExif, src);
```

```
            log.info(" --- Creating 25% image ---");
            File dest25 = new File(
                "chapter11/media-handling/src/main/resources/scottish_
                sky_25.jpg");
            resize(dest25, destNoExif, 0.25f);

            log.info(" --- Creating 50% image ---");
            File dest50 = new File(
                "chapter11/media-handling/src/main/resources/scottish_
                sky_50.jpg");
            resize(dest50, destNoExif, 0.5f);

            log.info(" --- Creating 75% image ---");
            File dest75 = new File(
                "chapter11/media-handling/src/main/resources/scottish_
                sky_75.jpg");
            resize(dest75, destNoExif, 0.75f);
        } catch (Exception e) {
            log.error("Something bad happened.", e);
        }
    }

    private static void resize(final File dest, final File src, final float percent)
        throws IOException {
        BufferedImage originalImage = ImageIO.read(src);
        int scaledWidth = (int) (originalImage.getWidth() * percent);
        int scaledHeight = (int) (originalImage.getHeight() * percent);

        BufferedImage outputImage = new BufferedImage(scaledWidth,
            scaledHeight, originalImage.getType());

        Graphics2D g2d = outputImage.createGraphics();
        g2d.drawImage(originalImage, 0, 0, scaledWidth, scaledHeight, null);
        g2d.dispose();
        outputImage.flush();
```

```
        ImageIO.write(outputImage, "jpg", dest);
    }
    ...
}
```

To make things easier, the `ImageIO` class utility methods come in handy for reading images from files, or writing them to a specific location. If you want to test that the resizing works, you can look in the `resources` directory.

The output files have already been named accordingly, but to make sure, you can double check in a file viewer. You should see something similar to what is depicted in Figure 11-9.

scottish_sky_25.jpg	43 KB
scottish_sky_50.jpg	120 KB
scottish_sky_75.jpg	218 KB
scottish_sky_noexif.jpg	1.1 MB
scottish_sky.jpg	1.1 MB

Figure 11-9. *Images resized using Java code*

The resulting images are not as high in quality as the original image, because compressing the pixels does not result in higher quality, but they do fit the sizes we intended.

Now that we have all these versions of the same image we can use them to create a multiresolution image using the `BaseMultiResolutionImage` class introduced in Java 9. An instance of this class is created from a set of images, all copy of a single image, but with different resolutions. This is why we created more than one resized copy of the image. A `BaseMultiResolutionImage` retrieves images based on specific screen resolutions and it is suitable for applications designed to be accessed from multiple devices. Let's see the code first and then explain the results.

```
package com.apress.bgn.ch11;

import org.apache.commons.imaging.formats.jpeg.exif.ExifRewriter;
import org.slf4j.Logger;
import org.slf4j.LoggerFactory;
```

CHAPTER 11 WORKING WITH FILES

```java
import javax.imageio.ImageIO;
import java.awt.*;
import java.awt.image.BaseMultiResolutionImage;
import java.awt.image.BufferedImage;
import java.io.*;
import java.util.List;

public class MediaDemo {
    private static final Logger log = LoggerFactory.getLogger(MediaDemo.
    class);

    public static void main(String... args) {
        File src = new File(
           "chapter11/media-handling/src/main/resources/scottish_sky.jpg");
        try {
            Image[] imgList = new Image[]{
                    ImageIO.read(dest25), // 1008 x 277
                    ImageIO.read(dest50), //2016 x 554
                    ImageIO.read(dest75), // 3024 x 831
                    ImageIO.read(src) // 4032 x 1108
            };

            log.info(" --- Creating multi-resolution image ---");
            File destVariant = new File(
                "chapter11/media-handling/src/main/resources/sky_variant.jpg");
            createMultiResImage(destVariant, imgList);
        } catch (Exception e) {
            log.error("Something bad happened.", e);
        }
    }

    private static void createMultiResImage(final File dest, final Image[]
    imgList)
        throws IOException {
        MultiResolutionImage mrImage = new BaseMultiResolutionImage(0,
        imgList);
```

```
        List<Image> variants = mrImage.getResolutionVariants();

        variants.forEach(System.out::println);

        Image img = mrImage.getResolutionVariant(700, 250);
        log.info("Most fit to the requested size<{},{}>: <{},{}>", 700, 250,
            img.getWidth(null), img.getHeight(null));

        if (img instanceof BufferedImage) {
            ImageIO.write((BufferedImage) img, "jpg", dest);
        }

    }
    ...
}
```

To clearly show which image is selected, the resolution of each image has a comment next to it. The BaseMultiResolutionImage instance is created from an array of Image instances. When getResolutionVariant(..) is called, the arguments are compared to the corresponding image properiest, and if both are less than equal to the values of one of the images, that image is returned. In the next code snippet, the code of the BaseMultiResolutionImage.getResolutionVariant(..) is depicted.

```
@Override
public Image getResolutionVariant(double destImageWidth,
                                  double destImageHeight) {

    checkSize(destImageWidth, destImageHeight);

    for (Image rvImage : resolutionVariants) {
        if (destImageWidth <= rvImage.getWidth(null)
                && destImageHeight <= rvImage.getHeight(null)) {
            return rvImage;
        }
    }
    return resolutionVariants[resolutionVariants.length - 1];
}
```

The previous code leads to two conclusions.

- Both the desired width and height that are given as arguments must be less or equal to the properties of one of the images the multiresolution image was created from; otherwise, the default image is returned—the one with the index given as argument for the base image index in the `BaseMultiResolutionImage` constructor. This means that getResolutionVariant(700, 250) returns image *dest25* because 700 <= 1008 && 250 <= 277 and (1008 x 277) is the (width x height) of this image. The call getResolutionVariant(700, 300) leads to image *src* being returned, because the previous condition is no longer evaluated to true while iterating the list, so the last image in the list is retuned, because the method exits through `return resolutionVariants[resolutionVariants.length - 1];`

- The array the `BaseMultiResolutionImage` instance is created from must be sorted in ascending order of the width and height of the images; otherwise, an image with the wrong dimensions is returned, because the decision algorithm is not that efficient.

So, if the algorithm is not efficient what can be done? It's simple: we can create our own `MultiResolutionImage` implementation that extends `BaseMultiResolutionImage` and overrides the `getResolutionVariant()` method. Since we know that all images are resized copies of the same image, this means width and height are proportional. So, an algorithm that always returns the variant of the image that is most suitable to the desired resolution can be written that does not really care about the order of the images in the array, and that it returns the image that fits most. So, the implementation might look similar to the following class.

```
package com.apress.bgn.ch11;

import java.awt.*;
import java.awt.image.BaseMultiResolutionImage;
import java.util.ArrayList;
import java.util.HashMap;
import java.util.Map;
```

```java
public class SmartMultiResolutionImage
    extends BaseMultiResolutionImage {

    public SmartMultiResolutionImage(int baseImageIndex,
        Image... resolutionVariants) {
        super(baseImageIndex, resolutionVariants);
    }

    @Override
    public Image getResolutionVariant(double destImageWidth,
                                      double destImageHeight) {
        checkSize(destImageWidth, destImageHeight);

        Map<Double, Image> result = new HashMap<>();

        for (Image rvImage : getResolutionVariants()) {
            double widthDelta = Math.abs(destImageWidth - rvImage.
            getWidth(null));
            double heightDelta = Math.abs(destImageHeight - rvImage.
            getHeight(null));
            double delta = widthDelta + heightDelta;
            result.put(delta, rvImage);
        }

        java.util.List<Double> deltaList = new ArrayList<>(result.keySet());
        deltaList.sort(Double::compare);

        return result.get(deltaList.get(0));
    }

    private static void checkSize(double width, double height) {
        if (width <= 0 || height <= 0) {
            throw new IllegalArgumentException(String.format(
                    "Width (%s) or height (%s) cannot be <= 0", width,
                    height));
        }
```

```
            if (!Double.isFinite(width) || !Double.isFinite(height)) {
                throw new IllegalArgumentException(String.format(
                        "Width (%s) or height (%s) is not finite", width,
                        height));
            }
        }
    }
}
```

The checkSize(..) method must be duplicated, as it is private and used inside getResolutionVariant(..), so it cannot be called inside a superclass, but that is a minor inconvenience to having an implementation that has a proper behavior. In the previous implementation, we no longer need a sorted array. Also, calls to getResolutionVariant(700, 250), getResolutionVariant(700, 300), getResolutionVariant(800, 250), getResolutionVariant(800, 400) all return image dest25.

```
Image[] imgList = new Image[]{
    ImageIO.read(src),      // 4032 x 1108
    ImageIO.read(dest75),   // 3024 x 831
    ImageIO.read(dest25),   // 1008 x 277
    ImageIO.read(dest50)    // 2016 x 554
};

log.info(" --- Creating multi-resolution image ---");
File destVariant = new File(
  "chapter11/media-handling/src/main/resources/sky_variant.jpg");
createMultiResImage(destVariant, imgList);
BufferedImage variantImg = ImageIO.read(destVariant);
BufferedImage dest25Img = ImageIO.read(dest25);
log.info("Are identical? {}", variantImg.equals(dest25Img));
...

private static void createMultiResImage(final File dest, final Image[] imgList)
      throws IOException {
    MultiResolutionImage mrImage = new SmartMultiResolutionImage(0, imgList);
```

CHAPTER 11   WORKING WITH FILES

```
    List<Image> variants = mrImage.getResolutionVariants();

    variants.forEach(i -> log.info(i.toString()));

    Image img = mrImage.getResolutionVariant(700, 400);
    log.info("Most fit to the requested size<{},{}>: <{},{}>", 700, 400,
        img.getWidth(null), img.getHeight(null));

    if (img instanceof BufferedImage) {
        ImageIO.write((BufferedImage) img, "jpg", dest);
    }
}
```

Running the log, the following is printed in the console.

```
INFO com.apress.bgn.ch11.MediaDemo -   --- Creating multi-resolution image
---
INFO com.apress.bgn.ch11.MediaDemo - BufferedImage@3c9d0b9d: type = 5
ColorModel:
  #... ByteInterleavedRaster: width = 4032 height = 1108 #numDataElements 3
  dataOff[0] = 2
INFO com.apress.bgn.ch11.MediaDemo - BufferedImage@64cd705f: type = 5
ColorModel:
  #... ByteInterleavedRaster: width = 3024 height = 831 #numDataElements 3
  dataOff[0] = 2
INFO com.apress.bgn.ch11.MediaDemo - BufferedImage@9225652: type = 5
ColorModel:
  #... ByteInterleavedRaster: width = 1008 height = 277 #numDataElements 3
  dataOff[0] = 2
INFO com.apress.bgn.ch11.MediaDemo - BufferedImage@654f0d9c: type = 5
ColorModel:
  #... ByteInterleavedRaster: width = 2016 height = 554 #numDataElements 3
  dataOff[0] = 2
INFO com.apress.bgn.ch11.MediaDemo - Most fit to the requested
size<700,400>: <1008,277>
INFO com.apress.bgn.ch11.MediaDemo - Are identical? false
```

Wait what? Why are the images not identical? Well, they do have the same resolution, but as objects are not identical, because drawing pixels is not really that precise. But if you really want to make sure, you could print the width and height of the two images, open them with an image viewer and notice that to the naked eye, they look identical.

```
log.info("variant width x height : {} x {}", variantImg.getWidth(),
    variantImg.getHeight());
log.info("dest25Img width x height : {} x {}", dest25Img.getWidth(),
    dest25Img.getHeight());
```

The code prints the width and height of the two images, making it obvious that the two images have the same dimensions, just as expected.

```
INFO com.apress.bgn.ch11.MediaDemo - variant width x height :  1008 x 277
INFO com.apress.bgn.ch11.MediaDemo - dest25Img width x height :  1008 x 277
```

Using JavaFX Image Classes

Aside from the Java Media API, which is centered on components of the `java.awt` package, another way to display and edit images is provided by JavaFX. The core class for the `javafx.scene.image` package is called `Image`, which handles images in a few common formats: PNG, JPEG, BMP, and GIF. JavaFX applications can display images using an instance of `javafx.scene.image.ImageView`. The part that I like most about this class is that the images can be also displayed scaled, without the original image being modified.

To create a `javafx.scene.image.Image` instance, all we need is a `FileInputStream` instance to read the image from the user-provided location, or a URL location given as `String`. The following code snippet creates a JavaFX application that displays an image with its original width and height, which can be accessed using methods in the `javafx.scene.image.Image` class.

```
package com.apress.bgn.ch11;

import javafx.application.Application;
import javafx.scene.Scene;
import javafx.scene.image.Image;
import javafx.scene.image.ImageView;
```

```java
import javafx.scene.layout.StackPane;
import javafx.stage.Stage;

import java.io.File;
import java.io.FileInputStream;

public class JavaFxMediaDemo extends Application {

    public static void main(String... args) {
        Application.launch(args);
    }

    @Override
    public void start(Stage primaryStage) throws Exception {
        primaryStage.setTitle("JavaFX Image Demo");
        File src = new File("chapter11/media-handling/src/main/resources/
        cover.png");
        Image image = new Image(new FileInputStream(src));

        ImageView imageView = new ImageView(image);
        imageView.setFitHeight(image.getHeight());
        imageView.setFitWidth(image.getWidth());
        imageView.setPreserveRatio(true);

        //Creating a Group object
        StackPane root = new StackPane();
        root.getChildren().add(imageView);
        primaryStage.setScene(new Scene(root,
            image.getWidth()+10,
            image.getHeight()+10));
        primaryStage.show();
    }
}
```

The Image instance cannot be added to the Scene of the JavaFX instance directly as it does not implement the Node interface, which is required to be implemented by all JavaFX elements that make a JavaFX application. That is why this instance must be wrapped in a javafx.scene.image.ImageView instance that is a class implementing node, which is a specialized class for painting images loaded with Image class.

CHAPTER 11   WORKING WITH FILES

This class resizes the displayed image with or without preserving the original aspect ratio by calling the setPreserveRatio(..) method with the appropriate argument: true to keep the original aspect ratio; false otherwise.

In the previous code, we use the values retuned by image.getWidth() and image.getHeight() to set the size of the ImageView object and the size of the Scene instance. But let's get creative and display the scaled image, still preserving the aspect ratio and also using a better-quality filtering algorithm when scaling the image using the smooth(..) method.

```
...
ImageView imageView = new ImageView(image);
imageView.setFitWidth(100);
imageView.setPreserveRatio(true);
imageView.setSmooth(true);
...
```

The ImageView class also supports a Rectangle2D viewport that rotates the image.

```
import javafx.geometry.Rectangle2D;
...
ImageView imageView = new ImageView(image);
Rectangle2D viewportRect = new Rectangle2D(2, 2, 600, 600);
imageView.setViewport(viewportRect);
imageView.setRotate(90);
...
```

Being an implementation of Node, ImageView supports clicking events, and it is easy to write some code to resize an image on click. Just take a look.

```
...
ImageView imageView = new ImageView(image);
imageView.setFitHeight(image.getHeight());
imageView.setFitWidth(image.getWidth());
imageView.setPreserveRatio(true);
root.getChildren().add(imageView);
imageView.setPickOnBounds(true);
```

```
imageView.setOnMouseClicked(mouseEvent -> {
    if(imageView.getFitWidth() > 100) {
        imageView.setFitWidth(100);
        imageView.setPreserveRatio(true);
        imageView.setSmooth(true);
    } else {
        imageView.setFitHeight(image.getHeight());
        imageView.setFitWidth(image.getWidth());
        imageView.setPreserveRatio(true);
    }
});
```

...

By calling onMouseClicked, we attached an `EventHandler<? super MouseEvent>` instance to the mouse-clicking event on `imageView`. The `EventHandler<T extends Event>` is a functional interface containing a single method named `handle`, and its concrete implementation is the body of the lambda expression in the previous code listing.

Since JavaFX was taken out of JDK 11, there is no real value in going over more image processing classes in this section. But if you are interested in learning more about this subject, this tutorial from Oracle should do the job: https://docs.oracle.com/javafx/2/image_ops/jfxpub-image_ops.htm. Also, as practice, you can try writing your own code, based on the code in the book, to add a mouse event that rotates the image.

And this is all the space that I can dedicate to playing with images in the Java. I hope you found this section useful and might get the chance to test your Java Media API skills in the future, if not for anything else, at least for cleaning EXIF data from your images.

Summary

This chapter has covered most of the information that you need to know to work with various types of files, and to serialize Java objects, save them to a file, and then recover them through deserialization. When writing Java applications, you typically need to save

CHAPTER 11   WORKING WITH FILES

data to files or read data from files and this chapter provides a wide list of components to do so. The following is a short summary of this chapter.

- how to use `File` and `Path` instances
- how to use utility methods in `Files` and `Paths`
- how to serialize/deserialize Java objects to/from binary, XML and JSON
- how to resize and modify images using the Java Media API
- how to use images in JavaFX applications

CHAPTER 12

The Publish/Subscribe Framework

All the programming concepts explained so far involved data that needed to be processed. Regardless of the form in which data is provided, the Java programs we've written so far took that data, modified it, and printed the results, whether to the console, to files, or to another software component. You could say that all of these components were communicating with each other and passing processed data from one to another. Figure 12-1 abstractly describes interactions among Java components in a program.

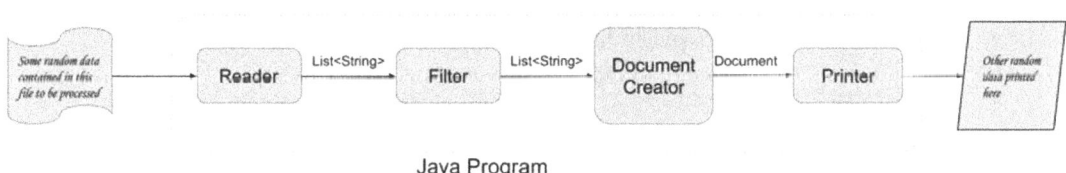

Figure 12-1. Interactions between Java components within a program

Each of the arrows is marked with the type of information being passed from one component to another. In Figure 12-1, you can identify a starting point where information enters the program (by being read by the Reader), and an end point where the information is printed to some output component by the Printer. So, you could say that the Reader provides the data, the Filter and the DocumentCreator are some internal processor, processing the data and the Printer is the consumer of the data.

What was described so far is resembles a **point-to-point (p2p) messaging model**, which describes a concept of one message being send to one consumer. The p2p model is specific to an Java API called Java Message Service (JMS) that supports the formal communication known as *messaging* between computers in a network. In the example that begins this chapter an analogy was made to show that communication between components of a Java Program works in a similar manner. And so, the design of a solution to implement a process as described in Figure 12-1 could be created by considering all components linked into a messaging style communication model. There is more than one communication model—Producer/Consumer, Publish/Subscribe, Sender/Receiver, each with its own specifics,[1] but this chapter is focused on **Publish/Subscribe** because it is the model that reactive programming is based on.

Reactive Programming and the Reactive Manifesto

Reactive programming is a declarative programming style that involves using data streams and propagation of change. You learned how to use streams in **Chapter 8**, so we're one step closer. Now all we must do is learn how to use reactive streams. Reactive programming involves using asynchronous data streams or event streams. Using reactive streams is not a new idea.

The Reactive Manifesto was first made public in 2014.[2] It made a request for software to be developed in such a way that *systems are responsive, resilient, elastic, and message driven*, in short they should be *reactive*. The following explains each of the four terms.

- **Responsive** should provide fast and consistent response times.
- **Resilient** should remain responsive in case of failure and be able to recover.
- **Elastic** should remain responsive and be able to handle various workloads.
- **Message driven** should communicate using asynchronous messages, avoid blocking and applying *back pressure* when necessary.

Systems designed this way are supposed to be more flexible, loosely coupled, and scalable, but at the same time they should be easier to develop, amendable to change and more tolerant of failure. But to accomplish all that, the systems need a common API for communication. Reactive Streams is an initiative to provide such a standard API for asynchronous, non-blocking stream processing that also supports back-pressure. We'll

---

[1] If you are interested more in communication models, you can search the web for *Enterprise Integration Patterns*.
[2] Read it at https://www.reactivemanifesto.org/

CHAPTER 12   THE PUBLISH/SUBSCRIBE FRAMEWORK

explain what *back-pressure* means in a moment. Let's start with the basics of reactive stream processing.

Any type of stream processing involves a producer of data, a consumer of data, and components in the middle between them that process the data. The direction of the data flow is from the producer to the consumer. The abstract schema of a system is depicted in Figure 12-2.

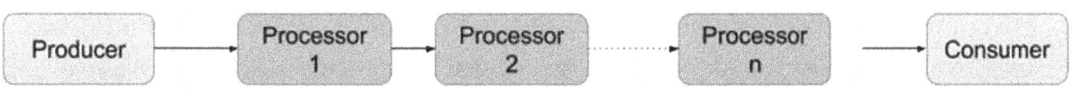

Figure 12-2. *Producer/Consumer system*

The system might end up in a pickle when the producer is faster than the consumer. So the extra data that cannot be processed must be dealt with. There is more than one way of doing that.

- The extra data is discarded (this is done in network hardware).
- The producer is blocked so the consumer has time to catch up.
- The data is buffered, but buffers are limited and if we have a fast producer and a slow consumer there is a danger of the buffer overflowing.
- By applying *back pressure*, which involves giving the consumer the power to regulate the producer and control how much data is produced. Back pressure can be viewed as a message being sent from the consumer to the producer to let it know it has to slow its data production rate. With this in mind, we can complete the design in Figure 12-2, which results in Figure 12-3.

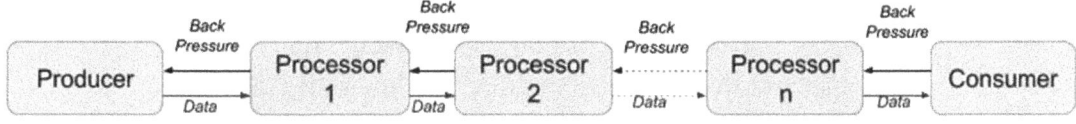

Figure 12-3. *Reactive Producer/Consumer system*

533

CHAPTER 12 THE PUBLISH/SUBSCRIBE FRAMEWORK

If producer, processors, and consumer are not synchronized, solving the problem of too much data by blocking until each one is ready to process it is not an option, as it would transform the system into a synchronous one. Discarding it is not an option either, and buffering is, well, unpredictable, so all we're left with for a reactive system is applying **non-blocking back-pressure**.

Writing applications that can be aggregated in reactive systems was not possible in Java before version 9, so developers had to make do with external libraries. A reactive application must be designed according to principle of reactive programming and use reactive streams for handling the data. The standard API for reactive programming was first described by the `reactive-streams` library that could be used with Java 8 as well. But in Java 9, the standard API was added to the JDK. Figure 12-4 shows the interfaces that are meant to be implemented by components with the roles defined previously. The reactive streams API is made of four very simple interfaces.

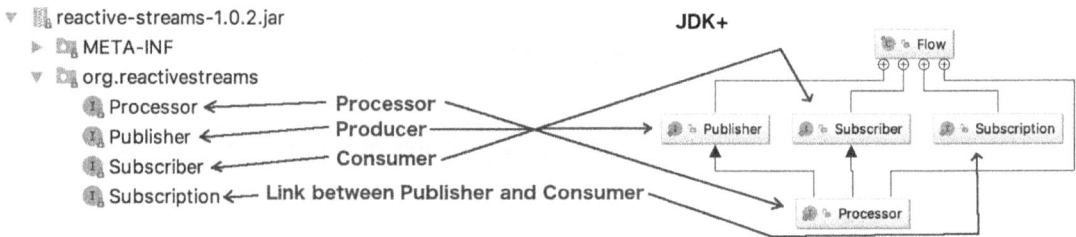

***Figure 12-4.** Reactive Streams interfaces*

- interface `Publisher<T>` exposes one method named `subscribe(Subscriber<? extendsT>)` that is called to add a `Subscriber` instance and produces elements of type T, which are consumed by the `Subscriber`.

- interface `Subscriber<R>`, consumes elements from the `Publisher` and exposes four methods that must be implemented to define concrete behavior of the instance depending on the event type received by the `Publisher` instance.

    - void `onSubscribe(Subscription)` is the first method called on a subscriber and this is the method that links the `Publisher` to the `Subscriber` instance using the `Subscription` argument, if this method throws an exception the following behavior is not guaranteed.

- void onNext(T) is the method invoked with a Subscription's next item to receive the data, if it throws an exception, the Subscription might be cancelled.

- void onError(Throwable) is the method invoked upon an unrecoverable error encountered by a Publisher or Subscription.

- void onComplete() is the method called when there is not more data to consume, thus no additional Subscriber method invocations occur.

- interface Processor<T,R> extends both Publisher<T> and Subscriber<R>, because it needs to consume data and produce it to send it further upstream.

- interface Subscription, its implementation should link the Publisher and the Subscriber and can be used to apply back-pressure by calling the request(long) to set he number of items to be produced and sent to the consumer. It also allows the cancellation of a flow by calling the cancel() method to tell a Subscriber to stop receiving messages.

In the JDK, all the previously listed interfaces are defined within the java.util.concurrent.Flow class. The name of this class is obvious in nature, as the previous interfaces are used to create flow-controlled components that can be linked together to create a reactive application. Aside from these four interfaces, there is a single JDK implementation, the java.util.concurrent.SubmissionPublisher<T> class implementing Publisher<T> that is a convenient base for subclasses that generate items and use the methods in this class to publish them.

The Flow interfaces are basic and can be used when writing reactive applications, but this requires a lot of work. Currently, there are multiple implementations by various teams that provide a more practical way to develop reactive applications. Using implementations of these interfaces, you can write reactive applications without needing to write the logic for synchronization of threads processing the data.

The following list is of the most well-known reactive streams API implementations.

- Project Reactor (https://projectreactor.io/) embraced by Spring for its Web Reactive Framework

- Akka Streams (https://doc.akka.io/docs/akka/current/stream/stream-flows-and-basics.html)

- MongoDB Reactive Streams Java Driver (http://mongodb.github.io/mongo-java-driver-reactivestreams/1.9/)

- Ratpack (https://ratpack.io/)

- RxJava (http://reactivex.io/)

And there are more, because in a big data world, reactive data processing is no longer a luxury, but a necessity.

This concludes the introduction into what reactive programming and what reactive streams are. It is about time we get down to the code.

Using the JDK Reactive Streams API

As the JDK provided interfaces for reactive programming are quite basic, implementing them to build something really useful is quite cumbersome, but nevertheless we will try. In this section, an application that generates an infinite number of integer values, filters these values, and selects the ones that are smaller than 127 is being built. For the ones that are even and between 98 and 122, we subtract 32 (basically converting small letters to uppercase). Then we convert them to a character and print them.

Clearly, the most basic solution is

```
private static final Logger log = LoggerFactory.getLogger(ReactiveMain.class);
private static final Random random = new Random();

public static void main(String... args) {

    while (true){
        int rndNo = random.nextInt(150);
        if (rndNo >=0 && rndNo < 127) {
            log.info("Initial value: {} ", rndNo);
            if(rndNo % 2 == 0 && rndNo >=98 && rndNo <=122) {
                rndNo -=32;
            }
            char res = (char) rndNo;
            log.info("Result: {}", res);
```

```
        } else {
            log.debug("Number {} discarded.", rndNo);
        }
    }
}
```

Each line of code in the previous code listing has a purpose, a desired outcome. This approach is called *imperative programming*, because it sequentially executes a series of statements to produce a desired output.

But this is not what we are aiming for. In this section, we implement a reactive solution using implementations of the JDK reactive interfaces. So we'll need the following.

- A publisher component that makes use of an infinite stream to generate random integer values. The class should implement the `Flow.Publisher<Integer>` interface.

- A processor that selects only integer values that can be converted to visible characters, let's say all characters with codes between [0,127). The class should implement the `Flow.Processor<Integer, Integer>`.

- A processor that modifies elements received, that are even, and between 98 and 122, by subtracting 32. This class should also implement the `Flow.Processor<Integer, Integer>`.

- A processor that transforms integer elements into the equivalent characters. This is a special type of processor that maps one value to another, of another type and should implement `Flow.Processor<Integer, Character>`.

- A subscriber that prints the received elements from the last processor in the chain. This class implements the `Flow.Subscriber<Character>` interface.

Let's start by declaring the `Publisher` that wraps around an infinite stream to produce values to be consumed. We implement the `Flow.Publisher<Integer>` interface, but provide a full concrete implementation to submit the elements asynchronously. To buffer them in case of need is a little much, so we'll make use of `SubmissionPublisher<Integer>` in our class. The code for the publisher is depicted next.

Chapter 12　The Publish/Subscribe Framework

```java
package com.apress.bgn.ch12.jdkstreams;

import java.util.Random;
import java.util.concurrent.Flow;
import java.util.concurrent.SubmissionPublisher;
import java.util.stream.IntStream;

public class IntPublisher implements Flow.Publisher<Integer> {
    private static final Random random = new Random();
    private final IntStream intStream = IntStream.generate(() -> random.nextInt(150));

    private final SubmissionPublisher<Integer>
        submissionPublisher = new SubmissionPublisher<>();

    @Override
    public void subscribe(Flow.Subscriber<? super Integer> subscriber) {
        submissionPublisher.subscribe(subscriber);
    }

    public void start() {
        intStream.forEach(element -> {
            submissionPublisher.submit(element);
            sleep();
        });
    }

    private void sleep() {
        try {
            Thread.sleep(1000);
        } catch (InterruptedException e) {
            throw new RuntimeException("could not sleep!");
        }
    }
}
```

As expected, we've provided an implementation for the `subscribe()` method, and in this case, we have to forward the subscriber to the internal `submissionPublisher`. Also, we've added a `start()` method that takes elements from the infinite `IntStream` and submits them using the internal `submissionPublisher`. The `IntStream` makes use of a `Random` instance to generate integer values in the [0,150] interval. This interval was chosen so we can see how values bigger than 127 are discarded by the first `Processor` instance connected to the publisher. To slow down the elements' submission, we added a call to `Thread.sleep(1000)` that basically guarantees one element per second is send up the chain.

The name of the first processor is `FilterCharProcessor` and makes use of an internal `SubmissionPublisher<Integer>` instance to send the elements it processes onward to the next processor. Exceptions thrown are forwarded using the `SubmissionPublisher<Integer>` also. The processor acts as a publisher, but as a subscriber as well, so the implementation on the `onNext(..)` method has to include a call to `subscription.request(..)` to apply back pressure. From the figures presented earlier in the chapter, you could see that the processor is basically a component that allows data flow in both directions, and it does that by implementing both `Publisher` and `Subscriber`.

The processor must subscribe to the publisher, and when the publisher's `subscribe(..)` method is called, it causes the `onSubscribe(Flow.Subscription subscription)` method to be invoked. The `subscription` must be stored locally, so that it can be used to apply back pressure. But when accepting a subscription, we must make sure that the field was not already initialized, because according to reactive streams specification there can only be one subscriber for a publisher; otherwise, the results are unpredictable. So if and when a new subscription arrives, it must be cancelled, and this is done by calling `cancel()`. The full code for the processor is depicted next.

```
package com.apress.bgn.ch12.jdkstreams;

import com.apress.bgn.ch12.dummy.BasicIntTransformer;
import org.slf4j.Logger;
import org.slf4j.LoggerFactory;

import java.util.concurrent.Flow;
import java.util.concurrent.SubmissionPublisher;
```

CHAPTER 12 THE PUBLISH/SUBSCRIBE FRAMEWORK

```java
public class FilterCharProcessor implements
     Flow.Processor<Integer, Integer> {

   private static final Logger log =
        LoggerFactory.getLogger(FilterCharProcessor.class);
   private final SubmissionPublisher<Integer>
       submissionPublisher = new SubmissionPublisher<>();
   private Flow.Subscription subscription;

   @Override
   public void subscribe(Flow.Subscriber<? super Integer> subscriber) {
       submissionPublisher.subscribe(subscriber);
   }

   @Override
   public void onSubscribe(Flow.Subscription subscription) {
       if (this.subscription == null) {
           this.subscription = subscription;
           // apply back pressure - request one element
           this.subscription.request(1);
       } else {
           subscription.cancel();
       }
   }

   @Override
   public void onNext(Integer element) {
       if (element >=0 && element < 127){
           submit(element);
       } else {
           log.debug("Element {} discarded.", element);
       }
       subscription.request(1);
   }

   @Override
   public void onError(Throwable throwable) {
       submissionPublisher.closeExceptionally(throwable);
   }
```

CHAPTER 12 THE PUBLISH/SUBSCRIBE FRAMEWORK

```java
    @Override
    public void onComplete() {
        submissionPublisher.close();
    }

    protected void submit(Integer element){
        submissionPublisher.submit(element);
    }
}
```

We have three processor classes to build, and aside from the code in the onNext(..) method body, the rest is boilerplate code that allows processor instances to be linked together in the flow we are designing. So it would be practical to wrap up this code in an AbstractProcessor that all processors needed for this solution can extend. As the last processor we need to implement needs to convert the received Integer value to a Character we keep this implementation generic regarding to the type of value being sent to the next processor or subscriber in the flow. The code is depicted next.

```java
package com.apress.bgn.ch12.jdkstreams;

import java.util.concurrent.Flow;
import java.util.concurrent.SubmissionPublisher;

public abstract class AbstractProcessor<T>
        implements Flow.Processor<Integer, T> {

    protected final SubmissionPublisher<T>
        submissionPublisher = new SubmissionPublisher<>();
    protected Flow.Subscription subscription;

    @Override
    public void subscribe(Flow.Subscriber<? super T> subscriber) {
        submissionPublisher.subscribe(subscriber);
    }
```

```java
    @Override
    public void onSubscribe(Flow.Subscription subscription) {
        if (this.subscription == null) {
            this.subscription = subscription;
            // apply back pressure - ask one or more than one
            this.subscription.request(1);
        } else {
            subscription.cancel();
        }
    }

    @Override
    public void onError(Throwable throwable) {
        submissionPublisher.closeExceptionally(throwable);
    }

    @Override
    public void onComplete() {
        submissionPublisher.close();
    }

    protected void submit(T element) {
        submissionPublisher.submit(element);
    }
}
```

This simplifies a lot the implementation of the `FilterCharProcessor` and the other processors as well.

```java
package com.apress.bgn.ch12.jdkstreams;

import org.slf4j.Logger;
import org.slf4j.LoggerFactory;

public class FilterCharProcessor extends AbstractProcessor<Integer> {
    private static final Logger log =
        LoggerFactory.getLogger(FilterCharProcessor.class);
```

```java
    @Override
    public void onNext(Integer element) {
        if (element >= 0 && element < 127) {
            submit(element);
        } else {
            log.debug("Element {} discarded.", element);
        }
        subscription.request(1);
    }
}
```

We have a publisher and a processor, now what ? We connect them of course. The dots (...) in the next code snippet, replace all the processors and the subscribers being connected to each other later in the chapter.

```java
package com.apress.bgn.ch12.jdkstreams;

public class ReactiveDemo {
    public static void main(String... args) {
        IntPublisher publisher = new IntPublisher();
        FilterCharProcessor filterCharProcessor = new FilterCharProcessor();

        publisher.subscribe(filterCharProcessor);
        ...
        publisher.start();
    }
}
```

The next processor implementation is the one that transforms lower case letters into upper case letters by subtracting 32. It can be easily implemented by extending `AbstractProcessor` as well.

```java
package com.apress.bgn.ch12.jdkstreams;

public class TransformerProcessor extends
     AbstractProcessor<Integer> {
```

CHAPTER 12 THE PUBLISH/SUBSCRIBE FRAMEWORK

```
    @Override
    public void onNext(Integer element) {
        if(element % 2 == 0 && element >=98 && element <=122) {
            element -=32;
        }
        submit(element);
        subscription.request(1);
    }
}
```

To plug in this processor into the flow, we need instantiate it and call the `filterCharProcessor.subscribe(..)` and provide this instance as an argument.

```
package com.apress.bgn.ch12.jdkstreams;

public class ReactiveDemo {
    public static void main(String... args) {
        IntPublisher publisher = new IntPublisher();
        FilterCharProcessor filterCharProcessor = new
        FilterCharProcessor();
        TransformerProcessor transformerProcessor = new
        TransformerProcessor();

        publisher.subscribe(filterCharProcessor);
        filterCharProcessor.subscribe(transformerProcessor);
        ...
        publisher.start();
    }
}
```

The next one to implement is the final processor needed for the solution. It converts an `Integer` value to a `Character` value. To keep the implementation as declarative as possible, the processor is provided the mapping function as an argument.

CHAPTER 12 THE PUBLISH/SUBSCRIBE FRAMEWORK

```java
package com.apress.bgn.ch12.jdkstreams;

import java.util.function.Function;

public class MappingProcessor extends
     AbstractProcessor<Character>  {
    private final Function<Integer, Character> function;

    public MappingProcessor(Function<Integer, Character> function) {
        this.function = function;
    }

    @Override
    public void onNext(Integer element) {
        submit(function.apply(element));
        subscription.request(1);
    }
}
```

And now, to plug it in.

```java
package com.apress.bgn.ch12.jdkstreams;

public class ReactiveDemo {
    public static void main(String... args) {
        IntPublisher publisher = new IntPublisher();
        FilterCharProcessor filterCharProcessor = new FilterCharProcessor();
         TransformerProcessor transformerProcessor = new
         TransformerProcessor();
         MappingProcessor mappingProcessor =
             new MappingProcessor(element -> (char) element.intValue());

        publisher.subscribe(filterCharProcessor);
        filterCharProcessor.subscribe(transformerProcessor);
        transformerProcessor.subscribe(mappingProcessor);
        ...
        publisher.start();
    }
}
```

CHAPTER 12 THE PUBLISH/SUBSCRIBE FRAMEWORK

The last component of this flow is the subscriber that does nothing more than print the values received from the transformerProcessor. The class implements the Flow.Subscriber<Character> and most of it is identical to the code we've isolated in the AbstractProcessor, but it is what it is.

```
package com.apress.bgn.ch12.jdkstreams;

import org.slf4j.Logger;
import org.slf4j.LoggerFactory;

import java.util.concurrent.Flow;

public class CharPrinter implements Flow.Subscriber<Character> {
    private static final Logger log =
        LoggerFactory.getLogger(CharPrinter.class);
    private Flow.Subscription subscription;

    @Override
    public void onSubscribe(Flow.Subscription subscription) {
        if (this.subscription == null) {
            this.subscription = subscription;
            this.subscription.request(1);
        } else {
            subscription.cancel();
        }
    }

    @Override
    public void onNext(Character element) {
        log.info("Result: {}", element);
        //apply back-pressure again
        subscription.request(1);
    }

    @Override
    public void onError(Throwable throwable) {
        log.error("Something went wrong.", throwable);
    }
```

```
        @Override
        public void onComplete() {
            log.info("Printing complete.");
        }
    }
}
```

So now that we have a subscriber, we can plug it in and run the application.

```
package com.apress.bgn.ch12.jdkstreams;

public class ReactiveDemo {
    public static void main(String... args) {
        IntPublisher publisher = new IntPublisher();
        FilterCharProcessor filterCharProcessor = new FilterCharProcessor();
        TransformerProcessor transformerProcessor = new
        TransformerProcessor();
        MappingProcessor mappingProcessor =
            new MappingProcessor(element -> (char) element.intValue());
        CharPrinter charPrinter = new CharPrinter();

        publisher.subscribe(filterCharProcessor);
        filterCharProcessor.subscribe(transformerProcessor);
        transformerProcessor.subscribe(mappingProcessor);
        mappingProcessor.subscribe(charPrinter);
        publisher.start();
    }
}
```

It would be nice if the subscribe method returns the caller instance so we could chain the subscribe(..) calls, but we work with what is provided for us. When the previous code is run, a log similar to the following is printed in the console.

```
..
DEBUG c.a.b.c.j.FilterCharProcessor - Element 149 discarded.
INFO  c.a.b.c.j.CharPrinter - Result: >
INFO  c.a.b.c.j.CharPrinter - Result: B
INFO  c.a.b.c.j.CharPrinter - Result: 4
INFO  c.a.b.c.j.CharPrinter - Result: Z
```

```
INFO  c.a.b.c.j.CharPrinter - Result: *
INFO  c.a.b.c.j.CharPrinter - Result: o
DEBUG c.a.b.c.j.FilterCharProcessor - Element 141 discarded.
INFO  c.a.b.c.j.CharPrinter - Result: 4
DEBUG c.a.b.c.j.FilterCharProcessor - Element 142 discarded.
INFO  c.a.b.c.j.CharPrinter - Result: Q
DEBUG c.a.b.c.j.FilterCharProcessor - Element 132 discarded.
..
```

The example uses an infinite `IntStream` to generate elements to be published, processed, and consumed. This leads to the execution program running forever, so you have to stop it manually. Another consequence of this is that the `onComplete()` methods will never be called. If we want to use them, we have to make sure the number of items being published is a finite one.

The support for reactive streams is thin in the JDK, even in version 11, released September 23, 2018. It was expected that more useful classes would be added in versions following Java 9, but apparently Oracle is focused on other aspects, such as reorganizing the module structure and deciding how to better monetize usage of the JDK, because two releases after there's still nothing new on the reactive front. That is why the next section covers a short example of reactive programming done with the Project Reactor library.

Reactive Streams Technology Compatibility Kit

When building applications that use reactive streams a lot of things can go wrong. To make sure that you are building a proper reactive application, you can use the **Reactive Streams Technology Compatibility Kit** project (also known as **TCK**) to write tests. This library contains classes that can test reactive implementations against the reactive streams specifications. TCK is intended to verify the interfaces contained in Java 9 (under `java.util.concurrent.Flow.*`) and for some reason the team that created the library decided to use TestNG as a testing library. The project sources are available on GitHub at https://github.com/reactive-streams/reactive-streams-jvm/tree/master/tck-flow, which contains four classes that have to be implemented to provide their

Flow.Publisher, Flow.Subscriber, Flow.Processor implementations for the test harness to validate. The four classes are

- FlowPublisherVerification tests Publisher implementations.

- FlowSubscriberWhiteboxVerification is used for whitebox testing Subscriber implementations and Subscription instances.

- FlowSubscriberBlackboxVerification is used for blackbox testing Subscriber implementations and Subscription instances.

- IdentityFlowProcessorVerification tests Processor implementations.

To make the purpose of each test clear, the library test methods names follow this pattern: TYPE_spec####_DESC where TYPE is one of *required, optional, stochastic, or untested*, which refers to the importance of the rule being tested, the number signs in spec#### represent the rule number with the first one being 1 for Publisher instances and the 2 for Subscribers and the DESC is a short explanation of the test purpose.

Let's see how we could test the IntPublisher that we defined previously. For this, we'll modify this class to allow the class to use a limited IntStream as a source.

```
package com.apress.bgn.ch12.jdkstreams;

import java.util.Random;
import java.util.concurrent.Flow;
import java.util.concurrent.SubmissionPublisher;
import java.util.stream.IntStream;

public class IntPublisher implements Flow.Publisher<Integer> {
    private static final Random random = new Random();
    protected final IntStream intStream;

    public IntPublisher(int limit) {
        intStream = limit == 0 ? IntStream.generate(() -> random.nextInt(150)) :
                IntStream.generate(() -> random.nextInt(150)).limit(30);
    }
    ...
}
```

CHAPTER 12   THE PUBLISH/SUBSCRIBE FRAMEWORK

We also need to provide access to the stream source of the IntStream so we can use it in our test. Now let's test our publisher by implementing the FlowPublisherVerification<Integer>.

```
package com.apress.bgn.ch12.jdkstreams;

import org.reactivestreams.tck.TestEnvironment;
import org.reactivestreams.tck.flow.FlowPublisherVerification;
import org.slf4j.Logger;
import org.slf4j.LoggerFactory;

import java.util.concurrent.Flow;

public class IntPublisherTest extends FlowPublisherVerification<Integer> {
    private static final Logger log =
        LoggerFactory.getLogger(FilterCharProcessor.class);

    public IntPublisherTest() {
        super(new TestEnvironment(300));
    }

    @Override
    public Flow.Publisher<Integer> createFlowPublisher(final long elements) {
        return new IntPublisher(30) {
            @Override
            public void subscribe(Flow.Subscriber<? super Integer>
            subscriber) {
                intStream.forEach(subscriber::onNext);
                subscriber.onComplete();
            }
        };
    }

    @Override
    public Flow.Publisher<Integer> createFailedFlowPublisher() {
        return new IntPublisher(0) {
            @Override
            public void subscribe(Flow.Subscriber<? super Integer>
            subscriber) {
```

CHAPTER 12 THE PUBLISH/SUBSCRIBE FRAMEWORK

```
            subscriber.onError(new RuntimeException(
                "There be dragons!"));
          }
        };
      }
    }
```

To make it clear, a `Publisher` implementation might not pass all the tests, because of design decisions that are specific to the application you are building. In our case, the `IntPublisher` is simplistic; and when running the `createFlowPublisher` method of all the executed tests, not many of them pass and most are ignored, as depicted in Figure 12-5.

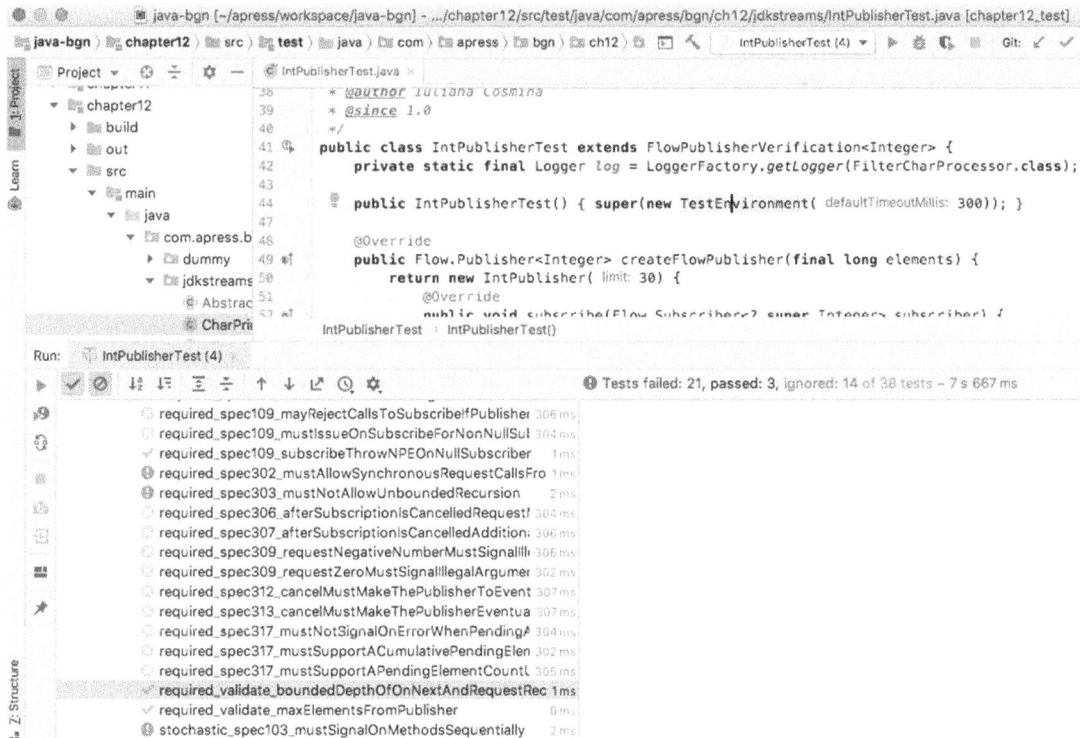

Figure 12-5. *Test NG Reactive Publisher*

The reason tests do not pass or are ignored is that the purpose of our implementation does not match those specific tests (e.g., `maySupportMultiSubscribe`, `maySignalLessThanRequestedAndTerminateSubscription`, and `mustSignalOnMethodsSequentially`).

We can test the processor and subscriber that we defined in the previous section by extending the testing classes, but I'll leave that as an exercise to you, because there is one more interesting thing I would like to cover in this chapter.

Using Project Reactor

As I've mentioned, the JDK support for reactive programming is scarce. Publishers, processors, and subscribers should function asynchronously and all that behavior must be implemented by the developer, which can be a bit of a pain. The only thing that the JDK is suitable for at the moment is providing a common interface between all the other already existing implementations. And there are a lot of them, providing a lot more useful classes for more specialized reactive components and utility methods to create and connect them easier. The one I personally fancy the most as a Spring aficionado is **Project Reactor**, the same one favored by the Spring development team.

Project Reactor is one of the first libraries for reactive programming and its classes provide a non-blocking stable foundation with efficient demand management for building reactive applications. It works with Java 8, but does provide adapter classes for JDK9 reactive streams classes that can be used within a JDK 11 project as well. Project Reactor is suitable for microservices applications and provides a lot more classes designed to make programming reactive application more practical than the JDK does. Project Reactor provides two main publisher implementations: `reactor.core.publisher.Mono<T>` which is a reactive stream publisher limited to publishing zero or one element and `reactor.core.publisher.Flux<T>`, which is a reactive stream publisher with basic flow operators.

The advantage of using Project Reactor is that we have a lot more classes and methods to work with. There are static factories that can create publishers and methods that allow operations to be chained way more easily.

The Project Reactor team did not like the name `Processor`, so the intermediary components are called **operators**.

If you look in the official documentation, you will most likely encounter the schema in Figure 12-6 .[3]

---

[3]Image source: Project Reactor Public API JavaDoc http://projectreactor.io/docs/core/release/api/reactor/core/publisher/Flux.html

CHAPTER 12   THE PUBLISH/SUBSCRIBE FRAMEWORK

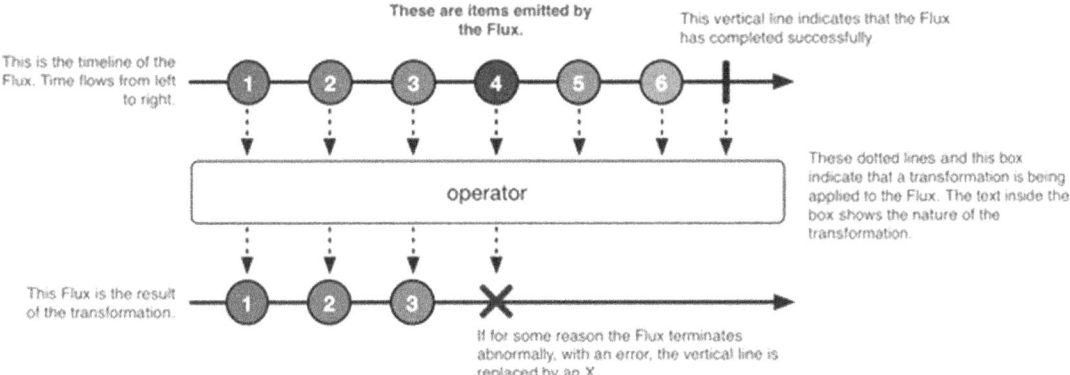

Figure 12-6. Project Reactor Flux Publisher implementation

Figure 12-6 is an abstract schema of how the `Flux` publisher works. It emits elements, throws exceptions, and completes when there are no more elements to publish. The Project Reactor team found a prettier way to draw it.

The drawing for the `Mono` implementation is similar (see http://projectreactor. io/docs/core/release/api/reactor/core/publisher/Mono.html).

But let's put that aside and look at a few code samples. Creating `Flux` instances is very easy using the multiple utility methods in this class. But before starting to publish elements, let's design a general subscriber that does nothing else than print values, because we need it to make sure our `Flux` publisher actually works.

To write a subscriber using Project Reactor API, you have multiple options. You can implement the `org.reactivestreams.Subscriber<T>` directly.

```
package com.apress.bgn.ch12.reactor;

import org.reactivestreams.Subscriber;
import org.reactivestreams.Subscription;
import org.slf4j.Logger;
import org.slf4j.LoggerFactory;

public class GenericSubscriber<T> implements Subscriber<T> {
    private static final Logger log =
        LoggerFactory.getLogger(GenericSubscriber.class);
    private Subscription subscription;
    @Override
```

```java
    public void onSubscribe(Subscription subscription) {
        if (this.subscription == null) {
            this.subscription = subscription;
            this.subscription.request(1);
        } else {
            subscription.cancel();
        }
    }

    @Override
    public void onNext(T element) {
        log.info("consumed {} ", element);
        subscription.request(1);
    }

    @Override
    public void onError(Throwable t) {
        log.error("Unexpected issue!", t);
    }

    @Override
    public void onComplete() {
        log.info("All done!");
    }
}
```

But, this can be avoided by either implementing `reactor.core.CoreSubscriber<T>`, the reactor base interface for subscribers, or even better, by extending `BaseSubscriber<T>` class, which provides basic subscriber functionality. The behavior of subscriber typical methods can be modified by overriding methods with then same name, but prefixed with hook. In the next code snippet, you can see how easy it is to write a subscriber using Project Reactor.

```java
package com.apress.bgn.ch12.reactor;

import org.slf4j.Logger;
import org.slf4j.LoggerFactory;
import reactor.core.publisher.BaseSubscriber;
```

```java
public class GenericSubscriber<T> extends BaseSubscriber<T> {
    private static final Logger log =
        LoggerFactory.getLogger(GenericSubscriber.class);

    @Override
    protected void hookOnNext(T value) {
        log.info("consumed {} ", value);
        super.hookOnNext(value);
    }
}
```

Ta, da! Now we have a subscriber class, let's create a reactive publisher that serves integers from an infinite integer stream to use an instance of this class.

```java
package com.apress.bgn.ch12.reactor;

import org.slf4j.Logger;
import org.slf4j.LoggerFactory;
import reactor.core.publisher.Flux;

import java.util.Random;
import java.util.stream.Stream;

public class ReactorDemo {
    private static final Logger log = LoggerFactory.getLogger(ReactorDemo.class);
    private static final Random random = new Random();

    public static void main(String... args) {
        Flux<Integer> intFlux = Flux.fromStream(
                Stream.generate(() -> random.nextInt(150))
        );

        intFlux.subscribe(new GenericSubscriber<>());
    }
}
```

If you run the code, you see that all the generated integer values are printed. A Flux can be created from a multiple of sources, including arrays and other publishers. And for special situations, to avoid returning a null value, an empty Flux can be created by calling the empty() method.

```
String[] names = {"Joy", "John", "Anemona", "Takeshi"};
Flux.fromArray(names).subscribe(new GenericSubscriber<>());

Flux<Integer> intFlux = Flux.empty();
intFlux.subscribe(new GenericSubscriber<>());
```

But the most awesome method is named just(..) and it is provided for Flux and Mono both. It takes one or more values and returns a publisher, a Flux or a Mono, depending on the type being called on.

```
Flux<String> dummyStr = Flux.just("one", "two", "three");
Flux<Integer> dummyInt = Flux.just(1,2,3);

Mono<Integer> one = Mono.just(1);
Mono<String> empty = Mono.empty();
```

Another method that you might find useful is concat(), which allows us to concatenate two Flux instances.

```
String[] names = {"Joy", "John", "Anemona", "Takeshi"};
Flux<String> namesFlux = Flux.fromArray(names);

 String[] names2 = {"Hanna", "Eugen", "Anthony", "David"};
Flux<String> names2Flux = Flux.fromArray(names2);
Flux<String> combined = Flux.concat(namesFlux, names2Flux);
combined.subscribe(new GenericSubscriber<>());
```

And another thing that you might like, remember how the IntPublisher class had to be slowed down using a Thread.sleep(1000) call? With Flux you do not need to do that, because there are two utility methods that combined lead to the same behavior.

```
Flux<Integer> infiniteFlux = Flux.fromStream(
     Stream.generate(() -> random.nextInt(150))
);
```

CHAPTER 12 THE PUBLISH/SUBSCRIBE FRAMEWORK

```
Flux<Long> delay = Flux.interval(Duration.ofSeconds(1));
Flux<Integer> delayedInfiniteFlux = infiniteFlux.zipWith(delay, (s,l) -> s);
delayedInfiniteFlux.subscribe(new GenericSubscriber<>());
```

The interval(..) method creates a publisher that emits long values starting with 0 incrementing at specified time intervals on the global timer. It receives an argument of type Duration. In the previous example, seconds were used. The zipWith(..) method zips the Flux instance received as a parameter. The *zip* operation is a specific stream operation that translates as both publishers emitting one element and combining these elements using a java.util.function.BiFunction<T, U, R>. In our case, the function discards the seconds element, and returns the elements of the calling stream slowed down by the generated seconds of the stream given as an argument.

The good part about the components provided by Project Reactor is that they return mostly the same type of objects they are being called on and this means they can be easily chained. A reactive piece of code equivalent to the previously JDK-based example can be written with reactor API as follows.

```
Flux<Integer> infiniteFlux = Flux.fromStream(
            Stream.generate(() -> random.nextInt(150))
    );

Flux<Long> delay = Flux.interval(Duration.ofSeconds(1));
Flux<Integer> delayedInfiniteFlux =
           infiniteFlux.zipWith(delay, (s, l) -> s);

delayedInfiniteFlux
    .filter(element -> (element >= 0 && element < 127))
    .map(item -> {
        if (item % 2 == 0 && item >= 98 && item <= 122) {
            item -= 32;
        }
        return item; })
    .map(element -> (char) element.intValue())
    .subscribe(new GenericSubscriber<>());
```

Most functions that you remember from the Stream API have been implemented for a reactive usage in Project Reactor, so if this code seems familiar, this is the reason why.

As proven with the code samples in this section, programming using reactive streams is way more practical using the Project Reactor API, so if you are ever in need of a reactive library you could consider this one first. You can find the official documentation at http://projectreactor.io/docs/core/milestone/reference/, it's good and full of examples. If ever Oracle decides to provide their own rich API for programming reactive applications using reactive streams, they will probably be too late to the table.

Summary

Reactive programming is not an easy topic, but it does seem to be the future of programming. What you have to keep in mind is that reactive implementations are quite useless with implementations that are not reactive. I mean, there is no use to design and use reactive components with non-reactive components, because you might introduce failure points and slow things down. For example, if you are using an Oracle database, there is no point in defining a repository class that returns elements using reactive streams, because an Oracle database does not support reactive access. So you add a reactive layer that provides extra implementation, because there are no real benefits in this case. But if your database of choice is MongoDB, you can use reactive programming confidently, because MongoDB databases support reactive access. Also, if you are building a web application with a ReactJS or angular interface, you can design your controller classes to provide data reactively to be displayed by the interface.

This chapter covered

- reactive programming
- the behavior of reactive streams
- JDK reactive streams support
- the Reactive Streams Technology Compatibility Kit
- Project Reactor components

CHAPTER 13

Garbage Collection

When executing Java code, objects are created, used and discarded repeatedly from memory. The process through which unused Java objects are discarded is called **memory management**, but is most commonly known as **garbage collection (GC)**. garbage collection was mentioned in **Chapter 5** as it was needed for explaining the difference between primitive and reference types, but in this chapter we go deep *under the hood* of the JVM to resolve yet another mystery of a running Java application.

When the Java garbage collector does its job properly, the memory is cleaned up, before new objects are created and it does not fill up, so you could say that the memory allocated to a program is *recycled*. Programs of low complexity, like the ones we've been writing so far do not require that much memory to function, but depending on their design (remember recursivity?) they could end up using more memory than it is available to them. In Java, the garbage collector runs automatically. In more low level languages, like **C** there is no automatic memory management, and the developer is responsible for writing the code to allocate memory as needed, and deallocate it when it is no longer needed. Although it seems practical to have automatic memory management, the garbage collector can be a problem if managed incorrectly. So this chapter provides enough information about the garbage collector to make sure it is used wisely, and when problems arise, at least you have a good place to start solving them.

Although some ways to tune the garbage collector will be covered in this chapter introduced, keep in mind that garbage collection tuning should not be necessary, a program should be written in such a way that creates only objects that are needed to perform its function and references are managed correctly, estimations should be done before the application is put into production and the maximum amount of memory needed by it should be known and configured before that. If the memory allocated to a Java program is not enough, there is usually something rotten in the implementation.

© Iuliana Cosmina 2018
I. Cosmina, *Java for Absolute Beginners*, https://doi.org/10.1007/978-1-4842-3778-6_13

CHAPTER 13 GARBAGE COLLECTION

Garbage Collection Basics

The Java automatic garbage collection is one of the major features of the of the Java Programming language. The JVM is a virtual machine used to execute Java programs. As the Java programs uses resources of the system the JVM is running on top of, it has to have a way to release those resources safely. This job is done by the garbage collector. To understand the garbage collector, we have to take a look at the JVM architecture.

Oracle Hotspot JVM Architecture

Over the years, some big companies have produced their own variations of the JVM (e.g., IBM) and now that Java is moving into the module age and rapid delivery style, more and more companies appear that maintain a specific version of the JDK/JVM (e.g., Azul), because migration to 9+ is difficult for big applications with legacy dependencies. Also, another important economic factor here is that Java is paid software as of January 1, 2019, and developers have to pay for the software they have developed, which many are going to call *bait and switch* as Oracle first said, *Here it is free now use it,* and then, *Now that you have developed your Java apps, you have to pay us.* If you think about it, it is the same thing as buying the ground your house is built on, and the bricks, and everything else. Because the only thing that is yours when building a Java application is the application purpose and the design; everything you are using to build it is part of the JDK, which belongs to Oracle.

Still, Oracle's HotSpot is by far the most commonly used JVM when it comes to garbage collection. This JVM provides a mature set of garbage collection options. Its architecture is depicted in Figure 13-1.

CHAPTER 13 GARBAGE COLLECTION

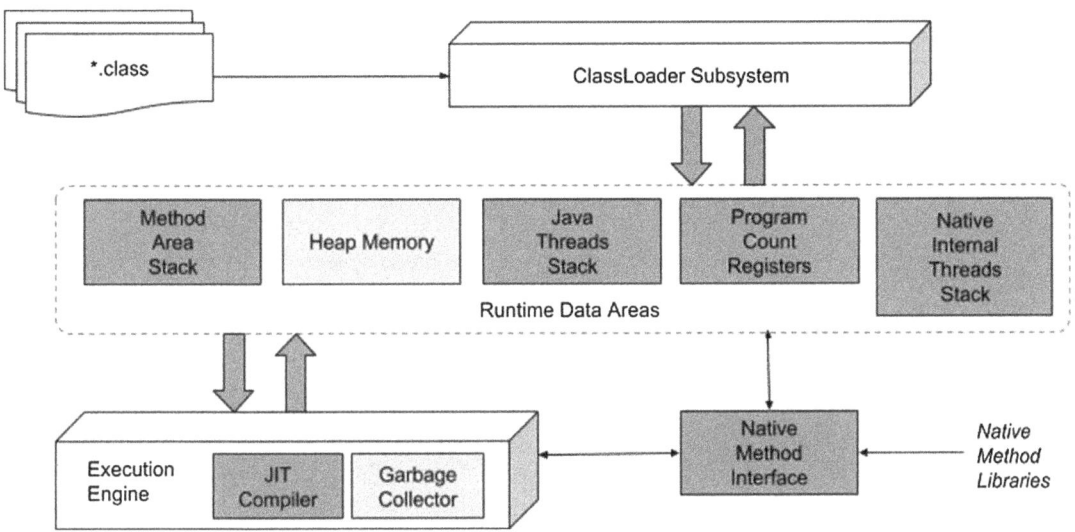

Figure 13-1. *Oracle HotSpot JVM Architecture*

The *heap* memory area is managed by the garbage collector, and is split into multiple zones. Objects are moved between these zones until being discarded. The zones are depicted in Figure 13-2 for old-fashioned garbage collector and the new style of garbage collector that follows the model of the current default garbage collector used by the JDK, the G1GC, introduced in JDK 8.

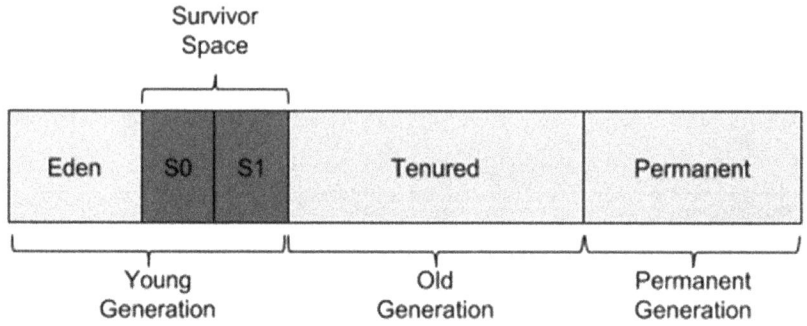

Figure 13-2. *The heap structure*

The G1GC is a next-generation garbage collector designed for machines with a lot of resources, which is why its approach to the partitioning of the heap is different. Its heap is partitioned into a set of equal-sized heap regions, each a contiguous range of virtual memory. Certain region sets are assigned the same roles (Eden, survivor, old) as in the older collectors, but there is not a fixed size for them. This provides greater flexibility in memory usage. You can read more about the different types of garbage collectors in the next section, for now the focus remain on the *heap* memory and its zones that are called *generations*.

When an application is running, objects created by it are stored in the **young generation** area. When an object is created it starts its life in a subdivision of this generation called **the Eden space**. When the Eden space is filled, this triggers a **minor garbage collection(minor GC run)** that cleans up this area of unreferenced objects, and moves referenced objects to the first survivor space (S0). The next time the Eden space is filled, another minor GC run is triggered, which again deletes unreferenced objects, and referenced objects are moved to the next survivor space (S1). The objects in S0 have been there for a minor GC run, so their age is incremented and they are moved to S1, so S0 and the Eden can be cleaned up. At the next minor GC run,

CHAPTER 13 GARBAGE COLLECTION

the operation is repeated again, but this time referenced objects are saved into the empty S0 and the older objects form S1, have their age incremented and moved here as well, so the S1 and Eden can be cleaned up. After the objects in survivor space reach a certain age, they are moved to the **old generation** space during minor GC runs.

The previous steps are depicted in Figure 13-3, and the o1 and o2 objects age until they are moved to the old generation area.

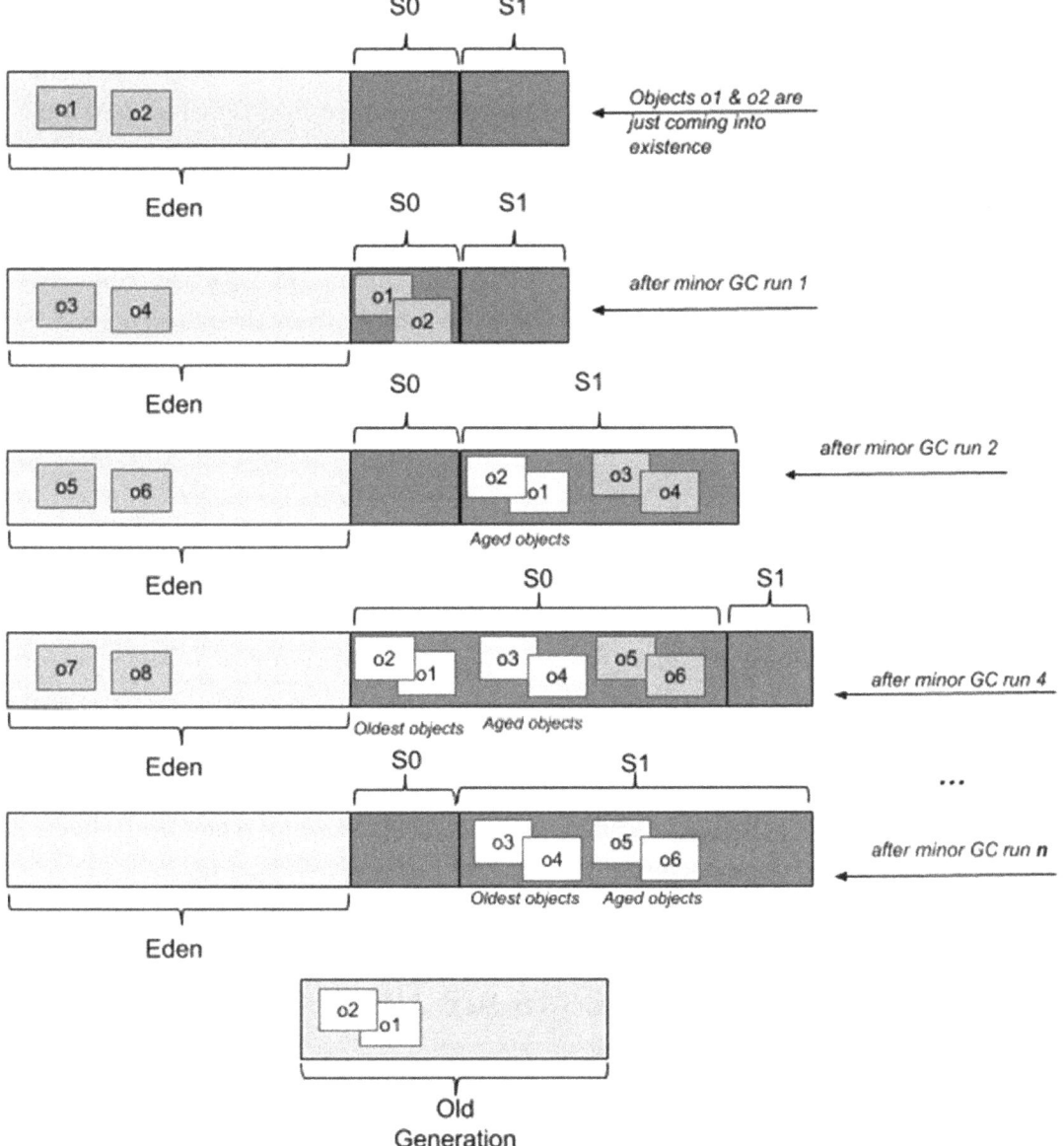

Figure 13-3. *Minor GC runs in the young generation space*

563

CHAPTER 13   GARBAGE COLLECTION

Minor GC collections happen until the old generation space is filled, which is when a **major garbage collection(major GC run)** is triggered. That deletes unreferenced objects, compacts the memory, and moves objects around so that the empty memory left is one big compact space. The *minor garbage collection* event is a *stop the world* event, this process basically takes over the run of the application and pauses its execution so it can free the memory. As the young generation space is small in size (as you see in the next section), the application pause is usually negligible. If no memory can be reclaimed from the young generation area after a minor GC run takes place, a major GC run is triggered.

The **permanent generation** area is reserved for JVM metadata such as classes and methods. This area is cleaned too from time to time to remove classes that are no longer used in the application. The cleanup of this area is triggered when there is no more available memory left in the heap.

The garbage collection process described up to this paragraph is specific to generational garbage collectors, such as the G1GC; but before JDK 8, garbage collection was done using an older garbage collector that uses an algorithm called **Concurrent Mark Sweep**. This type of garbage collector runs in parallel with the application marking used and unused zones of memory. Then it would delete unreferenced objects and would compact the memory into a contiguous zone by moving objects around. This process is inefficient and time consuming. Because as more and more objects were created, the garbage collection takes more and more time to be performed. But as most objects are short-lived, this is not really a problem. So the CMS garbage collector was OK for a while.

The G1GC has a similar approach, but after the mark phase is finished, G1 focuses on regions that are mostly empty to recover as much unused memory as possible. That is why this garbage collector is also called *garbage-first*. G1 also uses a pause prediction model to decide how many memory regions can be processed based on the pause time set for the application. Objects from the processed region are copied to a single region of the heap, thus realizing a memory compaction at the same time. Also G1GC does not have a fixed size for the eden and survivor spaces, it decides their size after every minor GC run.

How Many Garbage Collectors Are There?

The Oracle HotSpot JVM provides the following types of garbage collectors:

- **serial collector**: All garbage collection events are conducted serially in one thread. Memory compaction happens after each garbage collection.

- **parallel collector**: Multiple threads are used for minor garbage collection. A single thread is used for a major garbage collection and Old Generation compaction.

- **CMS (Concurrent Mark Sweep)**: Multiple threads are used for minor garbage collection using the same algorithm as the parallel GC. Major garbage collection is multithreaded, but CMS runs concurrently alongside application processes to minimize *stop the world* events. No memory compaction is done. This type of garbage collector is suitable for applications requiring shorter garbage collection pauses and that can afford to share processor resources with the garbage collector while the application is running. This was the default garbage collector until Java 8, when G1 was introduced officially as default.

- **G1 (garbage first)**: Introduced in Oracle JDK 7, update 4, was designed to permanently replace the CMS GC and is suitable for applications that can operate concurrently with CMS collector, need memory compaction, need more predictable GC pause durations, and do not require a much larger heap. The G1 collector is a server-style garbage collector, targeted for multiprocessor machines with large memories, and considering that most laptops now have at least eight cores and 16 GB RAM it is suitable for them. G1 has both concurrent (runs along with application threads—e.g., refinement, marking, cleanup) and parallel (multithreaded—e.g., stop the world) phases. Full garbage collections are still single threaded, but if tuned properly your applications should avoid full garbage collections.

- **Epsilon no-op collector**: Introduced in Java 11, this type of collector is a dummy GC that does not recycle or clean up the memory. When the heap is full, the JVM shuts down. This type of collector can be used for performance tests, for memory allocation analysis, VM interface testing, and extremely short-lived jobs and applications that are very limited when it comes to memory usage and developers must estimate the application memory footprint as precisely as possible.

CHAPTER 13 GARBAGE COLLECTION

OK, I've listed the garbage collector types, but how do we know which is the one used by our local JVM? There is more than one way. The simplest way is to add the -verbose:gc as a VM option when running a simple main class. Using Java 11 JDK, without any other configuration will print this in the console.

[0.016s][info][gc] Using G1

So it's clear; G1 garbage collector is used. We can see the details of this garbage collector by adding another VM option: -Xlog:gc*[1].

```
[0.012s][info][gc,heap] Heap region size: 1M
[0.017s][info][gc       ] Using G1
[0.017s][info][gc,heap,coops] Heap address: 0x0000000700000000, size: 4096 MB,
    Compressed Oops mode: Zero based, Oop shift amount: 3
[0.216s][info][gc,heap,exit ] Heap
[0.216s][info][gc,heap,exit ]  garbage-first heap   total 262144K, used 3072K
    [0x0000000700000000, 0x0000000800000000)
[0.216s][info][gc,heap,exit ]   region size 1024K, 4 young (4096K), 0
survivors (0K)
[0.216s][info][gc,heap,exit ]  Metaspace       used 7246K, capacity 7364K,
committed 7680K, reserved 1056768K
[0.216s][info][gc,heap,exit ]   class space    used 663K, capacity 709K,
committed 768K, reserved 1048576K
```

Now we can see the heap maximum size (4096 GB), the memory region size (1 M), and the size and occupation for each generation.

But we can tell JVM to use any of the garbage collectors listed previously by using their specific VM options.

- -XX:+UseSerialGC to use the serial GC (in this case, adding -verbose:gc -Xlog:gc* as the VM option) produces the following output.

---
[1]This VM option replaces deprecated -XX:+PrintGCDetails

CHAPTER 13 GARBAGE COLLECTION

[0.012s][info][gc] Using Serial
[0.012s][info][gc,heap,coops] Heap address: 0x0000000700000000, size: 4096 MB,
    Compressed Oops mode: Zero based, Oop shift amount: 3 [0.209s][info][gc,heap,exit] Heap
[0.209s][info][gc,heap,exit] def new generation   total 78656K, used 9794K
    [0x0000000700000000, 0x0000000705550000, 0x0000000755550000)
[0.209s][info][gc,heap,exit]   eden space 69952K, 14% used
    [0x0000000700000000, 0x0000000700990808, 0x0000000704450000)
[0.209s][info][gc,heap,exit]   from space 8704K,   0% used
    [0x0000000704450000, 0x0000000704450000, 0x0000000704cd0000)
[0.209s][info][gc,heap,exit]   to   space 8704K,   0% used
    [0x0000000704cd0000, 0x0000000704cd0000, 0x0000000705550000)
[0.209s][info][gc,heap,exit] tenured generation   total 174784K, used 0K
    [0x0000000755550000, 0x0000000760000000, 0x0000000800000000)
[0.209s][info][gc,heap,exit]   the space 174784K,   0% used
    [0x0000000755550000, 0x0000000755550000, 0x0000000755550200, 0x0000000760000000)
[0.209s][info][gc,heap,exit] Metaspace   used 7246K, capacity 7364K, committed 7680K,
    reserved 1056768K
[0.209s][info][gc,heap,exit]   class space   used 663K, capacity 709K, committed 768K,
    reserved 1048576K

- -XX:+UseParallelGC to use the serial GC (in this case, adding -verbose:gc -Xlog:gc* as the VM option) produces the following output.

[0.017s][info][gc] Using Parallel
[0.017s][info][gc,heap,coops] Heap address: 0x0000000700000000, size: 4096 MB,
    Compressed Oops mode: Zero based, Oop shift amount: 3 [0.231s][info][gc,heap,exit] Heap

567

```
[0.231s][info][gc,heap,exit ] PSYoungGen      total 76288K, used 9175K
 [0x00000007aab00000, 0x00000007b0000000, 0x0000000800000000)
[0.231s][info][gc,heap,exit ]   eden space 65536K, 14% used
  [0x00000007aab00000,0x00000007ab3f5f38,0x00000007aeb00000)
[0.231s][info][gc,heap,exit ]   from space 10752K, 0% used
  [0x00000007af580000,0x00000007af580000,0x00000007b0000000)
[0.231s][info][gc,heap,exit ]   to   space 10752K, 0% used
  [0x00000007aeb00000,0x00000007aeb00000,0x00000007af580000)
[0.231s][info][gc,heap,exit ] ParOldGen      total 175104K, used 0K
 [0x0000000700000000, 0x000000070ab00000, 0x00000007aab00000)
[0.231s][info][gc,heap,exit ]   object space 175104K, 0% used
  [0x0000000700000000,0x0000000700000000,0x000000070ab00000)
[0.231s][info][gc,heap,exit ] Metaspace      used 7245K, capacity
7364K, committed 7680K,
    reserved 1056768K
[0.231s][info][gc,heap,exit ] class space   used 663K, capacity
709K, committed 768K,
    reserved 1048576K
```

- -XX:+UseConcMarkSweepGC to use the serial GC (in this case, adding -verbose:gc -Xlog:gc* as the VM option) produces the following output.

```
[0.018s][info][gc] Using Concurrent Mark Sweep
[0.018s][info][gc,heap,coops] Heap address: 0x0000000700000000,
size: 4096 MB,
   Compressed Oops mode: Zero based, Oop shift amount: 3 [0.260s]
   [info][gc,heap,exit ] Heap
[0.260s][info][gc,heap,exit ] par new generation   total 78656K,
used 9794K
  [0x0000000700000000, 0x0000000705550000, 0x0000000729990000)
[0.260s][info][gc,heap,exit ]   eden space 69952K,  14% used
  [0x0000000700000000, 0x0000000700990850, 0x0000000704450000)
[0.260s][info][gc,heap,exit ]   from space 8704K,   0% used
  [0x0000000704450000, 0x0000000704450000, 0x0000000704cd0000)
[0.260s][info][gc,heap,exit ]   to   space 8704K,   0% used
  [0x0000000704cd0000, 0x0000000704cd0000, 0x0000000705550000)
```

CHAPTER 13   GARBAGE COLLECTION

```
[0.260s][info][gc,heap,exit ]   concurrent mark-sweep generation total
174784K,
     used 0K [0x0000000729990000, 0x0000000734440000,
     0x0000000800000000)
[0.260s][info][gc,heap,exit ]   Metaspace       used 7336K,
capacity 7428K, committed 7680K,
     reserved 1056768K
[0.260s][info][gc,heap,exit ]   class space     used 668K, capacity
709K, committed 768K,
     reserved 1048576K
```

- -XX:+UseG1GC, the default garbage collector, we already covered this one

- -XX:+UseEpsilonGC, the no-op garbage collector. If you see a message in the console that asks you to also add the -XX:+UnlockExperimentalVMOptions before the option to enable the Epsilon garbage collector, do so. This VM option is needed to unlock experimental features and at the moment when this book is being written this garbage collector is an experimental feature. Adding -verbose:gc -Xlog:gc* as the VM option produces the following output.

```
[0.013s][info][gc] Resizeable heap; starting at 256M, max: 4096M,
step: 128M
[0.013s][info][gc] Using TLAB allocation; max: 4096K
[0.013s][info][gc] Elastic TLABs enabled; elasticity: 1.10x
[0.013s][info][gc] Elastic TLABs decay enabled; decay time: 1000ms
[0.013s][info][gc] Using Epsilon
[0.013s][info][gc,heap,coops] Heap address: 0x0000000700000000, size:
4096 MB,
  Compressed Oops mode: Zero based, Oop shift amount: 3 [0.213s]
  [info][gc,heap,exit ] Heap
[0.213s][info][gc,heap,exit ] Epsilon Heap
[0.213s][info][gc,heap,exit ] Allocation space:
[0.213s][info][gc,heap,exit ]   space 262144K,   1% used
     [0x0000000700000000, 0x000000070030e8f0, 0x0000000710000000)
[0.213s][info][gc             ] Total allocated: 3130 KB
[0.213s][info][gc             ] Average allocation rate: 14691 KB/sec
```

569

CHAPTER 13 GARBAGE COLLECTION

The data printed for these garbage collectors has common elements, such as the size of heap, which is always 256 MB at the start of the application and has a maximum size of 4096 MB on my system. The eden and the young generation differ; the G1 uses 4096 KB for the young generation, whereas the CMS requires 78656 KB (a lot more).

The most interesting is the Epislon garbage collector, because as expected, it does not have a heap split into generation areas, as this type of garbage collector does not perform garbage collection at all. The **TLAB** is an acronym for *thread local allocation buffer*, which is the memory area where objects are stored. Only bigger objects are stored outside of TLABs. The TLABs are dynamically resized during the execution for each thread individually. So, if a thread allocates very much, the new TLABs that it gets from the heap increase in size. The minimum size of a TLAB can be controlled using two VM options: -XX:MinTLABSize.

For the small empty class that we ran with the previous VM options, this output is not really relevant, but you can play with these options when running the code from the next sections, because that is when the statistics printed here have some relevance.

Also, there is a VM option named -XX:+PrintCommandLineFlags that can be used when a class is run to depict configurations of the garbage collector: the number of threads it uses, heap size, and so on.

-XX:G1ConcRefinementThreads=8
-XX:GCDrainStackTargetSize=64
-XX:InitialHeapSize=268435456
-XX:MaxHeapSize=4294967296
-XX:+PrintCommandLineFlags
-XX:ReservedCodeCacheSize=251658240
-XX:+SegmentedCodeCache
-XX:+UseCompressedClassPointers
-XX:+UseCompressedOops -XX:+UseG1GC

Most of these VM options have obvious names that allow a developer to infer what they are used for. Also, there is the official documentation from Oracle. If you ever need to dissect the Oracle memory management, the article at www.oracle.com/technetwork/java/javase/tech/index-jsp-136373.html is very good.

Working with GC from the Code

For most applications garbage collection is not something a developer must really take into account. The JVM starts a GC thread that does its job without hindering the execution of the application (usually). But for developers who want to have more than Java basic skills, understanding how the Java garbage collection works and how can it be tuned is a must. The first thing that a developer must accept about Java garbage collection is that it cannot be controlled at runtime. As you see in the next section, there is a way to suggest the JVM that some memory cleaning is necessary, but there is no guarantee that a memory cleaning be performed. The only thing that can be done is specify some code to be run when an object is discarded.

Using the finalize() Method

Every Java class is automatically a subclass of the JDK `java.lang.Object` class. This class is at the root of the JDK hierarchy and is the root of all classes in an application. It provides a few useful methods that can be extended or overwritten to implement behavior specific to the subclass. The `equals()`, `hashcode()` and `toString()` were already mentioned. The `finalize()` method was deprecated in Java 9, but it was not removed from the JDK. This method is called by the garbage collector when there are no longer any references to that object in the code. Before we move forward, let's look at the following piece of code.

```
package com.apress.bgn.ch13;

import com.apress.bgn.ch13.util.NameGenerator;
import org.slf4j.Logger;
import org.slf4j.LoggerFactory;

import java.time.LocalDate;
import java.util.Random;

public class Main {
    private static final Logger log = LoggerFactory.getLogger(Main.class);
    private static NameGenerator nameGenerator = new NameGenerator();
    private static final Random rnd = new Random();
```

CHAPTER 13 GARBAGE COLLECTION

```
    public static void main(String... args) {
        while (true) {
            genSinger();
         }
    }

    private static void genSinger() {
        Singer s = new Singer(nameGenerator.genName(),
            rnd.nextDouble(), LocalDate.now());
        log.info("JVM created: {}", s.getName());
    }
}
```

The action performed by the code should be clear, even without knowing how the what the `NameGenerator` or the `Singer` class look like. The main method calls the `genSinger()` method in an infinite loop. This means that an infinite number of `Singer` instances is created. So, what happens? Will the code run? For how long? If you were able to reply these questions in your mind, my work here is complete. You can stop reading the book now. ☺

In **Chapter 5**, there were some figures representing the memory contents for a small program. Figure 13-4 represents how the Java heap and stack memory might look during the execution of the previous program.

CHAPTER 13   GARBAGE COLLECTION

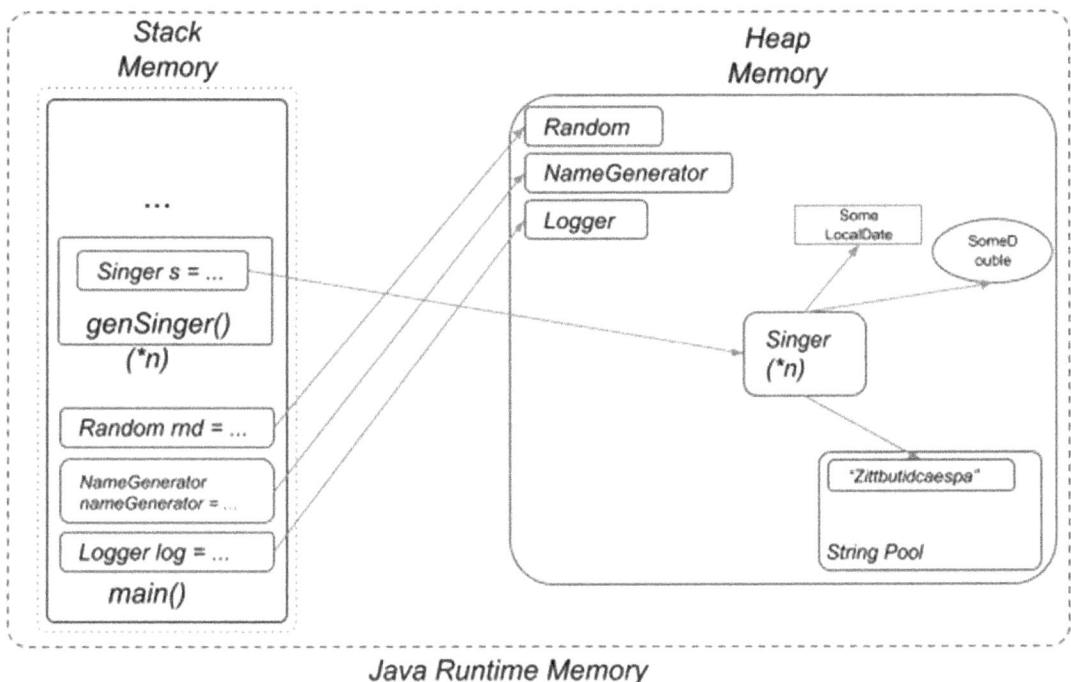

Figure 13-4. Java stack and heap memory during execution of the Main.class

Of course, only one genSinger() call was represented and only one Singer instance. When the main(..) method is called, references to the static instances are created, which will be relevant to the program until the end of its execution. Then, genSinger() methods is called repeatedly. Each of these methods has its own stack where it saves references to the objects created within the context of that method, in this case the Singer instance. This reference is used to print the name of the Singer instance that was created in the body of this method. Then the method terminates without returning the reference. This means that the instance that was created is no longer necessary, as it was created to be used only in the context of this method. When the execution of the genSinger() method ends, the reference to the Singer instance is discarded from the stack. The Singer instance still exists, in the heap memory, but can no longer be accessed from the program, thus it is no longer necessary to it. It now keeps a memory block occupied with its own contents, its references to other instances, in this case, a String, a Double and a LocalDate.

Considering that the genString() method is called an infinite number of times (in Figure 13-4 this is represented with the (*n)), more Singer instances are created, which keep the memory occupied. At some point, the program becomes unable to create others because there is no memory available.

This is where the garbage collector comes into the picture. The `Singer` instances that are no longer being referenced from the program (and thus unreachable) are considered garbage. Now you know where the name came from. These instances are no longer necessary and the memory can be safely cleaned up. The garbage collector is a cleanup thread that runs in parallel with the main execution thread. It occasionally deletes the unreferenced objects from the heap memory. And because the `finalize()` method is still available for use, we overwrite it for the `Singer` type to print a log message so that we can see when the garbage collector is destroying an instance, because before deleting an object from the heap memory the `finalize()` method of the object is called. The following code snippet depicts the `Singer` instance.

```java
package com.apress.bgn.ch13;

import org.slf4j.Logger;
import org.slf4j.LoggerFactory;

import java.io.*;
import java.time.LocalDate;
import java.util.Objects;

public class Singer implements Serializable {
    private static final Logger log = LoggerFactory.getLogger(Singer.class);
    private final long birthtime;

    private String name;
    private Double rating;
    private LocalDate birthDate;

    public Singer(String name, Double rating, LocalDate birthDate) {
        this.name = name;
        this.rating = rating;
        this.birthDate = birthDate;
        this.birthtime = System.nanoTime();
    }

    public String getName() {
        return name;
    }
```

```java
    @Override
    protected void finalize() throws Throwable {
        try {
            long deathtime = System.nanoTime();
            long lifespan =  (deathtime - birthtime) / 1_000_000_000;
            log.info("GC Destroyed: {} after {} seconds",  name, lifespan);
        } finally {
            super.finalize();
        }
    }
}
```

The **birthtime** field was added to calculate the time that passes between when an instance constructor is called and the time that the garbage collector calls the `finalize()` method; basically we are calculating the lifespan of the instance. As the time is counted in nanoseconds, we are dividing the difference by 10^9 to get the time in seconds.

The code sample used in this section gives the garbage collector a lot of work to do, as every `Singer` instance being created is being used very little before being discarded. If you run the code you will see a lot of log messages in the console, first a lot of messages about objects being created, but if you wait, messages about objects being discarded will appear as well. All output is directed to a file, because the IntelliJ IDEA console is based on a buffer that resets from time to time to prevent the editor from crashing. You have to stop the program manually, because the `while(true)` loop never ends, because its condition never evaluates to `false`. After you stopped the program, you notice a log file at the following location: `/chapter13/out/gc.log`. If you don't, modify the IntelliJ IDEA launcher for this class, add the `-Dlogback.configurationFile=chapter13/src/main/resources/logback.xml` VM option, and run it again.

The `gc.log` contents should look a lot like the snippet depicted next.

```
INFO  c.a.b.c.Main - JVM created: Ngvuamtkrfeavt
INFO  c.a.b.c.Main - JVM created: Weeqhwssuddcatm
INFO  c.a.b.c.Main - JVM created: Zrtfrjsjwhwlzh
INFO  c.a.b.c.Main - JVM created: Ymsdzcpkatryscf
INFO  c.a.b.c.Main - JVM created: T dkqgjujyz moj
INFO  c.a.b.c.Main - JVM created: Jjqzzetnwzi itu
INFO  c.a.b.c.Main - JVM created: Iuivwasfailc fi
```

```
INFO  c.a.b.c.Singer - GC Destroyed: Qtzr gwe ifujbn after 1 seconds
INFO  c.a.b.c.Main - JVM created: Djlui rbftvepf
INFO  c.a.b.c.Singer - GC Destroyed: Wzdwcc cqhisbbq after 0 seconds
INFO  c.a.b.c.Main - JVM created: Caqw iddgborajm
INFO  c.a.b.c.Singer - GC Destroyed: Ntiarzdzbhzolnn after 4 seconds
INFO  c.a.b.c.Main - JVM created: Crtayuigzccufqj
INFO c.a.b.c.Singer - GC Destroyed: Irsovagekpc hca after 0 seconds
INFO c.a.b.c.Singer - GC Destroyed: Hqkzodfrnhuhqwk after 0 seconds
INFO c.a.b.c.Singer - GC Destroyed: Norlcmkzjvkhiev after 0 seconds
INFO c.a.b.c.Singer - GC Destroyed: Gbjknkffngfaghf after 0 seconds
INFO c.a.b.c.Singer - GC Destroyed: Mhkn zpfogcc jm after 0 seconds
INFO c.a.b.c.Main - JVM created: Cningetinfmbunh
INFO c.a.b.c.Main - JVM created: Ipwomacdhzoywce
INFO c.a.b.c.Main - JVM created: Ydobktlzwcqvkfl
INFO c.a.b.c.Main - JVM created: Abjggajzbifghpa
INFO c.a.b.c.Main - JVM created: Hnwdvhnkwc rmbz
INFO  c.a.b.c.Main - JVM created: Hvcwmekbyhjfncc
INFO c.a.b.c.Singer - GC Destroyed: Rbefgb cmvlnfgm after 1 seconds
INFO c.a.b.c.Singer - GC Destroyed: Kusmvtkkikjtzzj after 1 seconds
INFO c.a.b.c.Singer - GC Destroyed: Ouybfhckbtkichc after 1 seconds
INFO c.a.b.c.Singer - GC Destroyed: Djzozlssperibka after 1 seconds
...
```

When you have the file, you can open it and start analyzing its contents. But because IntelliJ might not open such a big file, try to open it with a specialized text editor like Notepad++ or Sublime. Or, if you use a Unix/Linux operating system, open your console and use the grep command like this:

```
grep -a 'seconds' gc.log
```

This displays all log entries printed when the `finalize()` method is called. Then, you can select the name of an instance can do something like this:

```
$ grep -a 'Lybhpococssuoz' gc.log
INFO c.a.b.c.Main - JVM created: Lybhpococssuoz
INFO c.a.b.c.Singer - GC Destroyed: Lybhpococssuoz after 7 seconds
```

CHAPTER 13   GARBAGE COLLECTION

The time it takes for a Singer instance to be deleted from the heap varies, and this is because the GC is called randomly, the developer has no control over it. There is a way to explicitly request garbage collection to be done, well two ways. You can call the following.

System.gc() or
Runtime.getRuntime().gc();

This doesn't mean that the GC immediately start cleaning up the memory; it is more like a suggestion to the JVM that it should make an effort to recycle unused objects and reclaim unused memory, because it is needed.

Now, back to the finalize() method. It was marked as deprecated in Java 9. This method is meant to be overridden by classes that handle resources that are stored outside of the heap. The example is the I/O handling classes used to read resources as files or URLs and databases. The finalize() would be called by the JVM when an object can no longer be accessed by any alive thread of the running application to make sure that those resources were released and available for other external and unrelated programs to use.

** In older versions of Apache Tomcat (a Java based web server), there was a bug on Windows related to release of resources. When the server crashed or stopped, it couldn't be restarted because some of its log files were not released properly, and the new server instance could not get access to them to start writing the new log entries.

With the introduction of the java.lang. AutoCloseable interface in JDK 1.7, the finalize() method became less and less used. Also, another problem with this method is that the JVM cannot guarantee which thread call this method for any given object. So any thread that has access to it can call it, and we might end up with resources being released while the object is still needed. Also, what happens if the custom implementation is not correct, throws exceptions or does not releases resources properly? The finalize() method should be called only once by the JVM, but this cannot be guaranteed. Another downside is that finalize() calls, are not automatically chained, so an implementation of a finalize() method, must always explicitly call the finalize() method of the superclass. And another one for you: once finalize()

was called, there is no way to stop the method from executing or undo its effect, so you are basically left with a reference to an object that no longer has access to its resources. As you probably figured out by now, there is a lot of freedom given to the developer when it comes to implementing this method, and this means there is a lot of room for errors to happen.

This is why the finalization mechanism in Java is flawed and was deprecated in JDK 9 to discourage its use. Improper `finalize()` implementations could lead to: memory leaks (memory contents are not discarded), deadlocks (resource is blocked by two processes) and hangs(process is in a waiting state it cannot go out of). But, in order to help with memory management the `java.lang.ref.Cleaner` class was introduced. But before getting into that, I must show you how to check out the status of your memory programmatically.

Heap Memory Statistics

The `Runtime` class is useful when trying to interact with the internals of the JVM while a program is running. Its `gc()` method can be called to suggest to the JVM that the memory should be cleaned. A few chapters ago we used methods in this class to start processes from the Java code. There are three methods in this class that are useful to see the status of the memory assigned to a Java program.

- `runtime.maxMemory()` returns the maximum amount of memory the JVM attempts to use for its heap, if needed. The value returned by this method varies from machine to machine and is being set implicitly to a quarter of the total existing RAM memory on the machine, unless is set it is set explicitly by using the JVM option `-Xmx` followed by the amount of memory, (e.g., `-Xmx8G` allows the JVM to use a maximum of 8 GB of memory).

- `runtime.totalMemory()` returns the total amount of memory of the JVM. The value returned by this method varies from machine to machine too and is implementation-dependent, unless explicitly set by using the JVM option `-Xms` followed by the amount of memory (e.g., `-Xms1G` tells the JVM that is the initial size of its heap memory should be 1 GB of memory).

- `runtime.freeMemory()` returns an approximation of the amount of free memory for the Java virtual machine.

CHAPTER 13 GARBAGE COLLECTION

Using the runtime.totalMemory() and the runtime.freeMemory() methods, we can write some code to check how much of our memory is occupied at various times during the execution of the program. For this we create a class named MemAudit that uses the current logger to print memory values.

```
package com.apress.bgn.ch13.util;

import org.slf4j.Logger;

public class MemAudit {
    private static final long MEGABYTE = 1024L * 1024L;
    private static final Runtime runtime = Runtime.getRuntime();

    public static void printBusyMemory(Logger log) {
        long memory = runtime.totalMemory() - runtime.freeMemory();
        log.info("Occupied memory: {} MB", (memory / MEGABYTE));
    }

    public static void printTotalMemory(Logger log) {
        log.info("Total Program memory: {} MB", (runtime.totalMemory()/
        MEGABYTE));
        log.info("Max Program memory: {} MB", (runtime.maxMemory()/MEGABYTE));
    }
}
```

And the methods in this class are called during the execution of our program as it follows.

```
package com.apress.bgn.ch13;

import com.apress.bgn.ch13.util.NameGenerator;
import org.slf4j.Logger;
import org.slf4j.LoggerFactory;

import java.time.LocalDate;
import java.util.Random;
import static com.apress.bgn.ch13.util.MemAudit.printTotalMemory;
import static com.apress.bgn.ch13.util.MemAudit.printBusyMemory;
```

CHAPTER 13 GARBAGE COLLECTION

```java
public class Main {
    private static final Logger log = LoggerFactory.getLogger(Main.class);
    private static NameGenerator nameGenerator = new NameGenerator();
    private static final Random random = new Random();

    public static void main(String... args) {
        printTotalMemory(log);
        int count =0;
        while (true) {
            genSinger();
            count++;
            if (count % 1000 == 0) {
                printBusyMemory(log);
            }
        }
    }

    private static void genSinger() {
        Singer s = new Singer(nameGenerator.genName(),
            random.nextDouble(), LocalDate.now());
        log.info("JVM created: {}", s.getName());
    }

}
```

Now, after we delete the old log file, we should run it again, and leave it for a little while. And because it is impossible again to see the output, we'll use the grep method to extract all lines containing the memory word, and the result should look quite similar to the next listing.

```
$ grep -a 'memory' gc.log
INFO   c.a.b.c.Main - Total Program memory: 256 MB
INFO   c.a.b.c.Main - Max Program memory: 4096 MB
INFO   c.a.b.c.Main - Occupied memory: 5 MB
INFO   c.a.b.c.Main - Occupied memory: 3 MB
INFO   c.a.b.c.Main - Occupied memory: 4 MB
INFO   c.a.b.c.Main - Occupied memory: 5 MB
INFO   c.a.b.c.Main - Occupied memory: 5 MB
```

```
INFO  c.a.b.c.Main - Occupied memory: 4 MB
INFO  c.a.b.c.Main - Occupied memory: 4 MB
INFO  c.a.b.c.Main - Occupied memory: 7 MB
INFO  c.a.b.c.Main - Occupied memory: 8 MB
INFO  c.a.b.c.Main - Occupied memory: 8 MB
INFO  c.a.b.c.Main - Occupied memory: 9 MB
INFO  c.a.b.c.Main - Occupied memory: 7 MB
INFO  c.a.b.c.Main - Occupied memory: 3 MB
INFO  c.a.b.c.Main - Occupied memory: 15 MB
INFO  c.a.b.c.Main - Occupied memory: 7 MB
...
```

The max memory is 4096MB, which means my machine has a total of 16 GB of RAM, and the occupied memory is very little, not even close to the initial 256MB the JVM is given to use. If we want to see real memory being occupied we can modify the genSinger() method to return the created references and add them to a list.

```java
package com.apress.bgn.ch13;

import com.apress.bgn.ch13.util.NameGenerator;
import org.slf4j.Logger;
import org.slf4j.LoggerFactory;

import java.time.LocalDate;
import java.util.ArrayList;
import java.util.List;
import java.util.Random;

import static com.apress.bgn.ch13.util.MemAudit.printBusyMemory;
import static com.apress.bgn.ch13.util.MemAudit.printTotalMemory;

public class MemoryConsumptionDemo {
    private static final Logger log =
            LoggerFactory.getLogger(MemoryConsumptionDemo.class);
    private static NameGenerator nameGenerator = new NameGenerator();
    private static final Random random = new Random();
```

CHAPTER 13 GARBAGE COLLECTION

```java
    public static void main(String... args) {
        printTotalMemory(log);
        List<Singer> singers = new ArrayList<>();
        for (int i = 0; i < 1_000_000; ++i) {
            singers.add(genSinger());
            if (i % 1000 == 0) {
                printBusyMemory(log);
            }
        }
    }

    private static Singer genSinger() {
        Singer s = new Singer(nameGenerator.genName(),
            random.nextDouble(), LocalDate.now());
        log.info("JVM created: {}", s.getName());
        return s;
    }
}
```

After running the program, we can actually see the memory being used increasing gradually. A look in the log filtered magically by the *grep* command shows us that the program keeps the memory occupied until its end, since the references now are saved in to the List<Singer> instance.

```
$ grep -a 'memory' gc.log
INFO  c.a.b.c.MemoryConsumptionDemo - Total Program memory: 256 MB
INFO  c.a.b.c.MemoryConsumptionDemo - Max Program memory: 4096 MB
INFO  c.a.b.c.MemoryConsumptionDemo - Occupied memory: 13 MB
INFO  c.a.b.c.MemoryConsumptionDemo - Occupied memory: 16 MB
INFO  c.a.b.c.MemoryConsumptionDemo - Occupied memory: 18 MB
INFO  c.a.b.c.MemoryConsumptionDemo - Occupied memory: 21 MB
INFO  c.a.b.c.MemoryConsumptionDemo - Occupied memory: 4 MB
INFO  c.a.b.c.MemoryConsumptionDemo - Occupied memory: 6 MB
INFO  c.a.b.c.MemoryConsumptionDemo - Occupied memory: 9 MB
INFO c.a.b.c.MemoryConsumptionDemo - Occupied memory: 12 MB
INFO c.a.b.c.MemoryConsumptionDemo - Occupied memory: 15 MB
```

```
INFO c.a.b.c.MemoryConsumptionDemo - Occupied memory: 17 MB
INFO c.a.b.c.MemoryConsumptionDemo - Occupied memory: 20 MB
INFO c.a.b.c.MemoryConsumptionDemo - Occupied memory: 23 MB
INFO c.a.b.c.MemoryConsumptionDemo - Occupied memory: 26 MB
INFO c.a.b.c.MemoryConsumptionDemo - Occupied memory: 28 MB
...
INFO c.a.b.c.MemoryConsumptionDemo - Occupied memory: 428 MB
INFO c.a.b.c.MemoryConsumptionDemo - Occupied memory: 430 MB
INFO c.a.b.c.MemoryConsumptionDemo - Occupied memory: 433 MB
```

And as we print the occupied memory every 1000 steps, we can draw the conclusion that 1000 Singer instances occupy approximatively 2 MB. The code no longer uses an infinite loop to generate instances, if it would do that, at some point in time the program will abruptly crash throwing the following exception.

```
Exception in thread "main" java.lang.OutOfMemoryError: Java heap space
        at chapter.thirteen/com.apress.bgn.ch13.MemoryConsumptionDemo
            .genSinger(MemoryConsumptionDemo.java:64)
        at chapter.thirteen/com.apress.bgn.ch13.MemoryConsumptionDemo
            .main(MemoryConsumptionDemo.java:55)
```

Remember the value returned by the runtime.maxMemory()? On my machine, it was 4096MB. If I look in the console, right before the exception, I will see the following.

```
INFO  c.a.b.c.MemoryConsumptionDemo - Occupied memory: 4094 MB
INFO  c.a.b.c.MemoryConsumptionDemo - Occupied memory: 4094 MB
INFO  c.a.b.c.MemoryConsumptionDemo - Occupied memory: 4095 MB
INFO  c.a.b.c.MemoryConsumptionDemo - Occupied memory: 4095 MB
INFO  c.a.b.c.MemoryConsumptionDemo - Occupied memory: 4095 MB
```

So the JVM was struggling to create another Singer instance, but there was no more memory left. The last value printed before the exception was 4095MB, which is 1 MB less than 4096MB the maximum amount of memory that the JVM was allowed to use. So the poor JVM crashed because there was no more heap memory available. If a program ever ends like that, the problem is always in the design of the solution. Also the values for total and maximum memory for the JVM can influence the behavior of the GC as well.

The -Xms and -Xmx are important because they decide the initial and the maximum size of the heap memory. Configured properly they can increase performance, but when unsuitable values are used they have the adverse effect. For example, never set an initial size for the heap too small, because if there is not enough space to fit all objects created by the application the JVM has to allocate more memory, rebuilding the heap basically. So if this happens a few times during the application run, the overall time consumption is affected. The maximum size for the heap is very important, allocating too little might cause an application crash, allocating too much might hinder other programs from running. Deciding these values is usually done through repeated experiments and starting with JDK 11, the new **Epsilon** garbage collector comes in handy for this purpose.

If you want to learn more about GC tuning, the best documentation is the official one at `https://docs.oracle.com/javase/10/gctuning/toc.htm`.

So, now that you know what to expect from the GC, let's look at other methods of customizing its behavior so problems are avoided.

Using Cleaner

After the `finalize()` method is taken out of the JDK, if needed, classes can be developed to implement `java.lang.AutoCloseable` and provide an implementation for the `close()` method and make sure you use your objects in a `try-with-resources` statement. But if you want to avoid implementing the interface there is another way, use a `java.lang.ref.Cleaner` object. This class can be instantiated and objects can be registered to it together with an action to perform when the object is being discarded by the garbage collector. Using a `Cleaner` instance, the previous code can be rewritten as depicted in the next code listing.

```
package com.apress.bgn.ch13.cleaner;

import com.apress.bgn.ch13.util.NameGenerator;
import org.slf4j.Logger;
import org.slf4j.LoggerFactory;

import java.lang.ref.Cleaner;
import java.time.LocalDate;
import java.util.Random;

import static com.apress.bgn.ch13.util.MemAudit.printBusyMemory;
import static com.apress.bgn.ch13.util.MemAudit.printTotalMemory;
```

```java
public class CleanerDemo {
    private static final Logger log = LoggerFactory.getLogger(CleanerDemo.
    class);
    public static final Cleaner cleaner = Cleaner.create();
    private static NameGenerator nameGenerator = new NameGenerator();

    public static void main(String... args) {
        printTotalMemory(log);
        int count = 0;
        for (int i = 0; i < 100_000; ++i) {
            genActor();
            count++;
            if (count % 1000 == 0) {
                printBusyMemory(log);
                System.gc();
             }
        }
        //filling memory with arrays of String to force GC to clean up
        Actor objects
        for (int i = 1; i <= 10_000; i++) {
            String[] s = new String[10_000];
            try {
                Thread.sleep(1);
            } catch (InterruptedException e) {
            }
         }
    }

    private static Cleaner.Cleanable genActor() {
        Actor a = new Actor(nameGenerator.genName(), LocalDate.now());
        log.info("JVM created: {}", a.getName());
        Cleaner.Cleanable handle = cleaner.register(a,
            new ActorRunnable(a.getName(), log));
        return handle;
    }
```

```java
    static class ActorRunnable implements Runnable {
        private final String actorName;
        private final Logger log;

        public ActorRunnable(String actorName, Logger log) {
            this.actorName = actorName;
            this.log = log;
         }

        @Override
        public void run() {
            log.info("GC Destroyed: {} ", actorName);
        }
    }
}
```

Because we wanted to make it easier for you to browse the code, as all these sources are part of the same project, we are using here a class modelling an `Actor` instead of a `Singer`, but no worries, the implementation is quite similar. The `Cleaner` instance has a method named `register(..)` that is called to register the action to be performed when the object is cleaned. The action to be performed is specified as a `Runnable` instance, and the decision to create a class by implementing it, `ActorRunnable` in this example, was taken so we could save the name of the object to be destroyed into a field, without keeping a reference to the object to be destroyed; otherwise, the `Cleaner.Cleanable` handle would not be used by the GC during the execution of the program, as the object would appear as if it still had references to it.

The `cleaner.register(..)` method returns an instance of type `Cleaner.Cleanable` that explicitly performs the action by calling the `clean()` method. If you run the preceding code, the printed log would look similar to this:

```
INFO   c.a.b.c.c.CleanerDemo - Total Program memory: 256 MB
INFO   c.a.b.c.c.CleanerDemo - Max Program memory: 4096 MB
INFO   c.a.b.c.c.CleanerDemo - JVM created: Vgyfr uayznrtu
INFO   c.a.b.c.c.CleanerDemo - JVM created: Cowplkbzshwudhb
INFO   c.a.b.c.c.CleanerDemo - JVM created: Ijwqydlvzldequd
INFO   c.a.b.c.c.CleanerDemo - JVM created: Jfnjgopzmrdacim
INFO   c.a.b.c.c.CleanerDemo - JVM created: Tnnwizmtipgmvsz
```

```
INFO  c.a.b.c.c.CleanerDemo - JVM created: Wffuzkzrhrfjrsj
INFO  c.a.b.c.c.CleanerDemo - JVM created: Vlfsvprbtfytdzm
...
INFO  c.a.b.c.c.CleanerDemo - Occupied memory: 16 MB
INFO  c.a.b.c.c.CleanerDemo - JVM created: Vrjflltszakvzgp
INFO  c.a.b.c.c.CleanerDemo - JVM created: Ofu ugogizfwkci
...
INFO c.a.b.c.c.CleanerDemo - GC Destroyed: Dvhwsacmrytebor
INFO c.a.b.c.c.CleanerDemo - GC Destroyed: Sutwbmtegacrgvz
INFO c.a.b.c.c.CleanerDemo - GC Destroyed: Posqthfridobvit
INFO c.a.b.c.c.CleanerDemo - GC Destroyed: Bebmsdraphkpdbs
INFO c.a.b.c.c.CleanerDemo - GC Destroyed: Jrgekcgrkhcfkfv
INFO c.a.b.c.c.CleanerDemo - GC Destroyed: Ugffjeapvbjbqwz
INFO c.a.b.c.c.CleanerDemo - GC Destroyed: Mzkgezhkejfgc e
INFO c.a.b.c.c.CleanerDemo - JVM created: Rlamcgwypkktkah
INFO  c.a.b.c.c.CleanerDemo - GC Destroyed: Tefdzrt zqilo
...
```

So, the same result as using `finalize()` was obtained, but without implementing a deprecated method. As a good practice to take from here, if you are writing your application using Java 9+, avoid using `finalize()`, because this method is clearly on the path of being removed. Use `Cleaner` and you might have less of a hassle when upgrading the Java version your application is using.

Preventing GC from Deleting an Object

In the two previous sections, we focused on objects that are eligible for garbage collection. But in an application, there are objects that should not be discarded while the program runs, because they are needed. The most obvious references in our classes that were discarded only at the end of the execution were the static fields, and they are final, so they cannot be reinitialized.

```java
private static final Logger log = LoggerFactory.getLogger(CleanerDemo.
class);
public static final Cleaner cleaner = Cleaner.create();
private static NameGenerator nameGenerator = new NameGenerator();
private static final Random random = new Random();
```

CHAPTER 13 GARBAGE COLLECTION

The problem with these static values is that they occupy the memory. What if you need a big Map that contains a dictionary that is not needed when the application starts? To solve this, enter the Singleton design pattern. The Singleton pattern is a specific design of a class that ensures the class can only be instantiated once during the execution of the program. This is done by hiding the constructor (declare it private), and declaring a private static reference of the class type and a static method to return it. There is more than one way to write a class according to the Singleton pattern, but the most common way is depicted in the next code listing.

```java
package com.apress.bgn.ch13.util;

import org.slf4j.Logger;
import org.slf4j.LoggerFactory;

import java.util.HashMap;
import java.util.Map;

public final class SingletonDictionary {
    private static final Logger log =
        LoggerFactory.getLogger(SingletonDictionary.class);

    private static SingletonDictionary instance = new SingletonDictionary();

    private Map<String, String>  dictionary = new HashMap<>();

    private SingletonDictionary(){
        // init dictionary
        log.info("Starting to create dictionary: {}", System.
        currentTimeMillis());
        final NameGenerator keyGen = new NameGenerator(20);
        final NameGenerator valGen = new NameGenerator(200);
        for (int i = 0; i < 100_000; ++i) {
            dictionary.put(keyGen.genName(), valGen.genName());
         }
        log.info("Done creating dictionary: {}", System.currentTimeMillis());
    }
```

```
    public synchronized static SingletonDictionary getInstance(){
        return instance;

    }
}
```

In the code, we simulated a dictionary with 100,000 entries, all generated by a modified version of the `NameGenerator` class. Log messages were printed in its constructor to be really obvious when the instance is created. There are four things you have to remember about the **Singleton** pattern.

- The constructor must be private, as it should not be called outside the class.

- The class must contain a static reference to an object of its type that can be initialized in place by calling the private constructor.

- A method to retrieve this instance must be defined, so it has to be `static`.

- The method to retrieve the static instance also has to be `synchronized` so no two threads can call it at the same and gain access to the instance, because the core idea of the `Singleton` pattern is to allow the class to be instantiated only once during the duration of the execution of the program and ensure that no concurrent access is allowed, as it might lead to unexpected behavior. Also, there is an implementation version that initializes the instance in the method that retrieves it, so concurrent access might lead to more than one instance being created.

In a singleton class, a static reference to an instance is created and this static reference prevents the garbage collector from cleaning up this instance during the execution of the program. To test this, we'll write a main class that declares a `Cleaner` instance, and register a `Cleanable` for the `SingletonDictionary` instance. The main method creates a lot of `String` arrays to fill up the memory to convince the GC to delete the `SingletonDictionary` instance, and we'll even set its own reference to it to null.

```
package com.apress.bgn.ch13;

import com.apress.bgn.ch13.util.SingletonDictionary;
import org.slf4j.Logger;
import org.slf4j.LoggerFactory;
```

CHAPTER 13 GARBAGE COLLECTION

```java
import java.lang.ref.Cleaner;

public class SingletonDictionaryDemo {
    public static final Cleaner cleaner = Cleaner.create();
    private static final Logger log =
        LoggerFactory.getLogger(SingletonDictionaryDemo.class);

    public static void main(String... args) {
        log.info("Testing SingletonDictionary...");

        //filling memory with arrays of String to force GC
        for (int i = 1; i <= 10_000; i++) {
            String[] s = new String[10_000];
            try {
                Thread.sleep(1);
            } catch (InterruptedException e) {
            }
         }

        SingletonDictionary singletonDictionary =
                SingletonDictionary.getInstance();

        cleaner.register(singletonDictionary, ()-> {
            log.info("Cleaned up the dictionary!");
        });
        // we delete the reference
        singletonDictionary = null;

        //filling memory with arrays of String to force GC
        for (int i = 1; i <= 10_000; i++) {
            String[] s = new String[10_000];
            try {
                Thread.sleep(1);
            } catch (InterruptedException e) {
            }
        }
        log.info("DONE.");
    }
}
```

If we run the code and expect to see the "Cleaned up the dictionary!" message in the console, we're expecting in vain. That static reference in the SingletonDictionary will not allow GC to touch that object until the program ends. The static reference that we have in class SingletonDictionary is also called a **strong** reference, because it prevents the object from being discarded from memory.

Using Weak References

If there are strong references, we should be able to use weak references for objects that we want cleaned, right? Right. In Java, there are three classes that can be used to create a reference to an object that does not protect that object from garbage collection. This is useful for objects that are too big, and it makes it inefficient to keep them in memory. With this kind of objects it is worth the cost of time consumed to be reinitialized, because keeping them in memory would slow done the overall performance of the application.

The three classes are:

- java.lang.ref.SoftReference<T>: objects referred by these type of references are cleared at the discretion of the garbage collector in response to memory demand. Soft references are most often used to implement memory-sensitive caches.

- java.lang.ref.WeakReference<T>: objects referred by these type of references do not prevent their referents from being made finalizable, finalized, and then reclaimed. Weak references are most often used to implement canonicalizing mappings. Canonicalizing mapping refers to containers where weak references can be kept in and can be accessed by other objects, but their link to the container, does not prevent them from being collected.

- java.lang.ref.PhantomReference<T>: objects referred by these type of references are enqueued after the collector determines that their referents may otherwise be reclaimed. Phantom references are most often used to schedule post-mortem cleanup actions.

Our SingletonDictionary contains a Map<> that is the big object stored in memory. This map can be wrapped in a WeakReference, and we can write some logic that it should be reinitialized if it is not there when accessed. Because we need to access the map, the implementation changes a little, aside from wrapping the Map into a WeakReference. The new class, named WeakDictionary, is depicted in the following code listing.

```java
package com.apress.bgn.ch13.util;

import org.slf4j.Logger;
import org.slf4j.LoggerFactory;

import java.lang.ref.WeakReference;
import java.util.HashMap;
import java.util.Map;

public class WeakDictionary {
    private static final Logger log =
        LoggerFactory.getLogger(WeakDictionary.class);
    private static WeakDictionary instance = new WeakDictionary();
    private WeakReference<Map<Integer, String>> dictionary;
    private static Cleaner cleaner;

    private WeakDictionary() {
            cleaner = Cleaner.create();
        dictionary = new WeakReference<>(initDictionary());
    }

    public synchronized String getExplanationFor(Integer key) {
        Map<Integer, String> dict = dictionary.get();
        if (dict == null) {
            dict = initDictionary();
            dictionary = new WeakReference<>(dict);
            return dict.get(key);
        } else {
            return dict.get(key);
        }
    }

    public synchronized static WeakDictionary getInstance() {
        return instance;
    }
```

```
    private Map<Integer, String> initDictionary() {
        Map<Integer, String> dict = new HashMap<>();
        log.info("Starting to create dictionary: {}", System.
        currentTimeMillis());
        final NameGenerator keyGen = new NameGenerator(20);
        final NameGenerator valGen = new NameGenerator(200);
        for (int i = 0; i < 100_000; ++i) {
            dict.put(i, valGen.genName());
        }
        log.info("Done creating dictionary: {}", System.
        currentTimeMillis());
         cleaner.register(dict, ()-> log.info("Cleaned up the
         dictionary!"));
        return dict;
    }
}
```

The getExplanationFor accesses the map and gets the value corresponding a key. But before doing that, we have to check if the Map is still there. This is done by calling the get() method on the dictionary reference that is of type WeakReference<Map<Integer, String>>. If the map was not collected by the GC, the key is extracted and returned; otherwise, the Map is reinitialized and the weak reference is re-created.

The Cleaner instance was moved in the WeakDictionary class, and registered a Cleanable for the Map so we can see the map being collected. So, how do we test this? In a similar way we tested SingletonDictionary.

```
  package com.apress.bgn.ch13;

import com.apress.bgn.ch13.util.WeakDictionary;
import org.slf4j.Logger;
import org.slf4j.LoggerFactory;

public class WeakDictionaryDemo {
    private static final Logger log =
        LoggerFactory.getLogger(WeakDictionaryDemo.class);
```

CHAPTER 13   GARBAGE COLLECTION

```java
    public static void main(String... args) {
        log.info("Testing WeakDictionaryDemo...");

        //filling memory with arrays of String to force GC
        for (int i = 1; i <= 10_000; i++) {
            String[] s = new String[10_000];
            try {
                Thread.sleep(1);
            } catch (InterruptedException e) {
            }
         }
        WeakDictionary weakDictionary = WeakDictionary.getInstance();

        //filling memory with arrays of String to force GC
        for (int i = 1; i <= 10_000; i++) {
            String[] s = new String[10_000];
            try {
                Thread.sleep(1);
            } catch (InterruptedException e) {
            }
         }
        log.info("Getting val for 3 =  {}", weakDictionary.
        getExplanationFor(3));
        log.info("DONE.");
    }
}
```

So, after retrieving the WeakDictionary reference, a lot of String arrays are created to force GC to delete the map from memory. After that, we try to access the problematic map. Will it work?

```
INFO   c.a.b.c.WeakDictionaryDemo - Testing WeakDictionaryDemo...
INFO   c.a.b.c.u.WeakDictionary - Starting to create dictionary: 1536633126455
INFO   c.a.b.c.u.WeakDictionary - Done creating dictionary: 1536633126701
INFO   c.a.b.c.u.WeakDictionary - Cleaned up the dictionary!
```

```
INFO   c.a.b.c.u.WeakDictionary - Starting to create dictionary: 1536633139512
INFO   c.a.b.c.u.WeakDictionary - Done creating dictionary: 1536633139742
INFO   c.a.b.c.WeakDictionaryDemo - Getting val for 3 =  Ingermy...
INFO   c.a.b.c.WeakDictionaryDemo - DONE.
```

The log proves this works. And not only that, we can see the map being discarded by GC and then reinitialized when needed. This is the power of soft references.

Although the garbage collection process is un-deterministic, because it cannot be controlled much from the code, a Java program cannot tell it to start, pause or stop, but using the appropriate VM options we can control the resources it has and from the code using the proper implementation we can tell it what to collect or not and most of the times this is enough.[2]

Garbage Collection Exceptions and Causes

If objects cannot be discarded from the memory, an exception of type `OutOfMemoryError` is thrown. I'm not sure if you noticed, but this is not actually an exception. The exception class hierarchy was mentioned in **Chapter 5**. If you remember, in that hierarchy there was a class named `java.lang.Error` that implements `java.lang.Throwable`. These types of objects are thrown by a program when there is a critical issue that the program cannot recover from. The following is the full hierarchy of the `java.lang.OutOfMemoryError`.

```
java.lang.Object
    java.lang.Throwable
        java.lang.Error
            java.lang.VirtualMachineError
                java.lang.OutOfMemoryError
```

So, `OutOfMemoryError` is one of those ugly things you do not want thrown when your program is running, because this means your program is no longer running. In this case, it is not running because it has no memory left to store new objects being created.

---

[2] If you want more details about GC this article is on point: https://www.oracle.com/technetwork/tutorials/tutorials-1876574.html

This error is being thrown by the JVM when anything goes wrong when doing memory management. Although, the most common cause is that the heap memory is depleted, there are other causes.

When heap memory allocated to the JVM is depleted, the error has the following message:

```
Exception in thread "main" java.lang.OutOfMemoryError: Java heap space
```

But there is another message that you might see.

```
Exception in thread "main" java.lang.OutOfMemoryError: GC Overhead Limit Exceeded
```

This message is still related to the heap size. The error is thrown with this message when the data for the program barely fits the size of the heap, so the heap is almost full, which allows the GC to run, but because it cannot redeem any memory, the GC keeps running, and it is hindering the normal execution of the application. This message is added to the error when the GC spends 98% of execution time and the application spends the other 2%.

These two are the most common error messages you see when GC cannot do its job properly for whatever reason. A complete list can be found at `https://docs.oracle.com/javase/8/docs/technotes/guides/troubleshoot/memleaks002.html`, but since most GC issues relate to the heap size, G1GC mostly throws errors with the *Java heap space* message.

Summary

This section ends this book. When it comes to the Java ecosystem, there are a lot of books and tutorials on the Internet. This book only scratches the surface to give you a good starting point as a Java developer. The whole team that worked on it hopes it satisfies your needs and sparks your curiosity to find out more. Just keep in mind that there is no panacea solution to make sure the memory is always managed right regardless of the application scope. If you get in trouble, experimentation is always a step in determining the right collector for your JVM.

This chapter has covered the following topics.

- what garbage collection is and the steps involved
- how the heap memory is structured
- how many types of garbage collectors there are in the Oracle HotSpot JVM and how can we switch between them
- how to view a garbage collector configurations and statistics using VM options
- how to view the garbage collection in action using finalize and Cleaner
- how to stop the garbage collector from collecting important objects
- how to create objects that are easily collected using soft references

Index

A

Abstract Window Toolkit (AWT), 9, 14, 420–422
Access modifiers
    compilation error, 62
    member-level accessors, 60, 63
    package-private modifier, 61
    public class, 60
    top-level, 60
anonymous class, 285
anyMatch(..) method, 309
Apache Tomcat, 577
Arrays, 92
Assignment operator (=), 209–210
AudioType, 299

B

Binary operators, 217
Binary representation, 168–169
Binary serialization, 503–507
Bitwise operators, 227
    AND, 228, 230
    NOT, 227–228
    OR, 230–231
    XOR, 231–232
Boxing, 190
Bubble sort algorithm, 256, 267
Building blocks
    access modifiers, 60
    class, 56
    fields, 56
    JAR, 58
    library, 59
    methods, 56
    modules, 60
    package-info.java, 57

C

Checked exceptions, 143–144
Classes
    abstraction
        Actor class, 123
        Human class, 121–122
        Java compiler error, 122
        Musician class, 123
        parent class/superclass, 122
        subclass, 122
        UML diagram, IntelliJ IDEA, 123–124
    constructors, 117–120
    data encapsulation, 111–114
    fields, 108–110
    instantiation, 107–108
    methods, 115–117
    variables, 110–111
Comments, 107
Compact String, 187

INDEX

Concurrent mark sweep (CMS), 565
Constructors
    Actor class, 120
    Human instance, 117–119
    Musician class, 120
    polymorphism, 119
    return statement, 118
Control flow statements
    flowchart elements, 244
    if-else
        code, 248
        flowchart, Complex if-else, 247
        flowchart, missing else branch, 246
        IntelliJ IDEA launcher, 249
        parameters, 249
    using exception, 277–279
    using try catch, 277–278

D

Data encapsulation, 111–114
Debugging
    assertions
        java.lang.AssertionError, 346–347
        rules, 348
        VM options, 346
    breakpoints, 317
    definition, 317
    IntelliJ IDEA breakpoints, 348–349
    Java tools
        jcmd, 353–355
        jconsole, 355–358
        JMC, 359–362
        jps, 351–352
    logging
        main(..) method, 324
        merge sort, 319–322
        sort(..) method, 325
        sorting class hierarchy, 319
        System.out.print class family, 318
        System.out.print method, 322–324
    logging with JUL
        FileHandler class, 330
        IntelliJ IDEA, 334
        java.util.logging.ConsoleHandler, 329
        java.util.logging.Level class, 336
        java.util.logging.
            SimpleFormatter, 329
        logging libraries, 325
        logging output, 331
        log messages, 335
        MergeSort class, 326, 328
        SimpleFormatter, 330
        SorterJulDemo class, 326
        SortingJulDemo class, 329, 332–333
        StreamFormatter class, 329
        StringBuilder, 326
        WARNING, 335, 336
        XMLFormatter, 330
    SLF4J and Logback, 337
        ch.qos.logback.core.
            ConsoleAppender class, 340
        ch.qos.logback.core.FileAppender
            class, 341
        ch.qos.logback.core.rolling.
            RollingFileAppender, 342–343
        ch.qos.logback.core.rolling.
            RollingPolicy, 342
        configuration file, XML/Groovy, 339
        info.debug(..) logs, 339
        info.error(..) logs, 338
        info.warn(..) logs, 339
        logging implementation, 337, 339
        log.info(..) logs, 339
        LogManager, 337
        log.trace(..) logs, 339

    MergeSort class, 340
    <rollingPolicy> element, 343
    SortingSlf4jDemo class, 340–341
    SortingSlf4jDemo.main(..)
      method, 344
    StringBuilder, 344
    <timeBasedFileNamingAnd
      TriggeringPolicy>, 343
  SortingSlf4jDemo class, 349–351
  techniques, 317
Deserialization, 503
distinct() method, 306
Documentation, Javadoc
  @author tag, 398
  classes and variables, 397
  @deprecated tag, 403
  Doclet API, 407
  expression RTFM, 407
  Gradle javadoc task, 403–406
  HTML tags, 398
  IntelliJ IDEA, 406–407
  IntSorter interface, 398
  @link tag, 400, 402
  method declarations, 400–401
  Optional<T> interface, 399–400
  @param tags, 401
  @return tags, 401
  special tags, 397
  @throws tag, 402

E

Eden space, 562
Elvis operator, 241
empty() method, 295
Enums
  comment() method, 128
  field values, 126

  Gender enum, 125
  getComment(), 127
  Human class, 128, 129
  private modifier, 125
Epsilon no-op collector, 565
equals() method, 224
Exceptions
  checked, 143–144
  compiler error, 144
  definition, 139
  EmptyPerformerException, 143
  finally block, 144
  hierarchy, 140
  NullPointerException, 143
  PerformerGenerator, 142–143
  RuntimeException, 141
  StackOverFlowError, 140–141
  swallowing, 141
  throwable, 140
  try/catch block, 143–144
  unchecked, 143
Exchangeable Image File Format (EXIF)
      data, 514–517
Explicit type conversion, 212, 214

F

File handlers
  accept(..) method, 476
  canRead() and canWrite(), 475
  createNewFile(), 476
  createTempFile(prefix, suffix), 477
  deleteOnExit(), 477
  description, 471
  exists(), 477
  FileFilter, 476
  FilenameFilter, 476
  getAbsolutePath(), 473

INDEX

File handlers (*cont.*)
    getName(), 474
    getParent(), 474
    IOException, 478
    isFile(), 473
    isHidden(), 475
    lambda expressions, 476
    length(), 474
    list() method, 475
    listFiles(), 475
    pathnames, 473, 475
    printStats(..) method, 471–472
    rename(f), 478
    SecurityException, 477
    String value, 471
    URI, 474
FileInputStream, 489–492
FileOutputStream, 499–502
FilterCharProcessor, 539
Finite streams, 289
flatMap(..) method, 304–305
Flattening, 305
Floating-point types, 170
Flow.Processor, 549
Flow.Publisher, 549
FlowPublisherVerification
    <Integer>, 550
Flow.Subscriber, 549
forEach(..) method, 285, 301
Functional interfaces, 138

G

Garbage collection (GC)
    Cleaner instance, 584, 585
    cleaner.register() method, 586–587
    CMS, 564–565, 568
    code

    finalize() methods, 571, 574–575, 577
    genSinger() methods, 572, 573
    grep command, 576
    IntelliJ IDEA launcher, 575–576
deleting object, 587
eden space, 562
Epsilon no-op collector, 565, 569
exceptions and causes, 595–596
G1, 565, 569
garbage first (G1), 564
generations, 562
genSinger() method, 581–582
go() method, 578
grep method, 580, 582
head memory, 578, 583
heap structure, 561–562
Java heap and stack memory, 572–573
java.lang.ref.Cleaner object, 584
old generation space, 563
Oracle Hotspot JVM
    architecture, 560–561
parallel collector, 565, 567
permanent generation space, 564
runtime.freeMemory() method, 578
runtime.maxMemory()
    method, 578, 583
runtime.totalMemory() method, 578
serial collector, 564, 566
SingletonDictionary
    instance, 589, 590
Singleton pattern, 588–589
strong reference, 591
TLAB, 570
VM option, 566–568, 570
weak references, 591, 593–595
-Xms and -Xmx, 584
young generation space, 562–563

INDEX

Garbage first (G1), 565
generate(..) method, 290
Generics, 145–147
Git, 24, 38
Gradle, 24, 37–38, 85
Gradle multimodule-level structure, 87–88
Gradle project, 86, 88–89

H

Heavyweight components, 14
Hello World! class
    class declaration, 90
    configuration, 93–94
    IntelliJ IDEA editor, 89
    java.util.List, 94
    main() method, 90-92, 94
    package declaration, 90
    println() method, 95, 96

I

Identifiers, 106
Imperative programming, 537
Installation
    Download JDK button, 26
    Git, 38
    Gradle, 37–38
    JDK 8 *vs.* contents comparison, 28
    JDK 10 *vs.* JRE contents, 28
Integer primitives
    byte, 169
    int, 169
    long, 170
    short, 169
Integrated development environment (IDE), 23
Integration tests, 371
IntelliJ IDEA, 23, 41, 62, 88–89, 249

IntelliJ IDEA, HelloWorld project
    build menu, 76
    build project option, 76
    change directory, 79
    commands execution, 80
    compile, 77, 80
    configuration, 72
    create new project option, 70–71
    directory structure, 82
    HelloWorld.java file, 74, 79
    Java class, 75, 78–79
    Java module, 71
    Java 11 project, 71
    JRE, 78
    language level, 73
    menu option, 76
    modules, 73–74
    move class, 82
    object types, 76
    package option, 81
    project SDK, 73
    project settings, 73
    project view, 72
    refactor button, 82
    sandbox, 72
    src directory, 75
    terminal button, 79
Interactions, Java components, 531
Interface Publisher<T>, 534
Interfaces
    vs. abstract classes, 134
    annotations, 129, 137–139
    API, 135
    Artist interface, 133, 135
        compiler errors, 136
        isCreative method, 137
        Java broken hierarchy, 136
        Performer class, 135–136

INDEX

Interfaces (*cont.*)
    default methods, 135
    definition, 129
    diamond class hierarchy, 130
    marker, 129
    Musician and Actor classes, 129–130
    normal, 129
    Performer class, 129–133
Interface Subscriber<R>, 534
Intermediate operations, 282, 298
Internationalization
    contents of resource files, 444
    description, 442
    JavaFX, 446–449
    locale, 442
    property names, 445
    Resource Bundle IntelliJ IDEA editor, 444–445
    resource files, 443, 449
    Stage.close(), 449–450
International Software Testing Qualifications Board (ISTQB), 370
Interning, 184
IntPublisher class, 556
IntStream interface, 292

J, K

Jar hell, 60, 69
Java
    applications, 21
    code, 2–3
    conventions, 4
    Gradle, 3, 20, 22
    Hello World!, 2
    history, 1–2
    machine code, 9–10
    Node.js, 21
    portable, 8–9
    real applications in, 2
    Sun Microsystems
        automatic memory management, 7
        Duke, 5
        Green Team, 5
        Java logo, 7
        logo, 6
        multithreaded execution, 7
        portability, 7
        security, 7
    version 9, 21
Java Archives (JARs), 58
Java Architecture for XML Binding (JAXB), 507–510
Java building blocks, 59, 66
Java code, 100
Java coding conventions, 106
Java editors, 62
JavaFX
    applications, 526–529
    BorderPane, 438
    CellFactory, 439–440
    colored ComboBox demo, 441
    ComboBox, 438–440
    components, 432
    CSS style elements, 438
    graphics, 434
    GUI library, 432
    java.lang.IllegalAccessException, 433
    launch(...) method, 434
    ListCell declaration, 441
    modules, 432
    nodes, 434
    Oracle, 432
    Prism, 433
    properties, 434
    Quantum toolkit, 434

start(..) methods, 435
Swing and AWT, 433
TextArea, 438–439
Window Demo, 435–437
JAVA_HOME environment variable
   on Linux, 36–37
   on macOS, 35–36
   on Windows system
      dialog window, 31
      menu item, 30
      Path variable, 33
      system variable, 32, 34
Java IDE
   GitHub user, 42–43
   IntelliJ IDEA
      configure Git plugin, 41
      configure Gradle plugin, 41
      configure plugins dialog section, 40
      Gradle project view, 46
      IDE Feature Trainer plugin, 42
      java-for-absolute-beginners project, 43–45
   JetBrains, 39
Java keywords, 147–150
Java Media API
   BaseMultiResolutionImage class, 519–523
   BufferedImage, 517
   checkSize(..), 524
   EXIF data, 514–517
   getResolutionVariant(), 521, 522, 524–525
   image classes hierarchy, 513–514
   image file, 514
   ImageIO class, 519
   image storage formats, 513
   java.awt.Graphics2D, 517–519
   java.awt.Image class, 513–514
   output files, 519
   width and height of images, 526
Java Message Service (JMS), 531
Java Mission Control (JMC)
   description, 359
   flight recording menu and dialog window, 361–362
   Java Flight Recorder, 359
   Memory tab, 360–361
   Oracle article, 362
   SortingSlf4jDemo main class, 359
   start JMX console, 359–360
Java Native Interface (JNI), 29
Java 2 Platform, Enterprise Edition (J2EE), 11
Java 2 Platform, Micro Edition (J2ME), 11
Java 2 Platform, Standard Edition (J2SE), 11
Java Process API
   BufferedReader, 363
   children() method, 368
   creating, 362–363
   InputStream, 363
   JAVA_HOME environment variable, 366
   Linux shell commands, 367
   onExit(), 367
   parent() method, 368
   ProcessBuilder, 367–368
   ProcessDemo class, 366
   ProcessHandle, 364
   ProcessHandle.Info, 365
Java Runtime Environment (JRE), 10, 28
JavaScript Object Notation (JSON), 511–513
Java Server Pages (JSP), 455–456, 461, 463
Java Shell tool (JShell)
   code completion, 53
   defined, 49
   help, 50
   java.lang.String, 52

INDEX

Java Shell tool (JShell) (cont.)
    Java statements, 55
    JDK, 50
    + operator, 51
    Oracle, 55
    REPL, 49
    scratch variable, 51
    String method, 52
    string variable, 54
    variables, 51
    vars command, 54, 55
    verbose mode, 50
Java syntax
    comments, 107
    exceptions, 139–141, 143–145
    generics, 145–147
    grammar
        block delimiters, 105
        case sensitive, 103
        Java keywords, 104
        line terminators, 105
        variables, 104
    identifiers, 106
    import section, 101–103
    Java code, 100
    lambda expressions, 99
    languages, 99
    object types (*see* Object types)
    package declaration, 101
    variables, 106
java.util.Optional<T> instances, 295
java.util.stream.Stream.Builder<T>, 289
Java Virtual Machine (JVM), 29, 49
jcmd, 353–355
jconsole, 355–358
JDK reactive streams API
    AbstractProcessor, 541, 543, 546
        calling cancel(), 539

    FilterCharProcessor, 539, 542
    filterCharProcessor.subscribe(..), 544
    Flow.Publisher<Integer>
        interface, 537
    imperative programming, 537
    implementations, 537
    infinite IntStream, 548
    mapping function, 544–545
    processor/subscriber, flow, 541–542
    publisher subscribe(..), 539
    start() method, 539
    SubmissionPublisher
        <Integer>, 537–539
    subscribe(..) calls, 547
    subscribe() method, 539
    subscription.request(..), 539
    transformerProcessor, 546
JetBrains, 39
jlink, 67
jps, 351–352
JShell, 409
JSP Standard Tag
    Library (JSTL), 465–466
JUnit
    @AfterAll, 374
    @AfterEach, 375
    annotations, 374
    @BeforeAll, 374
    @BeforeEach, 374
    @DisplayName, 375
    FakeDBConnection
        Account instance, 378
        AccountRepoImpl, 378–380
        DbConnection implementation,
          380, 381
        deleteByHolder method, 382–384
        DerbyDBConnection, 378
        Map<String, Account>, 382

mocks
  classes, 393
  createAccount(..) method, 393, 394
  findOne(..) method, 395
  Gradle test reports, 395–396
  @InjectMocks and @Mock,
    394–395
  libraries, 395
  objects and variables, 395
  PowerMock, 393
pseudo test class, 375–376
  execution, 377
  junit-platform.properties, 376
  menu option, IntelliJ IDEA, 377
  testOne() method, 378
stubs
  AccountServiceImpl, 384
  assertThrows, 389–392
  createAccount(…)
    method, 385–386
  option field, 388
  repo stub, 387–388
  returned values and
    exceptions, 386
  test coverage, 387
  testNonNumericAmountVersion
    One() method, 389, 390
  write test, 388–389
@Test, 375

L

Lambda expression, 95
Last In, First Out (LIFO), 154
Lazy loading, 178
Looping statements, 257
  do-while
    code block execution, 268

    implementation, 268, 270–271
    vs. while flowcharts, 269
  for
    Arrays utility class, 263
    code, 257, 260–261
    condition, 259–260
    enhanced syntax, 262
    flowchart, 258
    square brackets, 258
Loops, breaking
  break statement, 271–273
  continue statement, 271, 273–274
  return statement, 271, 275–276

M

Maven repository, 85
Member-level accessors, 63
Methods, 115–117
Module descriptor, 64
Module hell, 60
Modules
  compile, manually, 84
  defined, 64
  directives, 67
  IDE generate, 83
  Java 9 project, 65, 66
  Java 10, 67
  java--list-modules, 66
  JDK, 64
  keywords, 67–68
  limit access, 69
  module-info.class descriptor, 84
  module-info.java, 64, 68
  public types, 68
  requires keyword, 68
  SimpleReader class, 65
Modulus operator, 222

INDEX

N

NetBeans, 23
NG reactive publisher, 551
Non-blocking back-pressure, 534
NullPointerException, 283
Numerical operators, 214

O

Object types
    classes (*see* Classes)
    enums, 125–128
    interfaces (*see* Interfaces)
Operators
    assignment, 209–210
    category, 207–208
    explicit conversion, 211–213
    numerical
        binary, 217, 219–223
        Elvis operator, 241
        logical, 233–237
        negation, 216
        relational, 223, 225–226
        shift, 238, 240–241
        sign, 215–216
        unary, 214–215
Oracle, 55
    JavaFX 2.0, 16
    Java SE 7, 15–16
    Java SE 8, 16–17
    Java SE 9, 17–18
    Java SE 10, 19
    Java SE 11, 20

P, Q

Package, 56, 81
Parallel collector, 565
parallelStream() method, 286
Path handlers
    compareTo(..) method, 479
    createFile(…), 482
    delete(..), 482
    getFileName(), 480
    getFileSystem(), 480
    getRoot(), 480
    IOException, 482
    java.nio.file.Path, 478
    Paths.get(fileURI), 478–479
    properties, 481
    resolve(..), 480
    sample code, 481
    toAbsolutePath(), 480
peek(..) method, 308, 310
Performer hierarchy, 211
Point-to-point (p2p) messaging model, 531
Polymorphism, 119
Primitive data types
    binary representation, 168–169
    boolean type, 165–166
    byte, 169
    char type, 166–167
    = (equals) operator, 159
    float and double, 170–171
    int, 169
    integer primitives, 167
    long, 170
    numeric types, 167–168
    numeric values, 171, 173
    real primitives, 170–171, 173
    short, 169
    stack, 160–161
    swap() method, 160
Project Jigsaw, 64
Project reactor

advantage, 552
empty() method, 556
Flux and Mono, 556
flux publisher implementation, 553
interval(..) method, 557
JDK-based implementation, 557
operators, 552
org.reactivestreams.
    Subscriber<T>, 553, 554
reactive publisher, 555
reactor.core.CoreSubscriber<T>, 554
subscriber, write, 553–554
Public class, 61

R

Reactive Manifesto, 532
Reactive producer/consumer system, 533
Reactive programming
    flow interfaces, 535
    producer/consumer system, 533
    reactive streams API, 534–535
    standard API, 534
    streams API implementations, 535–536
Reactive streams API
        implementations, 535–536
Reactive streams interfaces, 534–535
Reactive Streams Technology
        Compatibility Kit, 548, 550–551
Read-Eval-Print Loop (REPL), 49
Reading files, 482
    Files.readAllBytes(..), 484
    InputStream, 489–492
    Reader class
        BufferedReader, 485–486, 488
        Files.newBufferedReader, 489
        Files.newBufferedReader(Path)
            method, 487
        hierarchy, 488
        java.io.Closeable interface, 486
        lambda expressions, 487
        nullReader(), 489
        StringBuilder, 488
    Scanner class, 482
    utility methods, 484
Reading user data
    Scanner
        advantage, 412
        console.format(..), 419
        console methods, 418
        java.io.Console, 417
        long values, 416
        next..() methods list, 411–412
        ReadingUsingConsoleDemo, 420
        read value, 412–415
        sample code, 418–419
        System.in, 411
        templates, 419
        usage, 415–416
    System.in, 410–411
Real primitives
    boxing and unboxing, 173
    double, 171
    float, 170
    numeric values, 171, 173
Reference data types
    arrays
        initialization, 178–179
        int type, 179
        lazy loading, 178
        null keyword, 177–178
        square brackets, 179
    class and interface hierarchy, 174
    class constructor, 173
    collections, 196
    date time API, 191

INDEX

Reference data types (*cont.*)
    escaping characters, 187
    heap, 161–163
    java.lang.Thread class, 201–202
    lambda expressions, 205
    run() method, 202
    CounterRunnable code, 205
    runnable code, 204–205
    stack and heap memory, 174–176
    start() method, 203
    string, 183
    swap() method, 163–165
    Thread.currentThread() method, 205
    thread management, 206
    wrapper classes, 189
Regression tests, 371
Run-time polymorphism, 119

S

Serial collector, 564
Serialization, 502
    binary, 503–507
    JSON, 511–513
    XML, 507–511
sorted() operation, 313
Stack and heap memory
    add() method, 157
    definition, 153–154
    java.lang.String class, 154
    JVM parameters, 154
    main() method, 158
    object declaration, 156
    String Pool, 155
    variable declaration, 155–156
Stream API
    Consumer, 285–286
    creation
        from arrays, 287, 289
        collection interfaces and classes, 284
        empty streams, 289
        finite streams, 289
        IntStream instance, 292–293
        LongStream instances, 293
        stream of primitives, 292
        stream of strings, 294
    debugging, code, 310
        anyMatch(..), 309–310
        findAny(), 309–310
        peek(..), 310
    dropWhile, 292
    functions, 282
    interfaces, 293
    intermediate operation
        add(..), 289
        allMatch(..), 309–310
        anyMatch(..) method, 309
        collect(..) method, 303
        count(), 306
        distinct() method, 306
        filter(..) method, 302
        findAny(), 309–310
        findFirst(), 306
        flatMap(..) method, 304–305
        limit(..) method, 307
        map(..) method, 303
        noneMatch, 310
        Optimal<T> instance, 309
        parallelStream(), 286–287
        peek(..), 310
        sorted() method, 306
        toArray() method, 302
    iterate, 285
    java.util.function.Supplier, 290
    java.util.stream.BaseStream, 282

limit, 289–290, 307
NullPointerException, 283
Optimal, 309
Optional, 283, 295–298, 303–306, 309
parallel data processing, 282
range, 293
rangeClosed, 293
Stream, 281–294, 298–300
Stream.builder(), 289
Stream.generate(), 289
takeWhile, 291–292
terminal functions
    forEach and forEachOrdered, 300, 302
    sum and reduce, 307–308
terminal operations, 283
    min() and max(), 307
transform collections into streams, 283
String.format(..) method, 231–232
String Pool, 154, 183–184
    splitAsStream, 294
Sun Microsystem's Java Versions
    features, 11–12
    J2EE, 11
    J2ME, 11
    J2SE, 11
    J2SE 5.0, 12–13
    Java FX 1.0 SDK, 14
    Java official logo, 12
    JRE, 10
    Mac OS X, 13
    Oracle features, 14
Swing
    AWT model, 420–422
    border layout zones, 426
    components, 14
    FlowLayout, 427
    getInstalledLookAndFeels(), 429
    getValueIsAdjusting(), 429
    java.awt.BorderLayout, 425–426
    java.awt.event.ActionListener, 427
    javax.swing.JFrame, 423
    JComponent, 425
    JFrame, 424–425
    JFrame.EXIT_ON_CLOSE, 424
    JList<T> class, 428
    JScrollPane, 429
    JTextArea, 428
    ListSelectionListener implementation, 430, 431
    Operation System, 429
    UIManager class, 429
    Windows, 423, 431
Switch Statement
    code, 250–251
    flowchart, 252, 255–256
    NullPointerExceptions, 254–255

T

Terminal operations, 283, 298
Test-driven development (TDD), 371
Testing
    application
        account management, 373
        AccountRepo, 373
        AccountService, 373
        JUnit (see JUnit)
        Oracle RDBMS, 373
    development phase, 371
    Gradle module structure, 371–372
    integration tests, 371
    ISTQB, 370
    lifecycle of software application, 370
    regression tests, 371
    src directory, 372

INDEX

Testing (*cont.*)
  TDD, 371
  unit tests, 371
Thread local allocation buffer (TLAB), 570
toBinaryString method, 227

U, V

Unboxing, 190
Unchecked exceptions, 143
Uniform Resource Identifier (URI), 474
Unit tests, 371

W

Web application
  Apache Tomcat server, 451
  DateServlet, 467–468
  embedded Tomcat server, 453–454
  HttpServletRequest, 457–458
  index.jsp page, 463–466
  Internet, 451
  JavaScript, 468
  javax.servlet.http.HttpServlet, 456–457
  JSP scriptlets, directive tags, 463
  JSTL, 465–466
  network debugger view, Firefox, 452
  request method, 452–453
  resource/dynamic directory, 461
  SampleServlet, 461–462
  servers, 450
  servlets and JSP, 455–456
  structure, 460–461
  URL, context path value, 454–455
  urlPattern property, 457
  @WebServlet, 458–459
Writing files
  Files.write(..), 493–494
  Files.write(Path, byte[]), 492
  Files.writeString(..), 493
  OutputStream, 499–502
  Writer class
    BufferedWriter, 495, 498
    Files.newBufferedWriter(..), 497
    flush() method, 495
    hierarchy, 498
    nullWriter(), 499
    OutputStreamWriter, 499
    PrintWriter, 499
    String instances, 495, 496
    StringWriter, 499

X, Y

XML serialization, 507–511

Z

zipWith(..) method, 557

CPSIA information can be obtained
at www.ICGtesting.com
Printed in the USA
LVHW061534300119
605811LV00002B/4/P